CW00734112

The Breedon Book of

HORSE RACING RECORDS

The Breedon Book of

HORSE RACING RECORDS

Edward Abelson & John Tyrrel

The Breedon Books
Publishing Company
Derby

First published in Great Britain by
The Breedon Books Publishing Company Limited
44 Friar Gate, Derby DE1 1DA
1993

ISBN 1 873626 15 0

Printed and bound by Hillmans Printers, Frome, Somerset.
Cover printed by BDC Printing Services Ltd of Derby.
Racing results set by Saxon, Derby.
All photographs supplied by Hulton Picture Library.

All Races In Calendar Order

March
Champion Hurdle
Queen Mother Champion Chase
Triumph Hurdle
Cheltenham Gold Cup
Lincoln Handicap

April
Grand National
Fred Darling Stakes
Greenham Stakes
John Porter Stakes
Nell Gwyn Stakes
Earl of Sefton Stakes
Craven Stakes
Forte Mile
Gordon Richards Stakes
Thresher Classic Trial
Whitbread Gold Cup
Sagaro Stakes

May
One Thousand Guineas
Jockey Club Stakes
Two Thousand Guineas
Palace House Stakes
Chester Vase
Chester Cup
Ormonde Stakes
Lingfield Derby Trial Stakes
Musidora Stakes
Dante Stakes
Yorkshire Cup
Duke of York Stakes
Lockinge Stakes
Temple Stakes
Henry II Stakes
Brigadier Gerard Stakes

June
The Derby
Diomed Stakes
Coronation Cup
The Oaks
Queen Anne Stakes
Prince of Wales's Stakes
St James's Palace Stakes
Coventry Stakes
King Edward VII Stakes
Jersey Stakes
Queen Mary Stakes
Coronation Stakes
Royal Hunt Cup
Queen's Vase
Cork & Orrery Stakes
Ascot Gold Cup
Norfolk Stakes
Ribblesdale Stakes
Hardwicke Stakes
Wokingham Stakes
King's Stand Stakes
Criterion Stakes
Irish Derby

July
Eclipse Stakes
Lancashire Oaks
Princess of Wales's Stakes
Cherry Hinton Stakes
Falmouth Stakes
July Stakes
July Cup
Scottish Classic
King George VI & Queen Elizabeth Stakes
Princess Margaret Stakes
Beeswing Stakes
Gordon Stakes
Stewards' Cup
Sussex Stakes
Richmond Stakes
Vintage Stakes
Goodwood Cup
King George Stakes
Molecomb Stakes
Nassau Stakes

August
Rose of Lancaster Stakes
Hungerford Stakes
Geoffrey Freer Stakes
Solario Stakes
Juddmonte International Stakes
Yorkshire Oaks
Great Voltigeur Stakes
Ebor Handicap
Gimcrack Stakes
Nunthorpe Stakes
Lowther Stakes
Prestige Stakes
Beefeater Gin Celebration Mile

September
Haydock Park Sprint Cup
September Stakes
Portland Handicap
Park Hill Stakes
May Hill Stakes
Doncaster Cup
Kiveton Park Stakes
Champagne Stakes
St Leger
Flying Childers Stakes
Select Stakes
Ayr Gold Cup
Mill Reef Stakes
Cumberland Lodge Stakes
Queen Elizabeth II Stakes
Fillies' Mile
Royal Lodge Stakes
Diadem Stakes

October
Prix de l'Arc de Triomphe
Cheveley Park Stakes
Middle Park Stakes
Sun Chariot Stakes
Cambridgeshire Stakes
Jockey Club Cup
Supreme Stakes
Princess Royal Stakes
Cornwallis Stakes
Challenge Stakes
Dewhurst Stakes
Rockfel Stakes
Champion Stakes
Cesarewitch Stakes
Horris Hill Stakes
St Simon Stakes
Racing Post Trophy

November
November Handicap
Mackeson Gold Cup
Hennessy Gold Cup

December
King George VI Chase

Acknowledgements

The Jockey Club
in particular Jonathan Smith

All at The Thoroughbred
Breeders Association, Newmarket

The British Bloodstock Agency Ltd, Newmarket
in particular Chris Lloyd and Lyn Johnson

Greg Way

G.A.Thornbury

Ken Henhouse

Amy Hulley

Ginny Tyrrel

Caroline Williams

Mrs Jean Abelson

Introduction

WE ARE all familiar with the scene. A group of sporting friends are gathered in a bar, restaurant, club or at a dinner party. The topic turns to racing.

'Wonderful rider, Doug Smith,' says one of the chums. 'He was champion jockey five times and won five Doncaster Cups.'

'Seven,' comes the correction. 'Well, six anyway.'

'Surely not?' The discussion continues until someone suggests that it would be a good idea to check the record books. And soon the old sporting annuals are thumbed through to find the correct answer and settle the inevitable bets.

The Breedon Book of Horse Racing Records won't solve all arguments, of course, but it does provide a comprehensive record of the winners of the British Group races since their inception, giving the year, the winner, the jockey, trainer and owner, plus similar details for a selection of handicaps, overseas events and National Hunt races.

The records are introduced with a summary of the history of the race, its relative success and importance in the Racing Calendar. These jottings and comments are not intended to be exhaustive but rather to convey a general impression and bring out the flavour of the race.

Jockeys were not recorded in the Racing Calendar before 1826 and trainers, usually regarded as mere employees, an attitude stemming from the days of the training groom, do not appear in the Calendar until the mid-1930s. However, races included in the book have been traced from their foundation date, even where the trainer and jockey are not known. There were many walk-overs in the early days, when naturally no Starting Price was returned, and not all S/Ps were recorded.

In all cases, the present name of the race has been given, with notes on previous titles which have been altered through the years by historical necessity, expedience or the vagaries of sponsorship. For the latter, the commercial name is not included unless the sponsor founded the race or it has always been sponsored, for instance the Whitbread Gold Cup.

The races are in Calendar, or chronological, order and the National Hunt events likewise. The index gives the month in which the races are run and the term 'classic' is usually applied to English classic races. Foreign classics are described as such, *ie* Irish 1,000 Guineas.

The following have been, but are no longer, included in the Pattern, since it was started in 1971.

The Two Thousand Guineas Trial Stakes (Ascot and Salisbury)
The One Thousand Guineas Trial Stakes (Ascot and Salisbury)
The Blue Riband Trial Stakes (Epsom)
The Princess Elizabeth Stakes (Epsom)

John Tyrrel, Channel Four Racing's resident historian, (left) is a well-known face to racegoers. Edward Abelson (right), has made his mark as one of the sport's leading statisticians as well as having a great family connection through his father, who bred, owned and trained *National Spirit*.

The White Rose Stakes (Ascot)
The Cheshire Oaks (Chester)
The Dee Stakes (Chester)
The Lingfield Oaks Trial Stakes (Lingfield)
The Star Fillies' Stakes (Sandown)
The National Stakes (Sandown)
The Seaton Delaval Stakes (Newcastle)

Finally, a definition of the Group system which operates within the Pattern, itself an arrangement to inter-complement the major races of the principal European nations. Group 1 is of classic and other races of championship standard having international importance; Group 2 is the category of races immediately below championship standard, but also significant in an international context; and Group 3 takes in the remainder of the races, including classic trials, required to complete the series of tests for the best horses. These are mainly of domestic importance in each of the member countries but they attract overseas runners from time to time. Group 1 races are run without penalties on strict weight for age and sex terms, and penalties in Group 2 and 3 races are based on success in previous Pattern races. The member countries within the Pattern are Great Britain, France, Ireland, Germany and Italy.

John Tyrrel and Edward Abelson,
March 1993.

Flat Races

The Lincolnshire Handicap

The Lincolnshire Handicap has a history which has caused much confusion over the years. A race of that name was run for the first time over two miles in August 1849. In 1853, it was decided to stage a meeting on the Carholme in February, a fixture which was later moved to March. The card included a race called the Lincoln Spring Handicap, as opposed to the Lincolnshire Handicap, and this event was run over a mile and a half, reverting in distance to a mile in 1855.

Meanwhile the Lincolnshire Handicap continued to be run in the more agreeable climes of August until this meeting was abandoned in 1857, later re-emerging in the 1860s but without the original Lincolnshire.

In effect the old race became merged with the Spring Handicap in 1859, and this is the race which was to find considerable notoriety as the first leg of the Spring Double together with the Grand National.

The unpredictable nature of the latter speaks for itself and is described in another chapter, but in many ways the Lincolnshire was even more so. Eager punters spent the late winter months pouring over the weights for a handicap which frequently attracted more than thirty runners, all of whom had been out of action since the previous autumn. Speculation was not assisted by lack of knowledge of the draw and the hazards of the old barrier starting gate.

None the less, some spectacular gambles were landed. In 1940, Gordon Richards succeeded where he had failed since 1928 and won on *Quartier Maitre,* trained by Ivor Anthony and owned by Mrs Arthur Bendir, the wife of the chairman of Ladbrokes, a fact which may or may not have had some bearing on the starting price of 7/2 in a field of twenty-one.

In 1941, Dave Dick took the first leg of a long term spring Double when he won on *Gloaming* for the veteran trainer George Lambton. Dick's weight was 7st 4lb and the horse was not unfancied at 100/7. In 1956 Dick scaled 11st 3lb when winning the Grand National on E.S.B.

By 1943, the race had been transferred to Pontefract for the duration of the war. Cyril Ray, who enjoyed the rare if dubious distinction of being warned off as both a jockey and a trainer, won with *Lady Electra* at odds of 9/2. In the ownership of the late Phil Bull the mare later became known as 'The Idol of the North'.

The first post-war Lincolnshire went to *Langton Abbot,* trained by George Lambton's son Teddy and ridden by Tommy Weston at 7/1.

The late Manny Mercer rode the 100/1 chance *Jockey Treble,* to win from a field of 45 opponents in 1947, and the following year *Commissar* proved the best at 33/1 when a record 58 runners faced the starter.

In 1964, *Mighty Gurkha* won the last Lincolnshire to be run on the Carholme. The race was transferred to Doncaster and renamed the Lincoln. In recent years, the limitations of starting stalls have restricted the size of the fields to reasonable proportions, but the drainage problems of Town Moor's straight mile have if anything enhanced the unpredictability of the draw.

Run at Doncaster over 1 mile First Run 1853 Handicap

		Jockey	Trainer	Owner	Odds
1853	**Caurire**	T Clements	J Saxon	J Saxon	5/2
1854	**Georgey**	T Aldcroft	T Dawson	T Dawson	5/1
1855	**Saucebox**	G Fordham	T Parr	T Parr	Evens
1856	**Flageolet**	H Bray	G Drewe	Mr Elwes	6/1
1857	**Huntingdon**	W Grimmer	T Abrahams	Mr Mellish	12/1
1858	**Vandermulin**	T French	T Flintoff	E Clark	3/1
1859	**Bel Esperanza**	G Clements	John Dawson	J La Mert	–
1860	**Vigo**	G Fordham	–	Mr Lincoln	10/3
1861	**Benbow**	T Chaloner	J Scott	S Murland	16/1
1862	**Suburban**	A Edwards	John Dawson	Count Batthyany	7/1
1863	**Manrico**	S Adams	W Day	Lord Westmorland	8/1
1864	**Benjamin**	F Hunter	T Jennings	Comte F de Lagrange	100/30
1865	**Gaily**	C Carroll	J Osborne	J Osborne	20/1
1866	**Treasure Trove**	Barker	–	R Kirby	20/1
1867	**Vandervelde**	H Covey	John Dawson	Count Batthyany	33/1
1868	**Indigestion**	C Maidment	C Bloss	Sir C Legard	100/6
1869	**Sycee**	R Cameron	W Boyce	W Boyce	100/15
1870	**Royal Rake**	C Maidment	–	Lord Rendlesham	11/2
1871	**Vulcan**	G Jarvis	–	Mr Winchester	9/1
1872	**Guy Dayrell**	C Maidment	G Bloss	H Chaplin	100/6
1873	**Vestminster**	C Maidment	–	A E Hope	100/8
1874	**Tomahawk**	F Archer	W Goater	F Swindell	14/1
1875	**The Gunner**	E Rossiter	–	T Turner	30/1
1876	**Controversy**	H Constable	J Cannon	Lord Rosebery	33/1
1877	**Footstep**	W Hopkins	T Wadlow	Lord Wilton	100/6
1878	**Kaleidoscope**	T Glover	R Peck	R Peck	6/1
1879	**Touchet**	H Constable	J Cannon	Lord Rosebery	6/1
1880	**Rosy Cross**	S Mordan	J Martin	H Rymill	16/1
1881	**Buchanan**	J Gallon	A Taylor Snr	W S Crawfurd	100/8
1882	**Poulet**	J Goater	T Jennings	Comte F de Lagrange	20/1
1883	**Knight of Burghley**	C Wood	John Dawson Jnr	Jos Davis	8/1
1884	**Tonans**	C Wood	T Brown	J W Smith	5/1
1885	**Bendigo**	J Snowden	C Jousiffe	H T Barclay	11/4
1886	**Fulmen**	J Woodburn	J Hopper	R C Naylor	100/6
1887	**Oberon**	E Martin	A Taylor Snr	Duchess of Montrose	50/1

		Jockey	Trainer	Owner	Odds
1888	**Veracity**	S Chandley	E Weever	W J Legh	50/1
1889	**Wise Man**	T Loates	F Bates	Sir R Jardine	8/1
1890	**The Rejected**	F Rickaby	A Day	J O'Neill	18/1
1891	**Lord George**	J Woodburn	W Gibbons	Prince Soltykoff	100/9
1892	**Clarence**	F Allsopp	P Peck	Sir J Blundell Maple	6/1
1893	**Wolf's Crag**	W Bradford	C Archer	J W Smith	20/1
1894	**Le Nicham**	T Loates	A Hayhoe	Baron L de Rothschild	5/1
1895	**Euclid**	G Brown	W Viney	C Duncan	100/8
1896	**Clorane**	M Cannon	W T Robinson	A F Bassett	100/14
1897	**Winkfield's Pride**	M Cannon	W T Robinson	J C Sullivan	7/2
1898	**Prince Barcaldine**	N Robinson	W T Robinson	W M Clarke	4/1
1899	**General Peace**	O Madden	J Powney	P W Bewicke	100/7
1900	**Sir Geoffery**	M Cannon	C Archer	H Barnato	100/12
1901	**Little Eva**	O Madden	J Powney	F Bald	100/15
1902	**St Maclou**	G McGall	C Beatty	H McCalmont	100/8
1903	**Over Norton**	O Madden	C Waugh	E C Irish	100/7
1904	**Uninsured**	B Dillon	J Fallon	F Forester	9/2
1905	**Sansovino**	Wal Griggs	C Waugh	F Luscombe	100/9
1906	**Ob**	G Bellhouse	R Carter	M Ephrussi	20/1
1907	**Ob**	G Stern	R Carter	M Ephrussi	25/1
1908	**Kaffir Chief**	J H Martin	G Chaloner	F S Barnard	100/7
1909	**Duke of Sparta**	J Howard	A Sadler Jnr	A C Mandaras	20/1
1910	**Cinderello**	J Plant	W T Robinson	E F Schiff	9/1
1911	**Mercutio**	C Trigg	J Cannon	C Hibbert	100/12
1912	**Long Set**	W Higgs	J H Batho	S B Joel	13/2
1913	**Berrilldon**	H Robbins	H T Medcalfe	A E Barton	100/7
1914	**Outram**	R Stokes	S Pickering	P Nelke	25/1
1915	**View Law**	P Jones	J S Bramley	F Straker	6/1
1916	**Clap Gate**	E Gardner	F Barling	F Phillips	6/1
1917/18	**No Race**				
1919	**Royal Bucks**	G Hulme	R S Sievier	Lady Queensberry	100/7
1920	**Furious**	H Robbins	P Woodland	C C Hatry	33/1
1921	**Soranus**	B Carslake	E de Mestre	S B Joel	33/1
1922	**Granely**	S Donoghue	H Cottrill	J White	20/1
1923	**White Bud**	J Beasley	J McCall	J G Dingley	66/1
1924	**Sir Gallahad III**	F O'Neill	R Denman	J D Cohn	9/2
1925	**Tapin**	S Donoghue	C Bartholomew Jnr	A Eknayan	5/1
1926	**King of Clubs**	P Donoghue	W J Bellerby	W J Bellerby	100/1
1927	**Priory Park**	F Fox	C Peck	J B Joel	20/1
1928	**Dark Warrior**	R A Jones	W Earl	S B Joel	28/1
1929	**Elton**	K Robertson	H C Leader	Mrs R W Foster	100/1
1930	**Leonidas II**	H Southey	S H Darling	M Boussac	66/1
1931	**Knight Error**	F Fox	P Whitaker	A Wilson	100/9
1932	**Jerome Fandor**	W Christie	H Peacock	A McKinlay	40/1
1933	**Dorigen**	T Weston	G Lambton	G Lambton	25/1
1934	**Play On**	J Dines	J Russell	M Simon	100/9
1935	**Flamenco**	E Smith	J Jarvis	Lord Rosebery	8/1
1936	**Over Coat**	T Weston	J Russell	H Selby	10/1
1937	**Marmaduke Jinks**	D Smith	H Peacock	Mrs C Robinson	33/1
1938	**Phakos**	E Smith	J Jarvis	E Esmond	8/1
1939	**Squadron Castle**	V Mitchell	H Smallwood	S Oxenham	40/1
1940	**Quartier Maitre**	G Richards	I Anthony	Mrs A Bendir	7/2
1941	**Gloaming**	D Dick	G Lambton	S Raphael	100/7
1942	**Cuerdley**	J Taylor	R Renton	E Pilcher	3/1
1943	**Lady Electra**	R Colvern	C Ray	W Richardson	9/2
1944	**Backbite**	M Pearson	A Boyd	A Tully	33/1
1945	**Double Harness**	D Stansfield	C Elsey	J Hetherton	33/1
1946	**Langton Abbot**	T Weston	E Lambton	T Best	7/1
1947	**Jockey Treble**	E Mercer	W Smallwood	S Oxenham	100/1
1948	**Commissar**	W Rickaby	A Budgett	R Budgett	33/1
1949	**Fair Judgement**	E Smith	J Jarvis	C Gordon	6/1
1950	**Dramatic**	G Richards	G Todd	A E Saunders	7/1
1951	**Barnes Park**	J Sime	G Boyd	H Lane	33/1
1952	**Phariza**	D Forte	J Powell	C O-Lee	33/1
1953	**Sailing Light**	A Roberts	G Armstrong	Mrs M Farr	100/8
1954	**Nahar**	J Massard	A Head	Prince Aly Khan	100/7
1955	**Military Court**	E Mercer	H Wragg	Begum Aga Khan	8/1
1956	**Three Star II**	D W Morris	H Davison	G Graham	40/1
1957	**Babur**	E Hide	C Elsey	Capt S Lord	25/1
1958	**Babur**	E Britt	C Elsey	Capt S Lord	25/1
1959	**Marshal Pil**	P Robinson	S Hall	S Lip	15/2
1960	**Mustavon**	N McIntosh	S Ha	Mrs L McVey	8/1
1961	**Johns Court**	B Lee	E Cousins	K Wheldon	25/1
1962	**Hill Royal**	J Sime	E Cousins	D Murray	50/1
1963	**Monawin**	J Sime	R Mason	R Mason	25/1

		Jockey	Trainer	Owner	Odds
1964	**Mighty Gurkha**	P Robinson	E Lambton	Mrs G Lambton	33/1
1965	**Old Tom**	A Breasley	M H Easterby	J Ellis	22/1
1966	**Riot Act**	A Breasley	F Armstrong	Mrs J F C Bryce	8/1
1967	**Ben Novus**	P Robinson	W Hide	J N Peatt	22/1
1968	**Frankincense**	G Starkey	J Oxley	Lady Halifax	100/8
1969	**Foggy Bell**	A Barclay	Denys Smith	J Forrester	20/1
1970	**New Chapter**	A Barclay	F Armstrong	C P Goulandris	100/9
1971	**Double Cream**	E Hide	W Elsey	R F Dennis	30/1
1972	**Sovereign Bill**	E Hide	P Robinson	W Barr	9/2
1973	**Bronze Hill**	M Birch	M H Easterby	Mrs E Smith	50/1
1974	**Quizair**	M L Thomas	R Jarvis	W Macdonald	28/1
1975	**Southwark Star**	R Fox	G Peter-Hoblyn	T Hammond	33/1
1976	**The Hertford**	G Lewis	B Swift	B Shine	9/2
1977	**Blustery**	D McKay	M Smyly	R Lorenz	20/1
1978	**Captain's Wings**	M Wigham	R Boss	M House	13/2
1979	**Fair Season**	G Starkey	I Balding	J Berry	8/1
1980	**King's Ride**	G Baxter	W Wightman	D Clark	10/1
1981	**Saher**	R Cochrane	R Sheather	J C Smith	14/1
1982	**King's Glory**	B Crossley	P Mitchell	C Heard	11/1
1983	**Mighty Fly**	S Cauthen	D Elsworth	Mrs V Tory	14/1
1984	**Saving Mercy**	W R Swinburn	D Weld	M Benacerraf	14/1
1985	**Cataldi**	G Starkey	G Harwood	K Abdulla	10/1
1986	**K-Battery**	J Lowe	C Elsey	Mrs M Butler	25/1
1987	**Star of a Gunner**	J Reid	R J Holder	J Neville	9/1
1988	**Cuvee Charlie**	M Rimmer	H J Collingridge	R Davies	33/1
1989	**Fact Finder**	T Williams	R Akehurst	A D Spence	20/1
1990	**Evichstar**	A Munro	J Fitzgerald	G Meredith	33/1
1991	**Amenable**	Alex Greaves	T Barron	W G Spink	22/1
1992	**High Low**	J Quinn	W Haggas	B Haggas	16/1

Run at Lincoln 1853-1964, at Lingfield in 1916 and at Pontefract 1942-1944

The Fred Darling Stakes

Named in honour of the legendary trainer who produced no fewer than nineteen classic winners, the Fred Darling Stakes is often a good race in its own right but rarely a pointer to the future. In the last two seasons, however, the Fred Darling has indicated *Salsabil* (Guineas and Oaks 1990) and *Shadayid* (Guineas 1991).

Run at Newbury over 7 furlongs and 60 yards for 3 year-old fillies First Run 1949 Group 3

		Jockey	Trainer	Owner	Odds
1949	**Vale of Towy**	C Elliott	E Williams	Miss P Vaughan	7/2
1950	**Serocco**	G Richards	N Murless	J A Dewar	6/1
1951	**No Race**				
1952	**Refreshed**	G Richards	N Murless	J A Dewar	8/11
1953	**Rose Coral**	J Egan	G Brooke	Lady E Basset	5/1
1954	**Felise**	W Rickaby	J Jarvis	Lady Rosebery	4/1
1955	**Feria**	A Breasley	N Cannon	S Wingfield Digby	100/6
1956	**None Fairer**	W Snaith	H Cottrill	Maj L B Holliday	100/7
1957	**Sijui**	L Piggott	N Murless	Sir V Sassoon	20/1
1958	**Nicaria**	J Mercer	R J Colling	J J Astor	25/1
1959	**Rosalba**	J Mercer	R J Colling	J J Astor	6/4
1960	**Soldier's Song**	J Lindley	J Tree	J Tree	100/6
1961	**Who Can Tell**	R Elliott	W R Hern	Maj L B Holliday	5/1
1962	**Anassa**	J Lindley	J M Gosden	B Mavroleon	11/2
1963	**Gazpacho**	G Bougoure	P Prendergast	Mrs J R Mullion	7/1
1964	**Ela Marita**	G Bougoure	P Prendergast	J R Mullion	5/4
1965	**Night Appeal**	J Lindley	A Budgett	R Richmond-Watson	100/7
1966	**No Race**				
1967	**Royal Saint**	L Piggott	N Murless	Mrs V Hue-Williams	8/11
1968	**Raymonda**	G Starkey	J Oxley	Lady Halifax	100/6
1969	**Sea Lavender**	A Barclay	N Murless	J Hornung	9/4
1970	**Highest Hopes**	J Lindley	W R Hern	L B Holliday	4/11
1971	**Rotisserie**	A Murray	D Smith	H D H Wills	16/1
1972	**Miss Paris**	E Eldin	D Smith	J Pearce	6/4
1973	**Mysterious**	G Lewis	N Murless	G A Pope Jnr	4/1

		Jockey	Trainer	Owner	Odds
1974	**Northern Gem**	E Eldin	D Smith	B Roberts	14/1
1975	**Carnauba**	G Doleuze	L Turner	N B Hunt	4/1
1976	**Rowantree**	G Starkey	I Balding	J Berry	20/1
1977	**Durtal**	L Piggott	B Hills	R Sangster	8/13
1978	**Shapina**	G Baxter	P Cole	E A Badger	10/1
1979	**Topsy**	S Cauthen	H Wragg	R B Moller	2/1
1980	**Millingdale Lillie**	L Piggott	C Nelson	R Sangster	5/2
1981	**Marwell**	W R Swinburn	M Stoute	E J Loder	8/11
1982	**Slightly Dangerous**	S Cauthen	B Hills	A Clore	9/4
1983	**Goodbye Shelley**	J Lowe	S Norton	Mrs S Brook	9/1
1984	**Mahogany**	J Mercer	C Nelson	Mrs W Tulloch	5/4
1985	**Top Socialite**	W R Swinburn	M Stoute	Tjo Tek Tan	10/1
1986	**Maysoon**	W R Swinburn	M Stoute	M Al-Maktoum	11/2
1987	**Littlefield**	T Ives	I Balding	Mrs R M Chaplin	9/2
1988	**Bluebook**	S Cauthen	H Cecil	Lord Tavistock	5/1
1989	**Pass the Peace**	T Quinn	M Bell	C W Bell	11/8
1990	**Salsabil**	W Carson	J Dunlop	H Al-Maktoum	11/4
1991	**Shadayid**	W Carson	J Dunlop	H Al-Maktoum	8/11
1992	**Musicale**	P Eddery	H Cecil	R Sangster	8/11

Run as the Lambourn Stakes 1949-1954

The Greenham Stakes

Racing at Newbury was the brainchild of the trainer John Porter, the Henry Cecil of his day. Contemplating retirement and the near end of a career which had encompassed twenty-three classic winners including seven Derbies, like many rail travellers today he found himself gazing at a piece of land from a stationary train. The land in particular was at Newbury, and Porter decided it would make an excellent racecourse.

Porter lost no time in doing a deal with the landowner, and laying his plans before the Jockey Club. To his surprise, the Club refused to grant him a licence, on the grounds that there were too many fixtures already. There were in fact seventy-three, compared to the fifty-nine courses operating today. Legend has it that Porter emerged into Newmarket High Street and met King Edward VII taking his morning constitutional. Porter had trained eighteen winners for the monarch when the latter was Prince of Wales, and received a sympathetic royal ear when he explained his predicament.

The King promised to have a few words with the Stewards, and Porter duly received his licence.

The connection did not finish there. The Newbury track opened in the autumn of 1905, and the following spring the Greenham Stakes was inaugurated as a Two Thousand Guineas trial. In 1909, the King's *Minoru* defeated the odds-on favourite *Valens*, despite pessimism in the royal camp.

Edward VII's racing manager, Lord Marcus Beresford, reckoned that *Minoru* would have been overweighted with 7st 4lb in Stewards' Cup, but racing managers are not always good judges, as we have reason to know from their stewardship of some Middle Eastern interests today, and *Minoru* certainly proved Lord Marcus wrong by winning the Greenham under 9st 7lb and the Guineas along with the Derby.

Nowadays, the Greenham tends to highlight useful horses in the highest class rather than champions, with *Wollow* being the last classic winner, going on to take the Two Thousand Guineas in 1976, and *Mill Reef* won the Derby in 1971.

Horse racing at Newbury in 1992. The track was opened in 1905 and the Greenham Stakes was inaugurated the following spring.

Run at Newbury over 7 furlongs for 3 year-old colts & geldings First Run 1906 Group 3

		Jockey	Trainer	Owner	Odds
1906	**Rocketter**	W Higgs	S Darling	J H Greer	4/5
1907	**Donna Caterina**	W Higgs	P Peck	Lord Rosebery	10/1
1908	**Sir Toby**	D Maher	P Peck	Lord Rosebery	9/4
1909	**Minoru**	H Jones	R Marsh	HM The King	9/2
1910	**Bronzino**	F Fox	F Pratt	J A de Rothschild	33/1
1911	**Sydmonton**	S Donoghue	R C Dawson	Lord Carnarvon	11/2
1912	**Jingling Geordie**	F Wootton	S Darling	J Buchanan	10/11
1913	**Shogun**	F Wootton	R Wootton	E Hulton	4/5
1914	**Sunny Lake**	H Randall	R Marsh	HM The King	6/1
1915	**Let Fly**	E Huxley	F Leader	W Hall-Walker	11/4
	Sunfire	W Huxley	C Morton	J B Joel	6/1
1916	**Analogy**	J Childs	R C Dawson	E Hulton	8/1
1917/18	**No Race**				
1919	**Polygnotus**	S Donoghue	S Loates	S B Joel	7/1
1920	**Silvern**	S Donoghue	F Hartigan	Sir E Hulton	7/1
1921	**No Race**				
1922	**Weathervane**	H Jones	R Marsh	HM The King	5/2
1923	**Parth**	A Walker	J H Crawford	M Goculdas	8/1
1924	**Green Fire**	S Donoghue	C Morton	J B Joel	100/7
1925	**Sparus**	F Bullock	A Taylor Jnr	W M G Singer	10/1
1926	**Friar Wile**	J Childs	F Darling	Lord Woolavington	4/1
1927	**Lordland**	A Burns	R Gooch	W A Read	100/7
1928	**The Wheedler**	J Childs	F Darling	Duke of Portland	9/2
1929	**Sidonia**	R Perryman	T Cannon Jnr	A de Rothschild	20/1
1930	**Christopher Robin**	P Beasley	V Gilpin	G Loder	9/4
1931	**Link Boy**	R Dick	J Lawson	W M G Singer	5/1
1932	**Orwell**	R A Jones	J Lawson	W M G Singer	8/13
1933	**Harinero**	C Ray	R C Dawson	W Barnett	20/1
1934	**Zelina**	S Donoghue	Hugh Powney	Z Michalinos	33/1
1935	**Theft**	G Richards	Frank Butters	HH Aga Khan	2/5
1936	**Noble King**	R Perryman	Frank Butters	Sir A Butt	6/1
1937	**Fairford**	T Weston	H Cottrill	W Murray	11/2
1938	**Mirza II**	H Wragg	Frank Butters	HH Aga Khan	7/4
1939	**Fairstone**	C Richards	H Cottrill	Sir A Bailey	10/1
1940	**Tant Mieux**	G Richards	F Darling	Maharaja of Kolhapur	5/2
1941/48	**No Race**				
1949	**Star King**	D Smith	J C Waugh	W Harvey	4/9
1950	**Port o'Light**	T Gosling	W Nightingall	C C Matthews	6/1
1951	**No Race**				
1952	**Serpenyoe**	F Durr	W Smyth	Lady Irwin	7/1
1953	**March Past**	E Fordyce	K Cundell	Mrs G Trimmer-Thompson	11/8
1954	**Infatuation**	W Rickaby	V Smyth	Sir M McAlpine	Evens
1955	**Counsel**	J Mercer	R J Colling	Lord Astor	7/4
1956	**Ratification**	W H Carr	V Smyth	Sir M McAlpine	11/8
1957	**Pipe of Peace**	A Breasley	G Richards	S Niarchos	Evens
1958	**Paresa**	W Rickaby	R Day	Sir M McAlpine	15/2
1959	**Masham**	D Smith	G Brooke	A Ellis	11/10
1960	**Filipepi**	G Lewis	R Smyth	F Laker	100/8
1961	**Primus**	D Smith	G Richards	Sir G Dowty	7/4
1962	**Romulus**	W Swinburn	R F Johnson Houghton	C W Engelhard	9/4
1963	**Fighting Ship**	S Smith	J Jarvis	Lord Rosebery	15/2
1964	**Excel**	F Durr	T Gosling	L Sainer	8/1
1965	**Silly Season**	G Lewis	I Balding	P Mellon	100/30
1966	**No Race**				
1967	**Play High**	D Keith	W Nightingall	D W Molins	100/8
1968	**Heathen**	J Mercer	W R Hern	L B Holliday	10/1
1969	**Tower Walk**	M L Thomas	G Barling	V W Hardy	2/1
1970	**Gold Rod**	F Durr	R Akehurst	Mrs C A Dickson	2/1
1971	**Mill Reef**	G Lewis	I Balding	P Mellon	4/9
1972	**Martinmas**	P Waldron	I Balding	J Berry	12/1
1973	**Boldboy**	J Mercer	W R Hern	Lady Beaverbrook	16/1
1974	**Glen Strae**	A Murray	H R Price	K Maharaj	11/2
1975	**Mark Anthony**	L Piggott	C Brittain	M Lemos	11/2
1976	**Wollow**	G Dettori	H Cecil	C d'Alessio	10/11
1977	**He Loves Me**	A Kimberley	J Hindley	J Allbritton	14/1
1978	**Derrylin**	E Eldin	D Smith	Lady Sefton	4/1
1979	**Kris**	J Mercer	H Cecil	Lord H de Walden	11/10
1980	**Final Straw**	G Starkey	M Stoute	J Wigan	10/1
1981	**Another Realm**	G Starkey	F Durr	Mrs D Goldstein	5/1
1982	**Cajun**	L Piggott	H Cecil	J Stone	7/2
1983	**Wassl**	W Carson	J Dunlop	A Al-Maktoum	11/2

		Jockey	Trainer	Owner	Odds
1984	**Creag-an-Sgor**	J Mercer	C Nelson	Mrs W Tulloch	5/2
1985	**Bairn**	L Piggott	L Cumani	Sheikh Mohammed	11/10
1986	**Faustus**	S Cauthen	H Cecil	S Niarchos	5/1
1987	**Risk Me**	S Cauthen	P Kelleway	L H Norris	5/2
1988	**Zelphi**	P Eddery	J Tree	K Abdulla	9/2
1989	**Zayyani**	W Newnes	R F Johnson Houghton	HH Aga Khan	6/1
1990	**Rock City**	P Eddery	R Hannon	A F Budge Ltd	4/1
1991	**Bog Trotter**	L Piggott	W Haggas	B Haggas	4/1
1992	**Lion Cavern**	S Cauthen	A Fabre	Sheikh Mohammed	9/4

Run over 1 mile 1906-1940

The John Porter Stakes

Named after the founder of Newbury racecourse (see Greenham Stakes) the John Porter Stakes was inaugurated in 1928, six years after his death. The rather unhappily named *Ox and Ass* was the first winner from four opponents when the race was open to three-year-olds. Nowadays a contest for four-year-olds and upwards, there have been some notable winners in the post-war years including *Wilwyn* in 1953, previously the first victor from England 'across the herring pond' when he won the inaugural Washington International Stakes at Laurel Park.

Doutelle, owned by HM the Queen had the misfortune to be foaled into the same generation as *Crepello* and *Ballymoss,* but gained some compensation in the John Porter in 1958, going on to be a high class stallion before meeting with a fatal accident at the age of eight.

The 1960 winner *Aggressor* staked his chief claim to fame when defeating *Petite Etoile* in the King George VI and the Queen Elizabeth Stakes, on an occasion when Lester Piggott rode the most indifferent of more than a few indifferent races. *Charlottown,* the only Derby winner to triumph, succeeded in 1967 in a more sporting ownership than we would find nowadays when it is rare for winners of the premier classic to race into their fourth year.

Like *Doutelle, Meadowville* was unlucky enough to be a contemporary of a champion in the elegant form of *Nijinsky*. He gained compensation in the John Porter when the latter was contentedly cropping the blue grass of his stud in Kentucky. *Rock Roi,* who enjoyed the unenviable distinction of being disqualified from first place in two Ascot Gold Cups, had some consolation when winning the John Porter in 1972 and *Rheingold* made amends for a controversial and unlucky second in the Derby when taking the Prix de L'Arc de Triomphe in 1973.

Since then, although *Saddlers' Hall* went on to win the Coronation Cup in 1992, the list of winners has lacked some distinction and the race was downgraded from Group 2 to Group 3 in 1984.

The winner of the 1958 John Porter Stakes, HM The Queen's *Doutelle* with W.H.Carr up.

Run at Newbury over 1 mile 4 furlongs First Run 1928 Group 3

		Jockey	Trainer	Owner	Odds
1928	**Ox and Ass**	F Fox	L Cundell	G Drummond	7/2
1929	**Silver Hussar**	M Beary	R C Dawson	HH Aga Khan	100/30
1930	**Wedding Favour**	F Fox	D Waugh	Lord H de Walden	8/13
1931	**Birthday Book**	R Dick	J Lawson	Lord Astor	25/1
1932	**Corn Belt**	J Childs	C Boyd-Rochfort	M Field	9/2
1933	**Sarum**	B Carslake	N Scobie	Sir C Hyde	8/1
1934	**Felicitation**	G Richards	Frank Butters	HH Aga Khan	5/6
1935	**Night Owl**	C Richards	C Boyd-Rochfort	J H Whitney	7/2
1936	**St Botolph**	G Richards	G Digby	F W Dennis	20/1
1937	**Haulfryn**	G Richards	R Metcalfe	F Minoprio	7/4
1938	**Fair Copy**	R Perryman	C Leader	Lord Derby	2/9
1939/40	**No Race**				
1941	**Ruscus**	H Wragg	O Bell	Lord Londonderry	8/1
1942/48	**No Race**				
1949	**Solar Slipper**	E Smith	W Stephenson	J McGrath	4/6
1950	**Native Heath**	A Breasley	V Smyth	Sir M McAlpine	3/1
1951	**No Race**				
1952	**Neron**	E Mercer	H Wragg	Begum Aga Khan	7/2
1953	**Wilwyn**	E Mercer	G Colling	R C Boucher	7/4
1954	**Harwin**	W H Carr	J Dines	T Robinson	11/8
1955	**Entente Cordiale**	D Smith	G Colling	Lord Derby	5/4
1956	**Acropolis**	D Smith	G Colling	Lady Derby	2/7
1957	**China Rock**	F Durr	H Blagrave	H Blagrave	100/6
1958	**Doutelle**	W H Carr	C Boyd-Rochfort	HM The Queen	5/6
1959	**Cutter**	J Lindley	J Oxley	R D Hollingsworth	11/8
1960	**Aggressor**	J Lindley	J M Gosden	Sir H Wernher	11/8
1961	**High Perch**	J Lindley	J M Gosden	H Allen	6/4
1962	**Hot Brandy**	D Keith	W Nightingall	A Kennedy	4/1
1963	**Peter Jones**	E Smith	A Budgett	P Wright	4/1
1964	**Royal Avenue**	L Piggott	N Murless	C St George	100/8
1965	**Soderini**	G Lewis	S Ingham	L Lawrence	4/1
1966	**No Race**				
1967	**Charlottown**	J Lindley	G Smyth	Lady Z Wernher	4/6
1968	**Fortissimo**	G Lewis	R Fetherstonhaugh	V McCalmont	3/1
1969	**Crozier**	D Keith	P Walwyn	A D G Oldrey	15/8
1970	**Torpid**	B Taylor	J Oxley	R D Hollingsworth	6/1
1971	**Meadowville**	F Durr	M Jarvis	D Robinson	11/8
1972	**Rock Roi**	D Keith	P Walwyn	F Hue-Williams	6/4
1973	**Rheingold**	Y Saint-Martin	B Hills	H Zeisel	10/11
1974	**Freefoot**	L Piggott	H Wragg	R B Moller	13/2
1975	**Salado**	W Carson	P Mitchell	Mrs P Isaacs	33/1
1976	**Quiet Fling**	L Piggott	J Tree	J H Whitney	5/1
1977	**Decent Fellow**	L Piggott	G Balding	W Gilbride	4/1
1978	**Orchestra**	R Carroll	J Oxx	Lord Donoughmore	6/1
1979	**Icelandic**	C Roche	P Prendergast	P Prendergast	11/1
1980	**Niniski**	W Carson	W R Hern	Lady Beaverbrook	2/1
1981	**Pelerin**	B Taylor	H Wragg	Sir P Oppenheimer	16/1
1982	**Glint of Gold**	J Matthias	I Balding	P Mellon	7/2
1983	**Diamond Shoal**	S Cauthen	I Balding	P Mellon	7/2
1984	**Gay Lemur**	G Baxter	B Hobbs	Lady E Rosebery	20/1
1985	**Jupiter Island**	G Starkey	C Brittain	S Threadwell	11/2
1986	**Lemhill**	R Cochrane	M Blanshard	S Hinton	15/2
1987	**Rakaposhi King**	S Cauthen	H Cecil	Lord H de Walden	13/2
1988	**Alwasmi**	R Hills	H Thomson Jones	H Al-Maktoum	25/1
1989	**Unfuwain**	W Carson	W R Hern	H Al-Maktoum	4/9
1990	**Brush Aside**	S Cauthen	H Cecil	Sheikh Mohammed	9/2
1991	**Rock Hopper**	P Eddery	M Stoute	M Al-Maktoum	3/1
1992	**Saddler's Hall**	P Eddery	M Stoute	Lord Weinstock	9/4

Run over 1 mile 5 furlongs 1928-1935 and 1941 and 1 mile 2 furlongs 1936-1938

The Nell Gwyn Stakes

The Nell Gwyn Stakes, named after Charles II's favourite mistress and certainly the most famous, was not founded until 1962. Since then, the race has proved a decent pointer to the One Thousand Guineas, throwing up *One In a Million* (1979), *Fairy Footsteps* (1981), *Pebbles* (1984) and *Oh So Sharp* (1985) who also took the Oaks and the St Leger. Latterly, perhaps because of changing climatic conditions in East Anglia, the race has gone to more precocious animals who have subsequently failed in the classics.

Run at Newmarket over 7 furlongs for 3 year-old fillies First Run 1961 Group 3

		Jockey	Trainer	Owner	Odds
1961	**Verbena**	D Smith	G Brooke	D McCalmont	6/1
1962	**West Side Story**	E Smith	T E Leader	H J Joel	5/4
1963	**Amicable**	W H Carr	C Boyd-Rochfort	HM The Queen	100/7
1964	**Alborada**	G Starkey	J Oxley	Lady Halifax	9/4
1965	**Gently**	A Breasley	G Richards	W Hill	7/4
1966	**Hiding Place**	A Breasley	J Clayton	Lord Porchester	4/1
1967	**Cranberry Sauce**	G Moore	N Murless	J Hornung	7/4
1968	**Abbie West**	A Barclay	N Murless	Lady Sassoon	10/11
1969	**Anchor**	G Starkey	J Oxley	R D Hollingsworth	7/4
1970	**Obelisk**	A Barclay	N Murless	F Hue-Williams	6/1
1971	**Super Honey**	L Piggott	H R Price	Mrs M Slade	3/1
1972	**Carezza**	W Carson	B van Cutsem	Mrs J Olin	4/5
1973	**Caspian**	G Starkey	H Cecil	Mrs J Haines	4/7
1974	**Angels Two**	E Hide	W Elsey	J Cassar	11/1
1975	**Rose Bowl**	L Piggott	R F Johnson Houghton	Mrs C W Engelhard	7/4
1976	**Flying Water**	Y Saint-Martin	A Penna	D Wildenstein	15/8
1977	**Freeze the Secret**	G Dettori	L Cumani	L Gatto-Roissard	11/2
1978	**Seraphima**	P Eddery	P Walwyn	Mrs V Hue-Williams	9/2
1979	**One in a Million**	J Mercer	H Cecil	Helena Springfield Ltd	8/13
1980	**Evita**	J Mercer	H Cecil	Lord H de Walden	7/2
1981	**Fairy Footseps**	L Piggott	H Cecil	H J Joel	4/6
1982	**Chalon**	L Piggott	H Cecil	M Riordan	8/1
1983	**Favoridge**	P Eddery	G Wragg	E B Moller	13/8
1984	**Pebbles**	P Robinson	C Brittain	M Lemos	7/1
1985	**Oh So Sharp**	S Cauthen	H Cecil	Sheikh Mohammed	8/13
1986	**Sonic Lady**	W R Swinburn	M Stoute	Sheikh Mohmamed	13/8
1987	**Martha Stevens**	S Cauthen	H Cecil	Mrs P W Harris	4/1
1988	**Ghariba**	M Roberts	A Stewart	M Salem	11/2
1989	**Ensconce**	R Cochrane	L Cumani	Sheikh Mohammed	2/1
1990	**Heart of Joy**	W R Swinburn	M Stoute	J C Mabee	5/6
1991	**Crystal Gazing**	L Dettori	L Cumani	Mrs A L Chapman	6/4
1992	**A-To-Z**	M Hills	M Bell	B Cooper	8/1

The Earl of Sefton Stakes

Named after the 7th Earl, Senior Steward of the Jockey Club during the last War and the last of the line of the Molyneux family who were associated with Aintree for over 800 years (the 2nd and 3rd Earls were largely instrumental in laying out the Grand National course), the Earl of Sefton Stakes was founded in 1971.

The race has always attracted moderately sized but high class fields. The inaugural winner was *Pembroke Castle*, owned appropriately enough by Jim Joel, another stalwart of the Jockey Club. The following year *Pembroke Castle* finished second to *Lord David* and other notable winners include *Ela-Mana-Mou, Scottish Rifle, Gunner B* and *Kalaglow*, all subsequent winners of the Eclipse Stakes, and *Hawaiian Sound*, second in the 1978 Derby and perhaps a little unlucky.

Run at Newmarket over 1 mile 1 furlong First Run 1971 Group 3

		Jockey	Trainer	Owner	Odds
1971	**Pembroke Castle**	G Lewis	N Murless	H J Joel	7/2
1972	**Lord David**	L Piggott	S Ingham	G Marks	4/7
1973	**Scottish Rifle**	R Hutchinson	J Dunlop	A J Struthers	10/1
1974	**Owen Dudley**	G Lewis	N Murless	L Freedman	100/30
1975	**Jimsun**	J Mercer	H Jones	H Jones	6/1
1976	**Chil the Kite**	G Lewis	B Hobbs	Lady E Rosebery	7/2
1977	**Heaven Knows**	B Taylor	R Smyth	G Pritchard-Gordon	33/1
1978	**Gunner B**	J Mercer	H Cecil	Mrs P Barratt	7/2
1979	**Hawaiian Sound**	S Cauthen	H Cecil	R Sangster	5/4
1980	**Ela-Mana-Mou**	W Carson	W R Hern	S Weinstock	8/11
1981	**Hard Fought**	W R Swinburn	M Stoute	L B Holliday	9/2
1982	**Kalaglow**	G Starkey	G Harwood	A Ward	4/1
1983	**Ivano**	L Piggott	H Cecil	C d'Alessio	7/1
1984	**Legend of France**	J Mercer	H Cecil	D Wildenstein	4/1
1985	**King of Clubs**	P Eddery	I Balding	P Mellon	4/1
1986	**Supreme Leader**	P Robinson	C Brittain	M Lemos	7/2
1987	**K-Battery**	P Eddery	C Elsey	Mrs M C Butler	8/1
1988	**Media Starguest**	R Cochrane	L Cumani	R Duchossois	7/4
1989	**Reprimand**	S Cauthen	H Cecil	Sheikh Mohammed	9/2
1990	**Terimon**	R Cochrane	C Brittain	Lady Beaverbrook	20/1
1991	**Terimon**	M Roberts	C Brittain	Lady Beaverbrook	7/2
1992	**Sure Sharp**	S Cauthen	B Hills	Sheikh Mohammed	9/1

Run as the Rubbing House Stakes 1971-1972

Ridden by Greville Starkey, *Dancing Brave* won the 1986 Craven Stakes.

The Craven Stakes

The oldest of the Two Thousand Guineas trials, the inaugural winner of the Craven, *Thurio,* was owned by Prince Dimitri Soltykoff, a Russian who came to England after the Crimean War in 1856 and set up a private training establishment in Newmarket inevitably named Kremlin House. *Thurio* didn't go on to classic success, but the 1898 winner *Jeddah* won the Derby of that year at 100/1.

The winner in 1919, *Buchan* was one of the unluckiest horses ever in training. After his Craven victory, he was second in the Guineas by a neck and beaten by half a length in the Derby after a poor ride by J.J.Brennan and third in the St Leger. He won the Ascot Gold Cup only to be disqualified but gained compensation by winning the Eclipse twice.

Colombo went on to take the Guineas in 1934, only to lose the Derby due to pilot error. *My Babu* won the Guineas in 1948, but it was not until *Shadeed* in 1985 that the double was completed again, followed in recent years by *Dancing Brave, Doyoun* and *Tirol.*

Run at Newmarket over 1 mile for 3 year-old colts & geldings First Run 1878 Group 3

		Jockey	Trainer	Owner	Odds
1878	**Thurio**	E Rossiter	C Blanton	Prince Soltykoff	7/4
1879	**Discord**	C Wood	T Brown	R R Christopher	2/5
1880	**Fernandez**	C Morbey	J Porter	F Gretton	15/1
1881	**Cameliard**	T Cannon	J Cannon	Lord Rosebery	100/30
1882	**Laureate**	G Fordham	W Goater	W G Craven	7/2
1883	**Grandmaster**	F Archer	M Dawson	Lord Falmouth	2/1
1884	**Scot-free**	J Osborne Jnr	T Chaloner	J Foy	13/2
1885	**Esterling**	F Archer	M Dawson	R C Vyner	4/6
1886	**Grey Friars**	J Watts	J Enoch	Lord Zetland	3/1
1887	**The Baron**	F Webb	M Dawson	Mr Fern	4/9
1888	**Orbit**	T Cannon	J Porter	Duke of Westminster	21/10
1889	**Gay Hampton**	G Barrett	J Porter	W Low	100/12
1890	**Morion**	J Watts	R Marsh	Lord Hartington	9/2
1891	**Friar Lubin**	J Watts	J Enoch	Lord Zetland	75/20
1892	**The Lover**	G Barrett	G Blackwell	W Cooper	11/4
1893	**Harbinger**	M Cannon	J Ryan	D Baird	4/1
1894	**Sempronius**	M Cannon	J Ryan	D Baird	3/1
1895	**The Owl**	J Watts	Jos Day	Sir J Blundell Maple	5/4
1896	**Lord Hervey**	W Bradford	John Dawson Jnr	Lord Ilchester	100/12
1897	**Guernsey**	M Cannon	J Porter	Duke of Westminster	9/2

		Jockey	Trainer	Owner	Odds
1898	**Jeddah**	O Madden	R Marsh	J W Larnach	2/1
1899	**Solennis**	M Cannon	H Braime	F Alexander	2/5
1900	**Headpiece**	S Loates	John Dawson Jnr	Lord Ellesmere	5/1
1901	**Rigo**	O Madden	J Waugh	Mr Russel	3/1
1902	**Port Blair**	M Cannon	S Darling	J Gubbins	11/8
1903	**Countermark**	W Lane	R Day	Sir E Vincent	5/2
1904	**Airlie**	H Aylin	G Lambton	Lord Farquhar	7/1
1905	**St Oswald**	W Halsey	J Porter	Duke of Portland	100/12
1906	**His Eminence**	M Cannon	C Beatty	Lord H de Walden	100/30
1907	**Slieve Gallion**	W Higgs	S Darling	J H Greer	Evens
1908	**No Race**				
1909	**Howick**	W Halsey	H Braime	F Alexander	10/1
1910	**Neil Gow**	D Maher	P Peck	Lord Rosebery	4/6
1911	**Irish King**	D Maher	S Pickering	P Nelke	6/1
1912	**Jingling Geordie**	F Wootton	S Darling	J Buchanan	2/1
1913	**Sanquhar**	D Maher	P Peck	Lord Rosebery	6/4
1914	**Kennymore**	F O'Neill	A Taylor Jnr	Sir J Thursby	1/2
1915	**Rossendale**	J Clark	A T Hazleton	Sir J Thursby	10/1
1916	**Sir Dighton**	H Jones	R Marsh	HM The King	5/2
	Roi d'Ecosse	F Rickaby	H S Persse	D McCalmont	5/1
1917	**Dansellon**	R Watson	H S Persse	Sir H Meux	4/1
1918	**Benevente**	J Evans	R H Dewhurst	Lord Londonderry	5/2
1919	**Buchan**	J Brennan	A Taylor Jnr	W Astor	5/2
1920	**Daylight Patrol**	A Whalley	J Watson	A de Rothschild	5/2
1921	**No Race**				
1922	**Collaborator**	C Elliott	J Jarvis	Sir W Cooke	10/1
1923	**Light Hand**	F Bullock	A Taylor Jnr	Lord Astor	7/2
1924	**St Germans**	F Bullock	A Taylor Jnr	Lord Astor	100/30
1925	**Picaroon**	F Bullock	A Taylor Jnr	A R Cox	2/5
1926	**Harpagon**	C Elliott	J Jarvis	Sir G Bullough	3/1
1927	**Tattoo**	R Perryman	J Watson	A de Rothschild	100/6
1928	**Royal Minstrel**	J Childs	C Boyd-Rochfort	G P Gough	9/4
1929	**Cragadour**	R Perryman	R C Dawson	Lord Astor	10/11
1930	**Writ**	R Dick	J Lawson	Lord Astor	4/1
1931	**Philae**	T Weston	Lord G Dundas	Mrs L G Barbrook	100/8
1932	**Loaningdale**	J Childs	C Boyd-Rochfort	Lady Nunburnholme	Evens
1933	**Lochiel**	G Richards	F Darling	J A Dewar	7/4
1934	**Colombo**	W R Johnstone	T Hogg	Lord Glanely	30/100
1935	**Buckleigh**	G Richards	T Hogg	Lord Glanely	20/1
1936	**Monument**	P Beasley	C Boyd-Rochfort	Duke of Marlborough	11/2
1937	**Snowfall**	R Perryman	C Leader	Lord Derby	13/8
1938	**Challenge**	E Smith	J Jarvis	Sir L Phillips	3/1
1939	**Signal Light**	P Beasley	C Boyd-Rochfort	Mrs J Corrigan	8/1
1940	**Prince Tetra**	A Wragg	F Templeman	Lord Hirst	100/6
1941	**Morogoro**	H Wragg	F Darling	Maharani of Kolhapur	20/1
1942/45	**No Race**				
1946	**Gulf Stream**	H Wragg	W Earl	Lord Derby	1/8
1947	**Migoli**	D Smith	Frank Butters	HH Aga Khan	4/11
1948	**My Babu**	C Smirke	F Armstrong	Maharaja of Baroda	4/7
1949	**Moondust**	D Smith	Frank Butters	HH Aga Khan	7/1
1950	**Rising Flame**	G Littlewood	C Elsey	Lord Allendale	100/30
1951	**Claudius**	D Page	R Warden	Lady Fitzwilliam	20/1
1952	**Kara Tepe**	E Mercer	G Colling	F G Robinson	6/1
1953	**Oleandrin**	G Richards	H Leader	S Niarchos	4/1
1954	**Ambler II**	W H Carr	C Boyd-Rochfort	W Woodward Jnr	6/1
1955	**True Cavalier**	R Fawdon	H Leader	S Niarchos	8/1
1956	**Pirate King**	W Snaith	H Cottrill	Maj L B Holliday	100/8
1957	**Shearwater**	L Piggott	N Murless	G Loder	10/1
1958	**Bald Eagle**	W H Carr	C Boyd-Rochfort	H Guggenheim	7/2
1959	**Pindari**	L Piggott	N Murless	HM The Queen	6/1
1960	**Tudorich**	A Breasley	G Richards	T Lawley	11/4
1961	**Aurelius**	L Piggott	N Murless	Mrs V Lilley	8/1
1962	**High Noon**	E Hide	W Elsey	C Vyner	5/2
1963	**Crocket**	D Smith	G Brooke	D van Clief	4/11
1964	**Young Christopher**	R Sheather	F Maxwell	J McShane	100/7
1965	**Corifi**	G Lewis	S Ingham	Mrs S Jacobson	20/1
1966	**Salvo**	F Durr	H Wragg	G A Oldham	3/1
1967	**Sloop**	G Starkey	J Oxley	R D Hollingsworth	7/1
1968	**Petingo**	J Mercer	F Armstrong	M Lemos	2/5
1969	**Paddy's Progress**	A Barclay	N Murless	H J Joel	13/2
1970	**Tamil**	W Carson	B van Cutsem	Lord Derby	11/10
1971	**Levanter**	A Murray	H R Price	H Vickery	9/2
1972	**Leicester**	G Lewis	N Murless	H J Joel	8/1
1973	**My Drifter**	E Eldin	J Sutcliffe Jnr	R Watson	25/1
1974	**Numa**	P Eddery	P Walwyn	Mrs F Glazebrook	9/4
1975	**No Alimony**	P Eddery	P Walwyn	L Freedman	6/5

		Jockey	Trainer	Owner	Odds
1976	**Malinowski**	L Piggott	M V O'Brien	C St George	8/15
1977	**Limone**	G Starkey	G Harwood	D Allen	10/1
1978	**Admiral's Launch**	W Carson	W R Hern	R D Hollinsworth	2/1
1979	**Lyphard's Wish**	J Mercer	H Cecil	C d'Alessio	11/2
1980	**Tyrnavos**	E Hide	B Hobbs	G Cambanis	5/1
1981	**Kind of Hush**	S Cauthen	B Hills	A Shead	25/1
1982	**Silver Hawk**	A Murray	M Albina	M Fustok	11/2
1983	**Muscatite**	B Taylor	J Hindley	K Al-Said	7/2
1984	**Lear Fan**	G Starkey	G Harwood	A Salman	5/6
1985	**Shadeed**	W R Swinburn	M Stoute	M Al-Maktoum	9/4
1986	**Dancing Brave**	G Starkey	G Harwood	K Abdulla	11/8
1987	**Ajdal**	W R Swinburn	M Stoute	Sheikh Mohammed	6/5
1988	**Doyoun**	W R Swinburn	M Stoute	HH Aga Khan	100/30
1989	**Shaadi**	W R Swinburn	M Stoute	Sheikh Mohammed	5/2
1990	**Tirol**	P Eddery	R Hannon	John Horgan	9/2
1991	**Marju**	W Carson	J Dunlop	H Al-Maktoum	11/2
1992	**Alnasr Alwasheek**	S Cauthen	M Stoute	A Al-Maktoum	5/1

The Forte Mile

Founded in 1985 to fill a gap in the European Pattern, the Forte Mile became an immediate success when the brilliant filly *Pebbles* won the inaugural race. Arguably the best of her sex since the heady days of *Sceptre* and *Pretty Polly*, *Pebbles* won the 1,000 Guineas, became the first filly to win the Eclipse Stakes, going on to take the Champion Stakes and the Breeders' Cup Turf race in New York.

Soviet Star was a spectacular winner for France in 1988, and in 1991 *In The Groove* supplemented her three-year-old successes in the Irish 1,000 Guineas, the Juddmonte International and the Champion Stakes.

Run at Sandown Park over 1 mile First Run 1985 Group 2

		Jockey	Trainer	Owner	Odds
1985	**Pebbles**	S Cauthen	C Brittain	Sheikh Mohammed	11/8
1986	**Field Hand**	B Thomson	B Hills	R Sangster	11/2
1987	**Vertige**	A Cruz	P-L Biancone	D Wildenstein	8/1
1988	**Soviet Star**	C Asmussen	A Fabre	Sheikh Mohammed	5/4
1989	**Reprimand**	S Cauthen	H Cecil	Sheikh Mohammed	7/4
1990	**Markofdistinction**	L Dettori	L Cumani	G Leigh	9/2
1991	**In The Groove**	S Cauthen	D Elsworth	B Cooper	15/8
1992	**Rudimentary**	S Cauthen	H Cecil	Lord H de Walden	2/1

Run as the TrustHouse Forte Mile 1985-1991

The Gordon Richards Stakes

When the late Sir Gordon Richards received his knighthood in 1953 he became the first and so far the only professional rider to be so honoured.

Richards rode his first winner at Leicester in 1921. Some 4,869 victories later his career came to an end when he was thrown leaving the paddock at Sandown in 1954. Perhaps the greatest of the three leading jockeys of the twentieth century, Richards may have lacked the flamboyance of Steve Donoghue and the aggression of Lester Piggott, but his skill, dedication and above all his integrity and loyalty to his patrons made him champion jockey twenty-six times.

When Sir Gordon died in 1986, it was decided to rename the Westbury Stakes, founded in 1964, in his honour. Some fine horses have won, including *Connaught*, second in the Derby and winner of the Eclipse, *Brigadier Gerard* and *Hot Grove* defeated in the Derby by a neck by *The Minstrel*. The best winner since 1987 has been that fine racemare *Indian Skimmer*.

Gordon Richards, the 1948 champion jockey, meets two filmakers to discuss a movie of his life.

Left: Gordon Richards, wearing the colours of King George VI, after a race at Hurst Park in April 1949. *Right:* Now Sir Gordon Richards, the legendary jockey was a nostalgic visitor when Hurst Park closed in October 1962.

Run at Sandown Park over 1 mile 2 furlongs First Run 1963 Group 3

		Jockey	Trainer	Owner	Odds
1963	**Miralgo**	W Williamson	H Wragg	G A Oldham	7/2
1964	**Tacitus**	D Keith	W Nightingall	D W Molins	11/8
1965	**Goupi**	G Lewis	S Ingham	H Wingate	2/1
1966	**Super Sam**	B Taylor	J F Watts	G Cooper	8/13
1967	**Chinwag**	A Barclay	A Budgett	R Richardson-Watson	5/2
1968	**Sidon**	L Piggott	G Richards	Mrs D B Brewster	4/6
1969	**Remand**	J Mercer	W R Hern	J J Astor	6/4
1970	**Connaught**	A Barclay	N Murless	H J Joel	1/2
1971	**Arthur**	R Hutchinson	J Dunlop	Lady E Rosebery	3/1
1972	**Brigadier Gerard**	J Mercer	W R Hern	Mrs J Hislop	4/11
1973	**Scottish Rifle**	R Hutchinson	J Dunlop	A J Struthers	8/11
1974	**Funny Fellow**	G Lewis	H Wragg	R B Moller	3/1
	Tudor Rhythm	P Eddery	P Walwyn	Mrs D McCalmont	4/1
1975	**Never Return**	L Piggott	R Armstrong	Mrs T Hardin	9/4
1976	**Jolly Good**	G Lewis	B Hobbs	Mrs J Bricken	8/1
1977	**Lucky Wednesday**	J Mercer	H Cecil	C St George	9/2
1978	**Hot Grove**	W Carson	R F Johnson Houghton	Lord Leverhulme	7/4
1979	**Sexton Blake**	S Cauthen	B Hills	T Motley	7/2
1980	**Gregorian**	L Piggott	M V O'Brien	D Schwartz	11/4
1981	**Hard Fought**	W R Swinburn	M Stoute	L B Holliday	9/4
1982	**Princes Gate**	G Starkey	H Thomson Jones	H Al-Maktoum	10/1
1983	**Ivano**	L Piggott	H Cecil	C d'Alessio	4/6
1984	**Morcon**	W Carson	W R Hern	Lord Rotherwick	6/1
1985	**Elegant Air**	J Matthias	I Balding	P Mellon	8/1
1986	**Supreme Leader**	P Robinson	C Brittain	M Lemos	1/2
1987	**Allez Milord**	G Starkey	G Harwood	J Brody	15/8
1988	**Infamy**	R Cochrane	L Cumani	G Leigh	5/1
1989	**Indian Skimmer**	S Cauthen	H Cecil	Sheikh Mohammed	8/15
1990	**Dolpour**	W R Swinburn	M Stoute	HH Aga Khan	5/2
1991	**Noble Patriarch**	J Reid	J Dunlop	P S Winfield	7/1
1992	**Dear Doctor**	C Asmussen	J Hammond	H Chalhoub	6/1

Run as the Westbury Stakes 1963-1986

The Thresher Classic Trial Stakes

In our introduction to the Juddmonte International Stakes, we discuss two ways of becoming a sponsor, namely to take an existing race and add your name to it, or to found your own. The third method and the least attractive, is to take an existing race, chuck away the time-honoured title and parade the event as your own.

Despite these commerical ducks and drakes, the race formerly the Royal Stakes and until 1990 The Guardian Classic Trial has produced four Derby winners since 1979 including *Troy, Henbit, Shergar* and *Shahrastani.* The 1989 winner *Old Vic* won the Prix du Jockey Club and the Irish Derby.

Run at Sandown Park over 1 mile 2 furlongs for 3 year-old c & f First Run 1953 Group 3

		Jockey	Trainer	Owner	Odds
1953	**Mountain King**	E Smith	J A Waugh	J E Ferguson	8/1
1954	**Taw Valley**	E Smith	G Barling	Mrs J A P Martin	20/1
1955	**Peter Aegus**	W Rickaby	J Jarvis	J P Phillips	10/1
1956	**Pearl Orama**	A Breasley	S Ingham	Mrs S Jacobson	8/1
1957	**Sun Charger**	L Piggott	N Murless	B Hornung	7/1
1958	**Snow Cat**	L Piggott	N Murless	HM The Queen	11/2
1959	**Casque**	A Breasley	H Blagrave	H Blagrave	20/1
1960	**Marengo**	R Fawdon	M Marsh	H P Holt	6/1
1961	**Just Great**	G Lewis	S Ingham	Miss H Jacobson	7/2
1962	**Ferneley**	L Piggott	N Murless	G Loder	4/1
1963	**Raise You Ten**	W H Carr	C Boyd-Rochfort	P Widener	100/8
1964	**Oncidium**	E Smith	J A Waugh	Lord H de Walden	7/2
1965	**Nearside**	J Mercer	W R Hern	Lord Astor	11/8
1966	**Mehari**	D Smith	J Winter	D Prenn	10/1
1967	**Sun Rock**	L Piggott	N Murless	Mrs V Hue-Williams	9/4
1968	**Safety Match**	G Starkey	J Oxley	Lady Halifax	100/8
1969	**Shoemaker**	D Keith	P Walwyn	P Goulandris	11/2
1970	**Cry Baby**	A Barclay	N Murless	Lady Sassoon	9/1
1971	**L'Apache**	A Murray	T Gosling	S Threadwell	33/1
1972	**Pentland Firth**	P Eddery	G Barling	V W Hardy	5/2
1973	**Ksar**	W Carson	B van Cutsem	Lady Rotherwick	8/15
1974	**Bustino**	J Mercer	W R He	Lady Beaverbrook	5/2
1975	**Consol**	P Eddery	P Walwyn	A D G Oldrey	10/11
1976	**Riboboy**	J Mercer	W R Hern	Lady Beaverbrook	9/2
1977	**Artaius**	L Piggott	M V O'Brien	Mrs G Getty II	Evens
1978	**Whitstead**	B Taylor	H R Price	H Demetriou	9/2
1979	**Troy**	W Carson	W R Hern	Sir M Sobell	4/7
1980	**Henbit**	W Carson	W R Hern	Mrs A Plesch	9/4
1981	**Shergar**	W R Swinburn	M Stoute	HH Aga Khan	Evens
1982	**Peacetime**	P Eddery	J Tree	Beckhampton Ltd	9/2
1983	**Gordian**	G Starkey	G Harwood	S Niarchos	10/1
1984	**Alphabatim**	B Rouse	G Harwood	K Abdulla	4/1
1985	**Damister**	S Cauthen	J Tree	K Abdulla	10/11
1986	**Shahrastani**	W R Swimburn	M Stoute	HH Aga Khan	2/1
1987	**Gulf King**	P Cook	P Kelleway	Roldvale Ltd	25/1
1988	**Galitzin**	R Cochrane	C Brittain	C Elliot	11/2
1989	**Old Vic**	S Cauthen	H Cecil	Sheikh Mohammed	4/9
1990	**Defensive Play**	P Eddery	G Harwood	K Abdulla	7/4
1991	**Hailsham**	M Roberts	C Brittain	Sheikh Mohammed	3/1
1992	**Pollen Count**	S Cauthen	J Gosden	Sheikh Mohammed	5/1

Run as the Royal Stakes 1953-1970, the Ladbroke Classic Trial 1971-1973, the Classic Trial Stakes 1974-1980, the Guardian Classic Trial 1981-1990.

The Sagaro Stakes

Although founded when he was still alive, the Sagaro Stakes now serves to commemorate the finest stayer of his generation. Trained in France by Francois Boutin, his career record included three Ascot Gold Cups, the Grand Prix de Paris and the Prix du Cadran. When he completed his hat-trick at Ascot, ridden each time by Lester Piggott, he was purchased by the Horserace Betting Levy Board for £175,000 and retired to the National Stud at Newmarket, at the nomination fee of a paltry £700.

Sadly, the prejudice against staying blood narrowed his stallion career, the best of his crops being *Super Sunrise,* winner of the Chester Vase in 1982 and the 1983 Cambridgeshire winner *Sagamore. Sagaro* died in 1986.

The inaugural running of the Sagaro Stakes in 1983 had to be abandoned when the Ascot course became waterlogged, but the following year was won by the Ascot Gold Cup winner *Gildoran. Gildoran* also took the Gold Cup in 1985, after losing the Sagaro to *Longboat,* who in turn won the Gold Cup in 1986. The best winner of the Sagaro Stakes since then is probably *Sadeem,* awarded the Gold Cup in 1988 on the disqualification of *Royal Gait,* but a clear cut victor in his own right in 1989.

***Left:* Lester Piggott rides *Sagaro* to an easy victory in the 1975 Ascot Gold Cup. *Right:* Owner Mr G.A.Oldham proudly congratulates *Sagaro* after his Gold Cup triumph.**

Run at Ascot over 2 miles First Run 1978 Group 3

		Jockey	Trainer	Owner	Odds
1978	**Shangamuzo**	G Starkey	M Stoute	Mrs E Charles	12/1
1979	**Nicholas Bill**	P Waldron	H Candy	W Barnett	5/2
1980	**Pragmatic**	J Reid	R F Johnson Houghton	J Rowles	9/2
1981	**Nicholas Bill**	P Waldron	H Candy	R Barnett	Evens
1982	**Castelnau**	P Eddery	P Cole	Doublet Ltd	20/1
1983	**No Race**				
1984	**Gildoran**	S Cauthen	B Hills	R Sangster	11/2
1985	**Longboat**	W Carson	W R Hern	R D Hollingsworth	10/1
1986	**Valuable Witness**	P Eddery	J Tree	S Niarchos	10/11
1987	**Sadeem**	G Starkey	G Harwood	Sheikh Mohammed	100/30
1988	**Sergeyevich**	W Carson	J Dunlop	Mrs D Riley-Smith	7/1
1989	**Travel Mystery**	R Cochrane	M Pipe	Mrs J H Johnson	9/1
1990	**Teamster**	P Eddery	M Stoute	P Newton	7/2
1991	**Teamster**	P Eddery	M Stoute	P Newton	5/1
1992	**Al Mutahm**	L Dettori	J Old	W E Sturt	33/1

The Two Thousand Guineas & One Thousand Guineas

The turn of the century saw the three classic races, the Derby, Oaks and the St Leger firmly set in the Calendar as the top events in England with the exception of the long established Cup races.

The Jockey Club under the direction of the Steward, Sir Charles Bunbury decided to introduce two more races, both over one mile, one for three-year-old colts the other for fillies, although as with the Derby and St Leger, fillies could take part in the colts' contest. They were to be run at Newmarket.

The idea was to form what we would now call a pattern. Taking the age of three as the ideal time to test the championship potential of the thoroughbred, horses of both sexes were now asked to win over a mile in the late spring, a mile and a half in mid-summer and two miles in early September.

As the scheme developed, the latter distance was considered too far and the St Leger was reduced to a mile and three-quarters in 1813, following the founding of the Two Thousand Guineas in 1809.

The name of the race derived quite simply from the prize, 2,000 guineas was in effect a guaranteed sweepstake, irrespective of the number of subscribers. The inaugural running was won by *Wizard* in 1809, owned by the Yorkshire sportsman Christopher Wilson and ridden by Bill Clift. Five years later, the couple completed a unique double when Wilson's *Charlotte* won the first One Thousand Guineas with Clift once more in the plate.

Bill Clift was also a man from the Ridings, but from the opposite end of the social scale. Clift started life as a shepherd boy on the estate of Lord Rockingham and gained early experience riding in pony races organised to amuse the latter's house guests at the Marquis's home, Wentworth Woodhouse. Rockingham was impressed by his untutored skills and sent him to join his private stable, which was shortly to move to

Newmarket under the direction of the Marquis's trainer Christopher Scaife. Clift was not a polished rider, but he more than compensated for this deficiency with a severe use of the whip which would not be tolerated today.

By contrast, 'Kit' Wilson was described by James Rice in his 'History of the British Turf' as 'An English gentleman of the old school, keeping up the old customs and liberally dispensing hospitality at his residence at Oxton House, near Tadcaster'. Apart from his two Guineas winners, he also won the Derby and the St Leger in 1800 with *Champion.*

The new pattern did much to improve the speed of the breed, by the concentration on younger horses racing over shorter distances. Two-year-old racing had been well established by the time the July Stakes came into being in 1786, and at one time Newmarket boasted a yearling course of two furlongs and 147 yards, but this idea proved unpopular and the racing of yearlings was officially banned by the Jockey Club in 1859.

The Two Thousand was quickly recognised as the best 'trial' for the Derby. The first to complete the double was *Smolensko* in 1813, owned appropriately enough by Sir Charles Bunbury. It was Bunbury's last classic winner, but when he died in 1821 his work was well done. During the period of his administration, he had overseen the establishment of a classic pattern which would be copied in every corner of the racing world.

Since *Smolensko,* thirty-three horses have completed the Two Thousand Guineas-Derby double, and fifteen have gone on to take the St Leger and complete the Triple Crown named after the regal headgear of King Lear.

It used to be said that a winner-finding formula was 'fourth in the Guineas, first in the Derby'. The last to fit the pattern was *Generous* in 1991.

The One Thousand Guineas has produced only one filly capable of winning the Derby as well, when *Tagalie* won in 1912, but it has to be remembered

Frank Bullock (*above*) rode *Sauncy Sue* to victory in the 1925 One Thousand Guineas. Brownie Carslake (*below*) was aboard *Ferry* in 1918 and *Silver Urn* in 1922.

that even then few of her sex took on the colts at Epsom. An easier and more natural option was the Oaks, and fourty-five of the distaff side have succeeded at both Newmarket and on the downs, the first being *Neva* in 1817 and the latest *Salsabil* in 1990.

As always, there has been the odd whiff of scandal and concern. In 1864, Count Frederic de Lagrange's filly *Fille de l'Air* started 5/2 favourite for the Two Thousand Guineas but finished last, which was more than a little disappointing as she had won the Woodcote Stakes at Epsom, the Molecomb at Goodwood and the Criterion at Newmarket during a two-year-old career which had netted nine wins in all.

Her jockey Arthur Edwards did not enjoy a high reputation for integrity and the view of the racegoers who were convinced that she had not been allowed to run on her merits was enhanced by the comments of the correspondent of 'The Standard' who asserted 'I think a grosser robbery was never perpetrated on the Turf'.

Fillie de l'Air's subsequent victory in the Oaks resulted in the Count and Edwards having to be escorted from the course while the Filly's trainer Tom Jennings snr locked himself in a lavatory below the grandstand for the rest of the afternoon.

More recently, *Ribofilio's* abject failure when starting 15/8 favourite for the Two Thousand in 1969, when he was tailed off and eased to a canter in the final two furlongs, caused many to believe the colt had been nobbled, although dope tests proved negative and no explanation was ever forthcoming.

On a brighter note, *Brigadier Gerard's* victory in 1971 over *Mill Reef* and *My Swallow* was considered by most of those priveledged to witness the race to be one of the finest Guineas of modern times.

The Guineas races are the swallows of the Turf. Run in the fresh sweetness of spring, when the grass on Newmarket Heath is still emerald and the summer yet to come, there is a Browning Esque air of 'Oh, to be in England'.

One Thousand Guineas

Run at Newmarket over 1 mile for 3 year-old fillies First Run 1814 Group 1

		Jockey	Trainer	Owner	Odds
1814	**Charlotte**	W Clift	T Perren	C Wilson	11/5
1815	**filly by Selim**	W Clift	R Prince	Lord Foley	3/1
1816	**Rhoda**	S Barnard	R D Boyce	Duke of Rutland	3/1
1817	**Neva**	W Arnull	R D Boyce	G Watson	7/4
1818	**Corinne**	F Buckle	R Robson	J Udny	7/1
1819	**Catgut**	–	R Robson	Duke of Grafton	20/1
1820	**Rowena**	F Buckle	R Robson	Duke of Grafton	7/4
1821	**Zeal**	F Buckle	R Robson	Duke of Grafton	4/6
1822	**Whizgig**	F Buckle	R Robson	Duke of Grafton	2/5
1823	**Zinc**	F Buckle	R Robson	Duke of Grafton	4/6
1824	**Cobweb**	J Robinson	J Edwards	Lord Jersey	5/2
1825	**Tontine**	–	R Robson	Duke of Grafton	w.o.
1826	**Problem**	J B Day	R Robson	Duke of Grafton	5/1
1827	**Arab**	F Buckle	R Robson	Duke of Grafton	8/1
1828	**Zoe**	J Robinson	R Pettit	A Molony	6/5

Year	Winner	Jockey	Trainer	Owner	Odds
1829	**Young Mouse**	W Arnull	R D Boyce	Lord G H Cavendish	–
1830	**Charlotte West**	J Robinson	J Edwards	Lord Jersey	5/1
1831	**Galantine**	P Conolly	H Scott	Sir M Wood	10/1
1832	**Galata**	W Arnull	C Marson	Lord Exeter	1/2
1833	**Tarantella**	E Wright	John Robinson	T H Cookes	2/1
1834	**May Day**	J B Day	J Doe	Lord Berners	6/1
1835	**Preserve**	E Flatman	R Prince Jnr	C Greville	1/3
1836	**Destiny**	J B Day	J B Day	T Houldsworth	6/4
1837	**Chapeau d'Espagne**	J B Day	J B Day	Lord G Bentinck	2/5
1838	**Barcarolle**	E Edwards	W Edwards	Lord Albemarle	4/1
1839	**Cara**	G Edwards	C Marson	R Watt	7/4
1840	**Crucifix**	J B Day	J B Day	Lord G Bentinck	1/10
1841	**Potentia**	J Robinson	G Payne	S Batson	6/4
1842	**Firebrand**	S Rogers	J Kent Jnr	Lord G Bentinck	6/1
1843	**Extempore**	S Chifney Jnr	R Pettit	T Thornhill	7/1
1844	**Sorella**	J Robinson	W Butler Jnr	G Osbaldeston	10/1
1845	**Picnic**	W Abdale	J Kent Jnr	Duke of Richmond	5/2
1846	**Mendicant**	S Day	J B Day	J Gully	Evens
1847	**Clementina**	E Flatman	M Dilly	G Payne	5/2
1848	**Canezou**	F Butler	J Scott	Lord Stanley	5/1
1849	**Flea**	A Day	J Day	F Clarke	–
1850	**Lady Orford**	F Butler	W Beresford	Lord Orford	5/6
1851	**Aphrodite**	J Marson	A Taylor Snr	Sir J Hawley	5/6
1852	**Kate**	A Day	J Woolcott	J Sargent	4/1
1853	**Mentmore Lass**	J Charlton	W King	Baron M Rothschild	12/1
1854	**Virago**	J Wells	J B Day	H Padwick	1/3
1855	**Habena**	S Rogers	W Butler Jnr	Duke of Bedford	Evens
1856	**Manganese**	J Osborne Jnr	J Osborne	J W King	2/1
1857	**Imperieuse**	E Flatman	J Scott	J Scott	100/8
1858	**Governess**	T Ashmall	T Eskrett	G W Gratwicke	6/1
1859	**Mayonaise**	G Fordham	T Taylor	W S Crawfurd	9/2
1860	**Sagitta**	T Aldcroft	J Scott	Lord Derby	5/2
1861	**Nemesis**	G Fordham	W Harlock	G Fleming	10/1
1862	**Hurricane**	T Ashmall	J Scott	Lord Falmouth	11/2
1863	**Lady Augusta**	A Edwards	Jos Dawson	Lord Stamford	3/1
1864	**Tomato**	J Wells	J Hayhoe	Baron M de Rothschild	10/1
1865	**Siberia**	G Fordham	J Day	Duke of Beaufort	3/1
1866	**Repulse**	T Cannon	J Day	Marquis of Hastings	1/2
1867	**Achievement**	H Custance	J Dover	M Pearson	1/8
1868	**Formosa**	G Fordham	H Woolcott	W Graham	10/11
1869	**Scottish Queen**	G Fordham	J Day	Duke of Beaufort	100/8
1870	**Hester**	J Grimshaw	Jos Dawson	Jos Dawson	6/4
1871	**Hannah**	C Maidment	J Hayhoe	Baron M de Rothschild	2/1
1872	**Reine**	H Parry	T Jennings	C J Lefevre	20/1
1873	**Cecilia**	J Morris	M Dawson	Lord Falmouth	100/3
1874	**Apology**	J Osborne Jnr	W Osborne	J W King	5/2
1875	**Spinaway**	F Archer	M Dawson	Lord Falmouth	10/1
1876	**Camelia**	T Glover	T Cunnington	Comte F de Lagrange	4/1
1877	**Belphoebe**	H Jeffery	G Bloss	Lord Hartington	100/6
1878	**Pilgrimage**	T Cannon	J Cannon	Lord Lonsdale	4/5
1879	**Wheel of Fortune**	F Archer	M Dawson	Lord Falmouth	40/75
1880	**Elizabeth**	C Wood	Jos Dawson	T E Walker	9/2
1881	**Thebais**	G Fordham	A Taylor Snr	W S Crawfurd	5/6
1882	**St Marguerite**	C Wood	R Sherrard	W S Crawfurd	10/1
1883	**Hauteur**	G Fordham	T Jennings Jnr	C J Lefevre	9/4
1884	**Busybody**	T Cannon	T Cannon	G A Baird	85/40
1885	**Farewell**	G Barrett	J Porter	Duke of Westminster	20/1
1886	**Miss Jummy**	J Watts	R Marsh	Duke of Hamilton	3/1
1887	**Reve d'Or**	C Wood	A Taylor Snr	Duke of Beaufort	Evens
1888	**Briar-root**	W Warne	J Ryan	D Baird	100/9
1889	**Minthe**	J Woodburn	M Dawson	R C Vyner	4/1
1890	**Semolina**	J Watts	G Dawson	Duke of Portland	1/2
1891	**Mimi**	F Rickaby	M Dawson	N Fenwick	7/1
1892	**La Fleche**	G Barrett	J Porter	Baron M de Hirsch	1/2
1893	**Siffleuse**	T Loates	P Peck	Sir J Blundell Maple	33/1
1894	**Amiable**	W Bradford	G Dawson	Duke of Portland	100/8
1895	**Galeottia**	F Pratt	J Ryan	A W Cox	100/8
1896	**Thais**	J Watts	R Marsh	HRH the Prince of Wales	5/1
1897	**Chelandry**	J Watts	W Walters Jnr	Lord Rosebery	9/4
1898	**Nun Nicer**	S Loates	W Waugh	Sir J Blundell Maple	11/2
1899	**Sibola**	J F Sloan	J Huggins	Lord W Beresford	13/8
1900	**Winifreda**	S Loates	T Jennings Jnr	L Brassey	11/2
1901	**Aida**	D Maher	G Blackwell	Sir J Miller	13/8
1902	**Sceptre**	H Randall	R S Sievier	R S Sievier	1/2
1903	**Quintessence**	H Randall	J Chandler	Lord Falmouth	4/1

		Jockey	Trainer	Owner	Odds
1904	**Pretty Polly**	W Lane	P P Gilpin	E Loder	1/4
1905	**Cherry Lass**	G McCall	W T Robinson	W Hall-Walker	5/4
1906	**Flair**	B Dillon	P P Gilpin	Sir D Cooper	11/10
1907	**Witch Elm**	B Lynham	W T Robinson	W Hall-Walker	4/1
1908	**Rhodora**	L Lyne	J Allen	R Croker	100/8
1909	**Electra**	B Dillon	P P Gilpin	L Neumann	9/1
1910	**Winkipop**	B Lynham	W Waugh	W Astor	5/2
1911	**Atmah**	F Fox	F Pratt	J A de Rothschild	7/1
1912	**Tagalie**	L Hewitt	D Waugh	W Raphael	20/1
1913	**Jest**	F Rickaby	C Morton	J B Joel	9/1
1914	**Princess Dorrie**	W Huxley	C Morton	J B Joel	100/9
1915	**Vaucluse**	F Rickaby Jnr	F Hartigan	Lord Rosebery	5/2
1916	**Canyon**	F Rickaby Jnr	G Lambton	Lord Derby	9/2
1917	**Diadem**	F Rickaby Jnr	G Lambton	Lord D'Abernon	6/4
1918	**Ferry**	B Carslake	G Lambton	Lord Derby	50/1
1919	**Roseway**	A Whalley	F Hartigan	Sir E Hulton	2/1
1920	**Cinna**	W Griggs	T Waugh	Sir R W B Jardine	4/1
1921	**Bettina**	G Bellhouse	P Linton	W Raphael	33/1
1922	**Silver Urn**	B Carslake	H S Persse	B W Parr	10/1
1923	**Tranquil**	E Gardner	G Lambton	Lord Derby	5/2
1924	**Plack**	C Elliott	J Jarvis	Lord Rosebery	8/1
1925	**Saucy Sue**	F Bullock	A Taylor Jnr	Lord Astor	1/4
1926	**Pillion**	R Perryman	J Watson	A de Rothschild	25/1
1927	**Cresta Run**	A Balding	P P Gilpin	G Loder	10/1
1928	**Scuttle**	J Childs	W R Jarvis	HM The King	15/8
1929	**Taj Mah**	W Sibbritt	J Torterolo	S Guthmann	33/1
1930	**Fair Isle**	T Weston	Frank Butters	Lord Derby	7/4
1931	**Four Course**	C Elliott	F Darling	Lord Ellesmere	100/9
1932	**Kandy**	C Elliott	F Carter	E de Saint-Alary	33/1
1933	**Brown Betty**	J Childs	C Boyd-Rochfort	W Woodward	8/1
1934	**Campanula**	H Wragg	J Jarvis	Sir G Bullough	2/5
1935	**Mesa**	W R Johnstone	A Swann	P Wertheimer	8/1
1936	**Tide-way**	R Perryman	C Leader	Lord Derby	100/30
1937	**Exhibitionnist**	S Donoghue	J Lawson	Sir V Sassoon	10/1
1938	**Rockfel**	S Wragg	O Bell	Sir H Cunliffe-Owen	8/1
1939	**Galatea II**	R A Jones	J Lawson	R S Clark	6/1
1940	**Godiva**	D Marks	W R Jarvis	E Harmsworth	10/1
1941	**Dancing Time**	R Perryman	J Lawson	Lord Glanely	100/8
1942	**Sun Chariot**	G Richards	F Darling	HM The King	Evens
1943	**Herringbone**	H Wragg	W Earl	Lord Derby	15/2
1944	**Picture Play**	C Elliott	J E Watts	H J Joel	15/2
1945	**Sun Stream**	H Wragg	W Earl	Lord Derby	5/2
1946	**Hypericum**	D Smith	C Boyd-Rochfort	HM The King	100/6
1947	**Imprudence**	W R Johnstone	J Lieux	Mme P Corbiere	4/1
1948	**Queenpot**	G Richards	N Murless	Sir P Loraine	6/1
1949	**Musidora**	E Britt	C Elsey	N Donaldson	100/8
1950	**Camaree**	W R Johnstone	A Lieux	J Ternynck	10/1
1951	**Belle of All**	G Richards	N Bertie	H S Tufton	4/1
1952	**Zabara**	K Gethin	V Smyth	Sir M McAlpine	7/1
1953	**Happy Laughter**	E Mercer	J Jarvis	H D H Wills	10/1
1954	**Festoon**	A Breasley	N Cannon	J A Dewar	9/2
1955	**Meld**	W H Carr	C Boyd-Rochfort	Lady Z Wernher	11/4
1956	**Honeylight**	E Britt	C Elsey	Sir V Sassoon	100/6
1957	**Rose Royale II**	C Smirke	A Head	HH Aga Khan	6/1
1958	**Bella Paola**	S Boullenger	F Mathet	F Dupre	8/11
1959	**Petite Etoile**	D Smith	N Murless	Prince Aly Khan	8/1
1960	**Never Too Late II**	R Poincelet	E Pollet	Mrs H E Jackson	8/11
1961	**Sweet Solera**	W Rickaby	R Day	Mrs S Castello	4/1
1962	**Abermaid**	W Williamson	H Wragg	R More O'Ferrall	100/6
1963	**Hula Dancer**	R Poincelet	E Pollet	Mme P Widener	1/2
1964	**Pourparler**	G Bougoure	P Prendergast	Lady B Granard	11/2
1965	**Night Off**	W Williamson	W Wharton	Maj L B Holliday	9/2
1966	**Glad Rags**	P Cook	M V O'Brien	Mrs J P Mills	100/6
1967	**Fleet**	G Moore	N Murless	R C Boucher	11/2
1968	**Caergwrle**	A Barclay	N Murless	Mrs N Murless	4/1
1969	**Full Dress II**	R Hutchinson	H Wragg	R B Moller	7/1
1970	**Humble Duty**	L Piggott	P Walwyn	Lady J Ashcombe	3/1
1971	**Altesse Royale**	Y Saint-Martin	N Murless	F Hue-Williams	25/1
1972	**Waterloo**	E Hide	J W Watts	Mrs R Stanley	8/1
1973	**Mysterious**	G Lewis	N Murless	G A Pope Jnr	11/1
1974	**Highclere**	J Mercer	W R Hern	HM The Queen	12/1
1975	**Nocturnal Spree**	J Roe	H Murless	Mrs D O'Kelly	14/1
1976	**Flying Water**	Y Saint-Martin	A Penna	D Wildenstein	2/1
1977	**Mrs McArdy**	E Hide	M W Easterby	Mrs E Kettlewell	16/1
1978	**Enstone Spark**	E Johnson	B Hills	R A N Bonnycastle	35/1

The run-in to the 1981 One Thousand Guineas. Nearest the rails is Lester Pigoott on *Fairy Footsteps*. On his left is *Go Leasing* which took third place and in the extreme right of the picture is second-placed *Tolmi*.

		Jockey	Trainer	Owner	Odds
1979	**One in a Million**	J Mercer	H Cecil	Helena Springfield Ltd	Evens
1980	**Quick as Lightning**	B Rouse	J Dunlop	O Phipps	12/1
1981	**Fairy Footsteps**	L Piggott	H Cecil	H J Joel	6/4
1982	**On the House**	J Reid	H Wragg	Sir P Oppenheimer	33/1
1983	**Ma Biche**	F Head	Mme C Head	M Al-Maktoum	5/2
1984	**Pebbles**	P Robinson	C Brittain	M Lemos	8/1
1985	**Oh So Sharp**	S Cauthen	H Cecil	Sheikh Mohammed	2/1
1986	**Midway Lady**	R Cochrane	B Hanbury	H H Ranier	10/1
1987	**Miesque**	F Head	F Boutin	S Niarchos	15/8
1988	**Ravinella**	G W Moore	Mme C Head	Ecurie Aland	4/5
1989	**Musical Bliss**	W R Swinburn	M Stoute	Sheikh Mohammed	7/2
1990	**Salsabil**	W Carson	J Dunlop	H Al-Maktoum	6/4
1991	**Shadayid**	W Carson	J Dunlop	H Al-Maktoum	4/6
1992	**Hatoof**	W R Swinburn	Mme C Head	M Al-Maktoum	5/1

Two Thousand Guineas

Run at Newmarket over 1 mile for 3 year-old colts & fillies First Run 1809 Group 1

		Jockey	Trainer	Owner	Odds
1809	**Wizard**	W Clift	T Perren	C Wilson	4/5
1810	**Hephestion**	F Buckle	R Robson	Lord Grosvenor	5/1
1811	**Trophonius**	S Barnard	R D Boyce	R Andrew	5/2
1812	**Cwrw**	S Chifney Jnr	W Chifney	Lord Darlington	7/1
1813	**Smolensko**	H Miller	Crouch	Sir C Bunbury	7/4
1814	**Olive**	W Arnull	R D Boyce	C Wyndham	5/1
1815	**Tigris**	W Arnull	R D Boyce	Lord Rous	7/4
1816	**Nectar**	W Arnull	R D Boyce	Lord G H Cavendish	5/2
1817	**Manfred**	W Wheatley	R Stephenson	S Stonehewer	4/1
1818	**Interpreter**	W Clift	R Prince	Lord Foley	5/4

		Jockey	Trainer	Owner	Odds
1819	**Antar**	E Edwards	J Edwards	Sir J Shelley	4/1
1820	**Pindarrie**	F Buckle	R Robson	Duke of Grafton	Evens
1821	**Reginald**	F Buckle	R Robson	Duke of Grafton	11/10
1822	**Pastille**	F Buckle	R Robson	Duke of Grafton	4/6
1823	**Nicolo**	W Wheatley	J Rogers	J Rogers	5/1
1824	**Schahriar**	W Wheatley	–	J Haffenden	10/1
1825	**Enamel**	J Robinson	C Marson	Lord Exeter	7/4
1826	**Dervise**	J B Day	R Robson	Duke of Grafton	7/2
1827	**Turcoman**	F Buckle	R Robson	Duke of Grafton	5/1
1828	**Cadland**	J Robinson	R D Boyce	Duke of Rutland	5/2
1829	**Patron**	F Boyce	C Marson	Lord Exeter	1/8
1830	**Augustus**	P Conolly	C Marson	Lord Exeter	4/7
1831	**Riddlesworth**	J Robinson	J Edwards	Lord Jersey	1/5
1832	**Archibald**	A Pavis	–	J Peel	2/1
1833	**Clearwell**	J Robinson	–	Lord Orford	5/4
1834	**Glencoe**	J Robinson	J Edwards	Lord Jersey	6/1
1835	**Ibrahim**	J Robinson	J Edwards	Lord Jersey	1/7
1836	**Bay Middleton**	J Robinson	J Edwards	Lord Jersey	4/6
1837	**Achmet**	E Edwards	J Edwards	Lord Jersey	4/6
1838	**Grey Momus**	J B Day	J B Day	Lord G Bentinck	4/1
1839	**The Corsair**	W Wakefield	J Doe	Lord Lichfield	10/1
1840	**Crucifix**	J B Day	J B Day	Lord G Bentinck	8/11
1841	**Ralph**	J B Day	W Edwards	Lord Albemarle	5/2
1842	**Meteor**	W Scott	J Scott	J Bowes	6/4
1843	**Cotherstone**	W Scott	J Scott	J Bowes	1/3
1844	**The Ugly Buck**	J Day	J B Day	J B Day	2/7
1845	**Idas**	E Flatman	R Boyce Jnr	Lord Stradbroke	5/6
1846	**Sir Tatton Sykes**	W Scott	W Oates	W Scott	5/1
1847	**Conyngham**	J Robinson	J Day	Sir R Pigot	4/1
1848	**Flatcatcher**	J Robinson	H Stebbing	B Green	4/1
1849	**Nunnykirk**	F Butler	J Scott	A Nichol	5/6
1850	**Pitsford**	A Day	J Day	H Hill	5/2
1851	**Hernandez**	E Flatman	J Kent Jnr	Lord Enfield	5/1
1852	**Stockwell**	J Norman	W Harlock	Lord Exeter	10/1
1853	**West Australian**	F Butler	J Scott	J Bowes	4/6
1854	**The Hermit**	A Day	J Day	J Gully	12/1
1855	**Lord of the Isles**	T Aldcroft	W Day	J Merry	5/2
1856	**Fazzoletto**	E Flatman	J Scott	Lord Derby	5/1
1857	**Vedette**	J Osborne Jnr	G Abdale	Lord Zetland	5/2
1858	**Fitz-Roland**	J Wells	G Manning	Sir J Hawley	100/6
1859	**The Promised Land**	A Day	W Day	W Day	Evens
1860	**The Wizard**	T Ashmall	J Scott	A Nichol	20/1
1861	**Diophantus**	A Edwards	Jos Dawson	Lord Stamford	25/1
1862	**The Marquis**	T Ashmall	J Scott	S Hawke	5/1
1863	**Macaroni**	T Chaloner	J Godding	R C Naylor	10/1
1864	**General Peel**	T Aldcroft	T Dawson	Lord Glasgow	7/2
1865	**Gladiateur**	H Grimshaw	T Jennings	Comte F de Lagrange	7/1
1866	**Lord Lyon**	R Thomas	J Dover	R Sutton	4/7
1867	**Vauban**	G Fordham	J Day	Duke of Beaufort	5/2
1868	**Moslem**	T Chaloner	A Taylor Snr	W S Crawfurd	100/7
	Formosa	G Fordham	H Woolcott	W Graham	3/1
1869	**Pretender**	J Osborne Jnr	T Dawson	J Johnstone	3/1
1870	**Macgregor**	J Daley	J Waugh	J Merry	100/30
1871	**Bothwell**	J Osborne Jnr	T Dawson	J Johnstone	11/2
1872	**Prince Charlie**	J Osborne Jnr	Jos Dawson	Jos Dawson	2/1
1873	**Gang Forward**	T Chaloner	A Taylor Snr	W S Crawfurd	8/1
1874	**Atlantic**	F Archer	M Dawson	Lord Falmouth	10/1
1875	**Camballo**	J Osborne Jnr	M Dawson	H F C Vyner	7/2
1876	**Petrarch**	H Luke	John Dawson	Lord Dupplin	20/1
1877	**Chamant**	J Goater	T Jennings	Comte F de Lagrange	2/1
1878	**Pilgrimage**	T Cannon	J Cannon	Lord Lonsdale	2/1
1879	**Charibert**	F Archer	M Dawson	Lord Falmouth	25/1
1880	**Petronel**	G Fordham	J Cannon	Duke of Beaufort	20/1
1881	**Peregrine**	F Webb	R Peck	Duke of Westminster	15/2
1882	**Shotover**	T Cannon	J Porter	Duke of Westminster	10/1
1883	**Galliard**	F Archer	M Dawson	Lord Falmouth	9/2
1884	**Scot Free**	W Platt	T Chaloner	J Foy	3/1
1885	**Paradox**	F Archer	J Porter	W B Cloete	1/3
1886	**Ormonde**	G Barrett	J Porter	Duke of Westminster	7/2
1887	**Enterprise**	T Cannon	J Ryan	D Baird	2/1
1888	**Ayrshire**	J Osborne Jnr	G Dawson	Duke of Portland	8/1
1889	**Enthusiast**	T Cannon	J Ryan	D Baird	25/1
1890	**Surefoot**	J Liddiard	C Jousiffe	A W Merry	5/4
1891	**Common**	G Barrett	J Porter	Lord Alington	9/1
1892	**Bonavista**	W T Robinson	W A Jarvis	C D Rose	10/1
1893	**Isinglass**	T Loates	J Jewitt	H McCalmont	4/5

		Jockey	Trainer	Owner	Odds
1894	**Ladas**	J Watts	M Dawson	Lord Rosebery	5/6
1895	**Kirkconnel**	J Watts	Jos Day	Sir J Blundell Maple	10/1
1896	**St Frusquin**	T Loates	A Hayhoe	L de Rothschild	12/100
1897	**Galtee More**	C Wood	S Darling	J Gubbins	5/4
1898	**Disraeli**	S Loates	John Dawson	W Johnstone	100/8
1899	**Flying Fox**	M Cannon	J Porter	Duke of Westminster	5/6
1900	**Diamond Jubilee**	H Jones	R Marsh	HRH Prince of Wales	11/4
1901	**Handicapper**	W Halsey	F W Day	Sir E Cassel	33/1
1902	**Sceptre**	H Randall	R S Sievier	R S Sievier	4/1
1903	**Rock Sand**	J H Martin	G Blackwell	Sir J Miller	6/4
1904	**St Amant**	K Cannon	A Hayhoe	L de Rothschild	11/4
1905	**Vedas**	H Jones	W T Robinson	F de Wend-Fenton	11/2
1906	**Gorgos**	H Jones	R Marsh	A James	20/1
1907	**Slieve Gallion**	W Higgs	S Darling	J H Greer	4/11
1908	**Norman III**	O Madden	J Watson	A Belmont	25/1
1909	**Minoru**	H Jones	R Marsh	HM The King	4/1
1910	**Neil Gow**	D Maher	P Peck	Lord Rosebery	2/1
1911	**Sunstar**	G Stern	C Morton	J B Joel	5/1
1912	**Sweeper II**	D Maher	H S Persse	H B Duryea	6/1
1913	**Louvois**	J Reiff	D Waugh	W Raphael	25/1
1914	**Kennymore**	G Stern	A Taylor Jnr	Sir J Thursby	2/1
1915	**Pommern**	S Donoghue	C Peck	S B Joel	2/1
1916	**Clarissimus**	J Clark	W Waugh	Lord Falmouth	100/7
1917	**Gay Crusader**	S Donoghue	A Taylor Jnr	A W Cox	9/4
1918	**Gainsborough**	J Childs	A Taylor Jnr	Lady J Douglas	4/1
1919	**The Panther**	R Cooper	G Manser	Sir A Black	10/1
1920	**Tetratema**	B Carslake	H S Persse	D McCalmont	2/1
1921	**Craig an Eran**	J Brennan	A Taylor Jnr	Lord Astor	100/6
1922	**St Louis**	G Archibald	P P Gilpin	Lord Queensborough	6/1
1923	**Ellangowan**	C Elliott	J Jarvis	Lord Rosebery	7/1
1924	**Diophon**	G Hulme	R C Dawson	HH Aga Khan	11/2
1925	**Manna**	S Donoghue	F Darling	H E Morriss	100/8
1926	**Colorado**	T Weston	G Lambton	Lord Derby	100/8
1927	**Adam's Apple**	J Leach	H Cottrill	C W S Whitburn	20/1
1928	**Flamingo**	C Elliott	J Jarvis	Sir L Philipps	5/1

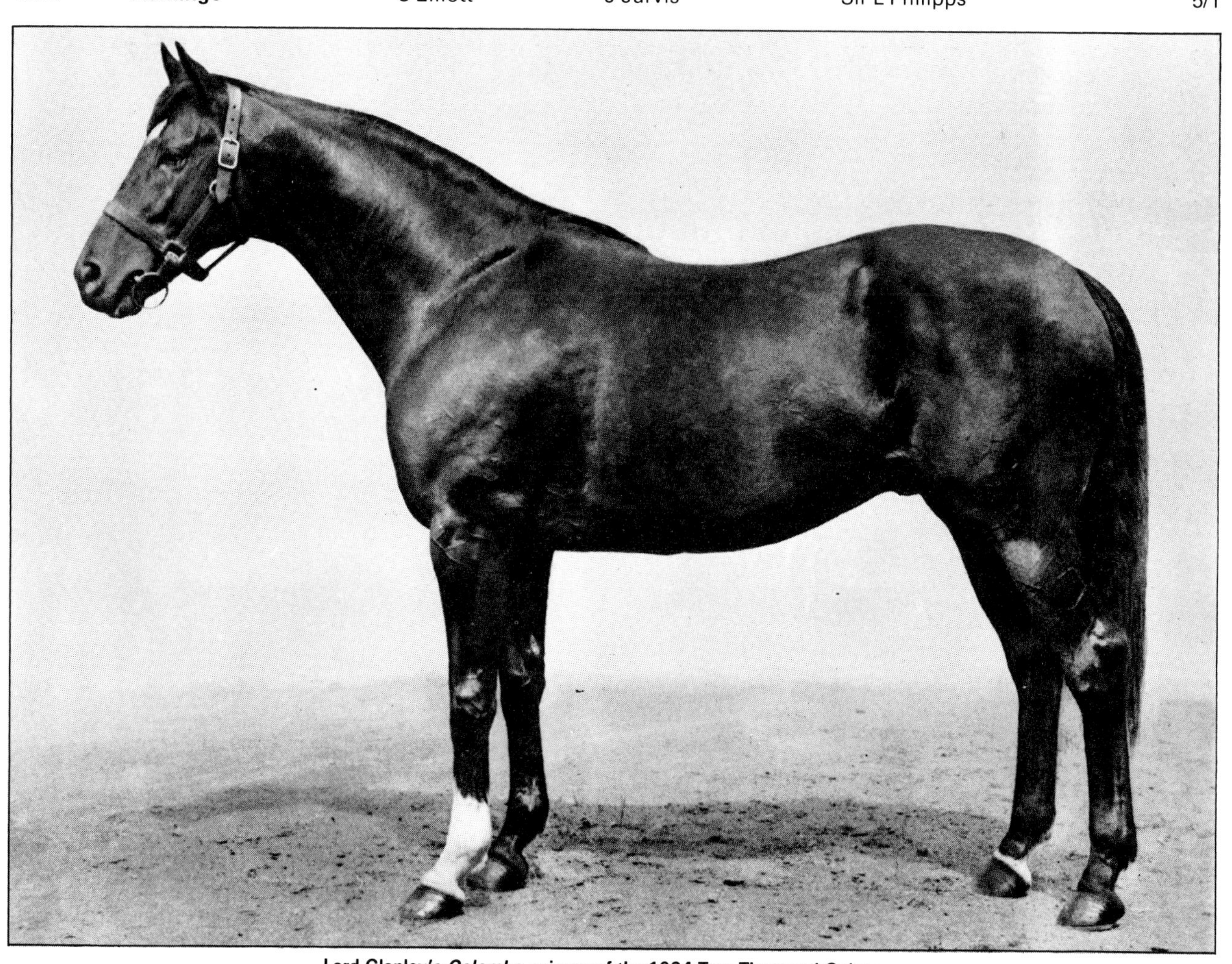

Lord Glanley's *Colombo*, winner of the 1934 Two Thousand Guineas.

		Jockey	Trainer	Owner	Odds
1929	**Mr Jinks**	H Beasley	H S Persse	D McCalmont	5/2
1930	**Diolite**	F Fox	F Templeman	Sir H Hirst	10/1
1931	**Cameronian**	J Childs	F Darling	J A Dewar	100/8
1932	**Orwell**	R A Jones	J Lawson	W M G Singer	Evens
1933	**Rodosto**	R Brethes	H Count	Princesse de Lucinge	9/1
1934	**Colombo**	W R Johnstone	T Hogg	Lord Glanely	2/7
1935	**Bahram**	F Fox	Frank Butters	HH Aga Khan	7/2
1936	**Pay Up**	R Dick	J Lawson	Lord Astor	11/2
1937	**Le Ksar**	C Semblat	F Carter	E de Saint-Alary	20/1
1938	**Pasch**	G Richards	F Darling	H E Morriss	5/2
1939	**Blue Peter**	E Smith	J Jarvis	Lord Rosebery	5/1
1940	**Djebel**	C Elliott	A Swann	M Boussac	9/4
1941	**Lambert Simnel**	C Elliott	F Templeman	Duke of Westminster	10/1
1942	**Big Game**	G Richards	F Darling	HM The King	8/11
1943	**Kingsway**	S Wragg	J Lawson	A E Saunders	18/1
1944	**Garden Path**	H Wragg	W Earl	Lord Derby	5/1
1945	**Court Martial**	C Richards	J Lawson	Lord Astor	13/2
1946	**Happy Knight**	T Weston	H Jelliss	Sir W Cooke	28/1
1947	**Tudor Minstrel**	G Richards	F Darling	J A Dewar	11/8
1948	**My Babu**	C Smirke	F Armstrong	Maharaja of Baroda	2/1
1949	**Nimbus**	C Elliott	G Colling	Mrs M Glenister	10/1
1950	**Palestine**	C Smirke	M Marsh	HH Aga Khan	4/1
1951	**Ki Ming**	A Breasley	M Beary	Ley On	100/8
1952	**Thunderhead II**	R Poincelet	E Pollet	E Constant	100/7
1953	**Nearula**	E Britt	C Elsey	W Humble	2/1
1954	**Darius**	E Mercer	H Wragg	Sir P Loraine	8/1
1955	**Our Babu**	D Smith	G Brooke	D Robinson	13/2
1956	**Gilles de Retz**	F Barlow	Mrs Johnson Houghton	A G Samuel	50/1
1957	**Crepello**	L Piggott	N Murless	Sir V Sassoon	7/2
1958	**Pall Mall**	D Smith	C Boyd-Rochfort	HM The Queen	20/1
1959	**Taboun**	G Moore	A Head	Prince Aly Khan	5/2
1960	**Martial**	R Hutchinson	P Prendergast	R N Webster	18/1
1961	**Rockavon**	N Stirk	G Boyd	T C Yuill	66/1
1962	**Privy Councillor**	W Rickaby	T A Waugh	G Glover	100/6
1963	**Only for Life**	J Lindley	J Tree	Miss M Sheriffe	33/1

Lester Piggott on *Ribofilio*, which failed miserably after starting 15/8 favourite for the 1969 Two Thousand Guineas.

		Jockey	Trainer	Owner	Odds
1964	**Baldric II**	W Pyers	E Fellows	Mrs H E Jackson	20/1
1965	**Niksar**	D Keith	W Nightingall	W Harvey	100/8
1966	**Kashmir II**	J Lindley	C Bartholemew	P Butler	7/1
1967	**Royal Palace**	G Moore	N Murless	H J Joel	100/30
1968	**Sir Ivor**	L Piggott	M V O'Brien	R Guest	11/8
1969	**Right Tack**	G Lewis	J Sutcliffe Jnr	J R Brown	15/2
1970	**Nijinsky**	L Piggott	M V O'Brien	C W Engelhard	4/7
1971	**Brigadier Gerard**	J Mercer	W R Hern	Mrs J Hislop	11/2
1972	**High Top**	W Carson	B van Cutsem	Sir J Thorn	85/40
1973	**Mon Fils**	F Durr	R Hannon	Mrs B Davis	50/1
1974	**Nonoalco**	Y Saint-Martin	F Boutin	Mme M F Berger	19/2
1975	**Bolkonski**	G Dettori	H Cecil	C d'Alessio	33/1
1976	**Wollow**	G Dettori	H Cecil	C d'Alessio	Evens
1977	**Nebbiolo**	G Curran	K Prendergast	N Schibbye	20/1
1978	**Roland Gardens**	F Durr	D Sasse	J Hayter	28/1
1979	**Tap on Wood**	S Cauthen	B Hills	A D Shead	20/1
1980	**Known Fact**	W Carson	J Tree	K Abdulla	14/1
1981	**To-Agori-Mou**	G Starkey	G Harwood	Mrs A Muinos	5/2
1982	**Zino**	F Head	F Boutin	G A Oldham	8/1
1983	**Lomond**	P Eddery	M V O'Brien	R Sangster	9/1
1984	**El Gran Senor**	P Eddery	M V O'Brien	R Sangster	15/8
1985	**Shadeed**	L Piggott	M Stoute	M Al-Maktoum	4/5
1986	**Dancing Brave**	G Starkey	G Harwood	K Abdulla	15/8
1987	**Don't Forget Me**	W Carson	R Hannon	James Horgan	9/1
1988	**Doyoun**	W R Swinburn	M Stoute	HH Aga Khan	4/5
1989	**Nashwan**	W Carson	W R Hern	H Al-Maktoum	3/1
1990	**Tirol**	M Kinane	R Hannon	John Horgan	9/1
1991	**Mystiko**	M Roberts	C Brittain	Lady Beaverbrook	13/2
1992	**Rodrigo de Triano**	L Piggott	P Chapple-Hyam	R Sangster	6/1

Michael Roberts urges home the grey *Mystiko* in the 1991 Two Thousand Guineas.

The Jockey Club Stakes

The Jockey Club Stakes, now run at the Newmarket Spring Meeting, was originally an autumn event and the inaugural winner, *Isinglass*, who took the Triple Crown in 1893 was supplementing his victories in the Princess of Wales's Stakes and the Eclipse. The following year *Isinglass* won the Ascot Gold Cup.

The new race could not have made a better start, and the classic winners *Persimmon, Sceptre, Rock Sand, St Amant* and *Lemberg* all followed suit. In 1926 *Foxlaw* caused an upset when beating his stable companion *Solariok*, the odds-on favourite. *Book Law* (1927) also won the St Leger, and *Toboggan* (1928) was the Oaks winner in that year. *Firdaussi* preceded his victory by winning the St Leger, a race in which his owner, the Aga Khan, was mob-handed with four runners all but one of which reached the frame.

Derby winner *St Paddy* scored in 1961, but since the conditions were changed to exclude three-year-olds in 1963, no classic winner has been successful, which is not surprising as so few stay in training as older horses.

Run at Newmarket over 1 mile 4 furlongs First Run 1894 Group 2

		Jockey	Trainer	Owner	Odds
1894	**Isinglass**	T Loates	J Jewitt	H McCalmont	2/5
1895	**Laveno**	M Cannon	J Ryan	J H Houldsworth	9/4
1896	**Persimmon**	J Watts	R Marsh	HRH the Prince of Wales	8/11
1897	**Love Wisely**	F Rickaby	A Taylor Jnr	W Bass	5/2
1898	**Cyllene**	S Loates	W A Jarvis	C D Rose	5/2
1899	**Flying Fox**	M Cannon	J Porter	Duke of Westminster	1/8
1900	**Disguise II**	M Cannon	S Darling	J R Keene	100/30
1901	**Pietermaritzberg**	M Cannon	J Porter	G Faber	4/1
1902	**Rising Glass**	W Halsey	C Beatty	H McCalmont	100/30
1903	**Sceptre**	F W Hardy	A Taylor Jnr	W Bass	5/4
1904	**Rock Sand**	D Maher	G Blackwell	Sir J Miller	5/2
1905	**St Amant**	K Cannon	T Cannon Jnr	L de Rothschild	100/7
1906	**Beppo**	W Higgs	F Pratt	J A de Rothschild	1/2
1907	**Sancy**	O Madden	A Taylor Jnr	W Bass	13/8
1908	**Siberia**	B Dillon	P P Gilpin	L Neumann	4/1
1909	**Phaleron**	B Dillon	W Waugh	Duke of Portland	7/2
1910	**Lemberg**	D Maher	A Taylor Jnr	A W Cox	1/3
1911	**Stedfast**	F Wootton	G Lambton	Lord Derby	1/2
1912	**Prince Palatine**	F O'Neill	H Beardsley	T Pilkington	5/1
1913	**Cantilever**	Wal Griggs	C Leader	Lord Harewood	6/1
1914	**Trois Temps**	J Clark	A Taylor Jnr	W Astor	5/1
1915	**Lanius**	Wal Griggs	P P Gilpin	L Neumann	5/2
1916	**Cannobie**	M Wing	W Waugh	Duke of Portland	100/7
1917	**No Race**				
1918	**Prince Chimay**	O Madden	A Taylor Jnr	W M Cazelet	20/1
1919	**No Race**				
1920	**Torelore**	B Carslake	H S Persse	Sir H Meux	2/1
1921	**Milenko**	W Lister	F Pratt	J A de Rothschild	4/1
1922	**Lady Juror**	F Lane	A Taylor Jnr	S Tattersall	13/8
1923	**Inkerman**	J Childs	A Taylor Jnr	R Walker	100/6
1924	**Teresina**	C Elliott	R C Dawson	HH Aga Khan	7/2
1925	**Tatra**	F Fox	R Gooch	Mrs H Cayzer	8/1
1926	**Foxlaw**	B Carslake	R Day	Sir A Bailey	20/1
1927	**Book Law**	H Jelliss	A Taylor Jnr	Lord Astor	4/6
1928	**Toboggan**	T Weston	Frank Butters	Lord Derby	3/1
1929	**Cyclonic**	C Elliott	B Jarvis	J S Courtauld	100/30
1930	**Pyramid**	T Weston	Frank Butters	Lord Derby	7/1
1931	**Shell Transport**	R Dick	J Lawson	W M Cazelet	8/1
1932	**Firdaussi**	M Beary	Frank Butters	HH Aga Khan	4/1
1933	**Tai-Yang**	G Richards	F Darling	H E Morriss	4/1
1934	**Umidwar**	F Fox	Frank Butters	HH Aga Khan	13/2
1935	**Plassy**	R Perryman	C Leader	Lord Derby	8/1
1936	**Precipitation**	R Perryman	C Boyd-Rochfort	Lady Z Wernher	9/2
1937	**Solfo**	T Lowrey	B Jarvis	J S Courtauld	9/1
1938	**Challenge**	E Smith	J Jarvis	Sir L Phillips	6/4
1939/44	**No Race**				
1945	**Black Peter**	S Wragg	J C Waugh	Mrs M Harvey	7/2
1946	**Rising Light**	D Smith	C Boyd-Rochfort	HM The King	6/1
1947	**Esprit de France**	D Smith	H Hartigan	HH Aga Khan	9/4
1948	**Alycidon**	D Smith	W Earl	Lord Derby	8/11
1949	**Dust Devil**	D Smith	Frank Butters	HH Aga Khan	1/3
1950	**Holmbush**	L Piggott	A Budgett	Sir D Bailey	5/1
1951	**Pardal**	W R Johnstone	C Semblat	M Boussac	4/6
1952	**Mister Cube**	E Mercer	J Jarvis	Sir A Jarvis	100/30
1953	**Buckhound**	G Richards	N Murless	B Hornung	7/2

		Jockey	Trainer	Owner	Odds
1954	**Brilliant Green**	E Smith	D Watson	J A de Rothschild	3/1
1955	**Nucleus**	L Piggott	C Jerdein	Miss D Paget	Evens
1956	**Kurun**	C Smirke	C Elliott	M Boussac	5/2
1957	**Court Harwell**	A Breasley	G Richards	J R Mullion	8/11
1958	**All Serene**	D Smith	N Bertie	HRH The Princess Royal	10/1
1959	**Court Prince**	L Piggott	N Murless	T Lilley	100/30
1960	**Prolific**	D Keith	W Nightingall	Mrs C Evans	10/11
1961	**St Paddy**	L Piggott	N Murless	Lady Sassoon	4/6
1962	**Gaul**	G Lewis	P Hastings-Bass	Lord Sefton	100/8
1963	**Darling Boy**	J Mercer	W R Hern	J J Astor	11/2
1964	**Fighting Ship**	P Robinson	J Jarvis	Lord Rosebery	5/1
1965	**Bal Masque**	W Pyers	E Fellows	Mrs H E Jackson	5/1
1966	**Alcalde**	D Smith	B van Cutsem	Lord Derby	7/2
1967	**Acrania**	J Lindley	G Harwood	R Zelker	100/30
1968	**Crozier**	D Keith	P Walwyn	A D G Oldrey	7/1
1969	**Torpid**	G Starkey	J Oxley	R D Hollingsworth	5/1
1970	**Queen of Twilight**	B Taylor	H Leader	Mrs L Smith	20/1
1971	**Meadowville**	F Durr	M Jarvis	D Robinson	4/6
1972	**Knockroe**	L Piggott	P Nelson	Mrs V McCalmont	4/1
1973	**Our Mirage**	F Durr	B Hills	Mrs S Enfield	15/8
1974	**Relay Race**	L Piggott	H Cecil	Sir R Macdonald-Buchanan	4/5
1975	**Shebeen**	G Baxter	B Hobbs	Sir K Butt	5/1
1976	**Orange Bay**	P Eddery	P Walwyn	C Vittadini	3/1
1977	**Oats**	P Eddery	P Walwyn	A D G Oldrey	9/4
1978	**Classic Example**	P Eddery	P Walwyn	F Hue-Williams	11/4
1979	**Obraztosvy**	B Taylor	H R Price	H Demetriou	5/1
1980	**More Light**	W Carson	W R Hern	R Budgett	4/1
1981	**Master Willie**	P Waldron	H Candy	R Barnett	2/1
1982	**Ardross**	L Piggott	H Cecil	C St George	Evens
1983	**Electric**	W R Swinburn	M Stoute	R Clifford-Turner	12/1
1984	**Gay Lemur**	G Baxter	B Hobbs	Lady E Rosebery	8/1
1985	**Kirmann**	S Cauthen	R F Johnson Houghton	HH Aga Khan	11/1
1986	**Phardante**	G Starkey	G Harwood	S Karmel	11/2
1987	**Phardante**	G Starkey	G Harwood	S Karmel	7/1
1988	**Almaarad**	W Carson	J Dunlop	H Al-Maktoum	13/2
1989	**Unfuwain**	W Carson	W R Hern	H Al-Maktoum	5/6
1990	**Roseate Tern**	L Dettori	L Cumani	P Brant	17/2
1991	**Rock Hopper**	P Eddery	M Stoute	M Al-Maktoum	8/11
1992	**Sapience**	R Cochrane	D Elsworth	W O'Gorman	40/1

Run over 1 mile 2 furlongs 1894-1900 and 1 mile 6 furlongs 1901-1962

The Palace House Stakes

Palace House, for some years unoccupied and in disrepair, but now awaiting renovation is one of the famous landmarks of Newmarket. Built on the site of the Palace of King Charles II and reputedly incorporating a passageway under Palace Street to Mistress Nell Gwyn's Cottage opposite, much of the yard dates back to Stuart times when it probably sheltered the King's hacks and coach horses. From the last quarter of the nineteenth century until quite recently, Palace House was the property of the Rothschild family, and many winners in the blue yellow colours, including *Hannah* who won the 1,000 Guineas, Oaks and St Leger in 1871 and *Favonixus*, who took the Derby in the same year, were trained there.

A frequent visitor to Palace House in the 1890s was the Prince of Wales, later King Edward VII and huge crowds would assemble in Palace Street when he arrived to dine with Mr Leopold de Rothschild.

The race usually attracts a good field of top-class sprinters, and among the most distinguished winners are *Be Friendly*, also the winner of the Vernons Sprint Cup at both two and three years of age, the Ayr Gold Cup and the King's Stand Stakes, *Tower Walk* who was second in the 2,000 Guineas before reverting to sprint distances, and *Perion* a tough and genuine horse who graduated from handicap to Pattern class.

Run at Newmarket over 5 furlongs First Run 1961 Group 3

		Jockey	Trainer	Owner	Odds
1961	**Galivanter**	R Elliott	W R Hern	Maj L B Holliday	15/8
1962	**Crisper**	W H Carr	W R Hern	Maj L B Holliday	4/1
1963	**Sammy Davis**	D Smith	G Brooke	J Hambro	9/4
1964	**Ruby Laser**	R Hutchinson	G Smyth	Duke of Norfolk	5/2
1965	**Runnymede**	D Keith	W Wightman	Miss F M Prior	7/2
1966	**Tamino**	R Hutchinson	J Dunlop	Duke of Norfolk	10/1
1967	**Heavenly Sound**	A Barclay	T A Waugh	N Barttelot	10/1
1968	**Mountain Call**	R Maddock	B van Cutsem	I E Kornberg	5/2
1969	**Be Friendly**	G Lewis	C Mitchell	P O'Sullevan	13/8
1970	**Tower Walk**	F Durr	G Barling	V W Hardy	7/4

		Jockey	Trainer	Owner	Odds
1971	**Communication**	L Piggott	W Marshall	G Van der Ploeg	10/1
1972	**Shiny Tenth**	J Mercer	D Marks	C Berlin	3/1
1973	**Brave Lad**	W Williamson	P Davey	D Robinsom	11/2
1974	**Singing Bede**	G Baxter	D Marks	Mrs C Grainger	9/2
1975	**Hot Spark**	J Roe	D Weld	R Tikkoo	12/1
1976	**Polly Peachum**	E Hide	M W Easterby	Mrs A Mears	11/10
1977	**Raga Navarro**	Y Saint-Martin	M Zilber	A Ben Lassin	100/30
1978	**Frimley Park**	R Currant	P Arthur	T Lyons	8/1
1979	**Vaigly Great**	G Starkey	M Stoute	T Sellier	5/6
1980	**Valeriga**	L Piggott	L Cumani	C d'Alessio	9/2
1981	**Standaan**	Y Saint-Martin	C Austin	A Richards	33/1
1982	**Lightning Label**	S Cauthen	P Kelleway	R Mandell	5/1
1983	**On Stage**	W Carson	W O'Gorman	A Foustok	9/4
1984	**Reesh**	M L Thomas	W O'Gorman	Yazid & Ahmed Ltd	5/1
1985	**Prince Sabo**	J Reid	Mrs S Swift	Mrs R Daniels	15/2
1986	**Double Schwartz**	B Thomson	C Nelson	R Sangster	12/1
1987	**Hallgate**	G Starkey	A Bailey	T Ramsden	7/2
1988	**Perion**	Paul Eddery	G Lewis	E & B Productions Ltd	6/4
1989	**Silver Fling**	J Matthias	I Balding	G Strawbridge	6/4
1990	**Statoblest**	L Dettori	L Cumani	R Duchossois	5/6
1991	**Elbio**	S Cauthen	P Makin	B Brackpool	9/4
1992	**Monde Bleu**	T Jarnet	A Fabre	D Wildenstein	8/1

The Chester Vase

Although the course does not resemble Epsom in any way, apart from being left handed, the tight turns of Chester make it an ideal test of the adaptability required for the Derby, assuming the aspirant can master the undulations of the Surrey course. *Papyrus, Hyperion, Windsor Lad, Henbit* and *Shergar* all won the Chester Vase over the full Derby distance.

As an early season race for three-year-old potential stayers, the Vase has indicated *Indiana,* St Leger winner in 1964, *Old Vic* who took the Prix du Jockey Club in 1989, and *Toulon,* victorious in the Leger of 1991.

The one that almost got away was *Alcide* in 1958. A rather sluggish win in the Vase was followed by a superb twelve-length beating of his opponents in the Lingfield Derby Trial. Money poured on him for Epsom, but eight days later he was found in his box with a rib broken by a vicious blow, which ensured that he did not run in the Derby, doubtless to the satisfaction of the bookmakers. *Alcide* then won the St Leger and at four the King George VI and the Queen Elizabeth Stakes. Since the 1958 Derby winner *Hard Ridden* was not in the same class, *Alcide* would have had the premiere classic at his mercy.

Run at Chester over 1 mile 4 fls 65 yds for 3 year-olds First Run 1907 Group 3

		Jockey	Trainer	Owner	Odds
1907	**Sancy**	O Madden	A Taylor Jnr	W Bass	100/8
	Earlston	C Heckford	S Loates	J B Joel	11/4
1908	**Galvani**	B Dillon	P P Gilpin	E Loder	4/11
1909	**St Ninian**	H Watts	M Gurry	H G Fenwick	9/2
1910	**Bayardo**	D Maher	A Taylor Jnr	A W Cox	1/5
1911	**Maaz**	E Piper	R Moreton	F Gretton	20/1
1912	**Lycaon**	F Wootton	C Morton	J B Joel	7/2
1913	**Cylba**	D Maher	S Pickering	P Nelke	8/1
1914	**Dan Russel**	F Bullock	G Lambton	Lord Derby	10/1
1915	**Esplandian**	C Dickens	J Butters	Sir B Sheffield	100/8
1916/18	**No Race**				
1919	**Air Raid**	J Childs	A Taylor Jnr	W M Cazelet	8/11
1920	**Buchan**	F Bullock	A Taylor Jnr	Lord Astor	6/4
1921	**No Race**				
1922	**Fodder**	J Shatwell	E de Mestre	S B Joel	10/1
1923	**Papyrus**	S Donoghue	B Jarvis	B Irish	Evens
1924	**Inkerman**	F Bullock	A Taylor Jnr	R Walker	4/9
1925	**Vermilion Pencil**	T Weston	R C Dawson	HH Aga Khan	7/4
1926	**Swift and Sure**	R A Jones	A Taylor Jnr	Lord Astor	3/1
1927	**Lone Knight**	A Burns	F Scott	Lady E Torrington	100/15
1928	**Hectare**	H Graves	C Doyle	R Walker	9/1
1929	**En Garde**	G Richards	J E Watts	W M G Singer	10/1
1930	**Pinxit**	A Burns	N Scobie	Sir C Hyde	11/2
1931	**Sandwich**	W Nevett	J Jarvis	Lord Rosebery	9/1
1932	**Bulandshar**	F Fox	Frank Butters	HH Aga Khan	5/2
1933	**Hyperion**	T Weston	G Lambton	Lord Derby	15/8

One of the horses to win the Chester Vase over the full Derby distance, *Hyperion* was successful in 1933.

		Jockey	Trainer	Owner	Odds
1934	**Windsor Lad**	F Fox	M Marsh	Maharaja of Rajpipla	3/1
1935	**Valerius**	T Weston	J Lawson	Sir A Bailey	4/1
1936	**Taj Akbar**	G Richards	Frank Butters	HH Aga Khan	7/1
1937	**Merry Mathew**	W Nevett	M Peacock	R Bownass	100/30
1938	**Cave Man**	C Richards	J Lawson	Lord Astor	8/1
1939	**Heliopolis**	T Weston	W Earl	Lord Derby	7/2
1940/45	**No Race**				
1946	**Sky High**	T Weston	W Earl	Lord Derby	9/4
1947	**Edward Tudor**	G Richards	F Darling	Mrs R Macdonald-Buchanan	5/6
1948	**Valognes**	E Britt	M Marsh	R Macdonald-Buchanan	4/1
1949	**Swallow Tail**	D Smith	W Earl	Lord Derby	2/5
1950	**Castle Rock**	D Smith	J Jarvis	Lord Rosebery	1/3
1951	**Supreme Court**	W R Johnstone	E Williams	Mrs T Lilley	9/4
1952	**Summer Rain**	E Mercer	J Jarvis	Lord Milford	7/4
1953	**Empire Honey**	E Mercer	J Jarvis	Lord Milford	11/10
1954	**Blue Rod**	D Greening	H Leader	D de Rougemont	33/1
1955	**Daemon**	J Wilson	P Prendergast	B Mavroleon	10/11
1956	**Articulate**	D Ryan	W Stephenson	J McGrath	5/1
1957	**King Babar**	P Robinson	P Prendergast	E More O'Ferrall	9/2
1958	**Alcide**	W Snaith	C Boyd-Rochfort	Sir H de Trafford	15/8
1959	**Fidalgo**	S Clayton	H Wragg	G A Oldham	10/1
1960	**Mr Higgins**	W H Carr	H Cottrill	P Winstone	10/1
1961	**Sovrango**	J Mercer	H Wragg	G A Oldham	7/1
1962	**Silver Cloud**	R Hutchinson	J Jarvis	T Blackwell	5/1
1963	**Christmas Island**	L Piggott	P Prendergast	Lord Ennisdale	100/8
1964	**Indiana**	J Mercer	J F Watts	C W Engelhard	11/4
1965	**Gulf Pearl**	J Lindley	J Tree	J H Whitney	7/1
1966	**General Gordon**	P Cook	J Jarvis	Lord Rosebery	6/1
1967	**Great Host**	D Lake	P Prendergast	L Gelb	2/1
1968	**Remand**	J Mercer	W R Hern	J J Astor	4/11
1969	**No Race**				
1970	**Politico**	A Barclay	N Murless	Mrs O Phipps	5/1
1971	**Linden Tree**	D Keith	P Walwyn	Mrs D McCalmont	11/2
1972	**Ormindo**	B Taylor	H Wragg	G A Oldham	12/1
1973	**Proverb**	E Johnson	B Hills	J Chandos-Pole	33/1

		Jockey	Trainer	Owner	Odds
1974	**Jupiter Pluvius**	J Gorton	B Hobbs	T Blackwell	11/2
1975	**Shantallah**	B Taylor	H Wragg	R More O'Ferrall	15/2
1976	**Old Bill**	B Taylor	H Wragg	R B Moller	33/1
1977	**Hot Grove**	L Piggott	R F Johnson Houghton	Lord Leverhulme	100/30
1978	**Icelandic**	C Roche	P Prendergast	P Prendergast	8/1
1979	**Cracaval**	S Cauthen	B Hills	A Shead	4/1
1980	**Henbit**	W Carson	W R Hern	Mrs A Plesch	Evens
1981	**Shergar**	W R Swinburn	M Stoute	HH Aga Khan	4/11
1982	**Super Sunrise**	P Cook	G Hunter	J Maxwell	10/1
1983	**No Race**				
1984	**Kaytu**	W Carson	W R Hern	R N Khan	11/2
1985	**Law Society**	P Eddery	M V O'Brien	S Niarchos	5/2
1986	**Nomrood**	T Quinn	P Cole	F Salman	11/2
1987	**Dry Dock**	W Carson	W R Hern	R D Hollingsworth	11/2
1988	**Unfuwain**	W Carson	W R Hern	H Al-Maktoum	1/3
1989	**Old Vic**	S Cauthen	H Cecil	Sheikh Mohammed	6/4
1990	**Belmez**	S Cauthen	H Cecil	Sheikh Mohammed	8/13
1991	**Toulon**	P Eddery	A Fabre	K Abdulla	9/4
1992	**Twist and Turn**	S Cauthen	H Cecil	Sheikh Mohammed	13/8

For 3 and 4 year-olds 1907-1958

The Chester Cup

Although the Chester Cup is now generally recognised as being run for the first time in 1824, the origins of the race can be traced back to the third year of the reign of Henry VII in 1511.

The original prize was a silver ball, which later in 1609 became a challenge bell and the race moved from Shrove Tuesday to St George's Day. After the Civil War, the eighth Earl of Derby restored the event and in 1683, it is claimed, the Duke of Monmouth won the 'Chester Cup' on his own horse, although it is probable that this race was run at nearby Wallesey, considered more of a course for gentlemen.

By the mid-eighteenth century it was the Chester City Plate sponsored by the City Corporation, and survived as such for another thirty-three years until the Municipal Capitals Reform Act made it illegal to provide prize money out of public funds, when the event was fused with the Tradesmen's Cup which had been founded in 1824.

When *The Doge of Venice* won the inaugural Tradesmen's Cup, it was a limited handicap with a scale down to only 8st 2lb but later a wider range of handicapping was introduced and soon the Cup became a heavier betting race than the Derby.

Perhaps the best story of the Chester Cup concerns a coup engineered by Lord George Bentinck in 1844, at that time managing the horses of the Duke of Richmond, and said to have netted £100,000. *Alice Hawthorn*, a superb racemare who won fifty-two races in seven seasons, won the Cup in 1842 under 6st but two years later had to give 5st 8lb to the Duke's *Red Deer*, the first three-year-old to win the Cup.

Despite several false starts, *Red Deer* made all to win by 'about fifty lengths'. Given the dimensions of the Chester course which is little over a mile round, *Alice Hawthorn* who finished second must have been negotiating the final bend as the winner past the post. *Red Deer's* jockey, Kitchener, weighed only 3st 4lb and the horse carried 4st. It took Kitchener another half a circuit to pull-up.

Not all jockeys appreciated the Chester 'soup-plate' in the days of unlimited fields, including the very first champion jockey, Nat Flatman, and perhaps the greatest of them all, Fred Archer. In modern times, the track is safer for man and beast, and the Chester Cup has become a haven for equine household names such as *Trelawny*, *Major Rose*, *Attivo*, *John Cherry*, *Donegal Prince* and *Sea Pigeon*, all winners of a tough handicap on a unique course steeped in history and exciting sport.

Run at Chester over 2 miles 4 furlongs and 97 yards First Run 1824 Handicap

		Jockey	Trainer	Owner	Odds
1824	**Doge of Venice**	T Nicholson	–	Sir T Stanley	6/4
1825	**Hymettus**	B Smith	R Robson	Lord Grosvenor	4/1
1826	**Brutandorf**	W Scott	–	J Clifton	5/1
1827	**Grenadier**	S Templeman	–	Sir T Stanley	3/1
1828	**Fylde**	G Nelson	–	J Clifton	7/2
1829	**Halston**	S Templeman	–	J Mytton	5/1
1830	**Felt**	R Johnson	–	Lord Derby	6/1
1831	**Independence**	S Darling	–	Mr Beardsworth	Evens
1832	**Colwick**	S Darling	–	Mr Beardsworth	9/4
1833	**Pickpocket**	S Darling	–	Sir R W Bulkeley	7/2
1834	**The Cardinal**	E Wright	–	Mr Miles	6/1
1835	**Birdlime**	T Lye	J Blenkhorn	E L Mostyn	7/4
1836	**Tanworth**	Spring	–	E Peel	10/1
1837	**General Chasse**	J Holmes	–	Sir J Boswell	5/2
1838	**King Cole**	C Marlow	–	T Walters	–
1839	**Cardinal Puff**	S Darling	J Scott	Lord Westminster	100/8
1840	**The Dey of Algiers**	E Flatman	W Cooper	J Peel	100/8
1841	**Cruiskeen**	N Stagg	–	Lord Milltown	18/1
1842	**Alice Hawthorn**	J Bumby	R Hesseltine	Mr Plummer	9/2
1843	**Millepede**	J Bumby	R Hesseltine	H Wormald	5/2

		Jockey	Trainer	Owner	Odds
1844	**Red Deer**	J Kitchener	J Kent Jnr	Duke of Richmond	7/2
1845	**Intrepid**	W Arthur	H Wadlow	J Skerratt	40/1
1846	**Corranna**	F Butler	W Boyce	G H Moore	40/1
1847	**St Lawrence**	W Ford	W Lumley	J S Drinkald	25/1
1848	**Peep o'Day Boy**	A Day	J Day	Lord Howth	7/1
1849	**Malton**	J Fenn	H Stebbing	H Stebbing	12/1
1850	**Mounseer**	G Dockeray	G Dockeray	Maj Pitt	16/1
1851	**Nancy**	J Kendall	G Noble	T Lister	12/1
1852	**Joe Miller**	J Goater	W Day	Mr Farrance	8/1
1853	**Goldfinder**	T Aldcroft	A Sait	W Palmer	30/1
1854	**Epaminondas**	G Fordham	W Smith	D Lane	25/1
1855	**Scythian**	J Wells	J B Day	H Padwick	10/1
1856	**One Act**	S Hibberd	W Day	J Parker	12/1
1857	**Leamington**	D Hughes	T Parr	F Higgins	6/1
1858	**Vanity**	T Withington	J Scott	Sir C Monck	30/1
1859	**Leamington**	J Wells	T Parr	F Higgins	5/1
1860	**St Albans**	G French	A Taylor Snr	Lord Ailesbury	5/1
1861	**Ben Webster**	L Snowden	J Saxon	Mr Barber	4/1
1862	**Tim Whiffler**	J Doyle	T S Dawson	Mr Jackson	25/1
1863	**Asteroid**	J Wells	G Manning	Sir J Hawley	11/2
1864	**Flash in the Pan**	J Morris	J Hughes	T Hughes	30/1
1865	**Dalby**	S Hibberd	J Warriner	W G Bennett	5/1
1866	**Dalby**	S Hibberd	J Warriner	W G Bennett	4/1
1867	**Beewsing**	Prior	–	A Heathcote	12/1
1868	**Paul Jones**	H Jeffery	F Balchin	G Hodgman	6/4
1869	**Knight of the Garter**	G Fordham	G Bloss	Lord Calthorpe	7/1
1870	**Our Mary Ann**	W Newhouse	D Hughes	T Hughes	25/1
1871	**Glenlivat**	G Jarvis	W H Scott	W H Scott	25/1
1872	**Inveresk**	J Griffiths	–	W Nicholl	100/8
1873	**Field Marshall**	J Griffiths	J Perren	J Bowes	100/6
1874	**Organist**	T Glover	M Dawson	R C Vyner	100/9
1875	**Freeman**	T Glover	R Peck	E Heneage	3/1
1876	**Tam o'Shanter**	J Thompson	F Bates	J Johnstone	9/1
1877	**Pageant**	T Glover	J Porter	F Gretton	100/6
1878	**Pageant**	T Cannon	J Porter	F Gretton	75/40
1879	**Reefer**	H Luke	John Dawson	Lord Dupplin	1,000/75
1880	**Fashion**	W Greaves	J Hayhoe	L de Rothschild	4/1
1881	**Windsor**	A F Weston	R Sherrard	Sir J Astley	100/8
1882	**Prudhomme**	A F Lemaire	J Cannon	Lord Rosebery	7/1
1883	**Biserta**	S Loates	A Hayhoe	L de Rothschild	7/2
1884	**Havock**	C Wood	C Jousiffe	C J Merry	4/1
1885	**Merry Prince**	S Loates	–	H B Craig	4/1
1886	**Eastern Emperor**	G Barrett	A Taylor Snr	Duke of Beaufort	5/1
1887	**Carlton**	G Barrett	A Taylor Snr	Lord E Somerset	9/4
1888	**Kinsky**	J Watts	C Jousiffe	J R G Homfray	7/2
1889	**Mill Stream**	T Loates	P Peck	J Blundell Maple	13/2
1890	**Tyrant**	S Chandley	W Walters	S J Baker	5/2
1891	**Vasistas**	G Barrett	J Porter	Baron M de Hirsch	9/4
1892	**Dare Devil**	J J Mullen	W I'Anson Jnr	C Perkins	11/2
1893	**Dare Devil**	J Fagan	W I'Anson Jnr	C Perkins	9/2
1894	**Queasitum**	T Loates	F Cole	Lord Penrhyn	5/2
1895	**Kilsallaghan**	F Finlay	J Jewitt	Capt J Machell	20/1
1896	**The Rush**	O Madden	J Waugh	G Dobell	8/1
1897	**Count Schomberg**	S Loates	W Leader	R Lebaudy	2/1
1898	**Up Guards**	S Chandley	A Sydney	H Pack	33/1
1899	**Uncle Mac**	F Finlay	F Lynham	Mr Teddy	100/8
1900	**Roughside**	J F Sloan	Sandever	C A Brown	7/1
1901	**David Garrick**	L Reiff	G Blackwell	P Lorillard	10/1
1902	**Carabine**	M Aylin	J Hornsby	J Collins	7/1
1903	**Vendale**	C Trigg	W Duke	G Thursby	10/1
1904	**Sandboy**	W Griggs	W T Robinson	W Hall-Walker	9/2
1905	**Imari**	W Saxby	S Pickering	W Low	100/8
1906	**Feather Bed**	A Templeman	J East	O W Rayner	11/4
1907	**Querido**	J Reiff	R Carter Jnr	M Caillault	9/4
1908	**Glacis**	F Wootton	G Lambton	Lord Derby	13/2
1909	**Santo Strato**	O Madden	J Watson	L de Rothschild	4/1
1910	**Elizabetta**	S Wootton	A Taylor Jnr	R Walker	8/1
1911	**Willonyx**	W Higs	S Darling	C E Howard	7/1
1912	**Rathlea**	C Foy	T Coulthwaite	T Nolan	8/1
1913	**The Guller**	J Ledson	J Osborne	H A Crallan	20/1
1914	**Aleppo**	C Foy	A Taylor Jnr	A W Cox	3/1
1915	**Hare Hill**	S Donoghue	W T Robinson	C B Ismay	11/2
1916/18	**No Race**				
1919	**Tom Pepper**	J Shatwell	J Rogers	R Walker	100/8
1920	**Our Stephen**	A Balding	V Hobbs	F Curzon	6/1

		Jockey	Trainer	Owner	Odds
1921	**No Race**				
1922	**Chivalrous**	G Smith	H Cottrill	Mrs S Whitburn	50/1
1923	**Chivalrous**	M Beary	H Cottrill	Mrs S Whitburn	100/14
1924	**Rugeley**	H Leach	R Moreton	F Gretton	10/1
1925	**Spithead**	T Weston	G Lambton	Lord Derby	6/1
1926	**Hidennis**	J Caldwell	H Leader	Mrs L H Walker	11/2
1927	**Dark Japan**	C Smirke	R C Dawson	HH Aga Khan	4/1
1928	**St Mary's Kirk**	W Alford	H S Persse	Sir H Meux	25/1
1929	**First Flight**	F Fox	F Leader	Lady Scarborough	9/1
1930	**Mountain Lad**	F Lane	R Gooch	H Sutton	20/1
1931	**Brown Jack**	M Beary	I Anthony	Sir H Wernher	100/8
1932	**Bonny Brighteyes**	J Dines	D Peacock	Mrs C Robinson	20/1
1933	**Dick Turpin**	G Richards	M Hartigan	R Watson	9/1
1934	**Blue Vision**	F Fox	I Anthony	M Evans	100/6
1935	**Damascus**	H Foster	G Lambton	G Lambton	10/1
1936	**Cho-sen**	J Dines	W Higgs	Mrs W Ahern	100/7
1937	**Faites vos Jeux**	P Maher	H Cottrill	Lady Nuttall	8/1
1938	**Mr Grundy**	C Richards	J Lawson	Sir A Bailey	10/1
1939	**Winnebar**	G Richards	F Templeman	Sir F Eley	100/8
1940/45	**No Race**				

Sir Frederick Eley's *Winnebar*, with Gordon Richards up, wins the 1939 Chester Cup by three lengths from Miss B.Jamieson's *Irish Stew*.

1946	**Retsel**	C Richards	G Todd	H Lester	4/1
1947	**Asmodee II**	T Burn	W Halsey	P Duboscq	10/1
1948	**Billett**	W Nevett	H Wragg	B Hilliard	5/1
1949	**John Moore**	A Carson	H Weatherill	W Chapman	25/1
1950	**Heron Bridge**	T Burns	D Rogers	J S Davies	11/2
1951	**Wood Leopard**	J Egan	R J Colling	Lord Durham	20/1
1952	**Le Tellier**	G Littlewood	G Barling	J Westoll	6/1
1953	**Eastern Emperor**	W Rickaby	J Jarvis	Lord Milford	2/1
1954	**Peperium**	E Britt	C Elsey	C Elsey	13/2
1955	**Prescription**	W Rickaby	J Jarvis	Lord Rosebery	8/1
1956	**Golovine**	P Robinson	H Wragg	Begum Aga Khan	9/2
1957	**Curry**	J Gifford	F Armstrong	F Honour	11/4
1958	**Sandiacre**	L Piggott	W Dutton	M Cowley	15/2
1959	**Agreement**	W H Carr	C Boyd-Rochfort	HM The Queen	3/1
1960	**Trelawny**	F Durr	S Mercer	Mrs L Carver	100/6
1961	**Hoy**	G Lewis	L Dale	C Spencer	15/2
1962	**Golden Fire**	D Yates	D Marks	Mrs G Ridley	7/1
1963	**Narratus**	D Yates	D Thom	D Symonds	8/1
1964	**Credo**	P Cook	P Prendergast	L Gelb	4/1
1965	**Harvest Gold**	F Durr	T Robson	T Marshall	11/2

		Jockey	Trainer	Owner	Odds
1966	**Aegean Blue**	L Piggott	R F Johnson Houghton	P S Emmett	22/1
1967	**Mahbub Aly**	P Cook	W R Hern	Lord Rotherwick	7/1
1968	**Major Rose**	L Piggott	H R Price	R Heaton	11/4
1969	**No Race**				
1970	**Altogether**	W Bentley	W Murray	W R Bolton	33/1
1971	**Random Shot**	F Durr	A Budgett	Mrs J Benskin	6/1
1972	**Eric**	A Cressy	V Cross	J Ismay	22/1
1973	**Crisalgo**	W Bentley	J A Turner	J Hanson	12/1
1974	**Attivo**	R Wernham	C Mitchell	P O'Sullevan	6/1
1975	**Super Nova**	E Johnson	W Hall	J Mitchell	11/2
1976	**John Cherry**	L Piggott	J Tree	J H Whitney	5/1
1977	**Sea Pigeon**	M Birch	M H Easterby	P Muldoon	7/1
1978	**Sea Pigeon**	M Birch	M H Easterby	P Muldoon	10/1
1979	**Charlotte's Choice**	W Carson	W Wightman	R Green	10/1
1980	**Arapahos**	S Cauthen	B Hills	R Sangster	7/2
1981	**Donegal Prince**	P Young	P Kelleway	J McGonagle	12/1
1982	**Dawn Johnny**	W R Swinburn	M Stoute	Sir G White	14/1
1983	**No Race**				
1984	**Contester**	G Baxter	P Cundell	P S Winfield	22/1
1985	**Morgans Choice**	W Carson	C J Hill	C J Hill	13/2
1986	**Western Dancer**	P Cook	C A Horgan	Mrs G R Stone	14/1
1987	**Just David**	M Roberts	A Stewart	A Leftwich	10/1
1988	**Old Hubert**	M L Thomas	A Bailey	T Ramsden	33/1
1989	**Grey Salute**	P Eddery	J Jenkins	T Hayward	7/1
1990	**Travelling Light**	A Munro	Mrs J R Ramsden	Mrs A E Sigsworth	5/2
1991	**Star Player**	L Dettori	J Baker	P Smith	9/2
1992	**Welshman**	J Quinn	M Blanshard	B Oxton	11/1

***John Cherry*, seen here winning the 1976 Cesarewitch, also took the Chester Cup that year.**

The Ormonde Stakes

The Ormonde Stakes, named after the 1886 Derby winner owned and bred at nearby Eaton Hall by the Duke of Westminster, was originally a two-year-old race over five furlongs. First run over the present distance of one mile five furlongs and seventy-five yards in 1936, it is doubtful if there can have been a better contest since.

Quashed, one of the gamest mares ever seen on a racecourse and later to defeat the American Triple Crown winner *Omaha* in the Ascot Gold Cup, beat another top-class stayer, *Cecil*, by a neck after a desperately hard race. Now confined to older horses, the Ormonde drew attention to the abilities of Derby winner *Tulyar* in 1952, and both *Blakeney* (Derby 1969) and *Teenoso* (Derby 1983) won as four-year-olds.

Run at Chester over 1 mile 5 furlongs 88 yards First Run 1936 Group 3

		Jockey	Trainer	Owner	Odds
1936	**Quashed**	R Perryman	C Leader	Lord Stanley	7/4
1937	**Young England**	W Nevett	M Peacock	R Bowmass	10/1
1938	**Senor**	J Crouch	R C Dawson	W Barnett	7/2
1939	**Tricameron**	A Tucker	L Robert	Baron E de Rothschild	7/1
1940/45	**No Race**				
1946	**High Stakes**	C Richards	J Lawson	Lord Astor	4/5
1947	**Turkish Tune**	W Wells	D Rogers	W Buckley	11/4
1948	**Goyama**	C Elliott	C Semblat	M Boussac	11/2
1949	**Alycidon**	D Smith	W Earl	Lord Derby	4/5
1950	**Oleins Grace**	C Elliott	D Rogers	P McCarthy	7/4

		Jockey	Trainer	Owner	Odds
1951	**Cagire II**	C Elliott	E Williams	Mrs E Williams	9/4
1952	**Tulyar**	D Smith	M Marsh	HH Aga Khan	13/8
1953	**Wyandank**	E Mercer	J Lawson	Miss M R Cox	9/1
1954	**Stem King**	D Smith	R Perryman	S Joel	4/1
1955	**North Cone**	E Smith	G Barling	Lord Ellesmere	4/1
1956	**Stephanotis**	K Gethin	H Leader	A Plesch	9/4
1957	**Hindu Festival**	T Gosling	P Prendergast	C F Myerscough	3/1
1958	**Doutelle**	W H Carr	C Boyd-Rochfort	HM The Queen	11/8
1959	**Primera**	L Piggott	N Murless	C Dracoulis	11/8
1960	**Light Horseman**	R Hutchinson	P Prendergast	Lord Ennisdale	4/1
1961	**Alcaeus**	A Breasley	P Prendergast	Sir R Brooke	4/11
1962	**Sovrango**	W Williamson	H Wragg	G A Oldham	11/10
1963	**Sovrango**	W Williamson	H Wragg	G A Oldham	11/4
1964	**Arctic Vale**	L Piggott	P Prendergast	Mrs E Goring	6/5
1965	**Indiana**	J Lindley	J F Watts	C W Engelhard	4/11
1966	**Biomydrin**	L Piggott	N Murless	Lady Sassoon	11/2
1967	**David Jack**	L Piggott	E Lambton	J Fisher	8/13
1968	**Hopeful Venture**	A Barclay	N Murless	HM The Queen	Evens
1969	**No Race**				
1970	**Blakeney**	E Johnson	A Budgett	A Budgett	9/4
1971	**Quayside**	L Piggott	Denys Smith	T Robson	6/4
1972	**Selhurst**	G Lewis	N Murless	H J Joel	9/4
1973	**Ormindo**	B Taylor	H Wragg	G A Oldham	13/2
1974	**Crazy Rhythm**	G Lewis	S Ingham	K Dodson	3/1
1975	**Rouser**	G Lewis	B Hobbs	Mrs J de Rothschild	11/8
1976	**Zimbalon**	J Mercer	W R Hern	R D Hollingsworth	13/8
1977	**Oats**	P Eddery	P Walwyn	A D G Oldrey	7/4
1978	**Crow**	P Eddery	P Walwyn	D Wildenstein	5/4
1979	**Remainder Man**	J Mercer	R Hollinshead	Mrs D Jardine	7/4
1980	**Niniski**	W Carson	W R Hern	Lady Beaverbrook	4/7
1981	**Pelerin**	B Taylor	H Wragg	Sir P Oppenheimer	11/8
1982	**Six Mile Bottom**	S Cauthen	H Wragg	E B Moller	12/1
1983	**No Race**				
1984	**Teenoso**	P Eddery	G Wragg	E B Moller	11/8
1985	**Seismic Wave**	B Thomson	B Hills	R Sangster	7/1
1986	**Brunico**	B Thomson	R Simpson	T Ramsden	33/1
1987	**Rakaposhi King**	S Cauthen	H Cecil	Lord H de Walden	1/3
1988	**Mr Pintips**	W Carson	W Hastings-Bass	Lord Halifax	20/1
1989	**Mountain Kingdom**	S Cauthen	C Brittain	Pin Oak Stable	4/6
1990	**Braashee**	M Roberts	A Stewart	M Al-Maktoum	6/1
1991	**Per Quod**	B Raymond	B Hanbury	H T McKnight	5/1
1992	**Saddlers' Hall**	P Eddery	M Stoute	Lord Weinstock	4/11

The Lingfield Derby Trial

The Lingfield Derby Trial was the brainchild of Fred Wilmot who was Clerk of the Course at Lingfield in 1932. The course resembles Epsom as no other, and the trial was an immediate success when *April the Fifth*, trained by actor Tom Walls famous for his appearances in Aldwych farces, went on to win the Derby. Since then the race has been the most successful Derby trial apart from the Two Thousand Guineas, producing seven winners of the premier classic, the latest being *Kahyasi* in 1988.

The trial has also been won by many other top-class animals including *Sayajirao*, winner of the Leger in 1947, *Aureole*, second in the Derby and winner of the Coronation Cup, the Hardwicke Stakes and the King George VI and Queen Elizabeth Stakes in 1954, *Cacoethes* and *Rock Hopper*.

Run at Lingfield Park over 1 mile 3 furlongs 106 yards for 3 year-olds First Run 1932 Group 3

		Jockey	Trainer	Owner	Odds
1932	**April the Fifth**	F Lane	T Walls	T Walls	6/1
1933	**Myosotis**	F Fox	J Lawson	W M G Singer	3/1
1934	**Medieval Knight**	G Richards	F Darling	J A Dewar	6/4
1935	**Field Trial**	F Fox	J Lawson	Lord Astor	7/1
1936	**Barrystar**	J Marshall	W Nightingall	F W Shenstone	3/1
1937	**Mid-day Sun**	M Beary	Fred Butters	Mrs G B Miller	7/2
1938	**Blandstar**	H Sprague	G Duller	Maharaja of Rajpipla	25/1
1939	**Hypnotist**	W Nevett	C Boyd-Rochfort	W Woodward	1/2
1940/45	**No Race**				
1946	**Fast and Fair**	C Richards	J Lawson	Lord Astor	4/1
1947	**Sayajirao**	E Britt	F Armstrong	Maharaja of Baroda	10/11
1948	**Black Tarquin**	W H Carr	C Boyd-Rochfort	W Woodward	8/11
1949	**Brown Rover**	W Cook	C Boyd-Rochfort	W Woodward	11/2
1950	**Tramper**	T Hawcroft	W Nightingall	C R Harper	100/7
1951	**North Carolina**	C Elliott	C Boyd-Rochfort	Mrs J Bryce	10/1

		Jockey	Trainer	Owner	Odds
1952	**Tulyar**	C Smirke	M Marsh	HH Aga Khan	4/1
1953	**Aureole**	W H Carr	C Boyd-Rochfort	HM The Queen	2/1
1954	**Rowston Manor**	D Smith	H Peacock	F Dennis	5/2
1955	**True Cavalier**	R Fawdon	H Leader	S Niarchos	3/1
1956	**Induna**	C Smirke	M Marsh	R Macdonald-Buchanan	10/1
1957	**Doutelle**	W H Carr	C Boyd-Rochfort	HM The Queen	11/4
1958	**Alcide**	W H Carr	C Boyd-Rochfort	Sir H de Trafford	2/1
1959	**Parthia**	W H Carr	C Boyd-Rochfort	Sir H de Trafford	4/11
1960	**Jet Stream**	D Smith	C Boyd-Rochfort	P Widener	100/8
1961	**Pardao**	W H Carr	C Boyd-Rochfort	Mrs C O Iselin	4/1
1962	**Pindaric**	R Elliott	T Masson	A B Askew	100/9
1963	**Duplation**	J Lindley	J M Gosden	Lady Wernher	100/7
1964	**Oncidium**	E Smith	J A Waugh	Lord H de Walden	11/2
1965	**Solstice**	J Lindley	J F Watts	C W Engelhard	20/1
1966	**Black Prince II**	B Taylor	J F Watts	E B Benjamin	20/1
1967	**Heave Ho**	W Williamson	S McGrath	Mrs T E Kelly	100/6
1968	**Laureate**	W Carson	B van Cutsem	Lord Derby	5/1
1969	**The Elk**	L Piggott	J Tree	Miss M Sheriffe	10/1
1970	**Meadowville**	G Lewis	M Jarvis	D Robinson	9/4
1971	**Homeric**	J Mercer	W R Hern	M Sobell	10/1
1972	**Charling**	J Lindley	G Smyth	Lady Z Wernher	6/1
1973	**Ksar**	W Carson	B van Cutsem	Lady Rotherwick	8/13
1974	**Bustino**	J Mercer	W R Hern	Lady Beaverbrook	13/8
1975	**Patch**	P Eddery	P Walwyn	C Vittadini	9/1
1976	**Norfolk Air**	R Hutchinson	J Dunlop	Miss E Rigden	9/1
1977	**Caporello**	E Eldin	G Pritchard-Gordon	J Hernandez	14/1
1978	**Whitstead**	B Taylor	H R Price	H Demetriou	4/5
1979	**Milford**	J Mercer	W R Hern	HM The Queen	4/11
1980	**Ginistrelli**	J Mercer	H Cecil	C St George	5/2
1981	**Riberetto**	P Robinson	R Boss	D McIntyre	66/1
1982	**Jalmood**	W Carson	J Dunlop	Sheikh Mohammed	11/8
1983	**Teenoso**	S Cauthen	G Wragg	E B Moller	9/2
1984	**Alphabatim**	B Rouse	G Harwood	K Abdulla	2/5
1985	**Slip Anchor**	S Cauthen	H Cecil	Lord H de Walden	10/11
1986	**Mashkour**	S Cauthen	H Cecil	Prince A Salman	7/4
1987	**Legal Bid**	S Cauthen	H Cecil	W S Farish III	5/6
1988	**Kahyasi**	R Cochrane	L Cumani	HH Aga Khan	5/6
1989	**Cacoethes**	G Starkey	G Harwood	Lady Harrison	5/2
1990	**Rock Hopper**	W R Swinburn	M Stoute	M Al-Maktoum	9/4
1991	**Corrupt**	C Asmussen	N Callaghan	K M Kalla	9/2
1992	**Assessor**	W R Swinburn	R Hannon	B E Nielsen	9/4

The Musidora Stakes

IN the immediate post-war years, trainers with top-class animals had to defend the major prizes against strong competition from France. It is ironic that nowadays those who train in the north have to fend off challenges from southern stables, but one who achieved both was the late Captain Charles Elsey. In 1949 he prepared *Musidora* to win both the 1,000 Guineas and The Oaks, in the latter race defeating M.Marcel Boussac's *Coronation. Musidora* was a failure as a broodmare, and the race named after her at York reflects her bravery in vanquishing *Coronation*, who went on to win the Prix de l'Arc de Triomphe by a neck.

The winners of the Musidora in the early days were of no special distinction, but the 1980 winner *Bireme* won the Oaks, *Indian Skimmer* (1987) took the Prix de Diane, *Diminuendo* the Oaks in 1988, as did *Snow Bride* a year later albeit on the disqualification of *Alyisa, In The Groove* went on to victory in the Irish 1,000 Guineas and the Juddmonte International at York after failing in the Oaks, while *All At Sea* was an outstanding filly in 1992.

Run at York over 1 mile 2+ furlongs for 3 year-old fillies First Run 1961 Group 3

		Jockey	Trainer	Owner	Odds
1961	**Ambergris**	L Piggott	H Wragg	Sir P Loraine	4/9
1962	**Fool's Gold**	W H Carr	C Boyd-Rochfort	J H Whitney	8/11
1963	**Noblesse**	G Bougoure	P Prendergast	Mrs J Olin	Evens
1964	**Ela Marita**	G Bougoure	P Prendergast	J R Mullion	20/21
1965	**Arctic Melody**	G Bougoure	P Prendergast Jnr	A Phelan	5/4
1966	**Orabella II**	B Taylor	H Leader	Mrs M Montgomerie	8/1
1967	**Palatch**	B Taylor	H Leader	C Vittadini	9/1
1968	**Exchange**	B Taylor	H Leader	R Midwood	11/4
1969	**Lovers Lane**	A Barclay	N Murless	M W Wickham-Boynton	9/2
1970	**Whitefoot**	J Lindley	H Wragg	R B Moller	7/4

Musidora pictured after winning the 1949 Oaks with Australian jockey Edgar Britt up.

		Jockey	Trainer	Owner	Odds
1971	**Catherine Wheel**	J Gorton	B Hobbs	T F Blackwell	10/11
1972	**Jakomima**	D Keith	P Walwyn	Sir W Pigott-Brown	4/1
1973	**Where You Lead**	E Hide	M V O'Brien	A Clore	10/1
1974	**Escorial**	L Piggott	I Balding	HM The Queen	4/5
1975	**Moonlight Night**	G Lewis	N Murless	H J Joel	9/1
1976	**Everything Nice**	G Lewis	B Hobbs	P Sinodhinos	9/4
1977	**Triple First**	E Hide	M Stoute	R Clifford-Turner	9/1
1978	**Princess of Man**	E Johnson	B Hills	R Sangster	8/1
1979	**Rimosa's Pet**	G Starkey	M Stoute	Sir C Clore	7/2
1980	**Bireme**	W Carson	W R Hern	R D Hollingsworth	5/1
1981	**Condessa**	D Gillespie	J Bolger	P Barrett	16/1
1982	**Last Feather**	S Cauthen	B Hills	M L Brosnan	7/4
1983	**Give Thanks**	D Gillespie	J Bolger	Mrs O White	13/8
1984	**Optimistic Lass**	W R Swinburn	M Stoute	Sheikh Mohammed	9/1
1985	**Fatah Flare**	S Cauthen	H Cecil	Sheikh Mohammed	10/1
1986	**Rejuvenate**	B Thomson	B Hills	K Abdulla	9/2
1987	**Indian Skimmer**	S Cauthen	H Cecil	Sheikh Mohammed	1/2
1988	**Diminuendo**	S Cauthen	H Cecil	Sheikh Mohammed	8/13
1989	**Snow Bride**	S Cauthen	H Cecil	M Al-Maktoum	4/1
1990	**In The Groove**	R Cochrane	D Elsworth	B Cooper	15/2
1991	**Gussy Marlowe**	M Roberts	C Brittain	Mrs J Van Geest	7/1
1992	**All At Sea**	P Eddery	H Cecil	K Abdulla	8/11

The Dante Stakes

Only two northern trained horses have won the Derby; *Pretender,* trained by Tom Dawson at Tupgill and ridden by the peerless John Osborne as the highlight of 46 years in the saddle, won at Epsom in 1869 and *Dante* took a wartime substitute race at Newmarket in 1945.

Unbeaten in six races at two, including the Middle Park and the Coventry, he was struck in the left eye a few days before the Two Thousand Guineas, which naturally held up his work and he was beaten by a neck by *Court Martial.* However in the Derby he reversed the form with the latter who could only finish third. *Dante* won with ease from a useful field including *Midas* who was second and *Chamossaire* who went on to win the St Leger, in which *Dante* did not run.

As a Derby trial, the Dante Stakes has produced four Epsom winners: *St Paddy* in 1960, *Shirley Heights* in 1978, *Shahrastani* in 1986 and *Reference Point* the following year. *Rheingold* won in 1972, and was certainly the unluckiest loser of the Derby in the decade, going down by inches in a very rough finish to *The Minstrel. Rheingold* gained compensation in the Prix de l'Arc de Triomphe in 1973.

Run at York over 1 mile 2+ furlongs for 3 year-olds First Run 1958 Group 2

		Jockey	Trainer	Owner	Odds
1958	**Bald Eagle**	W H Carr	C Boyd-Rochfort	H Guggenheim	11/10
1959	**Dickens**	W H Carr	C Boyd-Rochfort	Lady Z Wernher	100/8
1960	**St Paddy**	L Piggott	N Murless	Sir V Sassoon	8/11
1961	**Gallant Knight**	E Smith	T E Leader	H J Joel	3/1
1962	**Lucky Brief**	B Connorton	W Gray	W Cockerline	9/2
1963	**Merchant Venturer**	G Starkey	J Oxley	Sir F Robinson	9/2
1964	**Sweet Moss**	L Piggott	N Murless	Lady Sassoon	3/1
1965	**Ballymarais**	W Pyers	W Gray	W Stoker	10/1
1966	**Hermes**	G Starkey	J Oxley	R D Hollingsworth	3/1
1967	**Gay Garland**	R Hutchinson	H Wragg	A B Askew	100/7
1968	**Lucky Finish**	B Taylor	H Leader	C B Nathhorst	10/1
1969	**Activator**	M L Thomas	G Barling	Duke of Sutherland	6/1
1970	**Approval**	G Starkey	H Cecil	Sir H de Trafford	9/4
1971	**Fair World**	J Lindley	G Todd	J Dellal	6/1
1972	**Rheingold**	E Johnson	B Hills	H Zeisel	4/1
1973	**Owen Dudley**	G Lewis	N Murless	L Freedman	5/4
1974	**Honoured Guest**	G Lewis	N Murless	H J Joel	7/1
1975	**Hobnob**	W Carson	H Wragg	R B Moller	15/2
1976	**Trasi's Son**	E Hide	M Tate	J Hickman	50/1
1977	**Lucky Sovereign**	M L Thomas	H Wragg	R B Moller	20/1
1978	**Shirley Heights**	G Starkey	J Dunlop	Lord Halifax	10/1
1979	**Lyphard's Wish**	J Mercer	H Cecil	C d'Alessio	100/30
1980	**Hello Gorgeous**	J Mercer	H Cecil	D Wildenstein	4/1
1981	**Beldale Flutter**	P Eddery	M Jarvis	A Kelly	11/1
1982	**Simply Great**	L Piggott	H Cecil	D Wildenstein	11/10
1983	**Hot Touch**	P Eddery	G Wragg	E B Moller	11/1
1984	**Claude Monet**	S Cauthen	H Cecil	D Wildenstein	2/1
1985	**Damister**	P Eddery	J Tree	K Abdulla	5/1
1986	**Shahrastani**	W R Swinburn	M Stoute	HH Aga Khan	10/11
1987	**Reference Point**	S Cauthen	H Cecil	L Freedman	13/8
1988	**Red Glow**	P Eddery	G Wragg	E B Moller	7/1
1989	**Torjoun**	R Cochrane	L Cumani	HH Aga Khan	6/1
1990	**Sanglamore**	P Eddery	R Charlton	K Abdulla	11/2
1991	**Environment Friend**	G Duffield	J Fanshawe	W Gredley	11/2
1992	**Alnasr Alwasheek**	S Cauthen	M Stoute	A Al-Maktoum	8/1

The Yorkshire Cup

Founded in 1927 and run over two miles, the Yorkshire Cup soon became the first leg of the Cup race sequence, to be followed by the Ascot Gold Cup, the Goodwood Cup and the Doncaster Cup. Early winners were not especially distinguished but Lord Rosebery's *The Bastard* attracted much attention from jocular punters when winning in 1930. The origin of the name was Shakespearean, as *The Bastard* was out of a *Swynford* mare, *Swynford* being by *John O'Gaunt. The Bastard* was later exported to Australia, his great grandsire being the Australian champion *Carbine,* and the refined Antipodeans renamed him *The Buzzard.*

Pandofell won in 1961 before going on to victory in the Ascot Gold Cup and the Doncaster Cup, in spite of being a victim of the doping gangs, which were the scourge of racing in the Sixties, prior to the Goodwood Cup, but for which he may well have achieved a clean sweep of the Cup races.

HM The Queen's *Apprentice* won in 1965 before taking the Goodwood Cup, and the distance was reduced to a mile and three-quarters from 1966 onwards. In that season *Aunt Edith* won before becoming the first filly to win the King George and the Queen Elizabeth Stakes. The 1973 winner *Celtic Cone* became one of the best sires of National Hunt horses since the war, and the dual winner *Ardross* in 1981 and 1982 also won the Ascot Gold Cup twice and the Goodwood Cup.

Run at York over 1 mile 6 furlongs First Run 1927 Group 2

		Jockey	Trainer	Owner	Odds
1927	**Templestowe**	T Weston	R W Colling	H Stobart	3/1
1928	**Royal Pom**	G Baines	R Farquharson	Sir D Broughton	100/6
1929	**The Consul**	W Stephenson	W R Jarvis	Lord Lascelles	6/1
1930	**The Bastard**	H Wragg	J Jarvis	Lord Rosebery	11/2
1931	**The Scout II**	J Childs	C Boyd-Rochfort	W Woodward	5/2
1932	**Trimdon**	J Childs	J Lawson	C Lambton	9/4
1933	**Orpen**	R Perryman	Frank Butters	Sir A Butt	100/7
1934	**Within-the-law**	W Wells	J Cannon	Lady Yule	10/1
1935	**Felicitation**	F Fox	Frank Butters	HH Aga Khan	100/30
1936	**Valerius**	T Weston	J Lawson	Sir A Bailey	4/1
1937	**Silversol**	W Nevett	M Peacock	Sir R Sykes	5/1
1938	**Suzerain**	W Rickaby	T E Leader	A de Rothschild	7/2
1939	**Finis**	H Wragg	O Bell	Sir H Cunliffe-Owen	11/4
1940/44	**No Race**				
1945	**Kingstone**	D Smith	C Boyd-Rochfort	HM The King	1/2
1946	**Stirling Castle**	E Smith	J Lawson	A E Saunders	3/1
1947	**No Orchids**	H Blackshaw	M A H Everitt	M A H Everitt	8/1
1948	**Whiteway**	W T Evans	N Bertie	D Fitzgerald	8/1
1949	**Woodburn**	W Rickaby	C Elsey	Lord Allendale	13/8
1950	**Miraculous Atom**	W Nevett	S Hall	H Halmshaw	6/1
1951	**Orderly Ann**	A Carson	L Shedden	T B Watson	33/1
1952	**Eastern Emperor**	W Rickaby	J Jarvis	Lord Milford	11/8
1953	**Childe Harold**	J Brace	W Dutton	T H Farr	9/2
1954	**Premonition**	W H Carr	C Boyd-Rochfort	W P Wyatt	5/4
1955	**By Thunder!**	W Swinburn	F Armstrong	J Gerber	100/30
1956	**Romany Air**	W Rickaby	R Day	G Chesterman	100/8
1957	**Souverlone**	J Sime	H Peacock	R F Dennis	50/1
1958	**Brioche**	E Britt	C Elsey	W Humble	5/6
1959	**Cutter**	E Mercer	J Oxley	R D Hollingsworth	5/2
1960	**Dickens**	W H Carr	C Boyd-Rochfort	Lady Z Wernher	11/2
1961	**Pandofell**	L Piggott	F Maxwell	H W Daw	11/4
1962	**Sagacity**	W H Carr	C Boyd-Rochfort	Lady Cholmondeley	15/2
1963	**Honour Bound**	D Smith	F Rimell	E Gaze	9/2
1964	**Raise You Ten**	W H Carr	C Boyd-Rochfort	P Widener	5/1
1965	**Apprentice**	S Clayton	C Boyd-Rochfort	HM The Queen	33/1
1966	**Aunt Edith**	L Piggott	N Murless	J Hornung	4/5
1967	**Salvo**	R Hutchinson	H Wragg	G A Oldham	8/11
1968	**Sweet Story**	J Etherington	R D Peacock	Duke of Roxburghe	3/1
1969	**Quartette**	R Maddock	T Gosling	H L Vickery	100/8
1970	**Rangong**	A Barclay	N Murless	Lady Sassoon	4/6
1971	**Alto Volante**	B Taylor	F Maxwell	V Barclay	4/1
1972	**Knockroe**	L Piggott	P Nelson	V McCalmont	10/11
1973	**Celtic Cone**	G Starkey	F Cundell	Mrs S Hicks	7/1
1974	**Buoy**	J Mercer	W R Hern	R D Hollingsworth	11/8
1975	**Riboson**	J Mercer	W R Hern	Lady Beaverbrook	11/2
1976	**Bruni**	L Piggott	H R Price	C St George	7/4
1977	**Bright Finish**	L Piggott	J Tree	J H Whitney	100/30
1978	**Smuggler**	W Carson	W R Hern	Lord Porchester	4/1
1979	**Pragmatic**	J Reid	R F Johnson Houghton	J Rowles	12/1
1980	**Noble Saint**	L Piggott	R Armstrong	R Guest	10/1
1981	**Ardross**	L Piggott	H Cecil	C St George	2/1
1982	**Ardross**	L Piggott	H Cecil	C St George	2/5
1983	**Line Slinger**	E Hide	W Elsey	N Hetherton	33/1
1984	**Band**	W Carson	W R Hern	K Abdulla	9/4
1985	**Ilium**	R Hills	H Thomson Jones	H Al-Tajir	5/1
1986	**Eastern Mystic**	P Eddery	L Cumani	R W Harden	9/4
1987	**Verd-Antique**	S Cauthen	H Cecil	Sheikh Mohammed	7/4
1988	**Moon Madness**	P Eddery	J Dunlop	Duchess of Norfolk	6/5
1989	**Mountain Kingdom**	S Cauthen	C Brittain	Pin Oak Stable	2/1
1990	**Braashee**	M Roberts	A Stewart	M Al-Maktoum	11/8
1991	**Arzanni**	L Dettori	L Cumani	D Thompson	5/1
1992	**Rock Hopper**	P Eddery	M Stoute	M Al-Maktoum	100/30

Run over 2 miles 1927-1965.

Run as Yorkshire Autumn Cup in 1945

The Duke Of York Stakes

The Duke of York Stakes was first run in 1968 and named with typical English eccentricity as there was no Duke of York at the time. It is one of the Royal Dukedoms reserved for the children of the monarch and the last Duke of York before the title was conferred on HRH Prince Andrew following his marriage was HM King George VI.

Since 1974, the race has been something of a benefit for Mr Robert Sangster, as he has won six of the last eighteen runnings up to 1991, while *Boldboy*, one of the toughest sprinters seen since the war, is the senior winner at the age of seven in 1977.

Run at York over 6 furlongs First Run 1968 Group 3

		Jockey	Trainer	Owner	Odds
1968	**Hard Water**	J Mercer	J Sutcliffe Jnr	J R Brown	5/2
1969	**Great Bear**	R Hutchinson	J Dunlop	Lady S Fitzalan-Howard	5/2
1970	**Fluke**	G Duffield	J Oxley	R D Hollingsworth	11/4
1971	**The Brianstan**	L Piggott	J Sutcliffe Jnr	S Powell	Evens
1972	**Stilvi**	J Gorton	B Hobbs	G Cambanis	5/1
1973	**Abwah**	G Lewis	N Murless	L Freedman	9/1
1974	**Noble Mark**	W Carson	B Hills	R Sangster	4/1
1975	**Steel Heart**	L Piggott	D Weld	R Tikkoo	15/8
1976	**Three Legs**	G Dettori	L Cumani	M Boffa	8/1
1977	**Boldboy**	W Carson	W R Hern	Lady Beaverbrook	7/1
1978	**Private Line**	E Hide	C Brittain	G Greenwood	15/1
1979	**Thatching**	L Piggott	M V O'Brien	R Sangster	17/2
1980	**Flash N'Thunder**	S Cauthen	B Hills	R Sangster	5/1
1981	**King of Spain**	P Cook	P Cundell	Avon Industries Ltd	8/1
1982	**Jester**	S Cauthen	B Hills	R Sangster	4/1
1983	**Vorvados**	L Piggott	M Haynes	Miss F Gallichan	11/1
1984	**Gabitat**	R Curant	B Gubby	Brian Gubby Ltd	6/1
1985	**Chapel Cottage**	P Robinson	M Ryan	T Ramsden	3/1
1986	**Grey Desire**	K Darley	M Brittain	M Brittain	4/1
1987	**Handsome Sailor**	C Asmussen	B Hills	R Sangster	14/1
1988	**Handsome Sailor**	M Hills	B Hills	R Sangster	5/1
1989	**Indian Ridge**	S Cauthen	D Elsworth	Mrs A Coughlan	7/2
1990	**Lugana Beach**	S Cauthen	D Elsworth	R Richards	6/1
1991	**Green Line Express**	A Cruz	M Moubarak	Ecurie Fustok	7/2
1992	**Shalford**	M Roberts	R Hannon	D F Cock	6/1

The Lockinge Stakes

The Lockinge Stakes was founded in 1958 and represents the earliest opportunity in the Calendar for high-class three-year-olds to meet their elders. The first winner was HM The Queen's *Pall Mall*, winner of the 2,000 Guineas at odds of 20/1 and ridden by Doug Smith. The Boyd-Rochfort stable jockey Harry Carr, who usually partnered the Queen's horses, had elected to ride the stable-selected *Bald Eagle* who started favourite. *Pall Mall* won the Lockinge again, in the following season, and in a feat almost unthinkable today carried 9st 7lb into second place in the Royal Hunt Cup, conceding the winner *Faultless Speech* 20lb.

Brigadier Gerard's sire *Queen's Hussar* won in 1963, and the Brigadier duly franked the family fortunes in 1972. *Habitat* sprang a surprise in 1969 before going on to be one of the best horses of his generation, *Jimmy Reppin, Tower Walk, Lorenzaccio* and the Eclipse winner *Wolver Hollow* all finishing behind him at Newbury. *Habitat* also beat Guineas winner *Right Tack* and *Welsh Pageant* in the Prix du Moulin at Longchamp.

The versatile *Boldboy* won in 1974, but the most controversial race was in 1978. The record shows *Don* as a rare winner for the north, but the moral victor was *Jellaby*. The 11/4 favourite had all his rivals off the bit and struggling when inexplicably stumbling 100 yards from home and unseating his rider, the late Brian Taylor.

Run at Newbury over 1 mile First Run 1958 Group 2

		Jockey	Trainer	Owner	Odds
1958	**Pall Mall**	W H Carr	C Boyd-Rochfort	HM The Queen	4/6
1959	**Pall Mall**	W H Carr	C Boyd-Rochfort	HM The Queen	1/2
1960	**Sovereign Path**	L Piggott	R Mason	R Mason	7/4
1961	**Prince Midge**	D Keith	R J Colling	J J Astor	11/2
1962	**Superstition**	D W Morris	C Boyd-Rochfort	Mrs C O Iselin	100/30
1963	**Queen's Hussar**	A Breasley	T Corbett	Lord Carnarvon	9/2
1964	**The Creditor**	L Piggott	N Murless	Lady Sassoon	10/11
1965	**Young Christopher**	W Williamson	F Maxwell	J McShane	6/1
1966	**Silly Season**	G Lewis	I Balding	P Mellon	7/1
1967	**Bluerullah**	W Williamson	S McGrath	S McGrath	4/1
1968	**Supreme Sovereign**	R Hutchinson	H Wragg	Mrs R Hodges	5/6
1969	**Habitat**	R Hutchinson	R F Johnson Houghton	C W Engelhard	10/1
1970	**Welsh Pageant**	A Barclay	N Murless	H J Joel	8/13
1971	**Welsh Pageant**	G Lewis	N Murless	H J Joel	Evens
1972	**Brigadier Gerard**	J Mercer	W R Hern	Mrs J Hislop	1/4

Pall Mall, winner of the first two Lockinge Stakes with W.H.Carr aboard.

		Jockey	Trainer	Owner	Odds
1973	**Sparkler**	L Piggott	R Armstrong	Mrs M Mehl-Mulhens	7/2
1974	**Boldboy**	J Mercer	W R Hern	Lady Beaverbrook	15/8
1975	**No Race**				
1976	**El Rastro**	W Pyers	A Penna	D Wildenstein	9/2
1977	**Relkino**	W Carson	W R Hern	Lady Beaverbrook	4/1
1978	**Don**	B Rouse	W Elsey	E Ryan	5/1
1979	**Young Generation**	G Starkey	G Harwood	A Ward	4/1
1980	**Kris**	J Mercer	H Cecil	Lord H de Walden	4/9
1981	**Belmont Bay**	L Piggott	H Cecil	D Wildenstein	11/10
1982	**Motavato**	S Cauthen	B Hills	R Sangster	7/4
1983	**Noalcoholic**	G Duffield	G Pritchard-Gordon	W du Pont III	7/2
1984	**Cormorant Wood**	S Cauthen	B Hills	R J McAlpine	7/1
	Wassl	W Carson	J Dunlop	A Al-Maktoum	9/2
1985	**Prismatic**	Paul Eddery	H Cecil	Lord H de Walden	10/1
1986	**Scottish Reel**	W R Swinburn	M Stoute	Cheveley Park Stud	4/1
1987	**Then Again**	R Cochrane	L Cumani	R J Shannon	9/2
1988	**Broken Hearted**	T Quinn	P Cole	F Salman	8/1
1989	**Most Welcome**	Paul Eddery	G Wragg	Sir P Oppenheimer	9/1
1990	**Safawan**	W R Swinburn	M Stoute	Mrs D Thompson	5/1
1991	**Polar Falcon**	L Piggott	J Hammond	D Thompson	3/1
1992	**Selkirk**	R Cochrane	I Balding	G Strawbridge	5/2

The Temple Stakes

An essential part of the sprint pattern, the most distinguished winners in the early years were *Song,* later a good sire of sprinters, and *Raffingora,* winner of twenty races, many under huge weights. He won the Cherkley Sprint Handicap at Epsom in 53.89 seconds carrying 10st, the record being held by *Indigenous* at 53.60 but shouldering only 9st 5lb.

The outstanding winner in recent years was without question *Dayjur.* The Temple Stakes was followed by the King's Stand, the Nunthorpe, the Ladbroke Sprint Cup, the Prix de l'Abbaye and an extraordinary race for the Breeders' Cup sprint, when *Dayjur* hurdled the shadow of the time-keepers box sharply etched into the Belmont Park dirt track, with the race already won, and handed victory to the American filly *Safely Kept.*

Run at Sandown Park over 5 furlongs First Run 1965 Group 2

		Jockey	Trainer	Owner	Odds
1965	**Holborn**	A Breasley	R F Johnson Houghton	C W Engelhard	11/8
1966	**Polyfoto**	B Taylor	E Reavey	Mrs C J Reavey	8/1
1967	**Falcon**	L Piggott	R F Johnson Houghton	C W Engelhard	6/1
1968	**D'Urberville**	J Lindley	J Tree	J H Whitney	5/1
1969	**Song**	J Mercer	D Candy	B Jenks	2/1
1970	**Raffingora**	L Piggott	W Marshall	A G M Stevens	4/1
1971	**Mummy's Pet**	G Lewis	J Sutcliffe Jnr	L Goldschlager	5/6
1972	**Shoolerville**	L Piggott	F Armstrong	Mrs J F C Bryce	13/8
1973	**Saulingo**	W Williamson	P Davey	D Robinson	4/7
1974	**Bay Express**	B Taylor	P Nelson	P Cooper	11/2
1975	**Blue Cashmere**	F Durr	M Stoute	R Clifford-Turner	5/1
1976	**Lochnager**	E Hide	M W Easterby	C Spence	5/1
1977	**Vilgora**	S Perks	A Stevens	A Stevens	13/2
1978	**Oscilight**	B Rouse	J Sutcliffe Jnr	Mrs O Jackson	9/2
	Smarten Up	M L Thomas	W Wightman	Mrs R Kennard	14/1
1979	**Double Form**	J Reid	R F Johnson Houghton	Baroness H Thyssen	5/2
1980	**Sharpo**	B Rouse	J Tree	Mrs M Sheriffe	33/1
1981	**No Race**				
1982	**Mummy's Game**	T Ives	W O'Gorman	Rockhouse Stud	4/1
1983	**Fearless Lad**	L Piggott	R D Peacock	G Soulsby	5/4
1984	**Petorius**	W R Swinburn	M Stoute	Mrs I Phillips	4/1
	Reesh	M L Thomas	W O'Gorman	Yazid & Ahmed Ltd	9/2
1985	**Never So Bold**	S Cauthen	R Armstrong	E Kessly	9/4
1986	**Double Schwartz**	P Eddery	C Nelson	R Sangster	100/30
1987	**Treasure Kay**	W R Swinburn	P Makin	G W Yates	16/1
1988	**Handsome Sailor**	M Hills	B Hills	R Sangster	7/2
1989	**Dancing Dissident**	W R Swinburn	M Stoute	Sheikh Mohammed	3/1
1990	**Dayjur**	W Carson	W R Hern	H Al-Maktoum	11/2
1991	**Elbio**	W R Swinburn	P Makin	B Brackpool	11/8
1992	**Snaadee**	P Eddery	M Stoute	M Al-Maktoum	14/1

The Henry II Stakes

Sandown Park was laid down as a racecourse in 1875, on land originally occupied by Augustine Priory. This holy place was founded by King Henry II, a monarch who had trouble with the Irish, tiresome bishops, fractious children and his finances; all familiar problems to those in government and royal houses today.

As King Henry also held fiefdom over one third of France, it is appropriate that the inaugural winner of the Henry II Stakes was *Gaul*.

The miserly Group Three status awarded to the race is a reflection on the modern enthusiasm for precocity in breeding the thoroughbred. A glance at the list will show that the Henry II has been won by most of the finest stayers of modern times. If one had to choose an outstanding race, it would be *Fighting Charlie's* victory over the 1961 St Leger winner *Aurelius* and *Goupi* in 1966.

Run at Sandown Park over 2 miles First Run 1963 Group 3

		Jockey	Trainer	Owner	Odds
1963	**Gaul**	G Lewis	P Hastings-Bass	Lord Sefton	6/1
1964	**Fighting Ship**	P Robinson	J Jarvis	Lord Rosebery	5/2
1965	**Grey of Falloden**	J Mercer	W R Hern	Lord Astor	10/11
1966	**Fighting Charlie**	G Starkey	F Maxwell	Lady M Bury	9/4
1967	**Parbury**	R Hutchinson	D Candy	H P Holt	7/1
1968	**Chicago**	A Barclay	H Wragg	G A Oldham	7/2
1969	**Chicago**	R Hutchinson	H Wragg	G A Oldham	9/2
1970	**Ginger Boy**	W Wiliamson	J Hooton	Mrs J Vanden Bergh	1/4
1971	**Charlton**	J Mercer	W R Hern	HM The Queen	6/4
1972	**Hornet**	A Murray	G Todd	Mrs A Hurlstone	85/40
1973	**The Admiral**	G Lewis	N Murless	H J Joel	Evens
1974	**Ragstone**	R Hutchinson	J Dunlop	Duke of Norfolk	4/11
1975	**Zab**	J Mercer	W R Hern	Lady Beaverbrook	15/2
1976	**Sea Anchor**	J Mercer	W R Hern	R D Hollingsworth	100/30
1977	**Grey Baron**	G Lewis	B Hobbs	P Parnell	5/2
1978	**Smuggler**	W Carson	W R Hern	Lord Porchester	15/8
1979	**Buckskin**	J Mercer	H Cecil	D Wildenstein	10/11
1980	**Billion**	P Eddery	J Dunlop	N B Hunt	8/1
1981	**No Race**				
1982	**Ardross**	L Piggott	H Cecil	C St George	2/7
1983	**Ore**	L Piggott	W Musson	O Zawawi	5/4
1984	**Harly**	P Eddery	J Dunlop	N A Shuaib	11/1
1985	**Destroyer**	S Whitworth	K Brassey	D J Muir	9/1
1986	**Longboat**	W Carson	W R Hern	R D Hollingsworth	4/1
1987	**Saronicos**	T Ives	C Brittain	M Lemos	14/1

		Jockey	Trainer	Owner	Odds
1988	**Primitive Rising**	S Cauthen	H Cecil	S Niarchos	7/2
1989	**Sadeem**	G Starkey	G Harwood	Sheikh Mohammed	9/2
1990	**Teamster**	W R Swinburn	M Stoute	P Newton	2/1
1991	**Top of the World**	M Roberts	C Brittain	M Lemos	33/1
1992	**Drum Taps**	L Dettori	Lord Huntingdon	Y Asakawa	2/1

The Brigadier Gerard Stakes

Originally run in 1953 as the Coronation Stakes to commemorate the crowning of Her Majesty, the race was renamed in 1973 in honour of the champion racehorse who was beaten in only one of his eighteen starts.

On balance, the quality of the winners was better in the early years than in recent times; *Aggressor, Petite Etoile, Busted, Royal Palace* and *Connaught* all take the eye; but the Brigadier Gerard remains a race which usually produces strong fields and not a few surprises, as evidenced by *Stanerra's* 20/1 victory in 1983.

Brigadier Gerard, **who was beaten only once in 18 starts. The Coronation Stakes, first run in 1953, was renamed in honour of this great champion.**

Run at Sandown Park over 1 mile 2 furlongs First Run 1953 Group 3

		Jockey	Trainer	Owner	Odds
1953	**Guersant**	P Blanc	G Watson	Baron G de Rothschild	3/1
1954	**Chamier**	A Breasley	N Cannon	Mrs F L Vickermman	5/1
1955	**Chamier**	A Breasley	N Cannon	F Vickerman	5/4
1956	**Tribord**	J Massard	E Boullenger	Mme D Wildenstein	11/4
1957	**Gilles de Retz**	F Barlow	P Walwyn	A G Samuel	100/6
1958	**Arctic Explorer**	L Piggott	N Murless	G Loder	11/4
1959	**Aggressor**	J Lindley	J M Gosden	Sir H Wernher	7/2
1960	**Lucky Guy**	W Williamson	S McGrath	J McGrath Jnr	8/1
1961	**Petite Etoile**	L Piggott	N Murless	HH Aga Khan	4/9
1962	**Cipriani**	G Bougoure	P Prendergast	Lady H Svedjar	9/2
1963	**Tacitus**	G Lewis	W Nightingall	D W Molins	15/2
1964	**Tacitus**	D Keith	W Nightingall	D W Molins	13/2
1965	**Philanderer**	J Mercer	W Wharton	Maj L B Holliday	4/9
1966	**Super Sam**	J Lindley	J F Watts	G Cooper	6/1
1967	**Busted**	G Moore	N Murless	S Joel	3/1
1968	**Royal Palace**	A Barclay	N Murless	H J Joel	8/15
1969	**Connaught**	A Barclay	N Murless	H J Joel	6/5
1970	**Hotfoot**	J Gorton	B Hobbs	A Villar	8/1
1971	**Pembroke Castle**	G Lewis	N Murless	H J Joel	5/4
1972	**Stubb's Gazette**	E Eldin	D Smith	Mrs V McCalmont	13/2
1973	**Scottish Rifle**	R Hutchinson	J Dunlop	A J Struthers	5/4
1974	**Ksar**	W Carson	B van Cutsem	Lady Rotherwick	8/13
1975	**Rymer**	B Taylor	H Blagrave	H Blagrave	8/1
1976	**Anne's Pretender**	L Piggott	H R Price	Sir C Clore	2/1
1977	**Jellaby**	B Taylor	H R Price	E Alkhalifa	6/1
1978	**Gunner B**	J Mercer	H Cecil	Mrs P Barratt	2/1
1979	**Jellaby**	P Eddery	P Walwyn	R Denton	5/1
1980	**Gregorian**	L Piggott	M V O'Brien	D Schwartz	4/6
1981	**No Race**				
1982	**Kalaglow**	G Starkey	G Harwood	A Ward	Evens
1983	**Stanerra**	B Rouse	F Dunne	F Dunne	20/1
1984	**Adonijah**	L Piggott	H Cecil	K Abdulla	Evens
1985	**Commanche Run**	L Piggott	L Cumani	I Allan	11/10
1986	**Bedtime**	W Carson	W R Hern	Lord Halifax	5/2
1987	**Mtoto**	M Roberts	A Stewart	A Al-Maktoum	16/1
1988	**Highland Chieftain**	W Carson	J Dunlop	D R Hunnisett	16/1
1989	**Hibernian Gold**	G Starkey	G Harwood	K Nicklin	9/4
1990	**Husyan**	W Carson	P Walwyn	H Al-Maktoum	9/1
1991	**Stagecraft**	S Cauthen	M Stoute	Sheikh Mohammed	100/30
1992	**Opera House**	S Cauthen	M Stoute	Sheikh Mohammed	Evens

Run as the Coronation Stakes 1953-1972

The Derby

But for the inspiration of a disillusioned general, the Derby may never have been conceived. 'Gentleman' Johnny Burgoyne, soldier, playwright and politician married into the Derby family and leased his mansion in Surrey, a former ale-house known as The Oaks to the 12th Earl. He was also a keen racing buff and extremely interested in the experiment conducted by his old comrade in arms Anthony St Leger at Doncaster where the latter had founded a two mile race for three-year-old colts and fillies, which he had helped to devise.

The year was 1776 and Burgoyne was heavily involved in the American War of Independence. In 1778 political bungling forced him to surrender to the American forces at Saratoga, and worse, his wife had died during his absence.

He went to live with his nephew by marriage at the Oaks, and persuaded Derby to emulate St Leger and found a race over a mile and a half for three-year-old fillies to be run on the nearby course at Epsom.

Epsom during this period was a former spa town with some very dull racing taking place on Banstead Downs sponsored by local tradesmen for their own profit from booths and catering stalls. However, the new race proved an immediate sucess, especially for Lord Derby who owned the winner, *Bridget*, on 14 May 1779.

That evening, the Earl hosted a lavish dinner party. The guest list was distinguished; apart from Burgoyne, the table was graced by the playwright and politician Richard Brinsley Sheridan, the parliamentarian Charles James Fox and the Jockey Club Steward (in those days there was only one, the equivalent of the Senior Steward today) Sir Charles Bunbury.

Like so many Jockey Club men, Bunbury was a free thinker and joined Fox in the House of Commons to campaign against the slave trade.

But such thoughts were far from their minds as the gentlemen settled down to discuss another issue, namely a follow up to the Oaks. Eventually they came to plan race for three-year-old colts and fillies, to be run over one mile on the dog-leg course which in those days started half a mile east of Tattenham Corner. Colts were to carry 8st, fillies 7st 11lb. It but remained to find a name.

The idea was Burgoyne's but he demurred. Fox and Sheridan were not truly racing men, and it became a matter between Bunbury and Derby. Legend has it that the decision turned on the toss of a coin, but it is more likely that Bunbury, who would have preferred to run the race at Newmarket anyway, deferred to his host.

Bunbury received his satisfaction when *Diomed* won the inaugural Derby Stakes in his pink and white striped colours on Thursday, 4 May 1780. Second was *Budrow*, owned by 'Colonel' Dennis O'Kelly. An expatriate Irishman, former sedan chairman and wife of Charlotte Hayes, London's leading brothel keeper, he was not unnaturally socially spurned by Lord Derby and his friends but that did not prevent him from winning two out of the first five runnings of the Derby with the progeny of his great horse *Eclipse*.

In 1784 the distance became a mile and a half, as it is today, although the starting point has been moved twice since then. In 1848 at the suggestion of Lord George Bentinck, who considered that the punters in the stands had the right to a full view of the race, and again in 1872. Bentinck, who along with Bunbury and Admiral Rous was a prime influence on the Turf, left his mark on the Derby when he exposed the *'Running Rein'* scandal in 1844 in the depths of the 'Filthy Forties'. *Running Rein* was in fact a four-year-old called *Maccabeus* and it was due to Bentincks tireless efforts that the swindle was finally exposed and the race awarded to the runner-up *Orlando*, thus giving racing's first champion jockey Nat Flatman his only Derby winner.

In 1846, Bentinck decided to enter politics, and sold all his bloodstock including *Surplice*, winner of the Derby in 1848. The Derby meant more than anything to Bentinck who was found drenched in gloom the following morning in the House of Commons library by his party lieutenant Benjamin Disraeli.

Dizzy had recently received the Order of the Garter. Bentinck explained reason for his despondency, concluding 'You do not know what the Derby is'.

'Yes I do', replied Disraeli, pointing to the blue sash of his new Order,' it is the Blue Ribbon of the Turf'.

The years have bowdlerised this into Blue Riband, which is actually a mythical award for the fastest sea crossing of the Atlantic, but no matter; the Derby is the world's most famous horse race, much imitated (there were eighty-seven races world-wide calling themselves Derbies at the last count) but never equalled.

The roll of honour listed below speaks for itself. In its 214 year history the Derby has seen it all including the scandal and romance of *Hermit's* race in 1867, the tragedy of Emily Davison's death at Tattenham Corner in 1913, royal victories in 1788, 1896, 1900 and 1909, and the superb riding of Fred Archer, Steve Donoghue and Lester Piggott.

There can be little doubt that if the famous dinner party at The Oaks were to reconvene in ghostly form today, the last course they would choose for the three-year-old championship of the world would be Epsom, and it is equally certain that but for the Derby, the former spa town would be a dormitory suburb with the nearest racecourse at Kempton.

***Above:* Contemporary illustration of Fred Archer riding the 1881 Derby winner *Iroquois*. *Below:* King Edward VII pictured with his horse *Minoru*, winner of the 1909 Derby.**

Nonetheless, despite the switchback conformation of the track and competition from the Irish Derby together with the rise of all-aged European races such as the Arc de Triomphe, the King George VI and The Queen Elizabeth Stakes and the recent development of richly endowed American races, the Derby remains the ambition of everyone in flat racing; it is quite simply the one they all want to win.

Run at Epsom over 1 mile 4 furlongs for 3 year-old colts & fillies First Run 1780 Group 1

		Jockey	Trainer	Owner	Odds
1780	**Diomed**	S Arnull	R Teasdale	Sir C Bunbury	6/4
1781	**Young Eclipse**	C Hindley	–	D O'Kelly	10/1
1782	**Assassin**	S Arnull	F Neale	Lord Egremont	5/1
1783	**Saltram**	C Hindley	F Neale	J Parker	5/2
1784	**Serjeant**	J Arnull	–	D O'Kelly	3/1
1785	**Aimwell**	C Hindley	J Pratt	Lord Clermont	7/1
1786	**Noble**	J White	F Neale	T Panton	30/1
1787	**Sir Peter Teazle**	S Arnull	Saunders	Lord Derby	2/1
1788	**Sir Thomas**	W South	F Neale	HRH Prince of Wales	5/6
1789	**Skyscraper**	S Chifney	M Stephenson	Duke of Bedford	4/7

		Jockey	Trainer	Owner	Odds
1790	**Rhadamanthus**	J Arnull	J Pratt	Lord Grosvenor	5/4
1791	**Eager**	M Stephenson	M Stephenson	Duke of Bedford	5/2
1792	**John Bull**	F Buckle	J Pratt	Lord Grosvenor	4/6
1793	**Waxy**	W Clift	R Robson	Sir F Poole	12/1
1794	**Daedalus**	F Buckle	J Pratt	Lord Grosvenor	6/1
1795	**Spread Eagle**	A Wheatley	R Prince	Sir F Standish	3/1
1796	**Didelot**	J Arnull	R Prince	Sir F Standish	–
1797	**c by Fidget**	J Singleton	M Stephenson	Duke of Bedford	10/1
1798	**Sir Harry**	S Arnull	F Neale	J Cookson	7/4
1799	**Archduke**	J Arnull	R Prince	Sir F Standish	12/1
1800	**Champion**	W Clift	T Perren	C Wilson	7/4
1801	**Eleanor**	J Saunders	J Frost	Sir C Bunbury	5/4
1802	**Tyrant**	F Buckle	R Robson	Duke of Grafton	7/1
1803	**Ditto**	W Clift	J Lonsdale	Sir H Williamson	7/2
1804	**Hannibal**	W Arnull	F Neale	Lord Egremont	3/1
1805	**Cardinal Beaufort**	D Fitzpatrick	R D Boyce	Lord Egremont	20/1
1806	**Paris**	J Shepherd	R Prince	Lord Foley	5/1
1807	**Election**	J Arnull	R D Boyce	Lord Egremont	3/1
1808	**Pan**	F Collinson	J Lonsdale	Sir H Williamson	25/1
1809	**Pope**	T Goodisson	R Robson	Duke of Grafton	20/1
1810	**Whalebone**	W Clift	R Robson	Duke of Grafton	2/1
1811	**Phantom**	F Buckle	J Edwards	Sir J Shelley	5/1
1812	**Octavius**	W Arnull	R D Boyce	R Ladbroke	7/1
1813	**Smolensko**	T Goodisson	Crouch	Sir C Bunbury	Evens
1814	**Blucher**	W Arnull	R D Boyce	Lord Stawell	5/2
1815	**Whisker**	T Goodisson	R Robson	Duke of Grafton	8/1
1816	**Prince Leopold**	W Wheatley	W Butler	HRH The Duke of York	20/1
1817	**Azor**	J Robinson	R Robson	J Payne	50/1
1818	**Sam**	S Chifney Jnr	W Chifney	T Thornhill	7/2
1819	**Tiresias**	W Clift	R Prince	Duke of Portland	5/2
1820	**Sailor**	S Chifney Jnr	W Chifney	T Thornhill	7/2
1821	**Gustavus**	S Day	Crouch	J Hunter	2/1
1822	**Moses**	T Goodisson	W Butler	HRH The Duke of York	6/1
1823	**Emilius**	F Buckle	R Robson	J Udny	11/8
1824	**Cedric**	J Robinson	J Edwards	Sir J Shelley	9/2
1825	**Middleton**	J Robinson	J Edwards	Lord Jersey	7/4
1826	**Lap-dog**	G Dockeray	R Stephenson	Lord Egremont	50/1
1827	**Mameluke**	J Robinson	J Edwards	Lord Jersey	9/1
1828	**Cadland**	J Robinson	R D Boyce	Duke of Rutland	4/1
1829	**Frederick**	J Forth	J Forth	G W Gratwicke	40/1
1830	**Priam**	S Day	W Chifney	W Chifney	4/1
1831	**Spaniel**	W Wheatley	J Rogers	Lord Lowther	50/1
1832	**St Giles**	W Scott	J Webb	R Ridsdale	3/1
1833	**Dangerous**	J Chapple	I Sadler	I Sadler	30/1
1834	**Plenipotentiary**	P Conolly	G Payne	S Batson	9/4
1835	**Mundig**	W Scott	J Scott	J Bowes	6/1
1836	**Bay Middleton**	J Robinson	J Edwards	Lord Jersey	7/4
1837	**Phosphorus**	G Edwards	J Doe	Lord Berners	40/1
1838	**Amato**	J Chapple	Ralph Sherwood	Sir G Heathcote	30/1
1839	**Bloomsbury**	S Templeman	W Ridsdale	W Ridsdale	25/1
1840	**Little Wonder**	W Macdonald	W Forth	D Robertson	50/1
1841	**Coronation**	P Conolly	Painter	A T Rawlinson	5/2
1842	**Attila**	W Scott	J Scott	G Anson	5/1
1843	**Cotherstone**	W Scott	J Scott	J Bowes	13/8
1844	**Orlando**	E Flatman	W Cooper	J Peel	20/1
1845	**The Merry Monarch**	F Bell	J Forth	G W Gratwicke	15/1
1846	**Pyrrhus the First**	S Day	J B Day	J Gully	8/1
1847	**Cossack**	S Templeman	J Day	T Pedley	5/1
1848	**Surplice**	S Templeman	J Kent Jnr	Lord Clifden	Evens
1849	**The Flying Dutchman**	C Marlow	J Fobert	Lord Eglinton	2/1
1850	**Voltigeur**	J Marson	R Hill	Lord Zetland	16/1
1851	**Teddington**	J Marson	A Taylor Snr	Sir J Hawley	3/1
1852	**Daniel O'Rourke**	F Butler	J Scott	J Bowes	25/1
1853	**West Australian**	F Butler	J Scott	J Bowes	6/4
1854	**Andover**	A Day	J Day	J Gully	7/2
1855	**Wild Dayrell**	Robert Sherwood	J Rickaby	F L Popham	Evens
1856	**Ellington**	T Aldcroft	T Dawson	Admiral O Harcourt	20/1
1857	**Blink Bonny**	J Charlton	W I'Anson	W I'Anson	20/1
1858	**Beadsman**	J Wells	G Manning	Sir J Hawley	10/1
1859	**Musjid**	J Wells	G Manning	Sir J Hawley	9/4
1860	**Thormanby**	H Custance	M Dawson	J Merry	4/1
1861	**Kettledrum**	R Bullock	G Oates	C Towneley	16/1
1862	**Caractacus**	J Parsons	R Smith	C Snewing	40/1
1863	**Macaroni**	T Chaloner	J Godding	R C Naylor	10/1
1864	**Blair Athol**	J Snowden	W I'Anson	W I'Anson	14/1

Left: **Coach and four arrive at Epsom for the 1922 Derby Day meeting.** ***Right: Hyperion*** **restored to his temporary Epsom quarters after winning the 1933 Derby.**

		Jockey	Trainer	Owner	Odds
1865	**Gladiateur**	H Grimshaw	T Jennings	Comte F de Lagrange	5/2
1866	**Lord Lyon**	H Custance	J Dover	R Sutton	5/6
1867	**Hermit**	J Daley	G Bloss	H Chaplin	1,000/15
1868	**Blue Gown**	J Wells	J Porter	Sir J Hawley	7/2
1869	**Pretender**	J Osborne Jnr	T Dawson	J Johnstone	11/8
1870	**Kingcraft**	T French	M Dawson	Lord Falmouth	20/1
1871	**Favonius**	T French	J Hayhoe	Baron M de Rothschild	9/1
1872	**Cremorne**	C Maidment	W Gilbert	H Savile	3/1
1873	**Doncaster**	F Webb	R Peck	J Merry	45/1
1874	**George Frederick**	H Custance	T Leader	W S Cartwright	9/1
1875	**Galopin**	J Morris	John Dawson	Prince Batthyany	2/1
1876	**Kisber**	C Maidment	J Hayhoe	A Baltazzi	4/1
1877	**Silvio**	F Archer	M Dawson	Lord Falmouth	100/9
1878	**Sefton**	H Constable	A Taylor Snr	W S Crawfurd	100/12
1879	**Sir Bevys**	G Fordham	J Hayhoe	Baron L de Rothschild	20/1
1880	**Bend Or**	F Archer	R Peck	Duke of Westminster	2/1
1881	**Iroquois**	F Archer	J Pincus	P Lorillard	11/2
1882	**Shotover**	T Cannon	J Porter	Duke of Westminster	11/2
1883	**St Blaise**	C Wood	J Porter	Sir F Johnstone	11/2
1884	**St Gatien**	C Wood	Robert Sherwood	J Hammond	100/8
	Harvester	S Loates	J Jewitt	Sir J Willoughby	100/7
1885	**Melton**	F Archer	M Dawson	Lord Hastings	74/40
1886	**Ormonde**	F Archer	J Porter	Duke of Westminster	4/9
1887	**Merry Hampton**	J Watts	M Gurry	G A Baird	100/9
1888	**Ayrshire**	F Barrett	G Dawson	Duke of Portland	5/6
1889	**Donovan**	T Loates	G Dawson	Duke of Portland	8/11
1890	**Sainfoin**	J Watts	J Porter	Sir J Miller	100/15
1891	**Common**	G Barrett	J Porter	Sir F Johnstone	10/11
1892	**Sir Hugo**	F Allsopp	T Wadlow	Lord Bradford	40/1
1893	**Isinglass**	T Loates	J Jewitt	H McCalmont	4/9
1894	**Ladas**	J Watts	M Dawson	Lord Rosebery	2/9
1895	**Sir Visto**	S Loates	M Dawson	Lord Rosebery	9/1
1896	**Persimmon**	J Watts	R Marsh	HRH Prince of Wales	5/1
1897	**Galtee More**	C Wood	S Darling	J Gubbins	1/4
1898	**Jeddah**	O Madden	R Marsh	J W Larnach	100/1
1899	**Flying Fox**	M Cannon	J Porter	Duke of Westminster	2/5
1900	**Diamond Jubilee**	H Jones	R Marsh	HRH Prince of Wales	6/4
1901	**Volodyovski**	L Reiff	J Huggins	W C Whitney	5/2
1902	**Ard Patrick**	J H Martin	S Darling	J Gubbins	100/14
1903	**Rock Sand**	D Maher	G Blackwell	Sir J Miller	4/6
1904	**St Amant**	K Cannon	A Hayhoe	L de Rothschild	5/1
1905	**Cicero**	D Maher	P Peck	Lord Rosebery	4/11
1906	**Spearmint**	D Maher	P P Gilpin	E Loder	6/1
1907	**Orby**	J Reiff	F McCabe	R Croker	100/9
1908	**Signorinetta**	W Bullock	O Ginistrelli	O Ginistrelli	100/1
1909	**Minoru**	H Jones	R Marsh	HM The King	7/2

View of the 1949 Derby taken from at Mile Post. The race was won by *Nimbus* with Charlie Elliott aboard.

Brilliant sunshine, excited crowds, magnificent horses and the cries of the bookies – all make up the glory of Derby Day. This scene is from 1949.

		Jockey	Trainer	Owner	Odds
1910	**Lemberg**	B Dillon	A Taylor Jnr	A W Cox	7/4
1911	**Sunstar**	G Stern	C Morton	J B Joel	13/8
1912	**Tagalie**	J Reiff	D Waugh	W Raphael	100/8
1913	**Aboyeur**	E Piper	T Lewis	A P Cunliffe	100/1
1914	**Durbar II**	M MacGee	T Murphy	H B Duryea	20/1
1915	**Pommern**	S Donoghue	C Peck	S B Joel	11/10
1916	**Fifinella**	J Childs	R C Dawson	E Hulton	11/2
1917	**Gay Crusader**	S Donoghue	A Taylor Jnr	A W Cox	7/4
1918	**Gainsborough**	J Childs	A Taylor Jnr	Lady J Douglas	8/13
1919	**Grand Parade**	F Templeman	F Barling	Lord Glanely	33/1
1920	**Spion Kop**	F O'Neill	P P Gilpin	G Loder	100/6
1921	**Humorist**	S Donoghue	C Morton	J B Joel	6/1
1922	**Captain Cuttle**	S Donoghue	F Darling	Lord Woolavington	10/1
1923	**Papyrus**	S Donoghue	B Jarvis	B Irish	100/15
1924	**Sansovino**	T Weston	G Lambton	Lord Derby	9/2

The 1954 Derby winner *Never Say Die*, ridden by Lester Piggott, being led to the winner's enclosure.

		Jockey	Trainer	Owner	Odds
1925	**Manna**	S Donoghue	F Darling	H E Morriss	9/1
1926	**Coronach**	J Childs	F Darling	Lord Woolavington	11/2
1927	**Call Boy**	C Elliott	J E Watts	F Curzon	4/1
1928	**Felstead**	H Wragg	O Bell	Sir H Cunliffe-Owen	33/1
1929	**Trigo**	J Marshall	R C Dawson	W Barnett	33/1
1930	**Blenheim**	H Wragg	R C Dawson	HH Aga Khan	18/1
1931	**Cameronian**	F Fox	F Darling	J A Dewar	7/2
1932	**April the Fifth**	F Lane	T Walls	T Walls	100/6
1933	**Hyperion**	T Weston	G Lambton	Lord Derby	6/1
1934	**Windsor Lad**	C Smirke	M Marsh	Maharaja of Rajpipla	15/2
1935	**Bahram**	F Fox	Frank Butters	HH Aga Khan	5/4
1936	**Mahmoud**	C Smirke	Frank Butters	HH Aga Khan	100/8
1937	**Mid-day Sun**	M Beary	Fred Butters	Mrs G B Miller	100/7
1938	**Bois Roussel**	C Elliott	F Darling	P Beatty	20/1
1939	**Blue Peter**	E Smith	J Jarvis	Lord Rosebery	7/2
1940	**Pont l'Eveque**	S Wragg	F Darling	F Darling	10/1
1941	**Owen Tudor**	W Nevett	F Darling	Mrs R Macdonald-Buchanan	25/1
1942	**Watling Street**	H Wragg	W Earl	Lord Derby	6/1
1943	**Straight Deal**	T Carey	W Nightingall	Miss D Paget	100/6
1944	**Ocean Swell**	W Nevett	J Jarvis	Lord Rosebery	28/1
1945	**Dante**	W Nevett	M Peacock	Sir E Ohlson	100/30
1946	**Airborne**	T Lowrey	R Perryman	J E Ferguson	50/1
1947	**Pearl Diver**	G Bridgland	P Carter	Baron G de Waldner	40/1
1948	**My Love**	W R Johnstone	R Carver	HH Aga Khan	100/9
1949	**Nimbus**	C Elliott	G Colling	Mrs M Glenister	7/1
1950	**Galcador**	W R Johnstone	C Semblat	M Boussac	100/9
1951	**Arctic Prince**	C Spares	W Stephenson	J McGrath	28/1
1952	**Tulyar**	C Smirke	M Marsh	HH Aga Khan	11/2
1953	**Pinza**	G Richards	N Bertie	Sir V Sassoon	5/1
1954	**Never Say Die**	L Piggott	J Lawson	R S Clark	33/1
1955	**Phil Drake**	F Palmer	F Mathet	Mme L Volterra	100/8
1956	**Lavandin**	W R Johnstone	A Head	P Wertheimer	7/1
1957	**Crepello**	L Piggott	N Murless	Sir V Sassoon	6/4
1958	**Hard Ridden**	C Smirke	J M Rogers	Sir V Sassoon	18/1
1959	**Parthia**	W H Carr	C Boyd-Rochfort	Sir H de Trafford	10/1
1960	**St Paddy**	L Piggott	N Murless	Sir V Sassoon	7/1
1961	**Psidium**	R Poincelet	H Wragg	Mrs A Plesch	66/1
1962	**Larkspur**	N Sellwood	M V O'Brien	R Guest	22/1
1963	**Relko**	Y Saint-Martin	F Mathet	F Dupre	5/1
1964	**Santa Claus**	A Breasley	J M Rogers	J Ismay	15/8

Royal Palace wins the 1967 Derby with *Riboco* second.

Left: A dream come true for 19-year-old Walter Swinburn as he takes the Aga Khan's *Shergar* into the winner's enclosure after the 1981 Derby, Swinburn's first attempt at the race. *Right:* Willie Carson, rider of three Derby winners.

		Jockey	Trainer	Owner	Odds
1965	**Sea Bird II**	T P Glennon	E Pollet	J Ternynck	7/4
1966	**Charlottown**	A Breasley	G Smyth	Lady Z Wernher	5/1
1967	**Royal Palace**	G Moore	N Murless	H J Joel	7/4
1968	**Sir Ivor**	L Piggott	M V O'Brien	R Guest	4/5
1969	**Blakeney**	E Johnson	A Budgett	A Budgett	15/2
1970	**Nijinsky**	L Piggott	M V O'Brien	C W Engelhard	11/8
1971	**Mill Reef**	G Lewis	I Balding	P Mellon	100/30
1972	**Roberto**	L Piggott	M V O'Brien	J W Galbreath	3/1
1973	**Morston**	E Hide	A Budgett	A Budgett	25/1
1974	**Snow Knight**	B Taylor	P Nelson	Mrs N Phillips	50/1

		Jockey	Trainer	Owner	Odds
1975	**Grundy**	P Eddery	P Walwyn	C Vittadini	5/1
1976	**Empery**	L Piggott	M Zilber	N B Hunt	10/1
1977	**The Minstrel**	L Piggott	M V O'Brien	R Sangster	5/1
1978	**Shirley Heights**	G Starkey	J Dunlop	Lord Halifax	8/1
1979	**Troy**	W Carson	W R Hern	Sir M Sobell	6/1
1980	**Henbit**	W Carson	W R Hern	Mrs A Plesch	7/1
1981	**Shergar**	W R Swinburn	M Stoute	HH Aga Khan	10/11
1982	**Golden Fleece**	P Eddery	M V O'Brien	R Sangster	3/1
1983	**Teenoso**	L Piggott	G Wragg	E B Moller	9/2
1984	**Secreto**	C Roche	D V O'Brien	L Miglietti	14/1
1985	**Slip Anchor**	S Cauthen	H Cecil	Lord H de Walden	9/4
1986	**Shahrastani**	W R Swinburn	M Stoute	HH Aga Khan	11/2
1987	**Reference Point**	S Cauthen	H Cecil	L Freedman	6/4
1988	**Kahyasi**	R Cochrane	L Cumani	HH Aga Khan	11/1
1989	**Nashwan**	W Carson	W R Hern	H Al-Maktoum	5/4
1990	**Quest for Fame**	P Eddery	R Charlton	K Abdulla	7/1
1991	**Generous**	A Munro	P Cole	F Salman	9/1
1992	**Dr Devious**	J Reid	P Chapple-Hyam	S H Craig	8/1

The Derby was run over 1 mile from 1780 to 1783.

The Derby was run at Newmarket 1915-1918 and 1940-1945.

The Diomed Stakes

When one takes into consideration that *Diomed* won the inaugural Derby in 1780, it seems extraordinary that no one thought of naming a race after him until 1971, one hundred and ninety one years later. Better late than never, although the winners cannot claim any great distinction.

The best was almost certainly the first, *Sparkler*, who won four races at two and ran *Brigadier Gerard* to a head in the St James's Palace Stakes. The Italian bred *All Friends* was a dual winner in 1975 and 1976, and the Lincoln Handicap winner *Saher* triumphed in 1981.

Run at Epsom over 1 mile 110 yards First Run 1971 Group 3

		Jockey	Trainer	Owner	Odds
1971	**Sparkler**	L Piggott	F Armstrong	J R Mullion	Evens
1972	**Sallust**	J Mercer	W R Hern	Sir M Sobell	14/1
1973	**Owen Dudley**	G Lewis	N Murless	L Freedman	8/15
1974	**Averof**	L Piggott	C Brittain	M Lemos	11/10
1975	**All Friends**	P Cook	N Vigors	R Mendoza	20/1
1976	**All Friends**	P Cook	N Vigors	R Mendoza	10/1
1977	**Gunner B**	J Mercer	G Toft	Mrs P Barratt	12/1
1978	**Ovac**	J Mercer	H Cecil	F Aloisi	7/2
1979	**Spring in Deepsea**	G Starkey	L Cumani	S Fradkoff	4/1
1980	**Hardgreen**	L Piggott	M Stoute	Sir G White	9/4
1981	**Saher**	R Cochrane	R Sheather	J C Smith	9/2
1982	**Prima Voce**	B Raymond	R Armstrong	J Durham-Matthews	25/1
1983	**Lofty**	P Cook	H Thomson Jones	Mrs H Thomson Jones	5/1
1984	**Adonijah**	L Piggott	H Cecil	K Abdulla	4/5
1985	**Scottish Reel**	W R Swinburn	M Stoute	Sir G White	2/1
1986	**Pennine Walk**	P Eddery	J Tree	Miss M Niarchos	4/1
1987	**Lauries Warrior**	M Roberts	R Boss	L C James	10/1
1988	**Waajib**	M Roberts	A Stewart	H Al-Maktoum	15/8
1989	**Shining Steel**	S Cauthen	H Cecil	H J Joel	11/2
1990	**Eton Lad**	C Asmussen	N Callaghan	W Said	12/1
1991	**Sylva Honda**	A Munro	C Brittain	Eddy Grimstead Honda Ltd	20/1
1992	**Zaahi**	R Hills	H Thomson Jones	H Al-Maktoum	100/30

The Coronation Cup

Founded in 1902 to celebrate the Coronation of King Edward VII, one of the great royal racing buffs who won three Derbies with *Persimmon, Diamond Jubilee* and *Minoru*, the Coronation Cup deserves a better place in the Calendar than the present 'after the Lord Mayor's Coach' position of being run on the day after the Derby against a background of trash left on the Downs by the once-a-year punters, despite the Herculean efforts of the Epsom management to clean the scene.

That said it is always a good race and it has been won by many superb horses. Of the four animals who have triumphed twice, only one was a colt, *The White Knight* in 1907 and 1908. *The White Knight* was the outstanding stayer of his era. Bred in Ireland, he won the Newbury Autumn Cup in 1906 together with the Ascot Gold Vase, the Ascot Gold Cup in 1907 and 1908, and the Goodwood Cup in 1907.

The other dual winners were the triple classic heroine *Pretty Polly, Petite Etoile* (1,000 Guineas and Oaks) and *Triptych,*

Dual winner *Triptych*, who took the 1987 and 1988 Coronation Cups and was the first filly to win the Irish Two Thousand Guineas.

the much travelled mare who was the first filly to win the Irish 2,000 Guineas, in a career encompassing forty-one races, winning fourteen including twelve pattern events, nine of them Group One. Before she could give birth to a single foal, she was killed in a stupid accident at stud in America.

Run at Epsom over 1 mile 4 furlongs   First Run 1902   Group 1

		Jockey	Trainer	Owner	Odds
1902	**Osboch**	D Maher	R Marsh	Lord Wolverton	4/1
1903	**Valenza**	O Madden	F W Day	E Heinemann	10/1
1904	**Zinfandel**	M Cannon	C Beatty	Lord H de Walden	9/2
1905	**Pretty Polly**	O Madden	P P Gilpin	E Loder	4/9
1906	**Pretty Polly**	B Dillon	P P Gilpin	E Loder	2/11
1907	**The White Knight**	W Halsey	H Sadler	T Y L Kirkwood	7/1
1908	**The White Knight**	W Halsey	H Sadler	T Y L Kirkwood	2/1
1909	**Dean Swift**	Wal Griggs	C Morton	J B Joel	7/2
1910	**Sir Martin**	J H Martin	J Cannon	L Winans	5/1
1911	**Lemberg**	B Dillon	A Taylor Jnr	A W Cox	9/4
1912	**Stedfast**	F Rickaby	G Lambton	Lord Derby	11/4
1913	**Prince Palatine**	W Saxby	H Beardsley	T Pilkington	5/6
1914	**Blue Stone**	W Huxley	C Morton	J B Joel	7/1
1915	**Black Jester**	W Huxley	C Morton	J B Joel	4/7
1916	**Pommern**	S Donoghue	C Peck	S B Joel	4/9
1917	**Phalaris**	B Carslake	G Lambton	Lord Derby	Evens
1918	**No Race**				
1919	**He**	A Smith	F Barling	Lord Glanely	Evens
1920	**Manilardo**	J Childs	A Taylor Jnr	A R Cox	Evens
1921	**Silvern**	F O'Neill	F Hartigan	Sir E Hulton	11/4
1922	**Franklin**	S Donoghue	R C Dawson	Lord Carnarvon	2/1
1923	**Condover**	H Beasley	E Harper	Mrs A Bendir	11/4
1924	**Verdict**	S Donoghue	W Waugh	Lord Coventry	3/1
1925	**St Germans**	F Bullock	A Taylor Jnr	Lord Astor	11/4
1926	**Solario**	J Childs	R Day	Sir J Rutherford	2/1
1927	**Coronach**	J Childs	F Darling	Lord Woolavington	30/100
1928	**Apelle**	H Beasley	H S Persse	R McCreery	100/15
1929	**Reigh Count**	J Childs	–	Mrs J Hertz	10/1
1930	**Plantago**	C Ray	J Lawson	W M G Singer	100/30
1931	**Parenthesis**	F Fox	F Darling	Lord Woolavington	9/4

		Jockey	Trainer	Owner	Odds
1932	**Salmon Leap**	T Weston	G Lambton	Mrs A James	7/2
1933	**Dastur**	C Elliott	Frank Butters	HH Aga Khan	4/7
1934	**King Salmon**	H Wragg	O Bell	Sir R Brooke	7/4
1935	**Windsor Lad**	C Smirke	M Marsh	M Benson	1/2
1936	**Plassy**	R Perryman	C Leader	Lord Derby	11/8
1937	**Cecil**	T Weston	J Lawson	Sir A Bailey	100/8
	His Grace	G Richards	R C Dawson	J V Rank	100/9
1938	**Monument**	P Beasley	C Boyd-Rochfort	Duke of Marlborough	9/2
1939	**Scottish Union**	G Richards	N Cannon	J V Rank	85/40
1940	**No Race**				
1941	**Winterhalter**	D Smith	Frank Butters	HH Aga Khan	7/2
1942	**No Race**				
1943	**Hyperides**	E Smith	J Jarvis	Lord Rosebery	7/4
1944	**Persian Gulf**	R A Jones	C Boyd-Rochfort	Lady Z Wernher	5/2
1945	**Borealis**	H Wragg	W Earl	Lord Derby	5/2
1946	**Ardan**	C Elliott	C Semblat	M Boussac	5/6
1947	**Chanteur II**	R Brethes	H Count	W Hill	1/3
1948	**Goyama**	C Elliott	C Semblat	M Boussac	5/2
1949	**Beau Sabreur**	W Cook	C Brabazon	A B Macnaughton	9/4
1950	**Amour Drake**	R Poincelet	R Carver	Mme L Volterra	15/8
1951	**Tantieme**	J Doyasbere	F Mathet	F Dupre	2/7
1952	**Nuccio**	R Poincelet	A Head	HH Aga Khan	3/1
1953	**Zucchero**	L Piggott	W Payne	G Rolls	100/7
1954	**Aureole**	E Smith	C Boyd-Rochfort	HM The Queen	5/2
1955	**Narrator**	F Barlow	H Cottrill	Maj L B Holliday	100/30
1956	**Tropique**	P Blanc	G Watson	Baron G de Rothschild	13/8
1957	**Fric**	J Deforge	P Lallie	M Calmann	7/2
1958	**Ballymoss**	A Breasley	M V O'Brien	J McShain	Evens
1959	**Nagami**	L Piggott	H Wragg	Mrs A Plesch	5/4
1960	**Petite Etoile**	L Piggott	N Murless	Prince Aly Khan	1/3
1961	**Petite Etoile**	L Piggott	N Murless	HH Aga Khan	2/5
1962	**Dicta Drake**	Y Saint-Martin	F Mathet	Mme L Volterra	2/1
1963	**Exbury**	J Deforge	G Watson	Baron G de Rothschild	11/8
1964	**Relko**	Y Saint-Martin	F Mathet	F Dupre	4/6
1965	**Oncidium**	A Breasley	G Todd	Lord H de Walden	11/2
1966	**I Say**	D Keith	W Nightingall	L Freedman	10/1
1967	**Charlottown**	J Lindley	G Smyth	Lady Z Wernher	11/8
1968	**Royal Palace**	A Barclay	N Murless	H J Joel	4/9
1969	**Park Top**	L Piggott	B van Cutsem	Duke of Devonshire	11/4
1970	**Caliban**	A Barclay	N Murless	S Joel	8/1
1971	**Lupe**	G Lewis	N Murless	Mrs S Joel	5/2
1972	**Mill Reef**	G Lewis	I Balding	P Mellon	2/15
1973	**Roberto**	L Piggott	M V O'Brien	J Galbreath	4/9
1974	**Buoy**	J Mercer	W R Hern	R D Hollingsworth	4/1
1975	**Bustino**	J Mercer	W R Hern	Lady Beaverbrook	11/10
1976	**Quiet Fling**	L Piggott	J Tree	J H Whitney	5/2
1977	**Excellor**	G Dubroeucq	F Mathet	N B Hunt	13/8
1978	**Crow**	P Eddery	P Walwyn	D Wildenstein	9/4
1979	**Ile de Bourbon**	J Reid	R F Johnson Houghton	Sir P Oppenheimer	4/6
1980	**Sea Chimes**	L Piggott	J Dunlop	J Thursby	5/4
1981	**Master Willie**	P Waldron	H Candy	R Barnett	1/2
1982	**Easter Sun**	B Raymond	M Jarvis	Lady Beaverbrook	20/1
1983	**Be My Native**	L Piggott	R Armstrong	K Hsu	8/1
1984	**Time Charter**	S Cauthen	H Candy	R Barnett	100/30
1985	**Rainbow Quest**	P Eddery	J Tree	K Abdulla	8/15
1986	**Saint Estephe**	P Eddery	A Fabre	Y Houyvet	20/1
1987	**Triptych**	A Cruz	P-L Biancone	A Clore	4/5
1988	**Triptych**	S Cauthen	P-L Biancone	P Brant	11/8
1989	**Sheriff's Star**	R Cochrane	Lady Herries	Duchess of Norfolk	11/4
1990	**In The Wings**	C Asmussen	A Fabre	Sheikh Mohammed	15/8
1991	**In The Groove**	S Cauthen	D Elsworth	B Cooper	7/2
1992	**Saddlers' Hall**	W R Swinburn	M Stoute	Lord Weinstock	5/4

Run at Newmarket 1915-1917 and 1943-1945 and at Newbury in 1941.

Run over 1 mile in 1917.

The Oaks

Although senior by one year, the Oaks has inevitably been overshadowed by the Derby, even if the latter did not achieve great prominence until the victory of the Prince of Wales's *Sir Thomas* in 1788.

A race for three-year-old fillies over one and a half miles, the Oaks was founded in 1779. The inaugural event was won by Lord Derby's *Bridget*, by *Herod*, a descendant of *Byerley Turk*, who sired the winners of 1,042 races including the great *Highflyer*, himself a famous stallion. *Herod* lived too early to leave his mark on the classic races, but he sired *Faith* (1781) and *Maid of the Oaks* (1783) in addition to *Bridget*, thus providing three of the first five Oaks winners.

Maid of the Oaks was named by her owner Lord Grosvenor after a play written by Lord Derby's close friend and nephew by marriage, General Burgoyne to celebrate the former's engagement to Lady Elizabeth Hamilton in 1774. It was the period when racing at this level mostly consisted of the aristocracy taking on each other, and the names of Grosvenor, Derby, Bunbury, Cleremont, Egremont, Grafton, Rutland and Bedford dominate the first half century of Oaks history.

Sir Charles Bunbury's *Eleanor* was the first filly to win the Derby in 1801. Home bred, her trainer Cox was on his deathbed just before the premier classic. A parson was called to administer spiritual comfort and hear the dying man's last wish. With his final breath Cox whispered to the priest 'Depend on it, the *Eleanor* is a hell of mare', and slumped back dead.

Whether or not the cleric took advantage of this priceless advice is not recorded, but *Eleanor* won not only the Derby but the Oaks the next day, the first horse to complete the double. She continued racing until she was seven, often competing in minor events, which was not unusual for the period and is probably the only Derby or Oaks winner to have won at Huntingdon. Not surprisingly, she was a failure as a broodmare, a fate which frequently overtakes hard-raced fillies.

Only two other fillies completed the double on the Downs, *Blink Bonny* and *Signorinetta*. *Fifinella* won both races as wartime substitutes at Newmarket in 1916. *Blink Bonny* had a tough race in the Derby of 1857 but won the Oaks with ease. She ought to have won the St Leger for which she started an odds-on favourite, but was pulled by her jockey, John Charlton, at the instigation of a bookmaker called Jackson.

The story of *Signorinetta* is much more romantic. Her dam, *Signorina* was put in foal by *Chalureux*, unfashionable sire but considered by *Signorina's* Italian breeder, the Chevalier Ginistrelli, to be in love with her, forming the attachment as the stallion passed her Newmarket paddock for his daily exercise.

Love foal or not, *Signorinetta* won the 1908 Derby at 100/1 and the Oaks two days later at a less generous 3/1.

The St Leger has always been a good race for fillies, and no fewer than fourteen have completed the Epsom — Doncaster double including *Sceptre* (1902), *Pretty Polly* (1904) *Petite Etoile* (1959) and *Meld* (1955). *Sceptre* won four of the five classic races, failing only in the Derby in which she was fourth.

In more leisurely times the Epsom Summer Meeting was a four day affair like Ascot and Goodwood, running from Tuesday to Friday. Racing on Saturday was unthinkable — even the Grand National was run on a Friday, and Saturday was part of the old fashioned English weekend, otherwise known as a 'Friday-to-Monday'.

It took the power of the media, and in particular television to break this agreeable habit, with only Royal Ascot surviving in it's original form. At Epsom, the Tuesday card was re-distributed over the next four days, Derby Day became the first day of the meeting, an arrangement not always acceptable to foreign jockeys requiring experience of the course, and the Oaks became the centrepiece of Saturday.

Of course a strong Saturday card is important for television coverage, now a staple of many racecourses' income, but the old elegance of Epsom's Ladies' Day has gone. Happily the race for the Oaks remains as good as ever.

Above: **Contemporary painting of *The Byerley Turk*, whose descendent *Bridget* won the first Oaks in 1779. *Below:* One of the 14 fillies to complete the Oaks-St Leger double, *Pretty Polly*.**

Run at Epsom over 1 mile 4 furlongs for 3 year-old fillies First Run 1779 Group 1

		Jockey	Trainer	Owner	Odds
1779	**Bridget**	R Goodisson	Saunders	Lord Derby	5/2
1780	**Teetotum**	R Goodisson	–	T Douglas	6/4
1781	**Faith**	R Goodisson	J Pratt	Lord Grosvenor	4/1
1782	**Ceres**	S Chifney	J Pratt	Lord Grosvenor	4/7
1783	**Maid of the Oaks**	S Chifney	J Pratt	Lord Grosvenor	4/1

Mr R.S.Clark's *Galatea II* with R.A.Jones up, holds on to beat Mr Edward Esmond's *White Fox* by a head to win the 1939 Oaks.

		Jockey	Trainer	Owner	Odds
1784	**Stella**	C Hindley	–	P Burlton	20/1
1785	**Trifle**	J Bird	J Pratt	Lord Clermont	5/1
1786	**Yellow Filly**	J Edwards	R Prince	Sir F Standish	5/2
1787	**Annette**	D Fitzpatrick	J Watson	R Vernon	6/4
1788	**Nightshade**	D Fitzpatrick	F Neale	Lord Egremont	1/2
1789	**Tag**	S Chifney	F Neale	Lord Egremont	5/2
1790	**Hippolyta**	S Chifney	M Stephenson	Duke of Bedford	6/1
1791	**Portia**	J Singleton Jnr	M Stephenson	Duke of Bedford	5/2
1792	**Volante**	C Hindley	J Pratt	Lord Clermont	5/4
1793	**Celia**	J Singleton Jnr	M Stephenson	Duke of Bedford	5/2
1794	**Hermione**	S Arnull	Saunders	Lord Derby	5/2
1795	**Platina**	D Fitzpatrick	F Neale	Lord Egremont	3/1
1796	**Parissot**	J Arnull	R Prince	Sir F Standish	7/2
1797	**Nike**	F Buckle	J Pratt	Lord Grosvenor	15/8
1798	**Bellissima**	F Buckle	R Prince	J H Durand	6/4
1799	**Bellina**	F Buckle	J Pratt	Lord Grosvenor	5/2
1800	**Ephemera**	D Fitzpatrick	F Neale	Lord Egremont	9/4
1801	**Eleanor**	J Saunders	J Frost	Sir C Bunbury	1/2
1802	**Scotia**	F Buckle	R Robson	J Wastell	6/4
1803	**Theophania**	F Buckle	S King	Sir T Gascoigne	5/2
1804	**Pelisse**	W Clift	R Robson	Duke of Grafton	4/5
1805	**Meteora**	F Buckle	R Robson	Lord Grosvenor	7/2
1806	**Bronze**	W Edwards	R D Boyce	B Craven	10/1
1807	**Briseis**	S Chifney Jnr	R Robson	T Grosvenor	15/1
1808	**Morel**	W Clift	R Robson	Duke of Grafton	3/1
1809	**Maid of Orleans**	J Moss	R Robson	Gen Leveson Gower	100/6
1810	**Oriana**	W Peirse	W Peirse	Sir W Gerard	4/1
1811	**Sorcery**	S Chifney Jnr	R D Boyce	Duke of Rutland	3/1
1812	**Manuella**	W Peirse	W Peirse	W N W Hewett	20/1
1813	**Music**	T Goodisson	R Robson	Duke of Grafton	5/2
1814	**Medora**	S Barnard	R D Boyce	Duke of Rutland	10/1
1815	**Minuet**	T Goodisson	R Robson	Duke of Grafton	3/1
1816	**Landscape**	S Chifney Jnr	R Robson	Gen Leveson Gower	2/1
1817	**Neva**	F Buckle	R D Boyce	G Watson	Evens
1818	**Corinne**	F Buckle	R Robson	J Udny	5/2
1819	**Shoveler**	S Chifney Jnr	W Chifney	T Thornhill	2/1
1820	**Caroline**	H Edwards	R Stephenson	Lord Egremont	8/1
1821	**Augusta**	J Robinson	R Prince Jnr	Lord Exeter	20/11
1822	**Pastille**	H Edwards	R Robson	Duke of Grafton	7/2
1823	**Zinc**	F Buckle	R Robson	Duke of Grafton	5/6
1824	**Cobweb**	J Robinson	J Edwards	Lord Jersey	8/11
1825	**Wings**	S Chifney Jnr	R Robson	T Grosvenor	13/1
1826	**Lilias**	T Lye	J Forth	J Forth	15/1
1827	**Gulnare**	F Boyce	J Kent	Duke of Richmond	14/1
1828	**Turquoise**	J B Day	R Stephenson	Duke of Grafton	25/1
1829	**Green Mantle**	G Dockeray	C Marson	Lord Exeter	5/2
1830	**Variation**	G Edwards	R Pettit	S Stonehewer	28/1
1831	**Oxygen**	J B Day	R Stephenson	Duke of Grafton	12/1
1832	**Galata**	P Conolly	C Marson	Lord Exeter	9/4
1833	**Vespa**	J Chapple	H Scott	Sir M Wood	50/1

Sun Chariot with Gordon Richards up after winning the 1942 Oaks.

		Jockey	Trainer	Owner	Odds
1834	**Pussy**	J B Day	W Day	T Cosby	20/1
1835	**Queen of Trumps**	T Lye	J Blenkhorn	E L Mostyn	8/1
1836	**Cyprian**	W Scott	J Scott	J Scott	9/4
1837	**Miss Letty**	J Holmes	I Blades	T O Powlett	7/1
1838	**Industry**	W Scott	J Scott	Lord Chesterfield	9/2
1839	**Deception**	J B Day	W Treen	F Craven	8/13
1840	**Crucifix**	J B Day	J B Day	Lord G Bentinck	1/3
1841	**Ghuznee**	W Scott	J Scott	Lord Westminster	7/4
1842	**Our Nell**	T Lye	T Dawson	G Dawson	8/1
1843	**Poison**	F Butler	R Fisher	G S Ford	30/1
1844	**The Princess**	F Butler	J Scott	G Anson	5/1
1845	**Refraction**	H Bell	J Kent Jnr	Duke of Richmond	25/1
1846	**Mendicant**	S Day	J B Day	J Gully	9/4
1847	**Miami**	S Templeman	W Beresford	Sir J Hawley	9/1
1848	**Cymbra**	S Templeman	J Day	H Hill	7/1

		Jockey	Trainer	Owner	Odds
1849	**Lady Evelyn**	F Butler	T Taylor	Lord Chesterfield	3/1
1850	**Rhedycina**	F Butler	W Goodwin	G Hobson	6/1
1851	**Iris**	F Butler	J Scott	Lord Stanley	4/1
1852	**Songstress**	F Butler	J Scott	J Scott	2/1
1853	**Catherine Hayes**	C Marlow	M Dawson	J D Wauchope	5/4
1854	**Mincemeat**	J Charlton	W Goodwin	W Cookson	10/1
1855	**Marchioness**	S Templeman	J Scott	W H Rudston Read	12/1
1856	**Mincepie**	A Day	J Day	H Hill	5/2
1857	**Blink Bonny**	J Charlton	W I'Anson	W I'Anson	4/5
1858	**Governess**	T Ashmall	T Eskrett	G W Gratwicke	4/1
1859	**Summerside**	G Fordham	T Taylor	Lord Londesborough	4/1
1860	**Butterfly**	J Snowden	G Oates	R Eastwood	10/1
1861	**Brown Duchess**	L Snowden	J Saxon	J Saxon	100/7
1862	**Feu de Joie**	T Chaloner	J Godding	R C Naylor	20/1
1863	**Queen Bertha**	T Aldcroft	J Scott	Lord Falmouth	40/1
1864	**Fille de l'Air**	A Edwards	T Jennings	Comte F de Lagrange	6/4
1865	**Regalia**	J Norman	W Harlock	W Graham	20/1
1866	**Tormentor**	J Mann	C Blanton	B Ellam	5/1
1867	**Hippia**	J Daley	J Hayhoe	Baron M de Rothschild	11/1
1868	**Formosa**	G Fordham	H Woolcott	W Graham	8/11
1869	**Brigantine**	T Cannon	W Day	Sir F Johnstone	7/2
1870	**Gamos**	G Fordham	H Woolcott	W Graham	100/8
1871	**Hannah**	C Maidment	J Hayhoe	Baron M de Rothschild	6/5
1872	**Reine**	G Fordham	T Jennings	C J Lefevre	3/1
1873	**Marie Stuart**	T Cannon	R Peck	J Merry	2/1
1874	**Apology**	J Osborne Jnr	W Osborne	J W King	5/2
1875	**Spinaway**	F Archer	M Dawson	Lord Falmouth	5/4
1876	**Camelia**	T Glover	T Cunnington	Comte F de Lagrange	5/4
	Enguerrrande	Hudson	C Wetherall	A Lupin	4/1
1877	**Placida**	H Jeffery	J Marsh	J Fiennes	2/1
1878	**Jannette**	F Archer	M Dawson	Lord Falmouth	65/40
1879	**Wheel of Fortune**	F Archer	M Dawson	Lord Falmouth	1/3
1880	**Jenny Howlet**	J Snowden	W I'Anson Jnr	C Perkins	33/1
1881	**Thebais**	G Fordham	A Taylor Snr	W S Crawfurd	4/6
1882	**Geheimniss**	T Cannon	J Porter	Lord Stamford	4/6
1883	**Bonny Jean**	J Watts	J Cannon	Lord Rosebery	5/1
1884	**Busybody**	T Cannon	T Cannon	G A Baird	100/105
1885	**Lonely**	F Archer	W Gilbert Jnr	Lord Cadogan	85/40
1886	**Miss Jummy**	J Watts	R Marsh	Duke of Hamilton	Evens
1887	**Reve d'Or**	C Wood	A Taylor Snr	Duke of Beaufort	8/11
1888	**Seabreeze**	W T Robinson	J Jewitt	Lord Calthorpe	7/4
1889	**L'Abbesse de Jouarre**	J Woodburn	Robert Sherwood	Lord R Churchill	20/1
1890	**Memoir**	J Watts	G Dawson	Duke of Portland	100/30
1891	**Mimi**	F Rickaby	M Dawson	N Fenwick	4/7
1892	**La Fleche**	G Barrett	J Porter	Baron M de Hirsch	8/11
1893	**Mrs Butterwick**	J Watts	G Dawson	Duke of Portland	100/7
1894	**Amiable**	W Bradford	G Dawson	Duke of Portland	7/1
1895	**La Sagesse**	S Loates	M Gurry	Sir J Miller	5/1
1896	**Canterbury Pilgrim**	F Rickaby	G Lambton	Lord Derby	100/8
1897	**Limasol**	W Bradford	T Jennings Jnr	Lord Hindlip	100/8
1898	**Airs and Graces**	W Bradford	F W Day	W T Jones	100/8
1899	**Musa**	O Madden	H Enoch	D Baird	20/1
1900	**La Roche**	M Cannon	J Porter	Duke of Portland	5/1
1901	**Cap and Bells II**	M Henry	S Darling	F R Keene	9/4
1902	**Sceptre**	H Randall	R S Sievier	R S Sievier	5/2
1903	**Our Lassie**	M Cannon	C Morton	J B Joel	6/1
1904	**Pretty Polly**	W Lane	P P Gilpin	E Loder	8/100
1905	**Cherry Lass**	H Jones	W T Robinson	W Hall-Walker	4/5
1906	**Keystone II**	D Maher	G Lambton	Lord Derby	5/2
1907	**Glass Doll**	H Randall	C Morton	J B Joel	25/1
1908	**Signorinetta**	W Bullock	O Ginistrelli	O Ginistrelli	3/1
1909	**Perola**	F Wootton	G S Davies	W Cooper	5/1
1910	**Rosedrop**	C Trigg	A Taylor Jnr	Sir W Bass	7/1
1911	**Cherimoya**	F N Winter	C Marsh	W B Cloete	25/1
1912	**Mirska**	J Childs	T Jennings Jnr	J Prat	33/1
1913	**Jest**	F Rickaby	C Morton	J B Joel	8/1
1914	**Princess Dorrie**	W Huxley	C Morton	J B Joel	11/4
1915	**Snow Marten**	Wal Griggs	P P Gilpin	L Neumann	20/1
1916	**Fifinella**	J Childs	R C Dawson	E Hulton	8/13
1917	**Sunny Jane**	O Madden	A Taylor Jnr	W Astor	4/1
1918	**My Dear**	S Donoghue	A Taylor Jnr	A W Cox	3/1
1919	**Bayuda**	J Childs	A Taylor Jnr	Lady J Douglas	100/7
1920	**Charlebelle**	A Whalley	H Braime	A P Cunliffe	7/2
1921	**Love in Idleness**	J Childs	A Taylor Jnr	J Watson	5/1
1922	**Pogrom**	E Gardner	A Taylor Jnr	Lord Astor	5/4
1923	**Brownhylda**	V Smyth	R C Dawson	Vicomte de Fontarce	10/1

Left: The 1973 Oaks is won by *Mysterious* ridden by G.Lewis. *Right:* Willie Carson rides home *Bireme* in the 1980 Oaks, from *Vielle* and *The Dancer.*

		Jockey	Trainer	Owner	Odds
1924	**Straitlace**	F O'Neill	D Waugh	Sir E Hulton	100/30
1925	**Saucy Sue**	F Bullock	A Taylor Jnr	Lord Astor	30/100
1926	**Short Story**	R A Jones	A Taylor Jnr	Lord Astor	5/1
1927	**Beam**	T Weston	Frank Butters	Lord Durham	4/1
1928	**Toboggan**	T Weston	Frank Butters	Lord Derby	100/15
1929	**Pennycomequick**	H Jelliss	J Lawson	Lord Astor	11/10
1930	**Rose of England**	G Richards	T Hogg	Lord Glanely	7/1
1931	**Brulette**	C Elliott	F Carter	C W Birkin	7/2
1932	**Udaipur**	M Beary	Frank Butters	HH Aga Khan	10/1
1933	**Chatelaine**	S Wragg	F Templeman	E Thornton-Smith	25/1
1934	**Light Brocade**	B Carslake	Frank Butters	Lord Durham	7/4
1935	**Quashed**	H Jelliss	C Leader	Lord Stanley	33/1
1936	**Lovely Rosa**	T Weston	H Cottrill	Sir A Bailey	33/1
1937	**Exhibitionnist**	S Donoghue	J Lawson	Sir V Sassoon	3/1
1938	**Rockfel**	H Wragg	O Bell	Sir H Cunliffe-Owen	3/1
1939	**Galatea II**	R A Jones	J Lawson	R S Clark	10/11
1940	**Godiva**	D Marks	W R Jarvis	E Harmsworth	7/4
1941	**Commotion**	H Wragg	F Darling	J A Dewar	8/1
1942	**Sun Chariot**	G Richards	F Darling	HM The King	1/4
1943	**Why Hurry**	C Elliott	N Cannon	J V Rank	7/1
1944	**Hycilla**	G Bridgland	C Boyd-Rochfort	W Woodward	8/1
1945	**Sun Stream**	H Wragg	W Earl	Lord Derby	6/4
1946	**Steady Aim**	H Wragg	Frank Butters	Sir A Butt	7/1
1947	**Imprudence**	W R Johnstone	J Lieux	Mme P Corbiere	7/4
1948	**Masaka**	W Nevett	Frank Butters	HH Aga Khan	7/1
1949	**Musidora**	E Britt	C Elsey	N Donaldson	4/1
1950	**Asmena**	W R Johnstone	C Semblat	M Boussac	5/1
1951	**Neasham Belle**	S Clayton	G Brooke	Maj L B Holliday	33/1
1952	**Frieze**	E Britt	C Elsey	A M Keith	100/7
1953	**Ambiguity**	J Mercer	R J Colling	Lord Astor	18/1
1954	**Sun Cap**	W R Johnstone	R Carver	Mme R Forget	100/8
1955	**Meld**	W H Carr	C Boyd-Rochfort	Lady Z Wernher	7/4
1956	**Sicarelle**	F Palmer	F Mathet	Mme L Volterra	3/1
1957	**Carrozza**	L Piggott	N Murless	HM The Queen	100/8
1958	**Bella Paola**	M Garcia	F Mathet	F Dupre	6/4
1959	**Petite Etoile**	L Piggott	N Murless	Prince Aly Khan	11/2
1960	**Never Too Late II**	R Poincelet	E Pollet	Mrs H E Jackson	6/5
1961	**Sweet Solera**	W Rickaby	R Day	Mrs S Castello	11/4
1962	**Monade**	Y Saint-Martin	J Lieux	G Goulandris	7/1
1963	**Noblesse**	G Bougoure	P Prendergast	Mrs J Olin	4/11
1964	**Homeward Bound**	G Starkey	J Oxley	Sir F Robinson	100/7
1965	**Long Look**	J Purtell	M V O'Brien	J C Brady	100/7
1966	**Valoris**	L Piggott	M V O'Brien	C Clore	11/10
1967	**Pia**	E Hide	C Elsey	Countess M Batthyany	100/7
1968	**La Lagune**	G Thiboeuf	F Boutin	H Berlin	11/8

		Jockey	Trainer	Owner	Odds
1969	**Sleeping Partner**	J Gorton	D Smith	Lord Rosebery	100/6
1970	**Lupe**	A Barclay	N Murless	Mrs S Joel	100/30
1971	**Altesse Royale**	G Lewis	N Murless	F Hue-Williams	6/4
1972	**Ginevra**	A Murray	H R Price	C St George	8/1
1973	**Mysterious**	G Lewis	N Murless	G A Pope Jnr	13/8
1974	**Polygamy**	P Eddery	P Walwyn	L Freedman	3/1
1975	**Juliette Marny**	L Piggott	J Tree	J Morrison	12/1
1976	**Pawneese**	Y Saint-Martin	A Penna	D Wildenstein	6/5
1977	**Dunfermline**	W Carson	W R Hern	HM The Queen	6/1
1978	**Fair Salinia**	G Starkey	M Stoute	S Hanson	8/1
1979	**Scintillate**	P Eddery	J Tree	J Morrison	20/1
1980	**Bireme**	W Carson	W R Hern	R D Hollingsworth	9/2
1981	**Blue Wind**	L Piggott	D Weld	Mrs B Firestone	3/1
1982	**Time Charter**	W Newnes	H Candy	R Barnett	12/1
1983	**Sun Princess**	W Carson	W R Hern	Sir M Sobell	6/1
1984	**Circus Plume**	L Piggott	J Dunlop	Sir R McAlpine	4/1
1985	**Oh So Sharp**	S Cauthen	H Cecil	Sheikh Mohammed	6/4
1986	**Midway Lady**	R Cochrane	B Hanbury	H H Ranier	15/8
1987	**Unite**	W R Swinburn	M Stoute	Sheikh Mohammed	11/1
1988	**Diminuendo**	S Cauthen	H Cecil	Sheikh Mohammed	7/4
1989	**Snow Bride**	S Cauthen	H Cecil	M Al-Maktoum	13/2
1990	**Salsabil**	W Carson	J Dunlop	H Al-Maktoum	2/1
1991	**Jet Ski Lady**	C Roche	J Bolger	M Al-Maktoum	50/1
1992	**User Friendly**	G Duffield	C Brittain	W Gredley	5/1

The Oaks was run at Newmarket 1915-1918 and 1940-1945

The Queen Anne Stakes

Her Majesty Queen Anne, the last of the Stuart monarchs, was a neice of King Charles II and happily for generations of racegoers she inherited her uncle's love of the Turf. Her home life can hardly be described as pleasant, but she reigned during a period when peace came to her subjects following the Duke of Marlborough's victories at Blenheim and Ramillies and the Act of Union with Scotland.

Freed from involvement with tiresome foriegners, art, science, literature and sport all flourished during a renaissance of Great Britain. Commerce and agriculture also prospered, and it was against this background that Queen Anne drove out from Windsor Castle in the early summer of 1711 and decided that Ascot Heath was the ideal place for a racecourse.

So it became on 7 August 1711. Royal Ascot was founded and today the opening race of the meeting over the straight mile from the gates of Windsor Great Park where the Queen made her historic drive, is named in her memory.

Always a good race for milers slightly below classic class, the pristine turf usually produces a good result, except in 1974 when the first three home were all disqualified, namely *Confusion*, *Gloss* and *Royal Perogative*. Perhaps the names were indicative; at all events the stewards made history.

Run at Ascot over 1 mile First Run 1840 Group 2

		Jockey	Trainer	Owner	Odds
1840	**Flambeau**	J Robinson	W Boyce	Duke of Rutland	4/6
1841	**Flambeau**	J Robinson	W Boyce	Duke of Rutland	1/2
1842	**Satirist**	J Robinson	J Scott	Lord Westminster	5/4
1843	**Poison**	H Bell	R Fisher	G S Ford	4/1
1844	**Corranna**	J Robinson	W Boyce	R G Townley	1/2
1845	**The Libel**	W Arthur	H Wadlow	A W Hill	4/1
1846	**The Conjuror**	G Whitehouse	G Dockeray	E R Clark	5/4
1847	**Prussic Acid**	E Flatman	R Stephenson	Lord Orford	4/7
1848	**War Eagle**	J Marson	C Marson	E Bouverie	4/7
1849	**Collingwood**	E Flatman	French	P Rolt	1/4
1850	**Flatcatcher**	S Rogers	H Stebbing	W Stebbing	10/6
1851	**The Moor**	W Abdale	S Death	S Death	1/3
1852	**Officious**	E Flatman	J Kent Jnr	Duke of Richmond	7/2
1853	**Ariosto**	F Butler	G Bloss	Mr Mare	4/1
1854	**Crosslanes**	J Garvey	W Smith	D Lane	10/1
1855	**Coroner**	G Fordham	T Parr	T Parr	2/1
1856	**Spindle**	J Goater	W Goater	H Padwick	–
1857	**The Early Bird**	D Hughes	W Shirley	T Walker	7/1
1858	**Rosabel**	J Reeves	–	Mr Leppingwell	10/1
1859	**Sedbury**	W Boyce	T Parr	T Parr	5/2
1860	**Cock-a-hoop**	G Fordham	W Brown	R Ten Broeck	8/1
1861	**Buccaneer**	J Goater	R Milton	Lord Portsmouth	5/2
1862	**Duke Rollo**	G Fordham	G Manning	Sir J Hawley	5/2
1863	**Tippler**	F Adams	I Woolcot	Duke of St Albans	5/1
1864	**Auditor**	J Grimshaw	W Goater	Lord Westmorland	2/1

		Jockey	Trainer	Owner	Odds
1865	**Heir-in-Law**	F Adams	J Fobert	Capt Gray	4/1
1866	**Out and Outer**	H Parry	W Day	W Day	20/1
1867	**Black Diamond**	R Fry	M Dawson	J Merry	100/8
1868	**filly by Newminster**	T Cannon	W Day	Lord Annesley	–
1869	**Vagabond**	J Adams	J Porter	Sir J Hawley	2/1
1870	**Green Riband**	J Grimshaw	–	Mr Ray	–
1871	**Sir Hugo**	T French	–	J R Bruce	10/1
1872	**Como**	J Morris	C Peck	C Peck	100/7
1873	**Moorlands**	Mr W Bevill	–	W Bevill	4/1
1874	**Thunder**	J Goater	M Dawson	M Dawson	6/4
1875	**Conductor**	T Glover	–	R Pattinson	100/8
1876	**Jester**	Loates	W Marsh	F Harding	100/30
1877	**Plaisante**	W Johnson	T Jennings	T Jennings	8/1
1878	**Post Haste**	C Maidment	J Day	Lord Alington	3/1
1879	**Alchemist**	T Cannon	W Arnull	H E Beddington	6/1
1880	**Ragman**	J Goater	T Jennings	Comte F de Lagrange	3/1
1881	**Cradle**	F Archer	T Wadlow	Lord Wilton	60/100
1882	**Valentino**	G Fordham	A Hayhoe	L de Rothschild	10/11
1883	**Geheimniss**	F Archer	J Porter	Lord Alington	100/30
1884	**Legacy**	A Johnson	T Jennings	T Jennings	20/1
1885	**Toastmaster**	G Barrett	J Hopper	R C Naylor	100/15
1886	**Toastmaster**	F Archer	J Hopper	R C Naylor	5/2
1887	**No Race**				
1888	**Zest**	T Loates	T Jennings Jnr	T Jennings Jnr	20/1
1889	**Nasr-el-Din**	F Peake	T Jennings Jnr	T Jennings Jnr	6/1
1890	**True Blue II**	T Cannon	T Cannon	T Cannon	7/4
1891	**Caliche**	S Chandley	J Waugh	A B Carr	10/1
1892	**Tostig**	J Watts	C Morton	G Masterman	3/1
1893	**Workington**	J Watts	J Enoch	J Lowther	75/20
1894	**Best Man**	F Webb	John Dawson	W Johnstone	4/5
1895	**Worcester**	S Loates	W Leader	J Best	1/7
1896	**Worcester**	J Watts	J Cannon	B I Barnato	10/11
1897	**Kilcock**	J Watts	S Darling	J H Greer	1/6
1898	**Collar**	C Purkis	J Porter	Duke of Westminster	100/14
1899	**Good Luck**	C Purkis	J Porter	Duke of Westminster	100/8
1900	**colt by Torpedo**	T Loates	John Dawson Jnr	Sir S M Lockhart	6/1
1901	**Watershed**	J Reiff	J Huggins	W C Whitney	5/1
1902	**Rose Blair**	W Bray	S Darling	J Gubbins	9/4
1903	**Littleton**	T Miller	J Porter	W Low	5/2
1904	**Grey Plume**	J Jarvis	J Porter	Duke of Westminster	11/8
1905	**Nabot**	W Halsey	F Lambton	Sir E Cassel	8/11
1906	**Dean Swift**	H Randall	C Morton	J B Joel	11/4
1907	**Dean Swift**	H Randall	C Morton	J B Joel	6/1
1908	**Llangwm**	J H Martin	F Hartigan	B Walker	5/1
1909	**St Michan**	B Lynham	R H Dewhurst	J Daly	4/1
1910	**Whisk Broom**	J H Martin	A J Joyner	H P Whitney	1/3
1911	**Hornet's Beauty**	J H Martin	P P Peebles	Sir W Cooke	4/6
1912	**Berilldon**	C Foy	H T Medcalfe	A E Barton	33/1
1913	**Lomond**	F Wootton	R Wootton	E Hulton	3/1
1914	**Bridge of Orchy**	J Prout	G Lambton	A James	100/7
1915/18	**No Race**				
1919	**Ciceronnetta**	A Flanagan	A Taylor Jnr	A R Cox	11/10
1920	**Comrade**	F Bullock	P P Gilpin	E de St Alary	5/4
1921	**Plymstock**	H Wragg	A Taylor Jnr	Lord Astor	7/1
1922	**Collaborator**	C Elliott	J Jarvis	Sir W Cooke	2/1
1923	**Friar**	T Weston	W Waugh	Duke of Westminster	5/1
1924	**Brimstone**	W McLachlan Jnr	G Laing Ward	J White	100/8
1925	**Sunderland**	G Richards	F Barling	Lord Glanely	7/2
1926	**Bulger**	C Smirke	S Wootton	Mrs T Carthew	7/2
1927	**Sundry**	G Richards	D Waugh	Lord H de Walden	100/8
1928	**Fohanaun**	F N Winter	W Earl	S B Joel	5/2
1929	**Aristotle**	F Fox	F Darling	Lord Dewar	100/7
1930	**The Recorder**	C Richards	F Darling	J A Dewar	11/2
1931	**Coldstream**	G Richards	T Hogg	Lord Glanely	11/2
1932	**Unlikely**	H Wragg	F Hartigan	Baron F de Tuyll	100/8
1933	**Madagascar**	T Bartlam	R C Dawson	Lord Carnarvon	100/7
1934	**Spend a Penny**	E Smith	Frank Butters	Sir A Butt	9/1
1935	**Fair Trial**	G Richards	F Darling	J A Dewar	9/4
1936	**Hindoo Holiday**	D Smith	Frank Butters	HH Aga Khan	8/1
1937	**Tempest II**	B Carslake	V Beatty	A K Macomber	3/1
1938	**St Magnus**	R Perryman	C Leader	Lord Derby	7/1
1939	**Mac Kann**	W R Johnstone	W Cunnington	R Lazard	9/4
1940/45	**No Race**				
1946	**Royal Charger**	E Smith	J Jarvis	Sir J Jarvis	5/6
1947	**Woodruffe**	C Richards	F Darling	J A Dewar	7/1

		Jockey	Trainer	Owner	Odds
1948	**Solina**	J Doyasbere	P Moret	Mme P Moret	10/1
1949	**Pambidian**	G Richards	W Nightingall	C R Harper	7/4
1950	**Garrick**	T Burn	W Smyth	Duchess of Norfolk	20/1
1951	**Neron**	D Greening	H Wragg	Begum Aga Khan	100/6
1952	**Southborne**	G Richards	P Prendergast	A L Hawkins	7/1
1953	**Argur**	E Mercer	J Glynn	M Boussac	7/4
1954	**Upadee**	T Burns	B Gallivan	T McCairns	100/6
1955	**Golden Planet**	D Smith	F N Winter	P Bartholomew	7/1
1956	**Kandy Sauce**	D Smith	N Murless	Sir V Sassoon	10/1
1957	**Baron's Folly**	E Britt	P Beasley	H Leggat	100/7
1958	**Teynham**	D W Morris	G Colling	R C Boucher	15/2
1959	**Lucky Guy**	J Sime	S McGrath	J McGrath Jnr	100/8
1960	**Blast**	W Snaith	A Budgett	R Richmond-Watson	100/7
1961	**Amber Light**	D Smith	F N Winter	E R Hill	9/1
1962	**Nereus**	P Robinson	K Cundell	P N Robinson	8/1
1963	**Welsh Rake**	R Hutchinson	J Jarvis	J P Phillips	8/1
1964	**Princelone**	R Maddock	W Nightingall	A J Allen	100/8
1965	**Showdown**	D Smith	F N Winter	D Prenn	5/4
1966	**Tesco Boy**	R Hutchinson	S Ingham	J Cohen	8/1
1967	**Good Match**	D East	J Tree	G Dudley	6/1
1968	**Virginia Gentleman**	A Barclay	D Smith	J F Lewis	9/2
1969	**Town Crier**	D Keith	P Walwyn	E de Rothschild	11/2
1970	**Welsh Pageant**	A Barclay	N Murless	H J Joel	30/100
1971	**Roi Soleil**	R Hutchinson	C Bartholomew	Mrs D Riley-Smith	11/4
1972	**Sparkler**	L Piggott	F Armstrong	Mrs M Mehl-Mulhens	9/4
1973	**Sun Prince**	J Mercer	W R Hern	Sir M Sobell	3/1
1974	**Brook**	B Taylor	M Benetti	C Vittadini	12/1
1975	**Imperial March**	G Dettori	M V O'Brien	W F Mullady	2/1
1976	**Ardoon**	B Taylor	G Pritchard-Gordon	F Feeney	11/2
1977	**Jellaby**	B Taylor	H R Price	E Akhalifa	9/4
1978	**Radetzky**	E Hide	C Brittain	C Elliot	25/1
1979	**Baptism**	L Piggott	J Tree	J H Whitney	6/1
1980	**Blue Refrain**	B Rouse	C Benstead	Mrs L Wood	8/1
1981	**Belmont Bay**	L Piggott	H Cecil	D Wildenstein	4/1
1982	**Mr Fluorocarbon**	L Piggott	H Cecil	J McAllister	3/1
1983	**Valiyar**	P Eddery	H Cecil	G Vanian	10/1
1984	**Trojan Fen**	L Piggott	H Cecil	S Niarchos	9/4
1985	**Rousillon**	G Starkey	G Harwood	K Abdulla	11/4
1986	**Pennine Walk**	P Eddery	J Tree	Mrs S Niarchos	5/2
1987	**Then Again**	R Cochrane	L Cumani	R J Shannon	4/5
1988	**Waajib**	M Roberts	A Stewart	H Al-Maktoum	5/2
1989	**Warning**	P Eddery	G Harwood	K Abdulla	2/5
1990	**Markofdistinction**	L Dettori	L Cumani	G Leigh	7/1
1991	**Sikeston**	M Roberts	C Brittain	L Gaucci	9/1
1992	**Lahib**	W Carson	J Dunlop	H Al-Maktoum	100/30

Run as the Trial Stakes 1840-1929

The Prince of Wales's Stakes

The Prince of Wales's Stakes was inaugurated in 1862 when the then Prince, later Edward VII, took over many of the social duties of the monarch as his mother Queen Victoria mourned the death of Prince Albert in 1861. Principal winners in the early years included *Wheel of Fortune*, said by Fred Archer to be the best filly he ever rode and winner of the 1,000 Guineas and the Oaks, *Iroquois*, (ridden by Archer to win the Derby in 1881), *Galliard*, (the 2,000 Guineas winner in 1883), *Galtee More* (Guineas and Derby 1897), *Jeddah* (Derby 1898) and *Ard Patrick*, victorious in the 1902 Derby and despite finishing only second in the Prince of Wales's Stakes, took the race following a successful objection to the first past the post, *Cupbearer*.

The 1887 race won by *Claymore* owned by formidable Duchess of Montrose better known in Newmarket circles as old Six Mile Bottom, was reduced to a farce when a mounted policeman crossed the course during the race and interfered with a number of the runners and bringing down *Phil* with subsequent injury to the jockey Tom Cannon.

As horses were raced less frequently in the second quarter of the twentieth century, so fewer classic winners were asked to perform at both Epsom and Ascot. *Sansovino* (Derby 1924) and *Hyperion* (Derby 1933) were exceptions, and *Heliopolis*, third to *Blue Peter* in the 1939 Derby won the last Prince of Wales's Stakes before the outbreak of war. All three ran in the black and white colours of the 17th Earl of Derby.

When racing resumed, the Prince of Wales's Stakes did not, presumably because there was no elder son of the King, George VI, to hold the title, but the race was restored to the Calendar in 1968 prior to the investiture of the present Prince of Wales at Caernarfon in May 1969.

Happily enough the winner was *Royal Palace*, since when *Connaught*, *Brigadier Gerard* and the dual winner *Mtoto* have all added lustre to one of the most exciting events on the opening day of the Royal Meeting.

Run at Ascot over 1 mile 2 furlongs First Run 1862 Group 2

		Jockey	Trainer	Owner	Odds
1862	**Carisbrook**	S Rogers	R Boyce	R Boyce	10/1
1863	**Avenger**	A Edwards	Jos Dawson	Lord Stamford	100/8
1864	**Ely**	H Custance	T Olliver	W S Cartwright	5/1
1865	**Breadalbane**	H Custance	W I'Anson	H Chaplin	6/4
1866	**Rustic**	G Fordham	J Day	Duke of Beaufort	5/1
1867	**Vauban**	G Fordham	J Day	Duke of Beaufort	100/30
1868	**King Alfred**	J Daley	J Hayhoe	Baron M de Rothschild	4/1
1869	**Martyrdom**	G Fordham	G Bloss	Lord Calthorpe	5/1
1870	**King o'Scots**	W Hunt	Jos Dawson	Jos Dawson	10/1
1871	**King of the Forest**	J Snowden	R Peck	J Merry	11/2
1872	**Queen's Messenger**	T French	M Dawson	Lord Falmouth	9/2
1873	**Kaiser**	C Maidment	W Gilbert	H Savile	3/1
1874	**Leolinus**	T Osborne	–	Sir R W Bulkeley	2/1
1875	**Earl of Dartrey**	J Goater	W Gilbert	H Savile	100/7
1876	**Petrarch**	J Morris	John Dawson	Lord Dupplin	2/1
1877	**Glen Arthur**	A Dodge	P Price	W S Mitchell-Innes	7/4
1878	**Glengarry**	G Fordham	J Ryan	J H Houldsworth	9/1
1879	**Wheel of Fortune**	F Archer	M Dawson	Lord Falmouth	4/6
1880	**Zealot**	W McDonald	T Wadlow	Lord Bradford	10/1
1881	**Iroquois**	F Archer	J Pincus	P Lorillard	4/5
1882	**Quicklime**	C Wood	T Wadlow	Lord Bradford	5/6
1883	**Galliard**	F Archer	M Dawson	Lord Falmouth	9/4
1884	**Sir Reuben**	C Wood	J Jewitt	Lord Manners	5/1
1885	**Pepper and Salt**	G Barrett	A Taylor Snr	Duke of Beaufort	25/1
1886	**Button Park**	G Barrett	A Taylor Snr	Duke of Beaufort	6/1
1887	**Claymore**	F Barrett	A Taylor Snr	Duchess of Montrose	8/1
1888	**Ossory**	T Cannon	J Porter	Duke of Westminster	100/11
1889	**Donovan**	F Barrett	G Dawson	Duke of Portland	2/9
1890	**Alloway**	W Warne	J Ryan	J H Houldsworth	100/15
1891	**Melody**	J Watts	G Blackwell	D Cooper	11/10
1892	**Watercress**	G Barrett	J Porter	Baron M de Hirsch	100/8
1893	**Red Ensign**	T Loates	F Bates	Sir R Jardine	7/2
1894	**Contract**	W Bradford	Jos Day	Duchess of Montrose	4/1
1895	**Match Maker**	M Cannon	J Porter	Lord Alington	5/6
1896	**Shaddock**	M Cannon	J Porter	Duke of Westminster	11/4
1897	**Galtee More**	C Wood	S Darling	J Gubbins	1/33
1898	**Jeddah**	J Watts	R Marsh	J W Larnach	7/4
1899	**Manners**	M Cannon	J Porter	Duke of Portland	7/2
1900	**Simon Dale**	M Cannon	J Porter	Duke of Portland	1/4
1901	**Veronese**	F Rickaby	H Enoch	D Baird	5/2
1902	**Ard Patrick**	J H Martin	S Darling	J Gubbins	11/10
1903	**Mead**	H Jones	R Marsh	HM The King	5/4
1904	**Rydal Head**	M Cannon	J Porter	Duke of Westminster	6/4
1905	**Plum Centre**	M Cannon	J Porter	Sir F Johnstone	4/1
1906	**Sancy**	O Madden	A Taylor Jnr	W Bass	2/5
1907	**Qu'Appelle**	D Maher	G Chaloner	Lord Harewood	100/30
1908	**Santo Strato**	O Madden	J Watson	L de Rothschild	100/8
1909	**Bayardo**	D Maher	A Taylor Jnr	A W Cox	4/6
1910	**Greenback**	F Templeman	J F Hallick	Lord Villiers	Evens
1911	**Stedfast**	F Wootton	G Lambton	Lord Derby	1/5
1912	**Catmint**	D Maher	T Jennings Jnr	L Brassey	2/1
1913	**Louvois**	W Saxby	D Waugh	W Raphael	4/9
1914	**Marten**	F Rickaby	F Darling	J Buchanan	11/4
1915/18	**No Race**				
1919	**Dominion**	A Smith	F Barling	Lord Glanely	2/1
1920	**All Prince**	F Fox	R Day	Sir A Bailey	10/1
1921	**Polymestor**	S Donoghue	E de Mestre	S B Joel	3/1
1922	**Villars**	V Smyth	F Hunt	W Raphael	11/4
1923	**Eastern Monarch**	C Elliott	J Jarvis	Sir G Bullough	8/1
1924	**Sansovino**	T Weston	G Lambton	Lord Derby	4/9
1925	**Warminster**	G Archibald	G Sadler	Mrs W Raphael	5/4
1926	**Caissot**	T Weston	G Lambton	Lord Derby	3/1
1927	**Chantery**	H Jelliss	A Taylor Jnr	W M G Singer	7/2
1928	**Potocki**	F N Winter	W Earl	S B Joel	15/2
1929	**Lyme Regis**	J Childs	W R Jarvis	HM The King	10/1
1930	**Parenthesis**	F Fox	F Darling	Lord Woolavington	11/4
1931	**Sir Andrew**	P Beasley	C Boyd-Rochfort	W Woodward	10/1
1932	**Sigiri**	C Elliott	V Gilpin	E de St Alary	7/1
1933	**Hyperion**	T Weston	G Lambton	Lord Derby	1/2
1934	**Achtenan**	R Perryman	Frank Butters	T Lant	11/2
1935	**Assignation**	S Donoghue	L Cundell	Mrs C Glorney	100/8
1936	**Valerian**	T Weston	J Lawson	Sir A Bailey	20/1
1937	**Cold Scent**	T Weston	J Lawson	Sir A Bailey	9/2
1938	**L'Ouragan III**	R Brethes	H Count	Princesse de Lucinge	8/1
1939	**Heliopolis**	R Perryman	W Earl	Lord Derby	6/1

		Jockey	Trainer	Owner	Odds
1940/68	**No Race**				
1968	**Royal Palace**	A Barclay	N Murless	H J Joel	1/4
1969	**Connaught**	A Barclay	N Murless	H J Joel	11/10
1970	**Connaught**	A Barclay	N Murless	H J Joel	10/11
1971	**Arthur**	R Hutchinson	J Dunlop	Lady Rosebery	5/4
1972	**Brigadier Gerard**	J Mercer	W R Hern	Mrs J Hislop	1/2
1973	**Gift Card**	L Piggott	A Penna	Countess M Batthyany	7/2
1974	**Admetus**	M Philliperon	J Cunnington	Sir M Sobell	6/1
1975	**Record Run**	P Eddery	G Pritchard-Gordon	S Grey	12/1
1976	**Anne's Pretender**	L Piggott	H R Price	Sir C Clore	100/30
1977	**Lucky Wednesday**	J Mercer	H Cecil	C St George	5/6
1978	**Gunner B**	J Mercer	H Cecil	Mrs P Barratt	4/5
1979	**Crimson Beau**	L Piggott	P Cole	H Spearing	11/2
1980	**Ela-Mana-Mou**	W Carson	W R Hern	S Weinstock	100/30
1981	**Hard Fought**	W R Swinburn	M Stoute	L B Holliday	3/1
1982	**Kind of Hush**	S Cauthen	B Hills	A Shead	4/1
1983	**Stanerra**	B Rouse	F Dunne	F Dunne	7/1
1984	**Morcon**	W Carson	W R Hern	Lord Rotherwick	11/8
1985	**Bob Back**	B Raymond	M Jarvis	A Balzarini	33/1
1986	**English Spring**	P Eddery	I Balding	P Mellon	14/1
1987	**Mtoto**	R Hills	A Stewart	A Al-Maktoum	7/2
1988	**Mtoto**	M Roberts	A Stewart	A Al-Maktoum	8/15
1989	**Two Timing**	P Eddery	J Tree	K Abdulla	5/1
1990	**Batshoof**	P Eddery	B Hanbury	M Salem	2/1
1991	**Stagecraft**	S Cauthen	M Stoute	Sheikh Mohammed	6/4
1992	**Perpendicular**	W Ryan	H Cecil	Lord H de Walden	20/1

Run ovr 1 mile 5 furlongs from 1862-1939

The St James's Palace Stakes

The inaugural running of the St James's Palace Stakes, named after the Tudor former Royal Residence and still officially the Court (indeed the much coveted and unbuyable vouchers for the Royal Meeting are despatched from the Palace) did not make an auspicious start as the Derby winner, *Plenipotentiary* was allowed to walk-over.

Things could only improve, and in the latter half of the nineteenth century the winners included *Hermit*, victorious in the 'snowstorm' Derby of 1867, *Iroquois* and *Florizel II*, bred by the Prince of Wales and a full brother to the later King's classic winners *Persimmon* and *Diamond Jubilee*, all by *St Simon*.

A host of other classic conquerors followed suit, including *Sceptre* and the Triple Crown winners *Rock Sand* and *Bahram*, while *Rhodes Scholar*, taken out of the 1936 Derby as the track resembled the nearby A24, showed what a good thing he would have been by slamming the steel-legged Epsom hero *Mahmoud* in the St James's Palace Stakes.

Post-war, in the era of specialised milers, it is usually contested by horses which have won or been placed in the 2,000 Guineas, but no classic winner has won since *To-Agori-Mou* in 1981.

Run at Ascot over 1 mile for 3 year-old colts & fillies First Run 1834 Group 1

		Jockey	Trainer	Owner	Odds
1834	**Plenipotentiary**	–	G Payne	S Batson	w.o.
1835	**Ascot**	E Flatman	–	Lord Orford	2/5
1836/37	**No Race**				
1838	**Boeotian**	J B Day	–	Duke of Portland	–
1839	**Euclid**	P Conolly	R Pettit	T Thornhill	–
1840	**Scutari**	S Darling	–	Lord Exeter	4/6
1841	**Satirist**	W Scott	J Scott	Lord Westminster	w.o.
1842	**Misdeal**	S Rogers	J Kent Jnr	Lord G Bentinck	7/4
1843	**Ameer**	S Templeman	J Scott	Lord Westminster	7/4
1844	**Ionian**	–	W Cooper	J Peel	w.o.
1845	**Idas**	E Flatman	R Boyce Jnr	Lord Stradbroke	1/5
1846	**The Free Lance**	E Flatman	T Taylor	Lord Chesterfield	6/4
1847	**Montpensier**	S Templeman	C Peck	Sir R W Bulkeley	6/4
1848	**Glendower**	E Flatman	W Dilly	G Payne	1/4
1849	**Uriel**	F Butler	J Scott	Lord Stanley	1/6
1850	**Nutcracker**	C Marlow	W Harlock	Lord Exeter	3/1
1851	**The Ban**	J Marson	A Taylor Snr	Sir J Hawley	4/5
1852	**Daniel O'Rourke**	F Butler	J Scott	J Bowes	1/2
1853	**The Reiver**	G Whitehouse	M Dawson	Lord J Scott	Evens
1854	**Baalbec**	J Bumby	J Bumby	Mr Knowles	3/1
1855	**Paletot**	J Bartholomew	J Scott	Lord Derby	–
1856	**Pitapat**	J Bartholomew	W Channel	H Combe	4/5
1857	**Anton**	–	J Day	F Robinson	w.o.
1858	**Fitz-Roland**	J Wells	G Manning	Sir J Hawley	2/7
1859	**Cynricus**	S Rogers	I Woolcot	J Wyndham	Evens

Sceptre, **one of the great classic horses, pictured at the Newmarket Sales in July 1911.**

		Jockey	Trainer	Owner	Odds
1860	**Tom Bowline**	T Aldcroft	T Dawson	Lord Glasgow	6/5
1861	**Walloon**	A Edwards	Jos Dawson	Lord Stamford	4/5
1862	**Carisbrook**	–	R Boyce	R Boyce	w.o.
1863	**Gladstone**	A Edwards	M Dawson	J Merry	–
1864	**The Beadle**	H Grimshaw	A Taylor Snr	G Payne	4/5
1865	**Lazaretto**	–	J Godding	R C Naylor	w.o.
1866	**Staghound**	T Chaloner	A Taylor Snr	G Payne	Evens
1867	**Hermit**	H Custance	G Bloss	H Chaplin	1/20
1868	**The Earl**	G Fordham	J Day	Marquis of Hastings	2/7
1869	**Dunbar**	G Fordham	–	Mr Dyson	8/1
1870	**King Cole**	J Snowden	J Coates	Lord Zetland	–
1871	**Dalnacarnoch**	T Chaloner	A Taylor Snr	W S Crawfurd	10/11
1872	**Queen's Messenger**	T French	M Dawson	Lord Falmouth	2/5
1873	**Gang Forward**	T Chaloner	A Taylor Snr	W S Crawfurd	1/10
1874	**Leolinus**	T Osborne	–	Sir R W Bulkeley	2/1
1875	**Bay of Naples**	H Constable	T Leader	W S Cartwright	6/4
1876	**Great Tom**	F Archer	M Dawson	Lord Falmouth	2/5
1877	**Covenanter**	H Custance	W Goater	H Bird	100/30
1878	**Bonnie Scotland**	H Constable	J Cannon	Lord Rosebery	6/1
1879	**Rayon d'Or**	J Goater	T Jennings	Comte F de Lagrange	7/2
1880	**Bend Or**	G Fordham	R Peck	Duke of Westminster	30/100
1881	**Iroquois**	F Archer	J Pincus	P Lorillard	9/100
1882	**Battlefield**	F Archer	T Wadlow	Lord Bradford	4/1
1883	**Despair**	F Archer	W Gilbert	W Gilbert	11/8
1884	**Cambusmore**	F Archer	J Porter	Duke of Westminster	7/2
1885	**Sheraton**	J Osborne Jnr	T Wadlow	Lord Bradford	8/1
1886	**Althorp**	T Cannon	J Porter	Baron M de Hirsch	2/1
1887	**Florentine**	S Loates	J Jewitt	Lord Calthorpe	4/1
1888	**Ossory**	T Cannon	J Porter	Duke of Westminster	4/5
	Galore	F Webb	M Dawson	N Fenwick	–
1889	**Pioneer**	J Watts	M Gurry	G A Baird	4/6
1890	**Janissary**	T Loates	W Gray	H Milner	8/1
1891	**Common**	G Barrett	J Porter	Sir F Johnstone	1/40
1892	**St Angelo**	F Webb	Jos Day	H Milner	5/2
1893	**Phocion**	M Cnon	John Dawson Jnr	Lord Ellesmere	9/2
1894	**Florizel II**	T Loates	R Marsh	HRH the Prince of Wales	5/4
1895	**Troon**	G Chaloner	G Dawson	Duke of Portland	11/2
1896	**His Reverence**	T Loates	G Dawson	Duke of Portland	–
1897	**Vesuvian**	M Cannon	J Porter	Sir F Johnstone	40/85
1898	**Cap Martin**	F Rickaby	H Enoch	D Baird	2/1
1899	**Millennium**	O Madden	R Marsh	Duke of Devonshire	6/1

		Jockey	Trainer	Owner	Odds
1900	**Bonarosa**	L Reiff	F W Day	Sir E Cassel	100/30
1901	**Lauzun**	M Cannon	R Marsh	Duke of Devonshire	7/1
1902	**Sceptre**	F W Hardy	R S Sievier	R S Sievier	5/2
1903	**Rock Sand**	D Maher	G Blackwell	Sir J Miller	7/100
1904	**Challenger**	W Lane	S Darling	L Robinson	5/1
1905	**Cherry Lass**	H Jones	W T Robinson	W Hall-Walker	6/100
1906	**Black Arrow**	B Lynham	W T Robinson	W Hall-Walker	8/1
1907	**Slieve Gallion**	W Higgs	S Darling	J H Greer	1/20
1908	**Your Majesty**	Wal Griggs	C Morton	J B Joel	8/1
1909	**Minoru**	H Jones	R Marsh	HM The King	1/3
1910	**Lemberg**	D Maher	A Taylor Jnr	A W Cox	1/8
1911	**Stedfast**	F Wootton	G Lambton	Lord Derby	4/5
1912	**Tracery**	D Maher	J Watson	A Belmont	2/1
1913	**Roseworthy**	D Maher	H S Persse	A F Bassett	9/4
1914	**Carrickfergus**	J Clark	W T Robinson	W Hall-Walker	100/6
1915/18	**No Race**				
1919	**Grand Parade**	A Smith	F Barling	Lord Glanely	1/4
1920	**Allenby**	F Slade	P Linton	W Raphael	2/1
1921	**Craig an Eran**	F Bullock	A Taylor Jnr	Lord Astor	1/8
1922	**Captain Cuttle**	S Donoghue	F Darling	Lord Woolavington	1/4
1923	**Ellangowan**	C Elliott	J Jarvis	Lord Rosebery	3/1
1924	**Tom Pinch**	G Archibald	F Darling	Lord Woolavington	5/1
1925	**Zambo**	B Carslake	R C Dawson	HH Aga Khan	11/4
1926	**Coronach**	J Childs	F Darling	Lord Woolavington	1/6
1927	**Kincardine**	H Beasley	H S Persse	A Barclay	4/1
1928	**Royal Minstrel**	J Childs	C Boyd-Rochfort	G P Gough	9/4
1929	**Mr Jinks**	H Beasley	H S Persse	D McCalmont	6/4
1930	**Christopher Robin**	P Beasley	V Gilpin	G Loder	100/7
1931	**Cameronian**	F Fox	F Darling	J A Dewar	8/15
1932	**Andrea**	T Weston	P Whitaker	Duke of Marlborough	100/8
1933	**Canon Law**	R Dick	J Lawson	Lord Astor	9/2
1934	**Flamenco**	H Wragg	J Jarvis	Lord Rosebery	100/9
1935	**Bahram**	F Fox	Frank Butters	HH Aga Khan	1/8
1936	**Rhodes Scholar**	R Dick	J Lawson	Lord Astor	2/1
1937	**Goya II**	C Elliott	G Lambton	M Boussac	9/4
1938	**Scottish Union**	B Carslake	N Cannon	J V Rank	4/7
1939	**Admiral's Walk**	E Smith	J Jarvis	Sir J Jarvis	6/5
1940	**No Race**				
1941	**Orthodox**	D Smith	N Cannon	J V Rank	6/1
1942/45	**No Race**				
1946	**Khaled**	G Richards	Frank Butters	HH Aga Khan	2/1
1947	**Tudor Minstrel**	G Richards	F Darling	J A Dewar	6/100
1948	**Black Tarquin**	E Britt	C Boyd-Rochfort	W Woodward	5/1
1949	**Faux Tirage**	G Richards	N Murless	J A Dewar	11/10
1950	**Palestine**	C Smirke	M Marsh	HH Aga Khan	4/7
1951	**Turco II**	W H Carr	C Boyd-Rochfort	W Woodward	7/1
1952	**King's Bench**	G Richards	M Feakes	A Tompsett	3/1
1953	**Nearula**	E Britt	C Elsey	W Humble	4/6
1954	**Darius**	E Mercer	H Wragg	Sir P Loraine	Evens
1955	**Tamerlane**	A Breasley	N Bertie	Lord Porchester	8/11
1956	**Pirate King**	D Smith	H Cottrill	Maj L B Holliday	6/1
1957	**Chevastrid**	J Eddery	S McGrath	J McGrath	6/1
1958	**Major Portion**	E Smith	T E Leader	H J Joel	Evens
1959	**Above Suspicion**	W H Carr	C Boyd-Rochfort	HM The Queen	9/4
1960	**Venture VII**	G Moore	A Head	Prince Aly Khan	1/33
1961	**Tudor Treasure**	D Smith	J F Watts	Lord Derby	11/4
1962	**Court Sentence**	E Smith	T E Leader	H J Joel	100/8
1963	**Crocket**	D Smith	G Brooke	D van Clief	9/2
1964	**Roan Rocket**	L Piggott	G Todd	T Frost	5/4
1965	**Silly Season**	G Lewis	I Balding	P Mellon	5/1
1966	**Track Spare**	J Lindley	R Mason	R Mason	100/9
1967	**Reform**	A Breasley	G Richards	M Sobell	4/6
1968	**Petingo**	L Piggott	F Armstrong	M Lemos	10/11
1969	**Right Tack**	G Lewis	J Sutcliffe Jnr	J R Brown	4/6
1970	**Saintly Song**	A Barclay	N Murless	S Joel	11/10
1971	**Brigadier Gerard**	J Mercer	W R Hern	Mrs J Hislop	4/11
1972	**Sun Prince**	J Lindley	W R Hern	Sir M Sobell	7/4
1973	**Thatch**	L Piggott	M V O'Brien	J Mulcahy	Evens
1974	**Averof**	B Taylor	C Brittain	M Lemos	7/4
1975	**Bolkonski**	G Dettori	H Cecil	C d'Alessio	4/5
1976	**Radetzky**	P Eddery	C Brittain	C Elliott	16/1
1977	**Don**	E Hide	W Elsey	E Ryan	11/2
1978	**Jaazeiro**	L Piggott	M V O'Brien	R Sangster	5/2
1979	**Kris**	J Mercer	H Cecil	Lord H de Walden	11/10
1980	**Posse**	P Eddery	J Dunlop	O Phipps	11/2

		Jockey	Trainer	Owner	Odds
1981	**To-Agori-Mou**	G Starkey	G Harwood	Mrs A Muinos	2/1
1982	**Dara Monarch**	M Kinane	L Browne	Mrs L Browne	7/2
1983	**Horage**	S Cauthen	M McCormack	A Rachid	18/1
1984	**Chief Singer**	R Cochrane	R Sheather	J C Smith	85/40
1985	**Bairn**	L Piggott	L Cumani	Sheikh Mohammed	6/4
1986	**Sure Blade**	B Thomson	B Hills	Sheikh Mohammed	9/2
1987	**Half a Year**	R Cochrane	L Cumani	J C Mabee	11/2
1988	**Persian Heights**	P Eddery	G Huffer	Prince Y Saud	9/2
1989	**Shaadi**	W R Swinburn	M Stoute	Sheikh Mohammed	6/4
1990	**Shavian**	S Cauthen	H Cecil	Lord H de Walden	11/1
1991	**Marju**	W Carson	J Dunlop	H Al-Maktoum	7/4
1992	**Brief Truce**	M Kinane	D Weld	Moyglare Stud Farms Ltd	25/1

Run at Newmarket in 1941

The Coventry Stakes

In the days when two-year-olds with classic potential were throughly tested and exposed in top class races, as opposed to being allowed to coast home in obscure maidens at Nottingham and Yarmouth, the Coventry Stakes was the lynch-pin. Named after the 9th Earl of Coventry, Master of the Buckhounds, a post equivalent to Her Majesty's Representative nowadays, neither the inaugural winner *The Deemster* or *Danure* in 1891 proved to be classic material. *Milford,* who won at odds on the following year was doubtless laid out to score in the manner of his owner Lily Langtry, but it was a different story in 1893 when *Ladas* went on to take the Guineas and the Derby for Lord Rosebery.

The Earl was Prime Minister at the time, and he was warmly congratulated by his political colleagues, the only sour notes coming from Noncomformists, Liberals and Radicals. 'Plus ça change' . . .

Persimmon, Rock Sand and *St Amant* all followed in *Ladas's* hoofprints, while *The Tetrarch,* possibly the fastest horse ever seen on the English Turf, won by ten lengths in 1913. Between the wars, the 1927 winner *Fairway* was robbed of victory in the Derby by the yobs who pulled hairs from his tail by the handful on the walk to the start, but post-war *Big Game, Dante, Tudor Minstrel, Palestine* and *Martial* all maintained the classic tradition.

However, the last classic winner produced by the Coventry was *Mill Reef* in 1970, and the race is now more usually for high class and precocious two-year-olds bred for speed.

Mill Reef, **the last classic winner produced by the Coventry Stakes.**

Run at Ascot over 6 furlongs for 2 year-olds First Run 1890 Group 3

		Jockey	Trainer	Owner	Odds
1890	**The Deemster**	W T Robinson	J Jewitt	J B Leigh	9/4
1891	**Danure**	T Cannon	J Ryan	J H Houldsworth	8/1
1892	**Milford**	J Watts	S Pickering	Mr Jersey	4/7
1893	**Ladas**	A White	M Dawson	Lord Rosebery	6/4
1894	**Whiston**	S Chandley	J Waugh	G Dobell	100/6

		Jockey	Trainer	Owner	Odds
1895	**Persimmon**	J Watts	R Marsh	HRH the Prince of Wales	2/1
1896	**Goletta**	T Loates	A Hayhoe	L de Rothschild	11/4
1897	**Orzil**	W Bradford	T Jennings Jnr	L Brassey	9/2
1898	**Desmond**	T Loates	Robert Sherwood Jnr	Lord Dunraven	4/1
1899	**Democrat**	J F Sloan	J Huggins	Lord W Beresford	5/1
1900	**Good Morning**	L Reiff	S Darling	J H Greer	9/4
1901	**Sterling Balm**	O Madden	J Watts	Maj Joicey	2/1
1902	**Rock Sand**	D Maher	G Blackwell	Sir J Miller	6/4
1903	**St Amant**	K Cannon	A Hayhoe	L de Rothschild	5/1
1904	**Cicero**	D Maher	P Peck	Lord Rosebery	6/4
1905	**Black Arrow**	H Jones	W T Robinson	W Hall-Walker	2/9
1906	**Traquair**	D Maher	P Peck	Lord Rosebery	4/7
1907	**Prospector**	H Stokes	Sir C Nugent	D R Browning	7/2
1908	**Louviers**	G Stern	D Waugh	W Raphael	4/1
1909	**Admiral Hawke**	B Dillon	P P Gilpin	E Loder	20/1
1910	**Radiancy**	Wal Griggs	C Morton	J B Joel	100/7
1911	**Lady Americus**	S Donoghue	H S Persse	A H Ledlie	3/1
1912	**Shogun**	F Wootton	R Wootton	E Hulton	4/9
1913	**The Tetrarch**	S Donoghue	H S Persse	D McCalmont	30/100
1914	**Lady Josephine**	S Donoghue	J Fallon	W M Savill	5/4
1915	**Marcus**	H Jones	J Barrow	John Dawson Jnr	6/1
1916	**Diadem**	J H Martin	G Lambton	Lord D'Abernon	10/1
1917	**Benevente**	J H Martin	R H Dewhurst	Lord Londonderry	2/1
1918	**Bruff Bridge**	J Evans	John Dawson Jnr	Sir G Noble	9/1
1919	**Sarchedon**	J H Martin	P P Gilpin	J Buchanan	8/15
1920	**Milesius**	B Carslake	H Cottrill	E Kennedy	5/2
1921	**Pondoland**	J Shatwell	E de Mestre	S B Joel	5/4
1922	**Drake**	A Whalley	H Cottrill	Mrs S Whitburn	10/1
1923	**Knight of the Garter**	H Jones	R Marsh	HM The King	5/4
1924	**Iceberg**	F Lane	R Moreton	F Gretton	9/2
1925	**Colorado**	T Weston	G Lambton	Lord Derby	5/1
1926	**Knight of the Grail**	B Carslake	R Farquharson	Sir D Broughton	10/1
1927	**Fairway**	T Weston	Frank Butters	Lord Derby	7/1
1928	**Reflector**	R Perryman	J Watson	A de Rothschild	100/7
1929	**Diolite**	C Ray	F Templeman	Sir H Hirst	7/1
1930	**Lemnarchus**	F Fox	F Darling	Lord Ellesmere	9/2
1931	**Cockpen**	F Fox	F Darling	Lord Woolavington	13/8
1932	**Manitoba**	G Richards	F Darling	Lord Woolavington	13/8
1933	**Medieval Knight**	G Richards	F Darling	J A Dewar	8/13
1934	**Hiaran**	G Richards	Frank Butters	HH Aga Khan	4/9
1935	**Black Speck**	T Burns	H Cottrill	J V Rank	7/1
1936	**Early School**	R Dick	J Lawson	Lord Astor	11/4
1937	**Mirza II**	C Smirke	Frank Butters	HH Aga Khan	4/11
1938	**Panorama**	P Beasley	C Boyd-Rochfort	Mrs J Corrigan	2/9
1939	**Turkhan**	C Smirke	Frank Butters	Prince Aly Khan	100/8
1940	**No Race**				
1941	**Big Game**	H Wragg	F Darling	HM The King	2/9
1942	**Nasrullah**	G Richards	Frank Butters	HH Aga Khan	7/4
1943	**Orestes**	T Carey	W Nightingall	Miss D Paget	13/8
1944	**Dante**	W Nevett	M Peacock	Sir E Ohlson	11/8
1945	**Khaled**	G Richards	Frank Butters	HH Aga Khan	9/1
1946	**Tudor Minstrel**	G Richards	F Darling	J A Dewar	2/13
1947	**The Cobbler**	G Richards	F Darling	G Loder	4/5
1948	**Royal Forest**	C Richards	N Murless	R Macdonald-Buchanan	5/1
1949	**Palestine**	G Richards	Frank Butters	HH Aga Khan	1/2
1950	**Big Dipper**	W H Carr	C Boyd-Rochfort	Mrs J Bryce	2/1
1951	**King's Bench**	G Richards	M Feakes	A Tompsett	4/6
1952	**Whistler**	E Britt	P Nelson	Maharanee of Baroda	2/5
1953	**The Pie King**	T Gosling	P Prendergast	R Bell	11/2
1954	**Noble Chieftain**	F Barlow	H Cottrill	Maj L B Holliday	11/8
1955	**Ratification**	W H Carr	V Smyth	Sir M McAlpine	100/30
1956	**Messmate**	E Mercer	J Jarvis	Lord Milford	20/1
1957	**Amerigo**	E Smith	J A Waugh	Lord H de Walden	7/4
1958	**Hieroglyph**	W H Carr	C Boyd-Rochfort	Mrs J Hanes	10/1
1959	**Martial**	W Swinburn	P Prendergast	R Webster	11/10
1960	**Typhoon**	R Hutchinson	P Prendergast	N McCarthy	Evens
1961	**Xerxes**	D Smith	G Brooke	Mrs D McCalmont	9/2
1962	**Crocket**	D Smith	G Brooke	D van Clief	9/4
1963	**Showdown**	D Smith	F N Winter	Mrs D Prenn	6/1
1964	**Silly Season**	G Lewis	I Balding	P Mellon	13/2
1965	**Young Emperor**	L Piggott	P Prendergast	Mrs P Poe	9/4
1966	**Bold Lad**	D Lake	P Prendergast	Lady B Granard	4/6
1967	**Mark Royal**	A Breasley	P Norris	B Schmidt-Bodner	13/2
1968	**Murrayfield**	G Lewis	I Balding	Mrs P Hastings	15/2
1969	**Prince Tenderfoot**	W Williamson	P Prendergast	Mrs P Poe	15/8

		Jockey	Trainer	Owner	Odds
1970	**Mill Reef**	G Lewis	I Balding	P Mellon	4/11
1971	**Sun Prince**	J Mercer	W R Hern	M Sobell	20/1
1972	**Perdu**	J Lindley	T Corbett	A Holland	16/1
1973	**Doleswood**	F Durr	R Akehurst	F Tory	20/1
1974	**Whip It Quick**	G Lewis	W Marshall	G van der Ploeg	11/1
1975	**Galway Bay**	L Piggott	I Balding	J R Mullion	2/1
1976	**Cawston's Clown**	M L Thomas	N Adam	J Murrell	11/2
1977	**Solinus**	L Piggott	M V O'Brien	D Schwartz	7/4
1978	**Lake City**	B Taylor	H R Price	H Demetriou	7/1
1979	**Varingo**	B Taylor	H R Price	PTP Plant Hire Ltd	11/8
1980	**Recitation**	G Starkey	G Harwood	A Bodie	11/1
1981	**Red Sunset**	G Starkey	G Harwood	P Burns	14/1
1982	**Horage**	P Eddery	M McCormack	A Rachid	85/40
1983	**Chief Singer**	R Cochrane	R Sheather	J C Smith	20/1
1984	**Primo Dominie**	J Reid	B Swift	P Wetzel	4/7
1985	**Sure Blade**	B Thomson	B Hills	Sheikh Mohammed	3/1
1986	**Cutting Blade**	C Asmussen	L Piggott	M Fustok	11/1
1987	**Always Fair**	W R Swinburn	M Stoute	M Al-Maktoum	9/2
1988	**High Estate**	S Cauthen	H Cecil	H J Joel	10/11
1989	**Rock City**	W Carson	R Hannon	A F Budge Ltd	9/1
1990	**Mac's Imp**	A Munro	W A O'Gorman	Tamdown Ltd	2/1
1991	**Dilum**	A Munro	P Cole	F Salman	11/10
1992	**Petardia**	W R Swinburn	G Wragg	Moller Racing	5/1

Run at Newmarket 1915-1918 and 1941-1944

The King Edward VII Stakes

Known for many years as the 'Ascot Derby', the King Edward VII Stakes has provided compensation for horses defeated at Epsom such as *Pretendre* in 1966 after failing in the premiere classic behind *Charlottown, Connaught,* second at Epsom to *Sir Ivor* in 1968, *Great Wall* an unlucky fourth in *Nijinsky's* Derby in 1970, *Ela-Mana-Mou,* fourth to *Troy,* and *Cacoethes,* third to *Nashwan.*

It has also lent credence to the theory that Ascot comes too soon after Epsom for a horse to give of his or her best, as evidenced by *Mighty Flutter,* third to *Secreto* at Epsom in 1984 but a mighty flop at Ascot two weeks later when odds-on favourite.

Run at Ascot over 1 mile 4 furlongs for 3 year-old colts & geldings First Run 1834 Group 2

		Jockey	Trainer	Owner	Odds
1834	**Pussy**	J B Day	W Day	T Cosby	4/7
1835	**Griselda**	E Flatman	R Prince Jnr	C Greville	5/6
1836	**Lieutenant**	E Flatman	–	Sir F Collier	–
1837	**Mango**	E Flatman	M Dilly	C Greville	6/4
1838	**No Race**				
1839	**Bloomsbury**	S Rogers	W Ridsdale	W Ridsdale	1/5
1840	**Bokhara**	J Chapple	Ralph Sherwood	Sir G Heathcote	–
1841	**Coronation**	–	Painter	A T Rawlinson	w.o.
1842	**Envoy**	J Robinson	–	Duke of Bedford	4/1
1843	**Amorino**	J Chapple	Ralph Sherwood	Sir G Heathcote	7/2
1844	**The Miser Scarve**	E Flatman	T Taylor	Lord Chesterfield	7/4
1845	**Wood Pigeon**	S Mann	W Harlock	Lord Exeter	7/4
1846	**Bravissimo**	J Chapple	Ralph Sherwood	Sir G Heathcote	–
1847	**Conyngham**	A Day	J Day	Sir R Pigot	1/5
1848	**Distaffina**	F Butler	T Taylor	Lord Chesterfield	6/5
1849	**Repletion**	F Butler	S Death	Sir F Peacocke	4/1
1850	**Musician**	B Bartholomew	T Eskrett	G S Ford	2/1
1851	**Phlegethon**	C Marlow	W Harlock	Lord Exeter	–
1852	**Convulsion**	W Abdale	S Death	Maj Martyn	7/4
1853	**Ninnyhammer**	F Butler	W Smith	D Lane	Evens
1854	**Phaeton**	E Flatman	W Harlock	Lord Exeter	4/1
1855	**Pugnator**	S Rogers	W Butler Jnr	Duke of Bedford	3/1
1856	**Fly-by-Night**	J Bartholomew	J Scott	J Bowes	Evens
1857	**Sydney**	D Hughes	J Hayhoe	Baron M de Rothschild	6/5
1858	**Toxophilite**	E Flatman	J Scott	Lord Derby	2/9
1859	**Gamester**	T Ashmall	J Scott	Sir C Monck	7/4
1860	**The Wizard**	T Aldcroft	J Scott	A Nichol	1/5
1861	**Janus**	J Wells	J Hayhoe	Baron M de Rothschild	6/5
1862	**Carisbrook**	W Cresswell	R Boyce	R Boyce	Evens
1863	**Onesander**	A Edwards	Jos Dawson	Lord Stamford	2/1
1864	**Peon**	E Sharp	R Cotton	C Alexander	5/1
1865	**Celerimma**	T French	J Scott	Lord Falmouth	2/1
1866	**Staghound**	T Chaloner	A Taylor Snr	G Payne	10/1
1867	**The Palmer**	J Wells	J Porter	Sir J Hawley	Evens
1868	**The Earl**	G Fordham	J Day	Marquis of Hastings	4/7

		Jockey	Trainer	Owner	Odds
1869	**Pero Gomez**	J Wells	J Porter	Sir J Hawley	1/2
1870	**King Cole**	J Snowden	J Coates	Lord Zetland	6/4
1871	**Henry**	G Fordham	T Jennings	C J Lefevre	100/30
1872	**Drumochter**	T Chaloner	A Taylor Snr	W S Crawfurd	6/4
1873	**Gang Forward**	T Chaloner	A Taylor Snr	W S Crawfurd	2/5
1874	**Atlantic**	G Fordham	M Dawson	Lord Falmouth	2/5
1875	**Gilbert**	G Fordham	T Jennings	Comte F de Lagrange	6/1
1876	**Forerunner**	F Webb	R Peck	W Thorold	4/7
1877	**Silvio**	F Archer	M Dawson	Lord Falmouth	2/1
1878	**Insulaire**	J Goater	T Jennings	Comte F de Lagrange	6/4
1879	**Chippendale**	H Constable	T Wadlow	Lord Bradford	100/30
1880	**Mask**	T Cannon	C Blanton	Prince Soltykoff	1/2
1881	**Maskelyne**	J Goater	T Jennings	Comte F de Lagrange	10/1
1882	**Shotover**	T Cannon	J Porter	Duke of Westminster	1/3
1883	**Ladislas**	G Fordham	T Jennings Jnr	C J Lefevre	6/1
1884	**Brest**	F Webb	T Jennings Jnr	C J Lefevre	6/4
1885	**The Child of the Mist**	C Wood	J Porter	J T Mackenzie	7/4
1886	**St Mirin**	G Barrett	A Taylor Snr	Duchess of Montrose	5/2
1887	**Timothy**	C Wood	A Taylor Snr	Duchess of Montrose	2/1
1888	**Sheen**	J Woodburn	T Jennings	Prince Soltykoff	7/4
1889	**Morglay**	F Barrett	A Hayhoe	L de Rothschild	4/1
1890	**Battle-axe**	G Chaloner	J Jewitt	Lord Calthorpe	7/1
1891	**St Simon of the Rock**	M Cannon	Robert Sherwood	J T North	1/3
1892	**Llanthony**	G Barrett	F Bates	Sir R Jardine	6/5
1893	**Phocion**	J Watts	John Dawson Jnr	Lord Ellesmere	4/6
1894	**None the Wiser**	F Allsopp	Jos Day	Duchess of Montrose	7/2
1895	**Matchmaker**	M Cannon	J Porter	Lord Alington	4/7
1896	**Conroy**	M Cannon	J Porter	Duke of Westminster	4/9
1897	**Minstrel**	J Watts	R Marsh	Duke of Devonshire	1/10
1898	**Purser**	C Wood	W Gibbons	Prince Soltykoff	6/1
1899	**Frontier**	M Cannon	J Porter	Duke of Westminster	6/4
1900	**Ecton**	O Madden	R Marsh	Duke of Devonshire	5/1
1901	**Osboch**	M Cannon	R Marsh	Lord Wolverton	10/11
1902	**Flying Lemur**	M Cannon	J Porter	Duke of Westminster	8/11
1903	**Kroonstad**	W Halsey	John Dawson Jnr	Lord Ellesmere	9/4
1904	**Darley Dale**	M Cannon	J Porter	Duke of Portland	5/4
1905	**Pure Crystal**	H Randall	C Morton	J B Joel	100/7
1906	**Poussin**	W Higgs	C Beatty	Lord H de Walden	11/10
1907	**All Black**	H Jones	R Day	A Bailey	4/1
1908	**Dibs**	H Stokes	Sir C Nugent	J S Morrison	6/5
1909	**William the Fourth**	B Dillon	G S Davies	Lord Michelham	1/10
1910	**Decision**	F Wootton	G Lambton	Lord Derby	100/30
1911	**King William**	F Wootton	G Lambton	Lord Derby	2/1
1912	**Jaeger**	Wal Griggs	P P Gilpin	L Neumann	2/7
1913	**Pilliwinkle**	D Maher	A Taylor Jnr	W Astor	5/1
1914	**Corcyra**	H Jones	R H Dewhurst	Lord Londonderry	11/10
1915/18	**No Race**				
1919	**Old Bill**	H Jelliss	G Blackwell	L Montagu	5/1
1920	**Caligula**	J Childs	H Leader	Lord Wilton	10/1
1921	**Nippon**	F Bullock	B Jarvis	J P Hornung	5/1
1922	**Backwood**	J Brennan	H Cottrill	W E Whineray	100/8
1923	**Bold and Bad**	F Bullock	A Taylor Jnr	Lord Astor	5/4
1924	**Polyphontes**	W McLachlan	E de Mestre	S B Joel	5/2
1926	**Finglas**	G Archibald	P P Gilpin	E de St Alary	9/2
1927	**Buckfast**	J Evans	R Day	R D Cohen	4/1
1928	**Cyclonic**	R A Jones	B Jarvis	J S Courtauld	100/30
1929	**Horus**	C Elliott	J Jarvis	Sir L Philipps	7/1
1930	**Pinxit**	B Carslake	N Scobie	Sir C Hyde	9/4
1931	**Sandwich**	H Wragg	J Jarvis	Lord Rosebery	1/3
1932	**Dastur**	M Beary	Frank Butters	HH Aga Khan	4/9
1933	**Sans Peine**	E Smith	J Jarvis	E Esmond	20/1
1934	**Berestoi**	W Nevett	D Peacock	W Smith	4/1
1935	**Field Trail**	R Dick	J Lawson	Lord Astor	8/11
1936	**Precipitation**	P Beasley	C Boyd-Rochfort	Lady Z Wernher	2/1
1937	**Solfo**	T Lowrey	B Jarvis	J S Courtauld	8/11
1938	**Foroughi**	H Wragg	Frank Butters	HH Aga Khan	100/8
1939	**Hypnotist**	P Beasley	C Boyd-Rochfort	W Woodward	Evens
1940/45	**No Race**				
1946	**Field Day**	G Richards	Frank Butters	Prince Aly Khan	5/2
1947	**Migoli**	G Richards	Frank Butters	HH Aga Khan	1/4
1948	**Vic Day**	W R Johnstone	M D'Okhuysen	H Blagrave	13/2
1949	**Swallow Tail**	D Smith	W Earl	Lord Derby	4/5
1950	**Babu's Pet**	T Burn	G Duller	Maharaja of Baroda	20/1
1951	**Supreme Court**	C Elliott	E Williams	Mrs T Lilley	6/4
1952	**Castleton**	D Smith	T Carey	T Carey	100/6

		Jockey	Trainer	Owner	Odds
1953	**Skyraider**	R Poincelet	A Head	Prince Aly Khan	13/2
1954	**Rashleigh**	G Richards	N Murless	C Stuart	5/1
1955	**Nucleus**	L Piggott	C Jerdein	Miss D Paget	4/1
1956	**Court Command**	L Piggott	N Murless	Mrs T Lilley	100/7
1957	**Arctic Explorer**	L Piggott	N Murless	G Loder	6/1
1958	**Restoration**	W H Carr	C Boyd-Rochfort	HM The Queen	6/1
1959	**Pindari**	L Piggott	N Murless	HM The Queen	13/8
1960	**Atrax**	R Poincelet	H Nicholas	M Boussac	4/1
1961	**Aurelius**	G Lewis	P Hastings-Bass	Mrs V Lilley	20/1
1962	**Gaul**	G Lewis	P Hastings-Bass	Lord Sefton	20/1
1963	**Only for Life**	J Lindley	J Tree	Miss M Sheriffe	3/1
1964	**No Race**				
1965	**Convamore**	J Mercer	R Smyth	E More O'Ferrall	13/2
1966	**Pretendre**	P Cook	J Jarvis	J A C Lilley	1/2
1967	**Mariner**	G Starkey	J Oxley	R D Hollingsworth	8/1
1968	**Connaught**	A Barclay	N Murless	H J Joel	1/2
1969	**Vervain**	E Hide	P Nelson	D McCalmont	10/1
1970	**Great Wall**	W Williamson	A Breasley	D Sung	9/4
1971	**Seafriend**	J Mercer	P Prendergast	Mrs J R Mullion	3/1
1972	**Lord Nelson**	W Williamson	G Todd	T Frost	16/1
1973	**Klairvimy**	R F Parnell	D Weld	Mrs B Allen-Jones	10/1
1974	**English Prince**	P Eddery	P Walwyn	Mrs V Hue-Williams	8/11
1975	**Sea Anchor**	J Mercer	W R Hern	R D Hollingsworth	4/1
1976	**Marquis de Sade**	B Taylor	H R Price	C St George	6/1
1977	**Classic Example**	P Eddery	P Walwyn	F Hue-Williams	14/1
1978	**Ile de Bourbon**	J Reid	R F Johnson Houghton	D McCall	11/1
1979	**Ela-Mana-Mou**	G Starkey	G Harwood	Mrs A Muinos	11/10
1980	**Light Cavalry**	J Mercer	H Cecil	H J Joel	9/2
1981	**Bustomi**	W Carson	W R Hern	Lady Beaverbrook	13/2
1982	**Open Day**	W Carson	W R Hern	Sir M Sobell	100/30
1983	**Shareef Dancer**	W R Swinburn	M Stoute	M Al-Maktoum	10/1
1984	**Head for Heights**	W Carson	W R Hern	Sheikh Mohammed	5/1
1985	**Lanfranco**	S Cauthen	H Cecil	C St George	13/8
1986	**Bonhomie**	S Cauthen	H Cecil	Sheikh Mohammed	9/4
1987	**Love the Groom**	P Eddery	J Dunlop	Mrs V Gaucci del Bono	7/1
1988	**Sheriff's Star**	T Ives	Lady Herries	Duchess of Norfolk	9/2
1989	**Cacoethes**	P Eddery	G Harwood	Lady Harrison	8/13
1990	**Private Tender**	S Cauthen	H Cecil	Cliveden Stud	11/4
1991	**Saddlers' Hall**	L Piggott	M Stoute	Lord Weinstock	7/1
1992	**Beyton**	M Kinane	R Hannon	D F Cock	12/1

Run as the Ascot Derby 1834-1925

The Jersey Stakes

The Jersey Stakes came into being when the Old Triennial Stakes were discontinued after the first World War. The Triennial, as the name implies, was a three year cycle of races with the entries eligible to meet over five furlongs as two-year-olds, and extended to seven furlongs as three-year-olds and finally as four-year-olds over two miles.

The Jersey Stakes took on the second role and today is a race over seven furlongs for three-year-olds which at starting have not won a Group 1 or Group 2 race. Named after the Master of the Buckhounds between 1782-83, the 4th Earl of Jersey, the title was more significantly represented by the 8th Earl who originated the 'Jersey Act' in 1913 to protect the General Stud Book from the influence of American breeding; an act which had to be repealed in 1948 when it was realised that neither the 2,000 Guneas winner *My Babu* or the St Leger winner *Black Tarquin* were eligible for inclusion in the Stud Book.

Left: **'Nat' Flatman, winner of the first Jersey Stakes on *Borneo* in 1849. *Right:* Steve Donoghue, won in 1923 on *Friar* and in 1931 on *Oswald***

Run at Ascot over 7 furlongs for 3 year-olds First Run 1849 Group 3

		Jockey	Trainer	Owner	Odds
1849	**Borneo**	E Flatman	J Kent Jnr	Lord H G Lennox	10/1
1850	**No Race**				
1851	**Miserrima**	G Whitehouse	M Dawson	Lord J Scott	Evens
1852	**Songstress**	F Butler	J Scott	J Scott	Evens
1853	**Filbert**	E Flatman	W Harlock	Lord Exeter	8/1
1854	**Meteora**	A Day	J Scott	Lord Derby	2/1
1855	**Claret**	J Bartholomew	J Warriner	G Osbaldeston	6/1
1856	**Fly-by-Night**	J Bartholomew	J Scott	J Bowes	3/1
1857/58	**No Race**				
1859	**St Clarence**	J Charlton	–	G Osbaldeston	–
1860	**The Wizard**	–	J Scott	A Nichol	w.o.
1861	**Lupus**	G Fordham	J Scott	Lord Lincoln	–
1862	**No Race**				
1863	**Queen Bertha**	J Wells	J Scott	T Valentine	2/1
1864	**Blair Athol**	T Chaloner	W I'Anson	W I'Anson	–
1865	**Broomielaw**	H Custance	W I'Anson	H Chaplin	7/4
1866	**Janitor**	J Wells	J Hayhoe	Baron M de Rothschild	1/2
1867	**Vauban**	G Fordham	J Day	Duke of Beaufort	4/5
1868	**Vale Royal**	J Bumby	Jos Dawson	Lord Stamford	100/15
1869	**Duke of Beaufort**	T Cannon	J Stinton	E Brayley	2/5
1870	**Normanby**	T French	Jos Dawson	Lord Stamford	3/1
1871	**Ripponden**	C Maidment	W Gilbert	H Savile	1/5
1872	**Cremorne**	–	W Gilbert	H Savile	w.o.
1873	**The Laird of Holywell**	T Jennings Jnr	T Jennings	C J Lefevre	5/1
1874	**Volturno**	H Custance	T Leader	W S Cartwright	10/11
1875	**Ladylove**	F Archer	M Dawson	Lord Falmouth	8/100
1876	**Morning Star**	T Chaloner	A Taylor Snr	W S Crawfurd	10/1
1877	**Placida**	H Jeffery	J Marsh	J Fiennes	1/4
1878	**Jannette**	F Archer	M Dawson	Lord Falmouth	4/7
1879	**Dalnaspidal II**	G Fordham	A Taylor Snr	W S Crawfurd	5/1
1880	**Muncaster**	S Templeman	R Peck	Duke of Westminster	5/4
1881	**Limestone**	J Osborne Jnr	T Wadlow	Lord Bradford	2/1
1882	**Shotover**	T Cannon	J Porter	Duke of Westminster	w.o.
1883	**Galliard**	F Archer	M Dawson	Lord Falmouth	4/7
1884	**Talisman**	S Loates	A Hayhoe	L de Rothschild	2/1
1885	**Dandie Dimont**	C Wood	C Blanton	Prince Soltykoff	6/1
1886	**Mephisto**	C Wood	C Blanton	Prince Soltykoff	4/1
1887	**Jersey Lily**	R Chaloner	T Chaloner Jnr	J Snarry	20/1
1888	**Rada**	E Martin	M Dawson	Lord Falmouth	6/1
1889	**Cherry Bounce**	M Cannon	T Jennings	Prince Soltykoff	7/2
1890	**Blue-green**	G Barrett	J Porter	Duke of Westminster	1/3
1891	**Peter Flower**	F Rickaby	A B Sadler	Lord Durham	1/2
1892	**May Duke**	C Loates	T Leader	J Charlton	8/11
1893	**Prisoner**	R Chaloner	J Waugh	Lord Cadogan	5/1
1894	**Florizel II**	J Watts	R Marsh	HRH the Prince of Wales	6/4
1895	**Utica**	T Loates	A Hayhoe	L de Rothschild	11/10
1896	**Labrador**	M Cannon	J Porter	Duke of Westminster	7/4
1897	**Cortegar**	S Loates	W A Jarvis	C D Rose	2/1
1898	**Nun Nicer**	C Wood	W Waugh	Sir J Blundell Maple	2/1
1899	**Santa Casa**	S Loates	W A Jarvis	C D Rose	–
1900	**Rice**	J H Martin	Robert Sherwood Jnr	Sir R W Griffith	100/30
1901	**Veles**	J H Martin	Robert Sherwood Jnr	Sir R W Griffith	6/1
1902	**Fowling-piece**	C Jenkins	John Dawson Jnr	J Barrow	9/4
1903	**Rabelais**	K Cannon	R Marsh	A James	7/4
1904	**Henry the First**	O Madden	A Gilbert	J Musker	2/5
1905	**Polymelus**	M Cannon	J Porter	Lord Crewe	8/1
1906	**Troutbeck**	H Jones	W Waugh	Duke of Westminster	4/7
1907	**Acclaim**	W Higgs	S Darling	Duke of Devonshire	9/4
1908	**Rhodora**	L Lyne	J Allen	R Croker	2/1
1909	**Louviers**	D Waugh	D Waugh	W Raphael	2/9
1910	**Admiral Hawke**	W Saxby	P P Gilpin	E Loder	8/15
1911	**Alice**	H Jones	W Waugh	Lord Falmouth	2/1
1912	**Hector**	A Escott	H Escott	J L Dugdale	10/1
1913	**Light Brigade**	F Rickaby	G Lambton	Lord Derby	1/6
1914	**Sunny Lake**	H Jones	R Marsh	HM The King	2/1
1915/18	**No Race**				
1919	**Knight of the Air**	F Templeman	H S Persse	A E Barton	6/1
1920	**Tete a Tete**	I Strydom	Robert Sherwood Jnr	Lord Furness	7/2
1921	**Gask**	V Smyth	F Darling	Sir J Buchanan	5/1
1922	**Dragoon**	J Childs	A Taylor Jnr	W M G Singer	5/1
1923	**Friar**	S Donoghue	W Waugh	Duke of Westminster	9/4
1924	**Blue Pete**	E Gardner	J Platt	Sir W Cooke	100/8
1925	**Sherwood Starr**	C Smirke	R Day	Sir A Bailey	100/8
1926	**Review Order**	H Beasley	H S Persse	Lord Barnby	4/1
1927	**Kincardine**	H Beasley	H S Persse	B Walker	11/4

		Jockey	Trainer	Owner	Odds
1928	**Speyside**	J Childs	A E Wilson	F J Benson	100/7
1929	**Rattlin the Reefer**	G Richards	V Gilpin	Lord Woolavington	9/2
1930	**Paradine**	R A Jones	J Lawson	W M Cazelet	7/4
1931	**St Oswald**	S Donoghue	C Easterbee	E R Kewley	100/6
1932	**Limelight**	J Childs	W R Jarvis	HM The King	4/7
1933	**Fur Tor**	R A Jones	J Lawson	W M G Singer	2/1
1934	**Medieval Knight**	G Richards	F Darling	J A Dewar	5/4
1935	**Theft**	G Richards	Frank Butters	HH Aga Khan	11/4
1936	**Thankerton**	H Wragg	G Armstrong	Mrs J Shand	1/2
1937	**Lady of Shalott**	M Beary	R Adams	H R Mosenthal	100/7
1938	**Cave Man**	G Richards	J Lawson	Lord Astor	5/4
1939	**Fairstone**	M Beary	H Cottrill	Sir A Bailey	1/2
1940/45	**No Race**				
1946	**Sayani**	R Poincelet	J Lieux	Mme J Lieux	100/6
1947	**Nebuchadnezzar**	G Richards	F Darling	Sir P Loraine	4/6
1948	**Hyperbole**	T Weston	N Cannon	J V Rank	100/7
1949	**Star King**	D Smith	J C Waugh	W Harvey	9/2
1950	**Double Eclipse**	W H Carr	C Boyd-Rochfort	Lady Z Wernher	6/5
1951	**Royal Serenade**	C Elliott	H Wragg	Mrs G Kohn	3/1
1952	**Kara Tepe**	E Mercer	G Colling	F G Robinson	100/8
1953	**Rhinehart**	G Richards	D Candy	E O Kay	4/1
1954	**Marshal Ney**	W R Johnstone	W Byrne	J J Cosgrove	100/9
1955	**Windsor Sun**	J Eddery	S McGrath	J McGrath	100/8
1956	**Adare**	W R Johnstone	M V O'Brien	J Cosgrave	8/1
1957	**Quorum**	A Russell	W Lyde	T Farr	4/6
1958	**Faith Healer**	J Sime	P Beasley	W Harrison	11/2
1959	**Welsh Guard**	W H Carr	C Boyd-Rochfort	Mrs J Hanes	4/1
1960	**Red Gauntlet**	E Smith	T E Leader	H J Joel	100/8
1961	**Favorita**	L Piggott	N Murless	Mrs V Lilley	5/4
1962	**Catchpole**	D Smith	G Brooke	R F Dennis	13/2
1963	**The Creditor**	L Piggott	N Murless	Lady Sassoon	11/2
1964	**Young Christopher**	L Piggott	F Maxwell	J McShane	5/4
1965	**Fortezza**	F Durr	H Wragg	R B Moller	100/6
1966	**Vibrant**	P Robinson	E Lambton	Mrs G Lambton	4/1
1967	**St Chad**	G Moore	N Murless	Mrs N Murless	11/2
1968	**World Cup**	W Williamson	P Prendergast	J R Mullion	15/8
1969	**Crooner**	J Gorton	D Smith	Lord Rosebery	8/1
1970	**Fluke**	G Duffield	J Oxley	R D Hollingsworth	9/4
1971	**Ashleigh**	W Williamson	P Prendergast	Mrs P Poe	13/8
1972	**Proof Positive**	P Eddery	J Tree	J H Whitney	14/1
1973	**Pitskelly**	W Williamson	M Jarvis	D Robinson	15/2
1974	**Red Alert**	J Roe	D Weld	B Firestone	6/1
1975	**Gay Fandango**	L Piggott	M V O'Brien	A Clore	11/10
1976	**Gwent**	G Lewis	B Hobbs	A S R Villar	11/2
1977	**Etienne Gerard**	P Cook	M Stoute	P Phillips	25/1
1978	**Camden Town**	P Eddery	P Walwyn	Sir J Thorn	4/1
1979	**Blue Refrain**	B Rouse	C Benstead	Mrs L Wood	12/1
1980	**Hard Fought**	L Piggott	M Stoute	L B Holliday	15/8
1981	**Rasa Penang**	L Piggott	R Armstrong	U Wijewardene	11/1
1982	**Merlin's Charm**	S Cauthen	B Hills	R Sangster	9/1
1983	**Tecorno**	W Carson	W R Hern	Countess M Esterhazy	8/1
1984	**Miss Silca Key**	B Rouse	D Elsworth	E Aldridge Ltd	15/1
1985	**Pennine Walk**	P Eddery	J Tree	S Niarchos	9/2
1986	**Cliveden**	G Starkey	G Harwood	A Speelman	9/1
1987	**Midyan**	S Cauthen	H Cecil	Prince A A Faisal	11/2
1988	**Indian Ridge**	C Asmussen	D Elsworth	Mrs A Coughlan	10/1
1989	**Zilzal**	W R Swinburn	M Stoute	M Al-Maktoum	10/11
1990	**Sally Rous**	G Carter	G Wragg	Sir P Oppenheimer	20/1
1991	**Satin Flower**	S Cauthen	J Gosden	Sheikh Mohammed	12/1
1992	**Prince Ferdinand**	J Reid	M McCormack	Miss J Winch	6/1

Run as 2nd Year of the Triennial Stakes 1849-1918

The Queen Mary Stakes

The Queen Mary Stakes was founded in 1921 in honour of the consort of King George V. The inaugural winner, *Wild Mint*, was not destined to play a great part in the history of the thoroughbred, but the runner-up *Selene* was to be the dam of *Hyperion*, Derby winner in 1933 and one the most influential sires of the present century.

The 1922 winner *Cos* displayed the green and chocolate hoops of the Aga Khan for the first time at Ascot, but more significant was *Mumtaz Mahal's* victory in 1923. This filly, a daughter of *The Tetrarch* was brilliantly fast and won in a canter by ten lengths. She was one of the yearlings purchased on behalf of the Aga by the Hon.George Lambton and like *Cos* became a foundation mare of an equine dynasty which was to survive for forty years.

Her daughter *Mah Mahal* was the dam of the 1936 Derby winner *Mahmoud* as well as *Star of Iran*, sire of *Petite Etoile*, winner of the 1,000 Guineas and the Oaks in 1959. Twenty-six years after *Mumtaz Mahal* had won the Queen

Mary, her great-granddaughter *Diableretta* was victorious in 1949.

With the odd exception such as *Waterloo,* most of the fillies who win the Queen Mary are too fast and precocious to make classic material. Their usual role is to provide the essential element of speed on the distaff side of a classic-winning pedigree.

Run at Ascot over 5 furlongs for 2 year-old fillies First Run 1921 Group 3

		Jockey	Trainer	Owner	Odds
1921	**Wild Mint**	J Shatwell	H Cottrill	W E Whineray	8/1
1922	**Cos**	G Hulme	R C Dawson	HH Aga Khan	7/2
1923	**Mumtaz Mahal**	G Hulme	R C Dawson	HH Aga Khan	1/4
1924	**Margeritta**	G Archibald	F Darling	Lord Woolavington	2/1
1925	**Aloysia**	J Childs	W Jarvis	HM The King	5/1
1926	**Book Law**	R A Jones	A Taylor Jnr	Lord Astor	7/2
1927	**Stadacona**	H Beasley	H S Persse	D McCalmont	5/1
1928	**Arabella**	C Smirke	P P Gilpin	G Loder	Evens
1929	**Qurrat-al-Ain**	M Beary	R C Dawson	HH Aga Khan	8/11
1930	**Atbara**	P Beasley	V Gilpin	G Loder	20/1
1931	**Diamalt**	H Wragg	A Holland	Mrs V Sainsbury	100/9
1932	**Supervisor**	G Richards	F Darling	F Darling	3/1
1933	**Maureen**	G Richards	F Darling	Lord Woolavington	5/2
1934	**Caretta**	G Richards	F Darling	Lord Lonsdale	6/4
1935	**Fair Ranee**	S Donoghue	R C Dawson	Vicomte de Fontacre	100/8
1936	**Night Song**	P Beasley	C Boyd-Rochfort	J Whitney	4/1
1937	**Queen of Simla**	C Smirke	Frank Butters	HH Aga Khan	20/1
1938	**Belle Travers**	D Smith	Frank Butters	T Lant	3/1
1939	**Snowberry**	G Richards	F Darling	Lord Lonsdale	4/1
1940	**No Race**				
1941	**Sun Chariot**	H Wragg	F Darling	HM The King	11/8
1942	**Samovar**	M Beary	H S Persse	Lord Wyfold	100/6
1943	**Fair Fame**	F Lane	H Leader	Mrs B Lavington	15/2
1944	**Sun Stream**	H Wragg	W Earl	Lord Derby	100/30
1945	**Rivaz**	C Elliott	Frank Butters	HH Aga Khan	4/7
1946	**Apparition**	G Richards	F Darling	Mrs R Macdonald-Buchanan	11/8
1947	**Masaka**	C Smirke	Frank Butters	HH Aga Khan	4/1
1948	**Coronation V**	C Elliott	C Semblat	M Boussac	7/2
1949	**Diableretta**	W R Johnstone	Frank Butters	HH Aga Khan	7/4
1950	**Rose Linnet**	D Smith	R Day	Mrs A Johnston	10/1
1951	**Primavera**	E Mercer	J Jarvis	Lord Milford	100/6
1952	**Devon Vintage**	E Mercer	R J Colling	R C Boucher	100/8
1953	**Sybil's Niece**	E Mercer	J Jarvis	Lord Milford	100/6
1954	**Bride Elect**	F Barlow	H Cottrill	Maj L B Holliday	6/1
1955	**Weeber**	A Breasley	P Nelson	J Olding	10/1
1956	**Pharsalia**	L Piggott	H Cottrill	Maj L B Holliday	100/7
1957	**Abelia**	L Piggott	N Murless	B Hornung	11/2
1958	**A.20**	W Rickaby	F Sutherland	H Clifton	5/1
1959	**Paddy's Sister**	G Moore	P Prendergast	Mrs J R Mullion	15/8
1960	**Cynara**	W H Carr	H Wragg	G A Oldham	Evens
1961	**My Dream**	D Smith	G Brooke	D Robinson	2/1
1962	**Shot Silk**	D Smith	G Brooke	D Cripps	100/8
1963	**Lerida**	J Lindley	J A Waugh	Mrs R Macdonald-Buchanan	9/2
1964	**Brassia**	J Purtell	M V O'Brien	A Plesch	7/2
1965	**Visp**	J Lindley	J F Watts	E Benjamin	6/4
1966	**Petite Path**	J Lindley	R Mason	R Mason	33/1
1967	**Sovereign**	R Hutchinson	H Wragg	R B Moller	10/11
1968	**Grizel**	W Williamson	P Prendergast	W Stirling	5/2
1969	**Farfalla**	A Murray	D Smith	D van Clief	13/2
1970	**Cawston's Pride**	B Taylor	F Maxwell	L B Hall	2/1
1971	**Waterloo**	E Hide	J W Watts	Mrs R Stanley	9/2
1972	**Truly Thankful**	A Murray	H R Price	G van der Ploeg	14/1
1973	**Bitty Girl**	B Raymond	M Jarvis	D Robinson	11/2
1974	**Highest Trump**	J Roe	D Weld	Lord Petersham	5/2
1975	**Rory's Rocket**	A Murray	P Ashworth	Mrs W Slaytor	33/1
1976	**Cramond**	J Mercer	R Boss	Mrs S Eldin	25/1
1977	**Amaranda**	L Piggott	H Wragg	R B Moller	4/6
1978	**Greenland Park**	H White	W Hastings-Bass	Greenland Park Ltd	15/2
1979	**Abeer**	W Carson	J Tree	K Abdulla	7/1
1980	**Pushy**	J Mercer	H Cecil	Lord Tavistock	7/1
1981	**Fly Baby**	P Cook	R Hannon	Malden Farms Ltd	40/1
1982	**Widaad**	W R Swinburn	M Stoute	M Al-Maktoum	13/8
1983	**Night of Wind**	B Raymond	M McCormack	P Durkan	50/1
1984	**Hi-Tech Girl**	G Starkey	P Makin	Intercraft	16/1
1985	**Gwydion**	S Cauthen	H Cecil	S Niarchos	2/1
1986	**Forest Flower**	P Eddery	I Balding	P Mellon	9/4
1987	**Princess Athena**	W Carson	D Elsworth	J H Senn	9/1
1988	**Gloriella**	J Reid	J J McLoughlin	J J McLoughlin	8/1
1989	**Dead Certain**	S Cauthen	D Elsworth	G G Marten	8/1
1990	**On Tiptoes**	D McKeown	J P Leigh	J W Rowles	8/1

		Jockey	Trainer	Owner	Odds
1991	**Marling**	G Carter	G Wragg	E J Loder	11/4
1992	**Lyric Fantasy**	M Roberts	R Hannon	Lord Carnarvon	11/8

Run at Newmarket 1941-1944

The Coronation Stakes

Founded in 1840 a little belatedly to celebrate the crowning of Queen Victoria two years before, the Coronation Stakes sported some interestingly named fillies in the early years. *Spangle, Distaffina, Stitch* and *Lesbia* all catch the eye, but the event soon became an ideal hunting ground for horses which had run prominently in the 1,000 Guineas.

Nowadays it would be better named as the Consolation Stakes, as no classic winner has triumphed since *One In A Million* in 1979, but *Tolmi, Al Bahathri, Sonic Lady, Milligram* and *Marling* all succeeded after being placed at Newmarket.

Run at Ascot over 1 mile for 3 year-old fillies First Run 1840 Group 1

		Jockey	Trainer	Owner	Odds
1840	**Spangle**	Cotton	W Edwards	Lord Albemarle	5/2
1841	**Ghuznee**	W Scott	J Scott	Lord Westminster	w.o.
1842	**Celia**	S Mann	–	Lord Exeter	4/6
1843	**La Stimata**	J Chapple	Ralph Sherwood	Sir G Heathcote	5/1
1844	**The Princess**	E Flatman	J Scott	G Anson	1/8
1845	**Stitch**	E Flatman	T Taylor	Lord Chesterfield	4/7
1846	**Guaracha**	J Howlett	W Smith	G S Ford	–
1847	**Cosachia**	W Abdale	W Harlock	Lord Exeter	–
1848	**Distaffina**	E Flatman	T Taylor	Lord Chesterfield	2/1
1849	**Lady Evelyn**	E Flatman	T Taylor	Lord Chesterfield	2/5
1850	**filly by Slane**	F Butler	R Stephenson	Lord Orford	5/4
1851	**Barcelona**	E Flatman	W Dilly	C Greville	–
1852	**Iona**	F Butler	W Beresford	Lord Orford	2/1
1853	**Catherine Hayes**	C Marlow	M Dawson	Lord J Scott	1/5
1854	**Mishap**	J Marson	A Taylor Snr	J M Stanley	3/1
1855	**Alcyone**	R Pettit	W Butler Jnr	Duke of Bedford	11/2
1856	**Victoria**	J Bartholomew	J Scott	J Bowes	6/4
1857	**Beechnut**	G Fordham	W Harlock	Lord Exeter	–
1858	**Sunbeam**	R Chilman	J Prince	J Merry	4/7
1859	**Cantine**	L Snowden	A Taylor Snr	Lord Ailesbury	7/4
1860	**Allington**	J Daley	J Eskrett	G W Gratwicke	–
1861	**Queen of the Vale**	J Wells	J Hayhoe	Baron M de Rothschild	4/5
1862	**Polynesia**	H Custance	T Taylor	Lord Chesterfield	2/1
1863	**Lady Augusta**	A Edwards	Jos Dawson	Lord Stamford	4/5
1864	**Breeze**	J Wells	J Hayhoe	Baron M de Rothschild	2/5
1865	**Siberia**	G Fordham	J Day	Duke of Beaufort	5/2
1866	**Mother of Pearl**	E Payne	H Sopp	Mr Maund	12/1
1867	**Achievement**	T Chaloner	J Dover	M Pearson	30/100
1868	**Athena**	G Fordham	J Day	H Padwick	–
1869	**Martinique**	J Snowden	C Peck	Sir R W Bulkeley	4/7
1870	**Sunshine**	J Grimshaw	J Waugh	J Merry	1/2
1871	**Corisande**	C Maidment	J Hayhoe	Baron M de Rothschild	4/6
1872	**Highland Lassie**	T Chaloner	A Taylor Snr	W S Crawfurd	5/1
1873	**Marie Stuart**	T Cannon	R Peck	J Merry	1/3
1874	**Apology**	J Osborne Jnr	W Osborne	J W King	10/11
1875	**Maud Victoria**	H Constable	T Leader	W S Cartwright	5/2
1876	**Footstep**	H Custance	T Wadlow	Lord Wilton	9/4
1877	**Belphoebe**	J Goater	G Bloss	Lord Hartington	5/4
1878	**Redwing**	F Archer	M Dawson	Lord Falmouth	8/1
1879	**Lelia**	A F Lemaire	J Ryan	J H Houldsworth	10/1
1880	**L'Eclair**	H Luke	John Dawson	Prince Batthyany	10/1
1881	**Mazurka**	T Cannon	W Gilbert Jnr	Lord Cadogan	8/1
1882	**Rozle**	A F Lemaire	J Ryan	J H Houldsworth	20/1
1883	**Lovely**	T Cannon	J Porter	Sir F Johnstone	7/4
1884	**Sandiway**	F Archer	J Porter	Duke of Westminster	100/30
1885	**St Helena**	J Watts	J Enoch	Lord Zetland	4/1
1886	**Argo Navis**	C Wood	C Blanton	Prince Soltykoff	4/7
1887	**Heloise**	G Barrett	A Taylor Snr	Duchess of Montrose	4/1
1888	**Seabreeze**	W T Robinson	J Jewitt	Lord Calthorpe	4/7
1889	**Seclusion**	T Loates	C W Golding	H Milner	5/4
1890	**Heresy**	W T Robinson	J Jewitt	Lord Calthorpe	4/7
1891	**Cereza**	J Watts	J Porter	W B Cloete	8/1
1892	**Lady Hermit**	M Cannon	Robert Sherwood	J T North	2/1
1893	**Silene**	M Cannon	J Ryan	D Baird	100/30
1894	**Throstle**	M Cannon	J Porter	Sir F Johnstone	10/1

		Jockey	Trainer	Owner	Odds
1895	**Butterfly**	W Bradford	T Jennings Jnr	L Brassey	100/12
1896	**Helm**	M Cannon	J Porter	Duke of Westminster	11/2
1897	**Goletta**	K Cannon	A Hayhoe	L de Rothschild	100/12
1898	**Lowood**	M Cannon	J Porter	Duke of Westminster	7/4
1899	**Fascination**	O Madden	R Marsh	A James	4/1
1900	**Winifreda**	T Weldon	T Jennings Jnr	L Brassey	5/1
	Sainte Nitouche	F Rickaby	H Enoch	D Baird	5/1
1901	**Bella Galliana**	W Lane	P P Gilpin	R Walker	–
1902	**Doctrine**	W Halsey	F W Day	Sir E Cassel	–
1903	**Oriole**	D Maher	G Blackwell	Lord Rosebery	–
1904	**Pretty Polly**	W Lane	P P Gilpin	E Loder	1/5
1905	**Commune**	F W Hardy	W Goodwin	Duke of Devonshire	20/1
1906	**Keystone II**	D Maher	G Lambton	Lord Derby	8/13
1907	**Frugality**	H Jones	W Waugh	Lord Falmouth	7/4
1908	**Lesbia**	D Maher	G Blackwell	Sir D Cooper	7/4
1909	**Princesse de Galles**	H Jones	R Marsh	HM The King	100/30
1910	**Winkipop**	H Jones	W Waugh	W Astor	11/2
1911	**Knockfeerna**	Wal Griggs	P P Gilpin	E Loder	4/1
1912	**Polkerris**	F Wootton	C Peck	S B Joel	8/11
1913	**Prue**	D Maher	P Peck	Lord Rosebery	5/2
1914	**Wassilissa**	S Donoghue	R C Dawson	Lord Carnarvon	7/2
1915/18	**No Race**				
1919	**Flying Spear**	J Childs	A Taylor Jnr	W M G Singer	4/1
1920	**Cinna**	W Griggs	T Waugh	Sir R W B Jardine	2/1
1921	**Donna Branca**	F Bullock	B Jarvis	J S Courtauld	2/1
1922	**Pogrom**	B Carslake	A Taylor Jnr	Lord Astor	2/1
1923	**Paola**	V Smyth	R C Dawson	HH Aga Khan	7/2
1924	**Straitlace**	C Elliott	D Waugh	Sir E Hulton	3/1
1925	**Saucy Sue**	F Bullock	A Taylor Jnr	Lord Astor	1/10
1926	**Moti Mahal**	C Smirke	R C Dawson	HH Aga Khan	8/1
1927	**Book Law**	H Jelliss	A Taylor Jnr	Lord Astor	4/9
1928	**Toboggan**	T Weston	Frank Butters	Lord Derby	11/10
1929	**Daumont**	F Fox	F Darling	Lord Lonsdale	100/8
1930	**Qurrat-al-Ain**	M Beary	R C Dawson	HH Aga Khan	6/1
1931	**Sunny Devon**	R Dick	J Lawson	Lord Astor	3/1
1932	**Udaipur**	M Beary	Frank Butters	HH Aga Khan	6/1
1933	**Betty**	R Dick	J Lawson	Lord Astor	10/11
1934	**Foxcroft**	J Childs	C Boyd-Rochfort	M Field	5/1
1935	**Ankaret**	F Fox	Fred Butters	Mrs G B Miller	5/1
1936	**Traffic Light**	R Dick	J Lawson	Lord Astor	5/1
1937	**Gainsborough Lass**	E Smith	J Jarvis	Sir J Jarvis	4/1
1938	**Solar Flower**	G Richards	Frank Butters	Sir A Butt	100/9
1939	**Olein**	T Lowrey	B Jarvis	Lord Glanely	6/1
1940/45	**No Race**				
1946	**Neolight**	G Richards	F Darling	J A Dewar	15/8
1947	**Saucy Sal**	W R Johnstone	H Blagrave	Mrs G Blagrave	11/10
1948	**Fortuity**	E Britt	M Marsh	J Musker	20/1
1949	**Avila**	M Beary	C Boyd-Rochfort	HM The King	11/2
1950	**Tambara**	C Smirke	M Marsh	HH Aga Khan	6/5
1951	**Belle of All**	G Richards	N Bertie	H Tufton	15/8
1952	**Zabara**	K Gethin	V Smyth	Sir M McAlpine	6/5
1953	**Happy Laughter**	W Rickaby	J Jarvis	H D H Wills	7/4
1954	**Festoon**	J Mercer	N Cannon	J A Dewar	11/8
1955	**Meld**	W H Carr	C Boyd-Rochfort	Lady Z Wernher	4/9
1956	**Midget II**	W R Johnstone	A Head	P Wertheimer	5/6
1957	**Toro**	J Massard	A Head	W R Johnstone	3/1
1958	**St Lucia**	G Lewis	P Hastings-Bass	Lord Sefton	100/8
1959	**Rosalba**	J Mercer	R J Colling	J J Astor	11/8
1960	**Barbaresque**	G Moore	W Clout	W Guest	9/2
1961	**Aiming High**	L Piggott	N Murless	HM The Queen	100/8
1962	**Display**	G Bougoure	P Prendergast	Mrs B Granard	3/1
1963	**Fiji**	G Starkey	J Oxley	Lady Halifax	7/2
1964	**Ocean**	G Starkey	J Oxley	R D Hollingsworth	7/1
1965	**Greengage**	A Breasley	G Richards	R F Watson	5/4
1966	**Haymaking**	J Mercer	R F Johnson Houghton	C Nicholson	100/7
1967	**Fleet**	G Moore	N Murless	R C Boucher	15/8
1968	**Sovereign**	R Hutchinson	H Wragg	R B Moller	3/1
1969	**Lucyrowe**	D Keith	P Walwyn	L Freedman	15/8
1970	**Humble Duty**	D Keith	P Walwyn	Lady J Ashcombe	1/6
1971	**Magic Flute**	G Lewis	N Murless	Lord H de Walden	85/40
1972	**Calve**	E Hide	P J Prendergast	Lord Granard	12/1
1973	**Jacinth**	J Gorton	B Hobbs	Lady Butt	15/8
1974	**Lisadell**	L Piggott	M V O'Brien	J Mulcahy	7/2
1975	**Roussalka**	L Piggott	H Cecil	N Phillips	9/1
1976	**Kesar Queen**	Y Saint-Martin	A Breasley	R Tikkoo	7/2
1977	**Orchestration**	P Eddery	A J Maxwell	V McCalmont	12/1

***Marling*, winner of the 1992 Coronation Stakes, seen here beating *Selkirk* in that year's Sussex Stakes.**

		Jockey	Trainer	Owner	Odds
1978	**Sutton Place**	W Swinburn	D Weld	Mrs T Donahue	14/1
1979	**One in a Million**	J Mercer	H Cecil	Helena Springfield Ltd	10/11
1980	**Cairn Rouge**	A Murray	M Cunningham	D Brady	6/5
1981	**Tolmi**	E Hide	B Hobbs	G Cambanis	4/1
1982	**Chalon**	L Piggott	H Cecil	M Riordan	9/4
1983	**Flame of Tara**	D Gillespie	J Bolger	Miss P O'Kelly	11/2
1984	**Katies**	P Robinson	M Ryan	T Ramsden	11/2
1985	**Al Bahathri**	A Murray	H Thomson Jones	H Al-Maktoum	4/6
1986	**Sonic Lady**	W R Swinburn	M Stoute	Sheikh Mohammed	8/15
1987	**Milligram**	W R Swinburn	M Stoute	Helena Springfield Ltd	4/5
1988	**Magic of Life**	P Eddery	J Tree	S Niarchos	16/1
1989	**Golden Opinion**	C Asmussen	A Fabre	Sheikh Mohammed	7/2
1990	**Chimes of Freedom**	S Cauthen	H Cecil	S Niarchos	11/2
1991	**Kooyonga**	W J O'Connor	M Kauntze	M Haga	3/1
1992	**Marling**	W R Swinburn	G Wragg	E J Loder	8/11

The Royal Hunt Cup

Always one of the great gambles and a highlight of the Royal Meeting for shrewd punters looking for long odds, the first running in 1843 has typified the race since. *Knight of Whistle*, ridden by Nat Flatman won in the colours of Lord Chesterfield with *Garry Owen*, *Bourra Tomacha* and *Epaulette* finishing in a triple dead heat for second.

Nowadays, only smart handicappers have a chance and although contested by three-year-olds and upwards, four-year-olds have had the best record in recent times, usually horses of proven ability carrying high weights.

The quality of the race is indicated by *Buzzards Bay* (1982) who went on to win the Queen Elizabeth II Stakes. The biggest gamble in the past decade was on *Tender Heart* in 1980, from the Epsom stable of John Sutcliffe who also sent out *My Hussar* to win in 1977, while the most popular was *Colour Sergeant* who won for HM The Queen in 1992 when Royal fortunes were at a rather low ebb.

Run at Ascot over 1 mile First Run 1843 Handicap

		Jockey	Trainer	Owner	Odds
1843	**Knight of Whistle**	E Flatman	T Taylor	Lord Chesterfield	5/1
1844	**Bishop Romford's Cob**	C Marlow	C Peck	Sir R W Bulkeley	3/1
1845	**Evenus**	S Mann	R Boyce Jnr	Lord Stradbroke	10/1
1846	**Leaconfield**	T Carter	W Boyce	W Stanley	15/1
1847	**Tragical**	W Abdale	H Bradley	Count Batthyany	–
1848	**Conyngham**	J Robinson	J Day	Sir R Pigot	12/1
1849	**Collingwood**	F Butler	French	P Rolt	8/1
1850	**Hagley**	W Thick	–	Mr Higden	6/1
1851	**Sir Charles**	H Goater	W Day	H Robinson	–
1852	**Ephesus**	T Lye	I Day	Mr Waller	7/2
1853	**The Friar**	L Garvey	J Kent Jnr	Lord H G Lennox	6/1
1854	**Brocket**	A Day	J Scott	B Way	15/1
1855	**Chalice**	G Fordham	R Stephenson Jnr	Lord Clifden	100/8
1856	**Forbidden Fruit**	W Cresswell	J Scott	S Murland	4/1
1857	**Rosa Bonheur**	C Rayner	J Scott	Lord Londesborough	10/1
1858	**Hesperithusa**	T Chaloner	W Oates	R Eastwood	7/2
1859	**King at Arms**	G Britton	G Drewe	Col Pearson	–
1860	**Crater**	W Bottom	I Woolcot	J Sargent	20/1
1861	**Buccaneer**	J Goater	R Milton	Lord Portsmouth	6/1
1862	**Canary**	A Deacon	J Day	J Day	5/1
1863	**Victor**	J Morris	F Balchin	G Hodgman	3/1
1864	**Gem of the Sea**	H Grimshaw	W Goodwin	Mr Longfield	40/1
1865	**Gratitude**	H Covey	J Waugh	W Robinson	6/1
1866	**Attache**	H Parry	J Godding	G Angell	33/1
1867	**Jasper**	H Jeffery	J Hayhoe	Baron M de Rothschild	30/1
1868	**Satyr**	J Adams	J Porter	Sir J Hawley	10/1
1869	**See Saw**	G Fordham	T Wadlow	Lord Wilton	100/30
1870	**Judge**	W Newhouse	W Day	Sir F Johnstone	100/15
1871	**Valuer**	G Jarvis	W Day	Sir F Johnstone	11/2
1872	**Ripponden**	H Covey	W Gilbert	H Savile	100/8
1873	**Winslow**	G Fordham	–	G Clive	20/1
1874	**Lowlander**	H Constable	W Reeves	H Bird	4/1
1875	**Thuringian Prince**	C Wood	Jos Dawson	Jos Dawson	100/30
1876	**Hopbloom**	W Hopkins	C Blanton	Sir J Astley	100/3
1877	**Cradle**	W Hopkins	T Wadlow	Lord Wilton	100/15
1878	**Julius Caesar**	F Archer	Jos Dawson	Jos Dawson	10/1
1879	**The Mandarin**	C Wood	J Cannon	Capt J Machell	33/1
1880	**Strathern**	W Brockwell	T Chaloner	J Foy	40/1
1881	**Peter**	F Archer	R Sherrard	Sir J Astley	100/30
1882	**Sweetbread**	J Woodburn	J Jewitt	W Gerard	5/1
1883	**Elzevir**	C Wood	J Jewitt	W Gerard	5/1
1884	**Acrostic**	F Barrett	F Bates	R Jardine	100/7
1885	**Eastern Emperor**	J Tomlisson	A Taylor Snr	Duke of Beaufort	9/1
1886	**Despair**	C Loates	W Gilbert Jnr	W Gilbert Jnr	25/1
1887	**Gay Hermit**	C Wood	A Taylor Snr	Duchess of Montrose	5/1
1888	**Shillelagh**	G Chaloner	J Jewitt	Capt J Machell	11/2
1889	**Whitelegs**	W Blake	T Cannon	D Henty	10/1
1890	**Morion**	G Barrett	R Marsh	Lord Hartington	9/2
1891	**Laureate II**	M Cannon	T Brown	J Hammond	33/1
1892	**Suspender**	G Chaloner	J Jewitt	H McCalmont	25/1
1893	**Amandier**	T Loates	A Hayhoe	Baron L de Rothschild	7/1
1894	**Victor Wild**	R Harrison	J Hornsby	T Worton	50/1
1895	**Clorane**	M Cannon	W T Robinson	A F Bassett	100/12
1896	**Quarrel**	J Fagan	W Walters Jnr	Lord Rosebery	7/2
1897	**Knight of the Thistle**	F Allsopp	J Jewitt	H McCalmont	100/12
1898	**Jaquemart**	T Loates	J Watson	L de Rothschild	100/9
1899	**Refractor**	A Weatherell	J Waugh	D J Jardine	25/1
1900	**Royal Flush**	J Reiff	E Wishard	J A Drake	100/7
1901	**Stealaway**	J Childs	G Chaloner	J B Leigh	4/1
1902	**Solicitor**	S Loates	R C Dawson	Lord Carnarvon	9/1
1903	**Kunstler**	J Watts	A Hayhoe	L de Rothschild	33/1
1904	**Csardas**	G McCall	J Cannon	H Keswick	10/1
1905	**Andover**	B Lynham	H Braime	F Alexander	10/1
1906	**Dinneford**	O Madden	A Taylor Jnr	R Walker	100/15
1907	**Lally**	L Hewitt	T Lewis	W B Purefoy	100/6
1908	**Billy the Verger**	R Crisp	L Rooney	R B Dobell	100/9
1909	**Dark Ronald**	W H Williams	J A Clement	A Bailey	4/1
1910	**Bachelor's Double**	C Trigg	H S Persse	W W Bailey	5/1
1911	**Moscato**	A Sharpe	A Taylor Jnr	W M G Singer	100/6
1912	**Eton Boy**	C Trigg	H Carter	H P Nickalls	100/12
1913	**Long Set**	W Higgs	J H Batho	S B Joel	100/7
1914	**Lie-a-bed**	K Robertson	J East	J East	25/1
1915/18	**No Race**				
1919	**Irish Elegance**	F Templeman	H Cottrill	J White	7/1
1920	**Square Measure**	S Donoghue	J Rogers	R Walker	8/1

		Jockey	Trainer	Owner	Odds
1921	**Illuminator**	R Stokes	Sir C Nugent	E L Short	50/1
1922	**Varzy**	B Lynch	R Moreton	F Gretton	20/1
1923	**Weathervane**	S Ingham	R Marsh	HM The King	20/1
1924	**Dinkie**	W Alford	W Earl	Mrs R Jeffrey	50/1
1925	**Cockpit**	A Orme	S Pickering	P Nelke	100/6
1926	**Cross Bow**	R A Jones	A Taylor Jnr	Lord Astor	33/1
1927	**Asterus**	C Elliott	S H Darling	M Boussac	10/1
1928	**Priory Park**	B Carslake	C Peck	J B Joel	15/2
1929	**Songe**	H Wragg	O Bell	Lord Michelham	100/6
1930	**The McNab**	F Fox	F Darling	J A Dewar	100/7
1931	**Grand Salute**	G Richards	T Hogg	Lord Glanely	5/1
1932	**Totaig**	B Rosen	G Duller	V Emmanuel	33/1
1933	**Colorado Kid**	C Buckham	V Gilpin	G Loder	100/8
1934	**Caymanas**	C Ray	C Easterbee	C Ewing	50/1
1935	**Priok**	S Middleton	P Whitaker	H Barnard-Hankey	66/1
1936	**Guinea Gap**	R A Jones	H Cottrill	Lady Nuttall	28/1
1937	**Fairplay**	P Maher	P Allden	R Middlemas	18/1
1938	**Couvert**	C Richards	H Blagrave	H Blagrave	100/8
1939	**Caerloptic**	M Beary	H Cottrill	Sir A Bailey	100/8
1940	**No Race**				
1941	**Time Step**	F Herbert	J Anthony	J H Whitney	4/1
1942/45	**No Race**				
1945	**Battle Hymn**	P Maher	C Boyd-Rochfort	J H Whitney	20/1
1946	**Friar's Fancy**	E Smith	T E Leader	O Watney	15/2
1947	**Master Vote**	T Sidebotham	H Blagrave	H Blagrave	25/1
1948	**Master Vote**	W R Johnstone	H Blagrave	H Blagrave	100/7
1949	**Sterope**	J Caldwell	P Beasley	J Townley	100/6
1950	**Hyperbole**	A Breasley	N Cannon	J V Rank	10/1
1951	**Val d'Assa**	N Sellwood	H S Persse	D McCalmont	100/6
1952	**Queen of Sheba**	F Barlow	H S Persse	D McCalmont	100/7
1953	**Choir Boy**	D Smith	C Boyd-Rochfort	HM The Queen	100/6
1954	**Chivalry**	D Forte	T Rimell	P Hatvany	33/1
1955	**Nicholas Nickleby**	W Snaith	F Armstrong	J Gerber	50/1
1956	**Alexander**	W H Carr	C Boyd-Rochfort	HM The Queen	13/2
1957	**Retrial**	P Robinson	C Boyd-Rochfort	Lady Z Wernher	100/7
1958	**Amos**	P Boothman	S Mercer	L Carver	20/1
1959	**Faultless Speech**	G Lewis	H Wallington	H Wallington	8/1
1960	**Small Slam**	R Elliott	G Barling	P King	28/1
1961	**King's Troop**	G Lewis	P Hastings-Bass	Mrs P Hastings	100/7
1962	**Smartie**	J Sime	R Mason	R Mason	22/1
1963	**Spaniard's Close**	L Piggott	F N Winter	Mrs B Davis	25/1
1964	**Zaleucus**	D Smith	G Brooke	D McCalmont	100/7
1965	**Casabianca**	L Piggott	N Murless	J Hornung	100/9
1966	**Continuation**	J Roe	S McGrath	S McGrath	25/1
1967	**Regal Light**	G Sexton	S Hall	Mrs L Lazarus	100/9
1968	**Golden Mean**	F Durr	D Smith	S H Lee	28/1
1969	**Kamundu**	L Piggott	F Carr	J Banks	7/1
1970	**Calpurnius**	G Duffield	J W Watts	C W Engelhard	33/1
1971	**Picture Boy**	J Wilson	G Todd	K Mackenzie	11/1
1972	**Tempest Boy**	R Hutchinson	J Sutcliffe Jnr	P Hesse	20/1
1973	**Camouflage**	D Cullen	J Dunlop	J Edwards	14/1
1974	**Old Lucky**	W Carson	B van Cutsem	N B Hunt	8/1
1975	**Ardoon**	D Maitland	G Pritchard-Gordon	F Feeney	9/1
1976	**Jumping Hill**	L Piggott	N Murless	G A Pope Jnr	6/1
1977	**My Hussar**	W Carson	J Sutcliffe Jnr	L Goldschlager	10/1
1978	**Fear Naught**	M Wigham	J Etherington	W Norton	12/1
1979	**Pipedreamer**	P Waldron	H Candy	Mrs J Brookes	12/1
1980	**Tender Heart**	J Mercer	J Sutcliffe Jnr	Esal Commodities Ltd	13/2
1981	**Teamwork**	G Starkey	G Harwood	A Ward	8/1
1982	**Buzzards Bay**	J Mercer	H Collingridge	Mrs V McKinney	14/1
1983	**Mighty Fly**	S Cauthen	D Elsworth	Mrs V Tory	12/1
1984	**Hawkley**	T Williams	P Haslam	S Dinsmore	10/1
1985	**Come On The Blues**	C Rutter	C Brittain	Mrs C Pateras	14/1
1986	**Patriach**	T Quinn	J Dunlop	P S Winfield	20/1
1987	**Vague Shot**	S Cauthen	R F Casey	H J Senn	10/1
1988	**Governorship**	J Reid	C Nelson	R E A Bott Ltd	33/1
1989	**True Panache**	P Eddery	J Tree	K Abdulla	5/1
1990	**Pontenuovo**	G Bardwell	D Elsworth	W Mariti	50/1
1991	**Eurolink the Lad**	J Reid	J Dunlop	Eurolink Computers Ltd	25/1
1992	**Colour Sergeant**	D Harrison	Lord Huntingdon	HM The Queen	20/1

Run at Newbury in 1941

The Queen's Vase

Contrary to popular belief, Queen Victoria enjoyed racing, certainly in the early years of her reign. When, in 1838, she drove up the course dressed in pink and white, she donated a gold vase for a mile and a half race over the Swinley Course. This later became the Gold Cup Vase, but it was not until 1960 that it was known as the Queen's Vase; the distance had been extended to two miles.

The years to the turn of the century are peppered with the great equine names of Victorian racing. *Alice Hawthorn* (1844) was said to have 'an action like a hare and steal along the ground with her ears pricked'. In this way she won 52 of her 71 races. *Fisherman*, who won in 1856, was a stayer with an iron constitution who ran 121 times and won 70 of them including two Ascot Gold Cups. *Isonomy*, a horse with classic potential who's three-year-old career was curtailed to one victorious run in the Cambridgeshire Handicap in order to land a nice touch for his owner at 40/1, went on to be one of the finest Cup horses of all time, while *St Gatien* dead-heated for the Derby in 1884.

The dual winner in 1904 and 1905, *Bachelor's Button*, was one of only two animals to lower the colours of *Pretty Polly*. In modern times the most significant winners are probably *Parnell* and *Le Moss* in the seventies.

The Queen's Vase was originally a Group Three event, but was reduced to Listed status between 1986 and 1990, being restored to Group Three the following season.

Gordon Richards (right) and Tommy Weston (left). Weston won the Queen's Vase twice, in 1925 on *Kentish Knock* and 1933 on *Gainslaw*. Richards was successful in 1938 on *Foxglove II*.

Run at Ascot over 2 miles for 3 year-olds First Run 1838 Group 3

		Jockey	Trainer	Owner	Odds
1838	**Mecca**	P Conolly	C Marson	Lord Exeter	5/2
1839	**Mendizabal**	P Conolly	R Pettit	T Thornhill	1/2
1840	**St Francis**	J Robinson	R Pettit	R Pettit	2/1
1841	**Satirist**	E Flatman	J Scott	Lord Westminster	3/1
1842	**St Francis**	J Robinson	R Pettit	R Pettit	4/1
1843	**Gorhambury**	J Howlett	–	Col Charretie	8/1
1844	**Alice Hawthorn**	R Hesseltine	R Hesseltine	G Salvin	1/3
1845	**Sweetmeat**	G Whitehouse	H Wadlow	A W Hill	5/4
1846	**Grimston**	T Lye	T Dawson	T Dawson	5/1
1847	**The Hero**	A Day	J B Day	J B Day	9/2
1848	**Gardenia**	J Sharp	W Harlock	Lord Exeter	6/1
1849	**Glenalvon**	S Templeman	W Harlock	Lord Exeter	10/1
1850	**Mildew**	E Flatman	J Scott	R M Jaques	5/1
1851	**Cariboo**	E Flatman	W Harlock	Lord Exeter	1/3
1852	**Leopold**	J Charlton	J Scott	Baron M de Rothschild	6/1
1853	**Rataplan**	J Wells	W Wyatt	C Thelluson	6/4
1854	**The Hermit**	J Wells	J Day	J Gully	4/5
1855	**Oulston**	J Wells	J B Day	H Padwick	4/1
1856	**Fisherman**	J Quinton	T Parr	T Parr	5/4
1857	**Arsenal**	G Fordham	W Goater	H Padwick	2/1
1858	**Sedbury**	G Fordham	W Goater	H Padwick	5/1
1859	**Schism**	J Adams	W Day	W Day	10/1
1860	**Horror**	G Fordham	T Wadlow	Capt Christie	4/5
1861	**Parmesan**	T Aldcroft	Anthony Taylor	H Savile	5/1
1862	**Tim Whiffler**	R Bullock	T S Dawson	Mr Jackson	5/1
1863	**Adventurer**	G Clement	J Kendall	G Crook	7/4
1864	**Young Rapid**	W Atkins	W Goater	W G Craven	30/1
1865	**Eltham**	S Adams	J Waugh	W Robinson	4/6
1866	**Elland**	R Thomas	J Dover	R Sutton	5/1
1867	**Mail Train**	T Cannon	W Day	Sir F Johnstone	10/1
1868	**Blinkhoolie**	H Custance	G Bloss	H Chaplin	12/1
1869	**Thorwaldsen**	Hudson	T Dawson	J Johnstone	5/1
1870	**Siderolite**	J Wells	J Porter	Sir J Hawley	10/11
1871	**Christopher Sly**	W Gray	T Dawson	J Johnstone	8/1
1872	**Albert Victor**	T Chaloner	T Olliver	W S Cartwright	10/1
1873	**Thorn**	Busby	J Osborne	R N Batt	4/1
1874	**Organist**	J Griffiths	M Dawson	R C Vyner	11/8
1875	**Marie Stuart**	G Fordham	R Peck	J Merry	4/6
1876	**Thunder**	F Archer	M Dawson	H F C Vyner	2/1
1877	**Skylark**	F Archer	M Dawson	Lord Falmouth	4/1
1878	**Verneuil**	J Goater	T Jennings	Comte F de Lagrange	–
1879	**Isonomy**	T Cannon	J Porter	F Gretton	11/4
1880	**Chippendale**	J Osborne Jnr	T Wadlow	Lord Bradford	4/9
1881	**Ambassadress**	G Fordham	M Dawson	Lord Falmouth	7/1
1882	**Tristan**	G Fordham	T Jennings Jnr	C J Lefevre	1/3
1883	**Border Minstrel**	C Bowman	F Bates	J Johnstone	11/8
1884	**St Gatien**	C Wood	Robert Sherwood	J Hammond	3/1
1885	**Thebais**	F Archer	A Taylor Snr	Duchess of Montrose	2/11
1886	**Bird of Freedom**	F Archer	J Ryan	D Baird	3/1
1887	**Quilp**	A White	M Gurry	G A Baird	2/1
1888	**Exmoor**	J Watts	Robert Sherwood	W Blake	100/30
1889	**Morglay**	T Loates	A Hayhoe	L de Rothschild	8/15
1890	**Tyrant**	T Calder	W Walters	A M Singer	5/2
1891	**Mons Meg**	G Chaloner	G Blackwell	D Cooper	5/4
1892	**Martagon**	J Watts	J Ryan	D Baird	100/30
1893	**Convent**	F Allsopp	J Humphreys	Sir J Thursby	w.o.
1894	**Quaesitum**	G Chaloner	F Cole	Lord Penrhyn	5/1
1895	**Florizel II**	J Watts	R Marsh	HRH the Prince of Wales	5/6
1896	**Pride**	W Bradford	T Jennings Jnr	L Brassey	7/1
1897	**Count Schomberg**	S Loates	W Leader	R Lebaudy	Evens
1898	**The Rush**	O Madden	J Waugh	G Dobell	Evens
1899	**No Race**				
1900	**Solitaire**	L Reiff	F W Day	Sir E Cassel	3/1
1901	**Mackintosh**	S Loates	W Waugh	Sir J Blundell Maple	30/100
1902	**Ice-maiden**	F W Hardy	J Porter	G Faber	3/1
1903	**Zinfandel**	M Cannon	C Beatty	Lord H de Walden	11/10
1904	**Bachelor's Button**	W Halsey	C Peck	S B Joel	9/2
1905	**Bachelor's Button**	D Maher	C Peck	S B Joel	7/1
1906	**The White Knight**	W Higgs	Robert Sherwood Jnr	T Y L Kirkwood	11/4
1907	**Golden Measure**	D Maher	J D Edwards	J Buchanan	2/1
1908	**Pillo**	G Torterolo	S H Darling	J Buchanan	8/15
1909	**Amadis**	W Earl	W Waugh	Lord Falmouth	5/2
1910	**Charles O'Malley**	S Donoghue	T Lewis	A P Cunliffe	9/4
1911	**Martingale II**	H Jelliss	R H Dewhurst	Lord Cadogan	20/1
1912	**Tidal Wave**	A Whalley	A Sadler Jnr	P Ralli	4/1

		Jockey	Trainer	Owner	Odds
1913	**Shogun**	W Huxley	R Wootton	E Hulton	8/13
1914	**Glorvina**	J Prout	G Lambton	Lord Derby	100/8
1915/18	**No Race**				
1919	**Silonyx**	V Smyth	W Waugh	Duke of Portland	2/1
1920	**Kentish Cob**	J Childs	A Taylor Jnr	W M Cazelet	9/2
1921	**Copyright**	F Bullock	B Jarvis	J P Hornung	2/1
1922	**Golden Myth**	C Elliott	J Jarvis	Sir G Bullough	6/1
1923	**Puttenden**	J Childs	A Taylor Jnr	The Tetrarch	100/30
1924	**Audlem**	C Smirke	C Davis	C F Kenyon	100/7
1925	**Kentish Knock**	T Weston	G Lambton	A James	9/4
1926	**High Art**	R James	Lord G Dundas	Sir G Noble	20/1
1927	**Adieu**	M Beary	Wal Griggs	F W Horlock	100/6
1928	**Maid of Perth**	J Sirett	F Darling	Mrs G Drummond	3/1
1929	**Covendon**	P Beasley	T Waugh	A E Phillips	100/9
1930	**Trimdon**	R A Jones	J Lawson	C Lambton	6/4
1931	**Pomme d'Api**	M Beary	R C Dawson	HH Aga Khan	4/1
1932	**Silvermere**	F Lane	W Nightingall	Mrs C Rich	100/6
1933	**Gainslaw**	T Weston	F Leader	H Simms	5/4
1934	**Duplicate**	F Sharpe	N Scobie	Sir C Hyde	100/6
1935	**Flash Bye**	J Sirett	J Lawson	Lord Astor	8/1
1936	**Rondo**	P Maher	F Pratt	J A de Rothschild	20/1
1937	**Fearless Fox**	E Smith	J Jarvis	A Smith	11/8
1938	**Foxglove II**	G Richards	F Darling	P Beatty	4/1
1939	**Atout Maitre**	W Sibbritt	H Blagrave	H Blagrave	11/2
1940/45	**No Race**				
1946	**Look Ahead**	D Smith	C Boyd-Rochfort	Sir H de Trafford	20/1
1947	**Auralia**	D Smith	R Day	Mrs A Johnston	100/8
1948	**Estoc**	R Bertiglia	C Semblat	M Boussac	7/2
1949	**Lone Eagle**	D Smith	C Boyd-Rochfort	W Woodward	100/30
1950	**Fastlad**	F Palmer	P Carter	Baron de Waldner	100/6
1951	**Faux Pas**	E Smith	J Lawson	Mrs R Foster	6/1
1952	**Souepi**	C Elliott	G Digby	G Digby	100/7
1953	**Absolve**	L Piggott	V Smyth	Sir M McAlpine	20/1
1954	**Prescription**	E Smith	J Jarvis	Lord Rosebery	6/1
1955	**Prince Barle**	E Mercer	J Lawson	J Barker	11/2
1956	**French Beige**	G Littlewood	H Peacock	R F Dennis	100/8
1957	**Tenterhooks**	E Britt	C Elsey	Lord Allendale	6/1
1958	**Even Money**	A Breasley	M V O'Brien	C Palmer	9/4
1959	**Vivi Tarquin**	D Greening	S McGrath	J McGrath	100/8
1960	**Prolific**	D Keith	W Nightingall	Mrs C Evans	5/2
1961	**Black King**	E Hide	W Elsey	H J Joel	100/8
1962	**Pavot**	J Sime	P Prendergast	E More O'Ferrall	10/1
1963	**Hereford**	J Hunter	H Murless	Mrs W Macaulay	20/1
1964	**I Titan**	M Giovannelli	N Murless	Mrs V Hue-Williams	10/1
1965	**Beddard**	J Sime	H Murless	R Reynolds	9/1
1966	**Bally Russe**	A Breasley	N Murless	F Hue-Williams	5/1
1967	**The Accuser**	F Durr	W R Hern	Lord Rotherwick	15/2
1968	**Zorba II**	R Hutchinson	P Prendergast	C Clore	10/1
1969	**Tantivy**	A Barclay	W Elsey	N Hetherton	15/8
1970	**Yellow River**	T Carter	A Breasley	D Sung	20/1
1971	**Parnell**	R Hutchinson	S Quirke	R More O'Ferrall	7/1
1972	**Falkland**	G Starkey	H Cecil	Lord H de Walden	9/2
1973	**Tara Brooch**	P Eddery	S McGrath	J McGrath	10/1
1974	**Royal Aura**	P Eddery	P Walwyn	Mrs J Silcock	11/2
1975	**Blood Royal**	L Piggott	M V O'Brien	Mrs G Getty II	11/2
1976	**General Ironside**	L Piggott	H Cecil	G Weston	11/8
1977	**Millionaire**	P Eddery	P Walwyn	Mrs D McCalmont	8/1
1978	**Le Moss**	G Baxter	H Cecil	C d'Alessio	7/4
1979	**Buttress**	W Carson	W R Hern	HM The Queen	3/1
1980	**Toondra**	P Cook	M Jarvis	Lady Beaverbrook	15/2
1981	**Ore**	W Carson	K Prendergast	P Prendergast	15/2
1982	**Evzon**	L Piggott	C Brittain	M Lemos	16/1
1983	**Santella Man**	G Starkey	G Harwood	R Taiano	11/1
1984	**Baynoun**	W Carson	R F Johnson Houghton	HH Aga Khan	13/8
1985	**Wassl Merbayeh**	R Hills	H Thomson Jones	A Al-Maktoum	6/1
1986	**Stavordale**	M Roberts	H Thomson Jones	Mrs H Thomson Jones	33/1
1987	**Arden**	S Cauthen	H Cecil	Lord H de Walden	7/2
1988	**Green Adventure**	G Starkey	G Harwood	J Garcia-Roady	6/4
1989	**Weld**	B Raymond	W Jarvis	Lord H de Walden	16/1
1990	**River God**	S Cauthen	H Cecil	Sheikh Mohammed	6/4
1991	**Jendali**	S Cauthen	H Cecil	Sheikh Mohammed	15/2
1992	**Landowner**	R Cochrane	J Gosden	Sheikh Mohammed	8/1

For 3 year-olds and upwards from 1840-1986

The Cork and Orrery Stakes

First run in 1868 and named like many other Ascot races after a Master of the Buckhounds, Lord Cork, the Cork and Orrery is a tough sprint and one of the most competitive races at the Royal Meeting, although inevitably overshadowed by the Gold Cup run on the same day.

The record shows victories by most of the leading sprinters of their generation, but the race is not always kind to punters on an expensive 'Ladies' Day' an extreme example being *Kearney's* win in 1980 at 40/1.

Run at Ascot over 6 furlongs First Run 1868 Group 3

		Jockey	Trainer	Owner	Odds
1868	**Laneret**	G Fordham	W Goodwin	G Bryan	6/4
1869	**No Race**				
1870	**Normanby**	T French	Jos Dawson	Lord Stamford	5/4
1871	**Cymbal**	J Goater	–	G F Bentley	55/40
1872	**Prince Charlie**	T French	Jos Dawson	Jos Dawson	11/8
1873	**Prince Charlie**	T French	Jos Dawson	Jos Dawson	15/100
1874	**Prince Charlie**	H Parry	Jos Dawson	Jos Dawson	4/6
1875	**Lowlander**	H Parry	W Reeves	H Bird	10/11
1876	**Lowlander**	H Custance	W Reeves	H Bird	–
1877	**Ecossais**	J Goater	T Jennings	T Jennings	–
1878	**Trappist**	F Archer	J Cannon	Capt Prime	2/5
1879	**Hackthorpe**	F Archer	J Cannon	Lord Hastings	1/20
1880	**Valentino**	G Fordham	J Hayhoe	L de Rothschild	6/1
1881	**Charibert**	F Archer	M Dawson	H F C Vyner	1/3
1882	**Marden**	R Wyatt	R Wyatt	R S Evans	100/8
1883	**Despair**	F Archer	W Gilbert	W Gilbert	11/8
1884	**Geheimniss**	F Archer	J Porter	Lord Alington	4/9
1885	**Energy**	F Archer	A Taylor Jnr	Duchess of Montrose	1/4
1886	**Whitefriar**	F Archer	J Porter	Duke of Westminster	1/4
1887	**Whitefriar**	C Wood	R Sherrard	Sir G Chetwynd	9/4
1888	**Deuce of Clubs**	J Watts	C Jousiffe	C J Merry	5/4
1889	**Napoleon**	G Barrett	J Porter	W Low	Evens
1890	**Mephisto**	F Webb	T Jennings	Prince Soltykoff	13/8
1891	**Bel Demonio**	F Webb	W A Jarvis	C D Rose	9/2
1892	**Peter Flower**	–	A B Sadler	Lord Durham	w.o.
1893	**Shemer**	M Cannon	T Wadlow	H E Beddington	2/1
1894	**Northshampton**	M Cannon	Robert Sherwood	J T North	8/1
1895	**Grey Leg**	M Cannon	J Porter	Duke of Westminster	2/11
1896	**Speed**	M Cannon	C Waugh	Prince Soltykoff	Evens
1897	**Red Heart**	C Wood	G Platt	M D Rucker	1/20
1898	**St Lucia**	M Cannon	A Taylor Jnr	R C Garton	4/1
1899	**Oria**	J Dalton	A Gilbert	J Musker	6/4
1900	**Nattie**	O Madden	J Waugh	Mr Russel	–
1901	**Bridge**	K Cannon	G S Davies	A M Singer	6/4
1902	**Reine des Fleurs**	J Reiff	–	M Caillault	8/1
1903	**Lord Bobs**	W Lane	W Waugh	Sir J Blundell Maple	3/1
1904	**Cossack**	D Maher	F Leach	Sir J Miller	1/4
1905	**Delaunay**	O Madden	P P Gilpin	P P Gilpin	1/40
1906	**Queen's Holiday**	B Dillon	J Fallon	F Forester	w.o.
1907	**Rocketter**	W Higgs	S Darling	J H Greer	2/11
1908	**Llangwm**	D Maher	F Hartigan	B Walker	9/4
1909	**Hillside III**	J H Martin	A J Joyner	H P Whitney	–
1910	**New Castle II**	J H Martin	A J Joyner	H P Whitney	4/9
1911	**Golden Rod**	D Maher	S Pickering	P Nelke	5/2
1912	**Sunflower II**	F Wootton	C Morton	J B Joel	1/2
1913	**Hornet's Beauty**	J H Martin	F Leach	Sir W Cooke	1/9
1914	**Hornet's Beauty**	F Fox	C F Elsey	Sir W Cooke	11/8
1915/18	**No Race**				
1919	**Freesia**	F Templeman	A Sadler	Lord Jersey	7/4
1920	**Diadem**	S Donoghue	G Lambton	Lord Derby	1/4
1921	**Tete a Tete**	I Strydom	Robert Sherwood Jnr	Lord Furness	–
1922	**Pharmacie**	S Donoghue	H Cottrill	J White	1/5
1923	**Hamlet**	S Donoghue	C Morton	J B Joel	9/4
1924	**Hamlet**	S Donoghue	C Morton	J B Joel	4/1
1925	**Drake**	R A Jones	H Cottrill	Mrs S Whitburn	5/4
1926	**Diomedes**	J Leach	H Leader	S W Beer	1/6
1927	**Highborn II**	H Beasley	O Bell	Sir H Cunliffe-Owen	Evens
1928	**Zaretta**	H Wragg	V Beatty	V Beatty	100/6
1929	**Royal Minstrel**	J Childs	C Boyd-Rochfort	J H Whitney	4/11
1930	**Costaki Pasha**	M Beary	R C Dawson	HH Aga Khan	5/1
1931	**Grindleton**	H Beasley	L Cundell	J W Sharples	8/1
1932	**Slipper**	R Perryman	Frank Butters	Sir A Butt	13/8
1933	**The Divot**	R Dick	E Stedall	C Blundell	6/4
1934	**Solenoid**	J Caldwell	H Cottrill	J V Rank	11/4
1935	**Winandermere**	S Donoghue	L Cundell	Mrs C Glorney	7/2

		Jockey	Trainer	Owner	Odds
1936	**Bellacose**	P Beasley	R J Colling	P Dunne	7/2
1937	**Pherozshah**	D Smith	Frank Butters	HH Aga Khan	10/1
1938	**Ipsden**	S Wragg	O Bell	Lady Ludlow	6/4
1939	**Old Reliance**	E Smith	J Jarvis	Sir J Jarvis	8/1
1940/45	**No Race**				
1946	**Honeyway**	E Smith	J Jarvis	Lord Milford	5/6
1947	**The Bug**	C Smirke	M Marsh	N Wachman	11/10
1948	**Delirium**	C Smirke	J Leach	J T Coltman	7/4
1949	**Solonaway**	G Richards	M C Collins	R A Duggan	100/30
1950	**Abadan**	G Richards	H Hartigan	G Loder	9/4
1951	**Bob Cherry**	N Sellwood	H S Persse	Lord Sefton	13/8
1952	**Royal Serenade**	E Mercer	H Wragg	G N Bell	6/1
1953	**Blood Test**	G Richards	N Murless	G Loder	8/1
1954	**Key**	G Richards	N Murless	Mrs D M Fitzpatrick	5/4
1955	**Trouville**	W Rickaby	W Smyth	Lady Waterford	11/4
1956	**Grass Court**	W Elliott	K Cundell	Mrs C Evans	7/4
1957	**Matador**	E Smith	J A Waugh	S Joel	13/8
1958	**Right Boy**	L Piggott	W Dutton	G Gilbert	5/6
1959	**Right Boy**	L Piggott	H Rohan	G Gilbert	11/4
1960	**Tin Whistle**	L Piggott	H Rohan	B Grainger	8/13
1961	**Bun Penny**	D Smith	R Fetherstonhaugh	S Joel	2/1
1962	**Compensation**	J Lindley	E Lambton	Mrs G Lambton	4/1
1963	**El Gallo**	L Piggott	N Murless	C St George	20/1
1964	**No Race**				
1965	**Majority Blue**	W Williamson	J Oxx	Mrs B Aitken	100/8
1966	**Current Coin**	J Roe	J Oxx	H Leggat	100/30
1967	**Siliconn**	G Moore	T Corbett	C Pollock	5/2
1968	**Mountain Call**	L Piggott	B van Cutsem	I E Kornberg	8/15
1969	**Tudor Music**	F Durr	M Jarvis	D Robinson	4/1
1970	**Welsh Saint**	L Piggott	M V O'Brien	J P Phillips	15/8
1971	**King's Country**	F Head	G W Robinson	B Firestone	6/1
1972	**Parsimony**	W Carson	R F Johnson Houghton	E Holland-Martin	8/1
1973	**Balliol**	B Taylor	J Winter	D Prenn	100/30
1974	**Saritamer**	L Piggott	M V O'Brien	C St George	11/1
1975	**Swingtime**	W Carson	M V O'Brien	J Mulcahy	11/4
1976	**Gentilhombre**	P Cook	N Adam	T Robson	17/2
1977	**He Loves Me**	J Mercer	J Hindley	J Allbritton	20/1
1978	**Sweet Mint**	W Swinburn	N Meade	M Wright	20/1
1979	**Thatching**	L Piggott	M V O'Brien	R Sangster	6/1
1980	**Kearney**	W R Swinburn	G W Robinson	Mrs D MacGillycuddy	40/1
1981	**The Quiet Bidder**	W R Swinburn	R Hollinshead	Heathavon Stables	11/1
1982	**Indian King**	G Starkey	G Harwood	J Levy	9/2
1983	**Sylvan Barbarosa**	B Rouse	P Mitchell	Mrs B Wade	20/1
1984	**Committed**	B Thomson	D Weld	R Sangster	3/1
1985	**Dafayna**	W Carson	M Stoute	HH Aga Khan	8/1
1986	**Sperry**	Paul Eddery	P Walwyn	Y Nasib	5/1
1987	**Big Shuffle**	M Kinane	D Weld	Moyglare Stud Farm	8/1
1988	**Posada**	M Roberts	R F Johnson Houghton	T D Holland-Martin	11/2
1989	**Danehill**	W Carson	J Tree	K Abdulla	11/8
1990	**Great Commotion**	P Eddery	A Scott	M Al-Maktoum	5/1
1991	**Polish Patriot**	R Cochrane	G Harwood	R A Kirstein	5/1
1992	**Shalford**	M Roberts	R Hannon	D F Cock	2/1

Run as the All-Aged Stakes 1868-1925

The Ascot Gold Cup

The Ascot Gold Cup is the centre-piece of the Royal Meeting and the first of the races of the present day to be staged on the Heath. Founded in 1807, the winner of the inaugural race was *Master Jackey*, a three-year-old who won from three opponents. Useful by the standards of the period, he had won at Ascot only 24 hours earlier.

His owner was a Mr Durand, and the horse carried 6st 12lbs to win by half a length. The race was worth a hundred guineas and was run in the regal presence of King George III, Queen Charlotte and the Princesses Mary and Amelia, who were wearing Spanish mantles and gypsy hats. The Prince of Wales was attired in his favourite bottle-green.

By 1829 the race had gained much in prestige and the field included two Derby winners, an Oaks winner, a Leger winner and *Bobadilla*, the heroine of the 1828 Gold Cup. The winner was *Zinganee*, from the 1827 Derby winner *Mameluke*.

The Prince of Wales, by now George IV, had the option to purchase *Zinganee* but failed to do so, thus frustrating a long-held ambition to win the Gold Cup. Almost on his deathbed he decreed that future Gold Cups should be confined to members of the Jockey Club, Whites or Brooks, a measure which did little to enhance either the quality of the runners or the size of the fields.

His successor, William IV, took a more liberal view and the race was reopened to all-comers. Queen Victoria, who was keener on racing than her reputation suggests, saw her first Gold Cup as monarch when *Touchstone* won for the second time in 1838.

In 1844, Czar Nicholas I of Russia paid a State Visit and joined the Royal party at Ascot. The winner of the Gold Cup was an unnamed colt by *Defence*, owned by Lord Albemarle. As a gesture to the honoured guest, Albemarle named his horse *Emperor* and in return the Czar offered to present a plate worth £500, to be known as the Emperor's Plate in place of the Gold Cup.

Alas for the hopes of Victorian *glasnost*. The Emperor's Plate survived for only nine years, when a bloody war against Russia in the Crimea caused a hasty revision to the original name as *West Australian*, the first winner of the Triple Crown, won the Gold Cup at 6/4 on in the hands of Alfred Day.

Boiard was a French-trained winner in 1874 and the Prince of Wales, later Edward VII, won with his Derby winner *Persimmon* in 1897. In 1900, *Merman* won in the colours of the Prince's friend Lily Langtry and ridden by the jockey who was to change the style of race riding forever, Tod Sloan.

The new century brought controversy in the wake of the defeat, in 1906, of one of racing's greatest heroines, *Pretty Polly*. She was beaten by *Bachelor's Button*, something of an Ascot specialist and ridden by Danny Maher, the first American to be champion jockey in Britain. Many blamed *Pretty Polly's* loss on her jockey Bernard Dillon, who was to win the Derby on *Lemberg* and achieve greater notoriety as the husband of Marie Lloyd, but it is more likely that the brilliant racemare hated the conditions on a sweltering day and was irritated by a wart on her belly.

The most notable achievement in modern times was *Sagaro's* unique hat-trick in 1975, 1976 and 1977 ridden on each occasion by Lester Piggott. Nowadays the Gold Cup is open to geldings and under strong pressure from those who would reduce the distance of the Cup races, but it remains one of the unmissable events at Royal Ascot, the finest festival of racing in the Western world.

Above: **The first winner of the Triple Crown, *West Australian* won the Ascot Gold Cup in 1854.**
Below: **In 1897, the Prince of Wales's Derby winner *Persimmon* won the Gold Cup.**

Run at Ascot over 2 miles 4 furlongs First Run 1807 Group 1

		Jockey	Trainer	Owner	Odds
1807	**Master Jackey**	–	R Prince	J H Durand	2/1
1808	**Brighton**	–	–	W Fermor	–
1809	**Anderida**	–	R Robson	Gen Leveson Gower	2/1
1810	**Loiterer**	–	–	Lord Lowther	5/2
1811	**Jannette**	–	–	F Craven	4/5
1812	**Flash**	–	–	Lord Lowther	–
1813	**Lutzen**	–	–	J B Trevanion	6/4
1814	**Pranks**	–	–	S Batson	5/2
1815	**Aladdin**	–	W Butler	HRH The Duke of York	4/6
1816	**Anticipation**	–	W Chifney	T Thornhill	10/1
1817	**Sir Richard**	–	–	D Blake	–
1818	**Belville**	–	W Chifney	Lord Darlington	–
1819	**Anticipation**	–	–	A Goddard	1/3
1820	**Champignon**	–	–	T A Fraser	–
1821	**Banker**	–	W Butler	HRH The Duke of York	–
1822	**Sir Huldibrand**	–	–	J Ramsbottom	5/1
1823	**Marcellus**	W Wheatley	W Chifney	Lord Darlington	6/4
1824	**Bizarre**	W Arnull	R D Boyce	Lord G H Cavendish	–
1825	**Bizarre**	W Arnull	R D Boyce	Lord G H Cavendish	7/4
1826	**Chateau Margaux**	G Dockeray	R Stephenson	C Wyndham	4/6

		Jockey	Trainer	Owner	Odds
1827	**Memnon**	S Chifney Jnr	W Chifney	Lord Darlington	1/2
1828	**Bobadilla**	T Lye	R Pettit	A Molony	8/1
1829	**Zinganee**	S Chifney Jnr	W Chifney	Lord Chesterfield	2/1
1830	**Lucetta**	J Robinson	H Scott	Sir M Wood	4/1
1831	**Cetus**	J Robinson	H Scott	Sir M Wood	5/6
1832	**Camarine**	J Robinson	H Scott	Sir M Wood	11/8
1833	**Galata**	W Arnull	C Marson	Lord Exeter	1/3
1834	**Glaucus**	W Scott	J Scott	Lord Chesterfield	5/2
1835	**Glencoe**	J Robinson	J Edwards	Lord Jersey	5/6
1836	**Touchstone**	J B Day	J Scott	Lord Westminster	6/5
1837	**Touchstone**	W Scott	J Scott	Lord Westminster	1/2
1838	**Grey Momus**	W Day	J B Day	Lord G Bentinck	4/5
1839	**Caravan**	J Robinson	I Day	I Day	3/1
1840	**St Francis**	S Chifney Jnr	R Pettit	R Pettit	5/2
1841	**Lanercost**	W Noble	W I'Anson	W Ramsay	4/1
1842	**Beeswing**	D Cartwright	–	W Orde	7/1
1843	**Ralph**	J Robinson	W Edwards	Lord Albemarle	4/5
1844	**The Emperor**	G Whitehouse	W Edwards	Lord Albemarle	10/1
1845	**The Emperor**	G Whitehouse	W Edwards	Lord Albemarle	200/12
1846	**Alarm**	E Flatman	M Dilly	C Greville	3/1
1847	**The Hero**	A Day	J B Day	J B Day	6/4
1848	**The Hero**	A Day	J B Day	J B Day	1/2
1849	**Van Tromp**	C Marlow	J Fobert	Lord Eglinton	2/1
1850	**The Flying Dutchman**	C Marlow	J Fobert	Lord Eglinton	4/7
1851	**Woolwich**	J Marson	J Scott	A Campbell	7/4
1852	**Joe Miller**	G Mann	W Day	Mr Farrance	6/1
1853	**Teddington**	J Marson	A Taylor Snr	J M Stanley	4/1
1854	**West Australian**	A Day	J Scott	Lord Londesborough	4/6
1855	**Fandango**	T Ashmall	G Abdale	Lord Zetland	5/2
1856	**Winkfield**	J Bartholomew	S Death	S Walker	12/1
1857	**Skirmisher**	J Charlton	G Abdale	Lord Zetland	4/1
1858	**Fisherman**	J Wells	T Parr	J B Starkey	3/1
1859	**Fisherman**	W Cresswell	T Parr	F Higgins	7/4
1860	**Rupee**	H Grimshaw	Jos Dawson	Lord Stamford	3/1
1861	**Thormanby**	H Custance	M Dawson	J Merry	Evens
1862	**Asteroid**	J Wells	G Manning	Sir J Hawley	6/1
1863	**Buckstone**	A Edwards	M Dawson	J Merry	9/4
1864	**The Scottish Chief**	H Covey	M Dawson	J Merry	2/1
1865	**Ely**	H Custance	T Olliver	W S Cartwright	6/1
1866	**Gladiateur**	H Grimshaw	T Jennings	Comte F de Lagrange	2/5
1867	**Lecturer**	G Fordham	J Day	Marquis of Hastings	3/1
1868	**Blue Gown**	T Cannon	J Porter	Sir J Hawley	4/6
1869	**Brigantine**	F Butler	W Day	Sir F Johnstone	4/1
1870	**Sabinus**	R Rowell	–	J G Hessey	100/60
1871	**Mortemer**	G Fordham	T Jennings	C J Lefevre	Evens
1872	**Henry**	G Fordham	T Jennings	C J Lefevre	6/1
1873	**Cremorne**	C Maidment	W Gilbert	H Saville	8/11
1874	**Boiard**	Carver	–	H Delamarre	2/1
1875	**Doncaster**	G Fordham	R Peck	J Merry	1/2
1876	**Apology**	J Osborne Jnr	W Osborne	Mr Seabrook	5/2
1877	**Petrarch**	T Cannon	J Cannon	Lord Lonsdale	Evens
1878	**Verneuil**	J Goater	T Jennings	Comte F de Lagrange	100/15
1879	**Isonomy**	T Cannon	J Porter	F Gretton	2/1
1880	**Isonomy**	T Cannon	J Porter	F Gretton	4/9
1881	**Robert the Devil**	T Cannon	C Blanton	C Brewer	4/9
1882	**Foxhall**	T Cannon	W Day	J R Keene	4/7
1883	**Tristan**	G Fordham	T Jennings Jnr	C J Lefevre	4/7
1884	**St Simon**	C Wood	M Dawson	Duke of Portland	40/75
1885	**St Gatien**	C Wood	J Waugh	J Hammond	30/100
1886	**Althorp**	T Cannon	J Porter	Baron M de Hirsch	2/1
1887	**Bird of Freedom**	W Warne	J Ryan	D Baird	10/1
1888	**Timothy**	W T Robinson	J Jewitt	H McCalmont	4/1
1889	**Trayles**	W T Robinson	J Jewitt	W de la Rue	5/2
1890	**Gold**	F Webb	T Jennings	Prince Soltykoff	100/30
1891	**Morion**	J Watts	R Marsh	Lord Hartington	11/4
1892	**Buccaneer**	G Barrett	S Pickering	Lord Rosslyn	1/2
1893	**Marcion**	S Chandley	W Matthews	R C Vyner	5/4
1894	**La Fleche**	J Watts	R Marsh	Baron M de Hirsch	2/5
1895	**Isinglass**	T Loates	J Jewitt	H McCalmont	2/11
1896	**Love Wisely**	S Loates	A Taylor Jnr	W Bass	10/1
1897	**Persimmon**	J Watts	R Marsh	HRH Prince of Wales	40/85
1898	**Elf II**	E Watkins	R Count	J de Bremond	7/2
1899	**Cyllene**	S Loates	W A Jarvis	C D Rose	6/4
1900	**Merman**	J F Sloan	W T Robinson	Lady de Bathe	20/1
1901	**Santoi**	F Rickaby	F Davis	G Edwardes	11/10

Lord Milford's four-year-old Chestnut colt *Flyon* wins the 1939 Ascot Gold Cup by five lengths from Sir Abe Bailey's *Maranta*.

		Jockey	Trainer	Owner	Odds
1902	**William the Third**	M Cannon	J Porter	Duke of Portland	2/1
1903	**Maximum II**	A McIntyre	R Count	J de Bremond	6/4
1904	**Throwaway**	W Lane	H Braime	F Alexander	10/1
1905	**Zinfandel**	M Cannon	C Beatty	Lord H de Walden	2/5
1906	**Bachelor's Button**	D Maher	C Peck	S B Joel	7/1
1907	**The White Knight**	W Halsey	H Sadler	T Y L Kirkwood	Evens
1908	**The White Knight**	W Halsey	H Sadler	T Y L Kirkwood	4/7
1909	**Bomba**	F Fox	F Pratt	J A de Rothschild	25/1
1910	**Bayardo**	D Maher	A Taylor Jnr	A W Cox	7/4
1911	**Willonyx**	W Higgs	S Darling	C E Howard	5/4
1912	**Prince Palatine**	F O'Neill	H Beardsley	T Pilkington	2/1
1913	**Prince Palatine**	W Saxby	H Beardsley	T Pilkington	4/7
1914	**Aleppo**	F Fox	A Taylor Jnr	A W Cox	6/1
1915	**Apothecary**	E Lancaster	F Pratt	J A de Rothschild	6/5
1916	**No Race**				
1917	**Gay Crusader**	S Donoghue	A Taylor Jnr	A W Cox	8/100
1918	**Gainsborough**	J Childs	A Taylor Jnr	Lady J Douglas	2/5
1919	**By Jingo!**	G Hulme	J Rhodes	W de Pledge	3/1
1920	**Tangiers**	G Hulme	R C Dawson	Sir W Nelson	100/15
1921	**Periosteum**	F Bullock	B Jarvis	B Irish	4/1
1922	**Golden Myth**	C Elliott	J Jarvis	Sir G Bullough	8/1
1923	**Happy Man**	V Smyth	T Hogg	F Hardy	7/4
1924	**Massine**	A Sharpe	E Cunnington	H Ternynck	100/8
1925	**Santorb**	S Donoghue	J Rhodes	B Walker	10/1
1926	**Solario**	J Childs	R Day	Sir J Rutherford	4/6
1927	**Foxlaw**	B Carslake	R Day	Sir A Bailey	8/1
1928	**Invershin**	B Carslake	C Doyle	R Walker	100/8
1929	**Invershin**	R Perryman	G Digby	R Walker	8/1
1930	**Bosworth**	T Weston	Frank Butters	Lord Derby	3/1
1931	**Trimdon**	J Childs	J Lawson	C Lambton	3/1
1932	**Trimdon**	J Childs	J Lawson	C Lambton	15/2
1933	**Foxhunter**	H Wragg	J Jarvis	E Esmond	25/1
1934	**Felicitation**	G Richards	Frank Butters	HH Aga Khan	9/2
1935	**Tiberius**	T Weston	J Lawson	Sir A Bailey	100/30
1936	**Quashed**	R Perryman	C Leader	Lord Stanley	3/1
1937	**Precipitation**	P Beasley	C Boyd-Rochfort	Lady Z Wernher	2/1
1938	**Flares**	R A Jones	C Boyd-Rochfort	W Woodward	100/7
1939	**Flyon**	E Smith	J Jarvis	Lord Milford	100/6
1940	**No Race**				
1941	**Finis**	H Wragg	O Bell	Sir H Cunliffe-Owen	4/1
1942	**Owen Tudor**	G Richards	F Darling	Mrs R Macdonald-Buchanan	5/2
1943	**Ujiji**	G Richards	J Lawson	A E Allnatt	8/1
1944	**Umiddad**	G Richards	Frank Butters	HH Aga Khan	5/4
1945	**Ocean Swell**	E Smith	J Jarvis	Lord Rosebery	6/1
1946	**Caracalla**	C Elliott	C Semblat	M Boussac	4/9
1947	**Souverain**	M Lollierou	H Delavaud	F Schmitt	6/4
1948	**Arbar**	C Elliott	C Semblat	M Boussac	4/6
1949	**Alycidon**	D Smith	W Earl	Lord Derby	5/4
1950	**Supertello**	D Smith	J C Waugh	W Harvey	10/1
1951	**Pan II**	R Poincelet	E Pollet	E Constant	100/8
1952	**Aquino II**	G Richards	F Armstrong	Maharanee of Baroda	4/1
1953	**Souepi**	C Elliott	G Digby	G Digby	11/2
1954	**Elpenor**	J Doyasbere	C Elliott	M Boussac	100/8
1955	**Botticelli**	E Camici	Marc. della Rochetta	Marchesse della Rochetta	9/4
1956	**Macip**	S Boullenger	C Elliott	M Boussac	6/1

Royal Ascot – the first day of the 1965 meeting. Racegoers shelter from a cloudburst whilst a jockey gets on with his business.

		Jockey	Trainer	Owner	Odds
1957	**Zarathustra**	L Piggott	C Boyd-Rochfort	T Gray	6/1
1958	**Gladness**	L Piggott	M V O'Brien	J McShain	3/1
1959	**Wallaby II**	F Palmer	P Carter	Baron G de Waldner	9/4
1960	**Sheshoon**	G Moore	A Head	Prince Aly Khan	7/4
1961	**Pandofell**	L Piggott	F Maxwell	H W Drew	100/8
1962	**Balto**	F Palmer	M Bonaventure	A Reuff	7/4
1963	**Twilight Alley**	L Piggott	N Murless	Lady Sassoon	100/30
1964	**No Race**				
1965	**Fighting Charlie**	L Piggott	F Maxwell	Lady M Bury	6/1
1966	**Fighting Charlie**	G Starkey	F Maxwell	Lady M Bury	15/8
1967	**Parbury**	J Mercer	D Candy	H P Holt	7/1
1968	**Pardallo II**	W Pyers	C Bartholomew	Mme L Volterra	13/2
1969	**Levmoss**	W Williamson	S McGrath	S McGrath	15/8
1970	**Precipice Wood**	J Lindley	Mrs R Lomax	R J McAlpine	5/1
1971	**Random Shot**	G Lewis	A Budgett	Mrs G Benskin	11/1
1972	**Erimo Hawk**	P Eddery	G Barling	Y Yamamoto	10/1
1973	**Lassalle**	J Lindley	R Carver	Z Yoshida	2/1
1974	**Ragstone**	R Hutchinson	J Dunlop	Duke of Norfolk	6/4
1975	**Sagaro**	L Piggott	F Boutin	G A Oldham	7/4
1976	**Sagaro**	L Piggott	F Boutin	G A Oldham	8/15
1977	**Sagaro**	L Piggott	F Boutin	G A Oldham	9/4
1978	**Shangamuzo**	G Starkey	M Stoute	Mrs E Charles	13/2
1979	**Le Moss**	L Piggott	H Cecil	C d'Alessio	7/4
1980	**Le Moss**	J Mercer	H Cecil	C d'Alessio	3/1
1981	**Ardross**	L Piggott	H Cecil	C St George	30/100
1982	**Ardross**	L Piggott	H Cecil	C St George	1/5
1983	**Little Wolf**	W Carson	W R Hern	Lord Porchester	4/1
1984	**Gildoran**	S Cauthen	B Hills	R Sangster	10/1
1985	**Gildoran**	B Thomson	B Hills	R Sangster	5/2
1986	**Longboat**	W Carson	W R Hern	R D Hollingsworth	Evens
1987	**Paean**	S Cauthen	H Cecil	Lord H de Walden	6/1
1988	**Sadeem**	G Starkey	G Harwood	Sheikh Mohammed	7/2
1989	**Sadeem**	W Carson	G Harwood	Sheikh Mohammed	8/11
1990	**Ashal**	R Hills	H Thomson Jones	H Al-Maktoum	14/1
1991	**Indian Queen**	W R Swinburn	Lord Huntingdon	Sir G Brunton	25/1
1992	**Drum Taps**	L Dettori	Lord Huntingdon	Y Asakawa	7/4

Run at Newmarket 1917-1918 and 1941-1944

Left: Lester Piggot, 11 times a winner of the Gold Cup. *Right:* Willie Carson, successful twice.

Selection of headgear at Royal Ascot in 1981.

The Norfolk Stakes

The New Stakes, which was to become the Norfolk Stakes in 1973 in honour of one of racing's finest administrators was first won by *Rattan*, owned by the former fishmonger and professional gambler William Crockford, proprietor of the St James' club of the same name. *Rattan* went on to become a strong fancy for the 1844 Derby, the most scandalous ever run and 'won' by the ringer *Running Rein*. *Rattan* was blatantly stopped by his jockey Sam Rogers, who had backed another runner in the same race, and was subsequently warned off.

However, by the 1870s and through the early part of the present century, classic contenders were taking a hand including *Isinglass, Bayardo, Lemberg* and *Craganour,* first past the post in yet another controversial Derby in 1913, but subsequently disqualified.

In the late twenties and early thirties *Blenheim, Hyperion* and *Columbo* all demonstrated classic potential but since *My Babu's* victory in 1947 the race has, like so many others, become a vehicle for specialist breeding.

The 16th Duke of Norfolk was the Representative of both King George VI and the present Queen from 1945 to 1972 and was very much the father of modern Ascot. The administration of a racecourse must have been comfortably encompassed by a man who had organised two Coronations as the Earl Marshall of England, but his finest moment on the Royal Heath came when his home-bred *Ragstone* won the Gold Cup in 1974.

Run at Ascot over 5 furlongs for 2 year-olds First Run 1843 Group 3

		Jockey	Trainer	Owner	Odds
1843	**Rattan**	S Rogers	–	W Crockford	5/2
1844	**Old England**	J Day	J B Day	J B Day	2/1
1845	**Joy**	J Bartholomew	J Rogers	Lord Lonsdale	6/1
1846	**Slander**	W Abdale	J Kent Jnr	Lord G Bentinck	7/4
1847	**Assault**	E Edwards	H Stebbing	B Green	1/2
1848	**Garrick**	J Robinson	H Stebbing	B Green	5/4
1849	**Blarney**	W Day	W Day	J G Dixon	8/1
1850	**Citadel**	E Flatman	W Dilly	G Payne	5/2
1851	**Hobbie Noble**	G Whitehouse	M Dawson	Lord J Scott	5/6
1852	**Hybla**	J Mann	W Dilly	G Payne	–
1853	**Autocrat**	S Templeman	P Percy	R E Cooper	4/6
1854	**Monge**	A Day	W Ford	Mr Drinkald	8/1
1855	**Milton**	A Day	J Day	G W Fitzwilliam	2/1
1856	**Zaidee**	G Fordham	R Drewitt	M Dennett	–
1857	**Sedbury**	J Goater	W Goater	H Padwick	8/1
1858	**North Lincoln**	T Ashmall	J Hayhoe	Baron M de Rothschild	5/4
1859	**Rupee**	J Goater	W Goater	Mr Hamilton	10/1
1860	**Brown Duchess**	L Snowden	J Saxon	J Saxon	3/1
1861	**Alvediston**	A Day	W Day	W Day	4/1
1862	**Blue Mantle**	T Aldcroft	W Harlock	D Lane	2/1
1863	**Evelina**	J Wells	J Hayhoe	Baron M de Rothschild	4/1
1864	**Liddington**	J Adams	M Dawson	J Merry	4/7
1865	**Chibisa**	J Morris	Jos Dawson	Lord Stamford	10/1
1866	**Achievement**	H Custance	J Dover	M Pearson	2/5
1867	**Lady Elizabeth**	G Fordham	J Day	Marquis of Hastings	Evens
1868	**Belladrum**	G Fordham	M Dawson	J Merry	6/4
1869	**Temple**	R Marsh	–	J Barnard	100/6
1870	**Corisande**	G Fordham	J Hayhoe	Baron M de Rothschild	8/1
1871	**Helmet**	G Fordham	–	G Keswick	2/1
1872	**Marie Stuart**	J Morris	R Peck	J Merry	100/15
1873	**Ecossais**	G Fordham	T Jennings	C J Lefevre	4/6
1874	**Galopin**	J Morris	John Dawson	Prince Batthyany	6/4
1875	**Coltness**	T Osborne	J Ryan	J H Houldsworth	5/1
1876	**Rob Roy**	H Custance	C Blanton	J T Mackenzie	4/7
1877	**Bellicent**	H Constable	J Cannon	Lord Rosebery	100/6
1878	**Strathern**	T Cannon	W Arnull	H E Beddington	20/1
1879	**Oceanie**	J Morris	T Jennings	Comte F de Lagrange	Evens
1880	**Sir Charles**	T Glover	E Weever	W J Legh	5/1
1881	**Kermesse**	T Cannon	J Cannon	Lord Rosebery	Evens
1882	**Adriana**	A F Lemaire	J Ryan	J H Houldsworth	3/1
1883	**Wild Thyme**	G Fordham	T Jennings Jnr	C J Lefevre	5/2
1884	**Melton**	F Archer	M Dawson	Lord Hastings	5/1
1885	**Saraband**	C Wood	J Humphreys	J Blundell Maple	5/6
1886	**Enterprise**	G Barrett	J Ryan	D Baird	100/12
1887	**Friar's Balsam**	T Cannon	J Porter	Sir F Johnstone	13/8
1888	**Donovan**	F Barrett	G Dawson	Duke of Portland	Evens
1889	**Surefoot**	J Liddiard	C Jousiffe	A W Merry	5/4
1890	**Orvieto**	J Watts	J Ryan	J H Houldsworth	7/2
1891	**Goldfinch**	G Barrett	J Porter	Lord Alington	5/1
1892	**Isinglass**	G Chaloner	J Jewitt	H McCalmont	100/30
1893	**Wedding Bell**	T Loates	Robert Sherwood	Sir R W Griffith	–
1894	**Kissing Cup**	M Cannon	J Porter	Duke of Westminster	100/7
1895	**Roquebrune**	S Loates	M Gurry	Sir J Miller	2/1
1896	**Velasquez**	T Loates	W Walters Jnr	Lord Rosebery	11/10
1897	**Florio Rubattino**	M Cannon	J Jewitt	H McCalmont	20/1

		Jockey	Trainer	Owner	Odds
1898	**Flying Fox**	M Cannon	J Porter	Duke of Westminster	5/4
1899	**The Gorgon**	O Madden	R Marsh	A James	7/2
1900	**Bay Melton**	J F Sloan	A Gilbert	J Musker	6/1
1901	**Duke of Westminster**	S Loates	C Morton	R S Sievier	7/2
1902	**Sermon**	W Halsey	F W Day	Sir E Cassel	–
1903	**Montem**	W Halsey	R Marsh	Lord Wolverton	5/1
1904	**Llangibby**	W Lane	P P Gilpin	L Neumann	2/1
1905	**Colonia**	H Jones	W T Robinson	W Hall-Walker	6/1
1906	**Slieve Gallion**	W Higgs	S Darling	J H Greer	1/5
1907	**Sir Archibald**	L Lyne	H S Persse	A F Bassett	2/1
1908	**Bayardo**	B Dillon	A Taylor Jnr	A W Cox	7/1
1909	**Lemberg**	B Dillon	A Taylor Jnr	A W Cox	2/1
1910	**Seaforth**	H Randall	H S Persse	D McCalmont	5/2
1911	**Lomond**	F Wootton	R Wootton	E Hulton	5/1
1912	**Craganour**	W Saxby	W T Robinson	C B Ismay	3/1
1913	**Hapsburg**	F Herbert	W Halsey	Sir E Cassel	100/7
1914	**Let Fly**	H Jones	W T Robinson	W Hall-Walker	6/1
1915/18	**No Race**				
1919	**Orpheus**	F Leach Jnr	F Leach	H Cunliffe-Owen	7/1
1920	**Alan Breck**	A Smith	P P Gilpin	Sir J Buchanan	5/2
1921	**Scamp**	F Lane	F Templeman	Lord Jersey	100/15
1922	**Town Guard**	G Archibald	P P Gilpin	Lord Woolavington	7/1
1923	**Druid's Orb**	F Bullock	S H Darling	Lord Blandford	6/4
1924	**Black Friar**	G Archibald	F Darling	Lord Woolavington	7/4
1925	**Buckler**	T Weston	T Waugh	Sir R W B Jardine	100/8
1926	**Damon**	H Beasley	H S Persse	T F Ryan	9/2
1927	**Hakim**	C Smirke	R C Dawson	HH Aga Khan	6/1
1928	**Mr Jinks**	H Beasley	H S Persse	D McCalmont	9/4
1929	**Blenheim**	M Beary	R C Dawson	HH Aga Khan	7/2
1930	**Lighning Star**	S Donoghue	F Sneyd	J B Leigh	100/6
1931	**Spenser**	R A Jones	J Lawson	S Tattersall	15/2
1932	**Hyperion**	T Weston	G Lambton	Lord Derby	6/1
1933	**Colombo**	G Richards	T Hogg	Lord Glanely	10/11
1934	**Robin Goodfellow**	G Nicoll	H Cottrill	Sir A Bailey	50/1
1935	**Wyndham**	S Donoghue	D Snow	Miss D Paget	4/1
1936	**Le Grand Duc**	C Smirke	Frank Butters	HH Aga Khan	11/2
1937	**Ramtapa**	J Brennan	J Lawson	Sir A Bailey	100/8
1938	**Meadow**	T Weston	J Lawson	Sir A Bailey	8/1
1939	**Tant Mieux**	G Richards	F Darling	P Beatty	13/8
1940/45	**No Race**				
1946	**Petition**	H Wragg	Frank Butters	Sir A Butt	7/4
1947	**My Babu**	E Britt	F Armstrong	Maharaja of Baroda	8/13
	Delirium	C Smirke	J Leach	J Coltman	7/1
1948	**Makarpura**	C Smirke	F Armstrong	Maharaja of Baroda	100/30
1949	**Master Gunner**	K Gethin	P Thrale	D S Kennedy	11/10
1950	**Bay Meadows**	A Wragg	H Wragg	B J Hilliard	4/1
1951	**Bob Major**	W Rickaby	J Jarvis	Lord Rosebery	2/5
1952	**Blue Lamp**	D Smith	R Day	Mrs C Woodbridge	10/1
1953	**Hydrologist**	J Thompson	W Bellerby	Mrs A Brown	10/1
1954	**Tamerlane**	G Richards	N Bertie	Lord Porchester	7/2
1955	**Gratitude**	D Smith	H Cottrill	Maj L B Holliday	11/8
1956	**Skindles Hotel**	B Swift	P Prendergast	F Blackall	11/2
1957	**Pall Mall**	W H Carr	C Boyd-Rochfort	HM The Queen	6/1
1958	**Masham**	D Smith	G Brooke	A Ellis	8/1
1959	**Sound Track**	G Lewis	W Smyth	Duke of Norfolk	1/5
1960	**Floribunda**	R Hutchinson	P Prendergast	Mrs J R Mullion	2/7
1961	**Abermaid**	L Piggott	H Wragg	Sir P Loraine	3/1
1962	**Daybreak**	R Hutchinson	J Jarvis	Sir A Jarvis	13/8
1963	**Ballyamacad**	R Hutchinson	G Smyth	Duke of Norfolk	9/4
1964	**No Race**				
1965	**Tin King**	L Piggott	R F Johnson Houghton	C W Engelhard	4/7
1966	**Falcon**	L Piggott	R F Johnson Houghton	C W Engelhard	11/8
1967	**Porto Bello**	G Lewis	S Ingham	D Fermont	7/4
1968	**Song**	J Mercer	D Candy	B Jenks	8/1
1969	**Tribal Chief**	J Wilson	B Swift	J Swift	7/2
1970	**Swing Easy**	L Piggott	J Tree	J H Whitney	5/2
1971	**Phillip of Spain**	G Lewis	N Murless	Sir R Macdonald-Buchanan	9/4
1972	**Cade's Country**	G Cadwaladr	E Cousins	D Freeman	10/1
1973	**Habat**	P Eddery	P Walwyn	C Vittadini	7/4
1974	**Overtown**	E Eldin	D Smith	Sir H Calley	9/2
1975	**Faliraki**	L Piggott	M O'Toole	Mrs M O'Toole	6/1
1976	**Godswalk**	D Hogan	C Grassick	P Gallagher	8/13
1977	**Emboss**	L Piggott	R Boss	T Saud	11/4
1978	**Schweppeshire Lad**	G Starkey	M Stoute	M Madden	9/4
1979	**Romeo Romani**	B Taylor	H R Price	H Demetriou	7/2
1980	**Chummy's Special**	G Starkey	G Hunter	J Maxwell	11/2

		Jockey	Trainer	Owner	Odds
1981	**Day Is Done**	W Swinburn	D Weld	B Firestone	5/2
1982	**Brondesbury**	T Ives	W O'Gorman	A Foustok	8/11
1983	**Precocious**	L Piggott	H Cecil	Lord Tavistock	4/11
1984	**Magic Mirror**	L Piggott	M V O'Brien	S Niarchos	11/8
1985	**Marouble**	J Mercer	C Nelson	Countess of Lonsdale	20/1
1986	**Sizzling Melody**	R Hills	Lord J Fitzgerald	Mrs M Watt	5/1
1987	**Colmore Row**	B Raymond	W Jarvis	Mrs F G Allen	100/30
1988	**Superpower**	T Ives	W O'Gorman	Mrs P L Yong	Evens
1989	**Petillante**	R Hills	A Scott	P Newell	10/1
1990	**Line Engaged**	S Cauthen	D Elsworth	I Karageorgis	14/1
1991	**Magic Ring**	A Munro	P Cole	F Salman	7/4
1992	**Niche**	L Piggott	R Hannon	Lord Carnarvon	9/1

Run as the New Stakes 1843-1972

The Ribblesdale Stakes

Named after the Master of the Buckhounds from 1892 to 1895, the Ribblesdale Stakes was originally run over a mile and open to three and four-year-olds of either sex. The initial winner was *Milton*, ridden by a fifteen-year-old apprentice George Colling, indentured to his father Bob at Newmarket. Colling rode seventy-two winners that year, and was fifth to Steve Donoghue in the jockey's championship, but by 1922 increasing weight forced him to give up riding and move on to a distinguished career as a trainer, producing *Wilwyn* to win the inaugural Washington International at Laurel Park in 1952 and *Nimbus* to take the 2,000 Guineas and Derby in 1949.

Today, the distance extended to a mile and a half and confined to three-year-old fillies, it is the distaff equivalent of the King Edward VII Stakes, with the Oaks winner *Sleeping Partner*, Irish Oaks winner *Shoot a Line*, *Windmill Girl* and *Park Top* all gracing the roll of honour.

Run at Ascot over 1 mile 4 furlongs for 3 year-old fillies First Run 1919 Group 2

		Jockey	Trainer	Owner	Odds
1919	**Milton**	G Colling	R W Colling	C T Garland	Evens
1920	**Perion**	H Jones	H Sadler	Lord Penrhyn	5/4
1921	**The Yellow Dwarf**	B Carslake	H S Persse	Sir H Meux	5/1
1922	**Dry Toast**	B Carslake	H S Persse	J P Arkwright	11/4
1923	**Leighton Tor**	F Bullock	A Taylor Jnr	W M G Singer	11/8
1924	**Live Wire**	T Weston	G Lambton	Lord Wolverton	2/1
1925	**Glommen**	H Wragg	W Earl	S B Joel	100/30
1926	**Artist Glow**	C Elliott	Lord G Dundas	Mrs C Beatty	4/1
1927	**Foliation**	R A Jones	A Taylor Jnr	S Tattersall	4/5
1928	**O'Curry**	P Beasley	H S Persse	D Sullivan	4/1
1929	**Sir Cosmo**	J Childs	W Walters	Sir R Garton	6/4
1930	**Flying Argosy**	T Weston	Hugh Powney	W Vincent	7/4
1931	**Doctor Dolittle**	H Beasley	H S Persse	A F Basset	6/4
1932	**Rose en Soleil**	J Childs	D Waugh	Lord H de Walden	9/2
1933	**Versicle**	T Weston	G Lambton	Lord Stanley	100/8
1934	**The Blue Boy**	J Childs	M Hartigan	Sir W Portal	11/10
1935	**Easton**	G Richards	F Darling	Lord Woolavington	1/4
1936	**Can-Can**	P Evans	G Barling	T Blackwell	100/8
1937	**Rhodes Scholar**	R A Jones	J Lawson	Lord Astor	11/10
1938	**River Prince**	P Beasley	C Boyd-Rochfort	Duke of Marlborough	6/1
1939	**Ombro**	T Burns	C Boyd-Rochfort	Lord Portal	5/1
1940/48	**No Race**				
1948	**Sandastre**	G Richards	G Houghton	J Innes	4/1
1949	**Colonist II**	T Hawcroft	W Nightingall	W S Churchill	Evens
1950	**La Baille**	C Smirke	M Marsh	Mohamed Bey Sultan	15/2
1951	**Chinese Cracker**	A Breasley	H Blagrave	Mrs G Blagrave	7/4
1952	**Esquilla**	W R Johnstone	C Semblat	M Boussac	9/2
1953	**Skye**	W Rickaby	J Jarvis	Lord Rosebery	4/1
1954	**Sweet One**	W Rickaby	J Jarvis	Lord Milford	100/8
1955	**Ark Royal**	D Smith	G Colling	R D Hollingsworth	2/1
1956	**Milady**	C Smirke	M Marsh	H Holt	100/8
1957	**Almeria**	W H Carr	C Boyd-Rochfort	HM The Queen	13/8
1958	**None Nicer**	S Clayton	W R Hern	Maj L B Holliday	11/2
1959	**Cantelo**	E Hide	C Elsey	W Hill	5/4
1960	**French Fern**	G Lewis	J A Waugh	H Broughton	8/1
1961	**Futurama**	A Breasley	H Wragg	G A Oldham	9/2
1962	**Tender Annie**	G Bougoure	P Prendergast	Mrs J Bryce	5/4
1963	**Ostrya**	J Lindley	J A Waugh	Lord H de Walden	100/9
1964	**Windmill Girl**	A Breasley	A Budgett	Sir J Darrell	9/4
1965	**Bracey Bridge**	L Piggott	N Murless	M Wickham-Boynton	5/1

		Jockey	Trainer	Owner	Odds
1966	**Parthian Glance**	R Hutchinson	G Todd	Mrs W Riley-Smith	11/2
1967	**Park Top**	R Maddock	B van Cutsem	Duke of Devonshire	9/2
1968	**Pandora Bay**	M L Thomas	G Barling	C H Nathan	11/4
1969	**Sleeping Partner**	J Gorton	D Smith	Lord Rosebery	7/4
1970	**Parmelia**	A Barclay	N Murless	Lord H de Walden	9/1
1971	**Fleet Wahine**	G Starkey	H Thomson Jones	R Ohrstrom	9/1
1972	**Star Ship**	A Murray	H R Price	C St George	13/8
1973	**Miss Petard**	M L Thomas	R Jarvis	P Williams	12/1
1974	**Northern Princess**	A Kimberley	J Hindley	S Yoshida	9/2
1975	**Gallina**	L Piggott	M V O'Brien	S Fraser	7/1
1976	**Catalpa**	A Bond	H Cecil	Lord H de Walden	16/1
1977	**Nanticious**	W Swinburn	D Weld	Mrs B Firestone	15/2
1978	**Relfo**	C Roche	P Prendergast	Lord Granard	12/1
1979	**Expansive**	W Carson	W R Hern	HM The Queen	11/2
1980	**Shoot A Line**	W Carson	W R Hern	R Budgett	5/2
1981	**Strigida**	L Piggott	H Cecil	Lord H de Walden	5/1
1982	**Dish Dash**	B Raymond	R Armstrong	J F C Bryce	6/1
1983	**High Hawk**	W Carson	J Dunlop	Sheikh Mohammed	7/1
1984	**Ballinderry**	T Ives	J Tree	K Abdulla	9/2
1985	**Sally Brown**	W R Swinburn	M Stoute	R Cowell	7/1
1986	**Gull Nook**	P Eddery	J Dunlop	Lord Halifax	8/1
1987	**Queen Midas**	W Ryan	H Cecil	L Freedman	9/1
1988	**Miss Boniface**	C Asmussen	P Kelleway	P Kelleway	12/1
1989	**Alydaress**	S Cauthen	H Cecil	Sheikh Mohammed	4/1
1990	**Hellenic**	W R Swinburn	M Stoute	Lord Weinstock	6/1
1991	**Third Watch**	J Reid	J Dunlop	P G Goulandris	20/1
1992	**Armarama**	M Roberts	C Brittain	C Olley	5/4

Run over 1 mile for 3 & 4 year-olds from 1919-1939 and over 1 mile 4 furlongs for 3 year-olds 1949-1950

The Hardwicke Stakes

The Earl of Hardwicke, the Master of the Buckhounds who gave his name to the race, was not a lucky man. In 1878 he sustained serious injury in a fall while out with the Buckhounds, and in 1879 he resigned. Like many aristocrats of the period, he had been reduced to comparative penury in his efforts to entertain the easily bored Prince of Wales and he died in poor financial circumstances.

The most significant early winner was *Tristan*, French owned but trained at Newmarket. A versatile horse who won the July Cup over six furlongs in the year when he also won the Hardwicke, the Epsom Gold Cup (now the Coronation Cup) and the Champion Stakes. He won 26 races in all and is probably one of the few horses ever to have committed suicide, beating his head against his stable wall after being exported to Austria-Hungary.

Tristan's three successive wins is still a record, and is likely to remain so as three-year-olds are now excluded. The roll of honour shows that the Hardwicke was for many years considered to be a target for some of the best older horses, but the growth of international racing tends to mitigate against this nowadays.

Run at Ascot over 1 mile 4 furlongs First Run 1879 Group 2

		Jockey	Trainer	Owner	Odds
1879	**Chippendale**	J Osborne Jnr	T Wadlow	Lord Bradford	100/8
1880	**Exeter**	T Cannon	C Blanton	C Blanton	9/2
1881	**Peter**	F Archer	R Sherrard	Sir J Astley	5/4
1882	**Tristan**	G Fordham	T Jennings Jnr	C J Lefevre	8/13
1883	**Tristan**	F Webb	T Jennings Jnr	C J Lefevre	5/4
1884	**Tristan**	F Webb	T Jennings Jnr	C J Lefevre	100/30
1885	**Bendigo**	J Snowden	C Jousiffe	H T Barclay	4/6
1886	**Ormonde**	G Barrett	J Porter	Duke of Westminster	30/100
1887	**Ormonde**	T Cannon	J Porter	Duke of Westminster	4/5
1888	**Minting**	F Archer	M Dawson	R C Vyner	7/100
1889	**Gulliver**	F Rickaby	W A Jarvis	C D Rose	7/1
1890	**Amphion**	T Cannon	J Chandler	Gen Byrne	6/1
1891	**L'Abbesse de Jouarre**	M Cannon	Robert Sherwood	Lord Dunraven	5/6
1892	**St Damien**	J Woodburn	W A Jarvis	C D Rose	11/10
1893	**Watercress**	G Barrett	R Marsh	Baron M de Hirsch	60/100
1894	**Ravensbury**	M Cannon	W A Jarvis	C D Rose	6/1
1895	**Barbary**	S Loates	C W Golding	R Lebaudy	–
1896	**Shaddock**	M Cannon	J Porter	Duke of Westminster	11/8
1897	**Bay Ronald**	W Bradford	T Jennings Jnr	L Brassey	11/10
1898	**Collar**	O Madden	J Porter	Duke of Westminster	15/8
1899	**Ninus**	C Wood	G Platt	Prince Soltykoff	7/4
1900	**Boniface**	B Rigby	T Jennings Jnr	L Brassey	–
1901	**Merry Gal**	L Reiff	W T Robinson	W Hall-Walker	4/7
1902	**Joshua**	W Halsey	John Dawson Jnr	Lord Ellesmere	20/1
1903	**Sceptre**	F W Hardy	A Taylor Jnr	W Bass	10/11

		Jockey	Trainer	Owner	Odds
1904	**Rock Sand**	D Maher	G Blackwell	Sir J Miller	13/8
1905	**Bachelor's Button**	D Maher	C Peck	S B Joel	3/1
1906	**Wombwell**	J H Martin	W Waugh	Duke of Portland	10/1
1907	**Beppo**	W Higgs	F Pratt	J A de Rothschild	4/5
1908	**Bembo**	Wal Griggs	R C Dawson	Lord Carnarvon	7/1
1909	**Primer**	W Earl	W Waugh	Duke of Portland	10/1
1910	**Swynford**	F Wootton	G Lambton	Lord Derby	7/1
1911	**Swynford**	F Wootton	G Lambton	Lord Derby	4/11
1912	**Stedfast**	F Wootton	G Lambton	Lord Derby	2/9
1913	**Lancaster**	D Maher	T Cannon Jnr	C Lambton	4/1
1914	**Peter the Hermit**	R Watson	F Withington	H J King	7/1
1915/18	**No Race**				
1919	**Sir Douglas**	G Hulme	H S Persse	Sir H Meux	2/5
1920	**Black Gauntlet**	F Bullock	H East	Lord Wyfold	7/2
1921	**Franklin**	S Donoghue	R C Dawson	Lord Carnarvon	7/1
1922	**Welsh Spear**	G Archibald	P P Gilpin	Lord Queensborough	5/1
1923	**Chosroes**	G Smith	H S Persse	Sir H Meux	15/8
1924	**Chosroes**	G Archibald	H S Persse	Sir H Meux	10/1
1925	**Hurstwood**	V Smyth	A Taylor Jnr	S Tattersall	10/11
1926	**Lancegaye**	S Donoghue	A Taylor Jnr	W M G Singer	1/4
1927	**Coronach**	J Childs	F Darling	Lord Woolavington	30/100
1928	**Foliation**	R A Jones	J Lawson	S Tattersall	2/1
1929	**Posterity**	L Cordell	F Sneyd	Mrs C Glorney	5/1
1930	**Alcester**	J Childs	W R Jarvis	Lord Harewood	10/1
1931	**Orpen**	R A Jones	J Lawson	Sir J Rutherford	8/11
1932	**Goyescas**	S Donoghue	B Jarvis	M Boussac	9/2
1933	**Limelight**	J Childs	W R Jarvis	HM The King	7/1
1934	**Cotoneaster**	G Nicoll	F Templeman	E Thornton-Smith	9/1
1935	**J R Smith**	G Richards	C Boyd-Rochfort	M Field	4/1
1936	**Corrida**	C Elliott	J E Watts	M Boussac	8/1
1937	**Mid-day Sun**	M Beary	Fred Butters	Mrs G B Miller	2/1
1938	**Maranta**	T Weston	J Lawson	Sir A Bailey	11/4
1939	**Pointis**	D Smith	Frank Butters	Prince Aly Khan	100/8
1940/45	**No Race**				
1946	**Priam II**	C Elliott	C Semblat	M Boussac	4/11
1947	**Nirgal**	C Elliott	C Semblat	M Boussac	2/1
1948	**Sayjirao**	C Smirke	F Armstrong	Maharaja of Baroda	13/8
1949	**Helioscope**	J Sime	C Boyd-Rochfort	Lady Z Wernher	20/1
1950	**Peter Flower**	W Rickaby	J Jarvis	Lord Rosebery	6/5
1951	**Saturn**	D Smith	G Colling	Lord Derby	9/2
1952	**Dynamiter**	C Elliott	J Glynn	M Boussac	7/2
1953	**Guersant**	P Blanc	G Watson	Baron G de Rothschild	Evens
1954	**Aureole**	E Smith	C Boyd-Rochfort	HM The Queen	8/11
1955	**Elopement**	L Piggott	N Murless	Sir V Sassoon	–
1956	**Hugh Lupus**	W R Johnstone	N Murless	Lady Vernon	100/30
1957	**Fric**	J Deforge	J Lawson	M Calmann	11/10
1958	**Brioche**	E Britt	C Elsey	W Humble	7/2
1959	**Impatient**	J Lindley	J M Gosden	Sir H Wernher	10/1
1960	**Aggressor**	J Lindley	J M Gosden	Sir H Wernher	7/2
1961	**St Paddy**	L Piggott	N Murless	Sir V Sassoon	4/9
1962	**Aurelius**	A Breasley	N Murless	Mrs V Lilley	8/13
1963	**Miralgo**	W Williamson	H Wragg	G A Oldham	100/30
1964	**No Race**				
1965	**Soderini**	G Lewis	S Ingham	L Lawrence	3/1
1966	**Prominer**	D Lake	P Prendergast	J R Mullion	4/1
1967	**Salvo**	R Hutchinson	H Wragg	G A Oldham	7/4
1968	**Hopeful Venture**	A Barclay	N Murless	HM The Queen	4/6
1969	**Park Top**	G Lewis	B van Cutsem	Duke of Devonshire	11/8
1970	**Karabas**	L Piggott	B van Cutsem	Lord Iveagh	11/8
1971	**Ortis**	D Keith	P Walwyn	C Vittadini	9/2
1972	**Selhurst**	G Lewis	N Murless	H J Joel	11/4
1973	**Rheingold**	Y Saint-Martin	B Hills	H Zeisel	1/5
1974	**Relay Race**	L Piggott	H Cecil	Sir R Macdonald-Buchanan	10/11
1975	**Charlie Bubbles**	P Eddery	P Walwyn	L Sainer	12/1
1976	**Orange Bay**	P Eddery	P Walwyn	C Vittadini	9/2
1977	**Meneval**	L Piggott	M V O'Brien	Mrs G Getty II	2/1
1978	**Montcontour**	Y Saint-Martin	M Zilber	Mrs H Hausmann	25/1
1979	**Obraztsovy**	B Taylor	H R Price	R Sangster	9/4
1980	**Scorpio**	P Paquet	F Boutin	G A Oldham	2/1
1981	**Pelerin**	B Taylor	H Wragg	Sir P Oppenheimer	7/1
1982	**Critique**	L Piggott	H Cecil	G Vanian	7/2
1983	**Stanerra**	B Rouse	F Dunne	F Dunne	4/1
1984	**Khairpour**	S Cauthen	R F Johnson Houghton	G J Chittick	13/2
1985	**Jupiter Island**	L Piggott	C Brittain	Marchioness of Tavistock	85/40
1986	**Dihistan**	P Eddery	M Stoute	HH Aga Khan	11/2

		Jockey	Trainer	Owner	Odds
1987	**Orban**	S Cauthen	H Cecil	Prince A A Faisal	11/4
1988	**Almaarad**	W Carson	J Dunlop	H Al-Maktoum	6/1
1989	**Assatis**	P Eddery	G Harwood	K Abdulla	4/11
1990	**Assatis**	R Cochrane	G Harwood	S Harada	50/1
1991	**Rock Hopper**	P Eddery	M Stoute	M Al-Maktoum	5/6
1992	**Rock Hopper**	P Eddery	M Stoute	M Al-Maktoum	8/15

The Wokingham Stakes

The Wokingham Stakes is one of the most senior races at Royal Ascot. Named after what was then a nearby market town, it was first run in 1813 and the winner was the Duke of York's *Pointers.* For many years until 1873 the race was divided into classes, one of which was won in that year by a sixteen-year-old Fred Archer drawing 6st 10lb on *Merodach* for Mr C.S.Hardy.

Archer was to win again on *Trappist, Despair* and *Energy,* all names which ironically can be associated with his short and tragic life, despite his brilliance in the saddle.

The Wokingham was already becoming notorious as a betting medium, second only to the Royal Hunt Cup, but some good horses took part including *Glass Jug,* winner in 1903 and runner up to *Sceptre* in the Oaks the year before.

Surprisingly, it is much the case today and recent winners *Boone's Cabin* (1975) *Import* (1976), *Great Eastern* (1981) and *Petong* (1984) were all good class animals as their respective burdens of 10st, 9st 4lb, 9st 8lb and 9st 6lb would indicate.

Run at Ascot over 6 furlongs for 3-y-o & up First Run 1874 Handicap

		Jockey	Trainer	Owner	Odds
1874	**Josephine**	H Constable	–	W H Cooper	10/1
1875	**Albanus**	T Glover	–	R Pattinson	2/1
1876	**The Mandarin**	W Newhouse	–	Mr Jolliffe	4/1
1877	**Rosbach**	H Morgan	J Cannon	Lord Rosebery	4/1
1878	**Trappist**	F Archer	J Cannon	Capt Prime	7/2
1879	**Philippine**	A F Lemaire	C Blanton	A C Barclay	3/1
1880	**Warrior**	J Osborne Jnr	J Cannon	Capt J Machell	100/8
1881	**Wokingham**	G Barrett	F Bates	R Jardine	6/1
1882	**Wokingham**	C Bowman	F Bates	R Jardine	10/1
1883	**Despair**	F Archer	W Gilbert	W Gilbert	5/1
1884	**Energy**	F Archer	A Taylor Snr	Duchess of Montrose	4/1
1885	**Corunna**	J Wall	C Bloss	Lord Hartington	5/1
1886	**Loved One**	H Wilton	A Taylor Snr	Duchess of Montrose	7/1
1887	**Everitt**	T Loates	W Manser	Lord Ailesbury	100/8
1888	**Annamite**	P Bradbury	J Chandler	Sir W Throckmorton	10/1
1889	**Bret Harte**	F Peake	C W Golding	G Cleveland	100/12
1890	**Day Dawn**	W Bradford	T Wadlow	H T Fenwick	100/6
1891	**Rathbeal**	G Chaloner	J Jewitt	Capt J Machell	9/2
1892	**Hildebert**	W Bradford	G Blackwell	D Cooper	10/1
1893	**Pitcher**	H Huxtable	T Leader	C J F Fawcett	5/1
1894	**Oatlands**	O Madden	R Marsh	Duke of Devonshire	100/7
1895	**Hebron**	W Clayton	J Jewitt	C J Blake	100/14
1896	**Kilcock**	O Madden	S Darling	J H Greer	5/2
1897	**El Diablo**	C Wood	G Platt	M D Rucker	7/1
1898	**Minstrel**	O Madden	R Marsh	Duke of Devonshire	100/7
1899	**Eager**	M Cannon	J Ryan	A W Cox	9/4
1900	**Bridge**	J H Martin	W Halsey	W H Pawson	7/1
1901	**Rose Tree**	C Thorpe	E Corrigan	E Corrigan	33/1
1902	**His Lordship**	J Watts	C Morton	J B Joel	100/7
1903	**Glass Jug**	T Miller	C Beatty	Lord H de Walden	20/1
1904	**Out o'Sight**	M Cannon	F Hunt	J Sloncombe	100/12
1905	**Queen's Holiday**	B Dillon	J Fallon	F Forester	5/2
1906	**Golden Gleam**	W Higgs	R Marsh	A James	100/8
1907	**Forerunner II**	H Watts	Sir C Nugent	D R Browning	33/1
1908	**Portland Bay**	Wal Griggs	C Morton	J B Joel	100/8
1909	**Portland Bay**	Wal Griggs	C Morton	J B Joel	8/1
1910	**Galleot**	C Trigg	R H Dewhurst	A Bendon	20/1
1911	**Meleager**	J Evans	P P Gilpin	L Neumann	20/1
1912	**Borrow**	J H Martin	A J Joyner	H P Whitney	100/6
1913	**Braxted**	F Herbert	F Leach	Sir T R Dewar	100/7
1914	**Mount William**	E Gardner	R Farquharson	R Farqharson	100/7
1915/18	**No Race**				
1919	**Scatwell**	F Slade	F Barling	Lord Glanely	4/1
1920	**Golden Orb**	F Slade	J Jarvis	Sir W Cooke	7/4
1921	**Santaquest**	H Wragg	S Pickering	C E Hay	100/30
1922	**Proconsul**	A Whalley	H Cottrill	Mrs S Whitburn	25/1
1923	**Crowdennis**	B Carslake	H S Persse	P Cullinan	100/8
1924	**Pandarus**	W McLachlan Jnr	F Barling	H Benjamin	8/1
1925	**Compiler**	J Brennan	Sir C Nugent	L Schaverien	20/1
1926	**Capture Him**	J Thwaites	F Archer	Lord Glanely	20/1

		Jockey	Trainer	Owner	Odds
1927	**Nothing Venture**	J Leach	F Leach	Sir J Buchanan Jardine	100/6
1928	**Hera**	T Barber	J Platt	Sir W Cooke	100/6
1929	**Six Wheeler**	T Weston	C Elsey	H F Clayton	20/1
1930	**Grandmaster**	G Richards	T Hogg	Lord Glanely	5/1
1931	**Heronslea**	J Taylor	D Peacock	W Smith	100/30
1932	**Concerto**	H Wragg	O Bell	Sir H Cunliffe-Owen	9/2
1933	**Concerto**	H Wragg	O Bell	Sir H Cunliffe-Owen	4/1
1934	**Coroado**	H Gunn	W Easterby	F J Lundgren	11/4
1935	**Theio**	E Smith	J Jarvis	Sir L Phillips	33/1
1936	**Cora Deans**	S Donoghue	B Jarvis	Sir V Sassoon	7/1
1937	**Kong**	F Sharpe	N Scobie	Sir C Hyde	33/1
1938	**Bold Ben**	C Elliott	F Armstrong	A E Barry	9/1
1939	**America**	R A Jones	H Jelliss	F W Wilmot	20/1
1940/44	**No Race**				
1945	**Portamara**	D Smith	J Beary	D Morris	20/1
1946	**The Bug**	C Smirke	H Wellesley	N Wachman	7/1
1947	**Lucky Jordan**	J Sirett	A Boyd	Mrs G Gilroy	33/1
1948	**White Cockade**	J Sirett	T E Leader	R L Glasspool	33/1
1949	**The Cobbler**	G Richards	N Murless	G Loder	4/1
1950	**Blue Book**	E Britt	M Marsh	H E Morriss	100/6
1951	**Donore**	W H Carr	C Boyd-Rochfort	Sir H de Trafford	100/9
1952	**Malka's Boy**	L Piggott	W Nightingall	H Elvin	100/6
1953	**Jupiter**	J Sirett	P Beasley	Lord Lambton	22/1
1954	**March Past**	W Rickaby	K Cundell	Mrs G Trimmer-Thompson	15/2
1955	**The Plumber's Mate**	D Keith	H Smyth	Lord Ashcombe	25/1
1956	**Light Harvest**	J Mercer	J A Waugh	D Forster	100/6
1957	**Dionosio**	E Britt	C Elsey	P Bull	5/1
1958	**Magic Boy**	D Greening	M Bolton	D Miller	20/1
1959	**Golden Leg**	R Elliott	M Pope	E McAlpine	33/1
1960	**Silver King**	J Sime	S Hall	J Phang Jnr	15/2
1961	**Whistler's Daughter**	J Sime	S Hall	L Lucas	10/1
1962	**Elco**	W Williamson	D Whelan	T Langton	20/1
1963	**Marcher**	R Hutchinson	D Hanley	R Zelker	100/8
1964	**No Race**				
1965	**Nunshoney**	D East	G Beeby	G Todd	33/1
1966	**My Audrey**	G Cadwaladr	E Cousins	Mrs D Rosenfield	20/1
1967	**Spaniard's Mount**	D Smith	J Winter	B Schmidt-Bodner	100/6
1968	**Charicles**	D East	E Lambton	P Bull	100/7
1969	**Sky Rocket**	P Eddery	M Pope	A B Pope	20/1
1970	**Virginia Boy**	D McKay	D Smith	B Schmidt-Bodner	100/9
1971	**Whistling Fool**	D McKay	D Smith	B Schmidt-Bodner	11/2
1972	**Le Johnstan**	G Lewis	J Sutcliffe Jnr	S Powell	9/1
1973	**Plummet**	W Carson	J E Sutcliffe	M Myers	11/1
1974	**Ginnies Pet**	L Piggott	J E Sutcliffe	J Jackson	7/1
1975	**Boone's Cabin**	L Piggott	M V O'Brien	R Sangster	6/1
1976	**Import**	M L Thomas	W Wightman	H Cayzer	4/1
1977	**Calibana**	G Baxter	P Cole	E Badger	14/1
1978	**Equal Opportunity**	R Curant	P Arthur	P Wentworth	20/1
1979	**Lord Rochford**	B Raymond	B Swift	B Shine	16/1
1980	**Queen's Pride**	G Baxter	P Cole	Mrs L d'Ambrumenil	28/1
1981	**Great Eastern**	W Carson	J Dunlop	Mrs A J Struthers	16/1
1982	**Battle Hymn**	A Clark	G Harwood	Mrs D Abbott	16/1
1983	**Melindra**	A McGlone	D Elsworth	Miss A Winfield	7/1
1984	**Petong**	B Raymond	M Jarvis	T G Warner	11/1
1985	**Time Machine**	W Carson	P Hughes	T Harty	10/1
1986	**Touch of Grey**	M L Thonmas	D Thom	T Jennings	20/1
1987	**Bel Byou**	T Quinn	P Cole	F Salman	11/2
1988	**Powder Blue**	T Ives	P Makin	S McColl	28/1
1989	**Mac's Fighter**	C Asmussen	W O'Gorman	D McDonnell	16/1
1990	**Knight of Mercy**	P Eddery	R Hannon	M W Grant	16/1
1991	**Amigo Menor**	C Rutter	D Murray-Smith	F Glennon	14/1
1992	**Red Rosein**	G Carter	J Wilson	Exors of J S Gittins	33/1

First run in 1813 but in two or three classes until 1873

The King's Stand Stakes

The origins of the King's Stand Stakes lie in the vagaries of the English weather. In 1860 heavy rain made it impossible to run the two mile Royal Stand Plate. Accordingly it was renamed the Queen's Stand plate and the distance reduced to the only raceable part of the course, ie five furlongs.

In time, the Queen's Stand became the most important sprint of the Royal Meeting. *Diadem, Tetratema* and *Diomedes* were all natural and obvious winners in the twenties, but perhaps the finest was *Gold Bridge* in 1933 and 1934.

Gold Bridge had the reputation of being one of the most handsome sprinters seen on the racecourse between the wars, still thought by many to be the Golden Age of racing. As a two-year-old he raced in France, returning to join the Newmarket stable of Major 'Vandy' Beatty who prepared *Gold Bridge* not only for his double victory in the King's Stand but the Granville Stakes, also at Ascot, and the Nunthorpe at York as well as several other top class sprint events the names of which are now merely memories.

The race became the King's Stand on the accession of King Edward VII in 1901 but curiously did not revert to its original name when HM The Queen came to the throne in 1952. Formerly Group 1, the King's Stand was reduced to Group 2 in 1988 in order that the Vernon's Sprint Cup could be upgraded and improve the sprint pattern in the second half of the season. Doubtless Queen Victoria would not have been amused.

Run at Ascot over 5 furlongs First Run 1860 Group 2

		Jockey	Trainer	Owner	Odds
1860	**Queen of the Vale**	J Daley	J Hayhoe	Baron M de Rothschild	8/1
1861	**Buckstone**	J Hayward	M Dawson	J Merry	5/2
1862	**Shillelagh**	G Fordham	F Balchin	G Hodgman	4/1
1863	**Umpire**	J Adams	E Weever	Lord Coventry	5/1
1864	**Le Bearnais**	J Grimshaw	T Jennings	Comte F de Lagrange	5/2
1865	**Saccharometer**	G Fordham	Hayhoe	W Morris	3/1
1866	**Hippia**	A Peake	J Hayhoe	Baron M de Rothschild	8/1
1867	**Cecrops**	T French	–	G Fleming	5/1
1868	**Xi**	J Wells	J Porter	Sir J Hawley	5/2
1869	**Gertrude**	D Butler	M Dawson	Lord Falmouth	100/6
1870	**King of the Forest**	W Hunt	J Waugh	J Merry	9/4
1871	**Chopette**	J Wheeler	J Hayhoe	Baron M de Rothschild	4/1
1872	**Bertram**	J Jewitt	C Blanton	A C Barclay	4/1
1873	**Prince Charlie**	T French	Jos Dawson	Jos Dawson	4/11
1874	**Blenheim**	G Fordham	T Jennings	C J Lefevre	100/15
1875	**Tangible**	F Webb	H Woolcott	Sir G Chetwynd	9/4
1876	**Lowlander**	H Custance	W Reeves	H Bird	2/9
1877	**Springfield**	T Osborne	J Ryan	J H Houldsworth	8/15
1878	**Lollypop**	H Custance	R Marsh	Duke of Hamilton	8/100
1879	**Hackthorpe**	F Archer	J Cannon	Lord Hastings	2/9
1880	**Charibert**	F Webb	M Dawson	H F C Vyner	6/4
1881	**Ishmael**	J Osborne Jnr	F Bates	R Jardine	100/15
1882	**Eastern Empress**	F Archer	W Manser	W Gregory	4/6
1883	**Prince William**	E Martin	J Porter	Sir F Johnstone	4/1
1884	**Geheimniss**	F Archer	J Porter	Lord Alington	8/13
1885	**Glen Albyn**	C Loates	W G Stevens	G Arden	5/1
1886	**Financier**	S Howard	R Sherrard	O Williams	3/1
1887	**Crowberry**	W Warne	M Dawson	R C Vyner	1/2
1888	**Noble Chieftain**	T Weldon	T Clay	Lord Penrhyn	4/6
1889	**Formidable**	C Gray	R Marsh	Lord Dudley	5/2
1890	**Bumptious**	T Loates	A Hayhoe	L de Rothschild	5/6
1891	**Lady Caroline**	R Chaloner	W Gray	H Milner	–
1892	**Lady Lena**	C Loates	T Leader	J Charlton	11/10
1893	**Prince Hampton**	J Watts	P Peck	Sir J Blundell Maple	6/4
1894	**Best Man**	F Webb	John Dawson	W Johnstone	5/4
1895	**Woolsthorpe**	M Cannon	C Waugh	Prince Soltykoff	100/15
1896	**Wishard**	L Reiff	E Wishard	E Wishard	100/12
1897	**Woolsthorpe**	M Cannon	W Gibbons	Prince Soltykoff	6/1
1898	**Kilcock**	J Watts	S Darling	J H Greer	7/4
1899	**Kilcock**	S Loates	S Darling	S Darling	5/6
1900	**Eager**	M Cannon	P P Gilpin	L Neumann	7/4
1901	**Elizabeth M**	L Reiff	J Huggins	W C Whitney	Evens
1902	**Zanoni**	H Jones	F Leach	H J King	–
1903	**Sundridge**	M Cannon	C Morton	J B Joel	4/5
1904	**Sundridge**	M Cannon	C Morton	J B Joel	1/4
1905	**Delaunay**	O Madden	P P Gilpin	P P Gilpin	8/15
1906	**Thrush**	H Randall	E Robson	J Orr-Ewing	2/1
1907	**Camp Fire II**	D Maher	R Day	A Bailey	5/2
1908	**Foresight**	W Higgs	M Vasey	Lord Fitzwilliam	100/6
1909	**Foresight**	W Higgs	W J Costello	Lord Fitzwilliam	8/1
1910	**Spanish Prince**	H Randall	H Carter	H P Nickalls	100/7
1911	**Hornet's Beauty**	J H Martin	P P Peebles	Sir W Cooke	1/2
1912	**Great Surprise**	D Maher	W C Yapp	H Rhodes	4/6
1913	**Hornet's Beauty**	J H Martin	F Leach	Sir W Cooke	1/2
1914	**Adular**	N Spear	J Butters	Baron G Springer	5/1
1915/18	**No Race**				
1919	**Diadem**	S Donoghue	G Lambton	Lord D'Abernon	7/2
1920	**Diadem**	S Donoghue	G Lambton	Lord D'Abernon	5/6
1921	**Tetratema**	B Carslake	H S Persse	D McCalmont	6/5
1922	**King Sol**	S Donoghue	O Bell	J C Galstaun	9/2
1923	**Golden Boss**	C Elliott	S H Darling	A K Macomber	7/1
1924	**Golden Boss**	F O'Neill	S H Darling	A K Macomber	9/4
1925	**Diomedes**	J Leach	H Leader	S W Beer	1/2
1926	**Highborn II**	G Garner	F Carter	Sir H Cunliffe-Owen	7/2
1927	**Nice Prospect**	B Carslake	C Peck	J B Joel	6/1

		Jockey	Trainer	Owner	Odds
1928	**Chichester Cross**	C Smirke	C Howard	C Howard	20/1
1929	**Tag End**	H Wragg	C Peck	J B Joel	5/2
1930	**Oak Ridge**	H Beasley	L Cundell	F Cundell	11/8
1931	**Stingo**	H Wragg	W Lowe	D Gant	2/1
1932	**Lemnarchus**	G Richards	F Darling	Lord Ellesmere	7/2
1933	**Gold Bridge**	H Beasley	V Beatty	A K Macomber	11/10
1934	**Gold Bridge**	C Elliott	V Beatty	Lord Beatty	11/2
1935	**Shalfleet**	H Jelliss	H Leader	H Leader	5/4
1936	**Sweet Polly**	G Richards	L Cundell	L Long	7/1
1937	**Ticca Gari**	A Dupuit	Frank Butters	Prince Aly Khan	5/1
1938	**Foray**	P Beasley	C Boyd-Rochfort	M Field	3/1
1939	**Mickey The Greek**	H Wragg	H Leach	N Frieze	20/1
1940/45	**No Race**				
1946	**Vilmorin**	G Richards	J Lawson	J Read	10/1
1947	**Greek Justice**	G Richards	F Darling	J A Dewar	100/30
1948	**Squander Bug**	W Rickaby	M Collins	Mrs E Moss	33/1
1949	**Abernant**	G Richards	N Murless	R Macdonald-Buchanan	4/6
1950	**Tangle**	E Smith	W Payne	Lady Baron	3/1
1951	**Stephen Paul**	N Sellwood	H S Persse	J Olding	7/2
1952	**Easter Bride**	E Fordyce	T Rimell	W Rimell	7/1
1953	**Fairy Flax**	A Breasley	J Lawson	R Clark	20/1
1954	**Golden Lion**	B Swift	C Mitchell	W Barrett	10/1
1955	**Pappa Fourway**	W H Carr	W Dutton	Mrs E Goldson	4/7
1956	**Palariva**	R Poincelet	A Head	HH Aga Khan	6/1
1957	**Right Boy**	L Piggott	W Dutton	G Gilbert	4/1
1958	**Drum Beat**	A Breasley	W O'Gorman	J Gerber	2/1
1959	**Chris**	J Sime	W Nevett	H Hartley	9/4
1960	**Sound Track**	A Breasley	A S O'Brien	Lady Hemphill	8/1
1961	**Silver Tor**	G Lewis	R Fetherstonhaugh	S Joel	7/4
1962	**Cassarate**	N Sellwood	M V O'Brien	Countess M Batthyany	5/1
1963	**Majority Blue**	L Piggott	W O'Gorman	J Muldoon	100/8
1964	**No Race**				
1965	**Goldhill**	J Etherington	M H Easterby	R Johnson	10/1
1966	**Roughlyn**	G Cadwaladr	W D Francis	J Pickering	20/1
1967	**Be Friendly**	A Breasley	C Mitchell	P O'Sullevan	3/1
1968	**D'Urberville**	J Mercer	J Tree	J H Whitney	4/1
1969	**Song**	J Mercer	D Candy	B Jenks	Evens
1970	**Amber Rama**	Y Saint-Martin	F Mathet	A Plesch	4/1
1971	**Swing Easy**	L Piggott	J Tree	J H Whitney	7/1
1972	**Sweet Revenge**	G Lewis	T Corbett	Mrs B Attenborough	7/2
1973	**Abergwaun**	L Piggott	M V O'Brien	C St.George	7/4
1974	**Bay Express**	B Taylor	P Nelson	P Cooper	9/4
1975	**Flirting Around**	Y Saint-Martin	R Carver	Mrs A Hausmann	9/2
1976	**Lochnager**	E Hide	M W Easterby	C Spence	6/4
1977	**Godswalk**	L Piggott	M V O'Brien	R Sangster	4/6
1978	**Solinus**	L Piggott	M V O'Brien	D Schwartz	4/6
1979	**Double Form**	J Reid	R F Johnson Houghton	Baroness H Thyssen	12/1
1980	**African Song**	P Eddery	P Kelleway	G Kaye	10/1
1981	**Marwell**	W R Swinburn	M Stoute	E J Loder	5/4
1982	**Fearless Lad**	E Hide	R D Peacock	G Soulsby	10/1
1983	**Sayf El Arab**	M L Thomas	W O'Gorman	M Dabaghi	33/1
1984	**Habibti**	W Carson	J Dunlop	M Mutawa	4/5
1985	**Never So Bold**	L Piggott	R Armstrong	E Kessly	4/1
1986	**Last Tycoon**	C Asmussen	R Collet	R C Strauss	9/2
1987	**Bluebird**	C Asmussen	M V O'Brien	R Sangster	7/2
1988	**Chilibang**	W Carson	J Dunlop	Mrs H Heinz	16/1
1989	**Indian Ridge**	S Cauthen	D Elsworth	Mrs A Coughlan	9/4
1990	**Dayjur**	W Carson	W R Hern	H Al-Maktoum	11/2
1991	**Elbio**	S Cauthen	P Makin	B Brackpool	13/8
1992	**Sheikh Albadou**	W R Swinburn	A Scott	H Salem	7/2

Run as the Queen's Stand Plate/Stakes 1860-1900

The Criterion Stakes

In the mid 1830s the Criterion Stakes was a richly endowed two-year-old race, worth £910 to the winner. Probably named after a colt by *Chrysolite* out of *Hyaena* foaled in 1762, the race lapsed but the name was revived as a Listed race in the eighties and became Group 3 in 1986. The best winners since then have been *Cadeaux Genereux* (July Cup and the William Hill Sprint Championship) and *Rock City*, a winner of five pattern races, three of them as a juvenile, taking the Coventry Stakes, the July Stakes and the Gimcrack Stakes.

Run at Newmarket over 7 furlongs First Run 1978 Group 3

		Jockey	Trainer	Owner	Odds
1978	**Daring March**	G Duffield	J Bethell	Mrs D Shirley	25/1
1979	**Alert**	E Eldin	C Brittain	C Elliot	7/2
1980	**Captain Nick**	J Bleasdale	J Hindley	G Parkinson	14/1
1981	**Dalsaan**	E Hide	M Stoute	HH Aga Khan	6/4
1982	**Noalcoholic**	G Duffield	G Pritchard-Gordon	W du Pont III	100/30
1983	**Thug**	B Taylor	J Hindley	B Haggas	25/1
1984	**Grey Desire**	B Coogan	D Plant	M Brittain	12/1
1985	**Capricorn Belle**	R Guest	L Cumani	I Allan	10/1
1986	**Mister Wonderful**	T Ives	J Dunlop	Duchess of Norfolk	8/1
1987	**Linda's Magic**	W Carson	R Armstrong	J Bray	7/2
1988	**Cadeaux Genereux**	P Eddery	O Douieb	M Al-Maktoum	9/2
1989	**Zilzal**	W R Swinburn	M Stoute	M Al-Maktoum	1/4
1990	**Rock City**	B Raymond	R Hannon	A F Budge Ltd	Evens
1991	**La Grange Music**	W R Swinburn	J Fanshawe	D Thompson	10/1
1992	**Toussaud**	P Eddery	J Gosden	K Abdulla	7/1

The Irish Derby

The origins of the Irish Derby go back to 1817 when the rather comically named O'Darby Stakes was won by *Souvenir*. The race did not survive and was discontinued after 1824, to be succeeded by the Curragh Derby in 1848. The winner's name *Justice to Ireland* was not prophetic, and the event was short lived.

It was not until 1866 that the Irish Derby which we know today was established over an extended mile and three-quarters, reduced to twelve furlongs in 1872. The inaugural winner was *Selim*, owned by a Staffordshire based Englishman, James Cockin and ridden by an English jockey, Charlie Maidment. The Cockin/Maidment combination won again in 1867 but the Irish gained their first success the following year with 'Mr Holland's' *Madeira*, partnered by Denny Wynne. 'Holland' was the nom de course of the Bourke family of Irish industrialists based in the midland town of Roscrea.

The horse that did most to put the Irish Derby on the map was *Orby*, the first Irish-trained horse to win the Epsom Derby, albeit from a moderate field, going on to win easily at the Curragh. However, it was not until 1962 that the Irish Derby became a major international event, master-minded by Joe McGrath who had won at Epsom with *Arctic Prince* in 1951. Also a founding father of the Irish Hospitals Sweepstake, McGrath fused the Derby and the Sweep together to provide a prize of £50,027 compared to the £34,786 collected by *Larkspur* at Epsom a month before.

Shades of *Selim*; the first winner was the French horse *Tambourine II*, but McGrath's dream had come true and the Irish Derby became the obvious target for animals which had won or run prominently at Epsom.

In 1964 *Santa Claus* became the first horse since *Orby* to pull off the double, followed by *Nijinsky*, *Grundy*, *The Minstrel*, *Shirley Heights*, *Troy*, *Shergar*, *Shahrastani*, *Kahyasi* and *Generous*.

The first filly to win the Irish Derby since *Gallinaria* in 1900 was *Salsabil*, who defeated *Deploy*, the Epsom Derby winner *Quest for Fame* and subsequent King George winner *Belmez* in a race which many observers consider to be the best since the event achieved its present status.

***Nijinksy*, seen here winning the Two Thousand Guineas in 1970, also took that year's Irish Derby.**

Run at The Curragh over 1 mile 4 furlongs for 3 year-old colts & fillies First Run 1866 Group 1

		Jockey	Trainer	Owner	Odds
1866	**Selim**	C Maidment	–	J Cockin	5/4
1867	**Golden Plover**	C Maidment	–	J Cockin	7/4
1868	**Madeira**	D Wynne	–	Mr Holland	–
1869	**The Scout**	W Miller	–	J Johnstone	7/1
1870	**Billy Pitt**	W Canavan	T Connolly	P Keary	2/1
1871	**Maid of Athens**	T Broderick	P Doucie	Mr Williams	4/6
1872	**Trickstress**	W Miller	T Moran	A R Bourne	Evens
1873	**Kyrle Daly**	T Broderick	P Doucie	W Williams	4/1
1874	**Ben Battle**	E Martin	T Connolly	J W Denison	5/2
1875	**Innishowen**	G Ashworth	J Toon	J Cockin	2/1
1876	**Umpire**	P Lynch	J French	C Ryan	1/3
1877	**Redskin**	F Wynne	D Broderick	Capt Gubbins	5/1
1878	**Madame Dubarry**	F Wynne	F Martin	J W Denison	5/1
1879	**Soulouque**	J Connolly	T Connolly	W Dunne	100/30
1880	**King of the Bees**	F Wynne	D Broderick	W Brophy	100/8
1881	**Master Ned**	T Broderick	P Doucie	J A Cassidy	100/15
1882	**Sortie**	N Behan	P Doucie	J A Cassidy	5/1
1883	**Sylph**	J Connolly	J Dunne	C J Blake	10/1
1884	**Theologian**	J Connolly	W Behan	G Moore	7/1
1885	**St Kevin**	H Saunders	James Dunne	C J Blake	–
1886	**Theodemir**	J Connolly	G Moore	G Moore	100/15
1887	**Pet Fox**	T Kavanagh	H E Linde	H E Linde	6/1
1888	**Theodolite**	W Warne	G Moore	L H Jones	5/2
1889	**Tragedy**	Mr T Beasley	T G Gordon	J H Greer	3/1
1890	**Kentish Fire**	M Dawson	R Meredith	M A Maher	100/8
1891	**Narraghmore**	Mr T Beasley	C Archer	J D Wardell	4/5
1892	**Roy Neil**	M Dawson	R Meredith	R M Delamere	5/1
1893	**Bowline**	M Dawson	R Meredith	M A Maher	8/1
1894	**Blairfinde**	W T Garrett	S Darling	J Gubbins	2/1
1895	**Portmarnock**	W Clayton	S Jeffery	Capt J Machell	2/5
1896	**Gulsalberk**	A Aylin	S Jeffery	C J Blake	6/1
1897	**Wales**	T Fiely	W P Cullen	W P Cullen	4/1
1898	**Noble Howard**	T Moran	R Exshaw	S M Nolan	7/2
1899	**Oppressor**	A Anthony	S C Jeffery	T L Plunkett	4/7
1900	**Gallinaria**	Mr G W Lushington	D McNally	E Loder	6/1
1901	**Carrigavalla**	A Anthony	D McNally	A Summers	5/1
1902	**St Brendan**	D Condon	M Dawson	James Daly	3/1
1903	**Lord Rossmore**	J Dillon	J Fallon	A P Cunliffe	6/4
1904	**Royal Arch**	F Morgan	M Dawson	James Daly	5/2
1905	**Flax Park**	P Hughes	J Dunne	P J Dunne	5/1
1906	**Killeagh**	C Aylin	M Dawson	J Lowry	100/7
1907	**Orby**	W Bullock	F McCabe	R Croker	1/10
1908	**Wild Bouquet**	P Hughes	J Dunne	Sir E C Cochrane	6/1
1909	**Bachelor's Double**	A Sharples	M Dawson	J Lowry	Evens
1910	**Aviator**	John Doyle	P Behan	J Lonsdale	9/2
1911	**Shanballymore**	John Doyle	J Dwyer	J Kelly	6/1
1912	**Civility**	D Maher	B Kirby	J Reese	5/1
1913	**Bachelor's Wedding**	S Donoghue	H S Persse	Sir W E Nelson	6/4
1914	**Land of Song**	S Donoghue	H S Persse	E T Paterson	3/1
1915	**Ballaghtobin**	W Barrett	J Hunter	Lord Decies	7/2
1916	**Furore**	H Robbins	V Tabor	H Ellis	2/1
1917	**First Flier**	W Barrett	J J Parkinson	J J Parkinson	6/1
1918	**King John**	H Beasley	P P Gilpin	G Loder	1/3
1919	**Loch Lomond**	E M Quirke	J J Parkinson	Miss Cowhy	3/1
1920	**He Goes**	F Templeman	J Butters	H Whitworth	3/1
1921	**Ballyheron**	M Wing	J Hunter	R B Charteris	7/1
1922	**Spike Island**	G Archibald	P P Gilpin	G Loder	Evens
1923	**Waygood**	M Wing	W Halsey	W Raphael	6/1
1924	**Haine**	Jos Canty	C Davis	C F Kenyon	Evens
	Zodiac	G Archibald	P P Gilpin	G Loder	3/1
1925	**Zionist**	H Beasley	R C Dawson	HH Aga Khan	5/2
1926	**Embargo**	S Donoghue	C Bartholomew Jun	Maharaja of Rajpipla	4/5
1927	**Knight of the Grail**	M Beary	R Farquharson	Sir D Broughton	3/1
1928	**Baytown**	F Fox	N Scobie	Sir C Hyde	4/1
1929	**Kopi**	F N Winter	W Earl	S B Joel	4/5
1930	**Rock Star**	M Wing	W Nightingall	Sir M Wilson	5/1
1931	**Sea Serpent**	Jos Canty	P Behan	H S Gray	5/2
1932	**Dastur**	M Beary	Frank Butters	HH Aga Khan	4/7
1933	**Harinero**	C Ray	R C Dawson	W Barnett	4/1
1934	**Primero**	C Ray	R C Dawson	W Barnett	5/2
	Patriot King	G Bezant	F Pratt	J A de Rothschild	2/1
1935	**Museum**	S Donoghue	J T Rogers	Sir V Sassoon	100/8
1936	**Raeburn**	T Burns	J Lawson	S D Hollingsworth	8/1
1937	**Phideas**	S Donoghue	J T Rogers	Sir V Sassoon	4/7
1938	**Rosewell**	M Wing	A J Blake	D Sullivan	2/1
1939	**Mondragon**	Jos Canty	Jos Canty	P J Ruttledge	100/8
1940	**Turkhan**	C Smirke	Frank Butters	HH Aga Khan	4/11

Shergar won the 1981 Irish Derby with Lester Piggott aboard to complete a fine double. He also won that year's Derby with the young Walter Swinburn, shown here.

		Jockey	Trainer	Owner	Odds
1941	**Sol Oriens**	G Wells	A J Blake	J Dillon	9/4
1942	**Windsor Slipper**	M Wing	M Collins	J McGrath	2/7
1943	**The Phoenix**	Jos Canty	F S Myerscough	F S Myerscough	2/5
1944	**Slide On**	J Moylan	R Fetherstonhaugh	D McCalmont	4/7
1945	**Piccadilly**	J Moylan	R Fetherstonhaugh	D McCalmont	25/1
1946	**Bright News**	M Wing	D Rogers	J McVey Jnr	100/8
1947	**Sayajirao**	E Britt	F Armstrong	Maharaja of Baroda	Evens
1948	**Nathoo**	W R Johnstone	Frank Butters	HH Aga Khan	7/2
1949	**Hindostan**	W R Johnstone	Frank Butters	HH Aga Khan	7/1
1950	**Dark Warrior**	J W Thompson	P Prendergast	F More O'Ferrall	4/1
1951	**Fraise du Bois II**	C Smirke	H Wragg	Begum Aga Khan	5/2
1952	**Thirteen of Diamonds**	J Mullane	P Prendergast	A L Hawkins	10/1
1953	**Chamier**	W Rickaby	M V O'Brien	Mrs F L Vickerman	5/4
1954	**Zarathustra**	P Powell Jnr	M Hurley	T Gray	50/1
1955	**Panaslipper**	J Eddery	S McGrath	J McGrath	4/1
1956	**Talgo**	E Mercer	H Wragg	G A Oldham	9/2
1957	**Ballymoss**	T P Burns	M V O'Brien	J McShain	4/9
1958	**Sindon**	L Ward	M Dawson	Mrs A B Biddle	100/8
1959	**Fidalgo**	J Mercer	H Wragg	G A Oldham	1/2
1960	**Chamour**	G Bougoure	A S O'Brien	F W Burmann	3/1
1961	**Your Highness**	H Holmes	H Cottrill	Mrs S Joel	33/1
1962	**Tambourine II**	R Poincelet	E Pollet	Mrs H E Jackson	15/2
1963	**Ragusa**	G Bougoure	P Prendergast	J R Mullion	100/7
1964	**Santa Claus**	W Burke	J M Rogers	J Ismay	4/7
1965	**Meadow Court**	L Piggott	P Prendergast	G M Bell	11/10
1966	**Sodium**	F Durr	G Todd	R Sigtia	13/2
1967	**Ribocco**	L Piggott	R F Johnson Houghton	C W Engelhard	5/2
1968	**Ribero**	L Piggott	R F Johnson Houghton	C W Engelhard	100/6
1969	**Prince Regent**	G Lewis	E Pollet	Comtesse de la Valdene	7/2
1970	**Nijinsky**	L Ward	M V O'Brien	C W Engelhard	4/11
1971	**Irish Ball**	A Gilbert	P Lallie	E Littler	7/2
1972	**Steel Pulse**	W Williamson	A Breasley	R Tikkoo	16/1
1973	**Weavers' Hall**	G McGrath	S McGrath	S McGrath	33/1
1974	**English Prince**	Y Saint-Martin	P Walwyn	Mrs V Hue-Williams	8/1
1975	**Grundy**	P Eddery	P Walwyn	C Vittadini	9/10
1976	**Malacate**	P Paquet	F Boutin	Mrs M F Berger	5/1
1977	**The Minstrel**	L Piggott	M V O'Brien	R Sangster	11/10
1978	**Shirley Heights**	G Starkey	J Dunlop	Lord Halifax	5/4
1979	**Troy**	W Carson	W R Hern	Sir M Sobell	4/9
1980	**Tyrnavos**	A Murray	B Hobbs	G Cambanis	25/1

		Jockey	Trainer	Owner	Odds
1981	**Shergar**	L Piggott	M Stoute	HH Aga Khan	1/3
1982	**Assert**	C Roche	D V O'Brien	R Sangster	4/7
1983	**Shareef Dancer**	W R Swinburn	M Stoute	M Al-Maktoum	8/1
1984	**El Gran Senor**	P Eddery	M V O'Brien	R Sangster	2/7
1985	**Law Society**	P Eddery	M V O'Brien	S Niarchos	15/8
1986	**Shahrastani**	W R Swinburn	M Stoute	HH Aga Khan	Evens
1987	**Sir Harry Lewis**	J Reid	B Hills	H Kaskel	6/1
1988	**Kahyasi**	R Cochrane	L Cumani	HH Aga Khan	4/5
1989	**Old Vic**	S Cauthen	H Cecil	Sheikh Mohammed	4/11
1990	**Salsabil**	W Carson	J Dunlop	H Al-Maktoum	11/4
1991	**Generous**	A Munro	P Cole	F Salman	Evens
1992	**St Jovite**	C Roche	J Bolger	Mrs V K Payson	7/2

The Eclipse Stakes

When Sandown Park was founded by General Owen Williams and his brother Hwfa in 1875 as the first of the 'drawing room' courses which excluded hooligans and made racing safe for women, General Williams knew that the Royal patronage of his friend the Prince of Wales was not enough to secure a fickle future. He needed a top-class race and persuaded the Prince's friend Leopold de Rothschild to put up the money for the Eclipse Stakes.

De Rothschild duly stumped up and the race was first run in 1886, worth £10,000 at a time when the Derby was worth only £4,600.

The richest race ever run in Britain was won by *Bendigo,* owned by Major Hedworth T.Barclay, known to his many friends as 'Buck'. The Eclipse attracted class fields from its inception, among *Bendigo's* victims was *St Gatien,* the 1884 Derby winner. *Ayrshire,* an easy winner of the Derby in 1888, won the Eclipse the following year. *Orme* was the first dual winner, *Diamond Jubilee* was a Triple Crown and Eclipse winner for the Prince of Wales in 1900 but the best field was in 1903 when *Ard Patrick* and *Sceptre* beat that year's Derby winner *Rock Sand* into third place, the three horses having won seven classics between them.

Since then, the roll of honour, as with the Derby, speaks for itself. Run over what many consider to be the optimum distance of a mile and a quarter at the ideal time of the year, the Eclipse will always be one of the finest events in the Calendar, as befits a race named after perhaps the greatest racehorse ever.

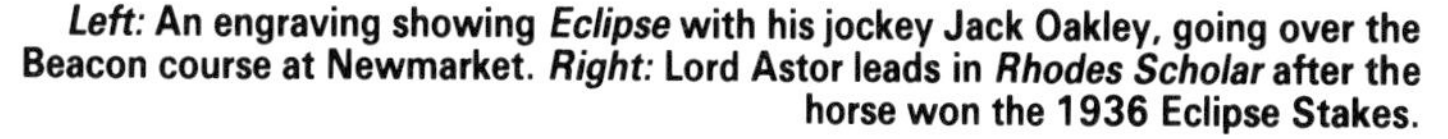

Left: **An engraving showing *Eclipse* with his jockey Jack Oakley, going over the Beacon course at Newmarket. *Right:* Lord Astor leads in *Rhodes Scholar* after the horse won the 1936 Eclipse Stakes.**

Run at Sandown Park over 1 mile 2 furlongs First Run 1886 Group 1

		Jockey	Trainer	Owner	Odds
1886	**Bendigo**	T Cannon	C Jousiffe	H T Barclay	6/4
1887	**No Race**				
1888	**Orbit**	T Cannon	J Porter	Duke of Westminster	9/4
1889	**Ayrshire**	F Barrett	G Dawson	Duke of Portland	4/5
1890	**No Race**				
1891	**Surefoot**	J Liddiard	G Moore	A W Merry	100/8
1892	**Orme**	G Barrett	J Porter	Duke of Westminster	5/4
1893	**Orme**	M Cannon	J Porter	Duke of Westminster	2/1
1894	**Isinglass**	T Loates	J Jewitt	H McCalmont	4/5
1895	**Le Justicier**	T French	W Webb	Baron A Schickler	6/1

		Jockey	Trainer	Owner	Odds
1896	**St Frusquin**	T Loates	A Hayhoe	L de Rothschild	1/2
1897	**Persimmon**	J Watts	R Marsh	HRH Prince of Wales	12/100
1898	**Velasquez**	C Wood	W Walters Jnr	Lord Rosebery	9/2
1899	**Flying Fox**	M Cannon	J Porter	Duke of Westminster	14/100
1900	**Diamond Jubilee**	H Jones	R Marsh	HRH Prince of Wales	7/4
1901	**Epsom Lad**	S Gomez	L Alvarez	J Buchanan	7/1
1902	**Cheers**	D Maher	W Goodwin	Duke of Devonshire	20/1
1903	**Ard Patrick**	O Madden	S Darling	J Gubbins	5/1
1904	**Darley Dale**	D Maher	J Porter	Duke of Portland	6/1
1905	**Val d'Or**	G Stern	R Denman	E Blanc	3/1
1906	**Llangibby**	D Maher	P P Gilpin	L Neumann	2/1
1907	**Lally**	B Dillon	T Lewis	W B Purefoy	5/1
1908	**Your Majesty**	Wal Griggs	C Morton	J B Joel	100/8
1909	**Bayardo**	D Maher	A Taylor Jnr	A W Cox	40/85
1910	**Lemberg**	B Dillon	A Taylor Jnr	A W Cox	5/4
	Neil Gow	D Maher	P Peck	Lord Rosebery	6/4
1911	**Swynford**	F Wootton	G Lambton	Lord Derby	10/11
1912	**Prince Palatine**	F O'Neill	H Beardsley	T Pilkington	5/1
1913	**Tracery**	A Whalley	J Watson	A Belmont	1/2
1914	**Hapsburg**	C Foy	W Halsey	Sir E Cassel	10/1
1915/18	**No Race**				
1919	**Buchan**	J Childs	A Taylor Jnr	W Astor	2/7
1920	**Buchan**	F Bullock	A Taylor Jnr	Lord Astor	5/2
1921	**Craig an Eran**	F Bullock	A Taylor Jnr	Lord Astor	2/7
1922	**Golden Myth**	C Elliott	J Jarvis	Sir G Bullough	8/1
1923	**Saltash**	J Brennan	A Taylor Jnr	Lord Astor	20/1
1924	**Polyphontes**	W McLachlan	W Earl	S B Joel	7/1
1925	**Polyphontes**	H Wragg	W Earl	S B Joel	11/4
1926	**Coronach**	J Childs	F Darling	Lord Woolavington	2/5
1927	**Colorado**	T Weston	Frank Butters	Lord Derby	10/11
1928	**Fairway**	T Weston	Frank Butters	Lord Derby	9/2

Coronach **leads the field during the 1926 Eclipse Stakes at Sandown Park.**

Lord Rosebery's *Blue Peter*, with E.Smith up, overtakes Mr W.Murray's *Glen Loan* to win the 1939 Eclipse Stakes.

		Jockey	Trainer	Owner	Odds
1929	**Royal Minstrel**	J Childs	C Boyd-Rochfort	J H Whitney	9/2
1930	**Rustom Pasha**	H Wragg	R C Dawson	HH Aga Khan	4/1
1931	**Caerleon**	T Weston	G Lambton	Lord Derby	25/1
1932	**Miracle**	H Wragg	J Jarvis	Lord Rosebery	10/1
1933	**Loaningdale**	J Childs	C Boyd-Rochfort	G Wilson	9/2
1934	**King Salmon**	H Wragg	O Bell	Sir R Brooke	4/1
1935	**Windsor Lad**	C Smirke	M Marsh	M Benson	4/7
1936	**Rhodes Scholar**	R Dick	J Lawson	Lord Astor	8/11
1937	**Boswell**	P Beasley	C Boyd-Rochfort	W Woodward	20/1
1938	**Pasch**	G Richards	F Darling	H E Morriss	13/8
1939	**Blue Peter**	E Smith	J Jarvis	Lord Rosebery	2/7
1940/45	**No Race**				
1946	**Gulf Stream**	H Wragg	W Earl	Lord Derby	8/13
1947	**Migoli**	C Smirke	Frank Butters	HH Aga Khan	7/2
1948	**Petition**	K Gethin	Frank Butters	Sir A Butt	8/1
1949	**Djeddah**	C Elliott	C Semblat	M Boussac	6/4
1950	**Flocon**	F Palmer	P Carter	Baron G de Waldner	100/9
1951	**Mystery iX**	L Piggott	P Carter	Mme E Esmond	100/8
1952	**Tulyar**	C Smirke	M Marsh	HH Aga Khan	1/3
1953	**Argur**	C Elliott	J Glynn	M Boussac	100/9
1954	**King of the Tudors**	K Gethin	W Stephenson	F Dennis	9/2
1955	**Darius**	L Piggott	H Wragg	Sir P Loraine	11/10
1956	**Tropique**	P Blanc	G Watson	Baron G de Rothschild	3/1
1957	**Arctic Explorer**	L Piggott	N Murless	G Loder	100/30
1958	**Ballymoss**	A Breasley	M V O'Brien	J McShain	8/11
1959	**Saint Crespin III**	G Moore	A Head	Prince Aly Khan	5/2
1960	**Javelot**	F Palmer	P Carter	Baron G de Waldner	4/1
1961	**St Paddy**	L Piggott	N Murless	Sir V Sassoon	2/13
1962	**Henry the Seventh**	E Hide	W Elsey	H J Joel	8/11
1963	**Khalkis**	G Bougoure	P Prendergast	Lord Elveden	7/4
1964	**Ragusa**	G Bougoure	P Prendergast	J R Mullion	4/6
1965	**Canisbay**	S Clayton	C Boyd-Rochfort	HM The Queen	20/1
1966	**Pieces of Eight**	L Piggott	M V O'Brien	Comtesse de la Valdene	15/2
1967	**Busted**	W Rickaby	N Murless	S Joel	8/1
1968	**Royal Palace**	A Barclay	N Murless	H J Joel	9/4

Royal Palace, **seen here winning the 1968 King George VI and Queen Elizabeth Stakes, also won the Eclipse Stakes that year.**

		Jockey	Trainer	Owner	Odds
1969	**Wolver Hollow**	L Piggott	H Cecil	Mrs C O Iselin	8/1
1970	**Connaught**	A Barclay	N Murless	H J Joel	5/4
1971	**Mill Reef**	G Lewis	I Balding	P Mellon	5/4
1972	**Brigadier Gerard**	J Mercer	W R Hern	Mrs J Hislop	4/11
1973	**Scottish Rifle**	R Hutchinson	J Dunlop	A J Struthers	15/8
1974	**Coup de Feu**	P Eddery	D Sasse	F Sasse	33/1
1975	**Star Appeal**	G Starkey	T Grieper	W Zeitelhack	20/1
1976	**Wollow**	G Dettori	H Cecil	C d'Alessio	9/4
1977	**Artaius**	L Piggott	M V O'Brien	Mrs G Getty II	9/2
1978	**Gunner B**	J Mercer	H Cecil	Mrs P Barratt	7/4
1979	**Dickens Hill**	A Murray	M O'Toole	Mme J Binet	7/4
1980	**Ela-Mana-Mou**	W Carson	W R Hern	S Weinstock	85/40
1981	**Master Willie**	P Waldron	H Candy	R Barnett	6/4
1982	**Kalaglow**	G Starkey	G Harwood	A Ward	11/10
1983	**Solford**	P Eddery	M V O'Brien	R Sangster	3/1
1984	**Sadler's Wells**	P Eddery	M V O'Brien	R Sangster	11/4
1985	**Pebbles**	S Cauthen	C Brittain	Sheikh Mohammed	7/2
1986	**Dancing Brave**	G Starkey	G Harwood	K Abdulla	4/9
1987	**Mtoto**	M Roberts	A Stewart	A Al-Maktoum	6/1
1988	**Mtoto**	M Roberts	A Stewart	A Al-Maktoum	6/4
1989	**Nashwan**	W Carson	W R Hern	H Al Maktoum	2/5
1990	**Elmaamul**	W Carson	W R Hern	H Al-Maktoum	13/2
1991	**Environment Friend**	G Duffield	J Fanshawe	W Gredley	28/1
1992	**Kooyonga**	W J O'Connor	M Kauntze	M Haga	7/2

Run at Kempton Park in 1973

Lancashire Oaks

The Lancashire Oaks was founded more in optimism than in hope as the war clouds were gathering in 1939 and first run at the Old Castle Irwell course in Manchester, then famed for the mist shrouded November Handicap at the bitter end of the flat season.

The track was closed in 1941 for the duration of the war and did not reopen until 1947. The first significant winner of the Lancashire Oaks was *Eyewash* in 1949, neatly named by *Blue Peter* out of *All Moonshine*. *Eyewash* became the dam of ten winners including *Collyria* winner of the Park Hill Stakes at Doncaster in 1959.

Mil's Bomb, who won in 1974 also took the Park Hill before being a very unlucky loser of the Sun Chariot Stakes at Newmarket and winning the Doonside Cup at four, while the well dubbed *One Over Parr* (by *Reform* out of *Seventh Bride* by *Royal Record*) completed the Cheshire Oaks — Lancashire Oaks double in 1975.

The best winners in recent times have been *Vielle*, who won the Nassau

Stakes at Goodwood and was second in the Oaks in 1980, and *Roseate Tern* who also won the Yorkshire Oaks and finished third in the Oaks at Epsom to the subsequently disqualifed *Aliysa* in 1989.

The race has been run at Haydock since the closure of Manchester in 1963.

Run at Haydock Park over 1 mile 4 furlongs for fillies First Run 1939 Group 3

		Jockey	Trainer	Owner	Odds
1939	**Cestria**	H Wragg	W R Jarvis	Sir R Brooke	2/1
1940/46	**No Race**				
1947	**Smoke Screen**	D Smith	W Earl	Lord Derby	5/2
1948	**Young Entry**	W Nevett	C Boyd-Rochfort	HM The King	5/4
1949	**Eyewash**	J Caldwell	P Beasley	M W Wickham-Boynton	11/8
1950	**Dutch Clover**	E Smith	P Beasley	G C Plummer	Evens
1951	**Dollarina**	P Evans	G Brooke	Maj L B Holliday	8/1
1952	**Stream of Light**	W H Carr	C Boyd-Rochfort	HM The Queen	Evens
1953	**Harvest Festival**	W Nevett	R Poole	J H Paine	100/8
1954	**Blue Prelude**	G Littlewood	W Bellerby	Mrs S L Glover	15/2
1955	**Jenny Lind**	E Britt	C Elsey	H J Joel	11/2
1956	**Hustle**	E Smith	T E Leader	H J Joel	11/2
1957	**Lobelia**	E Smith	H Leader	A Plesch	7/4
1958	**St Lucia**	G Lewis	P Hastings-Bass	Lord Sefton	11/10
1959	**Noble Lassie**	D Smith	W R Hern	Maj L B Holliday	20/1
1960	**Chota Hazri**	D Smith	H Wragg	Sir P Loraine	3/1
1961	**Irristable**	D Smith	G Brooke	R F Dennis	2/1
1962	**French Cream**	D Smith	G Brooke	R F Dennis	10/1
1963	**Red Chorus**	L Piggott	N Murless	J R Hindley	9/4
1964	**No Race**				
1965	**Without Reproach**	E Hide	W Elsey	E Hall	9/4
1966	**Royal Flirt**	D Smith	G Brooke	W M Lovejoy Jnr	9/2
1967	**The Nun**	J Mercer	W R Hern	J J Astor	9/2
1968	**Bringley**	B Taylor	H Leader	R Midwood	9/4
1969	**Gambola**	W Williamson	G Smyth	Lady Z Wernher	4/9
1970	**Amphora**	J Gorton	B Hobbs	J W Weston-Evans	11/10
1971	**Maina**	L Piggott	N Murless	H J Joel	1/2
1972	**Star Ship**	A Murray	H R Price	C St George	4/6
1973	**Istiea**	P Eddery	H Wragg	R More O'Ferrall	6/1
1974	**Mil's Bomb**	G Lewis	N Murless	L Freedman	85/40
1975	**One Over Parr**	P Eddery	P Walwyn	L Freedman	3/1
1976	**Centrocon**	P Waldron	H Candy	W Barnett	5/1
1977	**Busaca**	P Eddery	P Walwyn	Countess M Esterhazy	1/2
1978	**Princess Eboli**	G Lewis	B Hobbs	T F Blackwell	13/2
1979	**Reprocolor**	G Starkey	M Stoute	Helena Springfield Ltd	9/2
1980	**Vielle**	P Cook	B Hobbs	T F Blackwell	4/5
1981	**Rhein Bridge**	E Hide	J W Watts	R Sangster	10/1
1982	**Sing Softly**	L Piggott	H Cecil	Mrs P Harris	5/4
1983	**Give Thanks**	D Gillespie	J Bolger	Mrs O White	4/1
1984	**Sandy Island**	L Piggott	H Cecil	Lord H de Walden	5/6
1985	**Graecia Magna**	G Starkey	G Harwood	A Christodoulou	5/4
1986	**Park Express**	J Reid	J Bolger	P H Burns	13/2
1987	**Three Tails**	T Ives	J Dunlop	Sheikh Mohammed	6/4
1988	**Andaleeb**	P Eddery	J Tree	K Abdulla	100/30
1989	**Roseate Tern**	T Ives	W R Hern	Lord Carnarvon	7/4
1990	**Pharian**	L Dettori	C Brittain	S Manana	14/1
1991	**Patricia**	G Carter	H Cecil	C St George	11/1
1992	**Niodini**	Paul Eddery	M Stoute	Sheikh Mohammed	7/1

Run at Manchester 1939-1963 over 1 mile 3 furlongs.
For 3 year-old fillies only 1939-1990

The Princess of Wales's Stakes

The race was founded in 1894 in honour of the Princess Alexandra of Denmark, who became Princess of Wales on her marriage to the future Edward VII in 1862. The first winner *Isinglass* collected £1,916 for his victory in the hands of Tommy Loates.

The Princess of Wales's Stakes has always attracted select and high class fields. Another Triple Crown winner, *Rock Sand* won in 1904 and the neatly named *Lance Chest* took the race in successive years before the World War One darkened Europe for nearly half a decade. *Spearmint* had won the Derby for Major Eustace Loder, who also owned and bred *Pretty Polly*, and *Lance Chest* was by *Spearmint* out of *Chestnut Sunday*.

Lance Chest was no classic contender, but he had the pace to beat *Tagalie*, the last, and the only grey filly to win the Derby at Epsom.

Continuing standards resulted in the race being upgraded to Group 2 in 1978, the quality underlined by the victories of such as *Light Cavalry*, *Height of Fashion*, *Unfuwain* and *Rock Hopper*.

Run at Newmarket over 1 mile 4 furlongs First Run 1894 Group 2

		Jockey	Trainer	Owner	Odds
1894	**Isinglass**	T Loates	J Jewitt	H McCalmont	100/12
1895	**Le Var**	M Cannon	J Porter	Sir F Johnstone	5/6
1896	**St Frusquin**	T Loates	A Hayhoe	L de Rothschild	5/2
1897	**Velasquez**	J Watts	W Walters Jnr	Lord Rosebery	85/40
1898	**Goletta**	T Loates	A Hayhoe	L de Rothschild	100/8
1899	**Flying Fox**	M Cannon	J Porter	Duke of Westminster	4/6
1900	**Merry Gal**	J Reiff	W T Robinson	W Hall-Walker	100/30
1901	**Epsom Lad**	S Gomez	L Alvarez	J Buchanan	10/1
1902	**Veles**	J H Martin	Robert Sherwood Jnr	Sir R W Griffith	100/8
1903	**Ard Patrick**	M Cannon	S Darling	J Gubbins	1/2
1904	**Rock Sand**	D Maher	G Blackwell	Sir J Miller	6/100
1905	**St Denis**	D Maher	C Peck	S B Joel	11/4
1906	**Dinneford**	O Madden	A Taylor Jnr	R Walker	7/4
1907	**Polymelus**	D Maher	C Peck	S B Joel	7/4
1908	**Queen's Advocate**	O Madden	A Taylor Jnr	R Walker	2/1
1909	**Dark Ronald**	B Lynham	J A Clement	A Bailey	9/1
1910	**Ulster King**	S Donoghue	T Lewis	E A Wigan	Evens
1911	**Swynford**	F Wootton	G Lambton	Lord Derby	3/1
1912	**Lance Chest**	Wal Griggs	P P Gilpin	E Loder	20/1
1913	**Lance Chest**	Wal Griggs	P P Gilpin	E Loder	100/9
1914	**The Curragh**	J Clark	A Taylor Jnr	Lord Cadogan	Evens
1915	**Rossendale**	H Jones	A T Hazleton	Sir J Thursby	9/2
1916	**Nassovian**	N Spear	J Butters	J Sanford	2/5
1917	**No Race**				
1918	**Blink**	V Smyth	A Taylor Jnr	W Astor	1/5
1919	**Buchan**	J Childs	A Taylor Jnr	W Astor	1/10
1920	**Attilius**	G Hulme	R C Dawson	Sir W Nelson	11/2
1921	**Orpheus**	H Gray	F Leach	Sir H Cunliffe-Owen	11/10
1922	**Blandford**	G Hulme	R C Dawson	R C Dawson	11/10
1923	**Triumph**	J Childs	J Watson	A de Rothschild	7/1
1924	**Salmon Trout**	V Smyth	R C Dawson	HH Aga Khan	5/1
1925	**Solario**	J Childs	R Day	Sir J Rutherford	11/4
1926	**Tournesol**	J Childs	A Taylor Jnr	M Calmann	10/1
1927	**Colorado**	T Weston	Frank Butters	Lord Derby	4/1
1928	**Tourist**	J Dines	R Day	Sir A Bailey	100/6

Three furlongs from home in the 1939 Princess of Wales's Stakes. In the centre, R.Perryman is shaking up Lord Derby's *Heliopolis* before winning by three lengths. On the right is *Comptroller*, ridden by Gordon Richards, and on the left is *Challenge* with D.Smith up.

		Jockey	Trainer	Owner	Odds
1929	**Fairway**	T Weston	Frank Butters	Lord Derby	1/4
1930	**Press Gang**	F Fox	F Darling	Lord Woolavington	15/8
1931	**The Recorder**	F Fox	F Darling	J A Dewar	10/11
	Shell Transport	R Dick	J Lawson	W M Cazelet	6/1
1932	**Jacopo**	J Childs	C Boyd-Rochfort	M Field	4/1
1933	**Raymond**	G Richards	J Lawson	Sir A Bailey	7/1
1934	**Bright Bird**	F Fox	J Lawson	Lord Astor	7/4
1935	**Fairbairn**	G Richards	V Gilpin	G Loder	5/2
1936	**Taj Akbar**	C Smirke	Frank Butters	HH Aga Khan	4/1
1937	**Flares**	R A Jones	C Boyd-Rochfort	W Woodward	11/2
1938	**Pound Foolish**	G Richards	J Lawson	Lord Astor	3/1
1939	**Heliopolis**	R Perryman	W Earl	Lord Derby	4/6
1940/44	**No Race**				
1945	**Stirling Castle**	E Smith	J Lawson	A E Saunders	9/2
1946	**Airborne**	T Lowrey	R Perryman	J E Ferguson	9/4
1947	**Nirgal**	C Elliott	C Semblat	M Bousaac	13/8
1948	**Alycidon**	D Smith	W Earl	Lord Derby	100/8
1949	**Dogger Bank**	D Smith	W Earl	Lord Derby	100/9
1950	**Double Eclipse**	W H Carr	C Boyd-Rochfort	Lady Z Wernher	6/5
1951	**Pardal**	W R Johnstone	C Semblat	M Boussac	Evens
1952	**Zucchero**	L Piggott	W Payne	G Rolls	20/1
1953	**Rawson**	K Gethin	S Wootton	S Wootton	3/1
1954	**Woodcut**	E Smith	C Boyd-Rochfort	R W Sharples	5/1
1955	**Cobetto**	J Massard	C Semblat	Prince Aly Khan	9/1
1956	**Cash and Courage**	E Smith	S Hall	T West	9/4
1957	**Wake Up!**	D Smith	J F Watts	Lord Derby	9/4
1958	**Miner's Lamp**	W H Carr	C Boyd-Rochfort	HM The Queen	3/1
1959	**Primera**	L Piggott	N Murless	C Dracoulis	4/5
1960	**Primera**	L Piggott	N Murless	S Joel	9/4
1961	**Apostle**	L Piggott	S Ingham	Mrs D Montagu	4/6
1962	**Silver Cloud**	E Smith	J Jarvis	T Blackwell	5/1
1963	**Trafalgar**	A Breasley	G Richards	R F Watson	15/2
1964	**Carrack**	D Cullen	J Oxley	R D Hollingsworth	5/1
1965	**Lomond**	E Eldin	R Jarvis	W Ruane	10/1
1966	**Lomond**	E Eldin	R Jarvis	W Ruane	3/1
1967	**Hopeful Venture**	G Moore	N Murless	HM The Queen	13/8
1968	**Mount Athos**	R Hutchinson	J Dunlop	A J Struthers	3/1
1969	**Harmony Hall**	W Carson	G Smyth	Sir H Wernher	1/3
1970	**Prince Consort**	A Barclay	N Murless	H J Joel	2/1
1971	**Lupe**	G Lewis	N Murless	Mrs S Joel	8/13
1972	**Falkland**	G Starkey	H Cecil	Lord H de Walden	5/2
1973	**Our Mirage**	F Durr	B Hills	Mrs S Enfield	15/8
1974	**Buoy**	J Mercer	W R Hern	R D Hollingsworth	2/1
1975	**Libra's Rib**	W Carson	R F Johnson Houghton	Mrs J Rogers	8/1
1976	**Smuggler**	E Johnson	W R Hern	Lord Porchester	11/4
1977	**Lord Helpus**	L Piggott	B Hills	M Standen	5/1
1978	**Pollerton**	L Piggott	H Thomson Jones	Mrs R Vereker	7/1
1979	**Milford**	W Carson	W R Hern	HM The Queen	11/8
1980	**Nicholas Bill**	P Waldron	H Candy	W Barnett	12/1
1981	**Light Cavalry**	L Piggott	H Cecil	H J Joel	11/4
1982	**Height of Fashion**	W Carson	W R Hern	HM The Queen	4/1
1983	**Quilted**	W Newnes	M O'Toole	J Fluor	7/2
1984	**Head for Heights**	L Piggott	W R Hern	Sheikh Mohammed	100/30
1985	**Petoski**	W Carson	W R Hern	Lady Beaverbrook	8/1
1986	**Shardari**	W R Swinburn	M Stoute	HH Aga Khan	5/2
1987	**Celestial Storm**	R Cochrane	L Cumani	R Duchossois	13/8
1988	**Unfuwain**	W Carson	W R Hern	H Al-Maktoum	6/4
1989	**Carroll House**	W R Swinburn	M Jarvis	A Balzarini	10/1
1990	**Sapience**	P Eddery	J Fitzgerald	W H O'Gorman	11/2
1991	**Rock Hopper**	P Eddery	M Stoute	M Al-Maktoum	4/6
1992	**Saddlers' Hall**	P Eddery	M Stoute	Lord Weinstock	4/7

Run over 1 mile 1894-1901

The Cherry Hinton Stakes

The Cherry Hinton, for two-year-old fillies only and run over the last six furlongs of the Bunbury Mile at the Newmarket July Meeting, has provided classic winners notably *Pia* (Oaks), *Mysterious* (1,000 Guineas and Oaks) and *Diminuendo* (Oaks), but is usually won by the speedy type of filly examplified by *Devon Ditty*, winner in 1978 in addition to the Lowther Stakes at York, the Flying Childers Stakes at Doncaster and the Cheveley Park Stakes at Newmarket.

Eddie Hide aboard *Pia*, winner of the 1966 Cherry Hinton Stakes.

Run at Newmarket over 6 furlongs for 2 year-old fillies First Run 1947 Group 3

		Jockey	Trainer	Owner	Odds
1947	**Great Fun**	W H Carr	C Boyd-Rochfort	Sir H de Trafford	10/1
1948	**Ballisland**	C Smirke	R Warden	Lady M Fitzwilliam	2/1
1949	**Diableretta**	C Smirke	Frank Butters	HH Aga Khan	1/3
1950	**Marteline**	C Smirke	M Marsh	H E Morriss	20/1
1951	**Tikva**	C Elliott	E Williams	Mts I Esdaile	7/4
1952	**Omelia**	C Smirke	M Marsh	HH Aga Khan	4/7
	Pirouette	F Durr	W Smyth	Lady Irwin	5/1
1953	**Eastern Glamour**	G Richards	V Smyth	J R Mullion	10/1
1954	**Lucy Lufton**	W Snaith	F Armstrong	Sir R Brooke	11/4
1955	**No Race**				
1956	**Colonel's Lady**	E Smith	R Day	R Cohen	2/15

		Jockey	Trainer	Owner	Odds
1957	**Munch**	D Smith	R Jarvis	J Bartholomew	8/13
1958	**Fan Light**	E Mercer	G Colling	Lord Irwin	2/5
1959	**Panga**	E Smith	B van Cutsem	B van Cutsem	4/7
1960	**Sweet Solera**	W Rickaby	R Day	Mrs S Castello	4/5
1961	**Crepello's Daughter**	E Larkin	J Jarvis	J P Phillips	3/1
1962	**Tzigane**	A Breasley	G Richards	J Combe	13/8
1963	**Round Trip**	W Williamson	H Wragg	Mrs H Brown	5/1
1964	**Greengage**	A Breasley	G Richards	R F Watson	9/2
1965	**Chrona**	A Breasely	R F Johnson Houghton	H D H Wills	7/1
1966	**Pia**	E Hide	W Elsey	Countess M Batthyany	8/1
1967	**Cease Fire**	B Taylor	H Leader	Lord Willoughby de Broke	4/7
1968	**Symona**	G Starkey	H Leader	Mrs O H Hammond	2/1
1969	**Wild Wings**	R Hutchinson	J Dunlop	Duke of Norfolk	4/11
1970	**Hecla**	J Gorton	B Hobbs	H D H Wills	13/8
1971	**Padrona**	J Corton	D Smith	Lord Rosebery	7/2
1972	**Mysterious**	G Lewis	N Murless	G A Pope Jnr	5/4
1973	**Celestial Dawn**	B Taylor	J Winter	Mrs D McNab	4/1
1974	**Roussalka**	L Piggott	H Cecil	N Phillips	2/1
1975	**Everything Nice**	G Lewis	B Hobbs	P Sinodhinos	33/1
1976	**Ampulla**	W Carson	C Brittain	M Lemos	10/11
1977	**Turkish Treasure**	L Piggott	M V O'Brien	R Sangster	2/5
1978	**Devon Ditty**	G Starkey	H Thomson Jones	Sir E McAlpine	15/8
1979	**Mrs Penny**	J Matthias	I Balding	E Kronfeld	11/1
1980	**Nasseem**	J Reid	R F Johnson Houghton	HH Aga Khan	100/30
1981	**Travel On**	J Mercer	P Walwyn	R A Patrick	25/1
1982	**Crime of Passion**	W Newnes	D Laing	C Wright	12/1
1983	**Chapel Cottage**	E Hide	M W Easterby	R Sangster	7/2
1984	**Top Socialite**	W R Swinburn	M Stoute	Tjo Tek Tan	14/1
1985	**Storm Star**	B Raymond	I Balding	Princess L Ruspoli	Evens
1986	**Forest Flower**	T Ives	I Balding	P Mellon	4/5
1987	**Diminuendo**	S Cauthen	H Cecil	Sheikh Mohammed	6/4
1988	**Kerrera**	W R Swinburn	M Stoute	Sheikh Mohammed	5/4
1989	**Chimes of Freedom**	S Cauthen	H Cecil	S Niarchos	4/9
1990	**Chicarica**	W R Swinburn	J Gosden	Sheikh Mohammed	9/4
1991	**Musicale**	S Cauthen	H Cecil	R Sangster	9/2
1992	**Sayyedati**	M Roberts	C Brittain	M Obaida	6/4

The Falmouth Stakes

The 6th Viscount Falmouth had an astonishing record of success as an owner-breeder. He took up racing in 1857, and enjoyed his first classic victory with *Hurricane* in the 1,000 Guineas of 1862. Fifteen more classic winners were to follow until Lord Falmouth retired from the Turf in 1883, including the Derby with *Kingcraft* in 1870 and *Silvio* in 1877.

The race named in his honour is a Group 2 event originally for three-year-old fillies only but opened to older horses when Child's Bank took over as sponsors in 1974, and the Falmouth became known as the Child Stakes. Since then the three-year-olds have mostly been in command, the only four-year-olds to win being *Duboff* in 1976, *Rose Above* in 1979, the dual winner *Sonic Lady* who completed her double in 1987, and *Gussy Marlowe* in 1992.

Child's withdrew their support in 1991 and the race became the Falmouth Stakes once more.

Run at Newmarket over 1 mile for fillies First Run 1911 Group 2

		Jockey	Trainer	Owner	Odds
1911	**Alice**	H Jones	W Waugh	Lord Falmouth	1/10
1912	**Saucy Vixen**	F Herbert	T Jenkins	W N McMillan	20/1
1913	**Queen's Parade**	E Piper	T Lewis	F Forester	3/1
1914	**First Spear**	J Clark	A Taylor Jnr	W Astor	4/7
1915	**Silver Tag**	S Donoghue	R C Dawson	E Hulton	1/2
1916	**Eos**	F Bullock	G Lambton	Lord D'Abernon	7/1
1917	**No Race**				
1918	**Herself**	F Fox	R Day	D Fraser	11/10
1919	**Tomatina**	V Smyth	A Taylor Jnr	W M Cazalet	4/1
1920	**Lady Ava**	J Childs	A Taylor Jnr	W M Cazelet	8/1
1921	**Blue Lady**	J Childs	A Taylor Jnr	J Watson	5/4
1922	**Leighon Tor**	S Donoghue	A Taylor Jnr	W M G Singer	–
1923	**Shrove**	C Elliott	D Waugh	Sir E Hulton	15/100
1924	**Maid of Bath**	J Childs	A Taylor Jnr	Lady J Douglas	9/4
1925	**Bar Sinister**	R A Jones	H Cottrill	Mrs S Whitburn	4/1
1926	**Glasheen**	J Childs	C Boyd-Rochfort	R B Charteris	6/4
1927	**Hunt the Slipper**	J Childs	C Boyd-Rochfort	C Boyd-Rochfort	6/1
1928	**Mara**	M Beary	R C Dawson	Lord Carnarvon	5/1
1929	**Point Duty**	H Jelliss	J Lawson	Lord Astor	4/1
1930	**Theresina**	M Beary	R C Dawson	HH Aga Khan	4/1

		Jockey	Trainer	Owner	Odds
1931	**Pisa**	T Weston	G Lambton	Lord Derby	3/1
1932	**Pennycross**	R Dick	J Lawson	Lord Astor	9/4
1933	**Eclair**	J Childs	C Boyd-Rochfort	M Field	9/2
1934	**Mis Tor**	R A Jones	J Lawson	Mrs W M G Singer	11/4
1935	**Coppelia**	H Wragg	F Templeman	Lord Hirst	7/2
1936	**Crested Crane**	R A Jones	J Jarvis	Sir L Phillips	100/7
1937	**Tumbrel**	G Richards	F Darling	Lord Lonsdale	5/2
1938	**La-Li**	C Smirke	Frank Butters	HH Aga Khan	3/1
1939	**Bountiful**	R A Jones	J Lawson	A R Cox	10/1
1940	**No Race**				
1941	**Commotion**	H Wragg	F Darling	J A Dewar	6/5
1942/44	**No Race**				
1945	**Sweet Cygnet**	C Elliott	T Rimell	H Leven	7/1
1946	**Wheedler**	C Richards	J Lawson	Lord Astor	2/1
1947	**Mermaid**	E Smith	J Jarvis	Lord Rosebery	5/4
1948	**Goblet**	G Richards	N Murless	F Darling	11/8
1949	**Suntime**	E Britt	M Marsh	J Musker	4/5
1950	**Val d'Assa**	S Smith	H S Persse	D McCalmont	20/1
1951	**Red Shoes**	E Smith	J E Watts	H J Joel	20/1
1952	**Queen of Light**	E Smith	J E Watts	H J Joel	11/2
1953	**Happy Laughter**	W Rickaby	J Jarvis	H D H Wills	5/2
1954	**Sundry**	D Smith	G Colling	Lord Derby	5/1
1955	**Gloria Nicky**	A Breasley	N Bertie	Mrs R Digby	2/7
1956	**Following Breeze**	W Rickaby	N Bertie	C Nicholson	5/4
1957	**Sylphide**	L Piggott	N Murless	T Lilley	11/2
1958	**Court One**	D Smith	N Murless	HM The Queen	6/1
1959	**Crystal Palace**	E Smith	T E Leader	H J Joel	15/8
1960	**Green Opal**	L Piggott	N Murless	G Loder	9/4
1961	**Aphrodita**	J Mercer	H Wragg	G A Oldham	4/6
1962	**Tournella**	W Rickaby	F Sutherland	Mrs E N Hall	11/4
1963	**Crevette**	D Smith	G Brooke	Lady V Butt	6/1
1964	**Alborada**	G Starkey	J Oxley	Lady Halifax	8/11
1965	**Pugnacity**	J Mercer	W Wharton	Maj L B Holliday	4/5
1966	**Chrona**	L Piggott	R F Johnson Houghton	H D H Willis	9/1
1967	**Resilience II**	B Taylor	H Leader	C Vittadini	10/1
1968	**Ileana**	R Hutchinson	H Wragg	G A Oldham	7/4
1969	**Vital Match**	L Piggott	H Blagrave	H Blagrave	30/100
1970	**Caprera**	R Hutchinson	H Wragg	G A Oldham	15/8
1971	**Favoletta**	B Taylor	H Wragg	R B Moller	6/4
1972	**Waterloo**	E Hide	J W Watts	Mrs R Stanley	2/5
1973	**Jacinth**	J Gorton	B Hobbs	Lady Butt	2/5
1974	**Himawari**	F Morby	R F Johnson Houghton	J Kashiyama	9/1
1975	**Sauceboat**	G Lewis	N Murless	J Hornung	6/1
1976	**Duboff**	E Hide	B Hills	Mrs C Radclyffe	16/1
1977	**River Dane**	A Gibert	A Paus	R Sangster	11/8
1978	**Cistus**	W Carson	W R Hern	Sir M Sobell	4/7
1979	**Rose Above**	W Carson	M Cunningham	J O'Reilly	100/30
1980	**Stumped**	G Duffield	B Hobbs	A S R Villar	5/1
1981	**Star Pastures**	P Eddery	J Hindley	R Sangster	11/2
1982	**Chalon**	L Piggott	H Cecil	M Riordan	8/15
1983	**Royal Heroine**	W R Swinburn	M Stoute	R Sangster	2/1
1984	**Meis El-Reem**	S Cauthen	O Douieb	B Choucair	6/1
1985	**Al Bahathri**	A Murray	H Thomson Jones	H Al-Maktoum	6/5
1986	**Sonic Lady**	W R Swinburn	M Stoute	Sheikh Mohammed	4/9
1987	**Sonic Lady**	W R Swinburn	M Stoute	Sheikh Mohammed	11/10
1988	**Inchmurrin**	Paul Eddery	G Wragg	Sir P Oppenheimer	4/1
1989	**Magic Gleam**	P Eddery	A Scott	M Al-Maktoum	15/8
1990	**Chimes of Freedom**	S Cauthen	H Cecil	S Niarchos	4/6
1991	**Only Yours**	M Roberts	R Hannon	Mrs M Butcher	10/1
1992	**Gussy Marlowe**	M Roberts	C Brittain	Nrs J Van Geest	7/1

For 3 year-old fillies only 1911-1973.
Run as the Child Stakes 1975-1991

The July Stakes

The July Stakes is the oldest two-year-old race in the Calendar, and the original conditions stipulated that horses sired by *Eclipse* and *Highflyer* should carry three pounds extra. Run over an extended five furlongs of the Bunbury Course, the names of some the early winners reflect an imagination not found in some who own racehorses today.

Ostrich, Duckling and *Ringtail* all catch the eye, as do *Newmarket, Joke, Iodine, Gin* or quite simply *Loo.*

The fact that they were good enough to win belied the appelations given as scrawny foals, and although the race is nowadays dominated by precocity, in its heyday the *Flying Dutchman, Donovan* and *Sceptre* all went on to Turf immortality. The saddest reflection concerns *Lady Elizabeth*, the winner in 1867. She was a brilliant filly, trained by John Day, who had also prepared the 1839 winner *Crucifix* to go on to success in the 2,000 Guineas, the 1,000 Guineas and the Oaks.

Unhappily, *Lady Elizabeth* was owned by the dissolute Marquess of Hastings, who had squandered a fortune on the Turf and ran the filly mercilessly in order to maintain some degree of solvency. She won for him often enough, even surviving a hard fought decider after a deadheat and a match against a three-year-old, but unsurprisingly was useless at three, failing in the Derby and the Oaks, much to the disgust of the Epsom crowds who resented Hasting's harsh treatment of such a brave horse.

Perhaps the happiest winner was *Orlando* in 1843, who was awarded the 1844 Derby after the disqualification on the 'winner' running *Rein*, in fact a four-year-old named *Maccabaeus*.

Run at Newmarket over 6 furlongs for 2 year-old colts & geldings First Run 1786 Group 3

		Jockey	Trainer	Owner	Odds
1786	**Bullfinch**	–	J Pratt	Lord Clermont	4/1
1787	**Jubilator**	–	J Pratt	Lord Clermont	3/1
1788	**Seagull**	–	F Neale	T Panton	6/4
1789	**Ostrich**	–	F Neale	T Panton	7/4
1790	**filly by Saltram**	–	J Pratt	Lord Grosvenor	4/6
1791	**Trumpetta**	–	J Pratt	Lord Clermont	5/1
1792	**Cymbeline**	–	F Neale	HRH the Prince of Wales	3/1
1793	**filly by Trumpator**	–	J Pratt	Lord Grosvenor	2/1
1794	**colt by Volunteer**	–	M Stephenson	Duke of Bedford	4/5
1795	**colt by Anvil**	–	J Pratt	Lord Grosvenor	Evens
1796	**Emigrant**	–	–	W P Hamond	6/4
1797	**Young Spear**	–	T Perren	T Perren	5/4
1798	**Vivaldi**	–	–	R Heathcote	13/8
1799	**colt by Skyscraper**	–	–	W Golding	11/5
1800	**Flambeau**	–	R Robson	Duke of Grafton	3/1
1801	**Julia**	–	J Frost	Sir C Bunbury	5/2
1802	**Duckling**	–	R Robson	Duke of Grafton	5/2
1803	**Ringtail**	–	R D Boyce	Lord Stawell	3/1
1804	**Newmarket**	–	T Perren	C Wilson	13/8
1805	**Pantaloon**	–	T Perren	C Wilson	5/2
1806	**Little Sally**	–	T Perren	C Wilson	–
1807	**Susan**	–	B Atkinson	H F Mellish	3/1
1808	**Spindle**	–	T Perren	C Wilson	5/1
1809	**Cambric**	–	T Perren	C Wilson	5/2
1810	**Joke**	–	R Robson	Duke of Grafton	7/4
1811	**Cato**	–	R D Boyce	Lord Stawell	6/4
1812	**July**	–	–	Lord F G Osborne	7/4
1813	**Vittoria**	–	J Edwards	Sir J Shelley	6/4
1814	**Minuet**	–	R Robson	Duke of Grafton	4/1
1815	**Belvoirina**	–	R D Boyce	Duke of Rutland	7/1
1816	**Merrymaker**	–	R D Boyce	Lord Stawell	6/1
1817	**Loo**	–	R Robson	Duke of Grafton	5/2
1818	**Miracle**	–	R Prince	Lord Foley	5/2
1819	**Caroline**	–	R Stephenson	C Wyndham	4/1
1820	**Gustavus**	–	Crouch	J Hunter	100/6
1821	**The Stag**	–	–	Lord Rous	5/1
1822	**Palais Royal**	W Clift	R Prince	Lord Foley	7/4
1823	**Reformer**	W Clift	–	C Wilson	20/1
1824	**Red Gauntlet**	F Boyce	C Marson	Lord Exeter	10/1
1825	**Crusader**	F Boyce	–	J A S Wortley	7/2
1826	**Tom Thumb**	W Arnull	R Stephenson	C Wyndham	6/5
1827	**Scribe**	H Brown	–	J Rogers	–
1828	**Green Mantle**	F Boyce	C Marson	Lord Exeter	7/1
1829	**The Mummer**	J Robinson	H Scott	Sir M Wood	2/1
1830	**Zany**	J Robinson	R Pettit	S Stonehewer	7/4
1831	**Beiram**	W Arnull	C Marson	Lord Exeter	5/2
1832	**Forester**	T Robinson	–	J Hunter	15/1
1833	**Zulima**	E Pavis	R Pettit	S Stonehewer	9/1
1834	**Kate Kearney**	P Conolly	R Pettit	R Pettit	5/1
1835	**The Athenian**	J Robinson	W Chifney	W Chifney	6/4
1836	**Armenia**	E Flatman	–	Lord Orford	5/1
1837	**Mecca**	S Darling	C Marson	Lord Exeter	10/1
1838	**Bulwark**	J B Day	J Kent Jnr	Duke of Richmond	8/11
1839	**Crucifix**	J B Day	J B Day	Lord G Bentinck	5/6
1840	**Yorkshire Lad**	S Rogers	–	C Wilson	4/1
1841	**Chatham**	E Flatman	W Cooper	J Peel	3/1
1842	**Extempore**	R Pettit	R Pettit	T Thornhill	–
1843	**Orlando**	E Flatman	W Cooper	J Peel	1/2
1844	**Old England**	J Day	J B Day	J B Day	1/2
1845	**Queen Anne**	E Flatman	W Cooper	J Peel	4/1
1846	**Miami**	R Sly	W Beresford	Sir J Hawley	–
1847	**Iodine**	R Pettit	W Cooper	J Peel	5/1
1848	**The Flying Dutchman**	C Marlow	J Fobert	Lord Eglinton	4/7
1849	**Sweetheart**	S Templeman	J Day	T Pedley	5/4
1850	**Grecian**	A Day	J B Day	H Padwick	1/3

		Jockey	Trainer	Owner	Odds
1851	**Hobbie Noble**	G Whitehouse	M Dawson	Lord J Scott	4/9
1852	**The Reiver**	G Whitehouse	M Dawson	Lord J Scott	2/7
1853	**Marsyas**	R Basham	H Stebbing	Mr Knowles	3/1
1854	**The Bonnie Morn**	A Day	J Scott	J Bowes	1/10
1855	**Spindle**	J Wells	J B Day	H Padwick	–
1856	**Drumour**	J Wells	W Goater	H Padwick	5/2
1857	**Gin**	A Day	J Day	Duke of Beaufort	7/1
1858	**Cynricus**	S Rogers	I Woolcot	J Wyndham	100/8
1859	**Buccaneer**	J Goater	R Milton	Lord Portsmouth	6/4
1860	**Dictator**	S Rogers	J Fobert	H W Thomas	7/2
1861	**Tolurno**	G Fordham	T Parr	T Parr	9/4
1862	**Saccharometer**	T Aldcroft	W Channel	Lord Strathmore	2/1
1863	**Cambuscan**	A Edwards	Jos Dawson	Lord Stamford	5/1
1864	**Liddington**	J Adams	M Dawson	J Merry	Evens
1865	**Robin Hood**	G Fordham	R Milton	Lord Portsmouth	6/4
1866	**Achievement**	H Custance	J Dover	M Pearson	15/100
1867	**Lady Elizabeth**	G Fordham	J Day	Marquis of Hastings	4/5
1868	**Ryshworth**	C Maidment	W Gilbert	H Savile	2/1
1869	**Sunshine**	J Morris	J Waugh	J Merry	6/4
1870	**Hannah**	C Maidment	J Hayhoe	Baron M de Rothschild	10/1
1871	**Sir Amyas**	T Cannon	J Day	Lord Anglesey	2/1
1872	**Somerset**	T Cannon	W Day	Sir F Johnstone	3/1
1873	**Ecossais**	G Fordham	T Jennings	C J Lefevre	1/6
1874	**Camballo**	J Osborne Jnr	M Dawson	H F C Vyner	2/7
1875	**Levant**	G Fordham	J Cannon	Lord Rosebery	4/1
1876	**Warren Hastings**	J Goater	C Rayner	C Rayner	2/1
1877	**Strathfleet**	F Webb	R Peck	Duke of Westminster	100/15
1878	**Ruperra**	G Fordham	J Ryan	J H Houldsworth	8/11
1879	**Mask**	E Rossiter	C Blanton	Prince Soltykoff	4/1
1880	**Bal Gal**	F Archer	M Dawson	Lord Falmouth	4/5
1881	**Kermesse**	T Cannon	J Cannon	Lord Rosebery	5/6
1882	**Macheath**	C Wood	R Sherrard	W S Crawfurd	8/13
1883	**Queen Adelaide**	T Cannon	J Jewitt	Sir J Willoughby	Evens
1884	**Luminary**	F Webb	J Porter	Lord Alington	2/1
1885	**Kendal**	G Barrett	J Porter	Duke of Westminster	9/1
1886	**Enterprise**	F Archer	J Ryan	D Baird	85/40
1887	**Friar's Balsam**	T Cannon	J Porter	Sir F Johnstone	40/85
1888	**Donovan**	F Barrett	G Dawson	Duke of Portland	4/7
1889	**Loup**	J Watts	R Marsh	Duke of Hamilton	2/5
1890	**Beauharnais**	F Barrett	A Hayhoe	Baron L de Rothschild	8/11
1891	**Flyaway**	J Watts	J Jewitt	J B Leigh	2/1
1892	**Milford**	J Watts	S Pickering	Mr Jersey	4/7
1893	**Speed**	F Webb	T Fordham	Prince Soltykoff	1/6
1894	**Kirkconell**	S Loates	G Blackwell	W Cooper	2/7
1895	**Labrador**	M Cannon	J Porter	Duke of Westminster	6/1
1896	**Velasquez**	J Watts	W Walters Jnr	Lord Rosebery	2/11
1897	**Mousme**	M Cannon	R Marsh	HRH the Prince of Wales	4/11
1898	**Desmond**	T Loates	Robert Sherwood Jnr	Lord Dunraven	13/8
1899	**Captain Kettle**	F Allsopp	John Dawson	W Johnstone	–
1900	**Doricles**	T Loates	A Hayhoe	L de Rothschild	10/1
	Veles	J H Martin	Robert Sherwood Jnr	Sir R W Griffith	5/2
1901	**Sceptre**	S Loates	C Morton	R S Sievier	1/10
1902	**Hammerkop**	J H Martin	J Huggins	E Loder	10/1
1903	**Montem**	M Cannon	R Marsh	Lord Wolverton	2/1
1904	**Cicero**	D Maher	P Peck	Lord Rosebery	1/20
1905	**Gorgos**	H Jones	R Marsh	A James	7/4
1906	**Traquair**	D Maher	P Peck	Lord Rosebery	7/100
1907	**Pearl of the Loch**	H Jones	R Marsh	HM The King	100/8
1908	**Battleaxe**	B Dillon	G S Davies	J P Arkwright	13/8
1909	**Prince Rupert**	W Saxby	H S Persse	A F Bassett	4/1
1910	**St Anton**	D Maher	J Watson	L de Rothschild	8/1
1911	**White Star**	Wal Griggs	C Morton	J B Joel	10/1
1912	**Rock Flint**	D Maher	G Blackwell	H Beddington	3/1
1913	**Ambassador**	D Maher	R Day	Sir A Bailey	11/10
1914	**Roseland**	S Donoghue	H S Persse	A F Bassett	2/9
1915	**Figaro**	Wal Griggs	P P Gilpin	L Neumann	11/4
1916	**Grand Fleet**	J Childs	E de Mestre	Sir W J Tatem	4/9
1917	**No Race**				
1918	**Buchan**	R Colling	A Taylor Jnr	W Astor	1/2
1919	**Sarchedon**	J H Martin	P P Gilpin	J Buchanan	2/7
1920	**Monarch**	F Bullock	R S Sievier	Sir H Bird	13/8
1921	**Lembach**	F Bullock	R Day	E Moore	2/1
1922	**Legality**	G Hulme	R C Dawson	Lord Furness	4/5
1923	**Diophon**	G Hulme	R C Dawson	HH Aga Khan	7/1
1924	**Runnymede**	G Archibald	R Marsh	HM The King	100/8
1925	**Apple Sammy**	H Jelliss	B Jarvis	J P Hornung	4/1

Tommy Weston won the July Stakes aboard *Fairway* in 1927 and *Colorow* in 1932.

		Jockey	Trainer	Owner	Odds
1926	**The Satrap**	H Beasley	H S Persse	D McCalmont	2/5
1927	**Fairway**	T Weston	Frank Butters	Lord Derby	Evens
1928	**Mr Jinks**	H Beasley	H S Persse	D McCalmont	4/11
1929	**Teacup**	M Beary	R C Dawson	HH Aga Khan	30/100
1930	**Four Course**	F Fox	F Darling	Lord Ellesmere	15/8
1931	**Riot**	F Fox	F Darling	J A Dewar	7/1
1932	**Colorow**	T Weston	G Lambton	Mrs A James	9/2
1933	**Alishah**	M Beary	Frank Butters	HH Aga Khan	10/11
1934	**Hilla**	G Richards	Frank Butters	HH Aga Khan	20/21
1935	**Daytona**	E Smith	J Jarvis	Sir G Bullough	33/1
1936	**Foray**	P Beasley	C Boyd-Rochfort	M Field	9/4
1937	**Mirza II**	C Smirke	Frank Butters	HH Aga Khan	6/100
1938	**Prometheus**	R Perryman	T E Leader	A de Rothschild	3/1
1939	**colt by Colombo**	T Lowrey	B Jarvis	Lord Glanely	2/9
1940	**No Race**				
1941	**Ujiji**	M Beary	J Lawson	A E Allnatt	4/5
1942/43	**No Race**				
1944	**High Sheriff**	G Richards	F Darling	G Loder	2/5
1945	**Rivaz**	G Richards	Frank Butters	HH Aga Khan	1/6
1946	**Miss Stripes**	E Smith	H Jelliss	G C Gibson	13/8

		Jockey	Trainer	Owner	Odds
1947	**Masaka**	G Richards	Frank Butters	HH Aga Khan	4/5
1948	**Nimbus**	C Elliott	G Colling	Mrs M Glenister	3/1
1949	**Diableretta**	G Richards	Frank Butters	HH Aga Khan	1/40
1950	**Big Dipper**	W H Carr	C Boyd-Rochfort	Mrs J Bryce	Evens
1951	**Bob Major**	W Rickaby	J Jarvis	Lord Rosebery	2/5
1952	**Empire Honey**	E Mercer	J Jarvis	Lord Milford	20/1
1953	**Darius**	E Mercer	H Wragg	Sir P Loraine	7/4
1954	**Tamerlane**	G Richards	N Bertie	Lord Porchester	9/4
1955	**Edmundo**	A Breasley	N Bertie	Mrs R Digby	Evens
1956	**Earl Marshall**	E Mercer	J Jarvis	Lord Rosebery	7/2
1957	**Abelia**	L Piggott	N Murless	B Hornung	1/2
1958	**Greek Sovereign**	A Breasley	R Read	B Walsh	11/4
1959	**Sound Track**	W Rickaby	W Smyth	Duke of Norfolk	2/5
1960	**Favorita**	L Piggott	N Murless	Mrs V Lilley	100/30
1961	**Burning Thoughts**	W H Carr	W R Hern	Maj L B Holliday	3/1
1962	**Romantic**	A Breasley	N Murless	G Loder	4/11
1963	**Endless Honey**	R Hutchinson	J Jarvis	J P Phillips	100/8
1964	**Ragtime**	R Hutchinson	G Smyth	Duke of Norfolk	7/2
1965	**Sky Gipsy**	R Hutchinson	G Smyth	R Hibbert	11/8
1966	**Golden Horus**	L Piggott	W O'Gorman	Mrs D Solomon	2/1
1967	**Lorenzaccio**	G Moore	N Murless	C St George	5/1
1968	**Burglar**	R Hutchinson	J Dunlop	W Stirling	4/7
1969	**Huntercombe**	A Barclay	A Budgett	H Renshaw	9/4
1970	**Swing Easy**	L Piggott	J Tree	J H Whitney	10/11
1971	**Deep Diver**	F Durr	P Davey	D Robinson	4/1
1972	**Perdu**	J Lindley	T Corbett	A Holland	10/11
1973	**Dragonara Palace**	L Piggott	B Hills	Mrs B Stein	1/2
1974	**Auction Ring**	J Mercer	W R Hern	S Weinstock	7/1
1975	**Super Cavalier**	P Cook	G Hunter	J Maxwell	100/30
1976	**Sky Ship**	J Mercer	W R Hern	R D Hollingsworth	10/1
1977	**Royal Harmony**	G Lewis	B Hobbs	J Hambro	7/2
1978	**Main Reef**	J Mercer	H Cecil	H J Joel	5/4
1979	**Final Straw**	P Cook	M Stoute	J Wigan	14/1
1980	**Age Quod Agis**	J Mercer	H Cecil	D Wildenstein	11/4
1981	**End of the Line**	S Cauthen	B Hills	R Bonnycastle	16/1
1982	**Horage**	P Eddery	M McCormack	A Rachid	7/4
1983	**Superlative**	T Ives	W O'Gorman	Mrs P Yong	8/1
1984	**Primo Dominie**	J Reid	B Swift	P Wetzel	2/1
1985	**Green Desert**	W R Swinburn	M Stoute	M Al-Maktoum	7/2
1986	**Mansooj**	C Asmussen	N Callaghan	K Al-Said	25/1
1987	**Sanquirico**	S Cauthen	H Cecil	C St George	11/8
1988	**Always Valiant**	W Carson	N Callaghan	Dewfresh Mushrooms	9/1
1989	**Rock City**	W Carson	R Hannon	A F Budge Ltd	7/4
1990	**Mujtahid**	W Carson	R Armstrong	H Al-Maktoum	2/1
1991	**Showbrook**	B Raymond	R Hannon	A F Budge Ltd	13/8
1992	**Wharf**	P Eddery	H Cecil	K Abdulla	4/6

For all 2 year-olds 1784-1976.

Run at Windsor in 1944.

The July Cup

The July Cup is one of the finest races in the Calendar, for animals who are not merely sprinters, but exemplified by the inaugural winner *Springfield*. He was bred by Queen Victoria at the Hampton Court Stud and owned by J.H.Houldsworth, a Scotsman who never bet and raced purely for the love of the sport.

With *Springfield*, a 550 guineas purchase, he cannot have been disappointed. The bay with a white star, described as having 'great power and beauty' won 17 of the 18 races he contested, including the first two runnings of the July Cup and the Champion Stakes over a mile and a quarter.

Little has changed over the past 115 years. While out-and-out sprinters such as *Diomedes*, *The Bug*, *Hard Sauce* and *Pappa Fourway* have naturally had their say, recent winners have demonstrated their ability to stay longer distances, notably *Soviet Star*, *Royal Academy* and *Cadeaux Genereux*. A rarity outside the middle distance races, the July Cup combines the best of the present with the better traditions of the past.

Run at Newmarket over 6 furlongs First Run 1876 Group 1

		Jockey	Trainer	Owner	Odds
1876	**Springfield**	T Osborne	J Ryan	J H Houldsworth	1/4
1877	**Springfield**	T Osborne	J Ryan	J H Houldsworth	1/3
1878	**Trappist**	H Constable	J Cannon	Capt Prime	5/1
1879	**Phenix**	J Goater	T Jennings	Comte F de Lagrange	5/1
1880	**Charibert**	F Webb	M Dawson	H F C Vyner	5/4

		Jockey	Trainer	Owner	Odds
1881	**Charibert**	F Archer	M Dawson	H F C Vyner	6/5
1882	**Tristan**	F Archer	T Jennings Jnr	C J Lefevre	4/6
1883	**Clairvaux**	T Cannon	J Porter	Sir F Johnstone	5/2
1884	**Geheimniss**	F Archer	J Porter	Lord Alington	w.o.
1885	**Energy**	F Archer	J Jewitt	Capt J Machell	20/75
1886	**Melton**	F Archer	M Dawson	Lord Hastings	5/4
1887	**Ormonde**	T Cannon	J Porter	Duke of Westminster	3/100
1888	**Fullerton**	F Webb	R Marsh	Lord Dudley	1/4
1889	**Mephisto**	M Cannon	T Jennings	Prince Soltykoff	100/7
1890	**Queen of the Fairies**	R Colling	W Allen	Lord Penrhyn	7/1
1891	**Memoir**	J Watts	G Dawson	Duke of Portland	3/1
1892	**Workington**	J Watts	J Enoch	J Lowther	4/1
1893	**Prince Hampton**	F Webb	P Peck	Sir J Blundell Maple	10/11
1894	**Best Man**	F Webb	John Dawson	W Johnstone	1/5
1895	**Woolsthorpe**	M Cannon	C Waugh	Prince Soltykoff	13/8
1896	**Worcester**	M Cannon	J Cannon	B I Barnato	5/4
1897	**Kilcock**	J Watts	S Darling	J H Greer	w.o.
1898	**Ugly**	J Watts	R Marsh	Lord Wolverton	9/4
1899	**Eager**	M Cannon	J Ryan	A W Cox	30/100
1900	**Running Stream**	J Reiff	S Darling	F Keene	5/4
1901	**Lord Bobs**	S Loates	W Waugh	Sir J Blundell Maple	5/1
1902	**Sundridge**	M Cannon	J Cannon	Sir S Scott	3/1
1903	**Sundridge**	M Cannon	C Morton	J B Joel	1/25
1904	**Sundridge**	M Cannon	C Morton	J B Joel	13/8
1905	**Delaunay**	O Madden	P P Gilpin	P P Gilpin	1/50
1906	**Thrush**	H Randall	E Robson	J Orr-Ewing	8/100
1907	**Dinneford**	D Maher	A Taylor Jnr	R Walker	10/1
1908	**Lesbia**	D Maher	G Blackwell	Sir D Cooper	4/9
1909	**Jack Snipe**	W Higgs	S Darling	Lord Ilchester	3/1
1910	**Amore**	W Higgs	C Leader	J B Wood	7/1
1911	**Sunder**	D Maher	C Peck	S B Joel	15/100
1912	**Spanish Prince**	F Wootton	C Morton	J B Joel	4/9
1913	**Spanish Prince**	F Wootton	C Morton	J B Joel	11/10
1914	**Golden Sun**	W Huxley	C Morton	J B Joel	3/1
1915	**Volta**	S Donoghue	R C Dawson	Lord Carnarvon	Evens
1916	**Torloisk**	J Childs	R C Dawson	E Hulton	1/2
1917	**No Race**				
1918	**Irish Elegance**	F Fox	H Cottrill	J White	4/6
1919	**Diadem**	S Donoghue	G Lambton	Lord D'Abernon	9/100
1920	**Diadem**	G Colling	G Lambton	Lord D'Abernon	w.o.
1921	**Tetratema**	B Carslake	H S Persse	D McCalmont	2/9
1922	**Pharmacie**	S Donoghue	H Cottrill	J White	2/5
1923	**Golden Corn**	J Childs	C Boyd-Rochfort	M Field	–
1924	**Drake**	M Beary	H Cottrill	Mrs S Whitburn	6/4
1925	**Diomedes**	J Leach	H Leader	S W Beer	w.o.
1926	**Diomedes**	J Leach	H Leader	S W Beer	1/2
	Phalaros	T Weston	G Lambton	Mrs A James	2/1
1927	**Highborn II**	H Beasley	O Bell	Sir H Cunliffe-Owen	4/9
1928	**Golden Oracle**	J Childs	H I Ussher	H Whitworth	4/5
1929	**Tiffin**	F Fox	F Darling	Lord Ellesmere	Evens
1930	**Sir Cosmo**	G Swann	W Walters	Sir R Garton	11/10
1931	**Xandover**	C Elliott	F Holt	J Schwob	5/6
1932	**Concerto**	H Wragg	O Bell	Sir H Cunliffe-Owen	11/2
1933	**Myrobella**	G Richards	F Darling	Lord Lonsdale	4/6
1934	**Coroado**	H Gunn	W Easterby	F J Lundgren	5/2
1935	**Bellacose**	P Beasley	R J Colling	P Dunne	6/1
1936	**Bellacose**	P Beasley	R J Colling	P Dunne	Evens
1937	**Mickey the Greek**	H Wragg	H Leach	N Frieze	9/4
1938	**Shalfleet**	R Perryman	H Leader	J Walker	8/11
1939	**Portobello**	T Lowrey	R J Colling	P Dunne	10/1
1940	**No Race**				
1941	**Comatas**	W Nevett	O Bell	Miss K Farrar	13/2
1942/44	**No Race**				
1945	**Honeyway**	E Smith	J Jarvis	Lord Milford	8/11
1946	**The Bug**	C Smirke	H Wellesley	N Wachman	8/11
1947	**Falls of Clyde**	S Wragg	E Williams	Miss P Vaughan	100/30
1948	**Palm Vista**	E Smith	P Beasley	E Broadbelt	13/8
1949	**Abernant**	G Richards	N Murless	R Macdonald-Buchanan	2/11
1950	**Abernant**	G Richards	N Murless	R Macdonald-Buchanan	8/13
1951	**Hard Sauce**	G Richards	N Bertie	Sir V Sassoon	8/1
1952	**Set Fair**	E Smith	W Nightingall	C Bell	15/8
1953	**Devon Vintage**	G Richards	R J Colling	R C Boucher	11/4
1954	**Vilmoray**	W Snaith	B Bullock	A Green	6/4
1955	**Pappa Fourway**	W H Carr	W Dutton	Mrs E Goldson	1/6
1956	**Matador**	W Rickaby	J A Waugh	Mrs J Ferguson	11/2
1957	**Vigo**	L Piggott	W Dutton	T Farr	7/2

		Jockey	Trainer	Owner	Odds
1958	**Right Boy**	L Piggott	W Dutton	G Gilbert	4/5
1959	**Right Boy**	L Piggott	H Rohan	G Gilbert	11/10
1960	**Tin Whistle**	L Piggott	H Rohan	B Grainger	w.o.
1961	**Galivanter**	W H Carr	W R Hern	Maj L B Holliday	9/2
1962	**Marsolve**	W Rickaby	R Day	Sir M McAlpine	5/1
1963	**Secret Step**	G Lewis	P Hastings-Bass	P Mellon	2/1
1964	**Daylight Robbery**	A Breasley	A Budgett	R Budgett	100/9
1965	**Merry Madcap**	R Hutchinson	F Maxwell	Mrs H Frelinghuysen	100/8
1966	**Lucasland**	E Eldin	J A Waugh	J Baillie	100/6
1967	**Forlorn River**	B Raymond	W A Stephenson	Mrs W A Richardson	8/1
1968	**So Blessed**	F Durr	M Jarvis	D Robinson	7/2
1969	**Tudor Music**	F Durr	M Jarvis	D Robinson	4/5
1970	**Huntercombe**	A Barclay	A Budgett	H Renshaw	8/13
1971	**Realm**	B Taylor	J Winter	R C Boucher	11/2
1972	**Parsimony**	R Hutchinson	R F Johnson Houghton	E Holland-Martin	16/1
1973	**Thatch**	L Piggott	M V O'Brien	J Mulcahy	4/5
1974	**Saritamer**	L Piggott	M V O'Brien	C St George	11/4
1975	**Lianga**	Y Saint-Martin	A Penna	D Wildenstein	10/1
1976	**Lochnager**	E Hide	M W Easterby	C Spence	3/1
1977	**Gentilhombre**	P Cook	N Adam	J Murrell	10/1
1978	**Solinus**	L Piggott	M V O'Brien	D Schwartz	4/7
1979	**Thatching**	L Piggott	M V O'Brien	R Sangster	2/1
1980	**Moorestyle**	L Piggott	R Armstrong	Moores Furnishings Ltd	3/1
1981	**Marwell**	W R Swinburn	M Stoute	E J Loder	13/8
1982	**Sharpo**	P Eddery	J Tree	Miss M Sheriffe	13/2
1983	**Habibti**	W Carson	J Dunlop	M Mutawa	8/1
1984	**Chief Singer**	R Cochrane	R Sheather	J C Smith	15/8
1985	**Never So Bold**	S Cauthen	R Armstrong	E Kessly	5/4
1986	**Green Desert**	W R Swinburn	M Stoute	M Al-Maktoum	7/4
1987	**Ajdal**	W R Swinburn	M Stoute	Sheikh Mohammed	9/2
1988	**Soviet Star**	C Asmussen	A Fabre	Sheikh Mohammed	15/8
1989	**Cadeaux Genereux**	Paul Eddery	A Scott	M Al-Maktoum	10/1
1990	**Royal Academy**	J Reid	M V O'Brien	Classic Thoroughbred	7/1
1991	**Polish Patriot**	R Cochrane	G Harwood	R A Kirstein	6/1
1992	**Mr Brooks**	L Piggott	R Hannon	P Green	16/1

***Soviet Star* (left) was successful in the 1988 July Cup.**

The Scottish Classic

Originally run as the Mecca Bookmakers Scottish Derby, becoming the Scottish Classic in 1988, the race cannot be said to truly live up to either title. It is open to older horses, and the classics are confined to three-year-olds, and it is run over a mile and a quarter which is not a 'classic' distance. Falling as it does in mid-July, fields are usually small and the Classic is generally contested by animals described by Timeform as being 'not quite out of the top drawer', ie a little below true classic class. The best winner in recent years was probably *Kefaah*, fifth in the Derby proper, while earlier winners include *Little Wolf*, *Jalmood*, *Moon Madness* and *Ascot Knight*.

Run at Ayr over 1 mile 2 furlongs First Run 1979 Group 3

		Jockey	Trainer	Owner	Odds
1979	**Serge Lifar**	B Taylor	H R Price	Lord Carnarvon	5/6
1980	**Prince Roland**	S Cauthen	B Hills	R Swift	11/4
1981	**Little Wolf**	G Sexton	W R Hern	Lord Porchester	5/1
1982	**Jalmood**	S Cauthen	J Dunlop	Sheikh Mohammed	7/4
1983	**Dazari**	W R Swinburn	M Stoute	HH Aga Khan	5/2
1984	**Raami**	T Ives	W O'Gorman	A Fustok	9/4
1985	**Eagling**	Paul Eddery	H Cecil	Lord H de Walden	Evens
1986	**Moon Madness**	T Ives	J Dunlop	Duchess of Norfolk	4/7
1987	**Ascot Knight**	W R Swinburn	M Stoute	M Al-Maktoum	4/5
1988	**Kefaah**	R Cochrane	L Cumani	A Al-Maktoum	5/6
1989	**Scenic**	M Hills	B Hills	Sheikh Mohammed	5/2
1990	**Husyan**	W Carson	P Walwyn	H Al-Maktoum	4/1
1991	**Zoman**	A Munro	P Cole	F Salman	10/11
1992	**Sharpitor**	J Reid	W Jarvis	H Lopes	9/2

Run as the Scottish Derby 1979-1987.

Run over 1 mile 5 furlongs in 1979 and 1 mile 3 furlongs 1980-1986.

The King George VI and the Queen Elizabeth Stakes

The King George as it is popularly known, was first run in July 1951 as the King George VI and Queen Elizabeth Festival of Britain Stakes. The Festival was intended to commemorate the Great Exhibition at Crystal Palace in 1851 and encourage a nation still under the rigours of rationing and austerity six years after the war had ended.

There was no light at the end of that particular tunnel until Winston Churchill resumed his premiership in October 1951 and only the Festival Hall and the 'King George', renamed in memory of the King who died in 1952 remain as reminders of the period.

The inaugural running set the scene for the years to come. The winner, *Supreme Court* was a reject from the Fitzroy House stable of Marcus Marsh at Newmarket who had to make room for the horses of his principal patron, the Aga Khan. Trained by Evan Williams at Kingsclere, and ridden brilliantly by Charlie Elliott, probably the only jockey to truly master the short Ascot straight, *Supreme Court* beat a field including *Zucchero*, later a winner of the Coronation Cup, *Tantieme*, winner of the French Guineas and dual winner of the Prix de l'Arc de Triomphe, the Derby winner *Arctic Prince*, *Scratch II*, winner of the French Derby and the Doncaster St Leger, *Colonist II* (Jockey Club Cup and Ribblesdale Stakes), *Belle of All* (1,000 Guineas), *Aquino 11*, who won the Ascot Gold Cup in 1952, *Ki Ming* (2,000 Guineas) and *Wilwyn*, winner of the first Washington International Stakes.

Down the years since there have been many great races, with *Brigadier Gerard* winning his only race over one and a half miles to beat *Parnell* in 1972, *Dahlia's* dual victories in 1973 and 1974 and the celebrated confrontation between *Grundy* and *Bustino* the following year when *Dahlia*, by now temperamental and past her best was third.

It is interesting to reflect that an event conceived as a message of hope for the future has proved to be not merely that but one of the great races in the Calendar.

Run at Ascot over 1 mile 4 furlongs First Run 1951 Group 1

		Jockey	Trainer	Owner	Odds
1951	**Supreme Court**	C Elliott	E Williams	Mrs T Lilley	100/9
1952	**Tulyar**	C Smirke	M Marsh	HH Aga Khan	3/1
1953	**Pinza**	G Richards	N Bertie	Sir V Sassoon	2/1
1954	**Aureole**	E Smith	C Boyd-Rochfort	HM The Queen	9/2
1955	**Vimy**	R Poincelet	A Head	P Wertheimer	10/1
1956	**Ribot**	E Camici	U Penco	Marchese della Rocchetta	2/5
1957	**Montaval**	F Palmer	G Bridgland	R B Strassburger	20/1
1958	**Ballymoss**	A Breasley	M V O'Brien	J M McShain	7/4
1959	**Alcide**	W H Carr	C Boyd-Rochfort	Sir H de Trafford	2/1
1960	**Aggressor**	J Lindley	J M Gosden	Sir H Wernher	100/8
1961	**Right Royal V**	R Poincelet	E Pollet	Mme J Couturie	6/4
1962	**Match III**	Y Saint-Martin	F Mathet	F Dupre	9/2
1963	**Ragusa**	G Bougoure	P Prendergast	J R Mullion	4/1
1964	**Nasram II**	W Pyers	E Fellows	Mrs H E Jackson	100/7
1965	**Meadow Court**	L Piggott	P Prendergast	G M Bell	6/5

Left: Charlie Elliott, probably the only jockey to truly master the short Ascot straight. *Right:* A.Barclay aboard *Royal Palace* after their winning ride in the 1968 King George VI and Queen Elizabeth Stakes.

		Jockey	Trainer	Owner	Odds
1966	**Aunt Edith**	L Piggott	N Murless	J Hornung	7/2
1967	**Busted**	G Moore	N Murless	S Joel	4/1
1968	**Royal Palace**	A Barclay	N Murless	H J Joel	7/4
1969	**Park Top**	L Piggott	B van Cutsem	Duke of Devonshire	9/4
1970	**Nijinsky**	L Piggott	M V O'Brien	C W Engelhard	40/85
1971	**Mill Reef**	G Lewis	I Balding	P Mellon	8/13
1972	**Brigadier Gerard**	J Mercer	W R Hern	Mrs J Hislop	8/13
1973	**Dahlia**	W Pyers	M Zilber	N B Hunt	10/1
1974	**Dahlia**	L Piggott	M Zilber	N B Hunt	15/8
1975	**Grundy**	P Eddery	P Walwyn	C Vittadini	4/5
1976	**Pawneese**	Y Saint-Martin	A Penna	D Wildenstein	9/4
1977	**The Minstrel**	L Piggott	M V O'Brien	R Sangster	7/4
1978	**Ile de Bourbon**	J Reid	R F Johnson Houghton	D McCall	12/1
1979	**Troy**	W Carson	W R Hern	Sir M Sobell	2/5
1980	**Ela-Mana-Mou**	W Carson	W R Hern	S Weinstock	11/4
1981	**Shergar**	W R Swinburn	M Stoute	HH Aga Khan	2/5
1982	**Kalaglow**	G Starkey	G Harwood	A Ward	13/2
1983	**Time Charter**	J Mercer	H Candy	R Barnett	5/1
1984	**Teenoso**	L Piggott	G Wragg	E B Moller	13/2
1985	**Petoski**	W Carson	W R Hern	Lady Beaverbrook	12/1
1986	**Dancing Brave**	P Eddery	G Harwood	K Abdulla	6/4
1987	**Reference Point**	S Cauthen	H Cecil	L Freedman	11/10
1988	**Mtoto**	M Roberts	A Stewart	A Al-Maktoum	4/1
1989	**Nashwan**	W Carson	W R Hern	H Al-Maktoum	2/9
1990	**Belmez**	M Kinane	H Cecil	Sheikh Mohammed	15/2
1991	**Generous**	A Munro	P Cole	F Salman	4/6
1992	**St Jovite**	S Craine	J Bolger	Mrs V K Payson	4/5

The Princess Margaret Stakes

A Group Three event since 1986, presumably upgraded on the strength of victories by such fillies as *Tolmi, Royal Heroine, Desirable* and *Al Bahathri*, the Princess Margaret Stakes has proved a little disappointing since, the best being the superbly bred *Bluebook*, the winner in 1987 and also successful in the Fred Darling Stakes and the prix de Seine-et-Oise at Maisons-Lafitte.

Run at Ascot over 6 furlongs for 2 year-old fillies First Run 1946 Group 3

		Jockey	Trainer	Owner	Odds
1946	**Orum Blaze**	E Smith	H Jelliss	G H Fairhurst	7/2
1947	**Fair Dinah**	C Smirke	E Lambton	Mrs M Benson	6/5
1948	**Azolla**	G Richards	W Nightingall	Miss F Clark	5/1
1949	**Rose of Torridge**	D Smith	J Dines	J A P Martin	9/1
1950	**Par Avion**	J Thompson	W Bellerby	Mrs I Moss	7/4
1951	**Pareo**	W R Johnstone	C Semblat	M Boussac	7/4
1952	**Blue Ballas**	G Richards	R J Colling	W W Astor	10/11
1953	**Holwood**	D Smith	G Colling	R Stanley	4/1
1954	**Torbidora**	D Smith	C Elsey	C Nicholson	11/4
1955	**Persian Fair**	W Rickaby	W Smyth	E Digby	7/4
1956	**Taittinger**	E Britt	C Elsey	Sir V Sassoon	11/8
1957	**Medina**	A Breasley	S Ingham	A Aman	6/5
1958	**Parrotia**	L Piggott	N Murless	G Loder	8/15
1959	**Lady Advocate**	G Lewis	W Nightingall	Mrs W C Pegley	7/2
1960	**Abanilla**	J Mercer	H Wragg	Sir P Loraine	9/4
1961	**Parquetta**	L Piggott	H Wragg	Mrs J A Dewar	100/30
1962	**Palm Springs**	A Breasley	G Richards	J Gerber	4/1
1963	**High Powered**	S Clayton	S James	Maj L B Holliday	6/4
1964	**Attitude**	J Mercer	W R Hern	J J Astor	3/1
1965	**Soft Angels**	L Piggott	N Murless	Lady Sassoon	100/30
1966	**Fleet**	L Piggott	N Murless	R C Boucher	4/6
1967	**Photo Flash**	J Lindley	T E Leader	H J Joel	7/2
1968	**Star Story**	L Piggott	R F Johnson Houghton	Mrs D A Rasbotham	4/1
1969	**Red Velvet**	G Lewis	P Walwyn	Mrs D McCalmont	11/10
1970	**Boulevard**	E Hide	G Richards	M Sobell	100/7
1971	**Secret Kiss**	L Piggott	M Fogarty	Mrs M Fogarty	2/1
1972	**Fiery Diplomat**	L Piggott	M Fogarty	Mrs R Gallagher	13/8
1973	**Celestial Dawn**	B Taylor	J Winter	Mrs D McNab	4/1
1974	**Roussalka**	L Piggott	H Cecil	N Phillips	4/9
1975	**Outer Circle**	J Mercer	I Balding	D Willmot	7/4
1976	**Al Stanza**	L Piggott	R Armstrong	K Weihtag	3/1
1977	**Sarissa**	E Hide	E Weymes	Lord H de Walden	11/1
1978	**Devon Ditty**	G Starkey	H Thomson Jones	Sir E McAlpine	8/11
1979	**Luck of the Draw**	W Carson	W R Hern	Sir M Sobell	10/11
1980	**Tolmi**	E Hide	B Hobbs	G Cambanis	4/5
1981	**Circus Ring**	W R Swinburn	M Stoute	Snailwell Stud Co Ltd	4/6
1982	**Royal Heroine**	P Robinson	M Ryan	M Sinclair	4/1
1983	**Desirable**	L Piggott	B Hills	Mrs J M Corbett	4/6
1984	**Al Bahathri**	A Murray	H Thomson Jones	H Al-Maktoum	5/1
1985	**Kingscote**	P Eddery	J Tree	K Abdulla	5/2
1986	**Hiaam**	W R Swinburn	M Stoute	M Al-Maktoum	4/6
1987	**Bluebook**	S Cauthen	H Cecil	Lord Tavistock	13/8
1988	**Muhbubh**	R Hills	H Thomsom Jones	H Al-Maktoum	6/1
1989	**Pharaoh's Delight**	P Eddery	J P Hudson	Al-Deera Bloodstock Ltd	7/4
1990	**Cloche d'Or**	M Roberts	C Brittain	Mrs C Pateras	10/1
1991	**Bezelle**	P Shanahan	C Collins	J McNeill	6/1
1992	**Marina Park**	D McKeown	M Johnston	Laharna Ltd	100/30

The Beeswing Stakes

Named after one of the toughest racemares of all time who won fifty-one races including the Ascot Gold Cup, four runnings of the Doncaster Cup and won the Newcastle Cup on six occasions, the Beeswing Stakes was upgraded to Group Three from Listed status in 1986.

Confined to three-year-olds and upwards which at starting have not won a Group One or Group Two race, the best winner in recent years was probably *Salse*, a game and consistent horse in the finest traditions of *Beeswing*. *Salse* won the Beeswing Stakes as the first leg of a hat-trick of Group Three victories in the space of six weeks and two days, also taking the Hungerford Stakes and the Kiveton Park Stakes to add to his career record of eight wins, four seconds and a third from thirteen starts.

Run at Newcastle over 7 furlongs First Run 1977 Group 3

		Jockey	Trainer	Owner	Odds
1977	**In Haste**	J Lowe	J W Watts	F Buttery	11/1
1978	**John de Coombe**	G Baxter	P Cole	A H Warren	Evens
1979	**Jeroboam**	L Piggott	H Wragg	J Lilley	4/5
1980	**Kampala**	P Eddery	P Walwyn	Mrs D McCalmont	9/4
1981	**Milk of the Barley**	T Ives	W O'Gorman	Mrs I David	2/1
1982	**Silly Steven**	T Ives	R Hannon	S Bennett	6/1
1983	**Beaudelaire**	E Hide	M V O'Brien	R Sangster	8/11
1984	**Major Don**	E Hide	E Weymes	Mrs A Birkett	3/1
1985	**Sarab**	T Quinn	P Cole	F Salman	4/5
1986	**Hadeer**	S Cauthen	C Brittain	W Gredley	13/2
1987	**Farajullah**	G Carter	G Huffer	B Hamoud	16/1
1988	**Salse**	S Cauthen	H Cecil	Sheikh Mohammed	4/5
1989	**Great Commotion**	P Eddery	A Scott	M Al-Maktoum	4/6
1990	**Savahra Sound**	B Raymond	R Hannon	A F Budge Ltd	20/1
1991	**Bold Russian**	W Carson	B Hills	Lord White	11/2
1992	**Casteddu**	R Cochrane	J W Payne	E Landi	5/1

The Gordon Stakes

Named after the second Dukedom held by the Duke of Richmond, by virtue of the marriage of one of his ancestors like himself descended through the bastard line of Charles II's liaison with Louise de Kerouaille, Duchess of Portsmouth, the Gordon Stakes is essentially a race for good horses who lack the speed to win at Epsom but have the stamina to take the St Leger and other longer distance races, as typified by *Athens Wood*, fifth in the Derby and winner of the St Leger, *Commanche Run* and *Minster Son*, eighth in the Derby and a good winner of the St Leger from *Diminuendo* who had taken the Oaks.

The unluckiest horse to win the Gordon Stakes must surely be *Rock Roi*, the winner in 1970 who went on to be first past the post in the Ascot Gold Cup in 1971 and 1972, only to be disqualified on both occasions. A happier distinction is held by *Commanche Run*, who became Lester Piggott's twenty-eighth classic winner, thus theoretically beating Frank Buckle's record which had stood since 1827. However, Buckle's list could be incomplete, as the reader will see from the statistical tables that the rider of the winners of the 1819 and 1825 One Thousand Guineas are officially 'unknown'.

As both fillies, *Catgut* and *Tontine* were owned by the Duke of Grafton, for whom Buckle rode the winners of nine Guineas races, there must be a strong possibility that he was in the saddle on those occasions, and his true record may well be twenty-nine. However, since *Commanche Run's* win in 1984, he has ridden two more classic winners, taking the 2,000 Guineas on *Shadeed* and *Rodrigo de Triano*, thus establishing a clear total of 30 classic victories which is unlikely to be challenged.

Run at Goodwood over 1 mile 4 furlongs First Run 1902 Group 3

		Jockey	Trainer	Owner	Odds
1902	**Osbech**	W Halsey	P Peck	Lord Durham	8/11
1903	**Zinfandel**	M Cannon	C Beatty	Lord H de Walden	2/5
1904	**Delaunay**	W Lane	P P Gilpin	E Loder	1/10
1905	**Dinneford**	J Rogers	C Doyle	R Walker	6/1
1906	**Victorious**	D Maher	G Lambton	Lord Derby	9/4
1907	**Galvani**	B Dillon	P P Gilpin	E Loder	6/4
1908	**Putchamin**	O Madden	R Marsh	Lord Wolverton	10/1
1909	**Moscato**	C Trigg	A Taylor Jnr	W M G Singer	5/2
1910	**Cardinal Beaufort**	D Maher	R H Dewhurst	Mr St Aubyn	7/4
1911	**Prince Palatine**	S Donoghue	H Beardsley	T Pilkington	11/4
1912	**Fantasio**	W Earl	J Smith	W Hall-Walker	5/6
1913	**Augur**	Wal Griggs	P P Gilpin	E Loder	11/4
1914	**My Prince**	Wal Griggs	C Waugh	Lord St Davids	Evens
1915/18	**No Race**				
1919	**Sir Douglas**	G Hulme	H S Persse	H S Persse	4/7
1920	**The Alder**	J Childs	A Taylor Jnr	W M Cazelet	–
1921	**Stanislaus**	S Donoghue	G Lambton	Lord Derby	5/6
1922	**Tamar**	F Bullock	A Taylor Jnr	Lord Astor	1/5
1923	**Bold and Bad**	F Bullock	A Taylor Jnr	Lord Astor	4/7
1924	**Black Sheep**	F Bullock	A Taylor Jnr	Lord Astor	9/4
1925	**Kentish Knock**	T Weston	G Lambton	A James	11/8
1926	**Thistledown**	H Jelliss	B Jarvis	J P Hornung	7/4
1927	**Tiger Hill**	H Jelliss	C Leader	M Hughes	9/4
1928	**Cyclonic**	R A Jones	B Jarvis	J S Courtauld	9/2
1929	**Defoe**	F Fox	F Darling	Lord Woolavington	9/4

Gay Time **is led in after winning the Gordon Stakes at Goodwood in 1952 with Gordon Richards up.**

		Jockey	Trainer	Owner	Odds
1930	**Press Gang**	F Fox	F Darling	Lord Woolavington	1/2
	Ut Majeur	M Beary	R C Dawson	HH Aga Khan	5/2
1931	**Rose en Soleil**	R Perryman	D Waugh	Lord H de Walden	2/5
1932	**Firdaussi**	M Beary	Frank Butters	HH Aga Khan	4/6
1933	**Tavern**	G Richards	B Jarvis	J P Hornung	8/11
1934	**Bright Bird**	R Dick	J Lawson	Lord Astor	4/6
1935	**Bideford Bay**	E Smith	F Sneyd	A E Berry	4/1
1936	**Magnet**	G Richards	F Templeman	Lord Hirst	3/1
1937	**Perifox**	P Beasley	C Boyd-Rochfort	W Woodward	4/11
1938	**Valedictory**	P Beasley	C Boyd-Rochfort	J H Whitney	6/1
1939	**Wheatland**	T Burns	R C Dawson	W Barnett	11/4
1940/45	**No Race**				
1946	**Fast and Fair**	C Richards	J Lawson	Lord Astor	5/1
1947	**Merry Quip**	T Weston	N Cannon	J V Rank	4/11
1948	**Nathoo**	G Richards	Frank Butters	HH Aga Khan	7/2
1949	**Royal Forest**	G Richards	N Murless	R Macdonald-Buchanan	1/6
1950	**Foxoboro**	W Rickaby	V Smyth	C R Harper	100/9
1951	**Prinec D'Ouilly**	G Richards	R Warden	F Dupre	4/7
1952	**Gay Time**	G Richards	W Nightingall	HM The Queen	2/15
1953	**Prince Canaria**	D Smith	H Leader	Lady Bullough	1/3
1954	**Brilliant Green**	E Smith	D Watson	J A de Rothschild	5/2
1955	**Manati**	W H Carr	C Boyd-Rochfort	R W Sharples	100/8
1956	**Dacian**	W Snaith	H Cottrill	Maj L B Holliday	10/1
1957	**Pipe of Peace**	A Breasley	G Richards	S Niarchos	4/6
1958	**Guersillus**	E Hide	C Elsey	P Bull	13/8
1959	**Above Suspicion**	D Smith	C Boyd-Rochfort	HM The Queen	Evens

		Jockey	Trainer	Owner	Odds
1960	**Kipling**	G Lewis	P Hastings-Bass	Lord Sefton	6/1
1961	**Pardao**	W H Carr	C Boyd-Rochfort	Mrs C O Iselin	10/11
1962	**Gay Challenger**	R Hutchinson	J Oxx	Mrs M V Phillips	5/1
1963	**Tiger**	A Breasley	G Richards	M Sobell	100/30
1964	**Sweet Moss**	L Piggott	N Murless	Lady Sassoon	11/2
1965	**King Log**	R Hutchinson	G Todd	Mrs W Riley-Smith	4/1
1966	**Khalekan**	D Lake	P Prendergast	E More O'Ferrall	2/1
1967	**Sun Rock**	G Moore	N Murless	Mrs V Hue-Williams	11/4
1968	**Mount Athos**	R Hutchinson	J Dunlop	A J Struthers	4/7
1969	**Harmony Hall**	W Williamson	G Smyth	Sir H Wernher	5/1
1970	**Rock Roi**	G Lewis	P Walwyn	F Hue-Williams	3/1
1971	**Athens Wood**	G Starkey	H Thomson Jones	Mrs J Rogerson	7/4
1972	**Scottish Rifle**	R Hutchinson	J Dunlop	A J Struthers	4/6
1973	**Duke of Ragusa**	J Gorton	B Hobbs	Lord Rosebery	11/8
1974	**Grey Thunder**	W Carson	C Brittain	C Elliott	25/1
1975	**Guillaume Tell**	L Piggott	M V O'Brien	Mrs W Haefner	11/8
1976	**Smuggler**	J Mercer	W R Hern	Lord Porchester	7/2
1977	**Pollerton**	C Roche	P Prendergast	Mrs R Vereker	11/2
1978	**Sexton Blake**	E Hide	B Hills	T Motley	100/30
1979	**More Light**	W Carson	W R Hern	R Budgett	5/2
1980	**Prince Bee**	W Carson	W R Hern	Sir M Sobell	5/4
1981	**Bustomi**	W Carson	W R Hern	Lady Beaverbrrok	3/1
1982	**Electric**	G Starkey	M Stoute	R Clifford-Turner	25/1
1983	**John French**	L Piggott	H Cecil	C St George	4/1
1984	**Commanche Run**	L Piggott	L Cumani	I Allan	7/2
1985	**Kazaroun**	W R Swinburn	M Stoute	HH Aga Khan	10/1
1986	**Allez Milord**	G Starkey	G Harwood	J Brody	11/10
1987	**Love the Groom**	W Carson	J Dunlop	Mrs V Gaucci del Bono	6/4
1988	**Minster Son**	W Carson	W R Hern	Lady Beaverbrook	2/1
1989	**Warrshan**	W R Swinburn	M Stoute	Sheikh Mohammed	3/1
1990	**Karinga Bay**	B Rouse	Denys Smith	K Higson	13/2
1991	**Stylish Senor**	G Duffield	J Fanshawe	Dexa'Tex (Decorations) Ltd	11/4
1992	**Bonny Scot**	L Dettori	L Cumani	Lord Weinstock	6/1

The Stewards Cup

The Stewards Cup is one of the great betting races of the season, and although the records show that it was first run in 1840, in fact the history of the race traces to 1834. At that time the senior of the two stewards acting at the meeting presented a cup of about £100 in value for any race of their choosing. Over the years, the distances varied from one and a half miles to six furlongs, but the latter distance with handicap conditions proved the most popular, and so the Stewards Cup was founded.

The first winner of note was *Peter* in 1879. *Peter* had won the Middle Park in the previous year and was much fancied for the Derby until his nomination became void on the death of his owner General Peel. *Peter* was eventually acquired by Sir John Astley, and although the animal was of a quirky disposition, and several times let down his new owner when ridden by Charlie Wood, in the hands of Fred Archer he won the Royal Hunt Cup and the Hardwicke Stakes. However, not even Archer could persuade *Peter* to take part in the Goodwood Cup.

Over a century ago horses were expected to race over all distances. Today specialist breeding provides animals for a specific purpose, and a sprinter is one of the most rewarding horses to own. The horses can run frequently, the finish is usually close and exciting and the runners take a turn at winning depending on the handicap.

The Stewards Cup is no exception. Tony Villar's *Touch Paper* won a superb race in 1972, coming with a strong run in the centre of the course beat *Privateer* by a head. In 1980, the locally trained *Repetitious* emerged to defeat *Eagle Boy* with a short head to spare, but the best winner in recent times must the brilliant filly *Soba*.

Soba, unfashionably bred and the first northern trained winner for many years, made all the running to make the Stewards Cup the highlight of her eleven wins in 1982.

Run at Goodwood over 6 furlongs First Run 1840 Handicap

		Jockey	Trainer	Owner	Odds
1840	**Epirus**	W Scott	J Scott	J Bowes	–
1841	**Garry Owen**	E Flatman	–	G S Byng	3/1
1842	**Lady Adela**	J Chapple	–	Lord Jersey	6/1
1843	**Yorkshire Lady**	J Kitchener	J Kent Jnr	Lord G Bentinck	–
1844	**Sir Abstrupus**	C Wintringham	T Dawson	Capt O Harcourt	12/1
1845	**Psalmsinger**	J M Irvine	J Scott	Lord Stanley	100/6
1846	**Lady Wildair**	E Flatman	T Taylor	Lord Chesterfield	3/1
1847	**The Cur**	G Whitehouse	French	P Rolt	–
1848	**The Admiral**	J Sharp	J Rogers	H Lowther	–
1849	**Cotton Lord**	G Brown	J Kent Jnr	Lord Clifden	3/1
1850	**Turnus**	J Charlton	–	Count Hahn	3/1
1851	**Loadstone**	E Sharp	R Stephenson	Lord Clifden	9/4
1852	**Kilmeny**	J Barker	M Dawson	Lord J Scott	8/1
1853	**Long Bow**	F Butler	J Scott	Lord Derby	5/1
1854	**Pumicestone**	T Ashmall	T Taylor	Lord Wilton	5/1

		Jockey	Trainer	Owner	Odds
1855	**Clotilde**	R Quinton	M Dawson	Lord J Scott	25/1
1856	**New Brighton**	D Hughes	W May	F Fisher	–
1857	**Tournament**	G Fordham	R Drewitt	J Douglas	8/1
1858	**Glenmasson**	T French	I Woolcot	J Wyndham	7/1
1859	**Maid of Kent**	J Daley	J Eskrett	G W Gratwicke	10/1
1860	**Sweetsauce**	J Snowden	J Scott	Lord Annesley	20/1
1861	**Croagh Patrick**	H Taylor	T Cliff	Mr Murphy	7/1
1862	**Lady Clifden**	G Fordham	T Wadlow	Capt Christie	6/1
1863	**Birdhill**	J Judd	J Day	Duke of Beaufort	15/2
1864	**Marigold**	A Morgan	W Goater	Lord Westmorland	11/2
1865	**Out and Outer**	J Grimshaw	W Day	W Day	5/1
1866	**Sultan**	C Pratt	C Pratt	Maj Fridolin	12/1
1867	**Tibthorpe**	S Kenyon	–	J Drinkow	100/30
1868	**Vex**	F Butler	W Day	Sir F Johnstone	100/30
1869	**Fichu**	F Webb	R Peck	C Peck	20/1
1870	**Typhoeus**	J Morris	John Dawson	Count Batthyany	20/1
1871	**Anton**	J Crickmere	–	T E Case	33/1
1872	**Oxonian**	R Wyatt	–	Mr Richmond	20/1
1873	**Sister Helen**	J Lowe	–	Mr Eastlake	33/1
1874	**Modena**	F Archer	T Wadlow	Lord Wilton	10/1
1875	**Trappist**	F Archer	J Cannon	Capt Prime	100/7
1876	**Monaco**	H Luke	G Bloss	Lord Hartington	3/1
1877	**Herald**	Wainwright	E Weever	Sir W Throckmorton	8/1
1878	**Midlothian**	A F Lemaire	R Marsh	Duke of Hamilton	10/1
1879	**Peter**	C Wood	Jos Dawson	J T Best	100/8
1880	**Elf King**	G Fordham	A Taylor Snr	W S Crawfurd	10/1
1881	**Mazurka**	G Barrett	W Gilbert Jnr	Lord Cadogan	100/6
1882	**Lowland Chief**	F Webb	C Archer	Lord Ellesmere	100/9
1883	**Hornpipe**	C Wood	R Sherrard	Sir G Chetwynd	11/1
1884	**Sweetbread**	T Cannon	J Jewitt	W Gerard	8/1
1885	**Dalmeny**	E Martin	E Martin	F Morton	33/1
1886	**Crafton**	A Edwards	J Jewitt	Capt J Machell	100/3
1887	**Upset**	M Cannon	J Porter	J T Mackenzie	25/1
1888	**Tib**	W Blake	T Cannon	T Cannon	100/6
1889	**Dog Rose**	J Woodburn	W A Jarvis	A James	100/7
1890	**Marvel**	G Barrett	R Marsh	Lord Hartington	100/12
1891	**Unicorn**	O Madden	J Porter	W B Cloete	100/8
1892	**Marvel**	R Colling	R Marsh	Duke of Devonshire	1,000/45
1893	**Medora**	H Huxtable	Jos Day	Duchess of Montrose	100/6
1894	**Gangway**	W Bradford	P Peck	Sir J Blundell Maple	40/1
1895	**Wise Virgin**	H Toon	W T Robinson	A F Bassett	100/8
1896	**Chasseur**	F Rickaby	J Ryan	J Ryan	25/1
1897	**Amphora**	M Cannon	J Jewitt	H McCalmont	100/8
1898	**Altesse**	M Cannon	J Jewitt	J Jewitt	100/7
1899	**Northern Farmer**	F Finlay	J H Batho	H Bottomley	20/1
1900	**Royal Flush**	J Reiff	E Wishard	J A Drake	11/2
1901	**O'Donovan Rossa**	G Gibson	G S Davies	A M Singer	66/1
1902	**Mauvezin**	H Lewis	R C Dawson	Lord Carnarvon	10/1
1903	**Dumbarton Castle**	O Madden	J Powney	G A Prentice	4/1
1904	**Melayr**	W Griggs	W T Robinson	J M Kerne	33/1
1905	**Xeny**	F Bullock	J E Brewer	R H Henning	25/1
1906	**Rocketter**	W Higgs	S Darling	J H Greer	5/1
1907	**Romney**	H Watts	H Chandler	T Corns	10/1
1908	**Elmstead**	J Plant	C Morton	J B Joel	20/1
1909	**Mediant**	F O'Neill	A J Joyner	H B Duryea	10/1
1910	**Golden Rod**	H Randall	H S Persse	Mrs Morton-Jackson	20/1
1911	**Braxted**	F N Winter	F Leach	Sir T R Dewar	25/1
1912	**Golden Rod**	D Maher	S Pickering	P Nelke	9/1
1913	**Lord Annandale**	R Cooper	D Waugh	W Raphael	25/1
1914	**Lord Annandale**	S Donoghue	D Waugh	W Raphael	100/9
	Golden Sun	W Huxley	C Morton	J B Joel	10/1
1915	**Clap Gate**	P Allden	F Barling	Sir W Cooke	10/1
1916	**All Serene**	J Hulse	R H Dewhurst	Lord Savile	20/1
1917	**Trojan**	G Hulme	John Dawson Jnr	B Beckwith Smith	8/1
1918	**No Race**				
1919	**King Sol**	W Balding	J H Batho	H Cunliffe-Owen	100/7
1920	**Western Wave**	A Whalley	H Cottrill	W E Whineray	4/1
1921	**Service Kit**	T Weston	V Beatty	J Baylis	20/1
1922	**Tetrameter**	G Smith	H S Persse	Sir H McCalmont	10/1
1923	**Epinard**	E Haynes	H Leigh	P Wertheimer	7/2
1924	**Compiler**	W Lister	Sir C Nugent	L Schaverien	9/1
1925	**Defiance**	R Perryman	S Pickering	P Nelke	20/1
1926	**Perhaps So**	W McLachlan Jnr	C Boyd-Rochfort	Lady Nunburnholme	100/6
1927	**Priory Park**	B Carslake	C Peck	J B Joel	10/1
1928	**Navigator**	G Richards	T Hogg	Lord Glanely	8/1
1929	**Fleeting Memory**	R Perryman	W Earl	S B Joel	5/1

How fashions have changed. A section of the huge crowd at Goodwood in 1923.

The first post-war Goodwood and the finish of the 1946 Stewards Cup which was won by *Commissar* (no 10) from *Royal Charger* (behind) and *Port Vista* (extreme left).

		Jockey	Trainer	Owner	Odds
1930	**Le Phare**	M Beary	R C Dawson	HH Aga Khan	100/6
1931	**Poor Lad**	S Wragg	O Bell	Sir H Cunliffe-Owen	9/1
1932	**Solenoid**	T Barber	G Poole	Mrs C L Mackean	33/1
1933	**Pharacre**	F Fox	Fred Butters	A Wills	22/1
1934	**Figaro**	T Weston	J Leach	J Leach	100/7
1935	**Greenore**	S Wragg	O Bell	Lady Ludlow	7/1
1936	**Solerina**	E Smith	H Cottrill	C Mackean	10/1
1937	**Firozepore**	G Richards	F Darling	R B Strassburger	100/8
1938	**Harmachis**	P Evans	B Bullock	Mrs G Farrand	100/7
1939	**Knight's Caprice**	J Canty	R C Dawson	T Clarke	100/8

		Jockey	Trainer	Owner	Odds
1940	**No Race**				
1941	**Valthema**	K Robertson	Fred Butters	H Jennings	100/8
1942	**Sugar Palm**	T Carey	F Hartigan	A Bonsor	7/2
1943	**Sugar Palm**	T Carey	F Hartigan	A Bonsor	6/5
1944	**British Colombo**	T Bartlam	S Donoghue	H Kouyoumdjian	100/7
1945	**Happy Grace**	T Gosling	H Jelliss	Sir W Cooke	5/1
1946	**Commissar**	A Richardson	E Stedall	A Budgett	10/1
1947	**Closeburn**	G Richards	N Murless	R White	100/7
1948	**Dramatic**	E Smith	G Todd	A E Saunders	9/1
1949	**The Bite**	H Packham	J Wood	Mrs W Armstrong	33/1
1950	**First Consul**	E Britt	F Armstrong	Maharaja of Rajpipla	100/9
1951	**Sugar Bowl**	W Snaith	F Armstrong	J Gerber	100/6
1952	**Smokey Eyes**	C Smirke	R Jarvis	D Robinson	100/7
1953	**Palpitate**	W Snaith	F Armstrong	F Armstrong	5/1
1954	**Ashurst Wonder**	A Shrive	L Hall	R Merrick	50/1
1955	**King Bruce**	W Rickaby	P Hastings-Bass	W Tarry	100/6
1956	**Matador**	E Smith	J A Waugh	S Joel	100/8
1957	**Arcandy**	T Gosling	G Beeby	Mrs M Linde	100/7
1958	**Epaulette**	F Durr	W O'Gorman	J Gerber	33/1
1959	**Tudor Monarch**	G Lewis	W Nightingall	Sir W Churchill	25/1
1960	**Monet**	J Lindley	J Tree	Sir P Dunn	20/1
1961	**Skymaster**	A Breasley	G Smyth	W Kelly	100/7
1962	**Victorina**	W Williamson	P Nelson	Sir B Mountain	10/1
1963	**Creole**	E Smith	J Jarvis	Lord Rosebery	20/1
1964	**Dunme**	P Cook	R Read	J Simmons	9/1
1965	**Potier**	R Hutchinson	J Jarvis	T Blackwell	100/7
1966	**Patient Constable**	R Reader	R Smyth	I Allen	33/1
1967	**Sky Diver**	D Cullen	P Payne-Gallwey	J Fane	20/1
1968	**Sky Diver**	T Sturrock	P Payne-Gallway	J Fane	100/6
1969	**Royal Smoke**	M L Thomas	W O'Gorman	I Allen	100/7
1970	**Jukebox**	L Piggott	H Wallington	D Morris	100/6
1971	**Apollo Nine**	J Lindley	P Nelson	P Nelson	14/1
1972	**Touch Paper**	P Cook	B Hobbs	A Villar	25/1
1973	**Alphadamus**	P Cook	M Stoute	Mrs J Mountfield	16/1
1974	**Red Alert**	J Roe	D Weld	B Firestone	16/1
1975	**Import**	M L Thomas	W Wightman	H Cayzer	14/1
1976	**Jimmy The Singer**	E Johnson	B Lunness	Mrs S Bates	15/1
1977	**Calibina**	G Baxter	P Cole	E Badger	8/1
1978	**Ahonoora**	P Waldron	B Swift	E Alkhalifa	50/1
1979	**Standaan**	P Bradwell	C Brittain	A Richards	5/1
1980	**Repetitious**	A Clark	G Harwood	Mrs A Trimble	15/1
1981	**Crews Hill**	G Starkey	F Durr	C Henry	11/1
1982	**Soba**	D Nicholls	D Chapman	Mrs M Hills	18/1
1983	**Autumn Sunset**	W Carson	M Stoute	J McCaughey	6/1
1984	**Petong**	B Raymond	M Jarvis	T Warner	8/1
1985	**Al Trui**	M Wigham	S Mellor	M Saunders	9/1
1986	**Green Ruby**	J Williams	G Balding	Mrs E Weinstein	20/1
1987	**Madraco**	P Hill	P Calver	B Hampson	50/1
1988	**Rotherfield Greys**	N Day	C F Wall	Mrs D Gleeson	14/1
1989	**Very Adjacent**	D Gibson	G Lewis	J Lawrence	12/1
1990	**Knight of Mercy**	B Raymond	R Hannon	M Grant	14/1
1991	**Notley**	R Perham	R Hannon	D F Cock	14/1
1992	**Lochsong**	W Carson	I Balding	J C Smith	10/1

Run at Newmarket 1915-1917 and in 1941 and at Windsor 1942-1945

The Sussex Stakes

'I understand that Milton's 'Paradise Lost' is being revived and will appear in Derby Week and will be published under the title 'Paradox Lost' by Melton'. So ran a telegram of congratulation from Oscar Wilde, a man not known for his interest in the Turf but a close friend of the 20th Baron Hastings (not to be confused with the Marquess of Hastings) and owner of *Melton* who had just won the 1885 Derby from *Paradox* by a brilliant piece of riding from Fred Archer.

Paradox, the winner of the Guineas, gained compensation in the Grand Prix du Jockey Club, the Sussex Stakes and the Champion Stakes. Founded as a two-year-old race and run over six furlongs on a rather intermittent basis from 1841, there have been various changes in the conditions of the Sussex Stakes over the years. It became a three-year-old event in 1878 and was opened to four-year-olds in 1960. In 1975, the race became available to three-year-olds and upwards but only one horse above the age of four, the six-year-old *Noalcoholic* in 1983 has been successful.

The roll of honour includes both *Brigadier Gerard* and his sire *Queen's Hussar* along with many classic winners appropriate to one of the richest and most important mile races in Europe.

HM The Queen and HRH Princess Anne pictured at Goodwood in 1970.

Run at Goodwood over 1 mile First Run 1878 Group 1

		Jockey	Trainer	Owner	Odds
1878	**Clocher**	J Osborne Jnr	–	L Delatre	–
1879	**Rayon d'Or**	J Goater	T Jennings	Comte F de Lagrange	5/6
1880	**Mask**	T Cannon	C Blanton	Prince Soltykoff	Evens
1881	**Limestone**	F Archer	T Wadlow	Lord Bradford	6/4
1882	**Comte Alfred**	G Fordham	T Jennings Jnr	C J Lefevre	20/1
1883	**Ossian**	C Wood	R Sherrard	Sir G Chetwynd	11/1
1884	**Hermitage**	F Webb	T Jennings Jnr	C J Lefevre	2/1
1885	**Paradox**	F Archer	J Porter	W B Cloete	4/7
1886	**Chelsea**	J Goater	W Goater	G Lambert	100/8
1887	**Reve d'Or**	C Wood	A Taylor Snr	Duke of Beaufort	4/9
1888	**Zanzibar**	G Barrett	C W Golding	Duchess of Montrose	20/1
1889	**Enthusiast**	W Warne	J Ryan	D Baird	6/4
1890	**St Serf**	J Watts	G Dawson	Duke of Portland	2/5
1891	**Orvieto**	T Cannon	J Ryan	J H Houldsworth	10/11
1892	**Orme**	G Barrett	J Porter	Duke of Westminster	1/5
1893	**Harbinger**	M Cannon	J Ryan	D Baird	2/1
1894	**Matchbox**	J Watts	R Marsh	Baron M de Hirsch	15/100
1895	**Troon**	J Watts	G Dawson	Duke of Portland	9/2
1896	**Regret**	M Cannon	J Porter	Duke of Westminster	8/100
1897	**Ardeshir**	C Wood	J Waugh	Mr Theobalds	9/2
1898	**Dieudonne**	J Watts	R Marsh	Duke of Devonshire	3/1
1899	**Caiman**	M Cannon	J Huggins	Lord W Beresford	4/11
1900	**The Raft**	L Reiff	F W Day	A Bailey	4/5
1901	**Energetic**	O Madden	J Ryan	J H Houldsworth	9/2
1902	**Royal Lancer**	W Lane	W Waugh	Sir J Blundell Maple	2/1

Lord Glanely's filly *Olein* (left), which also won the Nassau Stakes on the last day, brings off the first half of a Goodwood double by winning the 1939 Sussex Stakes.

		Jockey	Trainer	Owner	Odds
1903	**Stephanas**	H Jones	R Marsh	A James	7/1
1904	**Mousqueton**	H Aylin	H Enoch	D Baird	4/1
1905	**Thrush**	H Randall	E Robson	J Orr-Ewing	1/2
1906	**Troutbeck**	H Jones	W Waugh	Duke of Westminster	1/4
1907	**Wool Winder**	W Halsey	H Enoch	E W Baird	1/5
1908	**White Eagle**	W Higgs	H S Persse	W Hall-Walker	4/7
1909	**Minoru**	H Jones	R Marsh	HM The King	2/5
1910	**Winkipop**	H Jones	W Waugh	W Astor	6/5
1911	**Stedfast**	F Wootton	G Lambton	Lord Derby	1/25
1912	**Tracery**	D Maher	J Watson	A Belmont	1/2
1913	**Sun Yat**	F Wootton	C Morton	J B Joel	5/4
1914	**Black Jester**	W Huxley	C Morton	J B Joel	4/9
1915/18	**No Race**				
1919	**Glanmerin**	S Donoghue	S Pickering	Lord H Vane-Tempest	8/13
1920	**Braishfield**	F Bullock	A Taylor Jnr	G H Deane	7/1
1921	**Sunblaze**	B Carslake	H S Persse	L Robinson	3/1
1922	**Diligence**	F Lane	A Sadler Jnr	Lord Lonsdale	Evens
1923	**Hurry Off**	B Carslake	H S Persse	Duke of Westminster	6/4
1924	**Burslem**	M Beary	H S Persse	Sir A Bailey	8/1
1925	**The Monk**	H Wragg	W Earl	S B Joel	7/2
1926	**Plimsol**	R A Jones	A Taylor Jnr	Lord Astor	9/2
1927	**Rosalia**	H Wragg	J H Crawford	Sir V Sassoon	11/2
1928	**Marconigram**	G Richards	F Darling	Lord Dewar	8/1
1929	**Le Phare**	M Beary	R C Dawson	HH Aga Khan	20/1
1930	**Paradine**	R A Jones	J Lawson	W M Cazalet	13/8
1931	**Inglesant**	R A Jones	J Lawson	S Tattersall	10/11
1932	**Dastur**	M Beary	Frank Butters	HH Aga Khan	8/15
1933	**The Abbot**	J Childs	W R Jarvis	HM The King	11/2
1934	**Badruddin**	F Fox	Frank Butters	HH Aga Khan	2/5
1935	**Hairan**	R Perryman	Frank Butters	HH Aga Khan	6/4
1936	**Corpach**	G Richards	J Lawson	Lord Astor	4/1
1937	**Pascal**	G Richards	F Darling	H E Morriss	5/2
1938	**Faroe**	R Perryman	C Leader	Lord Derby	20/1
1939	**Olein**	T Lowrey	B Jarvis	Lord Glanely	7/4
1940	**No Race**				
1941	**Eastern Echo**	M Beary	J Lawson	Lord Glanely	100/8
1942/45	**No Race**				
1946	**Radiotherapy**	G Richards	F Templeman	T Lilley	7/4
1947	**Combat**	G Richards	F Darling	J A Dewar	8/13
1948	**My Babu**	C Smirke	F Armstrong	Maharaja of Baroda	1/3
1949	**Krakatao**	G Richards	N Murless	Lord Feversham	2/11
1950	**Palestine**	C Smirke	M Marsh	HH Aga Khan	1/2
1951	**Le Sage**	G Richards	T Carey	S Sanger	6/4
1952	**Agitator**	G Richards	N Murless	J A Dewar	8/15
1953	**King of the Tudors**	C Spares	W Stephenson	F Dennis	11/10

		Jockey	Trainer	Owner	Odds
1954	**Landau**	W Snaith	N Murless	HM The Queen	6/4
1955	**My Kingdom**	D Smith	W Nightingall	J Armstrong	13/2
1956	**Lucero**	E Mercer	H Wragg	G A Oldham	8/1
1957	**Quorum**	A Russell	W Lyde	T Farr	10/11
1958	**Major Portion**	E Smith	T E Leader	H J Joel	8/11
1959	**Petite Etoile**	L Piggott	N Murless	Prince Aly Khan	1/10
1960	**Venture VII**	G Moore	A Head	HH Aga Khan	13/8
1961	**Le Levanstell**	W Williamson	S McGrath	J McGrath	100/7
1962	**Romulus**	W Swinburn	R F Johnson Houghton	C W Engelhard	9/1
1963	**Queen's Hussar**	R Hutchinson	T Corbett	Lord Carnarvon	25/1
1964	**Roan Rocket**	L Piggott	G Todd	T Frost	4/6
1965	**Carlemont**	R Hutchinson	P Prendergast	L Gelb	7/2
1966	**Paveh**	R Hutchinson	T Ainsworth	P Widener	5/1
1967	**Reform**	A Breasley	G Richards	M Sobell	Evens
1968	**Petingo**	L Piggott	F Armstrong	M Lemos	6/4
1969	**Jimmy Reppin**	G Lewis	J Sutcliffe Jnr	Mrs S Bates	7/4
1970	**Humble Duty**	D Keith	P Walwyn	Lady J Ashcombe	11/8
1971	**Brigadier Gerard**	J Mercer	W R Hern	Mrs J Hislop	4/6
1972	**Sallust**	J Mercer	W R Hern	Sir M Sobell	9/2
1973	**Thatch**	L Piggott	M V O'Brien	J Mulcahy	4/5
1974	**Ace of Aces**	J Lindley	M Zilber	N B Hunt	8/1
1975	**Bolkonski**	G Dettori	H Cecil	C d'Alessio	1/2
1976	**Wollow**	G Dettori	H Cecil	C d'Alessio	10/11
1977	**Artaius**	L Piggott	M V O'Brien	Mrs G Getty II	6/4
1978	**Jaazeiro**	L Piggott	M V O'Brien	R Sangster	8/13
1979	**Kris**	J Mercer	H Cecil	Lord H de Walden	4/5
1980	**Posse**	P Eddery	J Dunlop	O Phipps	8/13
1981	**Kings Lake**	P Eddery	M V O'Brien	Mme J Binet	5/2
1982	**On The House**	J Reid	H Wragg	Sir P Oppenheimer	14/1
1983	**Noalcoholic**	G Duffield	G Pritchard-Gordon	W du Pont III	18/1
1984	**Chief Singer**	R Cochrane	R Sheather	J C Smith	4/7
1985	**Rousillon**	G Starkey	G Harwood	K Abdulla	2/1
1986	**Sonic Lady**	W R Swinburn	M Stoute	Sheikh Mohammed	5/6
1987	**Soviet Star**	G Starkey	A Fabre	Sheikh Mohammed	3/1
1988	**Warning**	P Eddery	G Harwood	K Abdulla	11/10
1989	**Zilzal**	W R Swinburn	M Stoute	M Al-Maktoum	5/2
1990	**Distant Relative**	W Carson	B Hills	W Said	4/1
1991	**Second Set**	L Dettori	L Cumani	R Duchossois	5/1
1992	**Marling**	P Eddery	G Wragg	E J Loder	11/10

The Sussex stakes was first run in 1841 as a 2 year-old race.

In 37 years it was uncontested 25 times including 14 walk-overs. It became a 1 mile race for 3 year-olds in 1878.

For 3 year-olds only 1878-1959, 3 & 4 year-olds 1960-1974. Run at Newmarket in 1941.

The Richmond Stakes

As the record shows, the Richmond Stakes was 'farmed' by Fred Archer in the early years, since he rode the winner on six of the first eight occasions. The inaugural winner, *Jannette,* proved to be disappointing, but *Wheel of Fortune* won the 1,000 Guineas and the Oaks in a canter, *Bend Or* the Derby, and *Dutch Oven* took the St Leger at the incredible odds of 40/1, considering that she was ridden by Archer.

Amongst others, *Persimmon* and the brilliant, if eccentric, *Bayardo* continued the classic thread, but between the wars only *Manna* and *Mahmoud* aspired to the highest honours and since the war *Palestine,* the 2,000 Guineas winner in 1950 is the sole classic representative of the Richmond.

None the less, it remains one of the important two-year-olds races in the Calendar, and in 1983 one of the most controversial contests seen at Goodwood. *Vacarme,* 3/1 on favourite and ridden by Lester Piggott contrived to find himself boxed in during the final furlong in a field of nine. Meanwhile, *Crag-An-Sgor* was drifitng badly to the right and both he and *Vacarme* were judged to have interferred with *Godstone* in third, who was duly awarded the race with *Vacarme* disqualified and placed last. It cannot be said that it was one of Piggott's happiest moments in the saddle, but the man normally regarded as 'the punters friend' certainly helped the bookmakers by his moment of carelessness; *Godstone* was returned at 14/1.

Run at Goodwood over 6 furlongs for 2 year-old colts & geldings First Run 1877 Group 2

		Jockey	Trainer	Owner	Odds
1877	**Jannette**	F Archer	M Dawson	Lord Falmouth	2/1
1878	**Wheel of Fortune**	F Archer	M Dawson	Lord Falmouth	2/1
1879	**Bend Or**	F Archer	R Peck	Duke of Westminster	4/7
1880	**Bal Gal**	F Archer	M Dawson	Lord Falmouth	4/1
1881	**Dutch Oven**	F Archer	M Dawson	Lord Falmouth	6/1
1882	**Sigmophone**	T Cannon	J Day	T Cannon	100/30
1883	**Duke of Richmond**	F Webb	J Porter	Duke of Westminster	Evens
1884	**Rosy Morn**	F Archer	M Dawson	Duke of Portland	6/5
1885	**Sunrise**	T Cannon	J Ryan	J H Houldsworth	Evens
1886	**Panzerschiff**	J Watts	J Enoch	Lord Zetland	1/2

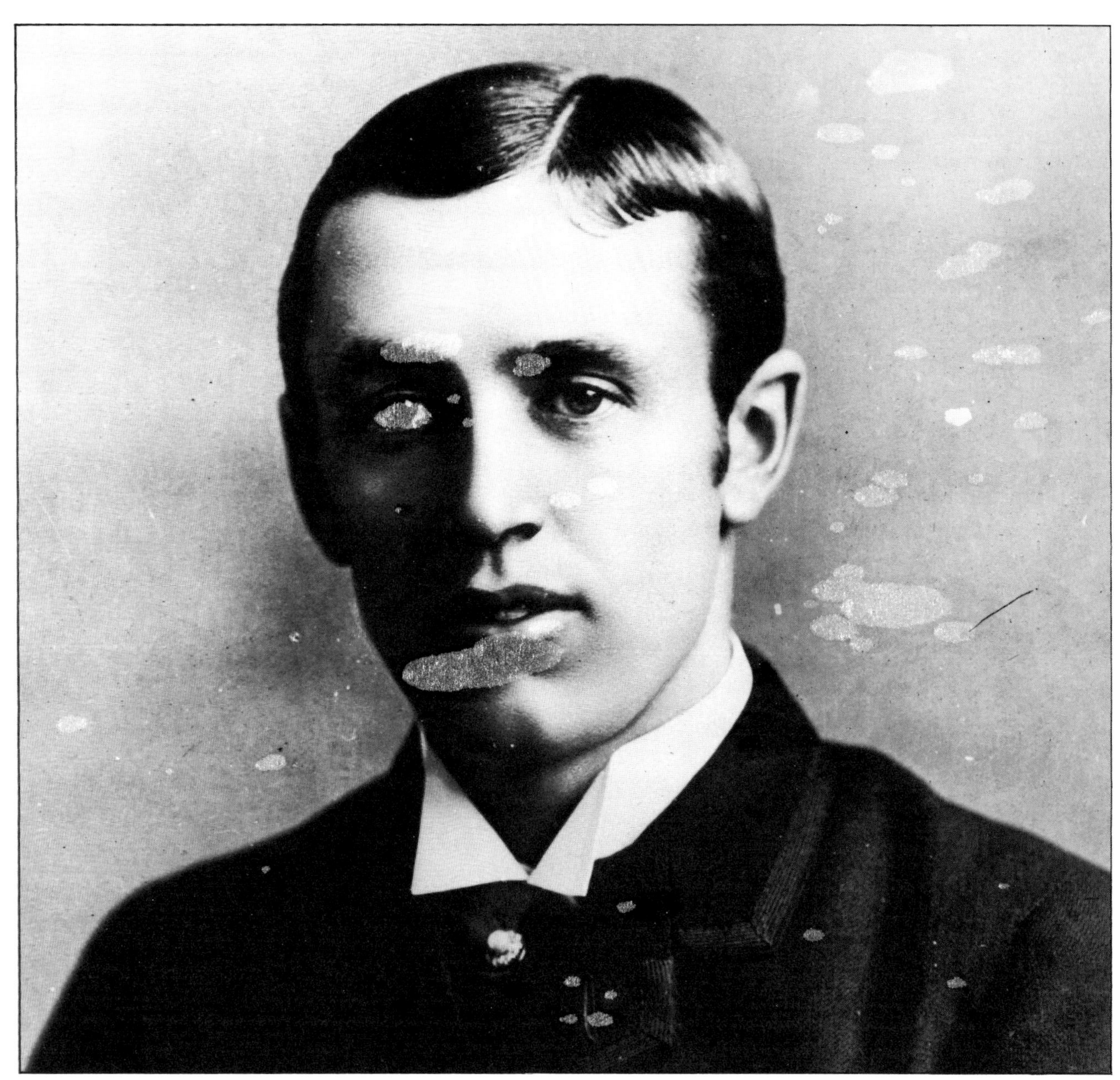

Fred Archer, the great jockey who won the Richmond Stakes for the first five years of the race's existence and then added a further victory in 1884.

		Jockey	Trainer	Owner	Odds
1887	**Friar's Balsam**	G Barrett	J Porter	Sir F Johnstone	1/25
1888	**Gulliver**	J Watts	W A Jarvis	C D Rose	2/1
1889	**Golden Gate**	M Cannon	T Cannon	E W Baird	6/1
1890	**Siphonia**	T Cannon	J Ryan	D Baird	4/9
1891	**Orme**	G Barrett	J Porter	Duke of Westminster	4/5
1892	**Inverdon**	M Cannon	J Ryan	J H Houldsworth	9/4
1893	**Galloping Dick**	M Cannon	J Ryan	D Baird	7/4
1894	**The Nipper**	F Finlay	R Marsh	Duke of Hamilton	100/7
1895	**Persimmon**	J Watts	R Marsh	HRH the PRince of Wales	1/2
1896	**Chillingham**	F Rickaby	P Peck	Lord Durham	100/6
1897	**Paladore**	W Bradford	T Jennings Jnr	L Brassey	5/4
1898	**St Gris**	T Loates	A Hayhoe	L de Rothschild	7/4
1899	**Winifreda**	W Bradford	T Jennings Jnr	L Brassey	7/4
1900	**Handicapper**	L Reiff	F W Day	Sir E Cassel	13/8
1901	**Duke of Westminster**	D Maher	C Morton	R S Sievier	4/7
1902	**Mead**	H Jones	R Marsh	HM The King	5/1
1903	**Queen's Holiday**	W Lane	W Waugh	Sir J Blundell Maple	7/4
1904	**Polymelus**	M Cannon	J Porter	Lord Crewe	5/2
1905	**Lally**	B Dillon	J Fallon	W B Purefoy	1/4
1906	**Weathercock**	B Dillon	P P Gilpin	E Loder	Evens
1907	**Bolted**	D Maher	R Day	D Fraser	3/1
1908	**Bayardo**	D Maher	A Taylor Jnr	A W Cox	1/3
1909	**Charles O'Malley**	W Saxby	T Lewis	A P Cunliffe	Evens
1910	**Pietri**	D Maher	J Watson	L de Rothschild	4/6
1911	**Sweeper II**	G Stern	H S Persse	H B Duryea	11/10

		Jockey	Trainer	Owner	Odds
1912	**Seremond**	C Trigg	J Butters	Sir B Sheffield	10/1
1913	**Black Jester**	F Wootton	C Morton	J B Joel	10/11
1914	**Pommern**	Wal Griggs	C Peck	S B Joel	10/1
1915/18	**No Race**				
1919	**Golden Guinea**	J H Martin	P P Gilpin	G Loder	4/5
1920	**Sunblaze**	B Carslake	H S Persse	L Robinson	4/7
1921	**Fodder**	B Carslake	E de Mestre	S B Joel	7/1
1922	**Bombay Duck**	G Hulme	R C Dawson	HH Aga Khan	10/11
1923	**Halcyon**	T Weston	G Lambton	Lord Derby	5/2
1924	**Manna**	B Carslake	F Darling	H E Morriss	6/4
1925	**Pantera**	H Wragg	W Earl	S B Joel	100/12
1926	**The Satrap**	H Beasley	H S Persse	D McCalmont	1/4
1927	**Gang Warily**	J Childs	F Darling	Mrs G Drummond	4/7
1928	**Rattlin The Reefer**	B Carslake	R Day	Sir A Bailey	6/1
1929	**Challenger**	F Fox	F Darling	Lord Dewar	9/2
1930	**Four Course**	F Fox	F Darling	Lord Ellesmere	8/13
1931	**Spenser**	R A Jones	J Lawson	S Tattersall	11/10
1932	**Solar Boy**	F Fox	F Templeman	Sir F Eley	6/1
1933	**Colombo**	S Donoghue	T Hogg	Lord Glanely	30/100
1934	**Bobsleigh**	T Weston	C Leader	Lord Derby	1/3
1935	**Mahmoud**	F Fox	Frank Butters	HH Aga Khan	2/1
1936	**Perifox**	P Beasley	C Boyd-Rochfort	W Woodward	5/2
1937	**Unbreakable**	P Beasley	C Boyd-Rochfort	J Widener	11/10
1938	**Chancery**	B Carslake	H Leader	J Walker	5/2
1939	**Moradabad**	C Smirke	Frank Butters	HH Aga Khan	10/11
1940/45	**No Race**				
1946	**Petition**	H Wragg	Frank Butters	Sir A Butt	1/5
1947	**Birthday Greetings**	J Simpson	H Jelliss	Miss D Paget	11/10
1948	**Star King**	S Wragg	J C Waugh	W Harvey	8/11
1949	**Palestine**	G Richards	Frank Butters	HH Aga Khan	6/100
1950	**Grey Sovereign**	W H Carr	G Beeby	J Measures	5/2
1951	**Gay Time**	A Breasley	N Cannon	J V Rank	100/7
1952	**Artane**	G Richards	P Prendergast	J O'Connell	13/8
1953	**The Pie King**	G Richards	P Prendergast	R Bell	8/13
1954	**Eubulides**	E Britt	C Elsey	P Bull	6/5
1955	**Ratification**	W Rickaby	V Smyth	Sir M McAlpine	11/8
1956	**Red God**	W H Carr	C Boyd-Rochfort	H Guggenheim	7/2
1957	**Promulgation**	E Smith	T E Leader	H J Joel	11/8
1958	**Hieroglyph**	W H Carr	C Boyd-Rochfort	Mrs J Hanes	9/4
1959	**Dollar Piece**	J Mercer	H Cottrill	P Winstone	100/6
1960	**Typhoon**	R Hutchinson	P Prendergast	N McCarthy	4/11
1961	**Sovereign Lord**	G Lewis	G Smyth	Duke of Norfolk	8/1
1962	**Romantic**	L Piggott	N Murless	G Loder	8/11
1963	**Gentle Art**	R Hutchinson	J Jarvis	Sir A Jarvis	8/11
1964	**Ragtime**	R Hutchinson	G Smyth	Duke of Norfolk	13/8
1965	**Sky Gipsy**	R Hutchinson	G Smyth	R Hibbert	3/1
1966	**Hambledon**	A Breasley	T Corbett	Lord Carnarvon	2/1
1967	**Berber**	A Breasley	G Richards	Sir M Sobell	8/11
1968	**Tudor Music**	F Durr	M Jarvis	D Robinson	5/1
1969	**Village Boy**	W Williamson	G Todd	Mrs A F Hurlstone	9/2
1970	**Swing Easy**	L Piggott	J Tree	J H Whitney	4/5
1971	**Sallust**	J Mercer	W R Hern	Sir M Sobell	2/1
1972	**Master Sing**	J Mercer	D Candy	B Jenks	13/8
1973	**Dragonara Palace**	L Piggott	B Hills	Mrs B Stein	4/9
1974	**Legal Eagle**	G Baxter	W Marshall	P Gallagher	4/1
1975	**Stand to Reason**	W Carson	B Hills	Lord Ranfurly	12/1
1976	**J O Tobin**	L Piggott	N Murless	G A Pope Jnr	8/11
1977	**Persian Bold**	L Piggott	A Ingham	R Vahabzadeh	4/6
1978	**Young Generation**	G Starkey	G Harwood	A Ward	12/1
1979	**Castle Green**	P Cook	M Stoute	Sir G White	20/1
1980	**Another Realm**	J Mercer	F Durr	Mrs D Goldstein	16/1
1981	**Tender King**	P Waldron	J Sutcliffe Jnr	Esal Commodities Ltd	11/4
1982	**Gallant Special**	L Piggott	R Armstrong	W R Hawn	4/6
1983	**Godstone**	G Sexton	P Haslam	Esal Commodities Ltd	14/1
1984	**Primo Dominie**	J Reid	B Swift	P Wetzel	10/11
1985	**Nomination**	T Quinn	P Cole	F Salman	8/1
1986	**Rich Charlie**	J Reid	C Nelson	R E A Bott Ltd	11/4
1987	**Warning**	P Eddery	G Harwood	K Abdulla	4/11
1988	**Heart of Arabia**	R Cochrane	C Brittain	S Manana	11/1
1989	**Contract Law**	B Raymond	W Jarvis	Kennet Valley Thoroughbred	9/2
1990	**Mac's Imp**	A Munro	W O'Gorman	Tamdown Ltd	2/1
1991	**Dilum**	A Munro	P Cole	F Salman	2/7
1992	**Son Pardo**	J Reid	R Hannon	NTC (Racing) Ltd	7/1

For all 2 year-olds 1877-1988

The Lanson Champagne Vintage Stakes

In the hands of the same sponsors since 1975 when it was known quite simply as the Lanson Champagne Stakes, the race was upgraded to Group 3 from Listed status in 1986. The first notable winner was *Troy* who went on to win the 1979 Derby. *Don't Forget Me* won the 2,000 Guineas in 1987 while *Generous*, third in 1990, joined *Troy* on the Epsom roll of honour the following year, as did the 1991 winner *Dr.Devious*.

Run at Goodwood over 7 furlongs for 2 year-olds First Run 1975 Group 3

		Jockey	Trainer	Owner	Odds
1975	**Riboboy**	J Mercer	W R Hern	Lady Beaverbrook	8/11
1976	**Sky Ship**	J Mercer	W R Hern	R D Hollingsworth	10/11
1977	**Conte Santi**	B Taylor	H R Price	H Demetriou	3/1
1978	**Troy**	W Carson	W R Hern	Sir M Sobell	2/1
1979	**Marathon Gold**	J Mercer	H Cecil	Mrs L Freedman	9/4
1980	**Church Parade**	W Carson	W R Hern	HM The Queen	8/13
1981	**Treboro**	G Starkey	G Harwood	A Ward	5/4
1982	**All Systems Go**	G Duffield	G Pritchard-Gordon	A Rudolf	5/1
1983	**Trojan Fen**	L Piggott	H Cecil	S Niarchos	4/11
1984	**Petoski**	J Mercer	W R Hern	Lady Beaverbrook	2/1
1985	**Faustus**	S Cauthen	H Cecil	S Niarchos	9/4
1986	**Don't Forget Me**	P Eddery	R Hannon	James Horgan	7/1
1987	**Undercut**	P Eddery	G Harwood	K Abdulla	Evens
1988	**High Estate**	S Cauthen	H Cecil	H J Joel	6/5
1989	**Be My Chief**	S Cauthen	H Cecil	P Burrell	8/15
1990	**Mukaddamah**	W Carson	P Walwyn	H Al-Maktoum	6/4
1991	**Dr Devious**	W Carson	P Chapple-Hyam	R Sangster	9/4
1992	**Maroof**	W Carson	R Armstrong	H Al-Maktoum	8/1

The Goodwood Cup

Originally this was a silver cup, first contested in 1808 and won by Mr Trevanion's *Bucephalus*. At that time the trophy was not perpetual and as *Bucephalus* won the Cup outright with victories in the next two years, it had to be replaced and thus founded the Gold Cup won by *Shoe-strings* in 1812.

Of *Shoe-strings* we know little, but it is hard not to be fond of a race won in consecutive years by *Cricketer* and *Stumps*, even if *Stumps* did enjoy a walk-over.

The first really top class animal to win the Cup was *Priam*, in 1831 and 1832. The Derby winner of 1830 also won the Eclipse Foot, which as the name implies is a hoof of the great horse set in gold and donated by King William IV. This prize was competed for on only four occasions and is now used as a snuff box on the dining table in the Jockey Club at Newmarket, but *Priam* will be remembered as one of the finest Derby winners of the nineteenth century, being beaten only twice in a long and hectic career.

By the 1850s, foreign owners began to make their mark in Britain. The American Richard Ten Broeck's *Prioress* was the first USA bred horse to win a race in England when she won the Cesarewitch in 1857. *Prioress* finished third in the Goodwood Cup in 1859, and Ten Broeck's *Starke* took the Goodwood Stakes in the same year and the Cup in 1861.

French invaders started to appear. *Jouvence* won the Cup in 1853, and *Monarque* triumphed in the colours of Count Frédéric de Lagrange in 1857.

Flageolet was another for the French in 1873, but the best of all was almost certainly *Kincsem*. Bred in Hungary, she won the Cup in 1878, was unbeaten in fifty-four races and must rate as one of the greatest fillies of the century.

St Simon, barred from the classics by the death of his owner-breeder the Hungarian Prince Gustavus Batthyany, won by twenty lengths as the climax of an eleven race career in 1884. Such was *St Simon's* strength that Fred Archer could not pull him up until the horse had run himself out.

In modern times, few witnesses will forget *Predominate's* win by a short head in 1961 after breaking down irrevocably with a mile to go. His jockey Eph Smith was prepared to surrender, but *Predominate* would have nothing of it and added the Cup to his three successive Goodwood Stakes victories.

Rock Roi gained compensation for his disqualification after finishing first in the Ascot Gold Cup in 1971, while the 1976 winner *Mr Bigmore* was owned by the former Newmarket trainer Teddy Lambton. Mr Lambton was a man of fluctuating fortunes and *Mr Bigmore* was named after the local bailiff.

Run at Goodwood over 2 miles First Run 1812 Group 3

		Jockey	Trainer	Owner	Odds
1812	**Shoe-strings**	–	–	J Cope	–
1813	**Camerton**	–	–	H Biggs	–
1814	**Banquo**	–	–	D Blake	–
1815	**No Race**				
1816	**Scarecrow**	–	R D Boyce	Lord Egremont	–
1817/24	**No Race**				
1825	**Cricketer**	G Edwards	R Stephenson	Lord Egremont	–
1826	**Stumps**	W Arnull	R Stephenson	Lord Egremont	w.o.
1827	**Link Boy**	F Boyce	J Kent	Duke of Richmond	2/1
1828	**Miss Craven**	F Boyce	J Kent	Duke of Richmond	–

Dark Japan, ridden by Charlie Smirke, winner of the Goodwood Cup in 1927. This shows them after they took the Chester Cup that year.

		Jockey	Trainer	Owner	Odds
1829	**Fleur de Lis**	J Robinson	–	D Radcliffe	8/1
1830	**Fleur de Lis**	G Nelson	–	HM The King	7/2
1831	**Priam**	P Conolly	W Chifney	Lord Chesterfield	6/5
1832	**Priam**	P Conolly	W Chifney	Lord Chesterfield	Evens
1833	**Rubini**	F Boyce	J Kent	J Kent	100/7
1834	**Glencoe**	J Robinson	J Edwards	Lord Jersey	4/1
1835	**Rockingham**	J Robinson	–	J Theobald	5/1
1836	**Hornsea**	W Scott	J Scott	Lord Chesterfield	4/5
1837	**Carew**	E Flatman	J Scott	Lord Chesterfield	5/1
1838	**Harkaway**	C Wakefield	–	T Ferguson	5/4
1839	**Harkaway**	G Calloway	–	T Ferguson	Evens
1840	**Beggarman**	J Robinson	–	HRH Duke of Orleans	14/1
1841	**Charles the Twelfth**	C Marson	J Scott	A Johnstone	11/2
1842	**Charles the Twelfth**	J Robinson	J Scott	A Johnstone	5/2
1843	**Hyllus**	F Butler	–	Mr Lichtwald	4/1
1844	**Alice Hawthorn**	F Templeman	R Hesseltine	G Salvin	1/3
1845	**Miss Elis**	W Abdale	J B Day	J Gully	2/1
1846	**Grimston**	T Lye	T Dawson	J O'Brien	2/1
1847	**The Hero**	J Day	J B Day	J B Day	4/5
1848	**Van Tromp**	C Marlow	J Fobert	Lord Eglinton	4/6
1849	**Canezou**	F Butler	J Scott	Lord Stanley	8/13
1850	**Canezou**	F Butler	J Scott	Lord Stanley	2/1
1851	**Nancy**	J Charlton	J Marson	Mr Martinson	2/1
1852	**Kingston**	E Flatman	H Stebbing	J B Morris	6/1
1853	**Jouvence**	T Sherwood	Ralph Sherwood	A Lupin	10/1

		Jockey	Trainer	Owner	Odds
1854	**Virago**	J Wells	J B Day	H Padwick	1/6
1855	**Baroncino**	G Fordham	W King	Baron M de Rothschild	5/4
1856	**Rogerthorpe**	G Fordham	J Day	H Hill	8/1
1857	**Monarque**	T Ashmall	T Jennings	Comte F de Lagrange	100/6
1858	**Saunterer**	J Osborne Jnr	J Prince	J Merry	7/1
1859	**The Promised Land**	H Bray	W Day	W Day	3/1
1860	**Sweetsauce**	J Charlton	J Scott	Lord Annesley	8/1
1861	**Starke**	G Fordham	R B Pryor	R Ten Broeck	8/1
1862	**Tim Whiffler**	R Bullock	T S Dawson	Lord W Powlett	7/2
1863	**Isoline**	T French	J Godding	R C Naylor	6/1
1864	**Dollar**	J Kitchener	–	A Lupin	10/1
1865	**Ely**	H Custance	T Olliver	W S Cartwright	4/1
1866	**The Duke**	G Fordham	J Day	Marquis of Hastings	Evens
1867	**Vauban**	H Parry	J Day	Duke of Beaufort	4/7
1868	**Speculum**	S Kenyon	M Dawson	Duke of Newcastle	4/1
1869	**Restitution**	J Daley	J Hayhoe	Baron M de Rothschild	5/1
1870	**Siderolite**	J Wells	J Porter	Sir J Hawley	9/4
1871	**Shannon**	Hunt	–	F Mouncey	50/1
1872	**Favonius**	C Maidment	J Hayhoe	Baron M de Rothschild	2/1
1873	**Flageolet**	H Huxtable	T Jennings	C J Lefevre	9/4
1874	**Doncaster**	F Webb	R Peck	J Merry	2/1
1875	**Aventuriere**	T Chaloner	A Taylor Snr	Lord Ailesbury	8/1
1876	**New Holland**	T Cannon	C Blanton	Prince Soltykoff	9/4
1877	**Hampton**	F Webb	R Peck	F G Hobson	3/1
1878	**Kincsem**	E Madden	–	E Blascovitz	5/2
1879	**Isonomy**	T Cannon	J Porter	F Gretton	5/4
1880	**Dresden China**	J Snowden	W I'Anson Jnr	C Perkins	–
1881	**Madame du Barry**	J Snowden	W I'Anson Jnr	C Perkins	5/2
1882	**Friday**	E Martin	R Marsh	Duke of Hamilton	20/1
1883	**Border Minstrel**	G Fordham	F Bates	J Johnstone	11/10
1884	**St Simon**	C Wood	M Dawson	Duke of Portland	7/100
1885	**Althorp**	G Barrett	J Porter	Baron M de Hirsch	60/100
1886	**The Bard**	C Wood	M Gurry	R Peck	–
1887	**Savile**	G Barrett	J Porter	Duke of Westminster	5/6
1888	**Rada**	T Loates	M Dawson	Lord Falmouth	9/4
1889	**Trayles**	W T Robinson	J Jewitt	W de la Rue	1/4
1890	**Philomel**	T Cannon	Robert Sherwood	J T North	Evens
1891	**Gonsalvo**	G Barrett	J Porter	J Gretton	5/4
1892	**Martagon**	J Watts	J Ryan	D Baird	8/11
1893	**Barmecide**	G Barrett	C Andrews	J Burton	4/1
1894	**Kilsallaghan**	T Loates	J Jewitt	Capt J Machell	9/4
1895	**Florizel II**	J Watts	R Marsh	HRH the Prince of Wales	9/100
1896	**Count Schomberg**	M Cannon	W Leader	R Lebaudy	w.o.
1897	**Count Schomberg**	S Loates	W Leader	R Lebaudy	11/10
1898	**King's Messenger**	O Madden	F Cole	Lord Penrhyn	4/1
1899	**Merman**	C Wood	W T Robinson	Lady de Bathe	6/5
1900	**Mazagan**	F Rickaby	H Enoch	D Baird	13/2
1901	**Fortunatus**	D Maher	R Marsh	A James	4/6
1902	**Perseus**	J Childs	R Marsh	A James	Evens
1903	**Rabelais**	J Watts	R Marsh	A James	5/4
1904	**Saltpetre**	W Lane	H Chandler	D Faber	5/2
1905	**Red Robe**	W Griggs	R Marsh	A James	100/12
1906	**Plum Tree**	O Madden	A Taylor Jnr	A W Cox	9/4
1907	**The White Knight**	W Halsey	H Sadler	W R Wyndham	5/4
1908	**Radium**	O Madden	J Watson	L de Rothschild	11/4
1909	**Carrousel**	C Trigg	F Leach	H J King	9/2
1910	**Magic**	F Rickaby Jnr	F Leach	H Beddington	20/1
1911	**Kilbroney**	Wal Griggs	C Waugh	Lord St David	4/1
1912	**Tullibardine**	E Wheatley	S Darling	J Buchanan	2/1
1913	**Catmint**	D Maher	T Jennings Jnr	L Brassey	100/8
1914	**Son-in-Law**	F Bullock	R Day	Sir A Bailey	9/4
1915/18	**No Race**				
1919	**Queen's Square**	S Donoghue	A Taylor Jnr	A R Cox	7/4
1920	**Mount Royal**	S Donoghue	H Leader	Lady Cunliffe-Owen	100/30
1921	**Bucks**	S Donoghue	R Day	Sir A Bailey	2/1
1922	**Flamboyant**	W Lister	R Day	Mrs G Robinson	1/3
1923	**Triumph**	J Childs	J Watson	A de Rothschild	4/5
1924	**Teresina**	V Smyth	R C Dawson	HH Aga Khan	9/4
1925	**Cloudbank**	S Donoghue	G Laing Ward	J White	10/1
1926	**Glommen**	H Wragg	W Earl	S B Joel	10/11
1927	**Dark Japan**	C Smirke	R C Dawson	HH Aga Khan	4/11
1928	**Kinchinjunga**	F Fox	R Gooch	H C Sutton	4/1
1929	**Old Orkney**	F Lane	R Gooch	J Murphy	11/2
1930	**Brown Jack**	S Donoghue	I Anthony	Sir H Wernher	4/9
1931	**Salmon Leap**	T Weston	G Lambton	Mrs A James	5/2

The runners jump off for the 1939 Goodwood Cup. This race, like the Stakes, starts and finishes in front of the stand.

		Jockey	Trainer	Owner	Odds
1932	**Brulette**	G Richards	F Darling	Lord Woolavington	5/2
1933	**Sans Peine**	E Smith	J Jarvis	E Esmond	20/1
1934	**Loosestrife**	G Richards	E Richards	P Johnson	11/2
1935	**Tiberius**	T Weston	J Lawson	Sir A Bailey	2/9
1936	**Cecil**	T Weston	J Lawson	Sir A Bailey	13/8
1937	**Fearless Fox**	E Smith	J Jarvis	A Smith	6/1
1938	**Epigram**	B Carslake	N Cannon	J V Rank	6/1
1939	**Dubonnet**	T Lowrey	B Jarvis	J P Hornung	6/4
1940/45	**No Race**				
1946	**Marsyas II**	C Elliott	C Semblat	M Boussac	1/3
1947	**Monsieur l'Amiral**	C Smirke	E Charlier	Mrs I Henderson	1/2
1948	**Tenerani**	E Camici	N Bertie	F Tesio	100/30
1949	**Alycidon**	D Smith	W Earl	Lord Derby	30/100
1950	**Val Drake**	R Poincelet	R Carver	Mme L Volterra	4/1
1951	**Pan II**	R Poincelet	E Pollet	E Constant	5/6
1952	**Medway**	D Smith	F N Winter	P Bartholemew	5/1
1953	**Souepi**	C Elliott	G Digby	G Digby	2/1
1954	**Blarney Stone**	W Rickaby	V Smyth	M McAlpine	13/2
1955	**Double Bore**	T Gosling	J Tree	J Tree	9/1
1956	**Zarathustra**	W H Carr	C Boyd-Rochfort	T Gray	10/11
1957	**Tenterhooks**	E Britt	C Elsey	Lord Allendale	2/1
1958	**Gladness**	L Piggott	M V O'Brien	J McShain	1/2
1959	**Dickens**	D Smith	C Boyd-Rochfort	Lady Z Wernher	9/4
1960	**Exar**	L Piggott	N Murless	C Vittadini	4/9
1961	**Predominate**	E Smith	T E Leader	H J Joel	11/4
1962	**Sagacity**	W H Carr	C Boyd-Rochfort	Lady Cholmondeley	5/1
1963	**Trelawny**	A Breasley	G Todd	Mrs L Carver	8/13
1964	**Raise You Ten**	S Clayton	C Boyd-Rochfort	P Widener	Evens
1965	**Apprentice**	S Clayton	C Boyd-Rochfort	HM The Queen	8/1
1966	**Gaulois**	R Hutchinson	C Boyd-Rochfort	HM The Queen	15/2
1967	**Wrekin Rambler**	A Breasley	G Richards	G Murphy	2/1
1968	**Ovaltine**	B Taylor	J F Watts	G Cooper	5/2
1969	**Richmond Fair**	J Gorton	B Hobbs	T Blackwell	5/4
1970	**Parthenon**	G Starkey	H Cecil	Sir R Macdonald-Buchanan	3/1
1971	**Rock Roi**	D Keith	P Walwyn	F Hue-Williams	4/6
1972	**Erimo Hawk**	P Eddery	G Barling	Y Yamamoto	10/11
1973	**Proverb**	E Johnson	B Hills	J Chandos-Pole	6/4
1974	**Proverb**	L Piggott	B Hills	J Chandos-Pole	4/5
1975	**Girandole**	L Piggott	M Stoute	J Hattersley	7/2
1976	**Mr Bigmore**	G Starkey	P Robinson	E Lambton	3/1
1977	**Grey Baron**	G Lewis	B Hobbs	P Parnell	11/4
1978	**Tug Of War**	B Rouse	D Whelan	Mrs Y Perry	20/1
1979	**Le Moss**	J Mercer	H Cecil	C d'Alessio	1/2
1980	**Le Moss**	J Mercer	H Cecil	C d'Alessio	4/7
1981	**Ardross**	L Piggott	H Cecil	C St George	2/9
1982	**Heighlin**	S Cauthen	D Elsworth	J Burr	8/1
1983	**Little Wolf**	W Carson	W R Hern	Lord Porchester	4/9
1984	**Gildoran**	S Cauthen	B Hills	R Sangster	9/4
1985	**Valuable Witness**	P Eddery	J Tree	S Niarchos	11/10
1986	**Longboat**	W Carson	W R Hern	R D Hollingsworth	1/3
1987	**Sergeyevich**	W Carson	J Dunlop	Mrs D Riley-Smith	Evens
1988	**Sadeem**	G Starkey	G Harwood	Sheikh Mohammed	4/6
1989	**Mazzacano**	P Eddery	G Harwood	A Ward	15/2
1990	**Lucky Moon**	W Carson	J Dunlop	Duchess of Norfolk	11/8
1991	**Further Flight**	M Hills	B Hills	S Wingfield Digby	9/2
1992	**Further Flight**	M Hills	B Hills	S Wingfield Digby	7/1

Run over 2 miles 5 furlongs 1812-1989, 2 miles 4 furlongs in 1990 and 2 miles from 1991

The King George V Stakes

Founded in 1911 to celebrate the Coronation of King George V, the King George is best described as a helter-skelter for top class horses. Certainly some remarkable animals have won. *Tetratema*, a son of the brilliant *The Tetrarch*, won the Two Thousand Guineas in 1920. He had little chance of staying the Derby distance on pedigree but was made favourite none the less. He was well beaten, as he was in the Eclipse Stakes but reverting to sprint distances won the King George twice along with the Kings Stand at Ascot and the July Cup.

Mumtaz Mahal, a foundation mare of the breeding empire created by the Aga Khan III in the twenties won in 1924 and *Diomedes*, one of the fastest horses of the inter-war period and owned by the successful gambler Sidney Beer, won in 1925 ridden by the stylish Jack Leach.

Indeed jockeyship in sprint races is of greater importance than might seem apparent in such pillar to post affairs. This was especially true in the days before the introduction of starting stalls when races could literally be won and lost at the old barrier start. It is no coincidence that the late Sir Gordon Richards won the King George six years in succession between 1947 and 1952.

Scene in the paddock before the start of the 1970 King George Stakes at Goodwood.

Run at Goodwood over 5 furlongs First Run 1911 Group 3

		Jockey	Trainer	Owner	Odds
1911	**Spanish Prince**	F Wootton	C Morton	J B Joel	10/1
1912	**Golden Rod**	D Maher	S Pickering	P Nelke	4/1
1913	**Hornet's Beauty**	J H Martin	F Leach	Sir W Cooke	4/1
1914	**Harmonicon**	J H Martin	A J Joyner	H P Whitney	11/8
1915/18	**No Race**				
1919	**Chiffre d'Amour**	B Carslake	H S Persse	Lord Furness	5/1
1920	**Tetratema**	B Carslake	H S Persse	D McCalmont	–
1921	**Tetratema**	B Carslake	H S Persee	D McCalmont	8/15
1922	**Roman Bachelor**	G Archibald	P P Gilpin	N Baring	7/1
1923	**Sicyon**	W McLachlan	E de Mestre	S B Joel	15/8
1924	**Mumtaz Mahal**	G Archibald	R C Dawson	HH Aga Khan	20/21
1925	**Diomedes**	J Leach	H Leader	S W Beer	11/10
1926	**Oojah**	B Carslake	W Earl	S B Joel	100/7
1927	**Endowment**	J Nolan	F Darling	Lord Lonsdale	7/2
1928	**Queen's Bower**	F Fox	R Gooch	E Harmsworth	5/2
1929	**Tiffin**	F Fox	F Darling	Lord Ellesmere	4/11
1930	**Stingo**	C Ray	W Lowe	D Gant	5/2
1931	**Stingo**	C Ray	W Lowe	D Gant	2/5
1932	**Clustine**	H Beasley	S H Darling	A K Macomber	5/1
1933	**Myrobella**	G Richards	F Darling	Lord Lonsdale	8/13
1934	**Old Riley**	J Childs	T Rintoul	H J Brueton	11/10
1935	**Strathcarron**	R A Jones	F N Winter	H Collins	9/2
1936	**Veuve Clicquot**	E Smith	J Jarvis	Sir J Jarvis	2/1
1937	**Veuve Clicquot**	E Smith	J Jarvis	Sir J Jarvis	11/8
1938	**Neuvy**	G Richards	Frank Butters	Prince Aly Khan	Evens
1939	**Mickey the Greek**	H Wragg	H Leach	N Frieze	13/2
1940	**No Race**				
1941	**Antecedent**	E Smith	J Jarvis	T F Blackwell	6/1
1942/45	**No Race**				
1946	**Honeyway**	E Smith	J Jarvis	Lord Milford	7/100
1947	**Daily Mail**	G Richards	W Nightingall	Miss D Paget	1/8
1948	**Royal Barge**	G Richards	P Allden	A E Allnatt	7/4
1949	**Abernant**	G Richards	N Murless	R Macdonald-Buchanan	30/100
1950	**Abernant**	G Richards	N Murless	R Macdonald-Buchanan	4/9
1951	**Bakshishi**	G Richards	H Wragg	Begum Aga Khan	100/30

		Jockey	Trainer	Owner	Odds
1952	**Royal Serenade**	G Richards	H Wragg	G M Bell	7/2
1953	**Fairy Flax**	A Breasley	J Lawson	R S Clark	6/1
1954	**Four of Spades**	W R Johnstone	G Beeby	A L Hawkins	100/30
1955	**Democratic**	A Breasley	P Prendergast	F More O'Ferrall	11/10
1956	**Palariva**	R Poincelet	A Head	HH Aga Khan	6/1
1957	**Refined**	D Smith	P Prendergast	Lady M van Cutsem	5/2
1958	**Right Boy**	L Piggott	W Dutton	G Gilbert	8/13
1959	**Right Boy**	L Piggott	H Rohan	H D H Wills	8/13
1960	**Bleep Bleep**	W H Carr	H Cottrill	Mrs M Turner	100/8
1961	**Floribunda**	R Hutchinson	P Prendergast	Mrs J R Mullion	4/6
1962	**La Tendresse**	G Bougoure	P Prendergast	Mrs P Poe	11/10
1963	**Secret Step**	A Breasley	P Hastings-Bass	P Mellon	11/10
1964	**Matatina**	L Piggott	F Armstrong	Mrs R C Wilson	Evens
1965	**Pugnacity**	L Piggott	W Wharton	Maj L B Holliday	9/4
1966	**Polyfoto**	B Taylor	E Reavey	Mrs C J Reavey	8/1
1967	**Right Strath**	J Mercer	W Nightingall	A J Allen	100/6
1968	**So Blessed**	F Durr	M Jarvis	D Robinson	4/5
1969	**Laser Light**	R Hutchinson	J Dunlop	Duke of Norfolk	2/1
1970	**Raffingora**	L Piggott	W Marshall	A G M Stevens	4/1
1971	**Constans**	L Piggott	J Tree	Miss M Sheriffe	9/4
1972	**Stilvi**	J Gorton	B Hobbs	G Cambanis	100/30
1973	**Sandford Lad**	A Murray	H R Price	C Olley	6/5
1974	**Singing Bede**	G Baxter	D Marks	Mrs C Grainger	12/1
1975	**Auction Ring**	J Mercer	W R Hern	S Weinstock	85/40
1976	**Music Boy**	G Starkey	B Lunness	Cheveley Park Stud	16/1
1977	**Scarcely Blessed**	R Hutchinson	R F Johnson Houghton	E Holland-Martin	6/1
1978	**Music Maestro**	G Starkey	M Stoute	R Clifford-Turner	6/1
1979	**Ahonoora**	G Starkey	F Durr	E Alkahlifa	Evens
1980	**Valeriga**	L Piggott	L Cumani	C d'Alessio	9/2
1981	**King of Spain**	P Cook	P Cundell	Avon Industries Ltd	4/1
1982	**Tina's Pet**	L Piggott	G Huffer	Cheveley Park Stud	6/1
1983	**Soba**	D Nicholls	D Chapman	Mrs M Hills	9/4
1984	**Anita's Prince**	L Piggott	R Lister	Mrs A Quinn	2/1
1985	**Primo Dominie**	W R Swinburn	M Stoute	Cheveley Park Stud	5/4
1986	**Double Schwartz**	P Eddery	C Nelson	R Sangster	6/4
1987	**Singing Steven**	B Rouse	R Hannon	S Bennett	14/1
1988	**Silver Fling**	P Eddery	I Balding	G Strawbridge	2/1
1989	**Statoblest**	R Cochrane	L Cumani	R Duchossois	11/1
1990	**Argentum**	J Reid	L J Holt	K F Khan	4/1
1991	**Title Roll**	W Carson	T Stack	R Sangster	8/1
1992	**Freddie Lloyd**	J Reid	N Callaghan	M Hill	5/1

Run at Newmarket in 1941

The Molecomb Stakes

Crucifix was the first winner of distinction, going on to take the 2,000 Guineas, 1,000 Guineas and the Oaks. *Fille de l'Air* won the Oaks, as did *La Fleche,* and the 1,000 Guineas also; she ought to have won the Derby, for which she started favourite at 11/10, but her jockey George Barrett was already showing the signs of mental instability which were to terminate his career. Sold to Sir Tatton Sykes via an agent, namely Lord Marcus Beresford, the mean old Yorkshireman was horrified to find himself with a bill for one of the finest mares in Europe amounting to 12,600 guineas, admittedly a large sum in 1896.

However, nothing can forgive Sir Tatton's conduct in allowing *La Fleche* to stand unattended in a horse box at Sledmere station for fourteen days. She was only saved from starvation by the local station master who fed her from the fodder drawn from his own smallholding. Her six foals later produced £21,000 for Sir Tatton.

Now open to colts, the Molecomb is these days a race for good class speedy two-year-olds, and few runners have classic pretensions.

Run at Goodwood over 5 furlongs for 2 year-olds First Run 1829 Group 3

		Jockey	Trainer	Owner	Odds
1829	**Convert**	F Boyce	J Kent	Duke of Richmond	–
1830	**filly by Emilius**	F Buckle Jnr	J Forth	J Forth	Evens
1831/32	**No Race**				
1833	**Defensive**	J Chapple	I Sadler	I Sadler	1/4
1834	**Waresti**	J B Day	J B Day	S Wreford	–
1835	**Elis**	E Flatman	R Prince Jnr	C Greville	4/6
1836	**Defender**	J Chapple	I Sadler	I Sadler	1/2
1837	**Grey Momus**	J B Day	J B Day	J Bowes	4/7
1838	**Wapiti**	J Day	J B Day	S Wreford	Evens
1839	**Crucifix**	J B Day	J B Day	Lord G Bentinck	1/4

		Jockey	Trainer	Owner	Odds
1840	**Decision**	S Darling	–	Capt Williamson	6/4
1841	**Barrier**	P Conolly	W Treen	W Treen	1/2
1842	**The Caster**	W Scott	J Scott	Lord Maidstone	1/3
1843	**The Ugly Buck**	J Day	J B Day	J B Day	1/5
1844	**Nutbourne**	J Day	J B Day	J Gully	7/2
1845	**Sting**	H Bell	J Forth	J Forth	6/4
1846	**Planet**	W Abdale	J Kent Jnr	Lord G Bentinck	7/4
1847	**Glendower**	E Flatman	M Dilly	G Payne	1/4
1848	**Mr Milner**	A Day	J Day	F Clarke	4/1
1849	**William the Conqueror**		J Kent Jnr	Lord H G Lennox	w.o.
1850	**Teddington**	S Templeman	A Taylor Snr	Sir J Hawley	5/1
1851	**Glenluce**	E Flatman	W Dilly	G Payne	–
1852	**Elmsthorpe**	A Day	J B Day	H Padwick	1/4
1853	**Andover**	A Day	J Day	J Gully	Evens
1854	**Polydore**	E Flatman	W Dilly	G Payne	2/1
1855	**Enchanter**	A Day	J Day	J Gully	1/2
1856	**Lambourn**	T Aldcroft	E Parr	E Parr	7/4
1857	**The Lord of Lorn**	T Aldcroft	J Prince	J Merry	4/6
1858	**Merryman**	E Flatman	A Taylor Snr	C Greville	5/2
1859	**Buccaneer**	J Goater	R Milton	Lord Portsmouth	2/7
1860	**Diophantus**	A French	Jos Dawson	Lord Stamford	1/2
1861	**Ace of Clubs**	J Osborne Jnr	J Scott	Lord Annesley	7/1
1862	**c by Lord of the Isle**	T Aldcroft	M Dawson	J Merry	4/1
1863	**Fille de L'Air**	A Watkins	T Jennings	Comte F de Lagrange	3/1
1864	**Koenig**	G Fordham	J Day	Duke of Beaufort	4/7
1865	**The Student**	A Edwards	M Dawson	J Merry	2/5
1866	**Marksman**	G Fordham	J Waugh	J Merry	5/1
1867	**Banditto**	T Cannon	W Day	Sir F Johnstone	5/2
1868	**Belladrum**	J Daley	M Dawson	J Merry	1/5
1869	**Mantilla**	T French	Jos Dawson	F Pryor	6/4
1870	**General**	H Custance	T Jennings	Comte F de Lagrange	2/7
1871	**Vanderdecken**	T French	G Bloss	Sir G Chetwynd	6/4
1872	**Somerset**	T Cannon	J Cannon	Lord Lonsdale	1/8
1873	**Packington**	J Goater	–	Mr Bruton	8/11
1874	**Craig Millar**	T Chaloner	A Taylor Snr	W S Crawfurd	3/1
1875	**Red Cross Knight**	H Jeffery	–	Mr Gerard	3/1
1876	**Shillelagh**	H Parry	J Hayhoe	H Baltazzi	2/1
1877	**Red Hazard**	F Archer	J Porter	F Gretton	4/6
1878	**colt by Cambuscan**	F Archer	J Cannon	Count Festetic	100/15
1879	**Brotherhood**	F Archer	W Arnull	H E Beddington	3/1
1880	**Paw Paw**	H Jeffery	J Pincus	P Lorillard	5/1
1881	**Adrastus**	H Jeffery	W Matthews	I Bate	20/1
1882	**St Blaise**	T Cannon	J Porter	Lord Alington	Evens
1883	**La Trappe**	F Archer	M Dawson	Lord Hastings	20/1
1884	**Luminary**	F Archer	J Porter	Lord Alington	2/7
1885	**The Devil to Pay**	T Bruckshaw	J Perren	J Bowes	25/1
1886	**Freedom**	F Archer	J Porter	Duke of Westminster	Evens
1887	**Friar's Balsam**	T Cannon	J Porter	Sir F Johnstone	w.o.
1888	**Seclusion**	G Barrett	C W Golding	Duchess of Montrose	2/5
1889	**Le Nord**	F Barrett	A Hayhoe	Baron L de Rothschild	1/4
1890	**Cleator**	J Watts	J Enoch	J Lowther	2/5
1891	**La Fleche**	G Barrett	J Porter	Baron M de Hirsch	1/3
1892	**Harbinger**	M Cannon	J Ryan	D Baird	–
1893	**La Nievre**	T Loates	A Hayhoe	Baron L de Rothschild	10/11
1894	**Bentworth**	W Bradford	W G Stevens	C Trimmer	Evens
1895	**Rampion**	M Cannon	J Porter	Duke of Westminster	100/30
1896	**Galtee More**	J Watts	S Darling	J Gubbins	2/9
1897	**Royal Footstep**	T Calder	W Waugh	Sir J Blundell Maple	11/10
1898	**Vara**	O Madden	R Marsh	Duke of Devonshire	1/6
1899	**O'Donovan Rossa**	J Watts	R Marsh	A James	Evens
1900	**Princess Melton**	L Reiff	A Gilbert	J Musker	2/5
1901	**filly by Melton**	J H Martin	A Gilbert	J Musker	5/1
1902	**Quintessence**	H Randall	J Chandler	Lord Falmouth	8/11
1903	**Islesman**	H Aylin	H Enoch	D Baird	5/2
1904	**Vedas**	G McCall	W T Robinson	F de Wend-Fenton	8/15
1905	**Colonia**	H Jones	W T Robinson	W Hall-Walker	2/1
1906	**My Pet II**	D Maher	D Waugh	W Raphael	4/7
1907	**Sea King**	W Griggs	T Waugh	Sir R W B Jardine	100/6
1908	**Perdiccas**	W Higgs	S Darling	Lord Rosebery	4/5
1909	**Tressady**	W Higgs	S Darling	J Buchanan	11/8
1910	**Beaurepaire**	H Jones	D Waugh	W Raphael	5/2
1911	**White Star**	F Wootton	C Morton	J B Joel	2/5
1912	**Rock Flint**	D Maher	G Blackwell	H Beddington	4/1
1913	**Black Jester**	F Wootton	C Morton	J B Joel	1/4
1914	**Redfern**	S Donoghue	A Taylor Jnr	Lord Cadogan	11/10

		Jockey	Trainer	Owner	Odds
1915/18	**No Race**				
1919	**Tetratema**	B Carslake	H S Persse	D McCalmont	1/2
1920	**Trash**	J Childs	A Taylor Jnr	J Watson	7/1
1921	**Lembach**	F Bullock	R Day	E Moore	5/2
1922	**Town Guard**	G Archibald	P P Gilpin	Lord Woolavington	1/11
1923	**Mumtaz Mahal**	G Hulme	R C Dawson	HH Aga Khan	1/40
1924	**Priory Park**	F Bullock	G T Clancy	C Howard	10/1
1925	**Review Order**	H Beasley	H S Persse	Lord Barnby	7/4
1926	**Shian Mor**	H Jelliss	B Jarvis	J S Courtauld	11/10
1927	**Black Watch**	G Richards	P P Gilpin	L Neumann	7/2
1928	**Belle Mere**	J Leach	F Leach	Sir J Buchanan Jardine	9/4
1929	**Diolite**	C Ray	F Templeman	Sir H Hirst	3/1
1930	**Jacopo**	J Childs	C Boyd-Rochfort	M Field	10/11
1931	**Safe Return**	F Fox	F Darling	Lord Woolavington	5/6
1932	**Betty**	R Dick	J Lawson	Lord Astor	5/2
1933	**Light Brocade**	B Carslake	Frank Butters	Lord Durham	8/1
1934	**La Gaite**	R Perryman	Frank Butters	HH Aga Khan	10/1
1935	**Crosspatch**	T Lowrey	B Jarvis	J S Courtauld	9/1
1936	**Bright Beam**	G Richards	F Darling	J A Dewar	13/8
1937	**Anne of Austria**	C Smirke	Frank Butters	HH Aga Khan	3/1
1938	**Money Down**	G Richards	F Darling	R B Strassburger	2/5
1939	**Allure**	M Beary	V Smyth	Sir M McAlpine	3/1
1940	**No Race**				
1941	**Feberion**	R Perryman	J Lawson	Lord Glanely	13/2
1942/45	**No Race**				
1946	**Rule Britannia**	H Wragg	W Earl	Lord Derby	33/1
1947	**Phaetonia**	G Richards	F Darling	J A Dewar	5/4
1948	**Integrity**	C Smirke	J Leach	Mrs J V Rank	7/2
1949	**Diableretta**	G Richards	Frank Butters	HH Aga Khan	1/8
1950	**Crawley Beauty**	G Richards	N Murless	G Loder	4/6
1951	**Tayeh**	G Richards	M Marsh	HH Aga Khan	9/4
1952	**Tessa Gillian**	W Rickaby	J Jarvis	Sir A Jarvis	5/4
1953	**Urshalim**	C Smirke	M Marsh	R B Moller	11/2
1954	**Brave Venture**	W Rickaby	J Jarvis	H D H Wills	100/6
1955	**Palariva**	R Poincelet	A Head	HH Aga Khan	4/9
1956	**Pharsalia**	W Snaith	H Cottrill	Maj L B Holliday	11/8
1957	**Abelia**	L Piggott	N Murless	B Hornung	1/5
1958	**Krakenwake**	A Breasley	N Bertie	F Alexander	11/4
1959	**Queensberry**	E Smith	J A Waugh	B Hornung	5/4
1960	**Cynara**	J Mercer	H Wragg	G A Oldham	2/9
1961	**La Tendresse**	R Hutchinson	P Prendergast	Mrs P Poe	Evens
1962	**Royal Indiscretion**	G Bougoure	P Prendergast	Mrs P Poe	11/8
1963	**Crimea II**	W H Carr	C Boyd-Rochfort	Mrs J Hanes	11/2
1964	**Regal Pink**	G Bougoure	P Prendergast	Mrs J Olin	5/2
1965	**Reet Lass**	B Connorton	W Gray	Mrs V Gray	100/9
1966	**Smooth**	L Piggott	R F Johnson Houghton	Mrs D A Rasbotham	9/2
1967	**Lowna**	G Moore	N Murless	Mrs N Murless	7/4
1968	**Flying Legs**	L Piggott	M Jarvis	D Robinson	4/1
1969	**Mange Tout**	B Foy	K Cundell	Mrs D Sieff	8/11
1970	**Cawston's Pride**	B Taylor	F Maxwell	L B Hall	1/5
1971	**Pert Lassie**	G Starkey	H Cecil	Mrs S Joel	4/7
1972	**Miss Slip**	J Lindley	W Marshall	Mrs I Hill	6/4
1973	**Bitty Girl**	B Raymond	M Jarvis	D Robinson	7/4
1974	**Lady Rowley**	L Piggott	N Callaghan	G Cooke	4/5
1975	**Hayloft**	L Piggott	R F Johnson Houghton	J Rowles	3/1
1976	**Be Easy**	R Hutchinson	J Dunlop	A Gooda	9/1
1977	**Hatta**	R Hutchinson	J Dunlop	Sheikh Mohammed	7/1
1978	**Greenland Park**	H White	W Hastings-Bass	Greenland Park Ltd	5/6
1979	**Keep Off**	W Carson	J Dunlop	Mrs J R Mullion	7/1
1980	**Marwell**	L Piggott	M Stoute	E J Loder	4/6
1981	**Prowess Prince**	L Piggott	E Eldin	S Liem	4/5
1982	**Kafu**	G Starkey	G Harwood	HH Yazid & A Al Saud Ltd	6/5
1983	**Precocious**	L Piggott	H Cecil	Lord Tavistock	30/100
1984	**Absent Chimes**	P Robinson	D Thom	B Hathaway	11/4
1985	**Hotbee**	T Williams	J Bridger	A G Speake	100/1
1986	**Gemini Fire**	S Cauthen	P Felgate	J D Abell	33/1
1987	**Classic Ruler**	J Reid	C Nelson	W Patterson	5/2
1988	**Almost Blue**	J Carroll	J Berry	A Shelton	10/1
1989	**Haunting Beauty**	P Eddery	J Etherington	Triangle Thoroughbreds	3/1
1990	**Poets Cove**	J Reid	W Carter	P R Cruden	11/2
1991	**Sahara Star**	J Reid	M Stoute	T Sellier	2/1
1992	**Millyant**	M Roberts	R Guest	Bradmill Ltd	9/2

For 2 year-old fillies only 1932-1980.

Run at Newmarket in 1941.

The Nassau Stakes

It is not surprising to find that most of the early runnings of the Nassau Stakes were dominated either by Lord George Bentinck, his patron the Duke of Richmond or his close friends George Payne and Charles Greville. In fact with the exception of Payne's animals, they were owned by Bentinck who was forced to run the horses in other colours in order to deceive his father, the 4th Duke of Portland who strongly disapproved of his son's gambling activities.

The 1881 Oaks and 1,000 Guineas winner *Thebais* and *La Flèche* were the outstanding winners in the last century and not surprisingly this race, originally for three-year-old fillies only, but opened to older fillies and mares in 1975, has produced some famous broodmares, notably *Selene* who's first foal *Sickle* was the progenitor of such famous horses as *Native Dancer* and *Sea Bird 11*. She was also the dam of *Hyperion*, and in more recent times *Roussalka* has produced *Ristna*, winner of the Sun Chariot Stakes and *Gayane*, a top class sprinter. *Roussalka's* other claim to fame is that she provided Lester Piggott with his three-thousandth winner on the flat in the Princess Margaret Stakes at Ascot in 1974.

Left: **A bay filly, *Coppelia* won the Nassau Stakes in 1935. *Right:* The next year the race was won by a chestnut *Barrowby Gem*. Both were ridden by Gordon Richards.**

Run at Goodwood over 1 mile 2 furlongs for fillies & mares   First Run 1840   Group 2

		Jockey	Trainer	Owner	Odds
1840	**Rosa Bianca**	J B Day	J B Day	Lord G Bentinck	1/3
1841	**Scarf**	S Darling	–	Lord Exeter	5/1
1842	**Dil-bar**	E Flatman	T Taylor	Lord Chesterfield	5/2
1843	**Mania**	E Flatman	M Dilly	G Payne	4/6
1844	**All round my Hat**	S Rogers	J Kent Jnr	Lord G Bentinck	6/1
1845	**Refraction**	H Bell	J Kent Jnr	Duke of Richmond	6/5
1846	**Princess Alice**	W Abdale	J Kent Jnr	Lord G Bentinck	4/6
1847	**Clementina**	E Flatman	W Dilly	G Payne	5/2
1848	**Canezou**	F Butler	J Scott	Lord Stanley	2/1
1849	**Clarissa**	E Flatman	W Dilly	C Greville	4/6
1850	**Nutmeg**	C Marlow	W Harlock	Lord Exeter	5/4
1851	**Anspach**	F Butler	J Kent Jnr	G W Gratwicke	7/1
1852	**Hirsuta**	E Flatman	W Dilly	G Payne	4/6
1853	**Mayfair**	F Butler	J Scott	Gen Anson	4/6
1854	**Virago**	J Wells	J B Day	H Padwick	–
1855	**Instructress**	T Ashmall	T Eskrett	M Magenis	Evens
1856	**Mincepie**	A Day	J Day	H Hill	2/1
1857	**Beechnut**	G Fordham	W Harlock	Lord Exeter	Evens
1858	**Go-ahead**	T Ashmall	J Scott	J Bowes	–
1859	**Cantine**	E Flatman	A Taylor Snr	Lord Ailesbury	1/4
1860	**Provision**	A Edwards	Jos Dawson	Lord Stamford	–
1861	**Pardalote**	A Edwards	Jos Dawson	Lord Stamford	4/7
1862	**Bertha**	A Edwards	Jos Dawson	Lord Stamford	Evens
1863	**Fantail**	W Boyce	R Boyce	R Boyce	4/6
1864	**Bradamante**	H Grimshaw	A Taylor Snr	C Greville	5/4
1865	**Peeress**	H Grimshaw	–	R W Cameron	12/1
1866	**Hebe**	J Norman	W Harlock	Lord Exeter	–
1867	**The Duchess**	T Cannon	–	W Edgar	2/1
1868	**Leonie**	T Chaloner	M Dawson	Duke of Hamilton	6/1
1869	**Morna**	J Adams	J Porter	Sir J Hawley	1/5
1870	**Agility**	J Osborne Jnr	W Osborne	J W King	4/7
1871	**Lady Atholstane**	G Fordham	–	G Keswick	4/1
1872	**Maid of Perth**	T French	–	R Long	6/4
1873	**Albani**	–	R Peck	J Merry	w.o.
1874	**Aventuriere**	T Chaloner	A Taylor Snr	Lord Ailesbury	5/2
1875	**Spinaway**	F Archer	M Dawson	Lord Falmouth	4/6
1876	**Zee**	J Goater	W Gilbert	H Savile	5/1
1877	**Lady Golightly**	F Archer	M Dawson	Lord Falmouth	1/2
1878	**Eue de Vie**	H Constable	T Leader	W S Cartwright	6/4
1879	**Reconciliation**	G Fordham	J Perren	J Bowes	6/4
1880	**Muriel**	F Archer	M Dawson	Lord Falmouth	3/1
1881	**Thebais**	G Fordham	A Taylor Snr	W S Crawfurd	4/6
1882	**St Marguerite**	C Wood	R Sherrard	W S Crawfurd	2/5
1883	**Spectre**	F Webb	J Porter	Duke of Westminster	5/4
1884	**Sandiway**	F Archer	J Porter	Duke of Westminster	4/6

		Jockey	Trainer	Owner	Odds
1885	**Armida**	F Archer	M Dawson	Lord Hastings	100/14
1886	**Miss Jummy**	J Watts	R Marsh	Duke of Hamilton	11/4
1887	**Maize**	T Cannon	J Ryan	D Baird	100/8
1888	**Zanzibar**	G Barrett	C W Golding	Duchess of Montrose	5/2
1889	**Wrinkle**	W T Robinson	J Jewitt	W de la Rue	2/1
1890	**Memoir**	J Watts	G Dawson	Duke of Portland	8/13
1891	**Haute Saone**	F Barrett	A Hayhoe	Baron L de Rothschild	2/5
1892	**La Fleche**	G Barrett	J Porter	Baron M de Hirsch	8/11
1893	**Harfleur II**	T Loates	A Hayhoe	Baron L de Rothschild	–
1894	**Throstle**	M Cannon	J Porter	Lord Alington	6/1
1895	**Butterfly**	W Bradford	T Jennings Jnr	L Brassey	–
1896	**Miss Fraser**	F Finlay	John Dawson Jnr	Lord Ellesmere	9/4
1897	**Perce Neige**	M Cannon	W Gibbons	Prince Soltykoff	5/6
1898	**Chinook**	C Wood	J Huggins	P Lorillard	7/2
1899	**Saint Lundi**	M Cannon	J Porter	Lord Crewe	7/2
1900	**Merry Gal**	L Reiff	W T Robinson	W Hall-Walker	Evens
1901	**Royal Summons**	M Cannon	W Waugh	Sir J Blundell Maple	6/1
1902	**Sceptre**	F W Hardy	R S Sievier	R S Sievier	2/1
1903	**Red Lily**	L Lyne	H Sadler	L Brassey	10/1
1904	**Pretty Polly**	W Lane	P P Gilpin	E Loder	1/33
1905	**Cherry Lass**	H Jones	W T Robinson	W Hall-Walker	1/9
1906	**Glasconbury**	D Maher	G Lambton	Lord Derby	4/9
1907	**Altitude**	D Maher	G Lambton	Lord Derby	5/1
1908	**Siberia**	B Dillon	P P Gilpin	L Neumann	1/20
1909	**Maid of the Mist**	D Maher	A Taylor Jnr	Sir W Bass	15/8
1910	**Winkipop**	H Jones	W Waugh	W Astor	4/6
1911	**Hair Trigger II**	F Wootton	G Lambton	A James	5/4
1912	**Belleisle**	D Maher	W Waugh	Lord Falmouth	–
1913	**Arda**	D Maher	B Jarvis	J P Hornung	11/4
1914	**First Spear**	J Clark	A Taylor Jnr	W Astor	4/6
1915/18	**No Race**				
1919	**Keysoe**	B Carslake	G Lambton	Lord Derby	13/8
1920	**Most Beautiful**	I Strydon	P Hartigan	A Bendon	5/1
1921	**Pompadour**	J Brennan	A Taylor Jnr	Lord Astor	7/4
1922	**Selene**	E Gardner	G Lambton	Lord Derby	1/2
1923	**Concertina**	F Bullock	A Taylor Jnr	Lord Astor	5/4
1924	**Straitlace**	C Elliott	D Waugh	Sir E Hulton	4/9
1925	**Saucy Sue**	F Bullock	A Taylor Jnr	Lord Astor	1/5
1926	**Foliation**	J Brennan	A Taylor Jnr	S Tattersall	11/4
1927	**Book Law**	H Jelliss	A Taylor Jnr	Lord Astor	2/5
1928	**La Sologne**	J Sirett	J Lawson	M Calmann	13/8
1929	**Nuwara Eliya**	R A Jones	J Lawson	S Tattersall	4/6
1930	**Quinine**	F Fox	F Darling	Lord Ellesmere	100/30
1931	**Suze**	R A Jones	A Molony	R S Clark	100/8
1932	**Ada Dear**	R Perryman	T Hogg	Lord Glanely	9/4
1933	**Solfatara**	G Richards	B Jarvis	Miss J B Courtauld	6/4
1934	**Zelina**	S Donoghue	Hugh Powney	Z Michalinos	4/5
1935	**Coppelia**	G Richards	F Templeman	Lord Hirst	9/2
1936	**Barrowby Gem**	G Richards	F Templeman	Sir F Eley	6/5
1937	**First Flight**	H Wragg	O Bell	Lord Londonderry	11/2
1938	**Valedah**	D Smith	Frank Butters	HH Aga Khan	100/8
1939	**Olein**	T Lowrey	B Jarvis	Lord Glanely	13/2
1940/45	**No Race**				
1946	**Wayward Belle**	E Smith	J Jarvis	Lord Milford	11/8
1947	**Wild Child**	T Lowrey	R Perryman	Mrs S Joel	11/2
1948	**Goblet**	G Richards	N Murless	F Darling	13/2
1949	**Jet Plane**	G Richards	J Lawson	Lord Astor	8/1
1950	**Flying Slipper**	W H Carr	C Boyd-Rochfort	Mrs W P Wyatt	8/1
1951	**Sea Parrot**	G Richards	N Murless	G Loder	7/4
1952	**Hortentia**	D Smith	G Colling	Lord Derby	11/2
1953	**Happy Laughter**	W Rickaby	J Jarvis	H D H Wills	5/6
1954	**Key**	W Smith	N Murless	Mrs D M FitzPatrick	4/1
1955	**Reel In**	A Breasley	N Cannon	G Fairlie	13/8
1956	**Dilettante**	D Smith	J F Watts	Lord Derby	6/1
1957	**Swallowswift**	E Mercer	G Golling	F Robinson	100/9
1958	**Darlene**	A Breasley	G Richards	Miss D Paget	100/30
1959	**Crystal Palace**	E Smith	T E Leader	H J Joel	3/1
1960	**Desert Beauty**	A Breasley	G Richards	R Evans	2/1
1961	**Rachel**	J Lindley	J M Gosden	E Covell	7/2
1962	**Nortia**	J Mercer	W R Hern	Maj L B Holliday	100/30
1963	**Spree**	J Lindley	J Tree	J Morrison	15/8
1964	**Cracker**	J Mercer	W Wharton	Maj L B Holliday	10/1
1965	**Aunt Edith**	L Piggott	N Murless	J Hornung	7/4
1966	**Haymaking**	L Piggott	R F Johnson Houghton	C Nicholson	13/2
1967	**Fair Winter**	J Mercer	D Candy	W Barnett	7/2

		Jockey	Trainer	Owner	Odds
1968	**Hill Shade**	A Barclay	N Murless	G A Pope Jnr	5/6
1969	**Lucyrowe**	F Durr	P Walwyn	L Freedman	1/2
1970	**Pulchra**	G Lewis	J Sirett	G Hager	20/1
1971	**Catherine Wheel**	G Lewis	B Hobbs	T Blackwell	4/1
1972	**Crespinall**	R Hutchinson	R Hannon	Mrs B Davis	25/1
1973	**Cheveley Princess**	L Piggott	H Wragg	R B Moller	15/2
1974	**Mil's Bomb**	G Lewis	N Murless	L Freedman	10/11
1975	**Roussalka**	L Piggott	H Cecil	N Phillips	9/4
1976	**Roussalka**	L Piggott	H Cecil	N Phillips	15/8
1977	**Triple First**	G Starkey	M Stoute	R Clifford-Turner	13/2
1978	**Cistus**	W Carson	W R Hern	Sir M Sobell	4/7
1979	**Connaught Bridge**	J Mercer	H Cecil	H Barker	5/1
1980	**Vielle**	G Baxter	B Hobbs	T F Blackwell	8/15
1981	**Go Leasing**	G Starkey	G Harwood	W Norton	15/2
1982	**Dancing Rocks**	P Eddery	H Wragg	Sir P Oppenheimer	12/1
1983	**Acclimatise**	G Baxter	B Hobbs	J Hambro	4/1
1984	**Optimistic Lass**	W R Swinburn	M Stoute	Sheikh Mohammed	5/2
1985	**Free Guest**	P Eddery	L Cumani	Fittocks Stud	11/2
1986	**Park Express**	J Reid	J Bolger	P H Burns	7/1
1987	**Nom de Plume**	S Cauthen	H Cecil	Sheikh Mohammed	11/4
1988	**Ela Romara**	P Eddery	G Wragg	Exors of E B Moller	10/1
1989	**Mamaluna**	G Starkey	G Harwood	A Christodoulou	9/1
1990	**Kartajana**	W R Swinburn	M Stoute	HH Aga Khan	11/2
1991	**Ruby Tiger**	T Quinn	P Cole	Mrs P Blacker	11/4
1992	**Ruby Tiger**	T Quinn	P Cole	Mrs P Blacker	2/1

For 3 year-old fillies only 1840-1974.

Run over 1 mile 1840-1899 and 1 mile 4 furlongs 1900-1910.

The Rose of Lancaster Stakes

The Rose of Lancaster Stakes has well justified its position in the Pattern since the first running in 1989. The winner, *Braiswick* won four other races at three including the Cheshire Oaks, the Sun Chariot Stakes and the E. P. Taylor Stakes at Woodbine, Toronto.

In 1990 *Defensive Play* also 'crossed the herring pond,' this time for the Man O'War Stakes at Belmont Park, after taking the Gaurdian Classic Trial in addition to the Rose of Lancaster, but the 1991 and 1992 winners cannot be said to be in quite the same category.

Run at Haydock Park over 1 mile 2 furlongs 130 yards First Run 1986 Group 3

		Jockey	Trainer	Owner	Odds
1986	**Wassl Touch**	W Carson	W R Hern	A Al-Maktoum	6/1
1987	**Free Fact**	W Carson	W R Hern	Lord Rotherwick	2/1
1988	**Galitzin**	S Cauthen	C Brittain	C Elliot	4/1
1989	**Braiswick**	G Carter	G Wragg	White Lodge Stud	7/1
1990	**Defensive Play**	P Eddery	G Harwood	K Abdulla	7/2
1991	**Lord of Tusmore**	A Munro	B Hills	W Said	10/1
1992	**Half a Tick**	C Rutter	P Cole	C J Wates	8/1

The Hungerford Stakes

A Group Three event designed to attract the speedier type of miler, the Hungerford Stakes is usually a competitive race and certainly the fields have not lacked quality, with *Romulus*, second in the Guineas and winner of the Sussex Stakes, the Queen Elizabeth II Stakes and the Prix du Moulin on the record sheet along with *Derring Do*, Champion Stakes winner *Silly Season*, *Welsh Pageant* and *Jimmy Reppin*, dual winner in 1968 and 1969 and one of the most popular and successful milers of the sixties.

Run at Newbury over 7 furlongs and 60 yards First Run 1949 Group 3

		Jockey	Trainer	Owner	Odds
1949	**Star King**	D Smith	J C Waugh	W Harvey	5/6
1950	**Hyperbole**	A Breasley	N Cannon	J V Rank	8/13
1951	**La Valeuse**	E Mercer	G Colling	M Glenister	5/1
1952	**Agitator**	G Richards	N Cannon	J A Dewar	1/5
1953	**Olga**	G Richards	N Murless	B Hornung	6/5
1954	**Tip the Bottle**	W H Carr	J Lawson	R S Clark	1/2
1955	**Princely Gift**	L Piggott	N Murless	Sir V Sassoon	2/1
1956	**High Bhan**	A Breasley	G Richards	A McIlhagga	Evens
1957	**Picture Light**	E Smith	T E Leader	H J Joel	100/30
1958	**Lovestone**	D Smith	H Murless	G Malone	2/1

		Jockey	Trainer	Owner	Odds
1959	**Agile**	G Bougoure	M V O'Brien	F W Burmann	5/2
1960	**Fagus**	A Breasley	G Richards	Mrs A Plesch	10/11
1961	**Eagle**	G Starkey	J Oxley	R D Hollingsworth	4/7
1962	**Romulus**	W Swinburn	R F Johnson Houghton	C W Engelhard	4/6
1963	**Dunce Cap**	D Smith	C Boyd-Rochfort	J H Whitney	9/4
1964	**Derring-Do**	A Breasley	A Budgett	Mrs H Renshaw	2/1
1965	**Roan Rocket**	L Piggott	G Todd	T Frost	1/2
1966	**Silly Season**	G Lewis	I Balding	P Mellon	10/11
1967	**St Chad**	G Moore	N Murless	Mrs N Murless	4/5
1968	**Jimmy Reppin**	G Lewis	J Sutcliffe Jnr	Mrs S Bates	10/11
1969	**Jimmy Reppin**	G Lewis	J Sutcliffe Jnr	Mrs S Bates	8/11
1970	**Zingari**	W Carson	R F Johnson Houghton	C W Engelhard	7/1
1971	**Welsh Pageant**	G Lewis	N Murless	H J Joel	10/11
1972	**Home Guard**	L Piggott	M V O'Brien	Mrs C W Engelhard	11/8
1973	**Brook**	P Eddery	P Walwyn	C Vittadini	6/1
1974	**Pitcairn**	R Hutchinson	J Dunlop	A J Struthers	7/2
1975	**Court Chad**	B Taylor	G Pritchard-Gordon	D Praznovsky	10/1
1976	**Ardoon**	B Taylor	G Pritchard-Gordon	F Feeney	13/2
1977	**He Loves Me**	A Kimberley	J Hindley	J Allbritton	7/1
1978	**Tannenberg**	J Mercer	H Cecil	Mrs S Arnold	11/2
1979	**Skyliner**	G Baxter	P Cole	D Rowland	10/1
1980	**Kampala**	P Eddery	P Walwyn	Mrs D McCalmont	5/4
1981	**Dalsaan**	W R Swinburn	M Stoute	HH Aga Khan	4/1
1982	**Pas de Seul**	P Eddery	D V O'Brien	R Sangster	13/2
1983	**Salieri**	L Piggott	H Cecil	C St George	7/2
1984	**Prego**	P Eddery	B Hills	R Sangster	15/1
1985	**Ever Genial**	S Cauthen	H Cecil	L Freedman	5/2
1986	**Hadeer**	S Cauthen	C Brittain	W Gredley	11/2
1987	**Abuzz**	T Ives	C Brittain	Mrs C Brittain	40/1
1988	**Salse**	S Cauthen	H Cecil	Sheikh Mohammed	9/4
1989	**Distant Relative**	M Hills	B Hills	W Said	5/1
1990	**Norwich**	M Hills	B Hills	Sheikh Mohammed	11/2
1991	**Only Yours**	M Roberts	R Hannon	Mrs M Butcher	11/2
1992	**Mojave**	W R Swinburn	M Stoute	Sultan Mohammed	16/1

Run over 1 mile 4 furlongs 1949

The Geoffrey Freer Stakes

There can be no more appropriate race in this compendium of Pattern Racing than the Geoffrey Freer Stakes. The race was founded by Freer in 1949 as the Oxfordshire Stakes, and renamed in his honour in 1969, the year after his death.

A brilliant handicapper for the Jockey Club since 1944, Geoffrey Freer restored Newbury after the devastation of the course which was used as a main American supply depot during World War Two. He was also engaged in racecourse management at Newmarket, Salisbury, Warwick and Manchester at various times, bred the grand-dam of *Ribot*, *Tofanella* and served on the original Pattern Race Committee set up by the late Duke of Norfolk in 1965.

The Geoffrey Freer Stakes is a fitting tribute to the man who always averred that 'racing should be fun'. The list of winners including the names of classic animals such as *Ridge Wood*, *Charlottown* and *Moon Madness*, together with some of the finest stayers ever to grace the Turf, speaks for itself.

Run at Newbury over 1 mile 5 furlongs and 60 yards First Run 1949 Group 2

		Jockey	Trainer	Owner	Odds
1949	**Ridge Wood**	G Richards	N Murless	G R H Smith	4/9
1950	**Tilloy**	E Britt	F Armstrong	Lord Carnarvon	5/2
1951	**Le Sage**	G Richards	T Carey	S Sanger	–
1952	**Westinform**	T Gosling	R Smyth	W T Wheeler	9/2
1953	**Harwin**	W H Carr	J Dines	T Robinson	3/1
1954	**Umberto**	K Gethin	P Thrale	J D C Brownlow	4/6
1955	**True Cavalier**	E Smith	H Leader	S Niarchos	11/8
1956	**Court Command**	L Piggott	N Murless	Mrs T Lilley	5/2
1957	**Court Harwell**	A Breasley	G Richards	J R Mullion	5/2
1958	**Owen Glendower**	G Lewis	P Hastings-Bass	Lord Sefton	13/8
1959	**Kalydon**	E Smith	B van Cutsem	B van Cutsem	Evens
1960	**High Hat**	W H Carr	W Nightingall	Sir W Churchill	7/1
1961	**Sagacity**	E Smith	C Boyd-Rochfort	Lady Cholmondeley	5/1
1962	**Sovrango**	W Williamson	H Wragg	G A Oldham	15/8
1963	**Sovrango**	W Williamson	H Wragg	G A Oldham	5/2
1964	**Sunseeker**	J Purtell	M V O'Brien	J C Brady	6/1
1965	**Court Gift**	S Clayton	B Hobbs	D Robinson	4/1
1966	**Charlottown**	J Lindley	G Smyth	Lady Z Wernher	11/8
1967	**Hopeful Venture**	G Moore	N Murless	HM The Queen	4/7
1968	**Levmoss**	B Taylor	S McGrath	S McGrath	100/6

		Jockey	Trainer	Owner	Odds
1969	**Rangong**	A Barclay	N Murless	Lady Sassoon	7/4
1970	**High Line**	J Mercer	D Candy	W Barnett	11/10
1971	**High Line**	J Lindley	D Candy	W Barnett	2/1
1972	**Sol'Argent**	J Lindley	T Gosling	Mrs G Harris	14/1
1973	**Attica Meli**	G Lewis	N Murless	L Freedman	9/1
1974	**Realistic**	P Eddery	H Blagrave	H Blagrave	14/1
1975	**Consol**	P Eddery	P Walwyn	A D G Oldrey	9/1
1976	**Swell Fellow**	A Kimberley	J Hindley	Lord J Crichton-Stuart	16/1
1977	**Valinsky**	L Piggott	M V O'Brien	Sir C Clore	8/13
1978	**Ile de Bourbon**	J Reid	R F Johnson Houghton	D McCall	11/8
1979	**Niniski**	W Carson	W R Hern	Lady Beaverbrook	7/4
1980	**Nicholas Bill**	P Waldron	H Candy	W Barnett	15/8
1981	**Ardross**	L Piggott	H Cecil	C St George	10/11
1982	**Ardross**	L Piggott	H Cecil	C St George	1/3
1983	**Khairpour**	J Reid	R F Johnson Houghton	HH Aga Khan	9/4
1984	**Baynoun**	S Cauthen	R F Johnson Houghton	HH Aga Khan	2/1
1985	**Shernazar**	W R Swinburn	M Stoute	HH Aga Khan	8/13
1986	**Bakharoff**	W Carson	G Harwood	K Abdulla	6/4
1987	**Moon Madness**	P Eddery	J Dunlop	Duchess of Norfolk	11/8
1988	**Top Class**	M Roberts	C Brittain	M Lemos	20/1
1989	**Ibn Bey**	T Quinn	P Cole	F Salman	9/2
1990	**Charmer**	L Dettori	C Brittain	Lady Beaverbrook	4/1
1991	**Drum Taps**	L Dettori	Lord Huntingdon	Lord Carnarvon	15/2
1992	**Shambo**	M Roberts	C Brittain	Mrs C Brittain	9/1

Run as the Oxfordshire Stakes 1949-1968

The Solario Stakes

The Solario Stakes is named in memory of a brilliant stayer who won the Ascot Gold Cup and six races in all. *Solario* was also the sire of the Derby winners *Midday Sun* and *Straight Deal* as well as *Exhibitionist* who took the 1,000 Guineas and the Oaks in 1937.

Elevated from Listed level in 1986 following the 1984 victory of *Oh So Sharp* who went on to win the 1,000 Guineas, the Oaks and the St Leger in 1985, the race has been more notable for subsequent failure ever since with the trio trained by Henry Cecil, *Sanquirico*, *High Estate* and *Be My Chief* all disappointing in their three-year-old careers along with *Shining Water* and *Radwell*.

Run at Sandown Park over 7 furlongs for 2 year-olds First Run 1947 Group 3

		Jockey	Trainer	Owner	Odds
1947	**Panair**	W Rickaby	H Wragg	C Sweeney	25/1
1948	**Suntime**	E Britt	M Marsh	J Musker	Evens
1949	**Scratch II**	C Elliott	C Semblat	M Boussac	7/4
1950	**Turco II**	W H Carr	C Boyd-Rochfort	W Woodward	10/11
1951	**Gay Time**	A Breasley	N Cannon	J V Rank	6/1
1952	**March Past**	L Piggott	K Cundell	Mrs G Trimmer-Thompson	9/2
1953	**Barton Street**	J Sime	S Hall	R A Smith	13/8
1954	**North Cone**	E Smith	G Barling	Lord Ellesmere	100/7
1955	**Castelmarino**	K Gethin	H Wallington	W Satinoff	5/2
1956	**Nagaika**	A Breasley	W Smyth	Sir R Fielden	100/30
1957	**Aggressor**	J Lindley	J M Gosden	Sir H Wernher	7/1
1958	**Pindari**	L Piggott	N Murless	HM The Queen	/
1959	**Intervener**	W Snaith	H Cottrill	S Joel	4/1
1960	**Dual**	J Lindley	J M Gosden	Sir H Wernher	7/1
1961	**Hidden Meaning**	E Smith	H Leader	K Grant	2/1
1962	**Happy Omen**	W H Carr	W R Hern	Maj L B Holliday	5/2
1963	**Penny Stall**	D Keith	W Nightingall	Lady Marks	33/1
1964	**Rehearsed**	R Hutchinson	J M Gosden	Sir H Wernher	5/2
1965	**Charlottown**	J Lindley	J M Gosden	Lady Z Wernher	3/1
1966	**Speed of Sound**	L Piggott	N Murless	F Hue-Williams	4/7
1967	**Remand**	L Piggott	W R Hern	J J Astor	8/15
1968	**Murrayfield**	G Lewis	I Balding	Mrs P Hastings	8/13
1969	**Miracle**	E Hide	G Richards	Lady Beaverbrook	11/8
1970	**Athens Wood**	G Starkey	H Thomson Jones	Mrs J Rogerson	2/1
1971	**Meadow Mint**	W Carson	F Armstrong	R Webster	6/4
1972	**Duke of Ragusa**	J Gorton	B Hobbs	Lord Rosebery	8/1
1973/74	**No Race**				
1975	**Over to You**	J Mercer	W R Hern	Sir M Sobell	10/1
1976	**Avgerinos**	P Eddery	P Walwyn	C Karpidas	6/1
1977	**Bolak**	P Eddery	P Walwyn	Countess of Esterhazy	9/2
1978	**Lyphard's Wish**	J Mercer	H Cecil	C d'Alessio	10/11
1979	**Rankin**	G Starkey	G Harwood	R Fennell	13/8
1980	**To-Agori-Mou**	G Starkey	G Harwood	Mrs A Muinos	8/11
1981	**Silver Hawk**	B Taylor	M Albina	I Moubarak	11/2
1982	**The Fort**	L Piggott	H Cecil	Mrs H Phillips	2/1

		Jockey	Trainer	Owner	Odds
1983	**Falstaff**	W Carson	W R Hern	Lord Porchester	5/4
1984	**Oh So Sharp**	L Piggott	H Cecil	Sheikh Mohammed	6/4
1985	**Bold Arrangement**	P Eddery	C Brittain	A Richards	5/1
1986	**Shining Water**	S Cauthen	R F Johnson Houghton	R Crutchley	20/1
1987	**Sanquirico**	S Cauthen	H Cecil	C St George	8/15
1988	**High Estate**	S Cauthen	H Cecil	H J Joel	4/7
1989	**Be My Chief**	S Cauthen	H Cecil	P Burrell	1/3
1990	**Radwell**	G Duffield	J Fanshawe	Lord Vestey	12/1
1991	**Chicmond**	G Duffield	Sir M Prescott	P G Goulandris	16/1
1992	**White Crown**	W R Swinburn	B Hanbury	S Suhail	9/4

The Juddmonte International Stakes

The sponsorship of races was inspired by the advent of commercial television in the mid-fifties. The benefits were twofold. The cost of the prize money donated would be far less than the equivalent air time bought at advertising rates, with the bonus of free coverage in the press, and the television coverage targeted the potential consumer to a fine degree.

There were also two ways of becoming a sponsor. You either took an existing race, for instance the Eclipse, and added your company's name to it as in Coral-Eclipse, or you founded your own, as did Whitbread, Hennessy and Vaux. Indeed, it was the success of the Vaux Gold Tankard at Redcar, for a time Europe's richest handicap, which persuaded Major Leslie Petch, who also presided over York as Clerk of the Course, to devise the Benson and Hedges Gold Cup.

Ill health forced Petch to resign in 1971, and it was his nephew John Sanderson who succeeded him and greeted HM The Queen on 15 August 1972 when she arrived for the inaugural running, the first Monarch to visit York races since Charles I, 339 years before.

It was indeed a dish to set before a Queen. Only five ran, but they included *Roberto,* winner of the most controversial Derby since 1913. Ridden by Lester Piggott, using his whip with a frequency which would ensure a long 'holiday' nowadays, he'd won a bumping match with *Rheingold* after Piggott had usurped the ride on *Roberto* from Bill Williamson in typical Piggott fashion. The Panamanian Braulio Baeza had the ride on *Roberto* in the Benson and Hedges, and *Rheingold* re-opposed on equal terms with Piggott in the saddle in place of his Derby rider, Ernie Johnson.

The 3-1 on favourite was the mighty *Brigadier Gerard,* at four years old the finest horse of his generation and unbeaten in fifteen races including the 2,000 Guineas, defeating *Mill Reef,* the Eclipse, the King George VI and Queen Elizabeth Stakes and the Champion Stakes.

Gold Rod and *Bright Beam* completed the field in a race on which, in the words of Raceform '*Roberto* was out of the stalls like a bat out of hell' and made all to hold off *Brigadier Gerard* by three lengths. Both first and second broke the course record and finished ten lengths clear of the third, *Gold Rod.*

Roberto's record stood for sixteen years until beaten by the subsequently disqualified *Persian Heights* in 1988 and the Benson and Hedges was soon established as one of the top middle-distance races in Europe, with *Dahlia* (1974 and 1975) *Wollow, Troy, Master Willie, Commanche Run, Triptych* and *In The Groove* on the roll of honour.

Not always a good race for favourites, there have been more than a few turn-ups. *Moulton* won in 1973 at 14/1, with a 6/4 on favourite *Rheingold* trailing in third, 33/1 chance *Relkino* beat 11/8 on favourite *Artaius* in 1977, and the enigmatic *Ile de Chypre* defeated the 5/2 on *Cacoethes* in 1989.

As the York August Meeting owes its position in the Calendar to the timing of the York Assizes, it comes at an awkward time in the career of the thoroughbred, especially three-year-olds often asked to take a step back in distance. The race has also had to endure the fluctuating fortunes of commerical sponsorship, with Benson and Hedges pulling out in 1986, when the Matchmaker bloodstock company took over for one year. The race was unsponsored in 1988 but Juddmonte, under the auspices of Prince Khaled Abdulla, took up the baton in 1989 and have held it since.

Run at York over 1 mile 2 furlongs First Run 1972 Group 1

		Jockey	Trainer	Owner	Odds
1972	**Roberto**	B Baeza	M V O'Brien	J W Galbreath	12/1
1973	**Moulton**	G Lewis	H Wragg	R B Moller	14/1
1974	**Dahlia**	L Piggott	M Zilber	N B Hunt	8/15
1975	**Dahlia**	L Piggott	M Zilber	N B Hunt	7/2
1976	**Wollow**	G Dettori	H Cecil	C d'Alessio	9/4
1977	**Relkino**	W Carson	W R Hern	Lady Beaverbrook	33/1
1978	**Hawaiian Sound**	L Piggott	B Hills	R Sangster	2/1
1979	**Troy**	W Carson	W R Hern	Sir M Sobell	1/2
1980	**Master Willie**	P Waldron	H Candy	W Barnett	13/2
1981	**Beldale Flutter**	P Eddery	M Jarvis	A Kelly	9/1
1982	**Assert**	P Eddery	D V O'Brien	R Sangster	4/5
1983	**Caerleon**	P Eddery	M V O'Brien	R Sangster	100/30
1984	**Cormorant Wood**	S Cauthen	B Hills	R J McAlpine	15/1
1985	**Commanche Run**	L Piggott	L Cumani	I Allan	5/1
1986	**Shardari**	W R Swinburn	M Stoute	HH Aga Khan	13/8
1987	**Triptych**	S Cauthen	P-L Biancone	A Clore	13/8
1988	**Shady Heights**	W Carson	R Armstrong	G Tong	7/2
1989	**Ile de Chypre**	A Clark	G Harwood	A Christodoulou	16/1
1990	**In The Groove**	S Cauthen	D Elsworth	B Cooper	4/1
1991	**Terimon**	M Roberts	C Brittain	Lady Beaverbrook	16/1
1992	**Rodrigo de Triano**	L Piggott	P Chapple-Hyam	R Sangster	8/1

Run as the Benson & Hedges Gold Cup 1972-1985, the Matchmaker International in 1986-1987, the International Stakes in 1988 and the Juddmonte International Stakes from 1989.

The Yorkshire Oaks

In the last century, the Yorkshire Oaks attracted a decent clutch of classic winners, and since the war has reasserted itself and now is frequently contested by winners of the Oaks proper, including *Frieze, Petite Etoile, Homeward Bound, Lupe, Mysterious, Fair Salinia, Circus Plume, Diminuendo,* and *User Friendly.*

, The most dramatic contest for the Yorkshire Oaks took place in August 1981. On the turn for home, *Silken Knot* ridden by Willie Carson broke both forelegs and pitched the jockey into the path of an eleven runner field. The plight of the filly was bad enough, but Carson became a human football, and was taken to hospital with severe injuries from which he happily recovered to maintain his position as one of the country's leading riders. His cheerful disposition has rightly ensured Carson a permanent place in the hearts of the racing public.

Run at York over 1 mile 4 furlongs for 3 year-old fillies First Run 1849 Group 1

		Jockey	Trainer	Owner	Odds
1849	**Ellen Middleton**	J Marson	R Hill	Lord Zetland	5/2
1850	**Brightonia**	F Butler	R Stephenson	J V Shelley	4/1
1851	**Vivandiere**	A Day	J Scott	R M Jaques	2/1
1852	**Adine**	E Flatman	W Dilly	C Greville	Evens
1853	**Mayfair**	A Day	J B Day	H Padwick	4/1
1854	**Virago**	J Wells	J B Day	H Padwick	–
1855	**Capucine**	J Marson	T Cunningham	T Turner	5/1
1856	**Victoria**	E Flatman	J Scott	J Bowes	2/1
1857	**Tasmania**	J Bumby	C Peck	Sir R W Bulkeley	7/4
1858	**The Argosy**	S Rogers	W Saunders	W Copeland	5/1
1859	**Bilberry**	T Withington	J Fobert	Capt Gray	–
1860	**Stockade**	T Aldcroft	J Scott	S Hawke	3/1
1861	**Brown Duchess**	L Snowden	J Saxon	J Saxon	4/9
1862	**Feu de Joie**	T Chaloner	J Godding	R C Naylor	6/1
1863	**Miss Armstrong**	J Snowden	J Watson	F Watt	6/1
1864	**Gondola**	J Snowden	J Watson	F Watt	–
1865	**Klarinska**	T Ashmall	J Scott	J Bowes	10/1
1866	**Lady Vane**	J Morris	T Dawson	J Johnstone	5/1
1867	**Ines**	G Fordham	J Day	Marquis of Hastings	100/30
1868	**Leonie**	T Chaloner	M Dawson	Duke of Hamilton	5/4
1869	**Toison d'Or**	G Fordham	J Scott	J Bowes	6/4
1870	**Gertrude**	T French	M Dawson	Lord Falmouth	100/8
1871	**Rebecca**	T French	–	J Hodson	10/1
1872	**Maid of Perth**	T French	–	R Long	Evens
1873	**Marie Stuart**	T Osborne	R Peck	J Merry	4/9
1874	**The Pique**	C Maidment	W Gilbert	H Savile	11/4
1875	**Spinaway**	F Archer	M Dawson	Lord Falmouth	1/5
1876	**Zee**	J Goater	W Gilbert	H Savile	2/1
1877	**Lady Golightly**	F Archer	M Dawson	Lord Falmouth	5/2
1878	**Jannette**	F Archer	M Dawson	Lord Falmouth	1/4
1879	**Wheel of Fortune**	F Archer	M Dawson	Lord Falmouth	1/3
1880	**Belfry**	G Fordham	–	C Bush	5/4
1881	**Thebais**	G Fordham	A Taylor Snr	W S Crawfurd	30/100
1882	**Dutch Oven**	F Archer	M Dawson	Lord Falmouth	4/9
1883	**Britomartis**	F Archer	M Dawson	Lord Falmouth	5/6
1884	**Clochette**	F Archer	M Dawson	Lord Lascelles	9/4
1885	**St Helena**	T Bruckshaw	J Enoch	Lord Zetland	15/8
1886	**Philosophy**	F Archer	M Gurry	R Peck	5/4
1887	**Reve d'Or**	C Wood	A Taylor Snr	Duke of Beaufort	1/4
1888	**Briar-root**	W Warne	J Ryan	D Baird	2/1
1889	**Antibes**	T Loates	C W Golding	H Milner	1/2
1890	**Ponza**	T Cannon	J Ryan	J H Houldsworth	4/9
1891	**Charm**	J Woodburn	W A Jarvis	A James	2/1
1892	**Gantlet**	J Watts	R Marsh	N Fenwick	5/2
1893	**Siffleuse**	J Watts	P Peck	Sir J Blundell Maple	5/4
1894	**Springray**	M Cannon	J Ryan	J H Houldsworth	6/1
1895	**Nighean**	S Loates	J Enoch	Lord Zetland	5/1
1896	**Helm**	M Cannon	J Porter	Duke of Westminster	4/5
1897	**Fortalice**	M Cannon	John Dawson Jnr	Lord Ellesmere	7/2
1898	**Fairmile**	S Loates	John Dawson Jnr	Lord Ellesmere	100/7
1899	**Victoria May**	O Madden	R Marsh	J W Larnach	2/1
1900	**La Roche**	M Cannon	J Porter	Duke of Portland	1/4
1901	**Santa Brigida**	F Rickaby	G Lambton	Lord Derby	5/1
1902	**Ice-maiden**	M Cannon	J Porter	G Faber	2/1
1903	**Hammerkop**	J H Martin	P P Gilpin	E Loder	6/4
1904	**Bitters**	W Lane	H Braime	F Alexander	5/4
1905	**Costly Lady**	D Maher	J E Brewer	L Robinson	1/6
1906	**Catnap**	G McCall	J Watson	L de Rothschild	2/1
1907	**Order of Merit**	B Lynham	W T Robinson	W Hall-Walker	4/1
1908	**Siberia**	B Dillon	P P Gilpin	L Neumann	4/6

		Jockey	Trainer	Owner	Odds
1909	**Collet Monte**	D Maher	G Lambton	Sir E Vincent	5/1
1910	**Winkipop**	H Jones	W Waugh	W Astor	1/8
1911	**Alice**	H Jones	W Waugh	Lord Falmouth	6/4
1912/18	**No Race**				
1919	**Mademoiselle Foch**	G Colling	R W Colling	J B Paget	10/1
1920	**Inflorescence**	E Wheatley	Hugh Powney	Sir E Cassel	6/1
1921	**Love in Idleness**	J Childs	A Taylor Jnr	J Watson	7/4
1922	**Sister-in-Law**	H Jones	A Taylor Jnr	S Tattersall	1/2
1923	**Splendid Jay**	F Bullock	A Taylor Jnr	Lord Astor	Evens
1924	**Blue Ice**	T Weston	G Lambton	Lord Derby	Evens
1925	**Brodick Bay**	T Weston	G Lambton	Lord Derby	3/1
1926	**Doushka**	C Smirke	R C Dawson	Lord Carnarvon	20/1
1927	**Gioconda**	G Richards	A Taylor Jnr	A R Cox	9/2
1928	**Rye Water**	P Beasley	H S Persse	J J Maher	8/1
1929	**Flittemere**	T Weston	Frank Butters	Lord Derby	7/4
1930	**Glorious Devon**	G Richards	T Hogg	Lord Glanely	9/4
1931	**Rackety Lassie**	J Dines	C Boyd-Rochfort	S Vlasto	100/6
1932	**Will o'the Wisp**	G Richards	F Darling	Lord Woolavington	13/8
	Nash Light	F Rickaby	T Hogg	Lord Glanely	6/1
1933	**Star of England**	G Nicholl	T Hogg	Lord Glanely	10/1
1934	**Dalmary**	F Fox	C Boyd-Rochfort	H Cayzer	11/8
1935	**Trigo Verde**	G Richards	N Cannon	J V Rank	11/10
1936	**Silversol**	W Nevett	M Peacock	M Peacock	8/1
1937	**Sculpture**	G Richards	J Lawson	Lord Astor	6/1
1938	**Joyce W**	W Nevett	J Lawson	Sir V Sassoon	11/2
1939	**Night Shift**	A Richardson	W Earl	Lord Derby	20/1
1940/45	**No Race**				
1946	**Live Letters**	T Weston	N Cannon	J V Rank	8/1
1947	**Ladycross**	W H Carr	C Boyd-Rochfort	Sir R Sykes	2/1
1948	**Angelola**	E Britt	C Boyd-Rochfort	HM The King	4/1
1949	**Unknown Quantity**	W Rickaby	J Jarvis	H D H Wills	3/1
1950	**Above Board**	E Smith	C Boyd-Rochfort	HM The King	100/30
1951	**Sea Parrot**	G Richards	N Murless	G Loder	13/2
1952	**Frieze**	E Britt	C Elsey	Capt A Keith	5/4
1953	**Kerkeb**	G Richards	M Marsh	HH Aga Khan	7/4
1954	**Feevagh**	K Gethin	W Stephenson	J McGrath	20/1

User Friendly, ridden by George Duffield, wins the 1992 Yorkshire Oaks.

		Jockey	Trainer	Owner	Odds
1955	**Ark Royal**	E Mercer	G Colling	R D Hollingsworth	Evens
1956	**Indian Twilight**	J Mercer	R J Colling	J J Astor	13/2
1957	**Almeria**	W H Carr	C Boyd-Rochfort	HM The Queen	11/10
1958	**None Nicer**	S Clayton	W R Hern	Maj L B Holliday	4/1
1959	**Petite Etoile**	L Piggott	N Murless	Prince Aly Khan	2/15
1960	**Lynchris**	W Williamson	J Oxx	Mrs E Fawcett	5/4
1961	**Tenacity**	A Breasley	G Richards	Mrs W Riley-Smith	7/1
1962	**West Side Story**	E Smith	T E Leader	H J Joel	2/1
1963	**Outcrop**	E Smith	G Barling	J Priestman	9/1
1964	**Homeward Bound**	G Starkey	J Oxley	Sir F Robinson	2/1
1965	**Mabel**	J Mercer	P Walwyn	G Williams	7/4
1966	**Parthian Glance**	L Piggott	G Todd	Mrs W R Smith	3/1
1967	**Palatch**	B Taylor	H Leader	C Vittadini	7/1
1968	**Exchange**	B Taylor	H Leader	Mrs R Midwood	7/2
1969	**Frontier Goddess**	D Keith	P Walwyn	C Spence	3/1
1970	**Lupe**	A Barclay	N Murless	Mrs S Joel	4/6
1971	**Fleet Wahine**	G Lewis	H Thomson Jones	R Ohrstrom	9/4
1972	**Attica Meli**	G Lewis	N Murless	L Freedman	13/2
1973	**Mysterious**	G Lewis	N Murless	G A Pope Jnr	4/6
1974	**Dibidale**	W Carson	B Hills	N Robinson	1/3
1975	**May Hill**	P Eddery	P Walwyn	G Williams	4/1
1976	**Sarah Siddons**	C Roche	P Prendergast	Mrs J R Mullion	100/30
1977	**Busaca**	P Eddery	P Walwyn	Countess M Esterhazy	5/1
1978	**Fair Salinia**	G Starkey	M Stoute	S Hanson	5/1
1979	**Connaught Bridge**	J Mercer	H Cecil	H Barker	9/2
1980	**Shoot A Line**	L Piggott	W R Hern	R Budgett	13/8
1981	**Condessa**	D Gillespie	J Bolger	P Barrett	5/1
1982	**Awaasif**	L Piggott	J Dunlop	Sheikh Mohammed	11/4
1983	**Sun Princess**	W Carson	W R Hern	Sir M Sobell	6/5
1984	**Circus Plume**	W Carson	J Dunlop	Sir R McAlpine	5/6
1985	**Sally Brown**	W R Swinburn	M Stoute	R Cowell	6/1
1986	**Untold**	G Starkey	M Stoute	Sheikh Mohammed	5/1
1987	**Bint Pasha**	T Quinn	P Cole	F Salman	5/1
1988	**Diminuendo**	S Cauthen	H Cecil	Sheikh Mohammed	3/10
1989	**Roseate Tern**	W Carson	W R Hern	Lord Carnarvon	11/2
1990	**Hellenic**	W Carson	M Stoute	Lord Weinstock	100/30
1991	**Magnificent Star**	A Cruz	M Moubarak	Ecurie Fustok	16/1
1992	**User Friendly**	G Duffield	C Brittain	W Gredley	8/11

The Great Voltigeur Stakes

Named after Lord Zetland's Derby and St Leger winner who came off second-best in the famous match at York with *The Flying Dutchman*, The Great Voltigeur Stakes was founded in 1950 as a stepping-stone to the St Leger. In the early days six horses completed the double, namely *Premonition, Alcide, St Paddy, Hethersett, Ragusa* and *Indiana*, but since the emergence of the Pattern in 1967, only three animals have gone on to win at Doncaster; *Athens Wood, Bustino* and *Reference Point*. Other notable winners have been the Arc de Triomphe victors *Rainbow Quest* and *Alleged*, the latter successful in Paris twice in 1977 and 1978.

Run at York over 1 mile 4 furlongs for 3 year-old colts & geldings First Run 1950 Group 2

		Jockey	Trainer	Owner	Odds
1950	**Castle Rock**	W Rickaby	J Jarvis	Lord Rosebery	5/6
1951	**Border Legend**	W Nevett	R D Peacock	Duke of Northumberland	4/1
1952	**Childe Harold**	J Brace	W Dutton	T Farr	7/4
1953	**Premonition**	W H Carr	C Boyd-Rochfort	W P Wyatt	4/5
1954	**Blue Sail**	W Rickaby	P Prendergast	G Bell	3/1
1955	**Acropolis**	D Smith	G Colling	Lady Derby	2/7
1956	**Hornbeam**	J Mercer	R J Colling	Lord Astor	6/4
1957	**Brioche**	E Britt	C Elsey	W Humble	100/6
1958	**Alcide**	W H Carr	C Boyd-Rochfort	Sir H de Trafford	3/1
1959	**Pindari**	L Piggott	N Murless	HM The Queen	11/10
1960	**St Paddy**	L Piggott	N Murless	Sir V Sassoon	4/11
1961	**Just Great**	A Breasley	S Ingham	Mrs J Allen	3/1
1962	**Hethersett**	F Durr	W R Hern	Maj L B Holliday	15/2
1963	**Ragusa**	G Bougoure	P Prendergast	J R Mullion	2/5
1964	**Indiana**	J Lindley	J F Watts	C W Engelhard	4/7
1965	**Ragazzo**	L Piggott	P Prendergast	E More O'Ferrall	13/8
1966	**Hermes**	G Starkey	J Oxley	R D Hollingsworth	15/2
1967	**Great Host**	W Williamson	P Prendergast	L Gelb	3/1
1968	**Connaught**	A Barclay	N Murless	H J Joel	1/3
1969	**Harmony Hall**	W Williamson	G Smyth	Sir H Wernher	4/6

		Jockey	Trainer	Owner	Odds
1970	**Meadowville**	L Piggott	M Jarvis	D Robinson	8/13
1971	**Athens Wood**	L Piggott	H Thomson Jones	Mrs J Rogerson	13/8
1972	**Our Mirage**	L Piggott	B Hills	N Cohen	11/4
1973	**Buoy**	J Mercer	W R Hern	R D Hollingsworth	11/10
1974	**Bustino**	J Mercer	W R Hern	Lady Beaverbrook	15/8
1975	**Patch**	P Eddery	P Walwyn	C Vittadini	6/4
1976	**Hawkberry**	C Roche	P Prendergast	L Gelb	4/1
1977	**Alleged**	L Piggott	M V O'Brien	J Fluor	5/2
1978	**Whitstead**	B Taylor	H R Price	H Demetriou	3/1
1979	**Noble Saint**	L Piggott	R Armstrong	R Guest	12/1
1980	**Prince Bee**	L Piggott	W R Hern	Sir M Sobell	4/6
1981	**Glint of Gold**	J Matthias	I Balding	P Mellon	Evens
1982	**Electric**	W R Swinburn	M Stoute	R Clifford-Turner	7/4
1983	**Seymour Hicks**	W Carson	J Dunlop	P Brant	11/2
1984	**Rainbow Quest**	P Eddery	J Tree	K Abdulla	Evens
1985	**Damister**	P Eddery	J Tree	K Abdulla	7/4
1986	**Nisnas**	T Quinn	P Cole	F Salman	6/1
1987	**Reference Point**	S Cauthen	H Cecil	L Freedman	1/14
1988	**Sheriff's Star**	T Ives	Lady Herries	Duchess of Norfolk	11/4
1989	**Zalazl**	S Cauthen	H Cecil	M Al-Maktoum	7/4
1990	**Belmez**	S Cauthen	H Cecil	Sheikh Mohammed	1/2
1991	**Corrupt**	P Eddery	N Callaghan	F M Kalla	5/1
1992	**Bonny Scot**	L Dettori	L Cumani	Lord Weinstock	11/8

The Ebor Handicap

Eboracum was the Roman name for York, where the Emperor Severus started racing in the year 208, at the place now known as the Knavesmire. The sport knew various locations in the next fifteen centuries, but by 1731 had resumed where it had begun. A site of public executions, including that of Dick Turpin in 1739, attendances dropped sharply when this practice ceased in 1801, and forty years later the fortunes of the Knavesmire were at a low ebb.

Only eight horses arrived to contest the spring meeting in May and John Orton, the newly appointed Clerk of the Course, inherited an unenviable responsibility. A man of many parts, Orton was a judge at seven northern courses and all the Scottish tracks, a journalist and the proprietor of a coffee house.

Realising the importance of handicaps to the betting public, Orton framed the Great Ebor Handicap over two miles with stakes of £20, £15 forfeit and £200 added money. Orton had judged his market well and when *Pagan* won the inaugural race in 1843 carrying 7st 13lb for Sim Templeman it was the dawn of a new era for York, although Orton's improvements to the course's facilities for spectators later reduced the distance of the Ebor to a mile and three-quarters.

Not all the Ebor winners have been merely handicappers. *Lily Agnes* (1875) won twenty-one races including the Doncaster Cup and the Northumberland Plate. She was an outstanding broodmare, producing the Derby winner *Ormonde* and *Ornament*, the dam of *Sceptre*.

Isonomy, the 1879 winner, also took the Ascot Gold Cup twice and completed a nap hand in the Cup races at Doncaster, Goodwood, Brighton and Manchester.

The outstanding winners in recent times have been the dual Champion Hurdler *Sea Pigeon* and the classically bred but ill-fated *Kneller*.

Run at York over 1 mile 6 furlongs First Run 1843 Handicap

		Jockey	Trainer	Owner	Odds
1843	**Pagan**	S Templeman	J Scott	Col Cradock	6/1
1844	**Godfrey**	J Berwick	T Dawson	J Meiklam	10/1
1845	**Coheiress**	W Abdale	R Hill	Lord Zetland	7/1
1846	**Arthur**	J Sharpe	W Shepherd	W Copeland	25/1
1847	**Mathematician**	T Donaldson	J B Day	J Gully	5/4
1848	**Meaux**	E Flatman	J Gill	S Fox	4/1
1849	**The Hero**	A Day	J B Day	J Powney	40/1
1850	**Mark Tapley**	J Arnold	T Dawson	T Dawson	5/1
1851	**Nancy**	J Charlton	J Marson	Mr Martinson	5/6
1852	**Adine**	E Rickards	W Dilly	C Greville	7/4
1853	**Pantomime**	T Olliver Jnr	T Eskrett	M Magenis	6/1
1854	**The Grand Inquisitor**	G Fordham	J Fobert	H Robinson	7/4
1855	**Vandal**	W Cresswell	J Scott	Sir C Monck	7/2
1856	**Warlock**	H Withington	J Scott	A Nichol	4/1
1857	**El Hakim**	W Little	J Fobert	W Robinson	50/1
1858	**Vedette**	J Osborne Jnr	G Abdale	Lord Zetland	5/2
1859	**Underhand**	T Aldcroft	J Fobert	G Forster	8/1
1860	**Pax**	A Edwards	T Dawson	Lord Glasgow	100/6
1861	**Rising Sun**	G Fordham	G Manning	Sir J Hawley	7/1
1862	**Makeshift**	C Hardcastle	T Dawson	Lord Glasgow	12/1
1863	**Golden Pledge**	J Loates	J Peace	H Owen	9/1
1864	**Raglan**	J Morris	J Day	J Powney	5/1
1865	**Verdant**	T Heartfield	F Balchin	G Hodgman	8/1
1866	**Westwick**	H Covey	J Scott	J Bowes	3/1
1867	**Mandrake**	R Cameron	T Dawson	J Johnstone	7/1

		Jockey	Trainer	Owner	Odds
1868	**Fair Wind**	W Platt	W H Scott	J Parker	33/1
1869	**Fortunio**	T Chaloner	J Fobert	Capt Gray	8/1
1870	**Paganini**	J Snowden	–	J Smith	100/8
1871	**Not Out**	D Butler	J Godding	S Myer	5/1
1872	**Albert Victor**	H Custance	T Olliver	W S Cartwright	100/12
1873	**Louise Victoria**	H Constable	T Leader	W S Cartwright	5/2
1874	**Chivalrous**	J Griffiths	J Perren	J Bowes	100/30
1875	**Lily Agnes**	W Wood	–	J Snarry	10/1
1876	**Lilian**	F Archer	W Gilbert	H Savile	100/30
1877	**Il Gladiatore**	J Morrell	M Dawson	M Dawson	5/1
1878	**Caerau**	A F Lemaire	T Leader	W S Cartwright	6/1
1879	**Isonomy**	T Cannon	J Porter	F Gretton	8/11
1880	**Novice**	G Bell	W Osborne	W Stevenson	6/1
1881	**Mother Shipton**	N Percival	H Hall	R Walker	8/1
1882	**Victor Emanuel**	J Osborne Jnr	W Osborne	H Bragg	6/1
1883	**Corrie Roy**	C Wood	J Porter	Sir F Johnstone	5/1
1884	**Ben Alder**	J Fagan	W I'Anson Jnr	W I'Anson Jnr	85/40
1885	**Mate**	F Archer	W Gilbert Jnr	Lord Cadogan	8/1
1886	**Le Caissier**	F Allsopp	J Humphreys	J Blundell Maple	100/30
1887	**Silence**	T Calder	Robert Sherwood	B Willyams	15/1
1888	**Nappa**	J Snowden	W Sanderson	W Sanderson	20/1
1889	**King Monmouth**	J Watts	J Enoch	J Lowther	5/2
1890	**Silver Spur**	T Loates	T Leader	J Charlton	6/1
1891	**Buccaneer**	J Woodburn	S Pickering	Lord Rosslyn	11/2
1892	**Alice**	S Chandley	H Hall	H Dyas	100/30
1893	**Senaputty**	W Bradford	Robert Sherwood	Lord Dunraven	8/1
1894	**Quilon**	S Loates	C W Golding	R Lebaudy	10/1
1895	**Llanthony**	F Finlay	F Bates	Sir R Jardine	6/1
1896	**Dingle Bay**	T Loates	G Lambton	Lord Derby	2/1
1897	**Harvest Money**	O Madden	W Raisin	E J Percy	4/1
1898	**Invincible II**	O Madden	G Blackwell	Sir J Miller	100/30
1899	**Cassock's Pride**	J Fagan	J D Edwards	J D Edwards	100/6
1900	**Jiffy II**	J Reiff	J Huggins	Lord W Beresford	4/1
1901	**Gyp**	O Madden	P P Peebles	P P Peebles	5/1
1902	**Wargrave**	J Hare	J H Batho	H Bottomley	20/1
1903	**McYardley**	O Madden	A Gilbert	J Musker	4/1
1904	**War Wolf**	W Higgs	J C Sullivan	J C Sullivan	9/2
1905	**The Page**	W Higgs	J C Sullivan	J C Sullivan	5/1
1906	**Golden Measure**	D Maher	J D Edwards	J Buchanan	7/4
1907	**Wuffy**	H Randall	R H Dewhurst	A Bendon	4/1
1908	**Rousay**	W Halsey	T Jennings Jnr	Capt Laing	11/8
1909	**Dibs**	W Higgs	Sir C Nugent	J S Morrison	9/2
1910	**Claretoi**	C Ringstead	J D Edwards	J D Edwards	40/1
1911	**Pillo**	W Saxby	W T Robinson	J Buchanan	100/12
1912	**Election**	W Huxley	J Dawson Jnr	W F Story	10/1
1913	**Junior**	W Huxley	E de Mestre	T Martin	2/1
1914/18	**No Race**				
1919	**Race Rock**	F Lane	T Cannon Jnr	Sir W Gilbey	100/7
1920	**Iron Hand**	E Crickmere	J Fergusson	H Whitworth	11/4
1921	**March Along**	B Carslake	G Lambton	Lord Derby	100/7
1922	**Flint Jack**	G Smith	O Bell	G J Plevins	5/1
1923	**Flint Jack**	H Gray	O Bell	G J Plevins	10/1
1924	**Marvex**	E Gardner	F Tash	Mrs Rudd	10/1
1925	**Chapeau**	G Richards	H O Madden	H O Madden	100/12
1926	**Pons Asinorum**	H Wragg	W Earl	S B Joel	5/2
1927	**Cap-a-pie**	W Freeman	Frank Butters	Lord Derby	100/7
1928	**Cinq-a-Sept**	J Childs	C Boyd-Rochfort	M Field	15/2
1929	**Bonny Boy II**	T Weston	V Gilpin	E de St Alary	100/8
1930	**Gentlemen's Relish**	J Dines	H S Persse	J Arkwright	20/1
	Coaster	F Fox	F Templeman	Sir H Hirst	100/8
1931	**Brown Jack**	S Donoghue	I Anthony	Sir H Wernher	10/1
1932	**Cat o'Nine Tails**	G Richards	R J Colling	Mrs J Carruthers	9/1
1933	**Dictum**	J Dines	T Rimell	Lady B Smith	8/1
1934	**Alcazar**	J Childs	C Boyd-Rochfort	W Woodward	10/1
1935	**Museum**	S Donoghue	J T Rogers	Sir V Sassoon	100/8
1936	**Penny Royal**	G Richards	F Templeman	E Thornton-Smith	100/8
1937	**Weathervane**	T Weston	J Lawson	Sir A Bailey	100/6
1938	**Foxglove II**	G Richards	F Darling	P Beatty	8/1
1939	**Owenstown**	J Taylor	M Peacock	Sir T Dixon	11/2
1940/43	**No Race**				
1943	**Yorkshire Hussar**	G Littlewood	C Elsey	J Hetherton	100/6
1944	**The Kernel**	P Evans	G Oxtoby	G Oxtoby	100/8
1945	**Wayside Inn**	H Wragg	W Earl	Lord Derby	20/1
1946	**Foxtrot**	E Britt	E Lambton	H E Morriss	3/1
1947	**Procne**	J Sime	C Elsey	H J Joel	8/1
1948	**Donino**	J Sime	A Cooper	W Cockerline	100/7

		Jockey	Trainer	Owner	Odds
1949	**Miraculous Atom**	W Nevett	S Hall	H Halmshaw	100/7
1950	**Cadzow Oak**	J Thompson	J Thwaites	G Renwick	100/8
1951	**Bob**	E Carter	C Elsey	J Hetherton	8/1
1952	**Signification**	H Jones	J Pearce	A Bird	10/1
1953	**Norooz**	R Fawdon	M Marsh	HH Aga Khan	100/9
1954	**By Thunder!**	W Swinburn	F Armstrong	J Gerber	7/1
1955	**Hyperion Kid**	P Robinson	H Wragg	Miss R Olivier	100/8
1956	**Donald**	D Smith	J Jarvis	Lord Rosebery	5/1
1957	**Morecambe**	J Sime	S Hall	J Bullock	100/8
1958	**Gladness**	L Piggott	M V O'Brien	J McShain	5/1
1959	**Primera**	L Piggott	N Murless	S Joel	6/1
1960	**Persian Road**	G Moore	J Tree	J H Whitney	18/1
1961	**Die Hard**	L Piggott	M V O'Brien	L Gardner	11/2
1962	**Sostenuto**	Don Morris	W Elsey	P Bull	9/1
1963	**Partholon**	J Sime	T Shaw	Mrs A Biddle	100/6
1964	**Proper Pride**	D Smith	W Wharton	Maj L B Holliday	28/1
1965	**Twelfth Man**	P Cook	H Wragg	R B Moller	6/1
1966	**Lomond**	E Eldin	R Jarvis	W Ruane	100/8
1967	**Ovaltine**	E Johnson	J F Watts	G Cooper	100/8
1968	**Alignment**	E Johnson	W Elsey	Lord Allendale	9/1
1969	**Big Hat**	R Still	D Hanley	Mrs M Tennant	40/1
1970	**Tintagel II**	L Piggott	R Sturdy	Mrs R Sturdy	6/1
1971	**Knotty Pine**	F Durr	M Jarvis	D Robinson	9/2
1972	**Crazy Rhythm**	F Durr	S Ingham	K Dodson	19/2
1973	**Bonne Noel**	C Roche	P Prendergast	Mrs P Poe	4/1
1974	**Anji**	T McKeown	J Sutcliffe Jnr	G Coleman	20/1
1975	**Dakota**	A Barclay	S Hall	G Reed	7/1
1976	**Sir Montagu**	W Carson	H R Price	Mrs S Enfield	11/4
1977	**Move Off**	J Bleasdale	J Calvert	W G Barker	9/1
1978	**Totowah**	P Cook	M Jarvis	Lady Beaverbrook	20/1
1979	**Sea Pigeon**	J J O'Neill	M H Easterby	P Muldoon	18/1
1980	**Shaftesbury**	G Starkey	M Stoute	J McCaughey	12/1
1981	**Protection Racket**	M Birch	J Hindley	S Fradkoff	15/2
1982	**Another Sam**	B Rouse	R Hannon	J Norman	16/1
1983	**Jupiter Island**	L Piggott	C Brittain	S Threadwell	9/1
1984	**Crazy**	W R Swinburn	G Harwood	Marshall Racing Ltd	10/1
1985	**Western Dancer**	P Cook	C Horgan	Mrs G Stone	20/1
1986	**Primary**	G Starkey	G Harwood	K Abdulla	6/1
1987	**Daarkom**	M Roberts	A Stewart	A Al-Maktoum	13/2
1988	**Kneller**	Paul Eddery	H Cecil	C St George	9/1
1989	**Sapience**	P Eddery	J Fitzgerald	Marquesa de Moratalla	15/2
1990	**Further Flight**	M Hills	B Hills	S Wingfield Digby	7/1
1991	**Deposki**	F Norton	M Stoute	W H Scott	12/1
1992	**Quick Ransom**	D McKeown	M Johnston	S Morrison	16/1

Run at Pontefract in 1943-1944

***Sea Pigeon*, winner of the 1979 Ebor Handicap, pictured here in 1973.**

General view of racing at York in 1934. The Gimcrack Stakes has been run here since 1846, although the horse after whom the race is named never won on the knavesmire.

The Gimcrack Stakes

In typical English style, the Gimcrack celebrates a horse that never actually won at York. He was a pony-sized grey animal who won twenty-six races from thirty-six starts over eleven years, including a walk-over. He measured no more than 14.2 hands, and in the days when horses were handicapped on size rather than ability, literally had the measure of his larger and slower opponents.

His portrait by Stubbs which hangs in the Jockey Club rooms at Newmarket is valued in telephone numbers, and the Gimcrack Club, formed in his honour in 1767 presents an annual dinner at which the owner of the Gimcrack winner traditionally makes a speech on the politics of racing.

Originally open to all two-year-olds, the race was restricted to colts and geldings in 1987. A high quality affair, surprisingly few classic winners have demonstrated their ability on the Knavesmire, although *Blink Bonny*, *Sansovino*, *Bahram*, *Palestine* and *Mill Reef* all catch the eye, the last being *Nebbiolo*, winner of the 2,000 Guineas in 1977 but destined never to win again.

Run at York over 6 furlongs for 2 year-old colts & geldings First Run 1846 Group 2

		Jockey	Trainer	Owner	Odds
1846	**Ellerdale**	T Lye	T Dawson	Capt O Harcourt	10/1
1847	**Tuscan**	A Day	J Day	T Pedley	2/1
1848	**Glauca**	E Flatman	W Dilly	G Payne	6/4
1849	**Mildew**	E Flatman	J Scott	R M Jaques	Evens
1850	**Aaron Smith**	C Marlow	H Wadlow	Lord Caledon	7/4
1851	**Trousseau**	J Sharp	J Day	T Pedley	7/4
1852	**Exact**	J Osborne Jnr	J Osborne	J Osborne	2/5
1853	**Barrel**	G Whitehouse	J Saxon	J Saxon	5/2
1854	**Nettle**	J Marson	E Gill	T Wilkinson	5/4
1855	**Mirage**	J Marson	M Wetherell	W C Harland	5/1
1856	**Blink Bonny**	A Robertson	W I'Anson	W I'Anson	5/6
1857	**Princess Royal**	E Flatman	J Saxon	J Saxon	7/1
1858	**Rainbow**	J Wells	J Prince	J Merry	5/4
1859	**Thormanby**	A Day	M Dawson	J Merry	4/6
1860	**Prudence**	H Grimshaw	J Scott	Sir C Monck	6/4

		Jockey	Trainer	Owner	Odds
1861	**Johnny Armstrong**	T Aldcroft	J Fobert	Mr Gordon	9/2
1862	**Le Marechal**	H Grimshaw	T Jennings	Comte F de Lagrange	5/1
1863	**Coastguard**	J Osborne Jnr	J Osborne	W Hudson	6/1
1864	**Wild Agnes**	J Osborne Jnr	J Osborne	J Osborne	2/1
1865	**Lord of the Vale**	J Osborne Jnr	–	R Cathcart	5/1
1866	**Blinkhoolie**	H Custance	G Bloss	H Chaplin	10/1
1867	**The Earl**	G Fordham	J Day	Marquis of Hastings	6/5
1868	**Lady Dewhurst**	J Snowden	J Watson	G Holmes	–
1869	**Hester**	H Grimshaw	Jos Dawson	Jos Dawson	6/1
1870	**Bothwell**	J Osborne Jnr	T Dawson	J Johnstone	4/7
1871	**Lilian**	C Maidment	W Gilbert	H Savile	9/4
1872	**Thorn**	J Osborne Jnr	J Osborne	R N Batt	2/1
1873	**Padoroshna**	T Chaloner	J Cannon	Lord Rosebery	9/2
1874	**Holy Friar**	J Osborne Jnr	W Osborne	J W King	1/20
1875	**Springfield**	T Osborne	J Ryan	J H Houldsworth	4/9
1876	**Constantine**	J Osborne Jnr	W Osborne	R Osborne	4/5
1877	**King Olaf**	F Archer	Jos Dawson	J Lowther	4/5
1878	**Amice**	J Goater	W Gilbert	H Savile	5/6
1879	**Duke of Cumberland**	F Archer	J Cannon	Lord Rosebery	Evens
1880	**Simnel**	J Osborne Jnr	F Bates	R Jardine	11/10
1881	**Pursebearer**	J Snowden	W I'Anson Jnr	C Perkins	5/6
1882	**The Golden Farmer**	C Wood	R Sherrard	W S Crawfurd	4/5
1883	**Juventus**	F Archer	M Dawson	R C Vyner	8/13
1884	**Thuringian Queen**	J Watts	J Enoch	J Lowther	4/9
1885	**Castor**	J Fagan	W I'Anson Jnr	W I'Anson Jnr	4/7
1886	**Lady Muncaster**	J Fagan	W I'Anson Jnr	J B Cookson	4/7
1887	**Derwentwater**	J Fagan	W I'Anson Jnr	H Robertson	100/15
1888	**Cheroot**	J Woodburn	J Enoch	J Lowther	3/1
1889	**Lockhart**	J Fagan	W I'Anson Jnr	W I'Anson Jnr	7/4
1890	**Royal Stag**	J Fagan	W I'Anson Jnr	W I'Anson Jnr	100/8
1891	**Therapia**	J Watts	T Leader	J Joicey	100/12
1892	**Peppercorn**	F Rickaby	T Leader	J Joicey	100/30
1893	**Styx**	T Loates	A Hayhoe	Baron L de Rothschild	5/1
1894	**Bentworth**	J Watts	W G Stevens	C Trimmer	8/13
1895	**Amphora**	T Loates	J Jewitt	H McCalmont	6/1
1896	**Silver Fox**	T Loates	T Leader	J Joicey	100/12
1897	**Mauchline**	J Fagan	W Walters Jnr	Lord Rosebery	7/1
1898	**Queen Fairy**	F Pratt	J Ryan	J Wallace	10/1
1899	**Dusky Queen**	O Madden	J Waugh	Mr Russel	13/8
1900	**Garb Or**	K Cannon	T Cannon Jnr	T S Jay	8/1
1901	**Sterling Balm**	D Maher	J Watts	Maj Joicey	5/1
1902	**Chaucer**	D Maher	G Lambton	Lord Derby	15/8
1903	**Barbette**	J Dalton	W I'Anson Jnr	H Sandford	11/4
1904	**Desiree**	W Lane	P P Gilpin	P P Gilpin	10/1
1905	**Colonia**	H Jones	W T Robinson	W Hall-Walker	2/1
1906	**Polar Star**	B Lynham	W T Robinson	W Hall-Walker	9/2
1907	**Royal Realm**	B Lynham	W T Robinson	W Hall-Walker	7/4
1908	**Blankney II**	W Higgs	D Waugh	W Raphael	7/1
1909	**Lily Rose**	B Lynham	J Fergusson	W Hall-Walker	100/8
1910	**Pietri**	D Maher	J Watson	L de Rothschild	8/15
1911	**Lomond**	F Wootton	R Wootton	E Hulton	40/85
1912	**Flippant**	W Saxby	R Wootton	E Hulton	2/1
1913	**Stornoway**	F Wootton	R Wootton	E Hulton	Evens
1914/18	**No Race**				
1919	**Southern**	F Fox	R Day	Sir A Bailey	7/2
1920	**Polemarch**	F Lane	R H Dewhurst	Lord Londonderry	5/1
1921	**Scamp**	F Lane	F Templeman	Lord Jersey	11/10
1922	**Town Guard**	G Archibald	P P Gilpin	Lord Woolavington	1/2
1923	**Sansovino**	T Weston	G Lambton	Lord Derby	5/4
1924	**Game Shot**	F Bullock	N Scobie	Sir C Hyde	100/30
1925	**Lex**	M Beary	R Day	Sir A Bailey	5/1
1926	**Bold Archer**	H Wragg	R Moreton	H Shaw	11/2
1927	**Black Watch**	G Richards	P P Gilpin	L Neumann	4/5
1928	**The Black Abbot**	G Richards	F Darling	Lord Dewar	11/8
1929	**Roral**	R Perryman	H S Persse	Sir A Bailey	4/1
1930	**Four Course**	F Fox	F Darling	Lord Ellesmere	8/15
1931	**Miracle**	H Wragg	J Jarvis	Lord Rosebery	4/7
1932	**Young Lover**	R Perryman	Frank Butters	Sir A Butt	100/8
1933	**Mrs Rustom**	M Beary	Frank Butters	HH Aga Khan	4/7
1934	**Bahram**	R Perryman	Frank Butters	HH Aga Khan	2/7
1935	**Paul Beg**	H Gunn	W Easterby	Lord Milton	20/1
1936	**Goya II**	C Elliott	G Lambton	M Boussac	6/1
1937	**Golden Sovereign**	T Weston	H Cottrill	Sir A Bailey	6/1
1938	**Cockpit**	R Perryman	C Leader	Lord Derby	7/4
1939	**Tant Mieux**	G Richards	F Darling	Prince Aly Khan	6/1

		Jockey	Trainer	Owner	Odds
1940/44	**No Race**				
1945	**Gulf Stream**	H Wragg	W Earl	Lord Derby	7/2
1946	**Petition**	H Wragg	Frank Butters	Sir A Butt	13/8
1947	**Black Tarquin**	W H Carr	C Boyd-Rochfort	W Woodward	3/1
1948	**Star King**	S Wragg	J C Waugh	W Harvey	15/2
1949	**Palestine**	G Richards	Frank Butters	HH Aga Khan	1/25
1950	**Cortil**	W R Johnstone	C Semblat	M Boussac	11/2
1951	**Windy City**	G Richards	P Prendergast	R Bell	5/4
1952	**Bebe Grande**	W Snaith	F Armstrong	J Gerber	7/2
1953	**The Pie King**	G Richards	P Prendergast	R Bell	1/3
1954	**Precast**	W Nevett	R D Peacock	F Ellison	25/1
1955	**Idle Rocks**	D Smith	G Brooke	D Robinson	8/1
1956	**Eudaemon**	E Britt	C Elsey	Mrs E Foster	8/1
1957	**Pheidippides**	D Smith	C Elsey	P Bull	100/8
1958	**Be Careful**	E Hide	C Elsey	W Hill	10/1
1959	**Paddy's Sister**	G Moore	P Prendergast	Mrs J R Mullion	4/11
1960	**Test Case**	E Larkin	J Jarvis	Sir A Jarvis	100/7
1961	**Sovereign Lord**	A Breasley	G Smyth	Duke of Norfolk	10/1
1962	**Crocket**	D Smith	G Brooke	D van Clief	2/5
1963	**Talahasse**	L Piggott	T Corbett	H Loebstein	11/8
1964	**Double Jump**	J Lindley	J Tree	C W Engelhard	Evens
1965	**Young Emperor**	L Piggott	P Prendergast	Mrs P Poe	5/6
1966	**Golden Horus**	J Mercer	W O'Gorman	Mrs D Solomon	7/1
1967	**Petingo**	L Piggott	F Armstrong	M Lemos	7/4
1968	**Tudor Music**	F Durr	M Jarvis	D Robinson	10/11
1969	**Yellow God**	F Durr	P Davey	D Robinson	7/2
1970	**Mill Reef**	G Lewis	I Balding	P Mellon	4/5
1971	**Wishing Star**	F Durr	P Davey	D Robinson	12/1
1972	**Rapid River**	T Kelsey	W A Stephenson	Mrs W Richardson	8/1
1973	**Giacometti**	A Murray	H R Price	C St George	11/10
1974	**Steel Heart**	L Piggott	D Weld	R Tikkoo	17/2
1975	**Music Boy**	J Seagrave	G Wainwright	K Mackey	14/1
1976	**Nebbiolo**	G Curran	K Prendergast	N Schibbye	2/1
1977	**Tumbledownwind**	G Lewis	B Hobbs	J Wilson	6/5
1978	**Stanford**	P Eddery	N Callaghan	D Cock	15/2
1979	**Sonnen Gold**	M Birch	M H Easterby	P Muldoon	5/1
1980	**Bel Bolide**	P Eddery	J Tree	K Abdulla	11/2
1981	**Full Extent**	J Lowe	S Norton	M Korn	13/2
1982	**Horage**	A Murray	M McCormack	A Rachid	8/13
1983	**Precocious**	L Piggott	H Cecil	Lord Tavistock	8/11
1984	**Doulab**	A Murray	H Thomson Jones	H Al-Maktoum	10/1
1985	**Stalker**	J Mercer	P Walwyn	P Featherston-Godley	17/2
1986	**Wiganthorpe**	W Carson	M W Easterby	R Sangster	9/2
1987	**Reprimand**	S Cauthen	H Cecil	Sheikh Mohammed	2/7
1988	**Sharp N'Early**	B Rouse	R Hannon	A F Budge Ltd	14/1
1989	**Rock City**	W Carson	R Hannon	A F Budge Ltd	1/2
1990	**Mujtahid**	W Carson	R Armstrong	H Al-Maktoum	1/2
1991	**River Falls**	B Raymond	R Hannon	A F Budge Ltd	9/4
1992	**Splendent**	A Munro	P Cole	F Salman	8/1

For all 2 year-olds 1846-1986

The Nunthorpe Stakes

One of the few races in the Calendar where two-year-olds can take on their seniors, the Nunthorpe started as a humble seller in 1903 and became the medium for some hefty gambles by trainers with smart juveniles receiving all the allowances. In 1922, the Nunthorpe became a condition race, since when only three two-year-olds have succeeded; *High Treason* in 1953, *My Beau* in 1954 and *Ennis* in 1956.

Two horses have won the race three times, *Tag End* from 1928 to 1930 and *Sharpo* from 1980 to 1982. In 1976 the Nunthorpe was rather pretentiously titled the William Hill Sprint Championship. Few single races can be regarded as championships, but nonetheless the event has been remarkable in recent years for the quality of the winners.

Sheikh Albadou was the most recent example, going on to win the Sprint in the Breeders' Cup staged at Churchill Downs, Kentucky in 1991, together with the King's Stand stakes and the Haydock Sprint Cup in 1992, but one of the punters' favourites was *Polyfoto*, the winner in 1965. *Polyfoto's* trainer Eddie Reavey had taken the wrong course on *Zahia* in the 1948 Grand National with only one fence to jump and the sporting Yorkshire crowd were happy to applaud his compensation for the one that got away. One who didn't get away was the brilliant filly *Lyric Fantasy* in 1992, who became the first two-year-old to win for 36 years and the first two-year-old filly to succeed. She was supplementing victories in the Queen Mary Stakes, the National Stakes and five in all but failed behind *Sayyedati* in the Cheveley Park Stakes. Her shrewd owner Breeder netted £340,000 Guineas for her at the December sales.

Lyric Fantasy, ridden by Michael Roberts, on the way to winning the 1992 Nunthorpe Stakes.

Run at York over 5 furlongs First Run 1922 Group 1

		Jockey	Trainer	Owner	Odds
1922	**Two Steps**	H Jones	A Taylor Jnr	S Tattersall	4/1
1923	**Golden Boss**	C Elliott	C Boyd-Rochfort	A K Macomber	4/6
1924	**Mumtaz Mahal**	G Archibald	R C Dawson	HH Aga Khan	Evens
1925	**Diomedes**	J Leach	H Leader	S W Beer	4/7
1926	**Highborn II**	J Childs	O Bell	Sir H Cunliffe-Owen	30/100
1927	**Highborn II**	J Childs	O Bell	Sir H Cunliffe-Owen	13/8
1928	**Tag End**	B Carslake	C Peck	J B Joel	30/100
1929	**Tag End**	F Fox	C Peck	J B Joel	4/1
1930	**Tag End**	B Carslake	C Peck	J B Joel	11/4
1931	**Portlaw**	H Beasley	H S Persse	Sir A Bailey	5/1
1932	**Greenore**	H Wragg	O Bell	Lady Ludlow	8/1
1933	**Concerto**	B Carslake	O Bell	Sir H Cuncliffe-Owen	6/1
1934	**Gold Bridge**	C Elliott	V Beatty	Lord Beatty	6/5
1935	**Shalfleet**	H Jelliss	H Leader	H Leader	9/4
1936	**Bellacose**	P Beasley	R J Colling	P Dunne	Evens
1937	**Ipsden**	S Wragg	O Bell	Lady Ludlow	7/1
1938	**Mickey the Greek**	H Wragg	H Leach	H Leach	5/1
1939	**Portobello**	G Richards	R J Colling	P Dunne	15/8
1940/41	**No Race**				
1942	**Linklater**	E Smith	W Smyth	A E Saunders	100/8
1943	**Linklater**	E Smith	W Smyth	A E Saunders	9/2
1944	**Sugar Palm**	C Elliott	F Hartigan	A Bonsor	8/1
1945	**Golden Cloud**	M Beary	E Lambton	Mrs G Lambton	100/8
1946	**The Bug**	C Smirke	M Marsh	N Wachman	4/6
1947	**The Como**	W H Carr	G Armstrong	Capt J Fielden	3/1
1948	**Careless Nora**	C Elliott	J Dines	G Frampton	6/4
1949	**Abernant**	G Richards	N Murless	R Macdonald-Buchanan	2/11
1950	**Abernant**	G Richards	N Murless	R Macdonald-Buchanan	7/100
1951	**Royal Serenade**	C Elliott	H Wragg	Mrs G Kohn	4/1
1952	**Royal Serenade**	G Richards	H Wragg	G Bell	4/6
1953	**High Treason**	D Greening	T E Leader	H J Joel	9/4
1954	**My Beau**	T Carter	P Prendergast	A Wimbush	7/1
1955	**Royal Palm**	W Snaith	F Armstrong	J Gerber	11/10
1956	**Ennis**	P Tulk	W Nightingall	C Harper	11/2
1957	**Gratitude**	W Snaith	H Cottrill	Maj L B Holliday	7/2

		Jockey	Trainer	Owner	Odds
1958	**Right Boy**	L Piggott	W Dutton	G Gilbert	8/100
1959	**Right Boy**	L Piggott	H Rohan	H D H Wills	4/9
1960	**Bleep-Bleep**	W H Carr	H Cottrill	Mrs M Turner	9/2
1961	**Floribunda**	R Hutchinson	P Prendergast	Mrs J R Mullion	4/1
1962	**Gay Mairi**	A Breasley	H Whiteman	A Macdonald	100/8
1963	**Matatina**	L Piggott	F Armstrong	Mrs R Wilson	7/2
1964	**Althrey Don**	R Maddock	H Rohan	J Done	3/1
1965	**Polyfoto**	J Wilson	E Reavey	Mrs C Reavey	20/1
1966	**Caterina**	L Piggott	F Armstrong	R F Scully	13/2
1967	**Forlorn River**	B Raymond	W A Stephenson	Mrs W A Richardson	6/1
1968	**So Blessed**	F Durr	M Jarvis	D Robinson	4/6
1969	**Tower Walk**	L Piggott	G Barling	V W Hardy	7/1
1970	**Huntercombe**	A Barclay	A Budgett	H Renshaw	5/4
1971	**Swing Easy**	L Piggott	J Tree	J H Whitney	2/1
1972	**Deep Diver**	W Williamson	P Davey	D Robinson	100/30
1973	**Sandford Lad**	A Murray	H R Price	C Olley	4/1
1974	**Blue Cashmere**	E Hide	M Stoute	R Clifford-Turner	18/1
1975	**Bay Express**	W Carson	P Nelson	P Cooper	100/30
1976	**Lochnager**	E Hide	M W Easterby	C Spence	4/5
1977	**Haveroid**	E Hide	N Adam	T Newton	10/1
1978	**Solinus**	L Piggott	M V O'Brien	D Schwartz	1/2
1979	**Ahonoora**	G Starkey	F Durr	E Alkhalifa	3/1
1980	**Sharpo**	P Eddery	J Tree	Miss M Sheriffe	3/1
1981	**Sharpo**	P Eddery	J Tree	Miss M Sheriffe	14/1
1982	**Sharpo**	S Cauthen	J Tree	Miss M Sheriffe	Evens
1983	**Habibti**	W Carson	J Dunlop	M Mutawa	13/8
1984	**Committed**	B Thomson	D Weld	R Sangster	5/1
1985	**Never So Bold**	S Cauthen	R Armstrong	E Kessly	4/6
1986	**Last Tycoon**	Y Saint-Martin	R Collet	R C Strauss	7/2
1987	**Ajdal**	W R Swinburn	M Stoute	Sheikh Mohammed	2/1
1988	**Handsome Sailor**	M Hills	B Hills	R Sangster	5/2
1989	**Cadeaux Genereux**	P Eddery	A Scott	M Al-Maktoum	11/10
1990	**Dayjur**	W Carson	W R Hern	H Al-Maktoum	8/11
1991	**Sheikh Albadou**	P Eddery	A Scott	H Salem	6/1
1992	**Lyric Fantasy**	M Roberts	R Hannon	Lord Carnarvon	8/11

Run at Newmarket 1942-1944. Run as the William Hill Sprint Championship from 1976-1989

The Lowther Stakes

The Lowther Stakes commemorates the man forever known in sporting circles as 'The Yellow Earl', Hugh Lowther, 5th Earl of Lonsdale. His interests were wide ranging and included racing, hunting, athletics, shooting, yachting and of course boxing, hence the Lonsdale Belt awarded to every champion.

He did not own any horses of note except *Royal Lancer* who won the St Leger in 1922 and was in fact leased to him by the National Stud as was the superb filly *Myrobella,* winner of eleven top class races over sprint distances and the dam of *Big Game* who took the 2,000 Guineas in 1942.

The Lowther Stakes has provided a share of classic winners including *Humble Duty, Enstone Spark* and foreign classics were claimed by *Al Bahathri* and *Culture Vulture.*

Another picture of *Pia* with Eddie Hide up. They combined again to take the 1966 Lowther Stakes.

Run at York over 6 furlongs for 2 year-old fillies   First Run 1946   Group 2

		Jockey	Trainer	Owner	Odds
1946	**Southernwood**	W Nevett	C Elsey	C H Grey	100/8
1947	**Woodflower**	W H Carr	C Boyd-Rochfort	Sir R Sykes	Evens
1948	**Shard Bridge**	T Lowrey	R A Jones	J F Emery	2/1
1949	**Corjeda**	C Elliott	C Semblat	M Boussac	1/3
1950	**Gamble in Gold**	W H Carr	C Boyd-Rochfort	Mrs W P Wyatt	11/8

		Jockey	Trainer	Owner	Odds
1951	**Constantia**	P Maher	R Jarvis	Lord Fairhaven	15/8
1952	**Royal Duchy**	C Elliott	P Prendergast	A L Hawkins	7/2
1953	**Crimson**	J Mercer	H Smyth	Mrs C Y Bennett	10/1
1954	**Our Betters**	C Smirke	H Thomson Jones	S Joel	4/1
1955	**La Fresnes**	D Smith	G Colling	Lord Derby	7/2
1956	**Pharsalia**	W Snaith	H Cottrill	Maj L B Holliday	7/4
1957	**Liberal Lady**	K Gethin	P Thrale	A Wakling	100/8
1958	**Fortune's Darling**	S Clayton	W R Hern	Maj L B Holliday	20/1
1959	**Queensberry**	E Smith	J A Waugh	B Hornung	10/11
1960	**Kathy Too**	R Hutchinson	P Prendergast	G Bradbury	9/2
1961	**La Tendresse**	R Hutchinson	P Prendergast	Mrs P Poe	2/7
1962	**Dunce Cap**	W H Carr	C Boyd-Rochfort	J H Whitney	6/1
1963	**Pourparler**	G Bougoure	P Prendergast	Lady B Granard	7/2
1964	**Pugnacity**	J Mercer	W Wharton	Maj L B Holliday	4/6
1965	**Reet Lass**	B Connorton	W Gray	Mrs V Gray	3/1
1966	**Pia**	E Hide	W Elsey	Countess M Batthyany	100/9
1967	**Sovereign**	R Hutchinson	H Wragg	R B Moller	1/9
1968	**Flying Legs**	F Durr	M Jarvis	D Robinson	9/4
1969	**Humble Duty**	D Keith	P Walwyn	Lady J Ashcombe	4/1
1970	**Cawston's Pride**	B Taylor	F Maxwell	L B Hall	8/100
1971	**Rose Dubarry**	A Murray	T A Waugh	H J Joel	5/2
1972	**Regardia**	J Lindley	T Corbett	B Attenborough	15/2
1973	**Bitty Girl**	B Raymond	M Jarvis	D Robinson	9/4
1974	**Cry of Truth**	J Gorton	B Hobbs	Mrs P Lawson-Johnston	8/13
1975	**Pasty**	P Eddery	P Walwyn	G P Williams	15/8
1976	**Icena**	B Taylor	H Thomson Jones	R Hutchinson	25/1
1977	**Enstone Spark**	F Durr	R Hannon	J H Hughes Farms Ltd	33/1
1978	**Devon Ditty**	G Starkey	H Thomson Jones	Sir E McAlpine	4/1
1979	**Mrs Penny**	J Matthias	I Balding	E Kronfeld	11/2
1980	**Kittyhawk**	L Piggott	W R Hern	Lord Porchester	10/11
1981	**Circus Ring**	W R Swinburn	M Stoute	Snailwell Stud Ltd	1/4
1982	**Habibti**	W Carson	J Dunlop	M Mutawa	4/1
1983	**Prickle**	L Piggott	H Cecil	P D Player	11/4
1984	**Al Bahathri**	A Murray	H Thomson Jones	H Al-Maktoum	11/10
1985	**Kingscote**	P Eddery	J Tree	K Abdulla	5/2
1986	**Polonia**	J Reid	J Bolger	H de Kwiatkowski	5/2
1987	**Ela Romara**	Paul Eddery	G Wragg	E B Moller	2/1
1988	**Miss Demure**	M Roberts	R Armstrong	Kennet Valley Thoro. Ltd	16/1
1989	**Dead Certain**	S Cauthen	D Elsworth	G G Martin	5/4
1990	**Only Yours**	B Raymond	R Hannon	Mrs M Butcher	8/1
1991	**Culture Vulture**	T Quinn	P Cole	C Wright	85/40
1992	**Niche**	L Piggott	R Hannon	Lord Carnarvon	2/1

The Prestige Stakes

This seven furlong race for two-year-old fillies was originally the Waterford Candelabra Stakes, and when upgraded to Group status in 1981 seemed to have made a auspicious start as a Pattern race when the winner *Stratospheric* looked potentially classic material. It was not to be; *Stratospheric* could finish only sixth in the 1,000 Guineas and after breaking blood vessels in training had to be put down.

Some useful fillies have won since, and *Bella Colora* finished third in the 1,000 Guineas in 1985, although *Musicale* was very disappointing in the Newmarket classic in 1992.

Run at Goodwood over 7 furlongs for 2 year-old fillies First Run 1975 Group 3

		Jockey	Trainer	Owner	Odds
1975	**Cappucilli**	L Piggott	H Cecil	C St George	15/2
1976	**Triple First**	G Starkey	M Stoute	R Clifford-Turner	7/1
1977	**Cistus**	W Carson	W R Hern	Sir M Sobell	7/2
1978	**Formulate**	M Roberts	H Cecil	Mrs D Butler	20/1
1979	**Schweppes Forever**	B Taylor	H R Price	Mrs M Butler	15/2
1980	**Fairy Footsteps**	P Eddery	H Cecil	H J Joel	4/1
1981	**Stratospheric**	P Eddery	J Dunlop	O Phipps	16/1
1982	**Flamenco**	J Matthias	I Balding	M Jenney	5/1
1983	**Shoot Clear**	W R Swinburn	M Stoute	R H Cowell	3/1
1984	**Bella Colora**	W R Swinburn	M Stoute	Helena Springfield Ltd	4/1
1985	**Asteroid Field**	B Thomson	B Hills	Sheikh Mohammed	11/1
1986	**Invited Guest**	S Cauthen	R Armstrong	Kinderhill Corporation	4/1
1987	**Obeah**	C Asmussen	B Hills	R Sangster	16/1
1988	**Life At The Top**	M Roberts	A Stewart	Mrs M Landi	5/1
1989	**Moon Cactus**	S Cauthen	H Cecil	Sheikh Mohammed	4/7
1990	**Jaffa Line**	S Cauthen	D Elsworth	Mrs P J Sheen	5/2
1991	**Musicale**	P Eddery	H Cecil	R Sangster	15/8
1992	**Love of Silver**	M Roberts	C Brittain	A Saeed	9/1

Run as the Waterford Candelabra Stakes from 1975-1988

The Beefeater Gin Celebration Mile

Originally the Wills Mile when founded in 1967, then the Goodwood Mile from 1971 to 1974 and the Waterford Crystal Mile between 1975 and 1988, this event is a good example of the confusion which can arise when races are staged by courses which consider commercialisation to be an over-riding factor.

However, no one could dispute the quality of the winners up to 1981, a period which saw victories by *Habitat* and four classic winners, *Humble Duty, Brigadier Gerard, Known Fact* and *To-Agori-Mou*, plus the champion miler *Kris*, who won a substitue race at Ascot. Unfortunately, this level has not been sustained in recent years, with the honourable exception of *Selkirk* in 1992.

Run at Goodwood over 1 mile First Run 1967 Group 2

		Jockey	Trainer	Owner	Odds
1967	**St Chad**	G Moore	N Murless	Mrs N Murless	9/4
1968	**Jimmy Reppin**	G Lewis	J Sutcliffe Jnr	Mrs S Bates	5/1
1969	**Habitat**	L Piggott	R F Johnson Houghton	C W Engelhard	9/2
1970	**Humble Duty**	D Keith	P Walwyn	Lady J Ashcombe	4/6
1971	**Brigadier Gerard**	J Mercer	W R Hern	Mrs J Hislop	1/6
1972	**Sallust**	J Mercer	W R Hern	Sir M Sobell	1/2
1973	**Jacinth**	J Gorton	B Hobbs	Lady Butt	2/5
1974	**Pitcairn**	R Hutchinson	J Dunlop	A J Struthers	4/9
1975	**Gay Fandango**	P Eddery	M V O'Brien	A Clore	5/1
1976	**Free State**	P Eddery	P Walwyn	Mrs D McCalmont	13/8
1977	**Be My Guest**	L Piggott	M V O'Brien	Mrs A Manning	6/4
1978	**Captain James**	J Mercer	S McGrath	S McGrath	25/1
1979	**Kris**	J Mercer	H Cecil	Lord H de Walden	30/100
1980	**Known Fact**	W Carson	J Tree	K Abdulla	5/2
1981	**To-Agori-Mou**	G Starkey	G Harwood	Mrs A Muinos	5/4
1982	**Sandhurst Prince**	G Starkey	G Harwood	J Thompson	7/4
1983	**Montekin**	B Rouse	J Dunlop	P Winfield	8/1
1984	**Rousillon**	G Starkey	G Harwood	K Abdulla	8/13
1985	**No Race**				
1986	**Then Again**	G Starkey	L Cumani	R J Shannon	8/1
1987	**Milligram**	W R Swinburn	M Stoute	Helena Springfield Ltd	5/2
1988	**Prince Rupert**	M Hills	B Hills	R Sangster	16/1
1989	**Distant Relative**	M Hills	B Hills	W Said	2/1
1990	**Shavian**	S Cauthen	H Cecil	Lord H de Walden	5/2
1991	**Bold Russian**	W Carson	B Hills	Lord White	100/30
1992	**Selkirk**	R Cochrane	I Balding	G Strawbridge	1/2

Run as the Wills Mile 1967-1970, the Goodwood Mile 1971-1974 and the Waterford Crystal Mile 1975-1988

***Selkirk*, ridden by Ray Cochrane, won the 1992 Beefeater Gin Celebration Mile.**

The Haydock Sprint Cup

Originally the Vernons November Sprint Cup and the brainchild of owner-breeder Robert Sangster who was heir to the Vernons Football Pools fortune, the race has had changes of conditions, course and date since 1966, when it was open to two-year-olds and upwards and run over a dog-leg six furlongs. In 1986, Haydock installed a straight six furlong track and the event was upgraded to Group One. For a time two-year-olds were not eligible, but were reinstated in 1989. In 1979 it was decided to run the sprint in early September in order to avoid the mists and heavy ground which caused abandonment in 1968.

The old course which started on a chute with a sharp left-hand turn was taxing for horse and rider. In theory this gave the advantage to those with a low draw, but the ground on the stands side in wet weather nullified the poorer surface on the inside track and many runners sacrificed lengths by crossing at the bend.

Put on the racing map by the exploits of Peter O'Sullevan's *Be Friendly* who won both the inaugural and the second running, sponsorship was taken over by Ladbrokes in 1988. They have now withdrawn, but the race remains to strengthen the sprint race pattern in the second half of the season.

Run at Haydock Park over 6 furlongs First Run 1966 Group 1

		Jockey	Trainer	Owner	Odds
1966	**Be Friendly**	C Williams	C Mitchell	P O'Sullevan	15/2
1967	**Be Friendly**	A Breasley	C Mitchell	P O'Sullevan	2/1
1968	**No Race**				
1969	**Tudor Music**	F Durr	M Jarvis	D Richardson	11/4
1970	**Golden Orange**	J Lindley	K Cundell	Lady Clifden	10/1
1971	**Green God**	L Piggott	M Jarvis	D Robinson	7/4
1972	**Abergwaun**	L Piggott	M V O'Brien	C St George	11/10
1973	**The Blues**	R Marshall	W Marshall	G van der Ploeg	10/1
1974	**Princely Son**	J Seagrave	K Cundell	W Sherman	8/1
1975	**Lianga**	Y Saint-Martin	A Penna	D Wildenstein	2/1
1976	**Record Token**	P Eddery	P Walwyn	Sir H Ingram	3/1
1977	**Boldboy**	W Carson	W R Hern	Lady Beaverbrook	Evens
1978	**Absalom**	M L Thomas	R Jarvis	Mrs C Alington	20/1
1979	**Double Form**	G Lewis	R F Johnson Houghton	Baroness H Thyssen	11/4
1980	**Moorestyle**	L Piggott	R Armstrong	Moores Furnishings Ltd	8/13
1981	**Runnett**	B Raymond	J Dunlop	Miss V Evans	6/1
1982	**Indian King**	G Starkey	G Harwood	J Levy	3/1
1983	**Habibti**	W Carson	J Dunlop	M Mutawa	8/13
1984	**Petong**	B Raymond	M Jarvis	T G Warner	11/1
1985	**Orojoya**	B Thomson	J Hindley	R Sangster	11/1
1986	**Green Desert**	W R Swinburn	M Stoute	M Al-Maktoum	5/4
1987	**Ajdal**	W R Swinburn	M Stoute	Sheikh Mohammed	8/11
1988	**Dowsing**	P Eddery	J Tree	K Abdulla	15/2
1989	**Danehill**	P Eddery	J Tree	K Abdulla	3/1
1990	**Dayjur**	W Carson	W R Hern	H Al-Maktoum	1/2
1991	**Polar Falcon**	C Asmussen	J Hammond	D Thompson	13/2
1992	**Sheikh Albadou**	B Raymond	A Scott	H Salem	9/4

Run as the Vernons November Sprint Cup 1966-1967, the Vernons Sprint Cup 1968-1988 and the Ladbroke Sprint Cup 1989-1991

The September Stakes

The September Stakes achieved Group status in 1983. Usually contested by top class animals perhaps just short of classic standard, it is an ideal stepping stone for the lucrative autumn campaign now on offer in Europe. The best race in recent times came in 1985, when the Derby winner *Slip Anchor* went down by half a length to the four-year-old *Shernazar*, also winner of the Alycidon Stakes and the Geoffrey Freer Stakes.

Run at Kempton Park over 1 mile 3 furlongs and 30 yards First Run 1979 Group 3

		Jockey	Trainer	Owner	Odds
1979	**Cracaval**	S Cauthen	B Hills	A Shead	20/1
1980	**More Light**	W Carson	W R Hern	R Budgett	7/4
1981	**Kind of Hush**	S Cauthen	B Hills	A Shead	9/2
1982	**Critique**	L Piggott	H Cecil	G Vanian	8/11
1983	**Lyphard's Special**	B Rouse	G Harwood	Lady Harrison	12/1
1984	**Bedtime**	W Carson	W R Hern	Lord Halifax	13/8
1985	**Shernazar**	W R Swinburn	M Stoute	HH Aga Khan	4/1
1986	**Dihistan**	W R Swinburn	M Stoute	HH Aga Khan	6/1
1987	**Knockando**	R Cochrane	L Cumani	M Boffa	2/1
1988	**Percy's Lass**	P Eddery	G Wragg	Exors of E B Moller	7/2
1989	**Assatis**	R Cochrane	G Harwood	K Abdulla	4/6
1990	**Lord of the Field**	W Newnes	J Toller	Duke of Devonshire	6/1
1991	**Young Buster**	W R Swinburn	G Wragg	Exors of E B Moller	11/4
1992	**Jeune**	R Cochrane	G Wragg	Sir R McAlpine	6/1

The Portland Handicap

The Portland Handicap is a tough sprint requiring skilful jockeyship, especially in the days when the extended five furlong course starting opposite the Red House was a dog-leg to the left after about halfway. One of the most distinguished winners was *Diomedes*, owned by the successful gambler Sidney Beer, trained by Harvey Leader at Newmarket and winner of the Portland under 9st 2lb in 1925.

Three years later *Tag End* won the first of two Portland Handicaps in the same season as this outstanding sprinter took the first of three runnings of the Nunthorpe Stakes.

In recent times, the race has been clouded in controversy. In 1986, theoretically 'good' ground was in fact so bad that it was impossible to use the starting stalls, obliging the starter to send off a twenty-three runner field by flag. Following the inevitable false start, six horses passed the winning post, and thus were ineligible for the re-run.

Worse was to follow. In 1989, *Madraco* fell bringing down two other runners, and after another horse running over the same course two days later also fell, the track was declared unsafe due to subsidence and the remainder of the meeting abandoned. In the long term, this resulted in the transfer of the St Leger to Ayr, the only classic race to be contested outside England.

Lester Piggott, 'a promiment young flat jockey', pictured in May 1952. Three years later he won the Portland Handicap for the first time, on *Princely Gift*.

Run at Doncaster over 5 furlongs   First Run 1855   Handicap

		Jockey	Trainer	Owner	Odds
1855	**Manganese**	T Chaloner	J Osborne	W H Brook	15/1
1856	**Lance**	J Wilberforce	W Weatherell	Mr Hind	10/1
1857	**Meta**	J Snowden	J Watson	W F Adamson	100/8
1858	**The Ancient Briton**	L Snowden	J Saxon	J Saxon	6/1
1859	**Tight-fit**	H Bray	T Taylor	W S Crawfurd	6/1
1860	**Tattoo**	J Doyle	J Fobert	H O'Hara	100/3
1861	**Lady Clifden**	L Snowden	T Wadlow	Capt Christie	10/1
1862	**Queen of Trumps**	H Grimshaw	–	C Rodgers	100/30
1863	**Welland**	G Fordham	W Goodwin	G Bryan	8/1
1864	**Persuasion**	J Grimshaw	J Peace	W Phillips	10/1
1865	**Kilkenny**	J Morris	W Goater	Lord Westmorland	5/2
1866	**Skylark**	C Carroll	C Peck	R H Jones	100/6
1867	**Bounceaway**	J Mann	C Blanton	Prince Soltykoff	7/1
1868	**Lady Zetland**	A Hammond	–	Mr Feaster	25/1
1869	**Argyle**	W Gray	T Dawson	J Johnstone	100/8
1870	**Oxonian**	R Wyatt	W Day	W Day	9/2
1871	**St Vincent**	C Loates	Jos Dawson	T V Morgan	11/8
1872	**Little Nell**	W Chaloner	John Dawson	Count Batthyany	8/1
1873	**Grand Flaneur**	G Mills	J Osborne	H Bragg	33/1
1874	**Geneveive**	J Thompson	–	F Douglas	100/8
1875	**Grand Flaneur**	W Chaloner	J Osborne	H Bragg	100/8
1876	**Lollypop**	H Huxtable	R Marsh	Duke of Hamilton	100/8
1877	**Rosbach**	H Constable	J Cannon	Lord Rosebery	6/1
1878	**Telescope**	J Snowden	–	W H Shaw	11/1
1879	**Hackthorpe**	F Archer	J Cannon	Lord Hastings	9/2
1880	**Discount**	W Greaves	J Greaves	Y R Graham	10/1
1881	**Mowerina**	F Archer	M Dawson	Duke of Portland	100/8
1882	**Martini**	C Wood	R Sherrard	W S Crawfurd	11/1
1883	**Lowland Chief**	F Webb	C Archer	Lord Ellesmere	8/1
1884	**Leeds**	C Wood	J Humphreys	R Crest	5/2
1885	**Dalmeny**	E Martin	E Martin	F Morton	8/1
1886	**Modwena**	J Woodburn	M Dawson	Duke of Portland	100/6
1887	**Lisbon**	T Loates	R Sherrard	O Williams	100/8
1888	**Goldseeker**	W Blake	W Walters	Mr Leybourne	5/2
1889	**Galloping Queen**	W Blake	A Hayhoe	L de Rothschild	9/1

		Jockey	Trainer	Owner	Odds
1890	**L'Abbesse de Jouarre**	J Watts	Robert Sherwood	Lord R Churchill	9/2
1891	**Tostig**	W Platt	C Morton	G Masterman	100/6
1892	**Marvel**	J Watts	R Marsh	Duke of Devonshire	100/8
1893	**Whisperer**	T Loates	J Jewitt	H McCalmont	7/1
1894	**Grey Leg**	M Cannon	J Porter	Duke of Westminster	8/1
1895	**Whiston**	S Chandley	J Waugh	G Dobell	100/9
1896	**Grig**	T Loates	A Hayhoe	L de Rothschild	100/9
1897	**Kilkerran**	N Robinson	R Marsh	Lord C Montague	10/1
1898	**Eager**	F Allsopp	J Ryan	A W Cox	6/1
1899	**Mazeppa**	S Loates	C Morton	C A Mills	9/4
1900	**Lucknow**	J F Sloan	R Marsh	HRH the Prince of Wales	4/1
1901	**Dieudonne**	D Maher	R Marsh	Duke of Devonshire	11/2
1902	**Gladwin**	C Trigg	Leigh	R Croker	10/1
1903	**Nabot**	W Lane	W Waugh	Sir J Blundell Maple	9/2
1904	**Santry**	J H Martin	R C Dawson	Lord Carnarvon	10/1
1905	**Xeny**	D Maher	J E Brewer	R H Henning	100/6
1906	**Nero**	F Wootton	P P Gilpin	L Neumann	100/8
1907	**Woolley**	F Wootton	R C Dawson	R C Dawson	10/1
1908	**The Welkin**	L Hewitt	G Edwards	J L Dugdale	7/1
1909	**Americus Girl**	D Maher	P P Peebles	A H Ledlie	9/2
1910	**Hallaton**	D Maher	R C Dawson	Capt N Allfrey	11/2
1911	**Stolen Kiss**	C Trigg	J R Renwick	G Renwick	100/7
1912	**Wethers Well**	S Donoghue	J Fallon	L Clow	8/1
1913	**Hornet's Beauty**	E Wheatley	F Leach	Sir W Cooke	9/2
1914	**Flying Orb**	C Trigg	P Hartigan	G Edwardes	100/8
1915/18	**No Race**				
1919	**Irish Elegance**	B Carslake	H Cottrill	J White	9/4
1920	**Pelops**	V Smyth	F Hunt	Z Michalinos	20/1
1921	**Glanmerin**	B Carslake	S Pickering	Lord Londonderry	6/1
1922	**Two Step**	H Jones	A Taylor Jnr	S Tattersall	100/7
1923	**Polydipsia**	W McLachlan	E de Mestre	S B Joel	100/8
1924	**Heverswood**	C Elliott	J Jarvis	Sir L Richardson	10/1
1925	**Diomedes**	J Leach	H Leader	S W Beer	5/2
1926	**Sunstone**	G Archibald	R Day	Sir A Bailey	100/8
1927	**Mayrian**	A Wragg	W Earl	S B Joel	100/6
1928	**Tag End**	B Carslake	C Peck	J B Joel	100/7
1929	**Tag End**	F Fox	C Peck	J B Joel	2/1
1930	**Polar Bear**	J Dines	H Cottrill	Mrs J B Joel	10/1
1931	**Xandover**	C Elliott	B Jarvis	J Schwob	11/4
1932	**Polar Bear**	B Carslake	C Peck	Mrs J B Joel	100/6
1933	**Valkyrie**	T Barber	C Leader	O Watney	100/7
1934	**Rosemary's Pet**	B Carslake	C Peck	J B Joel	6/1
1935	**Shalfleet**	H Jellis	H Leader	J Walker	8/1
1936	**Shalfleet**	H Jellis	H Leader	J Walker	10/1
1937	**Carissa**	S Donoghue	H Peacock	Sir V Sassoon	100/8
1938	**The Drummer**	D Smith	W Carr	W Carr	7/1
1939/40	**No Race**				
1941	**Comatas**	W Nevett	O Bell	Miss K Farrar	100/7
1942/45	**No Race**				
1946	**The Shah**	J Sime	B Bullock	D Scott	7/1
1947	**Good View**	M Beary	E Parker	A Halford	100/7
1948	**Gold Mist**	C Richards	N Murless	A Wills	20/1
1949	**Le Lavandou**	P Evans	G Houghton	J Innes	25/1
1950	**Paramount**	C Smirke	M Marsh	Sir H de Trafford	100/7
1951	**Reminiscence**	C Smirke	W Nightingall	Mrs J V Rank	100/6
1952	**Stephen Paul**	G Richards	H S Persse	J Olding	100/30
1953	**Reminiscence**	E Britt	J Ormston	L Bland	100/7
1954	**Vilmoray**	A Shrive	B Bullock	A Green	100/7
1955	**Princely Gift**	L Piggott	N Murless	Sir V Sassoon	5/2
1956	**Epaulette**	W Snaith	F Armstrong	J Gerber	8/1
1957	**Refined**	D Smith	P Prendergast	Lady M van Cutsem	9/1
1958	**Welsh Abbot**	S Clayton	W Nightingall	Sir W Churchill	100/9
1959	**New World**	D Greening	G Balding	R Shaw	25/1
1960	**Accompanist**	D W Morris	F Maxwell	Mrs A Palmer	7/1
1961	**Winna**	C Parkes	H Wragg	N Frieze	100/8
1962	**Harmon**	A Breasley	P Beasley	Mrs J Aspinall	9/1
1963	**Marcher**	R Hutchinson	D Hanley	R Zelker	100/6
1964	**Comefast**	E Hide	J Vickers	H Walton	9/1
1965	**Go Shell**	D Smith	B van Cutsem	Lord Derby	100/7
1966	**Audrey Joan**	A Barclay	E Cousins	Mrs D Rosenfield	20/1
1967	**Florescence**	W Williamson	F Armstrong	J R Mullion	100/9
1968	**Gold Pollen**	E Johnson	R Jarvis	W Gaskin	11/4
1969	**Mountain Call**	L Piggott	B van Cutsem	I E Kornberg	11/4
1970	**Virginia Boy**	D McKay	D Smith	B Schmidt-Bodner	9/1
1971	**Royben**	N Williamson	A Breasley	A Kennedy	13/2

		Jockey	Trainer	Owner	Odds
1972	**Privateer**	E Hide	W Wightman	D Colebrook	8/1
1973	**Supreme Gift**	J Wilson	B Swift	R Pritchard	100/30
1974	**Matinee**	F Durr	J Clayton	Lord Porchester	10/1
1975	**Walk By**	E Hide	W Wightman	Mrs F Fleetwood-Hesketh	9/1
1976	**Hei'land Jamie**	T McKeown	N Adam	W Paul	20/1
1977	**Jon George**	W Carson	M W Easterby	Mrs W Newsome	11/2
1978	**Goldhills Pride**	K Leason	T Craig	H Ford	8/1
1979	**Oh Simmie**	B Jones	R Hollinshead	D Coppenhall	10/1
1980	**Swelter**	P Robinson	F Durr	G Greenwood	8/1
1981	**Touch Boy**	T Ives	J Berry	G Mullins	16/1
1982	**Vorvados**	L Piggott	M Haynes	Miss F Gallichan	6/1
1983	**Out of Hand**	S Dawson	D Dale	J D Baxter	14/1
1984	**Dawn's Delight**	L Charnock	K T Ivory	K T Ivory	20/1
1985	**Lochtillum**	R Cochrane	J Douglas-Home	J Douglas-Home	14/1
1986	**Felipe Toro**	J Lowe	M H Easterby	R Warden	11/2
1987	**Dawn's Delight**	M Wigham	K T Ivory	K T Ivory	14/1
1988	**Roman Prose**	I Johnson	L G Cottrell	C M Brown	8/1
1989	**Craft Express**	R P Elliott	M Johnston	Mrs V G Rowland	25/1
1990	**Love Legend**	A Munro	D Arbuthnot	M Gliksten	12/1
1991	**Sarcita**	W Carson	D Elsworth	R Tooth	13/2
1992	**Lochsong**	W Carson	I Balding	J C Smith	4/1

Run at Newmarket in 1941

The Park Hill Stakes

Often referred to as 'The Fillies' St Leger', a complete misnomer in the style of 'The Fillies' Triple Crown' as of course the St Leger is open to fillies, the Park Hill Stakes is a race for the best staying females.

Not many classic winners take part nowadays, the last to win being *Pia* in 1967, while both *Shoot a Line* and *Swiftfoot* took the Irish Oaks. However, there is usually a good quality field, as exemplified by *Patricia*, the 1991 winner of the Lancashire Oaks, and the Prix de Pomone at Deauville prior to her victory at Doncaster.

After 1990 the race was opened to older horses, and the six-year-old *Sesame* finished third to *Patricia*. This move is unlikely to detract from the quality of the race and at the same time improving the fields numerically.

The saddest tale of the Park Hill came in 1902. *Sceptre*, who had won four classics for her gambling owner Robert Sievier including the St Leger, when she was described as 'all skin and bone' when she paraded in the paddock, was pulled out two days later and beaten in the Park Hill by *Elba*, whom she had left for dead in the Oaks and the Nassau Stakes. Seldom can a good servant have been so disgracefully treated. No one could say that of *User Friendly*, a superb filly who won in 'The Leger' 1992 after victories in the Oaks and the Irish Oaks.

Run at Doncaster over 1 ml 6 fls 127 yds for fillies and mares First Run 1839 Group 3

		Jockey	Trainer	Owner	Odds
1839	**Mickleton Maid**	W Scott	J Scott	J Bowes	–
1840	**Calypso**	S Templeman	T Dawson	C M St Paul	Evens
1841	**Disclosure**	T Lye	I Blades	T O Powlett	Evens
1842	**Sally**	S Templeman	J Scott	Col Cradock	7/4
1843	**Peggy**	S Templeman	J Scott	Col Cradock	6/4
1844	**Sorella**	J Day	W Butler Jnr	G Osbaldeston	3/1
1845	**Miss Sarah**	J Holmes	C Peck	Maj Yarburgh	Evens
1846	**Ennui**	E Flatman	J Blenkhorn	E L Mostyn	10/1
1847	**Ellerdale**	J Marson	T Dawson	Capt O Harcourt	4/6
1848	**Canezou**	F Butler	J Scott	Lord Stanley	1/4
1849	**Lady Evelyn**	E Flatman	T Taylor	Lord Chesterfield	4/5
1850	**Tiff**	S Templeman	A Taylor Snr	Sir J Hawley	–
1851	**Aphrodite**	J Marson	A Taylor Snr	Sir J Hawley	1/3
1852	**Bird on the Wing**	H Goater	G Arran	C A Parker	4/6
1853	**Mayfair**	J Wells	J B Day	H Padwick	5/1
1854	**Honeysuckle**	S Templeman	J Scott	A Nichol	7/2
1855	**Clotilde**	S Templeman	W Day	J Merry	–
1856	**Melissa**	J Marson	R Stephenson Jnr	Lord Clifden	4/7
1857	**Blink Bonny**	J Charlton	W I'Anson	W I'Anson	1/3
1858	**Hepatica**	T Ashmall	J Scott	Sir C Monck	4/1
1859	**Qui Vive**	J Osborne Jnr	G Abdale	Lord Zetland	2/1
1860	**Lady Trespass**	J Osborne Jnr	J Osborne	W Hudson	4/5
1861	**Brown Duchess**	L Snowden	J Saxon	J Saxon	1/6
1862	**Imperatrice**	R Bullock	G Oates	C Towneley	6/1
1863	**Fantail**	W Boyce	R Boyce	R Boyce	4/6
1864	**Battaglia**	G Noble	J Waugh	W Robinson	–
1865	**White Duck**	H Custance	T Dawson	Lord Glasgow	–
1866	**Lass o'Gowrie**	J Loates	Jos Dawson	F Pryor	–
1867	**filly by Wild Dayrell**	J Daley	Jos Dawson	Lord Stamford	6/1
1868	**Athena**	G Fordham	J Day	H Padwick	4/6

		Jockey	Trainer	Owner	Odds
1869	**Toison d'Or**	G Fordham	J Scott	J Bowes	11/8
1870	**Agility**	J Osborne Jnr	W Osborne	J W King	4/7
1871	**Hopbine**	T French	–	Mr Lee	6/4
1872	**Maid of Perth**	T French	–	R Long	2/1
1873	**Marie Stuart**	T Osborne	R Peck	J Merry	1/7
1874	**Aventuriere**	T Chaloner	A Taylor Snr	Lord Ailesbury	6/4
1875	**Skotzka**	J Griffiths	J Perren	J Bowes	–
1876	**Twine the Plaiden**	J Griffiths	J Perren	J Bowes	5/2
1877	**Lady Golightly**	F Archer	M Dawson	Lord Falmouth	1/5
1878	**Jannette**	F Archer	M Dawson	Lord Falmouth	1/4
1879	**Peace**	H Huxtable	John Dawson	C Alexander	7/1
1880	**Experiment**	J Osborne Jnr	W Osborne	J Whittaker	4/5
1881	**Bal Gal**	F Archer	M Dawson	Lord Falmouth	4/6
1882	**Shotover**	T Cannon	J Porter	Duke of Westminster	4/7
1883	**Britomartis**	F Archer	M Dawson	Lord Falmouth	4/1
1884	**Belinda**	J Osborne Jnr	C Archer	Lord Ellesmere	6/1
1885	**Hurry**	C Wood	M Dawson	Duke of Portland	8/1
1886	**Miss Jummy**	J Watts	R Marsh	Duke of Hamilton	6/1
1887	**Porcelain**	J Fagan	W I'Anson Jnr	C Perkins	9/4
1888	**Belle Mahone**	J Fagan	W I'Anson Jnr	C Perkins	7/1
1889	**Minthe**	J Osborne Jnr	M Dawson	R C Vyner	2/1
1890	**Ponza**	T Cannon	J Ryan	J H Houldsworth	2/1
1891	**Cereza**	J Watts	J Porter	W B Cloete	100/30
1892	**Gantlet**	J Watts	R Marsh	N Fenwick	7/4
1893	**Self Sacrifice**	R Colling	W I'Anson Jnr	P Buchanan	3/1
1894	**Amiable**	W Bradford	G Dawson	Duke of Portland	8/15
1895	**filly by Saraband**	T Calder	A Taylor Jnr	W Bass	4/1
1896	**Canterbury Pilgrim**	F Rickaby	G Lambton	Lord Derby	10/11
1897	**Galatia**	C Wood	F Cole	R Walker	6/1
1898	**Lowood**	M Cannon	J Porter	Duke of Westminster	Evens
1899	**Irish Ivy**	J Doyle	W Behan	E Peel	9/4
1900	**Goosander**	L Reiff	S Pickering	R Monro	7/2
1901	**St Aldegonde**	M Cannon	J Porter	Duke of Portland	5/1
1902	**Elba**	D Maher	G Blackwell	Lord Cadogan	10/1
1903	**Quintessence**	H Randall	J Chandler	Lord Falmouth	9/4
1904	**Pretty Polly**	W Lane	P P Gilpin	E Loder	1/25
1905	**Adula**	B Dillon	P P Gilpin	E Loder	4/7
1906	**Demure**	O Madden	J E Brewer	W Clark	13/8
1907	**Jubilee**	W Higgs	A Taylor Jnr	A W Cox	100/6
1908	**Siberia**	B Dillon	P P Gilpin	L Neumann	8/15
1909	**Electra**	B Dillon	P P Gilpin	L Neumann	13/8
1910	**Yellow Slave**	D Maher	S Pickering	P Nelke	9/2
1911	**Hair Trigger II**	F Wootton	G Lambton	A James	5/6
1912	**Eufrosina**	E Wheatley	S Darling	Lord Lonsdale	100/7
1913	**Arda**	D Maher	B Jarvis	J P Hornung	15/8
1914	**First Spear**	J Clark	A Taylor Jnr	W Astor	Evens
1915/18	**No Race**				
1919	**Flying Spear**	J Childs	A Taylor Jnr	W M G Singer	11/8
1920	**Redhead**	G Colling	G Lambton	Lord Derby	4/6
1921	**Love in Idleness**	J Childs	A Taylor Jnr	J Watson	1/5
1922	**Selene**	E Gardner	G Lambton	Lord Derby	7/100
1923	**Brownhylda**	V Smyth	R C Dawson	Vicomte de Fontarce	Evens
1924	**Charley's Mount**	V Smyth	R C Dawson	HH Aga Khan	4/5
1925	**Juldi**	B Carslake	R C Dawson	HH Aga Khan	7/2
1926	**Glasheen**	J Childs	C Boyd-Rochfort	R B Charteris	8/1
1927	**Cinq-a-Sept**	J Childs	C Boyd-Rochfort	M Field	11/2
1928	**Girandola**	J Childs	C Boyd-Rochfort	M Field	7/4
1929	**Nuwara Eliya**	R A Jones	J Lawson	S Tattersall	8/15
1930	**Glorious Devon**	G Richards	T Hogg	Lord Glanely	7/2
1931	**Volume**	F Lane	J Lawson	Lord Astor	8/1
1932	**Fury**	W Nevett	D Peacock	Sir E Hanmer	9/2
1933	**Typhonic**	G Richards	B Jarvis	J S Courtauld	7/2
1934	**Poker**	G Bezant	F Pratt	J A de Rothschild	7/2
1935	**Fox Lair**	S Donoghue	L Cundell	Mrs C Glorney	3/1
1936	**Traffic Light**	J Sirett	J Lawson	Lord Astor	11/10
1937	**Nadushka**	H Wragg	V Gilpin	G Fairhurst	10/1
1938	**Gainly**	M Beary	C Boyd-Rochfort	W Woodward	9/2
1939/40	**No Race**				
1941	**Bright Lady**	J Hine	V Hobbs	T Venn	11/2
1942/45	**No Race**				
1946	**Procne**	E Britt	C Elsey	Miss J Clayton	2/1
1947	**Mitrailleuse**	G Richards	R J Colling	Lord Astor	9/4
1948	**Vertencia**	M Beary	A Smyth	W Hill	100/8
1949	**Sea Idol**	E Smith	J Lawson	A Hedley	100/7
1950	**La Baille**	C Smirke	M Marsh	Mohamed Bey Sultan	100/6

		Jockey	Trainer	Owner	Odds
1951	**Verse**	A Breasley	N Cannon	J V Rank	10/1
1952	**Moon Star**	W H Carr	C Boyd-Rochfort	W Woodward	5/2
1953	**Kerkeb**	C Smirke	M Marsh	HH Aga Khan	9/2
1954	**Bara Bibi**	C Smirke	N Murless	HH Aga Khan	100/9
1955	**Ark Royal**	E Mercer	G Colling	R D Hollingsworth	1/4
1956	**Kyak**	E Mercer	G Colling	R D Hollingsworth	100/6
1957	**Almeria**	W H Carr	C Boyd-Rochfort	HM The Queen	2/7
1958	**Cutter**	E Mercer	G Colling	R D Hollingsworth	100/8
1959	**Collyria**	E Smith	N Murless	Sir V Sassoon	33/1
1960	**Sunny Cove**	A Breasley	G Richards	M Sobell	5/1
1961	**Never Say**	J Mercer	R J Colling	J J Astor	7/2
1962	**Almiranta**	W H Carr	J A Waugh	Lord H De Walden	7/2
1963	**Outcrop**	E Smith	G Barling	J Priestman	4/1
1964	**Cursorial**	J Mercer	W Wharton	Maj L B Holliday	100/6
1965	**Bracey Bridge**	L Piggott	N Murless	M Wickhan-Boynton	7/2
1966	**Parthian Glance**	L Piggott	G Todd	Mrs W Riley-Smith	4/5
1967	**Pia**	E Hide	W Elsey	Countess M Batthyany	7/2
	Pink Gem	G Moore	N Murless	H J Joel	2/1
1968	**Bringley**	B Taylor	H Leader	R Midwood	3/1
1969	**Aggravate**	E Johnson	A Budgett	L E van Moppes	8/1
1970	**Parmelia**	A Barclay	N Murless	Lord H de Walden	8/11
1971	**Example**	L Piggott	I Balding	HM The Queen	11/2
1972	**Attica Meli**	G Lewis	N Murless	L Freedman	5/4
1973	**Reload**	A Murray	H Wragg	R B Moller	100/30
1974	**Mil's Bomb**	G Lewis	N Murless	L Freedman	11/10
1975	**May Hill**	P Eddery	P Walwyn	G Williams	13/8
1976	**African Dancer**	A Murray	H Wragg	Sir P Oppenheimer	6/1
1977	**Royal Hive**	J Mercer	H Cecil	L Freedman	8/15
1978	**Idle Waters**	J Reid	R F Johnson Houghton	R Crutchley	9/1
1979	**Quay Line**	P Waldron	H Candy	W Barnett	3/1
1980	**Shoot A Line**	W Carson	W R Hern	R Budgett	1/2
1981	**Alma Ata**	T Ives	L Cumani	Mrs D Zurcher	25/1
1982	**Swiftfoot**	W Carson	W R Hern	Lord Rotherwick	4/6
1983	**High Hawk**	W Carson	J Dunlop	Sheikh Mohammed	2/1
1984	**Borushka**	K Darley	R F Johnson Houghton	HH Aga Khan	13/2
1985	**I Want To Be**	L Piggott	J Dunlop	Sheikh Mohammed	6/5
1986	**Rejuvenate**	B Thomson	B Hills	K Abdulla	8/1
1987	**Trampship**	P Eddery	B Hills	K Abdulla	7/2
1988	**Casey**	R Cochrane	L Cumani	G Leigh	14/1
1989	**Lucky Song**	S Cauthen	L Cumani	Mrs V K Bender	4/11
1990	**Madame Dubois**	S Cauthen	H Cecil	Cliveden Stud	2/1
1991	**Patricia**	S Cauthen	H Cecil	Sheikh Mohammed	11/8
1992	**Niodini**	Paul Eddery	M Stoute	Sheikh Mohammed	11/2

For 3 year-old fillies only from 1839-1990.

Run at Newmarket in 1941

The May Hill Stakes

The May Hill Stakes, is best known for the victory of Her Majesty's *Height of Fashion*, also winner of the Acomb Stakes and the then called Hoover Fillies' Mile at two.

At three, *Height of Fashion* won the Lupe Sakes and the Princess of Wales's Stakes, after which she was sold to Sheikh Hamdan Al-Maktoum for an amount well in excess of £1,000,000. Her poor performances in the King George VI and the Queen Elizabeth Stakes and the Yorkshire Oaks suggested that *Height of Fashion* had been well sold, until she became the dam of *Nashwan*, the 1989 Derby winner, which made her look something of a bargain by providing the Arabs with a success which Her Majesty has been seeking since 1953.

Midway Lady, the winner in 1985 went on to complete a classic double in the 1,000 Guineas and Oaks the following season.

Run at Doncaster over 1 mile for 2 year-old fillies First Run 1976 Group 3

		Jockey	Trainer	Owner	Odds
1976	**Triple First**	G Starkey	M Stoute	R Clifford-Turner	2/1
1977	**Tartan Pimpernel**	W Carson	W R Hern	HM The Queen	6/4
1978	**Formulate**	J Mercer	H Cecil	Mrs D Butler	6/4
1979	**The Dancer**	W Carson	W R Hern	J J Astor	9/2
1980	**Exclusively Raised**	G Starkey	M Stoute	Sir G White	15/8
1981	**Height of Fashion**	J Mercer	W R Hern	HM The Queen	4/6
1982	**Bright Crocus**	L Piggott	H Cecil	Mrs B Walters	6/1
1983	**Satinette**	W Carson	W R Hern	Lord Porchester	2/1
1984	**Ever Genial**	L Piggott	H Cecil	L Freedman	10/11
1985	**Midway Lady**	L Piggott	B Hanbury	H H Rainier	11/2

		Jockey	Trainer	Owner	Odds
1986	**Laluche**	S Cauthen	H Cecil	Sheikh Mohammed	7/4
1987	**Intimate Guest**	S Cauthen	H Cecil	Exors of F Hue-Williams	11/8
1988	**Tessla**	M Roberts	H Cecil	C St George	4/5
1989	**Rafha**	S Cauthen	H Cecil	Prince A Faisal	11/8
1990	**Majmu**	W Carson	J Gosden	H Al-Maktoum	6/1
1991	**Midnight Air**	P Eddery	H Cecil	M Poland	3/1
1992	**Marillette**	P Eddery	J Gosden	Sheikh Mohammed	4/1

The Doncaster Cup

The oldest of the three major Cup races, the Doncaster Cup was founded in 1801, but was run over many varying distances of up to four miles until 1926 when Lord Rosebery's mare *Bongrace* won over the present distance of two miles and a quarter. Lazy but talented, she needed a couple of reminders from the whip to keep her interested, and it was an unhappy chance that caused her jockey, Charlie Elliott, to drop his whip some way from home in the Oaks. Even so she won seven races as a three-year-old apart from the Doncaster Cup including the Jockey Club Cup.

It is interesting to note that *Bongrace's* time of 3mins 54secs compares well with the best recent time of 3mins 52.7secs set by *Protection Racket* in 1981. There are few horses who can stay exteme distances on the flat in the highest class and fields are invariably small, the record being fifteen as long ago as 1834 and have not exceeded nine in modern times.

Many superb stayers have won the Doncaster Cup, including *Brown Jack*, *Pandofell* and *Le Moss*, but surely the greatest was *Alycidon*. At three he won the Jockey Club Stakes easily, and the two-mile King George Stakes, then run at Ascot in October. It was the post-war period when French raiders seemed unbeatable, but *Alycidon* made mince-meat of the three overseas contenders headed by the Eclipse winner *Djeddah*.

The following season (1949) he won the Ormonde Stakes at Chester, the Corporation Stakes at Doncaster, the Ascot Gold Cup, the Goodwood Cup and climaxed his career with an eight lengths win in the Doncaster Cup.

In all these races he was ridden by Doug Smith, five times champion jockey and a master of long distance races. Smith won the Doncaster Cup no fewer than seven times and always said that one of his most treasured souvenirs was a few hairs pulled from *Alycidon's* tail.

Run at Doncaster over 2 miles 2 furlongs First Run 1801 Group 3

		Jockey	Trainer	Owner	Odds
1801	**Chance**	–	–	P Wentworth	3/1
1802	**Alonzo**	–	–	C Brandling	10/1
1803	**Remembrancer**	B Smith	J Smith	Lord Strathmore	1/2
1804	**Sir Oliver**	–	–	Lord Grey	4/1
1805	**Caleb Quotem**	–	C Scaife	Lord Fitzwilliam	7/2
1806	**colt by Hambletonian**	–	–	W Garforth	10/1
1807	**Scud**	–	–	Lord Monson	13/8
1808	**Laurel Leaf**	–	–	T Duncombe	8/1
1809	**Whitenose**	–	–	Lord Milton	6/1
1810	**Trophonius**	–	–	Lord Darlington	3/1
1811	**Grimakiln**	–	–	T Duncombe	–
1812	**Slender Billy**	–	–	J Glover	5/2
1813	**Viscount**	–	J Croft	Sir W Maxwell	2/5
1814	**Tramp**	–	T Sykes	R Watt	1/3
1815	**Catton**	–	–	Lord Scarborough	4/6
1816	**Filho da Puta**	–	J Scott	T Houldsworth	1/2
1817	**Fulford**	–	–	Col King	6/1
1818	**Rasping**	–	–	Duke of Leeds	–
1819	**Otho**	–	–	W Garforth	–
1820	**Juggler**	–	I Blades	T O Powlett	2/1
1821	**Consul**	–	–	J G Lambton	3/1
1822	**Euphrates**	J Robinson	–	J Dilly	2/1
1823	**Figaro**	T Lye	–	A Farquharson	4/7
1824	**Mercutio**	H Edwards	–	Duke of Leeds	5/1
1825	**Lottery**	G Nelson	–	Mr Whittaker	13/8
1826	**Fleur de Lis**	G Nelson	–	Sir M W Ridley	4/5
1827	**Mulatto**	T Lye	–	Lord Fitzwilliam	5/1
1828	**Laurel**	T Nicholson	–	Maj Yarburgh	4/1
1829	**Voltaire**	T Lye	J Smith	Lord Cleveland	5/2
1830	**Retriever**	T Lye	–	Lord Kelburne	–
1831	**The Sadler**	J Chapple	–	Mr Wagstaff	7/2
1832	**Galopade**	R Johnson	–	R Riddell	5/2
1833	**Rockingham**	T Nicholson	R Shepherd	R Watt	Evens
1834	**Tomboy**	R Johnson	–	W Orde	–
1835	**Touchstone**	W Scott	J Scott	Lord Westminster	3/1
1836	**Touchstone**	W Scott	J Scott	Lord Westminster	4/6
1837	**Beeswing**	D Cartwright	–	W Orde	6/5
1838	**Don John**	E Flatman	J Scott	Lord Chesterfield	1/2
1839	**Charles the Twelfth**	W Scott	J Scott	Maj Yarburgh	8/11
1840	**Beeswing**	D Cartwright	–	W Orde	8/1

		Jockey	Trainer	Owner	Odds
1841	**Beeswing**	D Cartwright	–	W Orde	–
1842	**Beeswing**	D Cartwright	–	W Orde	4/7
1843	**Alice Hawthorn**	R Hesseltine	R Hesseltine	H Wormald	5/2
1844	**Alice Hawthorn**	J Bumby	R Hesseltine	G Salvin	–
1845	**Sweetmeat**	G Whitehouse	H Wadlow	A W Hill	4/5
1846	**The Hero**	A Day	J B Day	J B Day	7/4
1847	**War Eagle**	S Mann	C Marson	E Bouverie	–
1848	**Chanticleer**	E Flatman	W I'Anson	J Merry	3/1
1849	**Canezou**	F Butler	J Scott	Lord Stanley	–
1850	**Voltigeur**	E Flatman	R Hill	Lord Zetland	–
1851	**The Ban**	J Arnold	A Taylor Snr	Sir J Hawley	5/2
1852	**Teddington**	J Marson	A Taylor Snr	J M Stanley	6/4
1853	**Hungerford**	J Charlton	W King	Baron M de Rothschild	4/6
1854	**Virago**	J Wells	J B Day	H Padwick	1/15
1855	**Rataplan**	A Cowley	W Wyatt	C Thellusson	5/2
1856	**Fandango**	J Marson	G Abdale	Lord Zetland	9/4
1857	**Vedette**	T Chaloner	G Abdale	Lord Zetland	4/5
1858	**Vedette**	J Osborne Jnr	G Abdale	Lord Zetland	4/7
1859	**Newcastle**	G Fordham	Jos Dawson	Lord Stamford	3/1
1860	**Sabreur**	T Chaloner	G Abdale	Lord Zetland	3/1
1861	**Kettledrum**	R Bullock	G Oates	C Towneley	5/1
1862	**Tim Whiffler**	R Bullock	T S Dawson	Lord W Powlett	4/6
1863	**Macaroni**	T Chaloner	J Godding	R C Naylor	1/2
1864	**General Peel**	H Covey	T Dawson	Lord Glasgow	6/5
1865	**Ackworth**	G Fordham	J Day	Marquis of Hastings	5/6
1866	**Rama**	S Kenyon	W Goater	Lord Westmorland	8/1
1867	**Achievement**	S Kenyon	J Dover	M Pearson	10/11
1868	**Mandrake**	J Osborne Jnr	T Dawson	J Johnstone	9/4
1869	**Good Hope**	W Gray	T Dawson	J Johnstone	–
1870	**Sornette**	T Handley	C Pratt	Maj Fridolin	Evens
1871	**Shannon**	Hunt	–	F Mouncey	5/4
1872	**Dutch Skater**	G Fordham	T Jennings	C J Lefevre	1/3
1873	**Uhlan**	C Maidment	W Gilbert	H Savile	100/30
1874	**Lily Agnes**	W Chaloner	–	J Snarry	30/100
1875	**Fraulein**	J Goater	W Goater	Mr Gomm	100/8
1876	**Craig Millar**	T Chaloner	A Taylor Snr	W S Crawfurd	4/1
1877	**Hampton**	F Webb	R Peck	F G Hobson	4/7
1878	**Pageant**	T Cannon	J Porter	F Gretton	Evens
1879	**Isonomy**	T Cannon	J Porter	F Gretton	15/100
1880	**Dresden China**	J Snowden	W I'Anson Jnr	C Perkins	4/5
1881	**Petronel**	F Archer	J Jewitt	Duke of Beaufort	4/11
1882	**Retreat**	C Wood	T Wadlow	Lord Bradford	8/1
1883	**Thebais**	C Wood	J Porter	Sir F Johnstone	w.o.
1884	**Louis d'Or**	T Cannon	A Hayhoe	Baron L de Rothschild	10/1
1885	**Hambledon**	J Fagan	W I'Anson Jnr	W I'Anson Jnr	9/4
1886	**The Bard**	C Wood	M Gurry	R Peck	1/8
1887	**Carlton**	G Barrett	A Taylor Snr	Lord E Somerset	4/11
1888	**Grafton**	G Barrett	R Sherrard	Sir G Chetwynd	5/2
1889	**Claymore**	F Webb	J Humphreys	Lord Howe	11/10
1890	**Tyrant**	T Calder	W Walters	A M Singer	4/11
1891	**Queen's Birthday**	J Watts	C Lund	Maj Joicey	40/85
1892	**Chesterfield**	C Loates	C W Golding	J T Davies	100/14
1893	**Prisoner**	M Cannon	J Waugh	Lord Cadogan	5/1
1894	**Sweet Duchess**	S Chandley	Robert Sherwood	Sir R W Griffith	7/4
1895	**Kilsallaghan**	M Cannon	J Jewitt	Capt J Machell	9/4
1896	**Laodamia**	E Hunt	T Lewis	W W Fulton	4/1
1897	**Winkfield's Pride**	M Cannon	W T Robinson	J C Sullivan	1/4
1898	**Pinfold**	C Wood	G Blackwell	Sir J Miller	7/2
1899	**Calveley**	M Cannon	J Porter	Duke of Westminster	4/9
1900	**King's Courier**	L Reiff	E Wishard	J A Drake	7/2
1901	**Merry Gal** **Sidus**	L Reiff	W T Robinson	W Hall-Walker	1/4
1902	**William the Third**	M Cannon	J Porter	Duke of Portland	1/10
1903	**Wavelet's Pride**	D Maher	J D Edwards	J D Edwards	7/1
1904	**Robert le Diable**	W Lane	R C Dawson	Lord Carnarvon	11/2
1905	**Bachelor's Button**	D Maher	C Peck	S B Joel	11/10
1906	**Velocity**	D Maher	P P Peebles	Mrs H V Jackson	7/4
1907	**Velocity**	H Jones	P P Peebles	Mrs H V Jackson	7/1
1908	**Radium**	O Madden	J Watson	L de Rothschild	7/1
1909	**Amadis**	O Madden	W Waugh	Lord Falmouth	100/30
1910	**Bronzino**	F Fox	F Pratt	J A de Rothschild	2/1
1911	**Lemberg**	F Wootton	A Taylor Jnr	A W Cox	4/9
1912	**Prince Palatine**	F O'Neill	H Beardsley	T Pilkington	1/20
1913	**Long Set**	W Higgs	J H Batho	S B Joel	1/2
1914	**Willbrook**	S Donoghue	C Leader	J Ryan	2/1
1915/18	**No Race**				

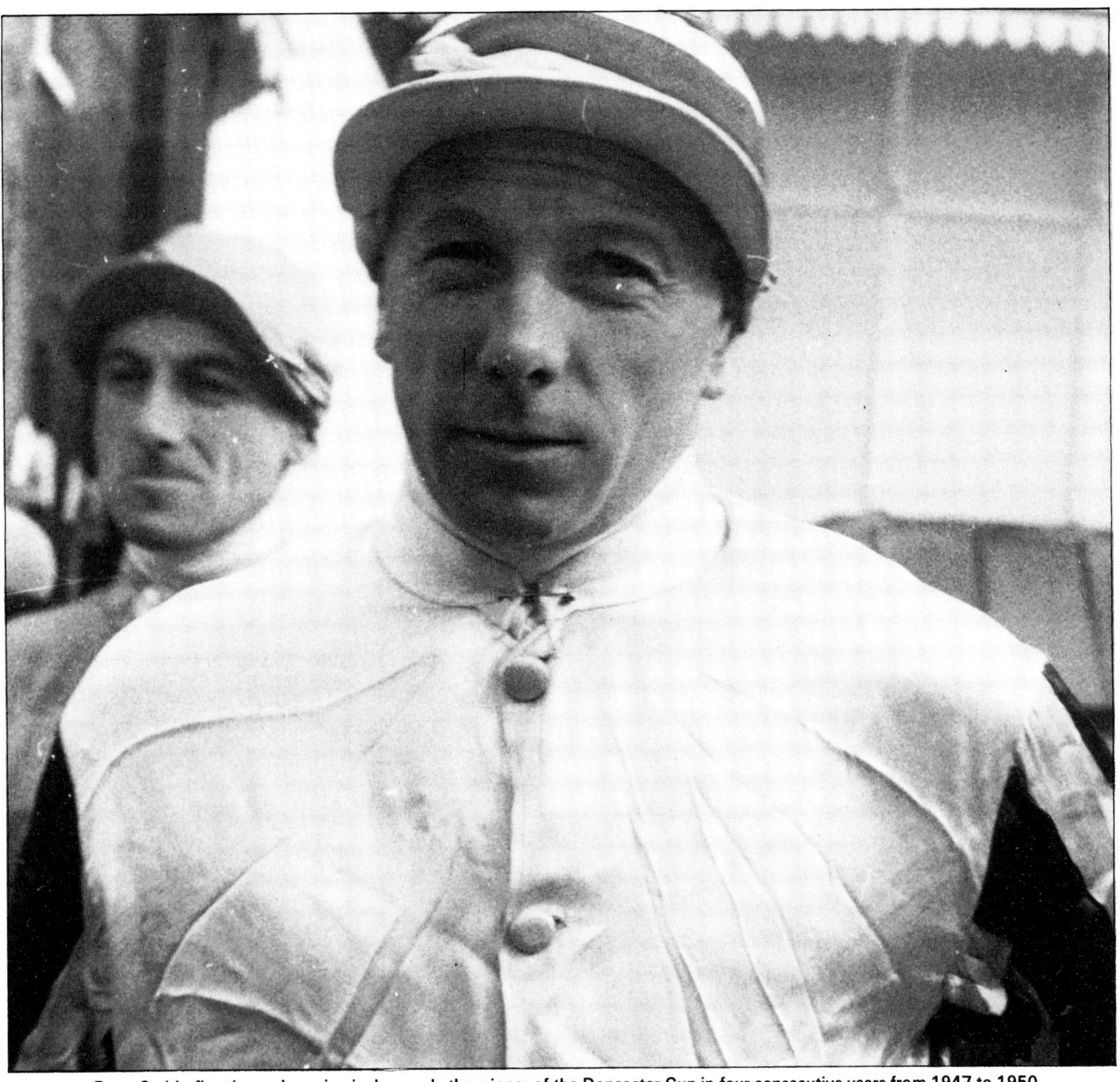

Doug Smith, five times champion jockey, rode the winner of the Doncaster Cup in four consecutive years from 1947 to 1950.

		Jockey	Trainer	Owner	Odds
1919	**Haki**	J Childs	A Taylor Jnr	W M Cazalet	1/7
1920	**Buchan**	F Bullock	A Taylor Jnr	W Astor	6/4
1921	**Flamboyant**	W Lister	R Day	Mrs G Robinson	6/1
1922	**Devizes**	C Elliott	J Jarvis	Sir W Cooke	8/11
1923	**Silurian**	T Weston	G Lambton	Lord Derby	5/4
1924	**Santorb**	S Donoghue	J Rhodes	B Walker	100/30
1925	**St Germans**	F Bullock	A Taylor Jnr	Lord Astor	6/1
1926	**Bongrace**	F Fox	J Jarvis	Lord Rosebery	9/4
1927	**Bythorne**	T Weston	Frank Butters	Lord Derby	5/2
1928	**Pons Asinorum**	F N Winter	W Earl	S B Joel	1/2
1929	**Athford**	M Beary	R C Dawson	W Barnett	4/5
1930	**Brown Jack**	J Childs	I Anthony	Sir H Wernher	11/10
1931	**Singapore**	G Richards	T Hogg	Lord Glanely	13/8
1932	**Foxhunter**	G Richards	J Jarvis	E Esmond	13/8
1933	**Colorado Kid**	G Richards	V Gilpin	G Loder	4/9
1934	**Alcazar**	J Childs	C Boyd-Rochfort	W Woodward	30/100
1935	**Black Devil**	J Childs	C Boyd-Rochfort	W Woodward	4/6
1936	**Buckleigh**	G Richards	T Hogg	Lord Glanely	7/2
1937	**Haulfryn**	G Richards	R Metcalfe	F Minoprio	7/4
1938	**Epigram**	B Carslake	N Cannon	J V Rank	7/4
1939/45	**No Race**				
1946	**Marsyas II**	C Elliott	C Semblat	M Boussac	1/7
1947	**Trimbush**	D Smith	P Vasey	Mrs F Senior	10/1
1948	**Auralia**	D Smith	R Day	Mrs A Johnston	6/1
1949	**Alycidon**	D Smith	W Earl	Lord Derby	2/7

		Jockey	Trainer	Owner	Odds
1950	**Aldborough**	D Smith	F Walwyn	Miss D Paget	6/1
1951	**Fast Fox**	F Palmer	P Carter	Baron G de Waldner	3/1
1952	**Aquino II**	G Richards	F Armstrong	Maharanee of Baroda	2/1
1953	**Souepi**	C Elliott	G Digby	G Digby	5/1
	Nick La Rocca	J Mercer	R J Colling	F Williams	100/7
1954	**Osborne**	W H Carr	C Boyd-Rochfort	W P Wyatt	5/1
1955	**Entente Cordiale**	D Smith	G Colling	Lord Derby	5/2
1956	**Atlas**	W H Carr	C Boyd-Rochfort	HM The Queen	11/4
1957	**French Beige**	G Littlewood	H Peacock	R F Dennis	5/1
1958	**Agreement**	D Smith	C Boyd-Rochfort	HM The Queen	25/1
1959	**Agreement**	W H Carr	C Boyd-Rochfort	HM The Queen	11/4
1960	**Exar**	L Piggott	N Murless	C Vittadini	6/100
1961	**Pandofell**	L Piggott	F Maxwell	H W Daw	9/4
1962	**Bonnard**	R Hutchinson	J Clayton	Marchese della Rocchetta	6/1
1963	**Raise You Ten**	D Smith	C Boyd-Rochfort	P Widener	5/1
1964	**Grey of Falloden**	J Mercer	W R Hern	Lord Astor	8/1
1965	**Prince Hansel**	D Yates	D Thom	J Barker	2/1
1966	**Piaco**	M L Thomas	G Barling	M Watney	11/8
1967	**Crozier**	F Durr	P Walwyn	A D G Oldrey	20/1
1968	**The Accuser**	J Mercer	W R Hern	Lord Rotherwick	2/1
1969	**Canterbury**	W Williamson	P Prendergast	J Olin	100/30
1970	**Magna Carta**	G Lewis	I Balding	HM The Queen	6/4
1971	**Rock Roi**	D Keith	P Walwyn	F Hue-Williams	4/11
1972	**Biskrah**	J Mercer	A Breasley	Lady Beaverbrook	4/1
1973	**Attica Meli**	G Lewis	N Murless	L Freedman	4/11
1974	**Proverb**	W Carson	B Hills	J Chandos-Pole	1/2
1975	**Crash Course**	A Kimberley	J Hindley	Mrs J Hindley	4/7
1976	**Sea Anchor**	J Mercer	W R Hern	R D Hollingsworth	2/5
1977	**Shangamuzo**	P Eddery	G Hunter	Mrs E Charles	33/1
1978	**Buckskin**	J Mercer	H Cecil	D Wildenstein	5/2
1979	**Le Moss**	J Mercer	H Cecil	C d'Alessio	4/11
1980	**Le Moss**	J Mercer	H Cecil	C d'Alessio	4/6
1981	**Protection Racket**	J Lowe	J Hindley	S Fradkoff	8/11
1982	**Ardross**	L Piggott	H Cecil	C St George	2/9
1983	**Karadar**	W R Swinburn	M Stoute	HH Aga Khan	2/1
1984	**Wagoner**	T Ives	P Walwyn	A D G Oldrey	10/1
1985	**Spicy Story**	S Cauthen	I Balding	P Mellon	7/4
1986	**Longboat**	W Carson	W R Hern	R D Hollingsworth	1/5
1987	**Buckley**	R Cochrane	L Cumani	Mrs A L Chapman	9/2
1988	**Kneller**	P Eddery	H Cecil	C St George	10/11
1989	**Weld**	W Carson	W Jarvis	Lord H de Walden	1/5
1990	**Al Maheb**	M Roberts	A Stewart	H Al-Maktoum	7/2
1991	**Great Marquess**	P Eddery	H Cecil	C St George	5/1
1992	**Further Flight**	M Hills	B Hills	S Wingfield Digby	8/15

Run over 4 miles 1801-1824, 2 miles 5 furlongs 1825-1890 and 2 miles 1 furlong 1908-1926.

The Kiveton Park Stakes

The first winner of the Kiveton Park Stakes when the race became Group Three in 1986 was *Hadeer*, a horse who failed to live up to his early promise as a two-year-old and at three, but won three pattern races including the Kiveton Park at four. A more consistent winner was *Salse* in 1988 and *Bog Trotter* found compensation for classic failure in the 2,000 Guineas in 1991. Like *Hadeer*, he is an inconsistent animal who owed a great deal to the tactical genius of his usual jockey, Lester Piggott.

Run at Doncaster over 7 furlongs First Run 1978 Group 3

		Jockey	Trainer	Owner	Odds
1978	**Green Girl**	G Duffield	P Kelleway	M Fine	33/1
1979	**Tap on Wood**	S Cauthen	B Hills	A Shead	11/4
1980	**Known Fact**	W Carson	J Tree	K Abdulla	4/6
1981	**Kittyhawk**	L Piggott	W R Hern	R Sangster	11/8
1982	**The Quiet Bidder**	W Carson	M Stoute	Mrs Heathcote	13/2
1983	**Annie Edge**	A Barclay	D H Jones	Mrs A Daniel	12/1
1984	**Sarab**	T Quinn	P Cole	Newgate Ltd	7/2
1985	**Lucky Ring**	W Carson	W R Hern	Sir M Sobell	11/2
1986	**Hadeer**	T Ives	C Brittain	W Gredley	10/1
1987	**Guest Performer**	C Asmussen	J Hills	R Sangster	16/1
1988	**Salse**	M Roberts	H Cecil	Sheikh Mohammed	8/15
1989	**Gold Seam**	W Carson	W R Hern	P Brant	9/4
1990	**Green Line Express**	L Dettori	M Moubarak	Ecurie Fustok	11/4
1991	**Bog Trotter**	L Piggott	W Haggas	B Haggas	11/2
1992	**Pursuit of Love**	R Cochrane	H Cecil	Lord H de Walden	4/1

The Champagne Stakes

For generations considered to be one of the leading classic pointers, and indeed the record shows this to be so even in the contemporary atmosphere of precocious breeding, the Champagne Stakes was increased in distance from six to seven furlongs in 1961. Formerly open to all two-year-olds, it was restricted to colts and geldings in 1988.

The last filly to win was *Ambergris* in 1960, subsequently second in the Oaks to *Sweet Solera*, but the heroine must be *Beeswing*, winner of over fifty races, including the Ascot Gold Cup, the Doncaster Cup four times and the Newcastle Cup on six occasions. The most appropriate winner was *Champagne* in 1853. Sadly *Champagne* (the horse) failed to live up to the sparkle.

Run at Doncaster over 7 furlongs for 2 year-old colts & geldings First Run 1823 Group 2

		Jockey	Trainer	Owner	Odds
1823	**Swiss**	W Scott	J Scott	Col Cradock	Evens
1824	**Memnon**	W Scott	R Shepherd	R Watt	5/4
1825	**King Catton**	J Jackson	–	Lord Kennedy	5/1
1826	**Moonshine**	G Edwards	–	Duke of Leeds	–
1827	**The Colonel**	W Scott	J Scott	E Petre	1/3
1828	**Cant**	T Lye	–	Lord Sligo	11/2
1829	**Bud**	J Forth	J Forth	J Forth	10/1
1830	**Frederica**	S Darling	–	T Houldsworth	8/1
1831	**Francesca**	W Scott	–	G Walker	6/1
1832	**Muley Moloch**	T Lye	J Smith	Lord Cleveland	6/1
1833	**Cotillon**	W Scott	–	G Walker	11/8
1834	**Coriolanus**	P Conolly	–	R Ridsdale	7/2
1835	**Beeswing**	D Cartwright	–	W Orde	6/1
1836	**Jereed**	W Scott	J Scott	Lord Chesterfield	1/2
1837	**Don John**	W Scott	J Scott	Lord Chesterfield	6/4
1838	**Eliza**	T Lye	–	Duke of Cleveland	–
1839	**Launcelot**	W Scott	J Scott	Lord Westminster	5/4
1840	**Kedge**	J Holmes	I Blades	T O Powlett	10/1
1841	**Attila**	W Scott	J Scott	G Anson	5/2
1842	**A British Yeoman**	S Templeman	–	G Blakelock	4/1
1843	**The Cure**	R Hesseltine	R Hesseltine	G Salvin	2/1
1844	**Lancashire Witch**	E Flatman	–	T Worthington	2/1
1845	**Princess Alice**	W Abdale	J Kent Jnr	Lord G Bentinck	8/1
1846	**Van Tromp**	J Marson	J Fobert	Lord Eglinton	2/1
1847	**Assault**	E Edwards	H Stebbing	B Green	2/3
1848	**The Flying Dutchman**	C Marlow	J Fobert	Lord Eglinton	5/2
1849	**The Italian**	S Templeman	T Dawson	J Meiklam	Evens
1850	**Aphrodite**	J Marson	A Taylor Snr	Sir J Hawley	6/4
1851	**Augur**	J Marson	R Hill	Lord Zetland	10/1
1852	**Vindex**	J Marson	J Scott	Sir C Monck	3/1
1853	**Champagne**	S Rogers	E Parr	G Osbaldeston	5/1
1854	**The Bonnie Morn**	J Marson	J Scott	J Bowes	1/3
1855	**Ellington**	T Aldcroft	T Dawson	Admiral O Harcourt	10/1
1856	**Tasmania**	J Holmes	R T Stephenson	Sir R W Bulkeley	–
1857	**Gildermire**	T Aldcroft	T Dawson	Admiral O Harcourt	2/1
1858	**Prelude**	J Osborne Jnr	J Scott	Sir C Monck	10/1
1859	**King of Diamonds**	G Fordham	W King	Baron M de Rothschild	9/1
1860	**Walloon**	A Edwards	Jos Dawson	Lord Stamford	10/1
1861	**The Marquis**	G Fordham	J Scott	S Hawke	8/11
1862	**Lord Clifden**	G Fordham	E Parr	Lord St Vincent	4/5
1863	**Ely**	T Aldcroft	T Olliver	W S Cartwright	Evens
1864	**Zambesi**	H Covey	M Dawson	J Merry	7/4
1865	**Redan**	J Grimshaw	E Parr	Lord St Vincent	w.o.
1866	**Achievement**	H Custance	J Dover	M Pearson	2/5
1867	**Virtue**	J Snowden	J Watson	G Holmes	7/1
1868	**Morna**	J Adams	J Porter	Sir J Hawley	8/1
1869	**Sunshine**	G Fordham	M Dawson	J Merry	40/75
1870	**King of the Forest**	J Snowden	J Waugh	J Merry	5/6
1871	**Cremorne**	C Maidment	W Gilbert	H Savile	30/100
1872	**Kaiser**	C Maidment	W Gilbert	H Savile	4/6
1873	**Napoleon III**	F Webb	–	F Fisher	7/1
1874	**Camballo**	J Osborne Jnr	M Dawson	H F C Vyner	7/4
1875	**Farnese**	F Archer	M Dawson	Lord Falmouth	5/4
1876	**Lady Golightly**	F Archer	M Dawson	Lord Falmouth	3/1
1877	**Clementine**	J Goater	T Jennings	Comte F de Lagrange	10/1
1878	**Charibert**	F Archer	M Dawson	Lord Falmouth	5/4
1879	**Evasion**	J Snowden	R Peck	Duke of Westminster	100/15
1880	**Bal Gal**	F Archer	M Dawson	Lord Falmouth	4/9
1881	**Kermesse**	T Cannon	J Cannon	Lord Rosebery	6/4
1882	**Hauteur**	G Fordham	T Jennings Jnr	C J Lefevre	10/1

		Jockey	Trainer	Owner	Odds
1883	**Superba**	F Archer	J Hopper	R Peck	4/6
1884	**Langwell**	F Archer	M Dawson	Duke of Portland	10/1
1885	**Minting**	F Archer	M Dawson	R C Vyner	1/3
1886	**Panzerschiff**	J Watts	J Enoch	Lord Zetland	40/95
	Grandison	G Barrett	C Archer	Lord Ellesmere	5/1
1887	**Ayrshire**	C Wood	G Dawson	Duke of Portland	5/4
1888	**Chitabob**	J Fagan	W I'Anson Jnr	C Perkins	1/2
1889	**Riviera**	T Loates	C W Golding	H Milner	6/5
1890	**Haute Saone**	W Platt	F Bates	F Bates	100/6
1891	**La Fleche**	G Barrett	J Porter	Baron M de Hirsch	2/5
1892	**The Prize**	J Watts	G Dawson	Duke of Portland	3/1
1893	**Ladas**	A White	M Dawson	Lord Rosebery	4/11
1894	**Solaro**	M Cannon	J Ryan	A W Cox	10/1
1895	**Omladina**	M Cannon	J Porter	Duke of Westminster	5/2
1896	**Velasquez**	J Watts	W Walters Jnr	Lord Rosebery	9/100
1897	**Ayah**	T Loates	A Hayhoe	L de Rothschild	20/1
1898	**Mark For'ard**	M Cannon	J Porter	W Low	10/1
1899	**Democrat**	J F Sloan	J Huggins	Lord W Beresford	1/2
1900	**Orchid**	J F Sloan	F Leach	H J King	2/1
1901	**Game Chick**	L Reiff	J Huggins	E Loder	5/2
1902	**Rock Sand**	D Maher	G Blackwell	Sir J Miller	1/3
1903	**Pretty Polly**	W Lane	P P Gilpin	E Loder	11/10
1904	**Galangal**	W Halsey	C Archer	E Dresden	10/1
	Vedriana	D Maher	G Lambton	Lord Derby	10/1
1905	**Achilles**	H Randall	F W Day	E L Heinemann	100/8
1906	**Slieve Gallion**	W Higgs	S Darling	J H Greer	1/4
1907	**Lesbia**	D Maher	G Blackwell	Sir D Cooper	7/2
1908	**Duke Michael**	O Madden	J Doyle	R Walker	100/8
1909	**Neil Gow**	D Maher	P Peck	Lord Rosebery	6/1
1910	**Pietri**	D Maher	J Watson	L de Rothschild	4/7
1911	**White Star**	G Stern	C Morton	J B Joel	6/4
1912	**Craganour**	W Saxby	W T Robinson	C B Ismay	15/8
1913	**The Tetrarch**	S Donoghue	H S Persse	D McCalmont	1/5
1914	**Redfern**	J Clark	A Taylor Jnr	Lord Cadogan	11/10
1915/18	**No Race**				
1919	**Tetratema**	B Carslake	H S Persse	D McCalmont	8/15
1920	**Lemonora**	J Childs	A Taylor Jnr	J Watson	4/1
1921	**Golden Corn**	J Childs	Hugh Powney	M Field	11/10
1922	**Drake**	M Beary	H Cottrill	Mrs S Whitburn	11/4
1923	**Mumtaz Mahal**	G Hulme	R C Dawson	HH Aga Khan	8/100
1924	**Bucellas**	H Jelliss	B Jarvis	J P Hornung	5/1
1925	**Coronach**	G Archibald	F Darling	Lord Woolavington	9/4
1926	**Damon**	H Beasley	H S Persse	T F Ryan	4/1
1927	**Fairway**	T Weston	Frank Butters	Lord Derby	4/9
1928	**Arabella**	J Childs	P P Gilpin	G Loder	7/4
1929	**Fair Diana**	F Fox	F Darling	Lord Woolavington	5/2
1930	**Portlaw**	H Beasley	H S Persse	Sir A Bailey	5/4
1931	**Orwell**	R A Jones	J Lawson	W M G Singer	1/4
1932	**Myrobella**	G Richards	F Darling	Lord Lonsdale	11/8
1933	**Blazonry**	R Perryman	D Waugh	Lord H de Walden	11/2
1934	**Kingsem**	S Donoghue	N Scobie	Sir C Hyde	8/1
1935	**Mahmoud**	F Fox	Frank Butters	HH Aga Khan	13/8
1936	**Foray**	P Beasley	C Boyd-Rochfort	M Field	7/4
1937	**Portmarnock**	P Beasley	C Boyd-Rochfort	Sir H de Trafford	11/2
1938	**Panorama**	P Beasley	C Boyd-Rochfort	Mrs J Corrigan	8/13
1939/40	**No Race**				
1941	**Big Game**	H Wragg	F Darling	HM The King	1/2
1942/45	**No Race**				
1946	**Petition**	H Wragg	Frank Butters	Sir A Butt	2/7
1947	**My Babu**	E Britt	F Armstrong	Maharaja of Baroda	21/20
1948	**Abernant**	G Richards	N Murless	R Macdonald-Buchanan	2/5
1949	**Palestine**	G Richards	Frank Butters	HH Aga Khan	1/9
1950	**Big Dipper**	W H Carr	C Boyd-Rochfort	Mrs J Bryce	4/7
1951	**Orgoglio**	E Britt	C Elsey	P Bull	100/8
1952	**Bebe Grande**	W Snaith	F Armstrong	J Gerber	4/9
1953	**Darius**	E Mercer	H Wragg	Sir P Loraine	7/4
1954	**Our Babu**	D Smith	G Brooke	D Robinson	100/8
1955	**Rustam**	D Smith	G Brooke	Lady Wyfold	8/15
1956	**Eudaemon**	E Britt	C Elsey	Mrs E Foster	5/2
1957	**Kelly**	J Purtell	N Cannon	J Olding	10/1
1958	**Be Careful**	E Hide	C Elsey	W Hill	4/7
1959	**Paddy's Sister**	G Moore	P Prendergast	Mrs J R Mullion	8/15
1960	**Ambergris**	J Lindley	H Wragg	Sir P Loraine	7/2
1961	**Clear Sound**	R Hutchinson	P Prendergast	Mrs M Sheehan	3/1
1962	**King of Babylon**	E Hide	W Elsey	R F Dennis	100/7
1963	**Talahasse**	A Breasley	T Corbett	H Loebstein	4/7
1964	**Hardicanute**	G Bougoure	P Prendergast	J R Mullion	7/1

		Jockey	Trainer	Owner	Odds
1965	**Celtic Song**	L Piggott	P Prendergast	M Rayne	2/1
1966	**Bold Lad**	D Lake	P Prendergast	Lady B Granard	8/11
1967	**Cheb's Lad**	B Connorton	W Gray	H Brown	7/1
1968	**Ribofilio**	L Piggott	R F Johnson Houghton	C W Engelhard	7/2
1969	**Saintly Song**	A Barclay	N Murless	S Joel	11/4
1970	**Breeder's Dream**	F Durr	M Jarvis	D Robinson	4/1
1971	**Crowned Prince**	L Piggott	B van Cutsem	F McMahon	11/10
1972	**Otha**	W Carson	B van Cutsem	N B Hunt	11/4
1973	**Giacometti**	A Murray	H R Price	C St George	8/11
1974	**Grundy**	P Eddery	P Walwyn	C Vittadini	13/8
1975	**Wollow**	G Dettori	H Cecil	C d'Alessio	11/4
1976	**J O Tobin**	L Piggott	N Murless	G A Pope Jnr	4/9
1977	**Sexton Blake**	W Carson	B Hills	T Motley	5/2
1978	**R B Chesne**	J Mercer	H Cecil	C St George	8/13
1979	**Final Straw**	P Cook	M Stoute	J Wigan	9/2
1980	**Gielgud**	J Mercer	H Cecil	C St George	11/2
1981	**Achieved**	P Eddery	M V O'Brien	R Sangster	11/4
1982	**Gorytus**	W Carson	W R Hern	Mrs J P Mills	8/13
1983	**Lear Fan**	A Clark	G Harwood	A Salman	1/4
1984	**Young Runaway**	G Starkey	G Harwood	S Niarchos	5/2
1985	**Sure Blade**	B Thomson	B Hills	Sheikh Mohammed	5/4
1986	**Don't Forget Me**	P Eddery	R Hannon	James Horgan	6/1
1987	**Warning**	P Eddery	G Harwood	K Abdulla	Evens
1988	**Prince of Dance**	W Carson	N Graham	Sir M Sobell	1/2
1989	**No Race**				
1990	**Bog Trotter**	N Day	W Haggas	B Haggas	8/1
1991	**Rodrigo de Triano**	W Carson	P Chapple-Hyam	R Sangster	11/8
1992	**Petardia**	W Carson	G Wragg	M Hills	11/2

For all 2 year-olds 1823-1987.
Run at Newbury in 1941.

The St Leger

It is an old Turf proverb which states that the fittest horse wins the Two Thousand Guineas, the luckiest horse wins the Derby but the best horse wins the St Leger.

This would still be true today if only the best horse ran in the St Leger. Unhappily, this is not always the case. The pattern of European racing has changed and now there are wider options for a top-class three-year-old, notably the Grand Prix de l'Arc de Triomphe, in the autumn of the year.

In the late eighteenth century, few horses raced under the age of five. Events were divided into heats run over distances of anything between two and four miles, and it could take all afternoon to decide one race, with the eventual winner covering twelve miles at racing pace, admittedly a little slower than it is now.

Racing at Doncaster dates back to Elizabethan times, and in 1776 was taking place on Cantley Common, nearby the present course at Town Moor, under the patronage of the Marquis of Rockingham when he wasn't detained by his duties as Prime Minister. Col. Anthony St Leger (properly pronounced Sellinger) lived not far from the course in his mansion at Park Hill. St Leger had the idea of a single race for three-year-olds, colts to carry 8st, fillies 7st 12lb, to be run over two miles with a sweeepstake of twenty-five guineas each.

A field of six went to post on 24 September 1776 for what was to be the world's first classic race. None of the runners were named, which was not unusual for the period, and Lord Rockingham's filly by *Sampson* beat St Leger's filly by *Trusty*, all of which goes to prove that fillies often have the edge in autumn races.

At this stage the race was unnamed, but not for long. Rockingham finally called his filly *Allabaculia*, and at a dinner party hosted by the Marquis at his seat at Wentworth Woodhouse in 1777 to discuss nominations for the 1778 race, Rockingham graciously proposed that the event should be named after St Leger. Some would have it that the dinner was at the Red Lion in Doncaster, but the social evidence suggests Wentworth.

That year the race was moved to Town Moor, where it has been ever since apart from wartime substitutes and the 1989 running at Ayr when the Doncaster track was unsafe, thus becoming the only classic staged outside of England.

***Blue Bonnett*, winner of the St Leger in 1842.**

The 1850 St Leger winner *Voltigeur*.

Fred Archer on the Triple Crown winner *Ormonde* which won the St Leger in 1886, one of several successes by Archer in this race.

The Leger did not achieve national importance until local owner Christopher Wilson's *Champion* completed the first Derby-St Leger double in 1800. Soon it was not only one of Britain's premier races but a great social event as well. Balls and houseparties for the gentry became a well established custom and every hostelry in Doncaster overflowed in every sense during Leger week.

The tradition of the eve of Leger dinner, still maintained today, dates back to 1803, and received the ultimate stamp of social approval in 1806 when the Prince of Wales, later George IV and his brother William, another future king attended race week.

They took lodgings in the town at 15 South Parade and the local population were amazed to see the First Gentleman of Europe standing on the balcony blowing his nose 'just like anybody else'.

In 1813, the distance was reduced to one mile six furlongs and 193 yards and despite a few minor alterations, remains much the same today.

In its long history, the Leger has seen plenty of heroes and not a few villains as well. The first Leger specialist was jockey John Mangle who rode five winners in the late eighteenth century. Known as 'Crying Jackie' because of his habit of bursting into tears if a close finish went against him, he could have made it six but for being disqualified on *Zanga* in 1789.

The great *Hambletonian*, a grandson of *Eclipse* won in 1795 and took the Doncaster Cup the following day. Things were not so savoury in 1819, when the Leger was run twice, as it was to be in 1823. Five horses were left at the start including *Agricola* the joint second favourite. The winner was *Antonio* at 33/1 and the angry crowd protested with such vehemence that the stewards ordered a re-run.

This time only ten took the field, with *Antonio* an absentee. *Sir Walter*, left the first time, ran out the winner. *Agricola* was unplaced and the whole affair reported to the Jockey Club, who decided that the result of the original race should stand.

The 1822 winner *Theodore* was so lame before the start that he went off at the extraordinary odds of 1,000 to 5, but that didn't stop him winning by four lengths and giving his jockey John Jackson his eighth Leger victory.

All of which was much to the chagrin of *Theodore's* owner, the Hon. Edward Petre, who sold all his bets on the winner in disgust before the race.

The favourite, *Swap*, was virtually tailed off in the hands of Will Scott, and the fact that Scott was apprenticed to James Croft, the trainer of *Theodore* may or may not have had some bearing on the result; certainly when the two horses met over the same course and distance three days later, *Swap* won easily from his now odds-on rival.

In 1834 Derby winner *Plenipotentiary* was doped so badly that he could barely get to the post, let alone win. It was becoming clear that the Turf was rapidly falling into disrepute, a decline which resulted in the 'Filthy Forties' (see Epsom). The man who cleansed the sport of corruption was Lord George Bentinck. Although enjoying the reputation of one of racing's greatest reformers, Bentinck was not averse to landing the odd touch himself and 1836 laid out *Elis* for a huge gamble in the St Leger.

Elis was trained in Sussex and knowing that the horse was still in his stable ten days before the race, and thinking that it would be impossible for the animal to walk the 250 miles to Yorkshire the bookmakers happily gave Bentinck 12/1 about his chances at Doncaster.

Elis didn't have to walk. Bentinck transported him the first-ever horsebox, pulled by six horses at the rate of eighty miles a day, and *Elis* arrived two days before the Leger, winning easily from *Scroggins* with *Beeswing* third.

The mid-nineteenth century on Town Moor was dominated by the Scott brothers, trainer John and jockey Will. John Scott trained forty-nine classic winners in all, including sixteen Legers, and Will rode nine, a record unlikely to be equalled, and achieved in spite of a massive addiction to the bottle.

The then Princess Victoria had made a visit in 1835 but otherwise the Leger lacked royal patronage until the future Edward VII became a regular visitor from 1876. He won the Leger with *Persimmon* and *Diamond Jubilee*.

West Australian's win in 1853 made him the first winner of the Triple Crown, the 2,000 Guineas, the Derby and the St Leger. Eight more were to follow by 1900, but only six horses have achieved this feat in the last ninety-two years, and none since *Nijinsky* in 1970.

It may be that the decline of the St Leger began at the turn of the century, but you would not have known it then with victories by *Sceptre, Pretty Polly, Bahram, Airborne* (the only grey to win both the Derby and the Leger) and *Meld* yet to come.

The writing was on the wall when the handicapper *Peleid* won in 1973. Many observers thought that the race should be opened to older horses on the French and Irish pattern, or the distance shortened. The decision not to tinker with either was justified when Her Majesty's *Dunfermline* completed the Oaks-St Leger double in 1977.

Others have followed, *Son of Love, Touching Wood, Commanche Run, Reference Point, Minster Son* and *User Friendly*. All top-class horses proving that the daddy of them all still retains its place in the classic pattern albeit not the force that it was to the modern, more commercial owner.

Run at Doncaster over 1 ml 6 fls 127 yds for 3 year-old colts & fillies First Run 1776 Group 1

		Jockey	Trainer	Owner	Odds
1776	**Allabaculia**	J Singleton	C Scaife	Lord Rockingham	1/2
1777	**Bourbon**	J Cade	–	W Sotheron	3/1
1778	**Hollandaise**	G Herring	J Rose	Sir T Gascoigne	5/2
1779	**Tommy**	G Lowry	J Rose	T Stapleton	Evens
1780	**Ruler**	J Mangle	–	W Bethel	5/2
1781	**Serina**	R Foster	J Lowther	W Radcliffe	–
1782	**Imperatrix**	G Searle	G Searle	H Goodricke	–
1783	**Phoenomenon**	A Hall	I Cape	Sir J Kaye	4/5
1784	**Omphale**	J Kirton	M Mason	J Coates	–
1785	**Cowslip**	G Searle	G Searle	R J Hill	–
1786	**Paragon**	J Mangle	J Mangle	Lord A Hamilton	20/1
1787	**Spadille**	J Mangle	J Mangle	Lord A Hamilton	2/1
1788	**Young Flora**	J Mangle	J Mangle	Lord A Hamilton	2/1
1789	**Pewett**	W Wilson	C Scaife	Lord Fitzwilliam	–
1790	**Ambidexter**	G Searle	G Searle	H Goodricke	5/1
1791	**Young Traveller**	J Jackson	J Hutchinson	J Hutchinson	3/1
1792	**Tartar**	J Mangle	J Mangle	Lord A Hamilton	25/1
1793	**Ninety-three**	W Peirse	–	J Clifton	15/1
1794	**Beningbrough**	J Jackson	J Hutchinson	J Hutchinson	2/1
1795	**Hambletonian**	R D Boyce	J Hutchinson	Sir C Turner	4/6
1796	**Ambrosio**	J Jackson	F Neale	J Cookson	4/7
1797	**Lounger**	J Shepherd	G Searle	G Crompton	–
1798	**Symmetry**	J Jackson	S King	Sir T Gascoigne	4/1
1799	**Cockfighter**	T Fields	T Fields	Sir H T Vane	4/6
1800	**Champion**	F Buckle	T Perren	C Wilson	2/1
1801	**Quiz**	J Shepherd	G Searle	H Goodricke	7/1
1802	**Orville**	J Singleton Jnr	C Scaife	Lord Fitzwilliam	5/1
1803	**Remembrancer**	B Smith	J Smith	Lord Strathmore	5/2
1804	**Sancho**	F Buckle	B Atkinson	H F Mellish	2/1
1805	**Staveley**	J Jackson	B Atkinson	H F Mlish	6/1
1806	**Fyldener**	T Carr	–	J Clifton	7/4
1807	**Paulina**	W Clift	C Scaife	Lord Fitzwilliam	8/1
1808	**Petronius**	B Smith	W Theakston	Duke of Hamilton	20/1
1809	**Ashton**	B Smith	W Theakston	Duke of Hamilton	15/8
1810	**Octavian**	W Clift	–	Duke of Leeds	12/1
1811	**Soothsayer**	B Smith	T Sykes	R O Gascoigne	6/1
1812	**Ottrington**	R Johnson	W Hesseltine	R Robb	100/1
1813	**Altisidora**	J Jackson	T Sykes	R Watt	5/2
1814	**William**	J Shepherd	W Theakston	Duke of Hamilton	7/1
1815	**Filho da Puta**	J Jackson	J Croft	Sir W Maxwell	Evens
1816	**The Duchess**	B Smith	J Croft	Sir B R Graham	12/1
1817	**Ebor**	R Johnson	J Lonsdale	H Peirse	20/1
1818	**Reveller**	R Johnson	J Lonsdale	H Peirse	4/1
1819	**Antonio**	T Nicholson	J Lonsdale	J Ferguson	33/1
1820	**St Patrick**	J Johnson	J Lonsdale	Sir E Smith	7/1
1821	**Jack Spigot**	W Scott	I Blades	T O Powlett	6/1
1822	**Theodore**	J Jackson	J Croft	E Petre	100/1
1823	**Barefoot**	T Goodisson	R Shepherd	R Watt	4/1
1824	**Jerry**	B Smith	J Croft	R O Gascoigne	9/1
1825	**Memnon**	W Scott	R Shepherd	R Watt	3/1
1826	**Tarrare**	G Nelson	S King	Lord Scarborough	20/1
1827	**Matilda**	J Robinson	J Scott	E Petre	10/1
1828	**The Colonel**	W Scott	J Scott	E Petre	3/1
1829	**Rowton**	W Scott	J Scott	E Petre	7/2
1830	**Birmingham**	P Conolly	T Flintoff	J Beardsworth	15/1
1831	**Chorister**	J B Day	J Smith	Lord Cleveland	20/1
1832	**Margrave**	J Robinson	J Scott	J Gully	8/1
1833	**Rockingham**	S Darling	R Shepherd	R Watt	7/1
1834	**Touchstone**	G Calloway	J Scott	Lord Westminster	40/1
1835	**Queen of Trumps**	T Lye	J Blenkhorn	E L Mostyn	8/11

		Jockey	Trainer	Owner	Odds
1836	**Elis**	J B Day	J Doe	Lord G Bentinck	7/2
1837	**Mango**	S Day Jnr	M Dilly	C Greville	13/2
1838	**Don John**	W Scott	J Scott	Lord Chesterfield	13/8
1839	**Charles the Twelfth**	W Scott	J Scott	Maj Yarburgh	4/6
1840	**Launcelot**	W Scott	J Scott	Lord Westminster	7/4
1841	**Satirist**	W Scott	J Scott	Lord Westminster	6/1
1842	**Blue Bonnet**	T Lye	T Dawson	Lord Eglinton	8/1
1843	**Nutwith**	J Marson	R Johnson	S Wrather	100/6
1844	**Faugh-a-Ballagh**	H Bell	J Forth	E J Irwin	7/2
1845	**The Baron**	F Butler	J Scott	G Watts	10/1
1846	**Sir Tatton Sykes**	W Scott	W Oates	W Scott	3/1
1847	**Van Tromp**	J Marson	J Fobert	Lord Eglinton	4/1
1848	**Surplice**	E Flatman	R Stephenson Jnr	Lord Clifden	9/4
1849	**The Flying Dutchman**	C Marlow	J Fobert	Lord Eglinton	4/9
1850	**Voltigeur**	J Marson	R Hill	Lord Zetland	8/13
1851	**Newminster**	S Templeman	J Scott	A Nichol	12/1
1852	**Stockwell**	J Norman	W Harlock	Lord Exeter	7/4
1853	**West Australian**	F Butler	J Scott	J Bowes	6/4
1854	**Knight of St George**	R Basham	R Longstaff	J B Morris	11/1
1855	**Saucebox**	J Wells	T Parr	T Parr	40/1
1856	**Warlock**	E Flatman	J Scott	A Nichol	12/1
1857	**Imperieuse**	E Flatman	J Scott	J Scott	100/6
1858	**Sunbeam**	L Snowden	J Prince	J Merry	15/1
1859	**Gamester**	T Aldcroft	J Scott	Sir C Monck	20/1
1860	**St Albans**	L Snowden	A Taylor Snr	Lord Ailesbury	8/1
1861	**Caller Ou**	T Chaloner	W I'Anson	W I'Anson	1,000/15
1862	**The Marquis**	T Chaloner	J Scott	S Hawke	100/30
1863	**Lord Clifden**	J Osborne Jnr	E Parr	Lord St Vincent	100/30
1864	**Blair Athol**	J Snowden	W I'Anson	W I'Anson	2/1
1865	**Gladiateur**	H Grimshaw	T Jennings	Comte F de Lagrange	8/13
1866	**Lord Lyon**	H Custance	J Dover	R Sutton	4/7
1867	**Achievement**	T Chaloner	J Dover	M Pearson	75/40
1868	**Formosa**	T Chaloner	H Woolcott	W Graham	100/30
1869	**Pero Gomez**	J Wells	J Porter	Sir J Hawley	3/1
1870	**Hawthornden**	J Grimshaw	Jos Dawson	T V Morgan	1,000/35
1871	**Hannah**	C Maidment	J Hayhoe	Baron M de Rothschild	9/4
1872	**Wenlock**	C Maidment	T Wadlow	Lord Wilton	8/1
1873	**Marie Stuart**	T Osborne	R Peck	J Merry	9/4
1874	**Apology**	J Osborne Jnr	W Osborne	J W King	4/1
1875	**Craig Millar**	T Chaloner	A Taylor Snr	W S Crawfurd	7/1
1876	**Petrarch**	J Goater	John Dawson	Lord Dupplin	5/1
1877	**Silvio**	F Archer	M Dawson	Lord Falmouth	65/40
1878	**Jannette**	F Archer	M Dawson	Lord Falmouth	5/2
1879	**Rayon d'Or**	J Goater	T Jennings	Comte F de Lagrange	3/1
1880	**Robert the Devil**	T Cannon	C Blanton	C Brewer	4/1
1881	**Iroquois**	F Archer	J Pincus	P Lorillard	2/1
1882	**Dutch Oven**	F Archer	M Dawson	Lord Falmouth	40/1
1883	**Ossian**	J Watts	R Marsh	Duke of Hamilton	9/1
1884	**The Lambkin**	J Watts	M Dawson	R C Vyner	9/1
1885	**Melton**	F Archer	M Dawson	Lord Hastings	40/95
1886	**Ormonde**	F Archer	J Porter	Duke of Westminster	1/7
1887	**Kilwarlin**	W T Robinson	J Jewitt	Lord Rodney	4/1
1888	**Seabreeze**	W T Robinson	J Jewitt	Lord Calthorpe	5/2
1889	**Donovan**	F Barrett	G Dawson	Duke of Portland	8/13
1890	**Memoir**	J Watts	G Dawson	Duke of Portland	10/1
1891	**Common**	G Barrett	J Porter	Sir F Johnstone	4/5
1892	**La Fleche**	J Watts	J Porter	Baron M de Hirsch	7/2
1893	**Isinglass**	T Loates	J Jewitt	H McCalmont	40/75
1894	**Throstle**	M Cannon	J Porter	Lord Alington	50/1
1895	**Sir Visto**	S Loates	M Dawson	Lord Rosebery	9/4
1896	**Persimmon**	J Watts	R Marsh	HRH Prince of Wales	2/11
1897	**Galtee More**	C Wood	S Darling	J Gubbins	1/10
1898	**Wildfowler**	C Wood	S Darling	J H Greer	10/1
1899	**Flying Fox**	M Cannon	J Porter	Duke of Westminster	2/7
1900	**Diamond Jubilee**	H Jones	R Marsh	HRH Prince of Wales	2/7
1901	**Doricles**	K Cannon	A Hayhoe	L de Rothschild	40/1
1902	**Sceptre**	F W Hardy	R S Sievier	R S Sievier	100/30
1903	**Rock Sand**	D Maher	G Blackwell	Sir J Miller	2/5
1904	**Pretty Polly**	W Lane	P P Gilpin	E Loder	2/5
1905	**Challacombe**	O Madden	A Taylor Jnr	W M G Singer	100/6
1906	**Troutbeck**	G Stern	W Waugh	Duke of Westminster	5/1
1907	**Wool Winder**	W Halsey	H Enoch	E W Baird	11/10
1908	**Your Majesty**	Wal Griggs	C Morton	J B Joel	11/8
1909	**Bayardo**	D Maher	A Taylor Jnr	A W Cox	10/11
1910	**Swynford**	F Wootton	G Lambton	Lord Derby	9/2

***Salmon Trout* wins the 1924 St Leger with B.Carslake up.**

		Jockey	Trainer	Owner	Odds
1911	**Prince Palatine**	F O'Neill	H Beardsley	T Pilkington	100/30
1912	**Tracery**	G Bellhouse	J Watson	A Belmont	8/1
1913	**Night Hawk**	E Wheatley	W T Robinson	W Hall-Walker	50/1
1914	**Black Jester**	Wal Griggs	C Morton	J B Joel	10/1
1915	**Pommern**	S Donoghue	C Peck	S B Joel	1/3
1916	**Hurry On**	C Childs	F Darling	J Buchanan	11/10
1917	**Gay Crusader**	S Donoghue	A Taylor Jnr	A W Cox	2/11
1918	**Gainsborough**	J Childs	A Taylor Jnr	Lady J Douglas	4/11
1919	**Keysoe**	B Carslake	G Lambton	Lord Derby	100/8
1920	**Caligula**	A Smith	H Leader	M Goculdas	100/6
1921	**Polemarch**	J Childs	T Green	Lord Londonderry	50/1
1922	**Royal Lancer**	R A Jones	A Sadler Jnr	Lord Lonsdale	33/1
1923	**Tranquil**	T Weston	C Morton	Lord Derby	100/9
1924	**Salmon Trout**	B Carslake	R C Dawson	HH Aga Khan	6/1
1925	**Solario**	J Childs	R Day	Sir J Rutherford	7/2
1926	**Coronach**	J Childs	F Darling	Lord Woolavington	8/15
1927	**Book Law**	H Jelliss	A Taylor Jnr	Lord Astor	7/4
1928	**Fairway**	T Weston	Frank Butters	Lord Derby	7/4
1929	**Trigo**	M Beary	R C Dawson	W Barnett	5/1
1930	**Singapore**	G Richards	T Hogg	Lord Glanely	4/1
1931	**Sandwich**	H Wragg	J Jarvis	Lord Rosebery	9/1
1932	**Firdaussi**	F Fox	Frank Butters	HH Aga Khan	20/1
1933	**Hyperion**	T Weston	G Lambton	Lord Derby	6/4
1934	**Windsor Lad**	C Smirke	M Marsh	M H Benson	4/9
1935	**Bahram**	C Smirke	Frank Butters	HH Aga Khan	4/11
1936	**Boswell**	P Beasley	C Boyd-Rochfort	W Woodward	20/1
1937	**Chulmleigh**	G Richards	T Hogg	Lord Glanely	18/1
1938	**Scottish Union**	B Carslake	N Cannon	J V Rank	7/1
1939	**No Race**				
1940	**Turkhan**	G Richards	Frank Butters	HH Aga Khan	4/1
1941	**Sun Castle**	G Bridgland	C Boyd-Rochfort	Lord Portal	10/1
1942	**Sun Chariot**	G Richards	F Darling	HM The King	9/4
1943	**Herringbone**	H Wragg	W Earl	Lord Derby	100/6
1944	**Tehran**	G Richards	Frank Butters	HH Aga Khan	9/2
1945	**Chamossaire**	T Lowrey	R Perryman	S Joel	11/2
1946	**Airborne**	T Lowrey	R Perryman	J E Ferguson	3/1
1947	**Sayajirao**	E Britt	F Armstrong	Maharaja of Baroda	9/2
1948	**Black Tarquin**	E Britt	C Boyd-Rochfort	W Woodward	15/2
1949	**Ridge Wood**	M Beary	N Murless	G R H Smith	100/7
1950	**Scratch II**	W R Johnstone	C Semblat	M Boussac	9/2

Mr J.V.Rank's *Scottish Union* which won the 1938 St Leger.

		Jockey	Trainer	Owner	Odds
1951	**Talma II**	W R Johnstone	C Semblat	M Boussac	7/1
1952	**Tulyar**	C Smirke	M Marsh	HH Aga Khan	10/11
1953	**Premonition**	E Smith	C Boyd-Rochfort	W P Wyatt	10/1
1954	**Never Say Die**	C Smirke	J Lawson	R S Clark	100/30
1955	**Meld**	W H Carr	C Boyd-Rochfort	Lady Z Wernher	10/11
1956	**Cambremer**	F Palmer	G Bridgland	R B Strassburger	8/1
1957	**Ballymoss**	T P Burns	M V O'Brien	J McShain	8/1
1958	**Alcide**	W H Carr	C Boyd-Rochfort	Sir H de Trafford	4/9
1959	**Cantelo**	E Hide	C Elsey	W Hill	100/7
1960	**St Paddy**	L Piggott	N Murless	Sir V Sassoon	4/6
1961	**Aurelius**	L Piggott	N Murless	Mrs V Lilley	9/2
1962	**Hethersett**	W H Carr	W R Hern	Maj L B Holliday	100/8
1963	**Ragusa**	G Bougoure	P Prendergast	J R Mullion	2/5
1964	**Indiana**	J Lindley	J F Watts	C W Engelhard	100/7
1965	**Provoke**	J Mercer	W R Hern	J J Astor	28/1
1966	**Sodium**	F Durr	G Todd	R J Sigtia	7/1
1967	**Ribocco**	L Piggott	R F Johnson Houghton	C W Engelhard	7/2
1968	**Ribero**	L Piggott	R F Johnson Houghton	C W Engelhard	100/30
1969	**Intermezzo**	R Hutchinson	H Wragg	G A Oldham	7/1
1970	**Nijinsky**	L Piggott	M V O'Brien	C W Engelhard	2/7
1971	**Athens Wood**	L Piggott	H Thomson Jones	Mrs J Rogerson	5/2
1972	**Boucher**	L Piggott	M V O'Brien	O Phipps	3/1
1973	**Peleid**	F Durr	C Elsey	W E Behrens	28/1
1974	**Bustino**	J Mercer	W R Hern	Lady Beaverbrook	11/10
1975	**Bruni**	A Murray	H R Price	C St George	9/1
1976	**Crow**	Y Saint-Martin	A Penna	D Wildenstein	6/1
1977	**Dunfermline**	W Carson	W R Hern	HM The Queen	10/1
1978	**Julio Mariner**	E Hide	C Brittain	M Lemos	28/1
1979	**Son of Love**	A Lequeux	R Collet	A Rolland	20/1
1980	**Light Cavalry**	J Mercer	H Cecil	H J Joel	3/1

Nijinsky, pictured here winning his first classic, the 1970 Two Thousand Guineas, also won the St Leger that year.

		Jockey	Trainer	Owner	Odds
1981	**Cut Above**	J Mercer	W R Hern	Sir J Astor	28/1
1982	**Touching Wood**	P Cook	H Thomson Jones	M Al-Maktoum	7/1
1983	**Sun Princess**	W Carson	W R Hern	Sir M Sobell	11/8
1984	**Commanche Run**	L Piggott	L Cumani	I Allan	7/4
1985	**Oh So Sharp**	S Cauthen	H Cecil	Sheikh Mohammed	8/11
1986	**Moon Madness**	P Eddery	J Dunlop	Duchess of Norfolk	9/2
1987	**Reference Point**	S Cauthen	H Cecil	L Freedman	4/11
1988	**Minster Son**	W Carson	N Graham	Lady Beaverbrook	15/2
1989	**Michelozzo**	S Cauthen	H Cecil	C St George	6/4
1990	**Snurge**	T Quinn	P Cole	M Arbib	7/2
1991	**Toulon**	P Eddery	A Fabre	K Abdulla	5/2
1992	**User Friendly**	G Duffield	C Brittain	W Gredley	7/4

Run over 2 miles 1776-1812, 1 mile 6 furlongs 193 yards 1813-1825 and 1 mile 6 furlongs 132 yards 1826-1970.

Run at Newmarket in 1915-1918 over 1 mile 6 furlongs and in 1942-1944 over 1 mile 6 furlongs 150 yards, at Thirsk in 1940 over 1 mile 7 furlongs, at Manchester in 1941 over 1 mile 6 furlongs, at York in 1945 over 1 mile 6 furlongs and at Ayr in 1989.

The Flying Childers Stakes

The Flying Childers Stakes was originally run as the Norfolk Stakes, and founded in 1967, but when that name was required by the Ascot Authority to rename the New Stakes in honour of the late Duke of Norfolk in 1973, it became the commemoration of *Flying Childers*, known as 'the fleetest horse that ever ran at Newmarket'. He was bred by Leonard Childers at Carr House near Doncaster, but was sold to the Duke of Devonshire, in whose straw livery he won the two matches on which his unbeaten reputation is based.

Sired by the *Darley Arabian*, one of the three founding horses of the modern thoroughbred line, *Flying Childers* own influence on the breed was profound.

The Flying Childers has been won by some superb horses in its brief history, including *Tower Walk, Tribal Chief, Mummy's Pet, Devon Ditty* and *Marwell*, but was downgraded to Group Two in 1979 since when the quality of the fields has inevitably declined slightly although *Green Desert*, the son of *Danzig* who is now one of the world's leading sires, won an exciting race from *Marouble* in 1985. The race has also thrown up a couple of surprises, with *Hittite Glory* at 100/1 in 1975 and *Poker Chip*, 33/1 winner in 1992.

The Flying Childers, 'the fleetest horse that ever ran at Newmarket'.

Run at Doncaster over 5 furlongs for 2 year-olds First Run 1967 Group 2

		Jockey	Trainer	Owner	Odds
1967	**D'Urbeville**	J Lindley	J Tree	J H Whitney	4/5
1968	**Tower Walk**	M L Thomas	G Barling	V W Hardy	6/4
1969	**Tribal Chief**	L Piggott	B Swift	J Swift	4/11
1970	**Mummy's Pet**	G Lewis	J Sutcliffe Jnr	L Goldschlager	5/6
1971	**Rose Dubarry**	A Murray	T A Waugh	H J Joel	11/8
1972	**Marble Arch**	L Piggott	T Curtin	N B Hunt	5/6
1973	**Gentle Thoughts**	L Piggott	T Curtin	N B Hunt	Evens
1974	**Hot Spark**	L Piggott	D Weld	R Tikkoo	9/2
1975	**Hittite Glory**	F Durr	A Breasley	R Tikkoo	100/1
1976	**Mandrake Major**	W Carson	Denys Smith	J van Geest	7/2
1977	**Music Maestro**	G Starkey	M Stoute	R Clifford-Turner	9/1
1978	**Devon Ditty**	G Starkey	H Thomson Jones	Sir E McAlpine	2/1
1979	**Abeer**	S Cauthen	J Tree	K Abdulla	5/1
1980	**Marwell**	G Starkey	M Stoute	E J Loder	4/11
1981	**Peterhof**	E Hide	M V O'Brien	R Sangster	2/1
1982	**Kafu**	G Starkey	G Harwood	HH Yazid & A Al Saud Ltd	8/15
1983	**Superlative**	T Ives	W O'Gorman	Mrs P L Yong	7/4
1984	**Prince Sabo**	J Reid	B Swift	Mrs R J Daniels	11/10
1985	**Green Desert**	L Piggott	M Stoute	M Al-Maktoum	Evens
1986	**Sizzling Melody**	R Hills	Lord J Fitzgerald	Mrs M Watt	6/4
1987	**Gallic League**	S Cauthen	B Hills	R Sangster	5/2
1988	**Shuttlecock Corner**	R Cochrane	P S Felgate	J D Abell	91/5
1989	**No Race**				
1990	**Distinctly North**	P Eddery	J Berry	R Sangster	6/4
1991	**Paris House**	J Carroll	J Berry	P E T Chandler	4/6
1992	**Poker Chip**	M Hills	I Balding	J C Smith	33/1

Run as the Norfolk Stakes 1967-1972

The Select Stakes

Run as the Valdoe Stakes from 1975 to 1965, the Select Stakes was established as a Group Three event in 1986, when the winner was *Dancing Brave*, considered an unlucky loser in the Derby but a convincing winner of the Prix de l'Arc de Triomphe.

The race has always attracted good class if small fields of animals prepared for a late season campaign. *Mtoto*, dual winner of the Eclipse won in 1988 and *In the Groove* was third in 1991. The previous winner of four Group races she was beaten in the Arc but was a desperately unlucky loser of the Champion Stakes after being given far too much to do by an uncharacteristic piece of pilot error by her American jockey Cash Asmussen.

Run at Goodwood over 1 mile 2 furlongs First Run 1965 Group 3

		Jockey	Trainer	Owner	Odds
1965	**Derring-Do**	A Breasley	A Budgett	Mrs H Renshaw	4/11
1966	**Antiquarian**	R Hutchinson	H Blagrave	H Blagrave	9/4
1967	**Haymaking**	L Piggott	R F Johnson Houghton	C Nicholson	13/8
1968	**No Race**				
1969	**Jimmy Reppin**	G Lewis	J Sutcliffe Jnr	Mrs S Bates	Evens
1970	**Northern Wizard**	G Lewis	W Marshall	Mrs R Nelson	10/1
1971	**Ortis**	D Keith	P Walwyn	C Vittadini	1/10
1972	**Wenceslas**	L Piggott	M V O'Brien	Mrs C W Engelhard	10/11
1973	**So Royal**	D Cullen	D Candy	A Portman	Evens
1974	**No Race**				
1975	**Escapologist**	E Johnson	A Budgett	Mrs L Culverwell	13/8
1976	**Obstacle**	P Waldron	H Candy	M Wyatt	11/1
1977	**Balmerino**	R Hutchinson	J Dunlop	R Stuart	6/1
1978	**Gunner B**	J Mercer	H Cecil	Mrs P Barratt	4/9
1979	**Bolide**	W Carson	W R Hern	Lord Rotherwick	13/8
1980	**Welsh Chanter**	J Mercer	H Cecil	H J Joel	4/1
1981	**Prince Bee**	J Mercer	W R Hern	Sir M Sobell	7/4
1982	**Peacetime**	P Eddery	J Tree	Beckhampton Ltd	3/1
1983	**Morcon**	W Carson	W R Hern	Lord Rotherwick	9/4
1984	**Bob Back**	B Raymond	M Jarvis	A Balzarini	8/1
1985	**Iroko**	B Rouse	M Stoute	Mrs A Plesch	7/2
1986	**Dancing Brave**	G Starkey	G Harwood	K Abdulla	–
1987	**Most Welcome**	Paul Eddery	G Wragg	E B Moller	6/4
1988	**Mtoto**	M Roberts	A Stewart	A Al-Maktoum	1/4
1989	**Legal Case**	L Dettori	L Cumani	Sir G White	7/4
1990	**Missionary Ridge**	R Cochrane	B Hills	Sir G White	9/2
1991	**Filia Ardross**	M Roberts	A Stewart	K E Rohde	11/2
1992	**Knifebox**	D Holland	J Gosden	Sheikh Mohammed	25/1

Run as the Valdoe Stakes 1965-1985. Run over 1 mile in 1965.

Run at Sandown in 1979.

The Ayr Gold Cup

As the noted historian on Northern and Scottish Turf affairs, John Fairfax-Blaekborough rightly pointed out, what the St Leger means to Yorkshire and the Northumberland Plate means to what used to be called Northumberland, the Ayr Gold Cup means to Scotland.

The race was originally confined to horses bred and trained in Scotland, and the inaugural event went to *Chancellor*, who won after competing in two heats of two miles each and went on to finish second in the next event, the Ayr Subscription of £50 divided into four heats of four miles. Thus *Chancellor* carried 8st 10lb over twenty miles at racing pace in one day.

Chancellor won again in 1805, after which the practice of running in heats was dropped, although the distance remained at two miles. The race became a handicap in 1855 and when the old course at Bellisle closed in 1907, the Gold Cup was run over the present track and became a six furlong event in 1908.

Perhaps the most notable event between the wars was the 1936 race, when Albert 'Midge' Richardson, a superb lightweight jockey, weighed out at 6st 13lb to win on *Marmaduke Jinks*. It was the lowest weight carried to victory since the race was run over six furlongs, and Richardson was not an apprentice, but a fully fledged jockey aged forty-two.

Nowadays the field tends to lack quality, but five recent winners stand out. *Be Friendly*, already described under the Haydock Sprint Cup won under 8st 9lb from thirty-two opponents in 1967 and in 1973 *Blue Cashmere* won before going on to prove to be a top-class sprinter in the following season's Nunthorpe and the Temple Stakes. *Roman Warrior* set a weight carrying record when getting up by a short head to beat *Import* and dead-heating with *Swingtime* for the Diadem Stakes at Ascot six days later, while the three-year-old *Vaigly Great* won under 9st 6lb in 1978. In 1992, *Lochsong* carrying 9st completed an historic treble in the Stewards' Cup. The Portland Handicap and the Ayr Gold Cup, a feat which may well never be repeated.

Run at Ayr over 6 furlongs First Run 1804 Handicap

		Jockey	Trainer	Owner	Odds
1804	**Chancellor**	–	–	Lord Cassillis	–
1805	**Chancellor**	–	–	Lord Cassillis	–
1806	**Young Newbyth**	–	–	R Baird	–
1807	**Juno**	–	–	Lord Cassillis	–
1808	**Young Daffodil**	–	–	Lord Montgomerie	–
1809	**Bit of Tartan**	–	–	Lord Eglinton	–
1810	**colt by John Bull**	–	–	Lord Montgomerie	–
1811	**Ayrshire Lass**	–	–	Lord Montgomerie	–
1812	**Ardrossan**	–	–	Lord Montgomerie	–
1813	**Snodgrass**	–	–	Lord Eglinton	–
1814	**Ardrossan**	–	J Croft	Sir W Maxwell	–
1815	**Marquis**	–	–	J Hunter Blair	–
1816	**Kate Kearney**	–	–	Lord Eglinton	–
1817	**Glengary**	–	–	Lord Eglinton	–
1818	**Sans Culottes**	–	–	Lord Eglinton	–
1819	**Monreith**	–	–	Lord Eglinton	–
1820	**Chance**	–	–	Lord Kelburne	–
1821	**colt by Stamford**	–	–	A Thompson	–
1822	**colt by Viscount**	–	J Croft	Sir W Maxwell	–
1823	**Lancer**	–	–	Mr Kennedy	–
1824	**Stratherne**	T Shepherd	–	Sir D Moncrieffe	–
1825	**Lancer**	–	–	Mr Kennedy	–
1826	**Robin Hood**	T Lye	–	R Baird	–
1827	**Dominie Skelp**	T Nicholson	–	R Baird	–
1828	**Mary**	J Jaques	–	Col Blair	–
1829	**Spadassin**	Boynton	–	Sir W Maxwell	1/3
1830	**Brunswick**	T Nicholson	–	Lord Elcho	–
1831	**Gondolier**	T Nicholson	–	Lord Elcho	–
1832	**Vyvyan**	J Robinson	–	Sir J Boswell	–
1833	**Philip**	S Templeman	–	Lord Elcho	–
1834	**Masetto**	T Nicholson	–	Sir J Boswell	–
1835	**Inheritor**	S Templeman	T Dawson	W Ramsay	–
1836	**Despot**	W Noble	T Dawson	W Ramsay	–
1837	**Despot**	J Cartwright	T Dawson	W Ramsay	–
1838	**Inheritor**	J Cartwright	T Dawson	W Ramsay	–
1839	**Lanercost**	J Cartwright	W I'Anson	W Ramsay	–
1840	**The Doctor**	W Noble	T Dawson	W Ramsay	–
1841	**Doctor Caius**	T Lye	T Dawson	Lord Eglinton	–
1842	**The Recorder**	W Noble	T Dawson	W Ramsay	–
1843	**The Shadow**	W Noble	T Dawson	W Ramsay	–
1844	**The Shadow**	H Robinson	T Dawson	W Ramsay	–
1845	**Inheritress**	–	T Dawson	J Meiklam	w.o.
1846	**Inheritress**	S Templeman	T Dawson	J Meiklam	–
1847	**Eryx**	J Prince	J Fobert	Lord Eglinton	–
1848	**Chanticleer**	H Robinson	W I'Anson	J Merry	–
1849	**Glen Saddel**	D Cartwright	J Fobert	Lord Eglinton	–
1850	**Elthiron**	–	J Fobert	Lord Eglinton	w.o.
1851	**Elthiron**	C Marlow	J Fobert	Lord Eglinton	–
1852	**Stilton**	T Lye	T Dawson	J Meiklam	–
1853	**Testator**	J Halliwell	J Halliwell	W Redfern	–

		Jockey	Trainer	Owner	Odds
1854	**Itch**	–	T Dawson	T Dawson	w.o.
1855	**John Dory**	J Halliwell	J Halliwell	W Redfern	–
1856	**The Assayer**	H Robertson	R I'Anson	J G Henderson	6/4
1857	**Gathercole**	F Bates	J Halliwell	J Sharpe	2/1
1858	**Trip the Daisy**	J Charlton	J Halliwell	W Sharpe	–
1859	**Susannah**	J Doyle	J Fobert	J T W Aspinall	Evens
1860	**Greta**	J Doyle	J Fobert	F W Whitehead	2/1
1861	**Bloomsbury**	Barron	–	Mr Rampling	–
1862	**Little Captain**	Blackburn	T S Dawson	T S Dawson	3/1
1863	**Bohemian**	J Snowden	J Watson	J Watson	6/4
1864	**Newchurch**	J Metcalf	W Bearpark	Mr Oliver	5/4
1865	**Nothing More**	Dixon	J Watson	J Watson	5/2
1866	**Fitzroy**	Walker	–	W Johnson	4/1
1867	**Miss Havelock**	T Cannon	W Day	Marquis of Hastings	3/1
1868	**Tabouret**	J Cameron	T Dawson	J Johnstone	1/2
1869	**Good Hope**	Hudson	T Dawson	J Johnstone	4/5
1870	**Lady of Lyons**	J Butters	J Waugh	J Merry	7/4
1871	**Irregularity**	Napier	–	Lord Eglinton	100/15
1872	**Alaric**	F Archer	J Ryan	J H Houldsworth	100/15
1873	**Lord Derby**	G Cooke	–	J Moffat	11/8
1874	**Servia**	H Morgan	–	R Forrester	3/1
1875	**Munden**	C Morbey	–	R Howett	5/1
1876	**Coltness**	H Huxtable	J Ryan	J H Houldsworth	4/5
1877	**Ivy**	W Macdonald	J Ryan	J H Houldsworth	6/2
1878	**Sutler**	A F Lemaire	R Marsh	Duke of Hamilton	Evens
1879	**Umbria**	J Fagan	W I'Anson Jnr	C Perkins	4/1
1880	**Strathblane**	J Gallon	Moran	Duke of Montrose	4/1
1881	**Heath Bird**	C Bowman	F Bates	R Jardine	4/1
1882	**Tita**	E Martin	H Hall	H Hall	10/1
1883	**Tibicen**	F Barrett	–	G F Lees	5/1
1884	**Perdita II**	W Lashmar	John Dawson	A Benholm	5/2
1885	**Daylight**	J Dorretty	–	J Brodie	100/9
1886	**Daylight**	J J Mullens	–	G Steel	8/1
1887	**Mirth**	S Chandley	F Bates	F Bates	9/2
1888	**Reverie**	H Falloon	J Ryan	W Gardner	6/1
1889	**Dazzle**	H Falloon	T Moran	Duke of Montrose	10/1
1890	**Dazzle**	W Wood	T Moran	Duke of Montrose	4/1
1891	**Dazzle**	J Weldon	W Allen	Duke of Montrose	11/2
1892	**Horton**	F W Lane	W Binnie	A H Laidlay	2/1
1893	**Once More**	S Chandley	H Hall	C J Cunningham	7/4
1894	**Mimram**	J Harrison	W Raisin	E J Percy	6/4
1895	**Linton**	S Chandley	H Hall	C J Cunningham	11/10
1896	**Athel**	F Finlay	W Binnie	R Ross	3/1
1897	**Athel**	F Finlay	W Binnie	R Ross	7/4
1898	**Gyp**	O Madden	D Peacock	J G Baird Hay	3/1
1899	**Portebella**	T Lofthouse	R W Armstrong	R W Armstrong	5/2
1900	**Child Waters**	A Adey	F Lynham	J Dawlish	3/1
1901	**Caedmon**	T Broom	J Ryan	J Wallace	10/1
1902	**Lovetin**	G McCall	Clements	Mr Ferns	2/1
1903	**Kirkbride**	T Heppell	D Peacock	W Chatterton	100/8
1904	**King's Birthday**	J McCall	J McCall	R Craig	9/4
1905	**Kilglass**	J Jarvis	C Beatty	Lord H de Walden	3/1
1906	**Cyrus**	E Wheatley	W E Elsey	T H Walker	9/2
1907	**Charis**	H Randall	Robert Sherwood Jnr	Sir R W Griffith	100/30
1908	**Raeberry**	R Crisp	G O McGregor	Duke of Montrose	5/1
1909	**Alwine**	J Clark	P W Bewicke	F Straker	11/2
1910	**Raeberry**	C Ringstead	G O McGregor	Duke of Montrose	11/2
1911	**Saucy John**	Wal Griggs	N H Scott	C O Hall	100/8
1912	**Grammont**	S Donoghue	J Fallon	J Fallon	4/1
1913	**Borrow**	J H Martin	A J Joyner	H P Whitney	7/2
1914/16	**No Race**				
1917	**Wayward**	A Smith	J Day	T C McGuffie	100/7
1918	**No Race**				
1919	**Beresina**	B Carslake	G Lambton	Lord Derby	7/4
1920	**Forest Guard**	T Burns	J Burns	J A McLaughlin	6/1
1921	**Self Sacrifice**	B Lynch	H Bazley	C F Kenyon	20/1
1922	**Soldennis**	C Elliott	Lord G Dundas	C L Mackean	Evens
1923	**Baydon**	J Stanton	D Peacock	Lord Wavertree	100/6
1924	**Westmead**	R Perryman	C Elsey	T Queen	100/6
1925	**Phalaros**	T Weston	G Lambton	Mrs A James	6/4
1926	**Lord Wembley**	S Donoghue	J Staunton	W A Wallis	8/1
1927	**Martenax**	J Taylor	D Peacock	Sir E Tate	10/1
1928	**Nothing Venture**	J Leach	F Leach	Sir J Buchanan Jardine	10/1
1929	**Tommy Atkins**	H Leach	F Leach	W T Sears	5/1
1930	**Heronslea**	J Taylor	D Peacock	W Smith	5/1

		Jockey	Trainer	Owner	Odds
1931	**Heronslea**	J Taylor	D Peacock	W Smith	8/1
1932	**Solenoid**	J Marshall	G Poole	Mrs C L Mackean	7/1
1933	**Ken Hill**	E Fox	T Green	Sir L Green	10/1
1934	**Figaro**	H Jelliss	J Leach	J Leach	7/2
1935	**Greenore**	S Wragg	O Bell	Lady Ludlow	5/1
1936	**Marmaduke Jinks**	A Richardson	H Peacock	Mrs C Robinson	20/1
1937	**Daytona**	M Beary	J Jarvis	Sir G Bullough	100/8
1938	**Old Reliance**	E Smith	J Jarvis	Sir J Jarvis	8/1
1939/45	**No Race**				
1946	**Royal Charger**	E Smith	J Jarvis	Sir J Jarvis	2/1
1947	**Kilbelin**	W H Carr	B Bullock	C Blyth	6/1
1948	**Como**	J Marshall	G Armstrong	J Fielden	10/1
1949	**Irish Dance**	E Britt	H Whiteman	H Stockdale	4/1
1950	**First Consul**	C Smirke	F Armstrong	Maharaja of Rajpipla	2/1
1951	**Fair Seller**	R Sheather	E Davey	E Davey	10/1
1952	**Vatellus**	H Jones	J Pearce	A Bird	10/1
1953	**Blue Butterfly**	E Mercer	H Wragg	F More O'Ferrall	11/2
1954	**Orthopaedic**	J Lindley	J M Gosden	Mrs M Moss	11/2
1955	**Hook Money**	W Elliott	A Budgett	R S Clark	4/1
1956	**Precious Heather**	E Hide	J M Gosden	A Bird	5/1
1957	**Jacintha**	E Larkin	W Lyde	G Munro	100/7
1958	**Rhythmic**	F Durr	W Dutton	A Straker	20/1
1959	**Whistling Victor**	J Sime	G Laurence	R Galloway	7/1
1960	**Dawn Watch**	C Parkes	E Cousins	W Kendrick	100/9
1961	**Klondyke Bill**	E Smith	C Benstead	A Comerford	100/8
1962	**Janeat**	B Henry	A Vasey	G Turnbull	25/1
1963	**Egualita**	F Durr	S Hall	R Sigtia	10/1
1964	**Compensation**	P Robinson	E Lambton	Mrs G Lambton	10/1
1965	**Kamundu**	G Cadwaladr	E Cousins	M Higgins	100/8
1966	**Milesius**	N McIntosh	G Boyd	G Boyd	25/1
1967	**Be Friendly**	G Lewis	C Mitchell	P O'Sullevan	100/8
1968	**Petite Path**	J Higgins	R Mason	Mrs R Mason	100/7
1969	**Brief Star**	C Parkes	E Cousins	R Sangster	10/1
1970	**John Splendid**	R Hutchinson	J Dunlop	A J Struthers	10/1
1971	**Royben**	W Williamson	A Breasley	A Kennedy	9/1
1972	**Swinging Junior**	R Hutchinson	N Angus	N Angus	14/1
1973	**Blue Cashmere**	E Johnson	M Stoute	R Clifford-Turner	7/1
1974	**Somersway**	D Cullen	W Wightman	T Parrington	16/1
1975	**Roman Warrior**	J Seagrave	N Angus	J Brown	8/1
1976	**Last Tango**	L Charnock	J Sutcliffe Jnr	R McRobert	6/1
1977	**Jon George**	B Raymond	M W Easterby	Mrs G Newsome	22/1
1978	**Vaigly Great**	G Starkey	M Stoute	T Sellier	5/1
1979	**Primula Boy**	W Higgins	W Bentley	Kavli Ltd	40/1
1980	**Sparkling Boy**	J Lowe	P Kelleway	R Orloff	15/1
1981	**First Movement**	M Miller	G Huffer	Mrs D Thompson	14/1
1982	**Famous Star**	Paul Eddery	M Albina	S Moubarak	13/2
1983	**Polly's Brother**	K Hodgson	M H Easterby	Mrs C Geraghty	11/1
1984	**Able Albert**	M Birch	M H Easterby	Mrs A Henson	9/1
1985	**Camps Heath**	W Woods	F Durr	A Whiteside	14/1
1986	**Green Ruby**	J Williams	G Balding	Mrs J Everitt	25/1
1987	**Not So Silly**	G Bardwell	A Bailey	T Ramsden	12/1
1988	**So Careful**	N Carlisle	J Berry	T Doherty	33/1
1989	**Joveworth**	J Fortune	M O'Neill	D C G Cooper	50/1
1990	**Final Shot**	J Lowe	M H Easterby	P Hurst	12/1
1991	**Sarcita**	B Doyle	D Elsworth	R Tooth	14/1
1992	**Lochsong**	F Arrowsmith	I Balding	J C Smith	10/1

Run over 2 miles 1806-1869, 1 mile + 1870-1907

The Mill Reef Stakes

Named after one of the great Derby winners, the Mill Reef Stakes struck classic gold immediately when the inaugural winner, *Mon Fils* went on to take the 1973 2,000 Guineas at the rewarding odds of 50/1.

However, the most appropriate winner was *Forest Flower*, owned by the American art collector Paul Mellon and carrying the *Mill Reef* colours in 1986. Although the ultimate loser of the controversial Cheveley Park Stakes in the

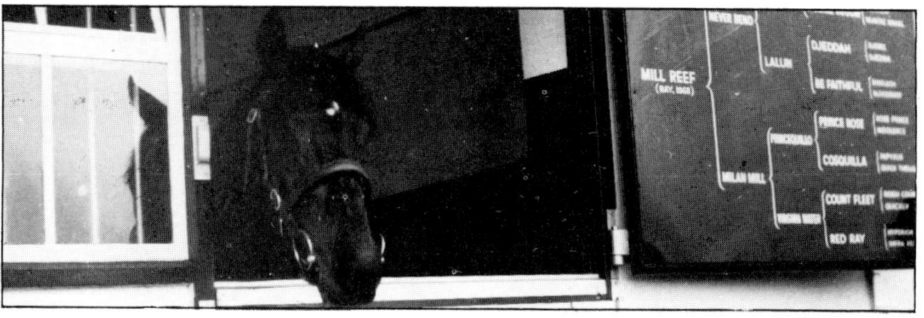

Mill Reef **at the National Stud.**

same year, *Forest Flower* won both the Cherry Hinton and the Queen Mary Stakes at two years and the Irish 1,000 Guineas at three.

The Mill Reef Stakes is sponsored by Paul Mellon's Rokeby Farms stud.

Run at Newbury over 6 furlongs for 2 year-olds First Run 1972 Group 2

		Jockey	Trainer	Owner	Odds
1972	**Mon Fils**	R Hutchinson	R Hannon	Mrs B Davis	6/1
1973	**Habat**	P Eddery	P Walwyn	C Vittadini	10/11
1974	**Red Cross**	P Eddery	P Walwyn	Mrs D McCalmont	13/8
1975	**Royal Boy**	B Raymond	M Jarvis	D Robinson	5/1
1976	**Anax**	G Lewis	B Hobbs	G Cambanis	4/1
1977	**Formidable**	P Eddery	P Walwyn	P Goulandris	13/8
1978	**King of Spain**	P Cook	P Cundell	J Hobhouse	9/1
1979	**Lord Seymour**	P Eddery	M Stoute	J McCaughey	9/2
1980	**Sweet Monday**	P Waldron	L Holt	J Redfern	9/1
1981	**Hays**	B Raymond	G Harwood	Prince Y Saud	5/2
1982	**Salieri**	L Piggott	H Cecil	C St George	11/4
1983	**Vacarme**	L Piggott	H Cecil	D Wildenstein	2/7
1984	**Local Suitor**	W Carson	W R Hern	Sheikh Mohammed	3/1
1985	**Luqman**	N Howe	P Walwyn	H Al-Maktoum	20/1
1986	**Forest Flower**	T Ives	I Balding	P Mellon	4/7
1987	**Magic of Life**	P Eddery	J Tree	S Niarchos	4/1
1988	**Russian Bond**	W Ryan	H Cecil	Sheikh Mohammed	2/5
1989	**Welney**	G Carter	G Wragg	Sir P Oppenheimer	9/1
1990	**Time Gentlemen**	W Carson	J Dunlop	Exors of Mrs A Ison	9/2
1991	**Showbrook**	W Carson	R Hannon	A F Budge Ltd	4/1
1992	**Forest Wind**	L Dettori	M Moubarak	Ecurie Fustok	11/2

The Cumberland Lodge Stakes

The Duke of Cumberland, second surviving son of King George II, was also Ranger of Windsor Forest, where he resided at Cumberland Lodge which was the home of his stud. Not the luckiest of soldiers despite being a Major-General at the age of 22, his military career is unhappily remembered by his excessive severity in putting down the Stuart rebellion in 1745 following the defeat of Prince Charles Edward at Culloden, but as a breeder he played the most important role in the development of the thoroughbred as we know the creature today.

Cumberland Lodge saw the birth of *Eclipse* and *Herod*, both brilliant racehorses and sires who jointly provided an extreme influence on later generations. He did not live to see *Eclipse* run, which was probably just as well since the Duke would hardly have approved of *Eclipse's* subsequent owner, the raffish 'Colonel' Dennis O'Kelly. He was one of the earliest members of the Jockey Club and certainly the first royal member.

The Cumberland Lodge is for stayers who are tough rather than exceptional, although the names of *Park Top*, *Doutelle* and *Aureole* all grace the winning list, along with the recalcitrant and eccentric *Knockroe* whom only Lester Piggott could have kidded to win twice in 1971 and 1972.

Run at Ascot over 1 mile 4 furlongs First Run 1951 Group 3

		Jockey	Trainer	Owner	Odds
1951	**Talma II**	W R Johnstone	C Semblat	M Boussac	1/5
1952	**Rawson**	K Gethin	S Wootton	S Wootton	4/6
1953	**Aureole**	E Smith	C Boyd-Rochfort	HM The Queen	8/13
1954	**Elopement**	C Smirke	N Murless	Sir V Sassoon	9/4
1955	**Daemon**	G Lewis	D Sherbrooke	B Mavroleon	4/1
1956	**Le Pretendant**	S Clayton	W Nightingall	Sir W Churchill	11/2
1957	**Doutelle**	W H Carr	C Boyd-Rochfort	HM The Queen	Evens
1958	**Mon Fetiche**	W Snaith	H Cottrill	S Joel	8/1
1959	**Aggressor**	J Lindley	J M Gosden	Sir H Wernher	11/8
1960	**High Perch**	J Lindley	J M Gosden	H Allen	4/9
1961	**Hot Brandy**	D Keith	W Nightingall	A Kennedy	–
1962	**Silver Cloud**	R Hutchinson	J Jarvis	T Blackwell	100/30
1963	**Wily Trout**	D Smith	C Weld	C Odlum	2/1
1964	**King Chesnut**	A Breasley	A Budgett	Mrs J Benskin	11/10
1965/67	**No Race**				
1968	**Chicago**	R Hutchinson	H Wragg	G A Oldham	5/2
1969	**Remand**	J Mercer	W R Hern	J J Astor	6/1
1970	**Park Top**	L Piggott	B van Cutsem	Duke of Devonshire	4/5
1971	**Knockroe**	L Piggott	P Nelson	V McCalmont	1/2
1972	**Knockroe**	L Piggott	P Nelson	V McCalmont	4/1
1973	**Scottish Rifle**	L Piggott	J Dunlop	A J Struthers	4/11
1974	**Shebeen**	G Baxter	B Hobbs	Sir K Butt	4/1
1975	**Calaba**	L Piggott	D Morley	Lord Fairhaven	11/2
1976	**Bruni**	L Piggott	H R Price	C St George	4/7
1977	**Orange Bay**	P Eddery	P Walwyn	C Vittadini	11/8
1978	**Fordham**	P Eddery	M V O'Brien	R Sangster	4/1
1979	**Main Reef**	J Mercer	H Cecil	H J Joel	9/4
1980	**Fingal's Cave**	P Eddery	J Dunlop	J R Mullion	9/2
1981	**Critique**	L Piggott	H Cecil	G Vanian	11/2
1982	**Lafontaine**	P Eddery	C Brittain	Mrs J Bigg	22/1

		Jockey	Trainer	Owner	Odds
1983	**Band**	W Carson	W R Hern	R D Hollingsworth	100/30
1984	**Bedtime**	W Carson	W R Hern	Lord Halifax	11/10
1985	**Shardari**	W R Swinburn	M Stoute	HH Aga Khan	Evens
1986	**Kazaroun**	W R Swinburn	M Stoute	HH Aga Khan	7/2
1987	**Moon Madness**	P Eddery	J Dunlop	Duchess of Norfolk	6/5
1988	**Assatis**	P Eddery	G Harwood	K Abdulla	11/4
1989	**Tralos**	P Eddery	G Harwood	K Abdulla	10/1
1990	**Ile de Nisky**	G Carter	G Huffer	Prince Y Saud	7/1
1991	**Drum Taps**	L Dettori	Lord Huntington	Lord Carnarvon	13/2
1992	**Opera House**	S Cauthen	M Stoute	Sheikh Mohammed	9/4

Run over 2 miles in 1951.

Run at Kempton in 1956, 1960 and 1963.

The Queen Elizabeth II Stakes

From the point of view of the racehorse owner, there can be few more satisfactory acquisitions than a top class miler. However, excluding the two Guineas races, there are only ten events in the Pattern catering for this type of animal, while the middle distance performers have no fewer than thirty-two.

The Queen Elizabeth II Stakes is outstanding amongst these limited opportunities. Founded in the mid-fifties and elevated to Group One status in 1987, the Guineas winners include *Brigadier Gerard* (twice), *Known Fact*, *To-Agori-Mou* and *Shadeed*. The consistent *Teleprompter* won in 1984 and was placed second in the next two years but perhaps the finest performance was that of the filly *Rose Bowl*. Carrying the famous Englehard colours made famous by *Nijinsky*, she won twice, in 1975 and 1976. Although only fourth in the Guineas as her jockey failed to secure a clear run twice inside the final two furlongs on the 7/4 favourite, her other victories in 1975 included the Champion Stakes in which she defeated *Allez France* and *Star Appeal*, both winners of the Prix de l'Arc de Triomphe.

Run at Ascot over 1 mile First Run 1955 Group 1

		Jockey	Trainer	Owner	Odds
1955	**Hafiz II**	R Poincelet	A Head	HH Aga Khan	9/4
1956	**Cigalon**	S Boullenger	M d'Okhuysen	Comte de Kerouara	8/1
1957	**Midget II**	A Breasley	A Head	P Wertheimer	5/6
1958	**Major Portion**	E Smith	T E Leader	H J Joel	1/3
1959	**Rosalba**	J Mercer	R J Colling	J J Astor	5/2
1960	**Sovereign Path**	W H Carr	R Mason	R Mason	13/8
1961	**Le Levanstell**	W Williamson	S McGrath	J McGrath	20/1
1962	**Romulus**	W Swinburn	R F Johnson Houghton	C W Engelhard	7/4
1963	**The Creditor**	L Piggott	N Murless	Lady Sassoon	5/4
1964	**Linacre**	L Piggott	P Prendergast	F More O'Ferrall	11/10
1965	**Derring-Do**	A Breasley	A Budgett	Mrs H Renshaw	9/4
1966	**Hill Rise**	L Piggott	N Murless	G A Pope Jnr	7/2
1967	**Reform**	A Breasley	G Richards	M Sobell	6/5
1968	**World Cup**	W Williamson	P Prendergast	J R Mullion	7/2
1969	**Jimmy Reppin**	G Lewis	J Sutcliffe Jnr	Mrs S Bates	13/8
1970	**Welsh Pageant**	A Barclay	N Murless	H J Joel	100/30
1971	**Brigadier Gerard**	J Mercer	W R Hern	Mrs J Hislop	2/11
1972	**Brigadier Gerard**	J Mercer	W R Hern	Mrs J Hislop	4/11
1973	**Jan Ekels**	J Lindley	G Harwood	A Bodie	5/1
1974	**No Race**				
1975	**Rose Bowl**	W Carson	R F Johnson Houghton	Mrs C W Engelhard	9/2
1976	**Rose Bowl**	W Carson	R F Johnson Houghton	Mrs C W Engelhard	13/8
1977	**Trusted**	W Carson	J Dunlop	Duchess of Norfolk	20/1
1978	**Homing**	W Carson	W R Hern	Lord Rotherwick	9/2
1979	**Kris**	J Mercer	H Cecil	Lord H de Walden	8/11
1980	**Known Fact**	W Carson	J Tree	K Abdulla	3/1
1981	**To-Agori-Mou**	L Piggott	G Harwood	Mrs A Muinos	5/4
1982	**Buzzards Bay**	W R Swinburn	H Collingridge	Mrs V McKinney	50/1
1983	**Sackford**	G Starkey	G Harwood	A Bodie	11/2
1984	**Teleprompter**	W Carson	J W Watts	Lord Derby	11/2
1985	**Shadeed**	W R Swinburn	M Stoute	M Al-Maktoum	9/4
1986	**Sure Blade**	B Thomson	B Hills	Sheikh Mohammed	6/5
1987	**Milligram**	P Eddery	M Stoute	Helena Springfield Ltd	6/1
1988	**Warning**	P Eddery	G Harwood	K Abdulla	9/4
1989	**Zilzal**	W R Swinburn	M Stoute	M Al-Maktoum	Evens
1990	**Markofdistinction**	L Dettori	L Cumani	G Leigh	6/1
1991	**Selkirk**	R Cochrane	I Balding	G Strawbridge	10/1
1992	**Lahib**	W Carson	J Dunlop	H Al-Maktoum	8/1

Run at Newbury in 1960 and 1963

The Fillies' Mile

The Fillies' Mile performs the same duty for fillies as the Racing Post Trophy does for colts, namely to provide a good test for animals of classic potential at middle distances. The unhappy vagaries of sponsorship have lead us from Green Shield in 1973 when the race was founded and won by Lester Piggott on Her Majesty's *Escorial*, through Argos, Hoover and Brent Walker and perhaps a scheme could be devised whereby Clerks of the Course encouraging first time sponsors could choose some generic, maybe geographical title which could survive the inevitable changes of name when the threads of commercial sponsorship are broken.

That said, the Fillies' Mile has served its purpose admirably. In 1976 *Dunfermline* was runner-up before going on to win the Oaks and the St Leger, *Scintillate*, fourth in 1978 won the Oaks, *Quick as Lightning* (1979) took the 1,000 Guineas the following season and *Height of Fashion*, the dam of *Nashwan*, won in 1981.

1985 was a vintage year when both first and second, in 1984 *Oh So Sharp* and *Helen Street* became classic winners, as did *Diminuendo* in 1988.

Run at Ascot over 1 mile for 2 year-old fillies First Run 1973 Group 1

		Jockey	Trainer	Owner	Odds
1973	**Escorial**	L Piggott	I Balding	HM The Queen	7/4
1974	**No Race**				
1975	**Icing**	C Roche	P Prendergast	Lady Iveagh	5/1
1976	**Miss Pinkie**	L Piggott	N Murless	H J Joel	5/1
1977	**Cherry Hinton**	L Piggott	H Wragg	R B Moller	10/11
1978	**Formulate**	J Mercer	H Cecil	Mrs D Butler	5/4
1979	**Quick as Lightning**	W Carson	J Dunlop	O Phipps	9/1
1980	**Leap Lively**	J Matthias	I Balding	P Mellon	9/2
1981	**Height of Fashion**	J Mercer	W R Hern	HM The Queen	15/8
1982	**Acclimatise**	A Murray	B Hobbs	J Hambro	3/1
1983	**Nepula**	B Crossley	G Huffer	S Al-Qemias	3/1
1984	**Oh So Sharp**	L Piggott	H Cecil	Sheikh Mohammed	6/5
1985	**Untold**	W R Swinburn	M Stoute	R H Cowell	6/4
1986	**Invited Guest**	S Cauthen	R Armstrong	Kinderhill Corporation	8/11
1987	**Diminuendo**	S Cauthen	H Cecil	Sheikh Mohammed	2/1
1988	**Tessla**	P Eddery	H Cecil	C St George	5/2
1989	**Silk Slippers**	M Hills	B Hills	R Sangster	10/1
1990	**Shamshir**	L Dettori	L Cumani	Sheikh Mohammed	11/2
1991	**Culture Vulture**	T Quinn	P Cole	C Wright	5/2
1992	**Ivanka**	M Roberts	C Brittain	A Saeed	6/1

Run as the Green Shield Stakes 1973, the Argos Stakes 1975-1977, the Hoover Fillies' Mile 1978-1989 and the Brent Walker Fillies' Mile 1990-1991

***Oh So Sharp*, ridden here by Steve Cauthen, won the 1984 Fillies' Mile with Lester Piggott up.**

The Royal Lodge Stakes

Before the last war there was no formal pattern, but it was generally accepted that few two-year-olds should be tested beyond seven furlongs, even late in the season. The most popular events for exposing classic potential were the Coventry, the winner usually becoming winter favourite for the Derby, the Queen Mary, the Norfolk (then the New Stakes), the July Stakes, the Richmond, the Gimcrack, the Champagne (Doncaster) the Middle and Cheveley Park and the Dewhurst.

It seemed logical, therefore that when the Royal Lodge was founded in 1946 on the day that *Gulf Stream* won the only Eclipse Stakes run at Ascot as Sandown swept away the debris of wartime military use, it should be a five furlong race. However, it soon became evident that precocious breeding would soon undermine the value of the old established juvenile races as classic trials, and the Royal Lodge was moved to September and extended to one mile from 1948.

The first classic winner to emerge was *Black Tarquin*, who took the St Leger in 1948. *Swallow Tail*, winner of the Royal Lodge in the same season, was a controversial third in the 1949 Derby but returned to Ascot for compensation in the King Edward VII Stakes.

The Royal Lodge has produced six classic successes in all, including three Derby winners, but none since 1978; possibly indicating a trend to keep horses with classic potential to less demanding minor events in their juvenile career.

Run at Ascot over 1 mile for 2 year-old colts & geldings First Run 1946 Group 2

		Jockey	Trainer	Owner	Odds
1946	**Royal Barge**	C Richards	J Lawson	A E Allnatt	8/15
1947	**Black Tarquin**	W H Carr	C Boyd-Rochfort	W Woodward	100/30
1948	**Swallow Tail**	D Smith	W Earl	Lord Derby	11/4
1949	**Tabriz**	G Richards	Frank Butters	HH Aga Khan	5/2
1950	**Fraise du Bois II**	C Smirke	H Wragg	HH Aga Khan	7/2
1951	**Khor-Mousa**	K Gethin	P Thrale	S Tate	100/7
1952	**Neemah**	C Smirke	M Marsh	HH Aga Khan	5/2
1953	**Infatuation**	G Richards	V Smyth	Sir M McAlpine	100/30
1954	**Solarium**	W Snaith	F Armstrong	J Ortiz-Patino	6/1
1955	**Royal Splendour**	A Breasley	W Nightingall	Mrs G Kohn	5/2
1956	**Noble Venture**	E Mercer	H Wragg	Begum Aga Khan	3/1
1957	**Pinched**	L Piggott	N Murless	Sir V Sassoon	Evens
1958	**Cantelo**	E Hide	C Elsey	W Hill	5/4
1959	**St Paddy**	L Piggott	N Murless	Sir V Sassoon	11/4
1960	**Beta**	E Larkin	J Jarvis	Lord Rosebery	9/4
1961	**Escort**	J Mercer	R J Colling	J J Astor	9/2
1962	**Star Moss**	E Smith	J A Waugh	H Broughton	5/1
1963	**Casabianca**	L Piggott	N Murless	B Hornung	4/1
1964	**Prominer**	G Bougoure	P Prendergast	J R Mullion	3/1
1965	**Soft Angels**	L Piggott	N Murless	Lady Sassoon	5/2
1966	**Royal Palace**	L Piggott	N Murless	H J Joel	6/4
1967	**Remand**	L Piggott	W R Hern	J J Astor	13/8
1968	**Dutch Bells**	A Murray	H R Price	G van der Ploeg	100/7
1969	**Domineering**	A Barclay	N Murless	G A Pope Jnr	13/2
1970	**Seafriend**	J Mercer	P Prendergast	Mrs J R Mullion	9/2
1971	**Yaroslav**	G Lewis	N Murless	Mrs V Hue-Williams	8/13
1972	**Adios**	G Lewis	N Murless	G Weston	10/1
1973	**Straight as a Die**	F Durr	B Hills	B Jenks	16/1
1974	**No Race**				
1975	**Sir Wimbourne**	L Piggott	M V O'Brien	Mrs A Manning	4/6
1976	**Gairloch**	B Taylor	H R Price	Miss V Hermon-Hodge	6/1
1977	**Shirley Heights**	G Starkey	J Dunlop	Lord Halifax	10/1
1978	**Ela-Mana-Mou**	G Starkey	G Harwood	Mrs A Muinos	10/1
1979	**Hello Gorgeous**	J Mercer	H Cecil	D Wildenstein	5/4
1980	**Robellino**	J Matthias	I Balding	Mrs J McDougald	4/1
1981	**Norwick**	J Mercer	G Harwood	A Bodie	12/1
1982	**Dunbeath**	L Piggott	H Cecil	M Riordan	5/2
1983	**Gold and Ivory**	S Cauthen	I Balding	P Mellon	25/1
1984	**Reach**	T Quinn	P Cole	F Salman	15/2
1985	**Bonhomie**	S Cauthen	H Cecil	Sheikh Mohammed	2/1
1986	**Bengal Fire**	M Roberts	C Brittain	N Phillips	14/1
1987	**Sanquirico**	S Cauthen	H Cecil	C St George	8/11
1988	**High Estate**	M Roberts	H Cecil	H J Joel	4/6
1989	**Digression**	P Eddery	G Harwood	K Abdulla	4/1
1990	**Mujaazif**	W R Swinburn	M Stoute	M Al-Maktoum	11/2
1991	**Made of Gold**	A Cruz	M Moubarak	Ecurie Fustok	4/1
1992	**Desert Secret**	P Eddery	M Stoute	M Al-Maktoum	12/1

For all 2 year-olds 1946-1986.

Run over 5 furlongs 1946-1947.

Run at Newbury in 1960 and 1963.

The Diadem Stakes

One of the best autumn races in the Calendar, the Diadem has been won by many superb horses over the years, including the inaurugal winner *The Bug*. It was not the most attractive of names, but *The Bug* was a versatile horse and won the one mile Knowsley Stakes at Liverpool in the days when Aintree staged flat racing, the Wokingham Stakes at Ascot in a canter, the July Cup at Newmarket, the Nunthorpe at York, returning to Ascot for the Diadem and the following season's Cork and Orrery Stakes. He was a favourite mount of Charlie Smirke.

Few classic winners revert to sprinting, but the 1951 Two Thousand Guineas victor *Ki Ming* did so in the Diadem. However, probably the best horse to win even in such a distinguished roll of honour, was *Pappa Fourway*. Bred to be a steeplechaser at the Ballykisteen Stud in Ireland, he was trained by Billy Dutton who won the 1928 Grand National on *Tipperary Tim*, the only horse to complete the course without falling.

Pappa Fourway won twelve races in all in two seasons and as a three-year-old was unbeaten in eight starts, including the Diadem in 1955.

Run at Ascot over 6 furlongs First Run 1946 Group 3

		Jockey	Trainer	Owner	Odds
1946	**The Bug**	C Smirke	M Marsh	N Wachman	5/4
1947	**Djelal**	C Elliott	C Semblat	M Boussac	5/1
1948	**Combined Operations**	T Burn	J Lawson	R Foster	2/5
1949	**Solonaway**	G Richards	A Smyth	R A Duggan	6/5
1950	**Abadan**	G Richards	N Murless	G Loder	30/100
1951	**Ki Ming**	A Breasley	M Beary	Ley On	–
1952	**Set Fair**	E Smith	W Nightingall	C W Bell	13/2
1953	**Rose Coral**	D Smith	G Brooke	Lady E Bassett	3/1
1954	**Set Fair**	A Breasley	W Nightingall	C W Bell	11/4
1955	**Pappa Fourway**	W H Carr	W Dutton	Mrs E Goldson	2/5
1956	**King Bruce**	A Breasley	P Hastings-Bass	W Tarry	100/7
1957	**Arcandy**	T Gosling	G Beeby	Mrs M Linde	7/4
1958	**Jack & Jill**	S Clayton	W Nightingall	E Littler	20/1
1959	**Jack & Jill**	W H Carr	W Nightingall	E Littler	6/1
1960	**Zanzibar**	W Rickaby	J Oxley	P Dunne	15/8
1961	**Satan**	J Mercer	T Shaw	Mrs A Biddle	100/8
1962	**La Belle**	W Williamson	H Wragg	Lady Noble	10/1
1963	**Sammy Davis**	D Smith	G Brooke	J Hambro	4/1
1964	**Ampney Princess**	F Durr	H Hannon	Mrs J Wood	25/1
1965	**Majority Blue**	W Williamson	J Oxx	Mrs B Aitken	3/1
1966	**Lucasland**	E Eldin	J A Waugh	J Baillie	7/2
1967	**Great Bear**	R Hutchinson	J Dunlop	Lady Fitzalan Howard	11/2
1968	**Secret Ray**	A Barclay	D Smith	A G Cornish	11/2
1969	**Song**	J Mercer	D Candy	H J Joel	7/4
1970	**Realm**	B Taylor	J Winter	R Boucher	11/8
1971	**Abergwaun**	L Piggott	M V O'Brien	C St George	15/2
1972	**Home Guard**	L Piggott	M V O'Brien	Mrs C W Engelhard	4/5
1973	**Boldboy**	J Mercer	W R Hern	Lady Beaverbrook	100/30
1974	**Saritamer**	L Piggott	M V O'Brien	C St George	11/10
1975	**Swingtime**	L Piggott	M V O'Brien	J Mulcahy	9/4
	Roman Warrior	J Seagrave	N Angus	J R Brown	5/2
1976	**Honeyblest**	G Baxter	D Smith	J Slade	8/1
1977	**Gentilhombre**	P Cook	N Adam	J Murrell	7/4
1978	**Creetown**	R Street	R Sheather	R Galpin	20/1
1979	**Absalom**	L Piggott	R Jarvis	Mrs C Alington	9/4
1980	**Sovereign Rose**	W Carson	W R Hern	Mrs P Pearce	7/1
1981	**Moorestyle**	L Piggott	R Armstrong	Moores Furnishings Ltd	Evens
1982	**Indian King**	G Starkey	G Harwood	J Levy	7/4
1983	**Salieri**	L Piggott	H Cecil	C St George	9/4
1984	**Never So Bold**	S Cauthen	R Armstrong	E Kessly	85/40
1985	**Al Sylah**	A Murray	H Thomson Jones	H Al-Maktoum	9/1
1986	**Hallgate**	G Starkey	Miss S Hall	Hippodromo Racing	11/4
1987	**Dowsing**	P Eddery	J Tree	K Abdulla	8/1
1988	**Cadeaux Genereux**	P Eddery	O Douieb	M Al-Maktoum	9/2
1989	**Chummy's Favourite**	L Dettori	N Callaghan	M Hill	40/1
1990	**Ron's Victory**	F Head	A J Falourd	J S Moss	13/2
1991	**Shalford**	A Cruz	R Hannon	D F Cock	10/1
1992	**Wolfhound**	S Cauthen	J Gosden	Sheikh Mohammed	4/1

Run at Kempton in 1956, 1960 and 1963

Prix de l'Arc de Triomphe

Of the international races to have emerged since the war, the 'Arc' as it is popularly known has been the one to catch the imagination of the racing public in a way unmatched by the Breeders' Cup, the Washington International, the Arlington Million or the Japan Cup.

The Arc's origins sprang from the aftermath of the first global conflict in 1920. Intended to compliment the Grand Prix de Paris also run at Longchamp, the idea was to attract the finest horses from around the world to meet in a final shake-out to decide the best middle-distance horse, at least in Europe.

Given the conditions in war-torn France in 1920, and in particular the understandable unreliability of the French railways by which a horse had no option but to travel, the inaugural running had little international quality, only two of the thirteen strong field coming from outside France.

However, one of these was *Comrade*, trained at Newmarket by Peter Gilpin and ridden by the Australian-born jockey Frank Bullock. Owned by a Frenchman, Evremond de Saint-Alary, *Comrade* duly won. *Ortello* won for Italy in 1929, as did *Crapom* in 1933. *Corrida*, trained in France by John Watts, won in 1936 and 1937 and is still the only mare to have won twice.

World War Two caused the cancellation of the race in 1939, but it was resumed in 1941 and 1942, moving to le Tremblay for the remainder of the war and returning to Longchamps in 1945.

Post-war, the first overseas winner was *Migoli*, in 1948, ridden by Charlie Smirke and trained by Frank Butters at Newmarket, but it was the great Italian horse *Ribot* who set the seal on the success of the Arc as the race was originally conceived. *Ribot*, who was actually foaled in England at the National Stud where his dam *Romanella* was waiting to visit *Ribot's* sire *Tenerani* once again, won sixteen races, thirteen of them in Italy and was never beaten.

Twice winner of the Arc, in 1955 and 1956, *Ribot* also won the King George VI and the Queen Elizabeth Stakes in 1956.

The Arc was a 'natural' for *Sea Bird II*, probably the finest Epsom Derby winner since the war, while controversy clouded *Sassafras's* victory over the Triple Crown winner *Nijinsky* in 1970. Various excuses were offered for *Nijinsky*, who had suffered a bout of ringworm before his victory in the St Leger, including the not entirely unjustified comment that his jockey Lester Piggott had left his challenge a little too late in the short Longchamp straight. In fact, the horse was probably just feeling the effects of a long and hard season, which he again demonstrated when beaten in the Champion Stakes under two weeks later.

Therein lies the dilemma of the Arc, or indeed any of the autumn 'internationals' listed in the opening paragraph. Should a classic or proven older horse be campaigned for the domestic season, or rested in mid-term? *Generous* is a case in point. The winner of what his owner fancifully chooses to call the modern 'Triple Crown', ie the Epsom Derby, the King George and the Irish Derby, he flopped in the Arc, as did *Troy*. On the other hand, *Dancing Brave* won the 2,000 Guineas, was second in the Derby, won the Eclipse Stakes by-passing the Irish Derby, took the King George and won the Arc triumphantly by a long-looking length and a half. Uneasy lies the head that trains the champion!

Run at Longchamp over 2,400 metres First Run 1920 Group 1

		Jockey	Trainer	Owner	Odds
1920	**Comrade**	F Bullock	P P Gilpin	E de Saint-Alary	34/10
1921	**Ksar**	G Stern	W R Walton	Mme E Blanc	115/10
1922	**Ksar**	F Bullock	W R Walton	Mme E Blanc	3/10
1923	**Parth**	F O'Neill	J H Crawford	A K Macomber	17/2
1924	**Massine**	A Sharpe	E Cunnington	H Ternynck	23/20
1925	**Priori**	M Allemand	P Carter	Comte G de Chavagnac	40/1
1926	**Biribi**	D Torterolo	J Torterolo	S Guthmann	5/2
1927	**Mon Talisman**	C Semblat	F Carter	E Martinez de Hoz	24/10
1928	**Kantar**	A Esling	R Carver	O Mills	32/10
1929	**Ortello**	P Caprioli	W Carter	G de Montel	13/1

***Ribot*, the claimed to the world's fastest racehorse, with E.Camici up, won the Prix de l'Arc de Triomphe is 1955 and 1956.**

		Jockey	Trainer	Owner	Odds
1930	**Motrico**	M Fruhinsholtz	M d'Okhuysen	Vicomte M de Rivaud	83/10
1931	**Pearl Cap**	C Semblat	F Carter	Mlle D Esmond	32/10
1932	**Motrico**	C Semblat	M d'Okhuysen	Vicomte M de Rivaud	38/10
1933	**Crapom**	P Caprioli	F Regoli	M Crespi	22/10
1934	**Brantome**	C Bouillon	L Robert	Baron E de Rothschild	11/10
1935	**Samos**	W Sibbritt	F Carter	E de St-Alary	19/1
1936	**Corrida**	C Elliott	J E Watts	M Boussac	4/5
1937	**Corrida**	C Elliott	J E Watts	M Boussac	Evens
1938	**Eclair au Chocolat**	C Bouillon	L Robert	Baron E de Rothschild	26/10
1939/40	**No Race**				
1941	**Le Pacha**	P Francolon	J Cunnington	P Gund	18/10
1942	**Djebel**	J Doyasbere	C Semblat	M Boussac	18/10
1943	**Verso II**	G Duforez	C Clout	Comte de Chambure	12/10
1944	**Ardan**	J Doyasbere	C Semblat	M Boussac	6/4
1945	**Nikellora**	W R Johnstone	R Pelat	Mme R Patureau	10/1

***Exbury* and Jean Deforge after their victory in the 1963 Prix de l'Arc de Triomphe.**

		Jockey	Trainer	Owner	Odds
1946	**Caracalla**	C Elliott	C Semblat	M Boussac	3/10
1947	**Le Paillon**	F Rochetti	W Head	Mme L Aurousseau	23/2
1948	**Migoli**	C Smirke	Frank Butters	HH Aga Khan	10/1
1949	**Coronation**	R Poincelet	C Semblat	M Boussac	37/10
1950	**Tantieme**	J Doyasbere	F Mathet	F Dupre	5/2
1951	**Tantieme**	J Doyasbere	F Mathet	F Dupre	17/10
1952	**Nuccio**	R Poincelet	A Head	HH Aga Khan	74/10
1953	**La Sorellina**	M Larraun	E Pollet	P Duboscq	65/4
1954	**Sica Boy**	W R Johnstone	P Pelat	Mme J Cochery	41/10
1955	**Ribot**	E Camici	U Penco	Marchese della Rochetta	9/1
1956	**Ribot**	E Camici	U Penco	Marchese della Rochetta	6/10
1957	**Oroso**	S Boullenger	D Lescalle	R Meyer	52/1
1958	**Ballymoss**	A Breasley	M V O'Brien	J McShain	39/10
1959	**Saint Crespin III**	G Moore	A Head	Prince Aly Khan	17/1
1960	**Puissant Chef**	M Garcia	C Bartholomew	H Aubert	14/1
1961	**Molvedo**	E Camici	A Maggi	E Verga	18/10
1962	**Soltikoff**	M Depalmas	R Pelat	Mme C del Duca	40/1
1963	**Exbury**	J Deforge	G Watson	Baron G Rothschild	36/10
1964	**Prince Royal II**	R Poincelet	G Bridgland	R Ellsworth	16/1
1965	**Sea Bird II**	T P Glennon	E Pollet	J Ternynck	12/10
1966	**Bon Mot III**	F Head	W Head	F W Burmann	53/10
1967	**Topyo**	W Pyers	C W Bartholemew	Mme L Volterra	82/1
1968	**Vaguely Noble**	W Williamson	E Pollet	Mrs R Franklyn	5/2
1969	**Levmoss**	W Williamson	S McGrath	S McGrath	52/1
1970	**Sassafras**	Y Saint-Martin	F Mathet	A Plesch	19/1
1971	**Mill Reef**	G Lewis	I Balding	P Mellon	7/10
1972	**San San**	F Head	A Penna	Countess M Batthyany	37/2
1973	**Rheingold**	L Piggott	B Hills	H Zeisel	77/10
1974	**Allez France**	Y Saint-Martin	A Penna	D Wildenstein	1/2
1975	**Star Appeal**	G Starkey	T Grieper	W Zeitelhack	119/1
1976	**Ivanjica**	F Head	A Head	J Wertheimer	71/10
1977	**Alleged**	L Piggott	M V O'Brien	R Sangster	38/10
1978	**Alleged**	L Piggott	M V O'Brien	R Sangster	14/10
1979	**Three Troikas**	F Head	Mme C Head	Mme A Head	88/10
1980	**Detroit**	P Eddery	O Douieb	R Sangster	67/10

Vaguely Noble **wins the 1968 Prix de l'Arc de Triomphe with W.Williamson up.**

Lester Piggott finally achieved victory in the Prix de l'Arc de Triomphe when he rode *Rheingold* to victory in 1973.

		Jockey	Trainer	Owner	Odds
1981	**Gold River**	G W Moore	A Head	J Wertheimer	53/10
1982	**Akiyda**	Y Saint-Martin	F Mathet	HH Aga Khan	43/4
1983	**All Along**	W R Swinburn	P-L Biancone	D Wildenstein	173/10
1984	**Sagace**	Y Saint-Martin	P-L Biancone	D Wildenstein	29/10
1985	**Rainbow Quest**	P Eddery	J Tree	K Abdulla	71/10
1986	**Dancing Brave**	P Eddery	G Harwood	K Abdulla	21/10
1987	**Trempolino**	P Eddery	A Fabre	P de Moussac	20/1
1988	**Tony Bin**	J Reid	L Camici	Mrs V Gaucci del Bono	14/1
1989	**Carroll House**	M Kinane	M Jarvis	A Balzarini	189/10
1990	**Saumarez**	G Mosse	N Clement	B McNall	15/1
1991	**Suave Dancer**	C Asmussen	J Hammond	H Chalhoub	37/10
1992	**Subotica**	T Jarnet	A Fabre	O Lecerf	88/10

Run at Le Tremblay 1943-1944 over 2,300 metres

Geoff Lewis waves as he is led in aboard *Mill Reef* after their 1971 Prix de l'Arc victory.

The Cheveley Park Stakes

Unlike the Middle Park Stakes, in recent years the Cheveley Park Stakes has maintained its reputation as a classic indicator. The race was founded in 1899 and named after the Newmarket estate of Col.Harry McCalmont, owner of the Triple Crown winner *Isinglass*. The first winner was *Lutetia*, ridden by Tod Sloan, the American who had changed the style of British race-riding. Sloan had learned the trick of balancing on the horse's withers rather than the English manner more typical of a hunting seat when 'carted' before a race at the Bay District track in San Francisco. Crouching over his mount's neck to regain control, Sloan discovered that the accidental redistribution of weight gave not only better steering, but enhanced the animal's freedom to stride.

Pretty Polly completed the Cheveley Park, Middle Park double in 1903 and *Fifinella*, the last filly to win the Derby (a wartime substitue at Newmarket in 1916) scored in 1915. *Scuttle*, who won in 1927 became H.M.King George V's sole classic winner in the One Thousand Guineas of 1928.

Since the second World War, eight fillies have returned to the Rowley Mile in the spring to win the One Thousand, the latest being the French trained *Ravinella* in 1988. The most controversial race in recent years was the 1986 running, when *Forest Flower* was first past the post in a field of five having given *Ministrella* a severe bump about two furlongs from home. An objection by *Minstrella's* rider John Reid fell on deaf ears with the Newmarket stewards, but an appeal to the Jockey Club succeeded in reversing the placings and Tony Ives, *Forest Flower's* jockey was stood down for twelve days. This decision caused much dissension at the time, but on the other hand it is not unreasonable to expect a rider to keep a horse straight in a five horse race with the width of the Bunbury Mile in which to manoeuvre.

NB The Cheveley Park in 1986 was run over the July Course as the stands on the Rowley Mile were being rebuilt.

Run at Newmarket over 6 furlongs for 2 year-old fillies First Run 1899 Group 1

		Jockey	Trainer	Owner	Odds
1899	**Lutetia**	J F Sloan	J Huggins	Lord W Beresford	1/2
1900	**Alruna**	F Rickaby	P Peck	Lord Durham	5/4
1901	**Punctilio**	O Madden	R Day	Sir E Vincent	10/1
1902	**Skyscraper**	W Halsey	J Watson	W Raphael	4/5
1903	**Pretty Polly**	W Lane	P P Gilpin	E Loder	8/100
1904	**Galantine**	O Madden	C Archer	E Dresden	Evens
1905	**Colonia**	W Higgs	W T Robinson	W Hall-Walker	4/9
1906	**Witch Elm**	B Lynham	W T Robinson	W Hall-Walker	4/5
1907	**Bracelet**	B Dillon	T Lewis	F Forester	4/6
1908	**Maid of the Mist**	O Madden	A Taylor Jnr	W Bass	4/1
1909	**Maid of Corinth**	B Dillon	A Taylor Jnr	Sir W Bass	5/1
1910	**Knockfeerna**	F O'Neill	P P Gilpin	E Loder	9/4
1911	**Belleisle**	H Jones	W Waugh	Lord Falmouth	10/11
1912	**Merula**	C Foy	W Waugh	Lord Falmouth	100/8
1913	**Shake Down**	E Wheatley	S Darling	J Buchanan	13/8

Tod Sloan, the American jockey who won the first Cheveley Park Stakes in 1899. Sloan taught British jockeys how to balance on the horse's withers rather than riding 'hunting style'.

		Jockey	Trainer	Owner	Odds
1914	**Lady of Asia**	H Jelliss	T Jennings Jnr	L Brassey	2/1
1915	**Fifinella**	S Donoghue	R C Dawson	E Hulton	1/10
1916	**Molly Desmond**	A Whalley	P P Gilpin	G Loder	6/4
1917	**Freesia**	J H Martin	A Sadler	Lord Jersey	2/1
1918	**Bayuda**	J Childs	A Taylor Jnr	Lady J Douglas	11/10
1919	**Bright Folly**	A Smith	F Barling	Lord Glanely	5/4
1920	**Romana**	F Bullock	B Jarvis	J P Hornung	6/1
1921	**Selene**	S Donoghue	G Lambton	Lord Derby	6/4
1922	**Paola**	G Hulme	R C Dawson	HH Aga Khan	2/1
1923	**Chronometer**	B Carslake	H S Persse	Duke of Westminster	11/4
1924	**Miss Gadabout**	F Bullock	A Taylor Jnr	Lord Astor	Evens
1925	**Karra**	C Elliott	J Jarvis	Lady Richardson	7/4
1926	**Nipisquit**	C Childs	C Leader	Lord Beaverbrook	10/1
1927	**Scuttle**	J Childs	W R Jarvis	HM The King	5/1
1928	**Tiffin**	G Richards	F Darling	Lord Ellesmere	Evens
1929	**Merry Wife**	H Wragg	R C Dawson	Lord Carnarvon	8/1
1930	**The Leopard**	B Carslake	N Scobie	Sir C Hyde	15/8
1931	**Concordia**	R A Jones	J Lawson	A R Cox	Evens
1932	**Brown Betty**	J Childs	C Boyd-Rochfort	W Woodward	2/1
1933	**Light Brocade**	B Carslake	Frank Butters	Lord Durham	11/8

		Jockey	Trainer	Owner	Odds
1934	**Lady Gabriel**	B Carslake	H S Persse	D Sullivan	13/8
1935	**Ferrybridge**	M Beary	M Hartigan	R Watson	5/1
1936	**Celestial Way**	B Carslake	G Lambton	H Cecil	3/1
1937	**Stafaralla**	H Wragg	Frank Butters	Prince Aly Khan	4/9
1938	**Seaway**	T Lowrey	B Jarvis	J S Courtauld	20/1
1939	**No Race**				
1940	**Keystone**	G Richards	F Darling	P Beatty	8/13
1941	**Perfect Peace**	H Wragg	J Lawson	Lord Glanely	2/1
1942	**Lady Sybil**	G Richards	W Pratt	M Benson	11/10
1943	**Fair Fame**	F Lane	H Leader	Nrs B Lavington	5/4
1944	**Sweet Cygnet**	C Elliott	T Rimell	H Leven	100/6
1945	**Neolight**	G Richards	F Darling	J A Dewar	13/8
1946	**Djerba**	C Elliott	C Semblat	M Boussac	9/2
1947	**Ash Blonde**	P Evans	R J Colling	Lord Astor	100/8
1948	**Pambidian**	G Richards	W Nightingall	C Harper	100/6
1949	**Corejada**	C Elliott	C Semblat	M Boussac	4/9
1950	**Belle of All**	G Richards	N Bertie	H Tufton	5/4
1951	**Zabara**	G Richards	V Smyth	Sir M McAlpine	10/11
1952	**Bebe Grande**	G Richards	F Armstrong	J Gerber	1/2
1953	**Sixpence**	G Richards	P Prendergast	A L Hawkins	4/1
1954	**Gloria Nicky**	A Breasley	N Bertie	Mrs R Digby	10/1
1955	**Midget II**	R Poincelet	A Head	P Wertheimer	Evens
1956	**Sarcelle**	A Breasley	N Cannon	K Mason	4/6
1957	**Rich and Rare**	E Mercer	J Jarvis	T Blackwell	5/1
1958	**Lindsay**	E Mercer	R D Peacock	F Ellison	100/8
1959	**Queensberry**	E Smith	J A Waugh	B Hornung	2/5
1960	**Opaline II**	G Moore	A Head	HH Aga Khan	11/10
1961	**Display**	R Hutchinson	P Prendergast	Lady B Granard	8/11
1962	**My Goodness Me**	E Smith	G Brooke	D Robinson	100/8
1963	**Crimea II**	W H Carr	C Boyd-Rochfort	Mrs J Haines	9/1
1964	**Night Off**	J Mercer	W Wharton	Maj L B Holliday	20/1
1965	**Berkeley Springs**	G Lewis	I Balding	P Mellon	100/8
1966	**Fleet**	L Piggott	N Murless	R C Boucher	5/2
1967	**Lalibela**	L Piggott	M V O'Brien	J B Philipps	5/1
1968	**Mige**	J Taillard	A Head	Mme P Wertheimer	5/2
1969	**Humble Duty**	D Keith	P Walwyn	Lady J Ashcombe	11/4
1970	**Magic Flute**	A Barclay	N Murless	Lord H de Walden	13/8
1971	**Waterloo**	E Hide	J W Watts	Mrs R Stanley	100/30
1972	**Jacinth**	J Gorton	B Hobbs	Lady Butt	9/2
1973	**Gentle Thoughts**	W Pyers	T Curtin	N B Hunt	9/1
1974	**Cry of Truth**	J Gorton	B Hobbs	Miss P Johnston	4/1
1975	**Pasty**	P Eddery	P Walwyn	G P Williams	9/1
1976	**Durtal**	L Piggott	B Hills	R Sangster	5/1
1977	**Sookera**	W Swimburn	D Weld	R Sangster	3/1
1978	**Devon Ditty**	G Starkey	H Thomson Jones	Sir E McAlpine	11/8
1979	**Mrs Penny**	J Matthias	I Balding	E Kronfeld	7/1
1980	**Marwell**	L Piggott	M Stoute	E J Loder	4/9
1981	**Woodstream**	P Eddery	M V O'Brien	R Sangster	5/2
1982	**Ma Biche**	F Head	Mme C Head	Mme A Head	11/4
1983	**Desirable**	S Cauthen	B Hills	Mrs J M Corbett	12/1
1984	**Park Appeal**	D Gillespie	J Bolger	P H Burns	4/1
1985	**Embla**	A Cordero	L Cumani	C St George	20/1
1986	**Minstrella**	J Reid	C Nelson	E P Evans	11/10
1987	**Ravinella**	G W Moore	Mme C Head	Ecurie Aland	9/2
1988	**Pass the Peace**	T Quinn	P Cole	B Bell	5/1
1989	**Dead Certain**	C Asmussen	D Elsworth	G G Marten	11/2
1990	**Capricciosa**	J Reid	M V O'Brien	R Sangster	7/1
1991	**Marling**	W R Swinburn	G Wragg	E J Loder	15/8
1992	**Sayyedati**	W R Swinburn	C Brittain	M Obaida	5/2

The Middle Park Stakes

The Middle Park Stakes was founded by William Blenkiron and named after his stud at Eltham in Kent. One of the earliest sponsors, he put up the £1,000 prize money in 1866 when *The Rake* won narrowly from *Achievement*, a filly who went on to win the One Thousand Guineas and the St Leger. Soon established as a classic trial, *Isinglass* (1892) and *Galtee More* (1896 won the Triple Crown, with nine classic winners by the turn of the century.)

In 1903, *Pretty Polly* won both the Middle Park and the Cheveley Park Stakes, unique achievement and impossible now as the Middle Park has been restricted to colts since 1987.

Bayardo, Lemberg, Tetratema, Call Boy, Bahram, Scottish Union, Djebel, Sun Chariot, Dante, Nearula, Our Babu, Brigadier Gerard and *Known Fact* have all demonstrated the value of the Middle Park as a stepping-stone to classic victory, but since *Known Fact* was awarded the race on the disqualification of *Nureyev* in the 1980 Two Thousand Guineas, only one classic winner has emerged — *Rodrigo de Triano.*

Run at Newmarket over 6 furlongs for 2 year-old colts First Run 1866 Group 1

		Jockey	Trainer	Owner	Odds
1866	**The Rake**	J Loates	Jos Dawson	F Pryor	4/1
1867	**Green Sleeve**	S Kenyon	J Porter	Sir J Hawley	100/8
1868	**Pero Gomez**	J Adams	J Porter	Sir J Hawley	3/1
1869	**Frivolity**	T Chaloner	Jos Dawson	W A Lyndon	8/1
1870	**Albert Victor**	J Morris	T Olliver	W S Cartwright	20/1
1871	**Prince Charlie**	W Hunt	Jos Dawson	Jos Dawson	11/1
1872	**Surinam**	J Osborne Jnr	C Peck	Sir R W Bulkeley	10/1
1873	**Newry**	F Webb	–	F Fisher	7/2
1874	**Floriform**	S Mordan	–	R Christophers	10/1
1875	**Petrarch**	J Goater	John Dawson	Mr Spencer	100/8
1876	**Chamant**	J Goater	T Jennings	Comte F de Lagrange	20/1
1877	**Beauclerc**	J Snowden	W I'Anson Jnr	C Perkins	5/1
1878	**Peter**	C Wood	Jos Dawson	J Peel	4/1
1879	**Beaudesert**	G Fordham	J Day	Lord Anglesey	65/40
1880	**St Louis**	G Fordham	A Taylor Snr	W S Crawfurd	11/4
1881	**Kermesse**	T Cannon	J Cannon	Lord Rosebery	Evens
1882	**Macheath**	C Wood	R Sherrard	W S Crawfurd	100/30
1883	**Busybody**	F Archer	M Dawson	G A Baird	15/8
1884	**Melton**	F Archer	M Dawson	Lord Hastings	10/1
1885	**Minting**	F Archer	M Dawson	R C Vyner	8/15
1886	**Florentine**	J Watts	J Jewitt	Lord Calthorpe	100/6
1887	**Friar's Balsam**	G Barrett	J Porter	Sir F Johnstone	4/9
1888	**Donovan**	F Barrett	G Dawson	Duke of Portland	11/8
1889	**Signorina**	G Barrett	O Ginistrelli	O Ginistrelli	4/6
1890	**Gouverneur**	J Woodburn	T Jennings Jnr	E Blanc	5/1
1891	**Orme**	G Barrett	J Porter	Duke of Westminster	8/15
1892	**Isinglass**	G Chaloner	J Jewitt	H McCalmont	10/1
1893	**Ladas**	A White	M Dawson	Lord Rosebery	1/5
1894	**Speedwell**	F Pratt	J Ryan	A W Cox	8/1
1895	**St Frusquin**	F Pratt	A Hayhoe	L de Rothschild	4/1
1896	**Galtee More**	M Cannon	S Darling	J Gubbins	5/1
1897	**Dieudonne**	O Madden	R Marsh	Duke of Devonshire	100/7
1898	**Caiman**	J F Sloan	J Huggins	Lord W Beresford	7/4
1899	**Democrat**	J F Sloan	J Huggins	Lord W Beresford	Evens
1900	**Floriform**	M Cannon	T Cannon Jnr	T S Jay	100/8
1901	**Minstead**	D Maher	G Chaloner	Lord Harewood	4/1
1902	**Flotsam**	D Maher	G Blackwell	Sir D Cooper	6/1
1903	**Pretty Polly**	W Lane	P P Gilpin	E Loder	2/1
1904	**Jardy**	G Stern	R Denman	E Blanc	5/4
1905	**Flair**	W Higgs	P P Gilpin	Sir D Cooper	11/4
1906	**Galvani**	B Dillon	P P Gilpin	E Loder	10/1
1907	**Lesbia**	D Maher	G Blackwell	Sir D Cooper	100/30
1908	**Bayardo**	D Maher	A Taylor Jnr	A W Cox	1/6
1909	**Lemberg**	D Maher	A Taylor Jnr	A W Cox	7/4
1910	**Borrow**	J H Martin	A J Joyner	H P Whitney	100/6
1911	**Absurd**	J H Martin	C Morton	J B Joel	7/1
1912	**Craganour**	W Saxby	W T Robinson	C B Ismay	11/8
1913	**Corcyra**	D Maher	R H Dewhurst	Lord Londonderry	11/8
1914	**Friar Marcus**	H Jones	R Marsh	HM The King	2/1
1915	**Argos**	Wal Griggs	P P Gilpin	L Neumann	9/4
1916	**North Star**	F Bullock	R Day	J B Joel	100/8
1917	**Benevente**	F Rickaby	R H Dewhurst	Lord Londonderry	8/11
1918	**Stefan the Great**	B Carslake	H S Persse	L Robinson	4/1
1919	**Tetratema**	B Carslake	H S Persse	D McCalmont	1/4
1920	**Monarch**	F Bullock	Wal Griggs	Sir H Bird	7/1
1921	**Golden Corn**	S Donoghue	Hugh Powney	M Field	2/7
1922	**Drake**	M Beary	H Cottrill	Mrs S Whitburn	4/11
1923	**Diophon**	G Hulme	R C Dawson	HH Aga Khan	2/1
1924	**Picaroon**	F Bullock	A Taylor Jnr	A R Cox	1/2
1925	**Lex**	M Beary	R Day	Sir A Bailey	100/12
1926	**Call Boy**	C Elliott	J E Watts	F Curzon	7/2
1927	**Pharamond**	T Weston	G Lambton	Lord Derby	100/30
1928	**Costaki Pasha**	M Beary	R C Dawson	HH Aga Khan	100/8
1929	**Press Gang**	F Fox	F Darling	Lord Woolavington	2/1
1930	**Portlaw**	H Beasley	H S Persse	Sir A Bailey	Evens
1931	**Orwell**	R A Jones	J Lawson	W M G Singer	4/11
1932	**Felicitation**	M Beary	Frank Butters	HH Aga Khan	3/1
1933	**Medieval Knight**	G Richards	F Darling	J A Dewar	100/30
1934	**Bahram**	F Fox	Frank Butters	HH Aga Khan	2/7
1935	**Abjer**	C Elliott	G Lambton	M Boussac	8/1
1936	**Fair Copy**	R Perryman	C Leader	Lord Derby	13/8
1937	**Scottish Union**	G Richards	N Cannon	J V Rank	10/1
1938	**Foxbrough II**	P Beasley	C Boyd-Rochfort	W Woodward	13/8
1939	**Djebel**	C Elliott	A Swann	M Boussac	9/1
1940	**Hyacinthus**	P Beasley	H S Persse	A Bassett	10/1

The Aga Khan's *Bahram*, winner of the 1934 Middle Park Stakes.

		Jockey	Trainer	Owner	Odds
1941	**Sun Chariot**	H Wragg	F Darling	HM The King	11/4
1942	**Ribbon**	E Smith	J Jarvis	Lord Rosebery	9/2
1943	**Orestes**	T Carey	W Nightingall	Miss D Paget	7/4
1944	**Dante**	W Nevett	M Peacock	Sir E Ohlson	2/5
1945	**Khaled**	G Richards	Frank Butters	HH Aga Khan	2/5
1946	**Saravan**	C Elliott	Frank Butters	Princess Aly Khan	100/8
1947	**The Cobbler**	G Richards	F Darling	G Loder	8/11
1948	**Abernant**	G Richards	N Murless	R Macdonald-Buchanan	1/7
1949	**Masked Light**	D Smith	N Scobie	E Wanless	2/7
1950	**Big Dipper**	W H Carr	C Boyd-Rochfort	Mrs J Bryce	2/5
1951	**King's Bench**	C Elliott	M Feakes	A Tompsett	7/2
1952	**Nearula**	E Britt	C Elsey	W Humble	13/2
1953	**Royal Challenger**	G Richards	P Beasley	A Gordon	4/1
1954	**Our Babu**	D Smith	G Brooke	D Robinson	6/1
1955	**Buisson Ardent**	D Smith	A Head	HH Aga Khan	9/2
1956	**Pipe of Peace**	A Breasley	G Richards	S Niarchos	8/1
1957	**Major Portion**	E Smith	T E Leader	H J Joel	11/2
1958	**Masham**	D Smith	G Brooke	A Ellis	2/1
1959	**Venture VII**	G Moore	A Head	Prince Aly Khan	1/4
1960	**Skymaster**	A Breasley	W Smyth	Duke of Norfolk	100/30

		Jockey	Trainer	Owner	Odds
1961	**Gustav**	J Londley	J Tree	J H Whitney	100/6
1962	**Crocket**	E Smith	G Brooke	D van Clief	5/4
1963	**Showdown**	D Smith	F N Winter	Mrs D Prenn	100/30
1964	**Spanish Express**	J Mercer	L Hall	Mrs G Marcow	9/1
1965	**Track Spare**	J Lindley	R Mason	R Mason	10/1
1966	**Bold Lad**	D Lake	P Prendergast	Lady B Granard	2/7
1967	**Petingo**	L Piggott	F Armstrong	M Lemos	1/4
1968	**Right Tack**	G Lewis	J Sutcliffe Jnr	J R Brown	11/2
1969	**Huntercombe**	E Johnson	A Budgett	H Renshaw	3/1
1970	**Brigadier Gerard**	J Mercer	W R Hern	Mrs J Hislop	9/2
1971	**Sharpen Up**	W Carson	B van Cutsem	Mrs B van Cutsem	5/6
1972	**Tudenham**	J Lindley	Denys Smith	L B Holliday	4/1
1973	**Habat**	P Eddery	P Walwyn	C Vittadini	4/6
1974	**Steel Heart**	L Piggott	D Weld	R Tikkoo	10/11
1975	**Hittite Glory**	F Durr	A Breasley	R Tikkoo	9/2
1976	**Tachypous**	G Lewis	B Hobbs	G Cambanis	5/1
1977	**Formidable**	P Eddery	P Walwyn	P Goulandris	15/8
1978	**Junius**	L Piggott	M V O'Brien	S Fraser	7/1
1979	**Known Fact**	W Carson	J Tree	K Abdulla	10/1
1980	**Mattaboy**	L Piggott	R Armstrong	R Tikkoo	7/1
1981	**Cajun**	L Piggott	H Cecil	J Stone	20/1
1982	**Diesis**	L Piggott	H Cecil	Lord H de Walden	10/11
1983	**Creag-an-Sgor**	S Cauthen	C Nelson	Mrs W Tulloch	50/1
1984	**Bassenthwaite**	P Eddery	J Tree	S Niarchos	7/2
1985	**Stalker**	J Mercer	P Walwyn	P Fetherston-Godley	9/2
1986	**Mister Majestic**	R Cochrane	R Williams	D A Johnson	33/1
1987	**Gallic League**	S Cauthen	B Hills	R Sangster	6/4
1988	**Mon Tresor**	M Roberts	R Boss	Mrs P Fitsall	8/1
1989	**Balla Cove**	S Cauthen	R Boss	H Cohen	20/1
1990	**Lycius**	C Asmussen	A Fabre	Sheikh Mohammed	13/8
1991	**Rodrigo de Triano**	W Carson	P Chapple-Hyam	R Sangster	Evens
1992	**Zieten**	S Cauthen	A Fabre	Sheikh Mohammed	5/2

Run at Nottingham in 1940

The Sun Chariot Stakes

Considering that she made a seventy-five per cent contribution to the record four classic winners owned by a monarch, King George VI, it seems odd that a race was not named after *Sun Chariot* until 1966. On her day one of the finest fillies ever to race and worthy of inclusion with *Sceptre, Pretty Polly* and *Meld* in the view of at least one distinguished racing historian, she had a fiery temperament which made her an extremely difficult ride for Gordon Richards and nearly cost her the Oaks, but she won the race easily enough in the end and the 1,000 Guineas and the St Leger as well.

All three races were on the July Course at Newmarket in 1942, and *Big Game* completed the quartet of classic victories for the King in the 2,000 Guineas.

The race was originally confined to three-year-old fillies, but was opened to older horses in 1974. Since then, only two senior animals have won; the dual winner *Free Guest* in 1984 and 1985 and the elegant *Indian Skimmer* in 1988.

Run at Newmarket over 1 mile 2 furlongs for fillies First Run 1966 Group 2

		Jockey	Trainer	Owner	Odds
1966	**Lucaya**	J Lindley	W Elsey	D Aykroyd	100/8
1967	**Cranberry Sauce**	G Moore	N Murless	J Hornung	7/2
1968	**Hill Shade**	A Barclay	N Murless	G A Pope Jnr	4/5
1969	**Lucyrowe**	D Keith	P Walwyn	L Freedman	4/6
1970	**Popkins**	L Piggott	H Wragg	R B Moller	4/7
1971	**Hill Circus**	G Lewis	N Murless	G A Pope Jnr	Evens
1972	**Sleat**	J Gorton	B Hobbs	H D H Wills	8/1
1973	**Cheveley Princess**	L Piggott	H Wragg	R B Moller	6/1
1974	**Sweet Farewell**	P Eddery	Sir H Nugent	C G St Lawrence	20/1
1975	**Duboff**	W Carson	B Hills	Mrs C Radcliffe	6/1
1976	**Ranimer**	A Gibert	P Head	Sir R McAlpine	9/1
1977	**Triple First**	G Starkey	M Stoute	R Clifford-Turner	7/1
1978	**Swiss Maid**	L Piggott	P Kelleway	M Fine	5/1
1979	**Topsy**	L Piggott	H Wragg	R B Moller	7/2
1980	**Snow**	L Piggott	K Prendergast	M Fraser	12/1
1981	**Home on the Range**	L Piggott	H Cecil	L Freedman	2/1
1982	**Time Charter**	W Newnes	H Candy	R Barnett	6/1
1983	**Cormorant Wood**	S Cauthen	B Hills	R J McAlpine	7/2
1984	**Free Guest**	D McHargue	L Cumani	M Boffa	2/1
1985	**Free Guest**	P Eddery	L Cumani	Fittocks Stud Ltd	13/8

		Jockey	Trainer	Owner	Odds
1986	**Dusty Dollar**	W Carson	W R Hern	M Al-Maktoum	7/2
1987	**Infamy**	R Cochrane	L Cumani	G Leigh	5/1
1988	**Indian Skimmer**	M Roberts	H Cecil	Sheikh Mohammed	40/85
1989	**Braiswick**	G Carter	G Wragg	White Lodge Stud	4/1
1990	**Kartajana**	W R Swinburn	M Stoute	HH Aga Khan	11/10
1991	**Ristna**	W Carson	J Gosden	G Strawbridge	4/1
1992	**Red Slippers**	L Dettori	L Cumani	Sheikh Mohammed	6/4

For 3 year-old fillies only 1966-1973

The Cambridgeshire Handicap

This is one of the toughest races in the Calendar, and they didn't come any tougher than *Lanercost*, the winner in 1841 of twenty-six races from forty starts, including the Ascot Gold Cup. Trained by Wm.I'Anson at Gullane, Lanercost won twice at Dumfries on 17 & 18 October 1839 and then was conveyed in a tiny horse-van which was much to small for him over 340 miles of rutted roads to Newmarket.

Not surprisingly, *Lanercost* was stiff and sore when he arrived four days before the Cambridgeshire. Unable to work, he was sweated in his box and won the race under 8st 9lb.

In the days when there were few opportunities, classic winners used to compete, but were usually weighted out with crushing burdens. None the less, *La Fleche* carried 8st 10lb to win in 1892 after taking the 1,000 Guineas, the Oaks and the St Leger. *Isonomy* (1878) went on to victory in two Ascot Gold Cups, and *Bendigo*, the inaugural Eclipse Stakes winner, won in 1883. In the same era, three horses achieved a feat unthinkable today and won both legs of the Autumn Double, the Cambridgeshire and the Cesarewitch, run over twice the distance, namely *Rosebery* (1876). *Foxhall* (1881) and *Plaisanterie* in 1885.

In 1935, *Commander 111* provided Basil Briscoe with some compensation for the bitter-sweet memories of *Golden Miller*, and the post-war hero of the Cambridgeshire is undoubtedly *Baronet*, winner in 1978 and 1980, and second in 1977 and 1981.

Run at Newmarket over 1 mile 1 furlong First Run 1839 Handicap

		Jockey	Trainer	Owner	Odds
1839	**Lanercost**	W Noble	W I'Anson	W Ramsay	9/2
1840	**Roscius**	J Chapple	–	W Graydon	–
1841	**Vulcan**	E Flatman	–	R Holmes	30/1
1842	**Ralph**	J Robinson	W Edwards	Lord Albemarle	11/1
1843	**Nat**	Simpson	–	B Eddison	15/1
1844	**Evenus**	E Flatman	R Boyce Jnr	Lord Stradbroke	30/1
1845	**Alarm**	E Flatman	M Dilly	C Greville	9/1
1846	**Prior of St Margarets**	A Day	J Scott	E Nunn	3/1
1847	**The Widow**	R Pettit	–	G Leigh	30/1
1848	**Dacia**	G Brown	W Cooper	J Peel	4/1
1849	**Raby**	J Arnold	T Dawson	J Meiklam	6/1
1850	**Landgrave**	J Chapple	J Kent Jnr	G W Gratwicke	5/2
1851	**Truth**	J Wells	W Saunders	E Phillips	40/1
1852	**Knight of the Shire**	Capt R Harding	W Dilly	Lord Bruce	6/1
1853	**Little David**	G Fordham	R Drewitt	W Smith	33/1
1854	**Scherz**	E Flatman	–	Baron Mollendorf	12/1
1855	**Sultan**	J Goater	W Day	Lord Anglesey	40/1
1856	**Malacca**	S Hibberd	T Parr	T Parr	10/1
1857	**Odd Trick**	G Fordham	T Parr	T Parr	12/1
1858	**Eurydice**	G Britton	J Dover	R Sutton	40/1
1859	**Red Eagle**	H Grimshaw	J Osborne	J Osborne	50/1
1860	**Weatherbound**	J Adams	W Day	F Swindell	9/4
1861	**Palestro**	Watkins	T Jennings	Comte F de Lagrange	100/6
1862	**Bathilde**	E Martin	T Taylor	Lord Chesterfield	25/1
1863	**Catch 'em Alive**	S Adams	W Day	W Day	4/1
1864	**Ackworth**	T Cannon	J Day	Marquis of Hastings	15/1
1865	**Gardevisure**	A Carter	J Dover	R Sutton	40/1
1866	**Actaea**	H Huxtable	R Drewitt	S Thellusson	20/1
1867	**Lozenge**	S Adams	–	Mr Fulke	22/1
1868	**See Saw**	G Fordham	T Wadlow	Lord Wilton	100/3
1869	**Vestminster**	J Gradwell	F Balchin	G Hodgman	100/8
1870	**Adonis**	F Lynham	–	Count Renard	6/1
1871	**Sabinus**	G Fordham	–	G Keswick	33/1
1872	**Playfair**	G Ashworth	J Porter	F Gretton	10/1
1873	**Montargis**	Carratt	–	Comte de Juigne	50/1
1874	**Peut-etre**	Rolfe	–	P Aumont	6/1
1875	**Sutton**	H Morgan	–	Mr Mannington	3/1
1876	**Rosebery**	H Constable	–	J Smith	4/1
1877	**Jongleur**	Rolfe	–	Prince D'Arenberg	100/3
1878	**Isonomy**	H Morgan	J Porter	F Gretton	40/1
1879	**La Merveille**	H Constable	J Cannon	Lord Rosebery	30/1
1880	**Lucetta**	W Greaves	C Blanton	Prince Soltykoff	100/6
1881	**Foxhall**	J Watts	W Day	J R Keene	10/1
1882	**Hackness**	S Loates	J Hopper	R Peck	100/12
1883	**Bendigo**	H Luke	C Jousiffe	H T Barclay	50/1

		Jockey	Trainer	Owner	Odds
1884	**Florence**	F Webb	Robert Sherwood	J Hammond	6/1
1885	**Plaisanterie**	Hartley	–	H Bouy	10/1
1886	**Sailor Prince**	A White	W G Stevens	W Gilbert Jnr	22/1
1887	**Gloriation**	T Glover	M Dawson	R C Vyner	40/1
1888	**Veracity**	T Calder	E Weever	W J Legh	20/1
1889	**Laureate**	W Warne	J Waugh	J Hammond	1,000/45
1890	**Alicante**	F Barrett	–	M Ephrussi	9/2
1891	**Comedy**	H Ibbett	T Lewis	W W Fulton	7/1
1892	**La Fleche**	G Barrett	J Porter	Baron M de Hirsch	7/2
1893	**Molly Morgan**	W Bradford	Robert Sherwood	Lord Dunraven	100/6
1894	**Indian Queen**	W Croft	E J Hobbs	E Hobson	25/1
1895	**Marco**	F Allsopp	T Chaloner Jnr	F Luscombe	9/1
1896	**Winkfield's Pride**	W T Robinson	W T Robinson	J C Sullivan	5/1
1897	**Comfrey**	K Cannon	W G Stevens	Sir W Ingram	25/1
1898	**Georgic**	S Chandley	F W Day	H C White	40/1
1899	**Irish Ivy**	K Cannon	W Behan	E Peel	20/1
1900	**Berrill**	J Thompson	P Behan	J C Sullivan	20/1
1901	**Watershed**	J Reiff	J Huggins	W C Whitney	25/1
1902	**Ballantrae**	J Watts	J Huggins	W C Whitney	9/4
1903	**Hackler's Pride**	J Jarvis	J Fallon	F Forester	6/1
1904	**Hackler's Pride**	B Dillon	J Fallon	F Forester	7/2
1905	**Velocity**	A Templeman	S Pickering	Mrs H V Jackson	7/2
1906	**Polymelus**	D Maher	C Peck	S B Joel	11/10
1907	**Land League**	W Higgs	Robert Sherwood Jnr	J G R Homfray	8/1
1908	**Marcovil**	L Hewitt	C Waugh	F Luscombe	50/1
1909	**Christmas Daisy**	C Ringstead	T Lewis	E A Wigan	100/7
1910	**Christmas Daisy**	S Donoghue	T Lewis	E A Wigan	7/1
1911	**Long Set**	H Jelliss	J H Batho	S B Joel	33/1
1912	**Adam Bede**	C Foy	J Cannon	L Winans	100/7
1913	**Cantilever**	H Southey	C Leader	Lord Harewood	33/1
1914	**Honeywood**	S Donoghue	C Peck	S B Joel	100/7
1915	**Silver Tag**	S Donoghue	R C Dawson	E Hulton	100/14
1916	**Eos**	V Smyth	G Lambton	Lord D'Abernon	10/1
1917	**Brown Prince**	P Jones	R Day	Sir A Bailey	100/6
1918	**Zinovia**	V Smyth	F Hunt	Z G Michalinos	9/2
1919	**Brigand**	E Crickmere	F Pratt	J A de Rothschild	25/1
1920	**No Race**				
1921	**Milenko**	B Lynch	F Pratt	J A de Rothschild	100/7
1922	**Re-echo**	A Whalley	C Leader	Sir E Paget	25/1
1923	**Verdict**	M Beary	W Waugh	Lord Coventry	100/7
1924	**Twelve Pointer**	B Carslake	H S Persse	Duke of Westminster	9/1
1925	**Masked Marvel**	W McLachlan Jnr	S H Darling	A K Macomber	100/8
1926	**Insight II**	J Thwaites	S H Darling	A K Macomber	50/1
1927	**Medal**	J Caldwell	S Wootton	Mrs T Carthew	20/1
	Niantic	W Stephenson	W Walters	J Sharp	25/1
1928	**Palais Royal II**	M Allemand	E Charlier	J Wittouck	5/1
1929	**Double Life**	J Dines	C Boyd-Rochfort	Lady Z Wernher	20/1
1930	**The Pen**	C Richards	M Hartigan	Mrs M Hartigan	50/1
1931	**Disarmament**	W Nevett	C Elsey	H Clayton	18/1
1932	**Pullover**	A Richardson	D Peacock	Mrs C Robinson	100/1
1933	**Raymond**	G Nicoll	J Lawson	Sir A Bailey	33/1
1934	**Wychwood Abbot**	R Perryman	T E Leader	O Watney	9/1
1935	**Commander III**	T Hawcroft	A Briscoe	G Foster	28/1
1936	**Dan Bulger**	T Weston	H Cottrill	Sir A Bailey	7/1
1937	**Artist's Prince**	A Richardson	J Dines	R Glover	13/1
1938	**Helleniqua**	B Guimard	W Webb	J Meller	50/1
1939(1)	**Gyroscope**	R Lacey	H Leader	Mrs H Leader	100/6
1939(2)	**Orichalque**	J Simpson	V Beatty	Lord Dufferin	25/1
1940	**Caxton**	P Evans	F Armstrong	T Rigg	100/7
1941	**Rue de la Paix**	T Carey	G Beeby	L A Abelson	18/1
1942	**No Race**				
1943	**Quartier-Maitre**	T Carey	T R Leader	L Lipton	8/1
1944	**Hunsingore**	H Wragg	R W Colling	Maj L B Holliday	6/1
1945	**Esquire**	G Packer	R W Colling	J Bueno	40/1
1946	**Sayani**	W R Johnstone	J Lieux	Mme J Lieux	25/1
1947	**Fairey Fulmar**	T Gosling	O Bell	G Tachmindji	28/1
1948	**Sterope**	D Schofield	P Beasley	J Townley	25/1
1949	**Sterope**	C Elliott	P Beasley	J Townley	25/1
1950	**Kelling**	D Smith	A Waugh	C Jarvis	100/7
1951	**Fleeting Moment**	A Breasley	T Bartlam	Mrs M Johnson	28/1
1952	**Richer**	K Gethin	S Ingham	G Baylis	100/6
1953	**Jupiter**	G Richards	P Beasley	Lord Lambton	100/6
1954	**Minstrel**	G Gaston	J Jarvis	Lord Rosebery	66/1
1955	**Retrial**	P Robinson	C Boyd-Rochfort	Lady Z Wernher	18/1
1956	**Loppylugs**	E Smith	J Beary	J Beary	100/7
1957	**Stephanotis**	W H Carr	J M Rogers	A Plesch	100/6
1958	**London Cry**	A Breasley	G Richards	M Sobell	22/1

		Jockey	Trainer	Owner	Odds
1959	**Rexequus**	N Stirk	G Boyd	J Adam	25/1
1960	**Midsummer Night II**	D Keith	P Hastings-Bass	P Mellon	40/1
1961	**Violetta III**	C Parkes	H Wragg	R B Moller	33/1
	Henry the Seventh	E Hide	W Elsey	H J Joel	100/8
1962	**Hidden Meaning**	A Breasley	H Leader	K Grant	7/1
1963	**Commander in Chief**	F Durr	E Cousins	H Whitehouse	100/7
1964	**Hasty Cloud**	J Wilson	H Wallington	G Walters	100/8
1965	**Tarqogan**	W Williamson	S McGrath	J McGrath	100/8
1966	**Dites**	D Maitland	H Leader	R Midwood	33/1
1967	**Lacquer**	R Hutchinson	H Wragg	R B Moller	20/1
1968	**Emerilo**	M L Thomas	P Allden	D Green	20/1
1969	**Prince de Galles**	F Durr	P Robinson	A Swift	5/2
1970	**Prince de Galles**	F Durr	P Robinson	A Swift	6/1
1971	**King Midas**	D Cullen	D Candy	Exors of H P Holt	10/1
1972	**Negus**	P Waldron	D Candy	R Watson	16/1
1973	**Siliciana**	G Lewis	I Balding	D Back	14/1
1974	**Flying Nelly**	L Maitland	W Wightman	S Digby	22/1
1975	**Lottogift**	R Wernham	D Hanley	A Richards	33/1
1976	**Intermission**	G Starkey	M Stoute	J H Whitney	14/1
1977	**Sin Timon**	A Kimberley	J Hindley	Lady B Ness	18/1
1978	**Baronet**	B Rouse	C Benstead	F Harris	12/1
1979	**Smartset**	J Reid	R F Johnson Houghton	G Ward	33/1
1980	**Baronet**	B Rouse	C Benstead	F Harris	22/1
1981	**Braughing**	S Cauthen	C Brittain	W Gredley	50/1
1982	**Century City**	J Mercer	L Cumani	I Allen	20/1
1983	**Sagamore**	M L Thomas	F Durr	E Naughton	35/1
1984	**Leysh**	J Lowe	S Norton	Prince Y Saud	33/1
1985	**Tremblant**	P Eddery	R V Smyth	K Abdulla	16/1
1986	**Dallas**	R Cochrane	L Cumani	R Duchossois	10/1
1987	**Balthus**	D McKeown	J Glover	E Bennett	50/1
1988	**Quinlan Terry**	G Duffield	Sir M Prescott	Lady Fairhaven	11/1
1989	**Rambo's Hall**	D McKeown	J Glover	B Dixon	15/1
1990	**Risen Moon**	S Cauthen	B Hills	R Sangster	7/1
1991	**Mellottie**	J Lowe	Mrs G R Reveley	Mrs J G Fulton	10/1
1992	**Rambo's Hall**	D McKeown	J Glover	B Dixon	9/2

Run in two classes in 1939.

Run at Nottingham in 1940.

The Jockey Club Cup

The first winner of the Jockey Club Cup, *Flagéolet* was a refugee from his native France where he found his contemporary *Boiard* to hot for him. *Boiard* also beat him in the Ascot Gold Cup, but *Flagéolet* found compensation in the Goodwood Cup and at Newmarket.

The last long distance Pattern race of the British season, the Jockey Club Cup is nowadays a little overshadowed at a time when thoughts are more on the future rather than the period which is drawing to its end. Many senior horses of quality are going into winter quarters and accordingly fields tend to be small and the contests do not always make the heart sing.

Run at Newmarket over 2 miles First Run 1873 Group 3

		Jockey	Trainer	Owner	Odds
1873	**Flageolet**	G Fordham	T Jennings	C J Lefevre	6/5
1874	**Gang Forward**	T Chaloner	A Taylor Snr	W S Crawfurd	5/4
1875	**Carnelion**	C Maidment	J Hayhoe	Sir A de Rothschild	7/1
1876	**Braconnier**	C Archer	T Jennings	Comte F de Lagrange	100/7
1877	**Verneuil**	C Wood	T Jennings	Comte F de Lagrange	100/30
1878	**Silvio**	F Archer	M Dawson	Lord Falmouth	5/4
1879	**Jannette**	F Archer	M Dawson	Lord Falmouth	8/1
1880	**Chippendale**	J Osborne Jnr	T Wadlow	Lord Bradford	4/7
1881	**Corrie Roy**	W Macdonald	A Taylor Snr	W S Crawfurd	10/1
1882	**Chippendale**	J Osborne Jnr	T Wadlow	Lord Bradford	8/1
1883	**Ladislas**	G Fordham	T Jennings Jnr	C J Lefevre	9/2
1884	**St Gatien**	C Wood	Robert Sherwood	J Hammond	1/8
1885	**St Gatien**	C Wood	J Waugh	J Hammond	1/10
1886	**St Gatien**	F Archer	J Waugh	J Hammond	8/11
1887	**Carlton**	G Barrett	A Taylor Snr	Lord E Somerset	w.o.
1888	**Reve d'Or**	T Cannon	A Taylor Snr	Duke of Beaufort	8/15
1889	**Sheen**	J Watts	T Jennings	Prince Soltykoff	15/100
1890	**Wild Monk**	G Barrett	A Taylor Snr	W Bass	w.o.
1891	**Patrick Blue**	J Woodburn	J Enoch	Lord Zetland	–
1892	**Buccaneer**	G Barrett	S Pickering	Lord Rosslyn	w.o.

		Jockey	Trainer	Owner	Odds
1893	**Lady Rosebery**	J Watts	S Pickering	Mr Jersey	Evens
1894	**Callistrate**	M Cannon	F Lynham	A Abeille	1/7
1895	**Florizel II**	J Watts	R Marsh	HRH the Prince of Wales	2/7
1896	**Canterbury Pilgrim**	F Allsopp	G Lambton	Lord Derby	20/21
1897	**Count Schomberg**	S Loates	W Leader	R Lebaudy	w.o.
1898	**Merman**	M Cannon	F Webb	Mr Jersey	11/10
1899	**Mazagan**	O Madden	H Enoch	D Baird	6/4
1900	**Osbech**	F Rickaby	P Peck	Lord Durham	Evens
1901	**King's Courier**	D Maher	John Dawson Jnr	Lord Ellesmere	7/2
1902	**Black Sand**	W Lane	L Alvarez	J Buchanan	9/2
1903	**Mead**	J E Watts	R Marsh	HM The King	9/4
1904	**Zinfandel**	M Cannon	C Beatty	Lord H de Walden	5/2
1905	**Pretty Polly**	B Dillon	P P Gilpin	E Loder	1/5
1906	**Bachelor's Button**	D Maher	C Peck	S B Joel	8/13
1907	**Radium**	B Lynham	J Watson	L de Rothschild	5/1
1908	**Radium**	O Madden	J Watson	L de Rothschild	1/6
1909	**Amadis**	O Madden	W Waugh	Lord Falmouth	1/25
1910	**Lagos**	D Maher	S Pickering	P Nelke	5/1
1911	**Willonyx**	W Higgs	S Darling	C E Howard	20/75
1912	**Aleppo**	A Whalley	A Taylor Jnr	A W Cox	–
1913	**Aleppo**	A Whalley	A Taylor Jnr	A W Cox	5/2
1914	**Son-in-Law**	F Bullock	R Day	Sir A Bailey	2/9
1915	**Son-in-Law**	F Bullock	R Day	Sir A Bailey	6/4
1916	**Hurry On**	J Childs	F Darling	J Buchanan	1/25
1917	**Brown Prince**	F Fox	R Day	Sir A Bailey	11/4
1918	**Queen's Square**	S Donoghue	A Taylor Jnr	A W Cox	4/5
1919	**Gay Lord**	A Whalley	H Cottrill	J White	–
1920	**No Race**				
1921	**Nippon**	F Fox	B Jarvis	J P Hornung	8/1
1922	**Bucks Hussar**	W Lister	R Day	Sir A Bailey	100/8
1923	**Tranquil**	T Weston	G Lambton	Lord Derby	1/5
1924	**Plack**	C Smirke	J Jarvis	Lord Rosebery	1/2
1925	**Bucellas**	A Orme	B Jarvis	J P Hornung	100/30
1926	**Bongrace**	T Weston	J Jarvis	Lord Rosebery	7/1
1927	**Mont Bernina**	C Bouillon	W Barker Jnr	Baron E de Rothschild	6/1
1928	**Invershin**	B Carslake	C Doyle	R Walker	1/5
1929	**Fairway**	T Weston	Frank Butters	Lord Derby	4/6
1930	**Brumeux**	G Richards	S H Darling	A K Macomber	21/20
1931	**Noble Star**	F Fox	L Cundell	F Cundell	Evens
1932	**Brulette**	G Richards	F Darling	Lord Woolavington	w.o.
1933	**Nitsichin**	H Wragg	P Thrale	D S Kennedy	11/8
1934	**Felicitation**	G Richards	Frank Butters	HH Aga Khan	1/4
1935	**Quashed**	T Weston	C Leader	Lord Stanley	5/4
1936	**Quashed**	R Perryman	C Leader	Lord Stanley	2/5
1937	**Buckleigh**	B Carslake	T Hogg	Lord Glanely	13/2
1938	**Foxglove II**	G Richards	F Darling	P Beatty	6/5
1939	**No Race**				
1940	**Atout Maitre**	C Elliott	H Blagrave	H Blagrave	5/2
1941	**No Race**				
1942	**Afterthought**	E Smith	J Jarvis	Lord Rosebery	11/4
1943	**Shahpoor**	G Richards	J Lawson	A E Allnatt	7/2
1944	**Ocean Swell**	E Smith	J Jarvis	Lord Rosebery	Evens
1945	**Amber Flash**	C Richards	R J Colling	Lord Astor	2/1
1946	**Felix II**	P Evans	W Halsey	Baron G de Waldner	100/7
1947	**Laurentis**	E Britt	G Houghton	H K Frost	15/2
1948	**Vic Day**	G Richards	H Blagrave	H Blagrave	w.o.
1949	**Vic Day**	G Richards	H Blagrave	H Blagrave	5/2
1950	**Colonist II**	T Gosling	W Nightingall	W S Churchill	8/11
1951	**Eastern Emperor**	W Rickaby	J Jarvis	Lord Milford	7/4
1952	**Blarney Stone**	W Rickaby	V Smyth	M McAlpine	25/1
1953	**Ambiguity**	J Mercer	R J Colling	Lord Astor	9/4
1954	**Yorick II**	P Blanc	G Watson	Baron G de Rothschild	9/4
1955	**Romany Air**	W Rickaby	R Day	G W Chesterman	8/1
1956	**Donald**	W Rickaby	J Jarvis	Lord Rosebery	Evens
1957	**Flying Flag II**	F Palmer	J Laumain	H Baranez	11/4
1958	**French Beige**	G Littlewood	H Peacock	R F Dennis	3/1
1959	**Vacarme**	A Breasley	N Bertie	M Goudchaux	7/2
1960	**Parthia**	W H Carr	C Boyd-Rochfort	Sir H de Trafford	10/11
1961	**Apostle**	E Hide	S Ingham	Mrs D Montagu	13/2
1962	**Pardao**	W H Carr	C Boyd-Rochfort	Mrs C O Iselin	2/1
1963	**Gaul**	G Lewis	P Hastings-Bass	Lord Sefton	2/1
1964	**Oncidium**	A Breasley	G Todd	Lord H de Walden	7/2
1965	**Goupi**	G Lewis	S Ingham	H Wingate	10/11
1966	**Hermes**	G Starkey	J Oxley	R D Hollingsworth	7/1
1967	**Dancing Moss**	G Lewis	R Fetherstonhaugh	D R Drewery	6/1

		Jockey	Trainer	Owner	Odds
1968	**Riboccare**	L Piggott	J Tree	C W Engelhard	100/7
1969	**High Line**	J Mercer	D Candy	W Barnett	5/2
1970	**High Line**	J Mercer	D Candy	W Barnett	100/30
1971	**High Line**	J Mercer	D Candy	W Barnett	8/11
1972	**Irvine**	L Piggott	H Cecil	C St George	3/1
1973	**Parnell**	W Carson	B van Cutsem	R More O'Ferrall	4/6
1974	**Petty Officer**	E Hide	A Budgett	Mrs J Benskin	7/2
1975	**Blood Royal**	L Piggott	M V O'Brien	Mrs G Getty II	11/10
1976	**Bright Finish**	L Piggott	M Stoute	J H Whitney	2/1
1977	**Grey Baron**	G Baxter	B Hobbs	P Parnell	6/4
1978	**Buckskin**	J Mercer	H Cecil	D Wildenstein	2/1
1979	**Nicholas Bill**	P Waldron	H Candy	W Barnett	5/1
1980	**Ardross**	L Piggott	K Prendergast	Exors of P Prendergast	5/6
1981	**Centroline**	P Waldron	H Candy	R Barnett	6/4
1982	**Little Wolf**	W Carson	W R Hern	Lord Porchester	9/4
1983	**Karadar**	W R Swinburn	M Stoute	HH Aga Khan	Evens
1984	**Old Country**	D McHargue	L Cumani	Mrs O Abegg	5/2
1985	**Tale Quale**	T Ives	H Candy	R Barnett	25/1
1986	**Valuable Witness**	P Eddery	J Tree	S Niarchos	4/5
1987	**Buckley**	R Cochrane	L Cumani	Mrs A L Chapman	8/1
1988	**Kneller**	P Eddery	H Cecil	C St George	4/6
1989	**Weld**	B Raymond	W Jarvis	Lord H de Walden	Evens
1990	**Great Marquess**	L Dettori	H Cecil	C St George	3/1
1991	**Further Flight**	M Hills	B Hills	S Wingfield Digby	7/4
1992	**Further Flight**	M Hills	B Hills	S Wingfield Digby	4/6

Run over 2 miles 2 furlongs 1873-1958 and 1 mile 4 furlongs 1959-1962.

Run at Nottingham in 1940 over 2 miles 4 furlongs.

The Supreme Stakes

If there was a prize for rather pretentiously named races, then Goodwood must take the palm. The Waterford Candelabra became the Prestige, the Valdoe, the Select, the Harroways and then Supreme. None of these appellations are really justified for Group Three events, and it is a particular shame in the case of the former Harroways, which is the name of the raceground where Goodwood was founded in 1801 after the Earl of Egremont forbade the races organised by the Sussex Militia in the grounds of his seat at Petworth Park.

Although the fields for the Supreme have been strong, the race has yet to live up to its name, a typical winner being the inconsistent *Osario* in 1991.

Run at Goodwood over 7 furlongs First Run 1981 Group 3

		Jockey	Trainer	Owner	Odds
1981	**Belmont Bay**	L Piggott	H Cecil	D Wildenstein	10/11
1982	**Hays**	G Starkey	G Harwood	A Salman	11/8
1983	**Larionov**	B Taylor	J Winter	Mrs P D Rossdale	14/1
1984	**Sarab**	T Quinn	P Cole	Newgate Ltd	15/8
1985	**Efisio**	W Carson	J Dunlop	Mrs M Landi	9/4
1986	**Sarab**	T Quinn	P Cole	F Salman	7/4
1987	**Asteroid Field**	M Hills	B Hills	Sheikh Mohammed	7/1
1988	**Fair Judgement**	J Reid	M V O'Brien	Sheikh Mohammed	7/4
1989	**Kerita**	P Eddery	R F Johnson Houghton	HH Aga Khan	7/1
1990	**Anshan**	P Eddery	J Gosden	Sheikh Mohammed	2/1
1991	**Osario**	M Roberts	R Hannon	J G Davis	20/1
1992	**Hazaam**	W R Swinburn	M Stoute	Sheikh Mohammed	7/1

Run as the Harroways Stakes in 1982-1986

The Princess Royal Stakes

The Princess Royal Stakes was founded in 1946 and named in honour of the daughter of King George V. Today we are fortunate to have another Princess Royal who's interest in racing and equestrianism generally is paramount, for whatever the politics of racing, it is evident that the sport has principally been maintained by royal patronage over the years.

A Group Three race for mares and fillies of three years old and upwards which have not won a Group One race, the fields have usually been more useful than distinguished, with some amusing names including *Nicky Nook, Mother Goose, Tenacity* and *Romantica* in the list of winners. The interesting case is *Snow Bride*, who certainly qualified to run when winning in 1989, but subsequently became a Group One winner when awarded the Oaks on the disqualification of *Aliysa* some eighteen months after the classic was run. As the Princess Royal is run in October, and the Oaks in June, *Snow Bride* was a Group One winner in retrospect at the time.

Run at Ascot over 1 mile 4 furlongs for fillies & mares   First Run 1946   Group 3

		Jockey	Trainer	Owner	Odds
1946	**Mehmany**	G Richards	Frank Butters	HH Aga Khan	Evens
1947	**Mombasa**	K Gethin	V Smyth	D Miln	13/8
1948	**Angelola**	E Britt	C Boyd-Rochfort	HM The King	9/4
1949	**Jet Plane**	G Richards	J Lawson	Lord Astor	7/4
1950	**Divinalh**	W R Johnstone	C Semblat	M Boussac	9/4
1951	**Verse**	C Smirke	N Cannon	J V Rank	7/1
1952	**Nicky Nook**	G Richards	P Beasley	J B Townley	9/2
1953	**Skye**	W Rickaby	J Jarvis	Lord Rosebery	3/1
1954	**Dust Storm**	E Mercer	G Colling	W A G Burns	11/4
1955	**Nemora**	E Mercer	H Wragg	G Egalis	4/5
1956	**Carezza**	W R Johnstone	P Prendergast	Lady H Svejdar	6/4
1957	**Nagaika**	W H Carr	W Smyth	H J Joel	5/1
1958	**Mother Goose**	W H Carr	W Nightingall	E Littler	3/1
1959	**Rose of Medina**	L Piggott	N Murless	J R Hindley	8/13
1960	**Green Opal**	L Piggott	N Murless	G Loder	3/1
1961	**Tenacity**	A Breasley	G Richards	Mrs W Riley-Smith	6/4
1962	**Romantica**	W Williamson	H Wragg	G A Oldham	5/2
1963	**Vhairi**	L Piggott	P Beasley	H Leggat	11/4
1964	**French Possession**	D Smith	G Brooke	R F Dennis	15/8
1965	**Bracey Bridge**	L Piggott	N Murless	M Wickham-Boynton	6/4
1966	**Predicament**	R Hutchinson	J Dunlop	Duke of Norfolk	1/6
1967	**Bamboozle**	L Piggott	F Armstrong	E C Bland	7/2
1968	**No Race**				
1969	**Seventh Bride**	D Keith	P Walwyn	L Freedman	6/1
1970	**Heavenly Thought**	J Mercer	W R Hern	Lord Rotherwick	20/1
1971	**Hill Circus**	G Lewis	N Murless	G A Pope Jnr	7/4
1972	**Attica Meli**	G Lewis	N Murless	L Freedman	6/4
1973	**Mandera**	L Piggott	J Tree	Mrs C W Engelhard	4/1
1974	**Shebeen**	G Baxter	B Hobbs	Sir K Butt	9/4
1975	**Shebeen**	G Baxter	B Hobbs	Sir K Butt	2/1
1976	**No Race**				
1977	**Aloft**	G Starkey	B Hills	Mrs J Burkhardt	20/1
1978	**Trillionaire**	P Eddeery	J Dunlop	N B Hunt	28/1
1979	**Alia**	S Raymont	J Tree	K Abdulla	10/1
1980	**Karamita**	L Piggott	M Stoute	HH Aga Khan	15/8
1981	**Flighting**	B Rouse	J Dunlop	A J Struthers	10/1
1982	**Believer**	B Rouse	J Dunlop	A Budgett	33/1
1983	**Sylph**	T Ives	J Tree	K Abdulla	9/2
1984	**One Way Street**	L Piggott	H Cecil	L Freedman	10/1
1985	**Free Guest**	R Guest	L Cumani	Fittocks Stud Ltd	9/4
1986	**Tashtiya**	W R Swinburn	M Stoute	HH Aga Khan	5/4
1987	**No Race**				
1988	**Banket**	B Rouse	J Dunlop	Lord Halifax	4/1
1989	**Snow Bride**	S Cauthen	H Cecil	M Al-Maktoum	15/8
1990	**Narwala**	P Eddery	L Cumani	HH Aga Khan	7/4
1991	**Always Friendly**	A Munro	H Candy	F Salman	5/1
1992	**Cunning**	L Dettori	L Cumani	Fittocks Stud Ltd	8/13

Run at Newbury in 1960 and 1963.

The Cornwallis Stakes

A Group Three affair for two-year-olds over five furlongs in October, the Cornwallis is an ideal test for potentially top-class sprinters who take on the best in their three-year-old season, possibly via some of the attractive races staged in the Paris autumn season, notably the Prix de l'Abbaye.

Some winners have had classic pretensions, such as *Cawston's Pride* and *Hallgate* in recent years, but invariably an unsurprising inability to stay has necessitated a return to sprint distances, usually with success. An unhappy exception was *Cawston's Pride*, a brilliant filly defeated by her temperament, but during a brief career as a broodmare produced *Cawston's Clown*, winner of the Coventry Stakes in 1976. The race was used as a modicum of a gamble by the Irish in 1992, when the winner *Up and At 'em*, received quite unnecessary attention from his rider's whip when the race was safely secured. No animal deserves to be flogged for pecuniary gain.

Run at Ascot over 5 furlongs for 2 year-olds   First Run 1946   Group 3

		Jockey	Trainer	Owner	Odds
1946	**Golden Hackle**	A Wragg	O Bell	Miss D Paget	3/1
1947	**Straight Play**	H Packham	H Smyth	R I Sainsbury	100/8
1948	**Burnt Brown**	M Beary	C Boyd-Rochfort	Lord Portal	7/4
1949	**Stella Polaris**	E Britt	M Marsh	J Musker	9/2
1950	**Par Avion**	J Thompson	W Bellerby	Mrs I Moss	11/10

		Jockey	Trainer	Owner	Odds
1951	**Sir Phoenix**	K Gethin	P Thrale	J D C Brownlow	100/8
1952	**Prince Canarina**	C Elliott	H Leader	Lady Bullough	9/4
1953	**Plainsong**	J Mercer	H Leader	D de Rougemont	6/1
1954	**Lark**	W Rickaby	J Jarvis	Lord Rosebery	3/1
1955	**Roman Conquest**	D Smith	G Brooke	Mrs D Matthews	5/4
1956	**Star Magic**	W H Carr	D Candy	L Hordern	2/1
1957	**Abelia**	L Piggott	N Murless	B Hornung	5/4
1958	**Rosalba**	J Mercer	R J Colling	J J Astor	11/4
1959	**Sing Sing**	D Smith	J F Watts	W Stirling	4/6
1960	**Favorita**	L Piggott	N Murless	Mrs V Lilley	11/10
1961	**Prince Tor**	W Rickbay	R Featherstonaugh	S Joel	–
1962	**Fair Astronomer**	G Bougoure	J Lenehan	J J Dolan	7/2
1963	**Derring-Do**	A Breasley	A Budgett	Mrs H Renshaw	8/13
1964	**Spaniard's Mount**	A Breasley	F N Winter	B Schmidt-Bodner	9/4
1965	**Tin King**	L Piggott	R F Johnson Houghton	C W Engelhard	8/11
1966	**Green Park**	J Lindley	J Tree	C W Engelhard	5/1
1967	**So Blessed**	F Durr	P Davey	D Robinson	4/5
1968	**No Race**				
1969	**Huntercombe**	A Barclay	A Budgett	H Renshaw	3/1
1970	**Cawston's Pride**	B Taylor	F Maxwell	L B Hall	4/5
1971	**Deep Diver**	W Williamson	P Davey	D Robinson	4/7
1972	**The Go-Between**	J Lindley	J Hindley	Mrs D Helmann	8/1
1973	**Splashing**	G Lewis	N Murless	Mrs D Wigan	5/1
1974	**Paris Review**	G Lewis	J Tree	J H Whitney	10/1
1975	**Western Jewel**	P Eddery	G Hunter	G Insoll	7/4
1976	**No Race**				
1977	**Absalom**	M L Thomas	R Jarvis	Mrs C Alington	5/6
1978	**Greenland Park**	W Carson	W Hastings-Bass	Greenland Park Ltd	7/4
1979	**Hanu**	G Starkey	A Breasley	R Tikkoo	14/1
1980	**Pushy**	J Mercer	H Cecil	Lord Tavistock	13/8
1981	**My Lover**	B Raymond	M Jarvis	R Milsom	2/1
1982	**Tatibah**	J Reid	R F Johnson Houghton	Mrs A Hoffberger	16/1
1983	**Petorius**	W R Swinburn	M Stoute	Mrs I Phillips	7/4
1984	**Doulab**	A Murray	H Thomson Jones	H Al-Maktoum	11/4
1985	**Hallgate**	K Hodgson	Miss S Hall	Hippodromo Racing	3/1
1986	**Singing Steven**	B Rouse	R Hannon	S Bennett	7/1
1987	**No Race**				
1988	**Hadif**	P Eddery	R Armstrong	H Al-Maktoum	9/1
1989	**Argentum**	J Reid	L J Holt	K F Khan	9/2
1990	**Mujadil**	S Cauthen	R Armstrong	H Al-Maktoum	9/4
1991	**Magic Ring**	A Munro	P Cole	F Salman	10/11
1992	**Up and At 'em**	B J Coogan	J Coogan	Mrs A Hughes	11/2

Run over 6 furlongs in 1946-1947 and 1 mile 1948-1956.
Run at Kempton in 1956, 1960 and 1963

***Cawston's Pride*, seen here winning the Queen Mary Stakes at Ascot in 1970, was one of the winners of the Cornwallis Stakes who had classic pretension.**

The Challenge Stakes

Founded in 1878 as 'The First Great Challenge Stakes', the race was run over six furlongs until 1977, when the distance was increased to seven parts of a mile. Two-year-olds were eligible to run up to 1985, when the present conditions were introduced.

Since the distance was extended, some notable milers have had their say including *Kris,* probably the best at that trip since *Brigadier Gerard, Noalchoholic* and the 2,000 Guineas winner *Mystiko.*

The tradition of parades for major races has surely become obsolete in the era of television coverage on an exhaustive scale when race-goers can see the action from every bar, enclosure and hospitality tent. It seems pointless to subject nervous juveniles and three-year-olds to an unneccessary ordeal, and many a top-class race has been lost in the parade, especially on hot or humid days.

Mystiko became very warm, before the Guineas and before the Derby, but at Newmarket he had the length of the Rowley Mile to recover, far from the madding crowd. At Epsom, no such chance was afforded him and although he patently failed to stay the mile and a half, what ever hope he may have had was literally evaporated before the off.

His subsequent victory in the Challenge Stakes, for which there is no parade, was some compensation.

Run at Newmarket over 7 furlongs First Run 1878 Group 2

		Jockey	Trainer	Owner	Odds
1878	**Lollypop**	H Custance	R Marsh	Duke of Hamilton	3/1
1879	**Rayon d'Or**	J Goater	T Jennings	Comte F de Lagrange	11/4
1880	**Thebais**	J Gallon	A Taylor Snr	W S Crawfurd	5/4
1881	**Nellie**	F Barrett	J Hayhoe	L de Rothschild	4/1
1882	**Energy**	H Luke	R Sherrard	W S Crawfurd	5/1
1883	**Busybody**	G Fordham	M Dawson	Lord Falmouth	7/4
1884	**Energy**	F Archer	A Taylor Snr	Duchess of Montrose	1/20
1885	**Modwena**	F Barrett	M Dawson	Duke of Portland	8/1
1886	**Mephisto**	T Cannon	T Jennings Jnr	Price Soltykoff	8/11
1887	**Kilwarlin**	W T Robinson	J Jewitt	Lord Rodney	1/3
1888	**Sandal**	W T Robinson	J Jewitt	Lord Calthorpe	4/6
1889	**Heaume**	T Loates	A Hayhoe	Baron L de Rothschild	Evens
1890	**Mephisto**	F Webb	T Jennings	Prince Soltykoff	5/4
1891	**Sir Frederick Roberts**	M Cannon	Robert Sherwood	J T North	–
1892	**St Angelo**	J Watts	Jos Day	H Milner	–
1893	**Dame President**	F Finlay	P Peck	Sir J Blundell Maple	5/1
1894	**Whittier**	F Finlay	J Waugh	Mr Russel	Evens
1895	**Amandier**	T Loates	A Hayhoe	Baron L de Rothschild	2/1
	Chasseur	F Pratt	J Ryan	J Ryan	7/1
1896	**Kilcock**	J Watts	S Darling	J H Greer	4/7
1897	**Kilcock**	J Watts	S Darling	J H Greer	w.o.
1898	**Heir Male**	O Madden	A Gilbert	Sir M FitzGerald	8/1
1899	**Fosco**	T Loates	A Hayhoe	L de Rothschild	w.o.
1900	**Sonatura**	C Jenkins	F W Day	Sir E Cassel	–
1901	**Sonatura**	W Halsey	F W Day	Sir E Cassel	9/2
1902	**Chacornac**	J H Martin	F Leach	J R Keene	6/1
1903	**Chacornac**	H Jones	F Leach	H J King	4/7
1904	**Delaunay**	O Madden	P P Gilpin	P P Gilpin	10/11
1905	**Thrush**	H Randall	E Robson	J Orr-Ewing	4/7
1906	**Rocketter**	W Higgs	S Darling	J H Greer	–
1907	**Succour**	H Jones	R H Dewhurst	R Kincaid-Smith	4/5
1908	**Succour**	H Randall	R H Dewhurst	R Kincaid-Smith	–
1909	**Sir Martin**	D Maher	J Cannon	L Winans	5/4
1910	**Jack Snipe**	W Higgs	S Darling	Lord Ilchester	11/4
1911	**Iron Mask II**	J H Martin	A J Joyner	H P Whitney	–
1912	**Hornet's Beauty**	W Huxley	F Leach	Sir W Cooke	2/1
1913	**Borrow**	D Maher	A J Joyner	H P Whitney	13/8
1914	**Hornet's Beauty**	F Fox	F Barling	Sir W Cooke	5/2
1915	**Golden Sun**	F Bullock	C Peck	J B Joel	–
1916	**King's Joker**	F Bullock	R Day	J B Joel	Evens
1917	**Phalaris**	F Rickaby	G Lambton	Lord Derby	2/9
1918	**Phalaris**	B Carslake	G Lambton	Lord Derby	w.o.
1919	**Diadem**	S Donoghue	G Lambton	Lord D'Abernon	2/9
1920	**Poltava**	S Donoghue	P Linton	W Raphael	6/4
1921	**Sunblaze**	B Carslake	H S Persse	L Robinson	11/8
1922	**Two Step**	H Jones	A Taylor Jnr	S Tattersall	–
1923	**Black Gown**	E Gardner	V Beatty	G C H Davy	2/1
1924	**Drake**	M Beary	H Cottrill	Mrs S Whitburn	6/4
1925	**Twelve Pointer**	H Beasley	H S Persse	Duke of Westminster	11/10
1926	**Diomedes**	J Leach	H Leader	S W Beer	2/5
1927	**Highborn II**	J Childs	O Bell	Sir H Cunliffe-Owen	1/6
1928	**Nice Prospect**	C Elliott	C Peck	J B Joel	8/13
1929	**Reedsmouth**	H Beasley	H S Persse	Lord Wyfold	4/6
1930	**Soloptic**	J Childs	C Boyd-Rochfort	C L Mackean	9/2
1931	**Portlaw**	H Beasley	H S Persse	Sir A Bailey	5/6
1932	**The Divot**	R Dick	E Stedall	C Blundell	7/4

		Jockey	Trainer	Owner	Odds
1933	**Myrobella**	G Richards	F Darling	Lord Lonsdale	8/15
1934	**Mate**	F Fox	I Anthony	A C Bostwick	10/1
1935	**Bellacose**	P Beasley	R J Colling	P Dunne	5/6
1936	**Solerina**	R A Jones	H Cottrill	Mrs C L Mackean	3/1
1937	**Ipsden**	S Wragg	O Bell	Lady Ludlow	6/4
1938	**Old Reliance**	E Smith	J Jarvis	Sir J Jarvis	Evens
1939/44	**No Race**				
1945	**Royal Charger**	E Smith	J Jarvis	Sir J Jarvis	6/1
1946	**Daily Double**	D Smith	C Boyd-Rochfort	Lady Z Wernher	–
1947	**Closeburn**	G Richards	N Murless	R White	4/7
1948	**The Cobbler**	G Richards	N Murless	G Loder	6/4
1949	**Combined Operations**	W H Carr	R Lawson	R Foster	5/1
1950	**Bob Cherry**	D Smith	H S Persse	Lord Sefton	100/30
1951	**Hard Sauce**	G Richards	N Bertie	Sir V Sassoon	4/5
1952	**Agitator**	G Richards	N Cannon	J A Dewar	9/4
1953	**Parakeet**	E Mercer	R Poole	T Holland-Martin	11/2
1954	**Princely Gift**	L Piggott	N Murless	Sir V Sassoon	2/1
1955	**Royal Palm**	W Snaith	F Armstrong	J Gerber	6/5
1956	**Coronation Year**	D Smith	A Thomas	A Thomas	8/1
1957	**Welsh Abbot**	E Hide	W Nightingall	Sir W Churchill	13/8
1958	**Logarithm**	E Hide	A Budgett	J Hobhouse	9/4
1959/67	**No Race**				
1967	**Forlorn River**	L Piggott	W A Stephenson	Mrs W A Richardson	6/4
1968	**Mountain Call**	L Piggott	B van Cutsem	I E Kornberg	2/1
1969	**Burglar**	R Hutchinson	J Dunlop	H D H Wills	9/2
1970	**Realm**	B Taylor	J Winter	R Boucher	13/8
1971	**Joshua**	J Mercer	A Kerr	G R Rickman	11/8
1972	**Abergwaun**	L Piggott	M V O'Brien	C St George	2/1
1973	**Boldboy**	J Mercer	W R Hern	Lady Beaverbrook	8/13
1974	**New Model**	P Eddery	H Cecil	C d'Alessio	100/30
1975	**Be Tuneful**	A Kimberley	J Hindley	Mrs J Hindley	7/2
1976	**Star Bird**	J P Lefevre	P Lallie	Sir E McAlpine	20/1
1977	**Boldboy**	W Carson	W R Hern	Lady Beaverbrook	11/8
1978	**Spence Bay**	J Mercer	S McGrath	Mrs R McGrath	8/1
1979	**Kris**	J Mercer	H Cecil	Lord H de Walden	4/9
1980	**Moorestyle**	L Piggott	R Armstrong	Moores Furnishings Ltd	2/5
1981	**Moorestyle**	L Piggott	R Armstrong	Moores Furnishings Ltd	8/15
1982	**Noalcoholic**	G Duffield	G Pritchard-Gordon	W du Pont III	5/2
1983	**Salieri**	L Piggott	H Cecil	C St George	13/8
1984	**Brocade**	G Starkey	G Harwood	G Leigh	5/4
1985	**Efisio**	W Carson	J Dunlop	Mrs M Landi	9/4
1986	**Lucky Ring**	W Carson	W R Hern	Sir M Sobell	20/1
1987	**Asteroid Field**	M Hills	B Hills	Sheikh Mohammed	4/1
1988	**Salse**	M Roberts	H Cecil	Sheikh Mohammed	4/6
1989	**Distant Relative**	M Hills	B Hills	W Said	Evens
1990	**Sally Rous**	G Carter	G Wragg	Sir P Oppenheimer	11/4
1991	**Mystiko**	M Roberts	C Brittain	Lady Beaverbrook	9/4
1992	**Selkirk**	R Cochrane	I Balding	G Strawbridge	5/6

Run over 6 furlongs 1878-1976

The Dewhurst Stakes

The race was founded in 1875 by Tom Gee, owner of the Dewhurst Stud in Sussex, who sponsored the first running as a race to point to horses with classic potential. In this Mr Gee was extraordinary successful, as the first winner was *Kisber* who went on to win the Derby and have a cottage named after him in Doris Street, Newmarket. The second winner, *Chamant* was destined to take the 2,000 Guineas; the third *Pilgrimage* triumphed in both the Guineas races and the fourth *Wheel of Fortune* won the 1,000 Guineas and the Oaks.

This pattern was continued until the first World War, but slackened in the twenties and thirties with the honorable exception of *Hyperion* while *Pinza* and *Crepello* in the mid-fifties were the most notable horses to win until *Nijinsky* and *Mill Reef*.

The seventies were to be a vintage period with *Grundy, Wollow* and *The Minstrel,* only to be followed by the blatant scandal of the failure of *Gorytus* in 1982. Although nothing was ever proven, the horse ran a lifeless race and was a spent force as a three-year-old.

El Gran Senor, Generous and *Dr Devious* have helped to maintain the prestige of the Dewhurst in recent years, and in spite of the modern trend to give potentially classic animals a 'quiet' first season, remains the top juvenile contest in the Calendar. *Zafonic's* win in 1992 was the most emphatic for many years, and he went into winter quarters the shortest-priced favourite for the 2,000 guineas since *Tudor Minstrel* in 1947.

Australian jockey Rae Johnstone, rode *Marsyad* to victory in the 1951 Dewhurst Stakes.

Run at Newmarket over 7 furlongs for 2 year-old colts & fillies First Run 1875 Group 1

	Jockey	Trainer	Owner		Odds
1875	**Kisber**	C Maidment	J Hayhoe	A Baltazzi	10/1
1876	**Chamant**	J Goater	T Jennings	Comte F de Lagrange	9/4
1877	**Pilgrimage**	H Constable	J Cannon	Lord Lonsdale	9/2
1878	**Wheel of Fortune**	F Archer	M Dawson	Lord Falmouth	1/2
1879	**Grace Cup**	E Rossiter	C Blanton	A C Barclay	Evens
1880	**Bal Gal**	F Archer	M Dawson	Lord Falmouth	3/1
1881	**Dutch Oven**	F Archer	M Dawson	Lord Falmouth	1/3
1882	**Ladislas**	Hampton	T Jennings Jnr	C J Lefevre	10/1
1883	**Queen Adelaide**	F Webb	J Jewitt	Sir J Willoughby	20/1
1884	**Paradox**	F Archer	J Porter	W B Cloete	2/1
1885	**Ormonde**	F Archer	J Porter	Duke of Westminster	4/11
1886	**Reve d'Or**	C Wood	A Taylor Snr	Duke of Beaufort	100/30
1887	**Friar's Balsam**	T Cannon	J Porter	Sir F Johnstone	3/100
1888	**Donovan**	F Barrett	G Dawson	Duke of Portland	30/100
1889	**Le Nord**	F Barrett	A Hayhoe	Baron L de Rothschild	4/7
1890	**Corstorphine**	F Rickaby	M Dawson	Lord Rosebery	2/1
1891	**Orme**	G Barrett	J Porter	Duke of Westminster	6/100
1892	**Meddler**	M Cannon	J Cannon	G A Baird	4/7
1893	**Matchbox**	M Cannon	J Porter	Lord Alington	8/11
1894	**Raconteur**	T Loates	J Jewitt	H McCalmont	2/1
1895	**St Frusquin**	F Pratt	A Hayhoe	L de Rothschild	4/7
1896	**Vesuvian**	M Cannon	J Porter	Sir F Johnstone	4/1
1897	**Hawfinch**	S Loates	J Porter	J Porter	
1898	**Frontier**	M Cannon	J Porter	Duke of Westminster	100/15
1899	**Democrat**	J F Sloan	J Huggins	Lord W Beresford	2/5
1900	**Lord Bobs**	S Loates	W Waugh	Sir J Blundell Maple	100/15
1901	**Game Chick**	J Reiff	J Huggins	E Loder	6/1
1902	**Rock Sand**	D Maher	G Blackwell	Sir J Miller	6/4
1903	**Henry the First**	O Madden	A Gilbert	J Musker	7/2
1904	**Rouge Croix**	F Bullock	J E Brewer	R H Henning	100/12
1905	**Picton**	W Higgs	G Edwards	J L Dugdale	7/1
1906	**My Pet II**	O Madden	D Waugh	W Raphael	9/4
1907	**Rhodora**	W Bullock	F McCabe	R Croker	100/7
1908	**Bayardo**	D Maher	A Taylor Jnr	A W Cox	75/20
1909	**Lemberg**	D Maher	A Taylor Jnr	A W Cox	4/11
1910	**King William**	F Wootton	G Lambton	Lord Derby	11/10
	Phryxus	D Maher	A Taylor Jnr	A W Cox	5/1
1911	**White Star**	F Wootton	C Morton	J B Joel	2/1
1912	**Louvois**	W Saxby	D Waugh	W Raphael	7/4
1913	**Kennymore**	A Whalley	A Taylor Jnr	Sir J Thursby	4/1
1914	**Let Fly**	S Donoghue	W T Robinson	W Hall-Walker	15/8
1915	**Atheling**	F Bullock	R C Dawson	E Hulton	11/10
1916	**Telephus**	S Donoghue	A Taylor Jnr	A W Cox	10/1
1917	**My Dear**	S Donoghue	A Taylor Jnr	A W Cox	11/10
1918	**Knight of Blyth**	A Whalley	F Leach	F Willey	2/1
1919	**Prince Galahad**	B Carslake	H S Persse	L Robinson	4/1
1920	**No Race**				
1921	**Lembach**	F Bullock	R Day	E Moore	Evens
1922	**Hurry Off**	B Carslake	H S Persse	Duke of Westminster	5/1
1923	**Salmon Trout**	G Hulme	R C Dawson	HH Aga Khan	4/1
1924	**Zionist**	V Smyth	R C Dawson	HH Aga Khan	1/4
1925	**Review Order**	H Beasley	H S Persse	Lord Barnby	4/11
1926	**Money Maker**	C Elliott	Lord G Dundas	Mrs C Beatty	8/1
1927	**Toboggan**	T Weston	Frank Butters	Lord Derby	4/9
1928	**Brienz**	R A Jones	J Lawson	S Tattersall	7/4
1929	**Grace Dalrymple**	F Fox	F Darling	Lord Dewar	5/2
1930	**Sangre**	H Beasley	H S Persse	W Chanler	11/10
1931	**Firdaussi**	M Beary	R C Dawson	HH Aga Khan	11/10
1932	**Hyperion**	T Weston	G Lambton	Lord Derby	100/7
1933	**Mrs Rustom**	M Beary	Frank Butters	HH Aga Khan	5/4
1934	**Hairan**	F Fox	Frank Butters	HH Aga Khan	8/13
1935	**Bala Hissar**	C Smirke	Frank Butters	HH Aga Khan	5/2
1936	**Sultan Mohamed**	G Richards	Frank Butters	Prince Aly Khan	20/1
1937	**Manorite**	E Smith	P Thrale	D Kennedy	20/1
1938	**Casanova**	P Beasley	C Boyd-Rochfort	Lady Z Wernher	8/11
1939	**No Race**				
1940	**Fettes**	G Richards	F Darling	Mrs R Macdonald-Buchanan	3/1
1941	**Canyonero**	T Carey	W Nightingall	F Bezner	13/8
1942	**Umiddad**	D Smith	Frank Butters	HH Aga Khan	6/4
1943	**Effervescence**	G Richards	R J Colling	Mrs M Hartigan	6/1
1944	**Paper Weight**	A Wragg	Frank Butters	Sir A Butt	11/8
1945	**Hypericum**	D Smith	C Boyd-Rochfort	HN The King	4/7
1946	**Migoli**	G Richards	Frank Butters	HH Aga Khan	5/1
1947	**Pride of India**	J Sime	J E Watts	H J Joel	5/2
1948	**Royal Forest**	G Richards	N Murless	R Macdonald-Buchanan	5/4
1949	**Emperor II**	C Elliott	C Semblat	M Boussac	7/2

Lord Derby's *Hyperion* won the 1932 Dewhurst Stakes.

		Jockey	Trainer	Owner	Odds
1950	**Turco II**	W H Carr	C Boyd-Rochfort	W Woodward	11/8
1951	**Marsyad**	W R Johnstone	C Semblat	M Boussac	7/1
1952	**Pinza**	G Richards	N Bertie	Sir V Sassoon	Evens
1953	**Infatuation**	K Gethin	V Smyth	Sir M McAlpine	11/8
1954	**My Smokey**	D Smith	J F Watts	Mrs D Robinson	7/2
1955	**Dacian**	W Snaith	H Cottrill	Maj L B Holliday	7/1
1956	**Crepello**	L Piggott	N Murless	Sir V Sassoon	1/2
1957	**Torbella III**	A Breasley	W Clout	Comte de Chambure	9/4
1958	**Billum**	E Hide	C Elsey	W Humble	6/1
1959	**Ancient Lights**	E Smith	T E Leader	H J Joel	100/7
1960	**Bounteous**	J Sime	P Beasley	Mrs H Leggat	2/1
1961	**River Chanter**	J Mercer	G Todd	R Sigtia	100/30
1962	**Follow Suit**	L Piggott	N Murless	G Loder	10/1
1963	**King's Lane**	J Sime	S Hall	L Chamberlain	10/1
1964	**Silly Season**	G Lewis	I Balding	P Mellon	13/2
1965	**Pretendre**	R Hutchinson	J Jarvis	J Lilley	11/2
1966	**Dart Board**	D Smith	G Richards	M Sobell	10/1
1967	**Hametus**	F Durr	W Nightingall	Lady Beaverbrook	100/9
1968	**Ribofilio**	L Piggott	R F Johnson Houghton	C W Engelhard	8/11
1969	**Nijinsky**	L Piggott	M V O'Brien	C W Engelhard	1/3
1970	**Mill Reef**	G Lewis	I Balding	P Mellon	4/7
1971	**Crowned Prince**	L Piggott	B van Cutsem	F McMahon	4/9
1972	**Lunchtime**	P Eddery	P Walwyn	R Poole	11/8
1973	**Cellini**	L Piggott	M V O'Brien	C St George	40/85
1974	**Grundy**	P Eddery	P Walwyn	C Vittadini	6/5
1975	**Wollow**	G Dettori	H Cecil	C d'Alessio	6/4
1976	**The Minstrel**	L Piggott	M V O'Brien	R Sangster	6/5
1977	**Try My Best**	L Piggott	M V O'Brien	R Sangster	4/6
1978	**Tromos**	J Lynch	B Hobbs	G Cambanis	11/4
1979	**Monteverdi**	L Piggott	M V O'Brien	R Sangster	15/8

		Jockey	Trainer	Owner	Odds
1980	**Storm Bird**	P Eddery	M V O'Brien	R Sangster	4/5
1981	**Wind and Wuthering**	P Waldron	H Candy	R Cyzer	11/1
1982	**Diesis**	L Piggott	H Cecil	Lord A de Walden	2/1
1983	**El Gran Senor**	P Eddery	M V O'Brien	R Sangster	7/4
1984	**Kala Dancer**	G Baxter	B Hanbury	R Tikkoo	20/1
1985	**Huntingdale**	M Hills	J Hindley	Mrs P Threlfall	12/1
1986	**Ajdal**	W R Swinburn	M Stoute	Sheikh Mohammed	4/9
1987	**No Race**				
1988	**Prince of Dance**	W Carson	N Graham	Sir M Sobell	6/4
	Scenic	M Hills	B Hills	Sheikh Mohammed	33/1
1989	**Dashing Blade**	J Matthias	I Balding	J C Smith	8/1
1990	**Generous**	T Quinn	P Cole	F Salman	50/1
1991	**Dr Devious**	W Carson	P Chapple-Hyam	L Gaucci	3/1
1992	**Zafonic**	P Eddery	A Fabre	K Abdulla	10/11

The Rockfel Stakes

The race is named in honour of *Rockfel*, a dark brown filly with a plain head and a lightish neck, described by some observers as lacking in quality. However, her breeding combined blue blood with a tough distaff line, being by the Derby winner *Felstead* out of a former selling plater *Rockliffe*, who ultimately won ten races in the course of three seasons of hard racing.

Rockfel was home bred by her owner Sir Hugo Cunliffe-Owen and like her dam started her career in selling races before going on to win the 1,000 Guineas and the Oaks in 1938.

Horses had to prove their worth in those days, and it is hard to imagine modern winners of the Rockfel Stakes starting their racing life in selling company. The best winner in recent years was *Musical Bliss*, who went on to take the 1,000 Guineas in 1989.

Run at Newmarket over 7 furlongs for 2 year-old fillies First Run 1981 Group 3

		Jockey	Trainer	Owner	Odds
1981	**Top Hope**	W R Swinburn	M Stoute	R Cowell	12/1
1982	**Saving Mercy**	B Taylor	J Hindley	M Benacerrat	14/1
1983	**Mahogany**	J Mercer	C Nelson	Mrs W Tulloch	4/1
1984	**Kashi Lagoon**	B Raymond	B Hanbury	R Tikkoo	9/2
1985	**Tralthee**	L Piggott	L Cumani	A Clore	9/1
1986	**At Risk**	S Cauthen	H Cecil	Mrs J W Hanes	4/1
1987	**No Race**	–			
1988	**Musical Bliss**	W R Swinburn	M Stoute	Sheikh Mohammed	85/40
1989	**Negligent**	M Hills	B Hills	Mrs J M Corbett	100/30
1990	**Crystal Gazing**	L Dettori	L Cumani	I Goldsmith	5/6
1991	**Musicale**	P Eddery	H Cecil	R Sangster	7/4
1992	**Yawl**	D Holland	B Hills	R D Hollingsworth	9/4

The Champion Stakes

In racing, no one race can be regarded as a 'championship', with the possible exception of the Derby. Champions establish themselves over a period of time and several races, earning the accolade by defeating the best around at the time.

However, it must be said that the Champion Stakes is well named, as a glance at the roll of honour will reveal. first run in 1877, five classic winners had scored by the end of the century. Many more were to follow, and since the war the Champion Stakes has become very much a fillies' race, in keeping with the physiology of the distaff side which often brings about a considerable improvement in performance in the autumn. Eighteen of the thirty-five races between 1957 and 1991 went to fillies.

But the finest winner in recent years must be a colt to be called a champion if any animal could. *Brigadier Gerard*, winner of the Champion Stakes for the second year running in 1972, was recording his seventeenth and final victory from eighteen starts, and the cheers that rang out over Newmarket Heath as 'the Brigadier' returned to unsaddle will be remembered for many years to come.

Run at Newmarket over 1 mile 2 furlongs First Run 1877 Group 1

		Jockey	Trainer	Owner	Odds
1877	**Springfield**	T Cannon	J Ryan	J H Houldsworth	11/8
1878	**Jannette**	F Archer	M Dawson	Lord Falmouth	4/6
1879	**Rayon d'Or**	J Goater	T Jennings	Comte F de Lagrange	5/4
1880	**Robert the Devil**	E Rossiter	C Blanton	C Brewer	11/10
1881	**Bend Or**	F Archer	R Peck	Duke of Westminster	4/6
1882	**Tristan**	F Archer	T Jennings Jnr	C J Lefevre	2/1
1883	**Tristan**	F Webb	T Jennings Jnr	C J Lefevre	7/4
1884	**Tristan**	F Webb	T Jennings Jnr	C J Lefevre	4/6
1885	**Paradox**	F Archer	J Porter	W B Cloete	12/100
1886	**Ormonde**	F Archer	J Porter	Duke of Westminster	1/100

		Jockey	Trainer	Owner	Odds
1887	**Bendigo**	J Watts	C Jousiffe	H T Barclay	1/3
1888	**Friar's Balsam**	G Barrett	J Porter	Sir F Johnstone	60/100
1889	**Gold**	D Hunt	T Jennings	Prince Soltykoff	100/8
1890	**Amphion**	T Cannon	J Chandler	Gen Byrne	4/7
1891	**Orion**	G Barrett	J Porter	Duke of Westminster	5/6
1892	**Orme**	G Barrett	J Porter	Duke of Westminster	1/3
1893	**Le Nicham**	T Loates	A Hayhoe	Baron L de Rothschild	1/4
1894	**La Fleche**	J Watts	R Marsh	Baron M de Hirsch	1/3
1895	**Laveno**	F Finlay	J Ryan	J H Houldsworth	4/9
1896	**Labrador**	M Cannon	J Porter	Duke of Westminster	9/2
1897	**Velasquez**	C Wood	W Walters Jnr	Lord Rosebery	1/2
1898	**Velasquez**	C Wood	C Wood	Lord Rosebery	4/11
1899	**Dieudonne**	M Cannon	R Marsh	Duke of Devonshire	7/1
1900	**Solitaire**	L Reiff	F W Day	Sir E Cassel	5/2
1901	**Osboch**	D Maher	R Marsh	Lord Wolverton	11/8
1902	**Veles**	J H Martin	Robert Sherwood Jnr	Sir R W Griffith	4/1
1903	**Sceptre**	F W Hardy	A Taylor Jnr	W Bass	1/33
1904	**Bachelor's Button**	W Halsey	C Peck	S B Joel	2/1
1905	**Pretty Polly**	D Maher	P P Gilpin	E Loder	2/5
1906	**Polymelus**	D Maher	C Peck	S B Joel	1/5
1907	**Galvani**	B Dillon	P P Gilpin	E Loder	100/30
1908	**Llangwm**	D Maher	W Waugh	B Walker	6/100
1909	**Bayardo**	D Maher	A Taylor Jnr	A W Cox	4/9
1910	**Lemberg**	D Maher	A Taylor Jnr	A W Cox	12/100
1911	**Lemberg**	F Wootton	A Taylor Jnr	A W Cox	w.o.
1912	**Stedfast**	F Wootton	G Lambton	Lord Derby	15/100
1913	**Tracery**	A Whalley	J Watson	A Belmont	5/6
1914	**Hapsburg**	C Foy	W Halsey	Sir E Cassel	5/6
1915	**Let Fly**	F Rickaby	F Leader	W Hall-Walker	7/1
1916	**Clarissimus**	F Bullock	W Waugh	Lord Falmouth	6/4
1917	**Gay Crusader**	S Donoghue	A Taylor Jnr	A W Cox	9/100
1918	**My Dear**	S Donoghue	A Taylor Jnr	A W Cox	11/10
1919	**Buchan**	J Brennan	A Taylor Jnr	W Astor	2/1
1920	**Orpheus**	F Leach Jnr	F Leach	Sir H Cunliffe-Owen	9/2
1921	**Orpheus**	H Gray	F Leach	Sir H Cunliffe-Owen	Evens
1922	**Franklin**	S Donoghue	R C Dawson	Lord Carnarvon	9/4
1923	**Ellangowan**	C Elliott	J Jarvis	Lord Rosebery	11/4
1924	**Pharos**	T Weston	G Lambton	Lord Derby	Evens
1925	**Picaroon**	F Bullock	A Taylor Jnr	A R Cox	–
1926	**Warden of the Marshes**	J Childs	F Darling	Lord Lonsdale	6/4
1927	**Asterus**	C Elliott	S H Darling	M Boussac	11/2
1928	**Fairway**	T Weston	Frank Butters	Lord Derby	4/9
1929	**Fairway**	T Weston	Frank Butters	Lord Derby	2/7
1930	**Rustom Pasha**	H Wragg	R C Dawson	HH Aga Khan	6/1
1931	**Goyescas**	C Elliott	B Jarvis	M Boussac	5/1
1932	**Cameronian**	G Richards	F Darling	J A Dewar	11/10
1933	**Dastur**	M Beary	Frank Butters	HH Aga Khan	2/5
	Chatelaine	G Richards	F Templeman	E Thornton-Smith	9/2
1934	**Umidwar**	F Fox	Frank Butters	HH Aga Khan	5/4
1935	**Wychwood Abbot**	R Perryman	T E Leader	O Watney	4/6
1936	**Wychwood Abbot**	R Perryman	T E Leader	O Watney	10/11
1937	**Flares**	P Beasley	C Boyd-Rochfort	W Woodward	Evens
1938	**Rockfel**	H Wragg	O Bell	Sir H Cunliffe-Owen	2/1
1939	**No Race**				
1940	**Hippius**	E Smith	J Jarvis	Lord Rosebery	100/8
1941	**Hippius**	E Smith	J Jarvis	Lord Rosebery	6/4
1942	**Big Game**	G Richards	F Darling	HM The King	11/10
1943	**Nasrullah**	G Richards	Frank Butters	HH Aga Khan	100/30
1944	**Hycilla**	W Nevett	C Boyd-Rochfort	W Woodward	10/1
1945	**Court Martial**	C Richards	J Lawson	Lord Astor	4/11
1946	**Honeyway**	E Smith	J Jarvis	Lord Milford	8/1
1947	**Migoli**	G Richards	Frank Butters	HH Aga Khan	Evens
1948	**Solar Slipper**	E Smith	H Smyth	J McGrath	6/1
1949	**Djeddah**	C Elliott	C Semblat	M Boussac	4/6
1950	**Peter Flower**	W Rickaby	J Jarvis	Lord Rosebery	3/1
1951	**Dynamiter**	C Elliott	C Semblat	M Boussac	100/8
1952	**Dynamiter**	C Elliott	J Glynn	M Boussac	4/5
1953	**Nearula**	E Britt	C Elsey	W Humble	4/1
1954	**Narrator**	F Barlow	H Cottrill	Maj L B Holliday	20/1
1955	**Hafiz II**	R Poincelet	A Head	HH Aga Khan	100/30
1956	**Hugh Lupus**	W R Johnstone	N Murless	Lady Vernon	3/1
1957	**Rose Royale II**	J Massard	A Head	Prince Aly Khan	5/2
1958	**Bella Paola**	G Lequeux	F Mathet	F Dupre	4/1
1959	**Petite Etoile**	L Piggott	N Murless	Prince Aly Khan	2/11
1960	**Marguerite Vernaut**	E Camici	U Penco	Marchesa della Rochetta	9/4
1961	**Bobar II**	M Garcia	R Corme	Mme G Courtois	100/8

***Swiss Maid*, ridden by Greville Starkey, wins the 1978 Champion Stakes from *Hawaiian Sound* (Piggott up) on the right and *Gunner B* (ridden by Joe Mercer) on the left.**

		Jockey	Trainer	Owner	Odds
1962	**Arctic Storm**	W Williamson	J Oxx	Mrs E Carroll	6/1
1963	**Hula Dancer**	J Deforge	E Pollet	Mme P Widener	9/2
1964	**Baldric II**	W Pyers	E Fellows	Mrs H E Jackson	7/2
1965	**Silly Season**	G Lewis	I Balding	P Mellon	100/8
1966	**Pieces of Eight**	L Piggott	M V O'Brien	Comtesse de la Valdene	5/4
1967	**Reform**	A Breasley	G Richards	M Sobell	100/30
1968	**Sir Ivor**	L Piggott	M V O'Brien	R Guest	8/11
1969	**Flossy**	J Deforge	F Boutin	H Berlin	100/7
1970	**Lorenzaccio**	G Lewis	N Murless	C St George	100/7
1971	**Brigadier Gerard**	J Mercer	W R Hern	Mrs J Hislop	1/2
1972	**Brigadier Gerard**	J Mercer	W R Hern	Mrs J Hislop	1/3
1973	**Hurry Harriet**	J Cruguet	P Mullins	M Thorp	33/1
1974	**Giacometti**	L Piggott	H R Price	C St George	4/1
1975	**Rose Bowl**	W Carson	R F Johnson Houghton	Mrs C W Engelhard	11/2
1976	**Vitiges**	P Eddery	P Walwyn	Mme M Laloun	22/1
1977	**Flying Water**	Y Saint-Martin	A Penna	D Wildenstein	9/1
1978	**Swiss Maid**	G Starkey	P Kelleway	M Fine	9/1
1979	**Northern Baby**	P Paquet	F Boutin	Mme A d'Estainville	9/1
1980	**Cairn Rouge**	A Murray	M Cunningham	D Brady	6/1
1981	**Vayrann**	Y Saint-Martin	F Mathet	HH Aga Khan	15/2
1982	**Time Charter**	W Newnes	H Candy	R Barnett	9/2
1983	**Cormorant Wood**	S Cauthen	B Hills	R J McAlpine	18/1
1984	**Palace Music**	Y Saint-Martin	P-L Biancone	N B Hunt	18/1
1985	**Pebbles**	P Eddery	C Brittain	Sheikh Mohammed	9/2
1986	**Triptych**	A Cruz	P-L Biancone	A Clore	4/1
1987	**Triptych**	A Cruz	P-L Biancone	A Clore	6/5
1988	**Indian Skimmer**	M Roberts	H Cecil	Sheikh Mohammed	8/15
1989	**Legal Case**	R Cochrane	L Cumani	Sir G White	5/1
1990	**In The Groove**	S Cauthen	D Elsworth	B Cooper	9/2
1991	**Tel Quel**	T Jarnet	A Fabre	Sheikh Mohammed	16/1
1992	**Rodrigo de Triano**	L Piggott	P Chapple-Hyam	R Sangster	11/8

The Cesarewitch Handicap

Known to countless cockney punters as the Caesar-Witch, the race bears the anglicised name of the Tsarevich, later Emperor Alexander II of Russia, and titled in his honour after the future Czar had donated £300 to the Jockey Club.

Now the second leg of the autumn double, although originally the first, the Cesarewitch was founded in the same year as the Cambridgeshire, and like the latter was in the early days a happy hunting ground for classic winners stumped for choice at the back-end. Derby winner *Bloomsbury* was second in 1840, and the Epsom hero *St Gatien* won in 1884. As late as 1935 the Oaks winner *Quashed* was running in long distance handicaps, finishing third at Newmarket.

Often described as a race starting in Cambridgeshire and finishing in Suffolk, when in fact the horses simply pull up in Suffolk, the distance and testing nature of the course make the Cesarewitch a tough race for the top weights. The best performances have been *Willonyx* carrying 9st 5lb in 1911, *Grey of Falloden* (9st 6lb in 1964), *John Cherry* (9st 13lb in 1976), *Centurion* (9st 8lb in 1978, a heavy burden for a three-year-old) and *Double Dutch* (9st 10lb in 1989). *Vintage Crop* landed a gamble for the Irish when winning under 9st 6lb in 1992.

Run at Newmarket over 2 miles 2 furlongs   First Run 1839   Handicap

		Jockey	Trainer	Owner	Odds
1839	**Cruiskeen**	N Stagg	–	Lord Milltown	3/1
1840	**Clarion**	J Robinson	–	S Herbert	100/3
1841	**Illiona**	R West	J B Day	Lord Palmerston	4/1
1842	**Arcanus**	T Day	J B Day	F Clarke	10/1
1843	**Corranna**	W Boyce	W Boyce	R G Townley	20/1
1844	**Faugh-a-Ballagh**	H Bell	J Forth	E J Irwin	6/1
1845	**The Baron**	E Flatman	J Scott	G Watts	5/1
1846	**Wits End**	T Donaldson	J Day	S Wreford	30/1
1847	**Caurouch**	G Abdale	J Osborne	W Disney	30/1
1848	**The Cur**	S Rogers	J Rogers	W S Crawfurd	5/1
1849	**Legerdemain**	E Hiett	J Scott	Lord Stanley	10/1
1850	**Glauca**	J Chapple	W Dilly	G Payne	66/1
1851	**Mrs Taft**	S Steggles	J Rogers	C Bevill	–
1852	**Weathergauge**	J Wells	T Parr	T Parr	4/1
1853	**Haco**	G Palmer	W Day	A Williams	50/1
1854	**Muscovite**	E Flatman	W Dilly	C Greville	3/1
1855	**Mr Sykes**	F Bates	T Flintoff	E Clark	15/2
1856	**Vengeance**	T Aldcroft	E Elliott	Mr Edwards	9/1
1857	**Pryoress**	G Fordham	W Brown	R Ten Broeck	30/1
1858	**Rocket**	H Custance	–	G Lambert	14/1
1859	**Artless**	Drew	J Godding	Sir W Booth	5/6
1860	**Dulcibella**	A Sadler	W Day	W Day	6/1
1861	**Audrey**	H Custance	–	W Bevill	100/1
1862	**Hartington**	J Grimshaw	W Treen	J Smith	14/1
1863	**Lioness**	H Covey	M Dawson	J Merry	5/2
1864	**Thalestris**	J Grimshaw	W Day	Lord Coventry	7/1
1865	**Salpinctes**	F Scorey	H Goater	Capt King	11/2
1866	**Lecturer**	S Hibberd	J Fobert	H Wilkinson	9/1
1867	**Julius**	T Chaloner	M Dawson	Duke of Newcastle	12/1
1868	**Cecil**	R Wyatt	J Nightingall	Maj Pemberton	5/1
1869	**Cherie**	F Webb	J Godding	R C Naylor	20/1
1870	**Cardinal York**	H Parry	Jos Dawson	F Pryor	20/1
1871	**Corisande**	C Maidment	J Hayhoe	Baron M de Rothschild	12/1
1872	**Salvanos**	F Archer	M Dawson	J Radcliff	11/1
1873	**King Lud**	T Bruckshaw	J Cannon	Lord Lonsdale	1,000/45
1874	**Aventuriere**	T Glover	A Taylor Snr	Lord Ailesbury	25/1
1875	**Duke of Parma**	E Rossiter	C Blanton	Prince Soltykoff	4/1
1876	**Rosebery**	F Archer	–	J Smith	100/14
1877	**Hilarious**	J Macdonald	F Bates	R Jardine	100/30
1878	**Jester**	H Luke	John Dawson	R C Naylor	20/1
1879	**Chippendale**	W McDonald	T Wadlow	Lord Bradford	22/1
1880	**Robert the Devil**	T Cannon	C Blanton	C Brewer	9/1
1881	**Foxhall**	W McDonald	W Day	J R Keene	9/2
1882	**Corrie Roy**	C Wood	R Sherrard	W S Crawfurd	9/2
1883	**Don Juan**	E Martin	W Goater	G Lambert	11/2
1884	**St Gatien**	C Wood	Robert Sherwood	J Hammond	9/1
1885	**Plaisanterie**	Hartley	–	H Bouy	100/15
1886	**Stone Clink**	W Glover	M Dawson	R C Vyner	100/3
1887	**Humewood**	W T Robinson	J Jewitt	Lord Rodney	85/20
1888	**Tenebreuse**	T Cannon	–	P Aumont	10/1
1889	**Primrose Day**	W Wood	W Goater	W Goater	100/9
1890	**Sheen**	F Webb	T Jennings	Prince Soltykoff	1,000/30
1891	**Ragimunde**	R Chaloner	A Taylor Snr	Duke of Beaufort	25/1
1892	**Burnaby**	J Doyle	E J Hobbs	E Hobson	7/1
1893	**Red Eyes**	T Loates	J Cannon	C Morbey	6/1
	Cypria	W Pratt	T Jennings Jnr	T Jennings Jnr	66/1

As late as 1935, Oaks winner *Quashed* was running in long-distance handicaps and finished third at Newmarket.

		Jockey	Trainer	Owner	Odds
1894	**Childwick**	W Bradford	P Peck	Sir J Blundell Maple	4/1
1895	**Rockdove**	C Ward	J Jewitt	C J Blake	10/1
1896	**St Bris**	K Cannon	J Porter	W Low	10/1
1897	**Merman**	J Sharples	F Webb	Mr Jersey	100/7
1898	**Chaleureux**	O Madden	G Blackwell	Sir J Miller	75/20
1899	**Scintillant**	F Wood	W A Jarvis	R A Oswald	6/1
1900	**Clarehaven**	W Halsey	P P Gilpin	L Neumann	6/1
1901	**Balsarroch**	M Aylin	J Ryan	J H Houldsworth	25/1
1902	**Black Sand**	K Cannon	L Alvarez	J Buchanan	8/1
1903	**Grey Tick**	F Hunter	A Taylor Jnr	W Bass	20/1

Fet, the 1936 winner of the Cesarewitch, is just beaten here by *Elmstead*, with E.Smith up, in a two-mile stayers' handicap at Gatwick in 1937.

		Jockey	Trainer	Owner	Odds
1904	**Wargrave**	J Sharples	J H Batho	H Bottomley	5/1
1905	**Hammerkop**	B Dillon	P P Gilpin	E Loder	100/14
1906	**Mintagon**	C Trigg	W I'Anson Jnr	J Hill	5/1
1907	**Demure**	F Wootton	J E Brewer	W Clark	4/1
1908	**Yentoi**	F Fox	F Darling	Lady de Bathe	100/6
1909	**Submit**	J Plant	C Morton	J B Joel	33/1
1910	**Verney**	F Wootton	P P Gilpin	L Neumann	7/1
1911	**Willonyx**	W Higgs	S Darling	C E Howard	9/2
1912	**Warlingham**	G Clout	T Goodgames	R S Sievier	33/1
1913	**Fiz-Yama**	F Herbert	J G Morris	C Wadia	50/1
1914	**Troubadour**	C Dickens	W Halsey	Sir E Cassel	66/1
1915	**Son-in-Law**	F Bullock	R Day	Sir A Bailey	100/9
1916	**Sanctum**	S Donoghue	H S Persse	W Raphael	9/4
1917	**Furore**	H Robbins	V Tabor	H Ellis	100/7
1918	**Air Raid**	O Madden	A Taylor Jnr	W M Cazalet	25/1
1919	**Ivanhoe**	A Whalley	H Cottrill	J White	100/6
1920	**Bracket**	S Donoghue	R Day	Mrs G Robinson	8/1
1921	**Yutoi**	H Jelliss	Lord G Dundas	Mrs R L Burnley	100/8
1922	**Light Dragoon**	T Pryor	E Harper	F Forester	7/1
1923	**Rose Prince**	G Archibald	S H Darling	A K Macomber	25/1
1924	**Charley's Mount**	T Pryor	R C Dawson	HH Aga Khan	100/1
1925	**Forseti**	H Beasley	S H Darling	A K Macomber	20/1
1926	**Myra Gray**	L Read	J Scott	J Davis	50/1
1927	**Eagles Pride**	J Dines	E Martin	F T Halse	9/1
1928	**Arctic Star**	R Perryman	V Tabor	Sir M Wilson	9/1
1929	**West Wicklow**	C Richards	L Todd	D Leahy	15/2
1930	**Ut Majeur**	M Beary	R C Dawson	HH Aga Khan	100/8
1931	**Noble Star**	F Fox	L Cundell	F Cundell	100/6
1932	**Nitsichin**	M Beary	P Thrale	D Kennedy	10/1
1933	**Seminole**	F Fox	C Boyd-Rochfort	J Widener	100/6
1934	**Enfield**	J Sirett	C Boyd-Rochfort	M Field	7/1
1935	**Near Relation**	E Smith	Frank Butters	Sir A Butt	22/1
1936	**Fet**	A Richardson	H Hedges	S Freeman	10/1
1937	**Punch**	S Wragg	V Tabor	T Westhead	17/1
1938	**Contrevent**	A Tucker	H Count	Princess de Lucinge	100/7
1939	**Cantatrice II**	D Smith	Frank Butters	Sir A Butt	7/2
1940	**Hunter's Moon IV**	G Richards	F Darling	E Esmond	100/8
1941	**Filator**	S Wragg	O Bell	Lady Cunliffe-Owen	100/9
1942	**No Race**				
1943	**Germanicus**	H Wragg	H Jelliss	T Lant	6/5

		Jockey	Trainer	Owner	Odds
1944	**No Race**				
1945	**Kerry Piper**	E Britt	F Armstrong	Sir H Bruce	25/1
1946	**Monsieur l'Amiral**	H Wragg	E Charlier	H Barnard-Hankey	33/1
1947	**Whiteway**	W Evans	W Pratt	Capt D Fitzgerald	100/8
1948	**Woodburn**	E Britt	C Elsey	Lord Allendale	100/9
1949	**Strathspey**	E Smith	N Cannon	J V Rank	25/1
1950	**Above Board**	E Smith	C Boyd-Rochfort	HM The King	18/1
1951	**Three Cheers**	E Mercer	P Thrale	C Croft	17/2
1952	**Flush Royal**	W Nevett	J Fawcus	G MacLean	33/1
1953	**Chantry**	K Gethin	S Ingham	S Ingham	4/1
1954	**French Design**	D Smith	G Todd	S Banks	100/6
1955	**Curry**	P Tulk	F Armstrong	F Honour	100/6
1956	**Prelone**	E Hide	W Hide	A Allen	20/1
1957	**Sandiacre**	D Smith	W Dutton	T Farr	100/8
1958	**Morecambe**	J Sime	S Hall	J Bullock	15/2
1959	**Come to Daddy**	D Smith	W Lyde	T Farr	6/1
1960	**Alcove**	D Smith	J F Watts	Lord Derby	100/30
1961	**Avon's Pride**	E Smith	W R Hern	Maj L B Holliday	100/8
1962	**Golden Fire**	D Yates	D Marks	G Ridley	25/1
1963	**Utrillo**	J Sime	H R Price	J Gerber	100/8
1964	**Grey of Falloden**	J Mercer	W R Hern	Lord Astor	20/1
1965	**Mintmaster**	J Sime	A Cooper	E Collington	13/2
1966	**Persian Lancer**	D Smith	H R Price	Lord Belper	100/7
1967	**Boismoss**	E Johnson	M W Easterby	J Gordon-Spriggs	13/1
1968	**Major Rose**	L Piggott	H R Price	R L Heaton	9/1
1969	**Floridian**	D McKay	L Shedden	A Patchett	20/1
1970	**Scoria**	D McKay	C Crossley	J Lang	33/1
1971	**Orosio**	G Lewis	H Cecil	C St George	5/1
1972	**Cider With Rosie**	M L Thomas	S Ingham	A Mullings	14/1
1973	**Flash Imp**	T Cain	R Smyth	Mrs O Negus-Fancy	25/1
1974	**Ocean King**	T Carter	A Pitt	V Lawson	25/1
1975	**Shantallah**	B Taylor	H Wragg	R More O'Ferrall	7/1
1976	**John Cherry**	L Piggott	J Tree	J H Whitney	13/2
1977	**Assured**	P Waldron	H Candy	Mrs G Kent	10/1
1978	**Centurion**	J Matthias	I Balding	J Berry	9/2
1979	**Sir Michael**	M Rimmer	G Huffer	Cheveley Park Stud	10/1
1980	**Popsi's Joy**	L Piggott	M Haynes	V Lawson	10/1
1981	**Halsbury**	J Mercer	P Walwyn	A D G Oldrey	14/1
1982	**Mountain Lodge**	W Carson	J Dunlop	Lord Halifax	9/1
1983	**Bajan Sunshine**	B Rouse	R Simpson	P C Green	7/1
1984	**Tom Sharp**	S Dawson	W Wharton	M J Yarrow	40/1
1985	**Kayudee**	A Murray	J Fitzgerald	Kenton Utilities	7/1
1986	**Orange Hill**	R Fox	J Tree	R J McCreery	20/1
1987	**Private Audition**	G Carter	M Tompkins	P Betts (Holdings) Ltd	50/1
1988	**Nomadic Way**	W Carson	B Hills	R Sangster	6/1
1989	**Double Dutch**	W Newnes	Miss B Sanders	L Fuller	15/2
1990	**Trainglot**	W Carson	J Fitzgerald	Marquesa de Moratalla	13/2
1991	**Go South**	N Carlisle	J Jenkins	R Joachim	33/1
1992	**Vintage Crop**	W R Swinburn	D Weld	M Smurfit	5/1

Run over 2 miles 24 yards 1939-1941 and 1943

The Horris Hill Stakes

The Horris Hill was originally open to fillies, and indeed the first winner was *Lone Victress* in 1949, but as no filly had won since *Sentier* in 1968, it was decided to restrict the race to colts and geldings from 1987.

Nowadays the race is regarded as something of a classic pointer with victories by *Charlottown* and *Tirol*, winners of the Derby and 2,000 Guinea respectively. One of the best winners was *Supreme Court*, victorious in 1950 but who held no classic engagements. Nowadays, he would surely have been 'supplemented' at considerable cost, since at three years old *Supreme Court* won the White Lodge Stakes at Hurst Park, the Chester Vase, the King Edward VII Stakes at Royal Ascot and finally the Festival of Britain King George VI and Queen Elizabeth Stakes, defeating a vintage field.

In this race, his last appearance on a racecourse, he was superbly ridden by Charlie Elliott who ignored the blistering early pace dictated by his more illustrious rivals cutting each others' throats, and pounced late to win at odds of 100/9.

Run at Newbury over 7 furlongs and 60 yards for 2 year-old colts & geldings First Run 1949 Group 3

		Jockey	Trainer	Owner	Odds
1949	**Lone Victress**	T Hawcroft	W Nightingall	R W Hall	1/3
1950	**Supreme Court**	C Elliott	E Williams	Mrs T Lilley	5/2
1951	**H.V.C.**	T Gosling	R Smyth	Mrs H V Cozens	3/1
1952	**Baldaquin**	W H Carr	I Anthony	Lady Z Wernher	100/6
1953	**Court Splendour**	G Richards	N Murless	Mrs T Lilley	2/1

		Jockey	Trainer	Owner	Odds
1954	**Royal Palm**	A Breasley	F Armstrong	J Gerber	11/10
1955	**Clarification**	W Rickaby	V Smyth	Sir M McAlpine	8/1
1956	**Persuader**	E Smith	H Cottrill	Maj L B Holliday	5/6
1957	**Alcide**	W H Carr	C Boyd-Rochfort	Lord H de Trafford	5/1
1958	**Seascape**	E Smith	T E Leader	H J Joel	1/7
1959	**Ironic**	W H Carr	D Candy	L A Hordern	100/8
1960	**Gallant Knight**	E Smith	T E Leader	H J Joel	4/5
1961	**Valentine**	D Smith	G Brooke	D McCalmont	9/4
1962	**Scholar Gypsy**	R Hutchinson	R Jarvis	K Butt	10/1
1963	**Atbara**	A Breasley	G Richards	R Macdonald-Buchanan	15/8
1964	**Foothill**	J Mercer	W R Hern	T Egerton	7/1
1965	**Charlottown**	J Lindley	J M Gosden	Lady Z Wernher	11/10
1966	**Alcan**	B Raymond	H Cottrill	Mrs S Joel	13/2
1967	**Dalry**	R Poincelet	P Prendergast	J R Mullion	11/8
1968	**Sentier**	A Breasley	K Cundell	R Deen	11/2
1969	**Double First**	J Lindley	J Tree	C W Engelhard	8/1
1970	**Good Bond**	A Murray	H R Price	J Etherington	11/2
1971	**Disguise**	L Piggott	B Hills	Lord Porchester	3/1
1972	**Long Row**	E Eldin	R Jarvis	Mrs F Allen	11/2
1973	**Welsh Harmony**	E Eldin	D Smith	J Pearce	8/1
1974	**Corby**	P Eddery	P Walwyn	R Hibbert	11/2
1975	**State Occasion**	P Eddery	P Walwyn	Mrs D McCalmont	4/1
1976	**Fair Season**	G Starkey	I Balding	J Berry	15/2
1977	**Derrylin**	E Eldin	D Smith	Lady Sefton	5/2
	Persian Bold	L Piggott	A Ingham	R Vahabzadeh	5/2
1978	**Kris**	J Mercer	H Cecil	Lord H de Walden	5/6
1979	**Super Asset**	J Mercer	H Cecil	M Riordan	Evens
1980	**Kalaglow**	G Starkey	G Harwood	J Vanner	3/1
1981	**Montekin**	P Eddery	J Dunlop	P Winfield	9/4
1982	**No Race**				
1983	**Elegant Air**	S Cauthen	I Balding	P Mellon	4/1
1984	**Efisio**	W Carson	J Dunlop	Mrs M Landi	7/2
1985	**Celtic Heir**	W Ryan	G Pritchard-Gordon	W du Pont III	20/1
1986	**Naheez**	P Eddery	D Elsworth	K Al-Said	5/2
1987	**Glacial Storm**	C Asmussen	B Hills	R Sangster	14/1
1988	**Gouriev**	M Roberts	P Makin	R W Dilley	20/1
1989	**Tirol**	P Eddery	R Hannon	John Horgan	6/1
1990	**Sapieha**	W R Swinburn	J Fanshawe	Baron G de Geer	5/2
1991	**Lion Cavern**	S Cauthen	A Fabre	Sheikh Mohammed	4/9
1992	**Beggarman Thief**	R Cochrane	J Gosden	L Knight	5/1

The St Simon Stakes

Imaginatively framed as a race for three-year-olds and upwards which have not won a Group One race since their juvenile days, the St Simon has proved to be a rewarding consolation stakes for some extremely good horses, even if none have been able to match the supremacy of the bay horse who gave his name to the event.

St Simon was not entered for any of the classic races, but won the Ascot Gold Cup by twenty lengths in 1884 and the Goodwood Cup by the same distance. He won nine races in all and enjoyed the rare distinction of being one of the few horses to 'cart' Fred Archer on the Newmarket gallops. At stud he sired the winners of 571 races worth £553,158 including the Derby winners *Persimmon* and *Diamond Jubilee*. His trainer, Mat Dawson who trained six Derby winners always maintained that he had trained only one good horse in his life; *St Simon*.

Run at Newbury over 1 mile 4 furlongs First Run 1969 Group 3

		Jockey	Trainer	Owner	Odds
1969	**Rangong**	G Lewis	N Murless	Lady Sassoon	7/2
1970	**Politico**	G Lewis	N Murless	Mrs O Phipps	8/13
1971	**Frascati**	B Taylor	N Murless	H J Joel	2/1
1972	**Knockroe**	E Eldin	P Nelson	V McCalmont	11/2
1973	**Ballyhot**	B Taylor	J Winter	D Prenn	20/1
1974	**Never Return**	W Carson	R Armstrong	Mrs T Hardin	100/30
1975	**Dakota**	A Barclay	S Hall	G Reed	11/8
1976	**Mart Lane**	B Raymond	S McGrath	S McGrath	8/1
1977	**Hot Grove**	W Carson	R F Johnson Houghton	Lord Leverhulme	2/1
1978	**Obraztsovy**	B Taylor	H R Price	H Demetriou	9/4
1979	**Main Reef**	P Eddery	H Cecil	H J Joel	100/30
1980	**Shining Finish**	S Cauthen	J Tree	V Stein	5/1
1981	**Little Wolf**	G Sexton	W R Hern	Lord Porchester	7/4
1982	**No Race**				
1983	**Jupiter Island**	P Robinson	C Brittain	S Threadwell	3/1

		Jockey	Trainer	Owner	Odds
1984	**Gay Lemur**	G Baxter	B Hobbs	Lady E Rosebery	10/1
1985	**Shardari**	W R Swinburn	M Stoute	HH Aga Khan	Evens
1986	**Jupiter Island**	A Murray	C Brittain	Lord Tavistock	6/1
1987	**Lake Erie**	W R Swinburn	M Stoute	R Sangster	8/1
1988	**Upend**	R Cochrane	H Cecil	P D Player	6/1
1989	**Sesame**	G Hind	D Morley	C Spence	14/1
1990	**Down the Flag**	B Raymond	B Hanbury	M Kura	5/1
1991	**Further Flight**	M Hills	B Hills	S Wingfield Digby	6/1
1992	**Up Anchor**	A Munro	P Cole	F Salman	25/1

***St Simon*, winner of both the Ascot Gold Cup and Goodwood Cup by 20 lengths in 1884. He gave his name to an imaginatively-framed race.**

The Racing Post Trophy

Founded in 1961, the Racing Post Trophy is the last Group One race of the season. Originally called the Timeform Gold Cup and the brainchild of Phil Bull who started The Timeform organisation in the early forties the race was designed to test potentially staying two-year-olds over a mile as the traditional trials such as the Middle Park and the Coventry Stakes fell increasingly to precocity of breeding.

Despite several changes of name and sponsor, the Racing Post Trophy, known as the Observer Gold Cup from 1965, the William Hill Futurity from 1976 and taking its present title in 1989, has more than justified Bull's far-sighted design. The inaugural winner, *Miralgo*, did not win at three years old but became a top-class middle-distance performer at four, taking the Hardwicke Stakes and running second in both the Eclipse and the King George VI and the Queen Elizabeth Stakes. More importantly, two horses he defeated at Doncaster, *Hethersett* and *Larkspur* went on to win the St Leger and the Derby respectively.

The 1962 winner *Noblesse* also won the Oaks by ten lengths, *Vaguely Noble* (1967) the Prix de L'Arc de Triomphe, *High Top* (1971) the 2,000 Guineas and *Linden Tree* (1970) was inferior only to *Mill Reef* in the Derby.

It only remained for the race to throw up a Derby winner, and *Reference Point* (1986) was the animal. Trained by Henry Cecil and ridden by Steve Cauthen, who had spurned him at Doncaster and allowed Pat Eddery the ride, preferring *Suhailie*, *Reference Point* won at Epsom by one and a half lengths going away, having made all.

Run at Doncaster over 1 mile for 2 year-old colts & fillies First Run 1961 Group 1

		Jockey	Trainer	Owner	Odds
1961	**Miralgo**	W Williamson	H Wragg	G A Oldham	10/1
1962	**Noblesse**	G Bougoure	P Prendergast	Mrs J Olin	11/10
1963	**Pushful**	W H Carr	S Meaney	Maj L B Holliday	100/6
1964	**Hardicanute**	W Williamson	P Prendergast	J R Mullion	13/8
1965	**Pretendre**	R Hutchinson	J Jarvis	J Lilley	6/1
1966	**Ribocco**	L Piggott	R F Johnson Houghton	C W Engelhard	4/9
1967	**Vaguely Noble**	W Williamson	W Wharton	L B Holliday	8/1
1968	**The Elk**	W Pyers	J Tree	Miss M Sheriffe	10/1
1969	**Approval**	D Keith	H Cecil	Sir H de Trafford	5/1
1970	**Linden Tree**	D Keith	P Walwyn	Mrs D McCalmont	25/1
1971	**High Top**	W Carson	B van Cutsem	Sir J Thorn	11/2
1972	**Noble Decree**	L Piggott	B van Cutsem	N B Hunt	8/1
1973	**Apalachee**	L Piggott	M V O'Brien	J Mulcahy	Evens
1974	**Green Dancer**	F Head	A Head	Mme P Wertheimer	7/2
1975	**Take Your Place**	G Dettori	H Cecil	C d'Alessio	4/1
1976	**Sporting Yankee**	P Eddery	P Walwyn	William Hill Racing	9/2
1977	**Dactylographer**	P Eddery	P Walwyn	P Niarchos	100/30
1978	**Sandy Creek**	C Roche	C Collins	A McClean	15/1
1979	**Hello Gorgeous**	J Mercer	H Cecil	D Wildenstein	11/8
1980	**Beldale Flutter**	P Eddery	M Jarvis	A Kelly	14/1
1981	**Count Pahlen**	G Baxter	B Hobbs	Mrs A Villar	25/1
1982	**Dunbeath**	L Piggott	H Cecil	M Riordan	4/7
1983	**Alphabatim**	G Starkey	G Harwood	K Abdulla	9/2
1984	**Lanfranco**	L Piggott	H Cecil	C St George	100/30
1985	**Bakharoff**	G Starkey	G Harwood	K Abdulla	2/1
1986	**Reference Point**	P Eddery	H Cecil	L Freedman	4/1
1987	**Emmson**	W Carson	W R Hern	Sir Michael Sobell	7/1
1988	**Al Hareb**	W Carson	N Graham	H Al-Maktoum	100/30
1989	**Be My Chief**	S Cauthen	H Cecil	P Burrell	4/7
1990	**Peter Davies**	S Cauthen	H Cecil	C St George	2/1
1991	**Seattle Rhyme**	C Asmussen	D Elsworth	H Senn	2/1
1992	**Armiger**	P Eddery	H Cecil	K Abdulla	5/4

Run at Newcastle in 1989

Run as the Timeform Gold Cup 1961-1964, the Observer Gold Cup 1965-1975 and the William Hill Futurity 1976-1988.

The November Handicap

'Fing's Aint What They Used To Be' in the words of the musical comedy song, and that is certainly true of the November Handicap, originally the Manchester November Handicap and run at the Castle Irwell course which closed in 1963. Founded in 1876, in its heyday the race was one of the great gambles on the dying day of the season, matched only by the Lincolnshire Handicap which had started proceedings seven months before. The fact that the latter was usually run in freezing conditions with no form available and the former invariably took place in a dense fog with little of the running visible, probably speaks volumes about the sagacity of the punter, but while the Lincoln has retained a good deal of its status, the November Handicap is now little more than run-of-the mill.

However, the early days provided some notable races. The 1902 winner *St Maclou* had beaten *Sceptre* in the Lincoln, in 1935 *Free Fare* used the race as a stepping stone to victory in the Champion Hurdle in 1937 and twice the November Handicap has provided a champion jockey with his farewell victory, *Las Vegas* doing the honours for Harry Wragg in 1946 and *Bold Rex* likewise for Joe Mercer in 1985.

Perhaps the most remarkable achievement was recorded by *Operatic Society* in 1959. The eventual winner of thirty races from seventy starts, he was set to carry 8st 9lb as a three-year-old in a field of forty-nine, charged the tapes and unseated his rider, Ken Gethin, ran lose for a mile and when reunited with Ken Gethin won the race by a length.

Run at Manchester over 1 mile 4 furlongs First Run 1876 Handicap

		Jockey	Trainer	Owner	Odds
1876	**Polonaise**	A Dodge	J Perren	J Bowes	5/2
1877	**Hopbloom**	W Chesterman	T Goddard	Duke of Montrose	4/1
1878	**Belphoebe**	H Jeffery	G Bloss	Lord Hartington	3/1
1879	**Mars**	J E Jones	H Hall	W Brown	25/1
1880	**Madame du Barry**	H Morgan	W I'Anson Jnr	C Perkins	12/1
1881	**Gladstone**	C Bowman	J Porter	Lord Alington	7/1
1882	**Boswell**	A F Lemaire	C Archer	Lord Ellesmere	100/1
1883	**Corrie Roy**	C Wood	J Porter	Sir F Johnstone	4/1
1884	**Keir**	J Watts	A Taylor Snr	Duchess of Montrose	5/2
1885	**Raffaello**	H Luke	O Ginistrelli	O Ginistrelli	50/1
1886	**Stourhead**	E Martin	A Taylor Snr	A Taylor Snr	11/4
1887	**Carlton**	G Barrett	A Taylor Snr	Lord E Somerset	20/1
1888	**Claymore**	F Allsopp	J Humphreys	Lord Howe	20/1
1889	**Fallow Chat**	H Luke	M Dawson	R C Vyner	100/6
1890	**Parlington**	S Loates	A Taylor Snr	Duke of Beaufort	6/1
1891	**Lily of Lumley**	G Chaloner	W Matthews	R C Vyner	100/11
1892	**Paddy**	G W Gough	J Humphreys	Sir J Thursby	100/7
1893	**Golden Drop**	S Chandley	H Hall	M Peacock	40/1
1894	**Ravensbury**	H Barker	J Jewitt	Capt J Machell	20/1
1895	**Ivor**	H Grimshaw	W Nightingall	C Hibbert	18/1
1896	**Telescope**	K Cannon	T Wadlow	W M G Singer	7/1
1897	**Asterie**	H Chapman	Robert Sherwood Jnr	Sir R W Griffith	100/8
1898	**Chaleureux**	O Madden	G Blackwell	Sir J Miller	8/1
1899	**Proclamation**	J F Sloan	John Dawson Jnr	Lord Ellesmere	25/1
1900	**Lexicon**	T Heppell	J Cannon	B Gottschalk	40/1
1901	**Carabine**	A Adey	G Hornsby	J Collins	100/7
1902	**St Maclou**	M Cannon	C Beatty	H McCalmont	9/1
1903	**Switch Cap**	R McIntyre	S Pickering	B Ellam	25/1
1904	**No Race**				
1905	**Ferment**	T Jennings	J Watson	A Belmont	25/1
1906	**Spate**	W Saxby	E Robson	J Orr-Ewing	100/7
1907	**Baltinglass**	W Halsey	P P Gilpin	E Loder	8/1
1908	**Old China**	G McCall	J Fagan	A Bell	20/1
1909	**Admiral Togo III**	F Wootton	A Taylor Jnr	Baroness M de Brienen	100/7
1910	**The Valet**	H Jelliss	J Cannon	L Winans	9/1
1911	**Ultimus**	S Donoghue	J Fallon	A Gorham	9/4
1912	**Wagstaff**	C Foy	F Pratt	E Dresden	8/1
1913	**Dalmatian**	C Foy	J Cannon	L Winans	10/1
1914	**Wardha**	P Jones	D Peacock	D J Jardine	9/1
1915/16	**No Race**				
1917	**Planet**	E Lancaster	J Cannon	L Winans	4/1
1918	**No Race**				
1919	**King John**	E Wheatley	P P Gilpin	G Loder	13/2
1920	**Pomme de Terre**	H Robbins	Lord G Dundas	Lord Zetland	3/1
1921	**Blue Dun**	B Carslake	P W Bewicke	F Straker	7/2
1922	**Torelore**	B Carslake	H S Persse	Sir H Meux	6/1
1923	**No Race**				
1924	**Cloudbank**	M Beary	G Laing Ward	J White	100/9
1925/26	**No Race**				
1927	**Old Orkney**	S Donoghue	A H Macauley	J Murphy	8/1
1928	**Saracen**	S Donoghue	B Jarvis	J S Courtauld	6/1
1929	**Promptitude**	W Stephenson	T Rimell	J D Robertson	33/1
1930	**Glorious Devon**	G Richards	T Hogg	Lord Glanely	25/1
1931	**North Drift**	C Dowdall	M Vasey	J Downing	8/1
1932	**Hypostyle**	A Richardson	H Fergusson	Mrs C Beatty	20/1
1933	**Jean's Dream**	J Dines	D Peacock	A Boazman	20/1
1934	**Pip Emma**	E Smith	J Jarvis	Lord Rosebery	100/7
1935	**Free Fare**	S Wragg	E Gwilt	B Warner	22/1
1936	**Newton Ford**	W Nevett	M Peacock	M Boazman	100/8
1937	**Solitaire**	J Taylor	H Peacock	Sir E Hoyle	25/1
1938	**Pappageno II**	G Richards	M Hartigan	G Hartigan	100/7
1939	**Tutor**	E Smith	J Jarvis	Lord Rosebery	9/2
1940	**Beinn Dearg**	W Nevett	H Peacock	Lord Zetland	9/1
1941	**Crown Colony**	C Richards	J Lawson	Lord Glanely	100/6
1942	**Golden Boy**	D Smith	W Carr	W Carr	10/1
1943	**Mad Carew**	J Sime	P Vasey	Mrs W Robottom	33/1
1944	**Kerry Piper**	C Spares	F Armstrong	Sir H Bruce	25/1
1945	**Oatflake**	E Britt	F Armstrong	W Barnett	100/8
1946	**Las Vegas**	H Wragg	A Boyd	Sir W Chaytor	20/1
1947	**Regret**	J Walker	P Vasey	Mrs F Senior	66/1
1948	**Sports Master**	D Greening	J Beary	D Morris	20/1
1949	**Fidonia**	W H Carr	E Parker	A Halford	40/1
1950	**Coltbridge**	J Sime	S Hall	D Thomson	100/6
1951	**Good Taste**	W Nevett	S Hall	J Bullock	28/1
1952	**Summer Rain**	P Evans	J Jarvis	Lord Milford	100/6

The field gets away for the 1938 November Handicap at Manchester. The winner, *Pappageno II*, ridden by Gordon Richards, is immediately under the chimney-pot to the right centre of the picture. Richards is wearing a dark cap.

		Jockey	Trainer	Owner	Odds
1953	**Torch Singer**	D Ward	S Hall	J Hanson	40/1
1954	**No Race**				
1955	**Tearaway**	W Bentley	S Hall	J Hanson	40/1
1956	**Trentham Boy**	J Gifford	J M Gosden	T Degg	100/6
1957	**Chief Barker**	D Walker	H R Price	N Cohen	33/1
1958	**Paul Jones**	J Mercer	A Budgett	P Wright	100/7
1959	**Operatic Society**	K Gethin	C Benstead	R Agars-Walker	18/1
1960	**Dalnamein**	H Greenaway	S Hall	J Phang	28/1
1961	**Henry's Choice**	E Hide	P Beasley	W Harrison	100/8
1962	**Damredub**	M Germon	J M Gosden	T Degg	20/1
1963	**Best Song**	J Lindley	J M Gosden	H Allen	100/7
1964	**Osier**	D Smith	B van Cutsem	D Montague	20/1
1965	**Concealdem**	R Hutchinson	J M Gosden	G Taylor	100/8
1966	**Polish Warrior**	A Barclay	A Budgett	P Wright	100/6
1967	**Bugle Boy**	A Barclay	A Budgett	Miss E Rigden	22/1
1968	**Zardia**	R Still	A Vasey	S Gillat	25/1
1969	**Tintagel II**	L Piggott	R Sturdy	Mrs R Sturdy	15/2
1970	**Saraceno**	G Sexton	H Wragg	G A Oldham	15/2
1971	**Misty Light**	J Mercer	F Armstrong	R Scully	25/1
1972	**King Top**	W Carson	J Oxley	Lady Halifax	6/1
1973	**Only for Jo**	I Jenkinson	R Smyth	D Toomey	13/1
1974	**Gritti Palace**	R Fox	P Robinson	Mrs J Fisher	7/2
1975	**Mr Bigmore**	G Starkey	P Robinson	E Lambton	100/30
1976	**Gale Bridge**	B Taylor	H R Price	J Byrne	10/1
1977	**Sailcloth**	M L Thomas	W Hastings-Bass	Lord Porchester	13/2
1978	**Eastern Spring**	M Wigham	L Cumani	Miss F Vittadini	17/2
1979	**Morse Code**	P Cook	J Dunlop	A Budgett	11/2
1980	**Path of Peace**	J Bleasdale	C Thornton	Miss L Gold	14/1
1981	**Lafontaine**	G Duffield	C Brittain	Mrs J Bigg	16/1
1982	**Double Shuffle**	G Duffield	G Pritchard-Gordon	D Sieff	12/1
	Turkoman	D McKay	D Sasse	M Pote	20/1
1983	**Azir**	G Starkey	G Harwood	Yazid & Ahmed Ltd	10/1
1984	**Abu Kadra**	W R Swinburn	M Stoute	M Salem	25/1
1985	**Bold Rex**	J Mercer	J Dunlop	Lord Granard	20/1
1988	**Young Benz**	M Birch	M H Easterby	T Bennett	12/1
1989	**Firelight Fiesta**	B Raymond	B Hanbury	Mrs J Lamb	9/2
1990	**Azzaam**	W Carson	J Dunlop	H Al-Maktoum	7/1
1991	**Hieroglyphic**	W Carson	J Gosden	R Sangster	11/4
1992	**Turgenev**	D Holland	J Gosden	Sheikh Mohammed	10/1

Run at Manchester 1876-1963 except 1942-1945 when run at Pontefract.

Run over 1 mile 6 furlongs 1876-1902.

National Hunt Races

The Mackeson Gold Cup

Run in mid-November, the Mackeson was the third of the three principal National Hunt races framed specifically to cash in on the advertising available to drinks and tobacco companies as racing gained in popularity as a television sport. Costing only a fraction of the charge for comparable airtime via commercial slots, and given the couch-potato punter snug by his or her fireside relaxing from the gentle pleasances of flat racing, the appeal was obvious.

The pioneers in the field, Whitbread and Hennessy had opted for long-distance races. Sensibly, Mackeson went for a two mile chase when the race was founded in 1960. However, specialist two mile chasers are spectacular but thin on the ground, and the distance was increased to two and a half miles in 1970.

The vintage years were the early ones when *Fortria* won two of the first three runnings and the ill-fated *Dunkirk*, who broke his heart attempting to defeat *Arkle* in the King George VI Chase on Boxing Day in 1965, won under the crushing burden of 12st 7lb.

As the quality of the short-distance steeplechaser has declined with the introduction of more and more flat race bloodlines, so has the quality of the race, although the names of *Bula*, a former dual champion hurdler second in 1976 carrying 12st 1lb, and the gallant *Pegwell Bay*, tragically killed at Sandown in 1992 after a fine career, stand out.

***Dunkirk*, winner of the 1965 Mackeson Gold Cup.**

Run at Cheltenham over 2 miles 4 furlongs First Run 1960

		Jockey	Trainer	Owner	Odds
1960	**Fortria**	P Taaffe	T Dreaper	G Ansley	8/1
1961	**Scottish Memories**	C Finnegan	A Thomas	G Sanderson	9/2
1962	**Fortria**	P Taaffe	T Dreaper	G Ansley	5/1
1963	**Richard of Bordeaux**	H Beasley	F Walwyn	J Schilizzi	20/1
1964	**Super Flash**	S Mellor	F Cundell	A Wood	8/1
1965	**Dunkirk**	W Rees	P Cazalet	W Whitbread	11/10
1966	**Pawnbroker**	P Broderick	W A Stephenson	C McCulloch	7/2
1967	**Charlie Worcester**	J Gifford	H R Price	Mrs H R Price	7/1
1968	**Jupiter Boy**	E Harty	F Rimell	J Liley	9/1
1969	**Gay Trip**	T Biddlecombe	F Rimell	A Chambers	8/1
1970	**Chatham**	K White	F Rimell	C Knott	33/1
1971	**Gay Trip**	T Biddlecombe	F Rimell	A Chambers	8/1
1972	**Red Candle**	J Fox	G Vallance	Mrs C O'Shea	20/1
1973	**Skymas**	T Murphy	B Lusk	M Magee	7/1
1974	**Bruslee**	A Turnell	M Scudamore	Mrs D R Davies	2/1
1975	**Clear Cut**	D Greaves	M Camacho	J Hemingway	13/2
1976	**Cancello**	D Atkins	N Crump	W Burdon	4/1
1977	**Bachelor's Hall**	M O'Halloran	P Cundell	P Harris	11/2
1978	**Bawnogues**	C Smith	M Tate	Mrs H Lawlor	5/1
1979	**Man Alive**	R Barry	G W Richards	J Ennis	6/1

		Jockey	Trainer	Owner	Odds
1980	**Bright Highway**	G Newman	M J O'Brien	G Strawbridge	5/1
1981	**Henry Kissinger**	P Barton	D Gandolfo	J Mansworth	5/1
1982	**Fifty Dollars More**	R Linley	F Winter	Sheikh A A Khamsin	11/1
1983	**Pounentes**	N Doughty	W McGhie	W McGhie	7/1
1984	**Half Free**	R Linley	F Winter	Sheikh A A Khamsin	5/2
1985	**Half Free**	R Linley	F Winter	Sheikh A A Khamsin	9/2
1986	**Very Promising**	R Dunwoody	D Nicholson	P Green	7/1
1987	**Beau Ranger**	M Perrett	M Pipe	White Bros (Taunton)	13/2
1988	**Pegwell Bay**	P Scudamore	T Forster	A K Barlow	6/1
1989	**Joint Sovereignty**	G McCourt	P Hobbs	G J Giddy	10/1
1990	**Multum in Parvo**	N Williamson	J Edwards	A Parker	12/1
1991	**Another Coral**	R Dunwoody	D Nicholson	M R Deeley	15/2
1992	**Tippimg Tim**	C Llewellyn	N Twiston-Davies	Mrs J Mould	11/2

Run at Haydock Park in 1976

The Hennessy Gold Cup

The Hennessy was originally run at Cheltenham for the first three seasons, moving to Newbury in 1960. The decade which later became known as 'the pendulum years' may have had some unhappy social consequences but it was certainly a vintage period for great steeplechasers; *Mandarin, Mill House, Arkle* and *Stalbridge Colonist* amongst others such as *Rondetto* and *Spanish Steps*.

The Hennessy attracted them all, and there were two especially fascinating races in 1963 and 1966. In the former event, *Mill House*, the winner of the Cheltenham Gold Cup, met *Arkle* for the first time, conceding five pounds. *Mill House* won easily enough with *Arkle* only third having slipped on landing three from home, but he was never to defeat the great Irish champion again.

In 1966, *Arkle* attempted to give *Stalbridge Colonist* two and a half stone. He failed by half a length in one of the most exciting races ever seen at Newbury, largely due to a fine piece of race riding by Stan Mellor on the grey.

Today the Hennessy is firmly established as the centrepiece of the National Hunt autumn campaign much as the Whitbread Gold Cup is regarded as the spring climax. Modern breeding and climatic change have altered the winter sport considerably since the fifties but the race sponsored by the Anglo-French family firm with a racing connection going back to 1909 when *Lutteur III* won the Grand National in the Hennessy colours, remains a firm favourite with the punters even after *Sibton Abbey's* shock 40/1 win in 1992, which was a record starting price for the race.

Michael Scudamore (left) watches unhappily as *Stalbridge Colonist*, ridden by Stan Mellor, completes the final fence in the two-horse Limpsfield Handicap Chase at Lingfield in March 1966. *Stalbridge Colonist* won the Hennessey Gold Cup that year, in a vintage decade for great steeplechasers.

Run at Newbury over 3 miles 2 furlongs 82 yards First Run 1957

		Jockey	Trainer	Owner	Odds
1957	**Mandarin**	G Madden	F Walwyn	Mme K Hennessy	8/1
1958	**Taxidermist**	Mr J Lawrence	F Walwyn	Mrs P Hastings	10/1
1959	**Kerstin**	S Hayhurst	C Bewicke	G Moore	4/1
1960	**Knucklecracker**	D Ancil	D Ancil	L Marler	100/7
1961	**Mandarin**	G W Robinson	F Walwyn	Mme K Hennessy	7/1
1962	**Springbok**	G Scott	N Crump	Lord Joicey	15/2
1963	**Mill House**	G W Robinson	F Walwyn	W Gollings	15/8
1964	**Arkle**	P Taaffe	T Dreaper	Duchess of Westminster	5/4
1965	**Arkle**	P Taaffe	T Dreaper	Duchess of Westminster	1/6
1966	**Stalbridge Colonist**	S Mellor	K Cundell	R Blundell	25/1
1967	**Rondetto**	J King	R Turnell	A Mitchell	100/8
1968	**Man of the West**	G W Robinson	F Walwyn	D Drewry	20/1
1969	**Spanish Steps**	J Cook	E Courage	E Courage	7/1
1970	**Border Mask**	D Mould	P Cazalet	Mrs A Arnold	7/1
1971	**Bighorn**	D Cartwright	C Vernon Miller	J Vernon Miller	7/1
1972	**Charlie Potheen**	R Pitman	F Walwyn	Mrs B Heath	10/1
1973	**Red Candle**	J Fox	G Vallance	Mrs C O'Shea	12/1
1974	**Royal Marshall II**	G Thorner	T Forster	J Sumner	11/2
1975	**April Seventh**	A Turnell	R Turnell	Mrs B Meehan	11/1
1976	**Zeta's Son**	I Watkinson	P Bailey	M Buckley	12/1
1977	**Bachelor's Hall**	M O'Halloran	P Cundell	P Harris	11/2
1978	**Approaching**	R Champion	J Gifford	D Wigan	3/1
1979	**Fighting Fit**	R Linley	K M Oliver	Mrs L Carr	15/2
1980	**Bright Highway**	G Newman	M J O'Brien	G Strawbridge	11/4
1981	**Diamond Edge**	W Smith	F Walwyn	S Loughridge	9/2
1982	**Bregawn**	G Bradley	M Dickinson	J Kennelly	9/4
1983	**Brown Chamberlin**	J Francome	F Winter	Mrs B Samuel	7/2
1984	**Burrough Hill Lad**	J Francome	Mrs J Pitman	R S Riley	100/30
1985	**Galway Blaze**	M Dwyer	J Fitzgerald	Mrs R Formby	11/2
1986	**Broadheath**	P Nicholls	D Barons	M Marsh	6/1
1987	**Playschool**	P Nicholls	D Barons	R Cottle	6/1
1988	**Strands of Gold**	P Scudamore	M Pipe	Ind. Twine Man Co Ltd	10/1
1989	**Ghofar**	H Davies	D Elsworth	Sir H Dundas	5/1
1990	**Arctic Call**	J Osborne	O Sherwood	B T Stewart-Brown	5/1
1991	**Chatam**	P Scudamore	M Pipe	B Nolan	10/1
1992	**Sibton Abbey**	A Maguire	F Murphy	G Hubbard	40/1

Run at Cheltenham 1957-1959

April Seventh **(2), the winner, is neck and neck with *Collingwood*, who finished second, as they come to the last fence in the 1975 Hennessey Gold Cup.**

The King George VI Chase

The King George VI Chase has enjoyed an unusual history, to say the least. It was originally an optional selling chase over three miles, an option seller being a race in which an owner may enter a horse to be sold or claimed in the usual way, but might opt for the choice of running inviolate of those conditions. If so the horse was burdened with considerably more weight than those of his rivals which could change hands.

The Manor Optional Selling chase, as it was known, was still in the Calendar for the late February meeting of 1937, but events beyond the minor issues of racing were playing their part. Edward VIII had become King in January 1936, but a matrimonial and constitutional crisis forced his abdication in the December of the same year.

The Kempton Park executive had planned a race in tribute to the new monarch, only to find themselves in the same position as the manufacturers of Coronation memorabilia with 'Edward VIII' stamped all over them. Using commendable presence of commercial mind only rivalled by the Desert Orchid industry today, they turned the Manor Optional Selling Chase into the King George VI Steeplechase worth £500 to the winner, plus a piece of plate worth £50 to the successful trainer.

These prizes were not attractive even by the standards of the time, but all the top horses entered including *Golden Miller, Reynoldstown* and *Royal Mail.* In the end *Golden Miller* defected, preferring to pick up a prize of £127 by winning the Optional Selling Chase at Birmingham on the Monday before the King George. *Reynoldstown* declined as well and it was left to *Southern Hero,* a dual Scottish Grand National winner to beat *Royal Mail,* who was to win the Grand National the following month.

When racing resumed after the war the race was moved to Boxing Day from its original February date. The advantage was that it would no longer be a severe test too close to Cheltenham and Liverpool; the disadvantage the harsh mid-winter weather common at the time, and the post-Christmas sloth of a nation happy before blazing fires with 'hairs of the dog' in their hands.

The gamble paid off. The crowds turned up to have a breath of sharp winter air and a break from the relation infested homestead, and the race itself read like a Who's Who of the sport. The winner *Rowland Roy,* was trained by Fulke Walwyn, three times champion amateur jockey and rider of *Reynoldstown* to win the Grand National in 1936. *Rowland Roy's* jockey Bryan Marshall had survived a bullet in the neck during the Normandy landings and was soon to be champion jockey. The rider of the second, *Klaxton,* was Ron Smyth who rode three champion Hurdlers to victory, including the peerless *National Spirit,* while the fearless amateur Dickie Black had ridden *Fortina* to win the Cheltenham Gold Cup.

The race became a traditional Londoner's day out, as the Derby had been for generations. The list of winners abounds with equine heroes, *Cottage Rake* winning in 1948, *Manicou* for Her Majesty in 1950 and *Mandarin* in '57 and '59. Another dual winner, was *Halloween,* along with *Pendil, Captain Christy* and *Silver Buck. Wayward Lad* won three times, *Arkle* only once, but he was crippled on his second attempt.

Today it will take some years to allow *Desert Orchid's* four wins to slip into the mists of time. More significant pointers to the future are the victories of *Nupsala* in 1987 and *The Fellow* in both 1991 and 1992. Both French-trained, they represent the new breed of jumping horse to which British racing will have to adapt in the fullness of time, and perhaps a little earlier in the case of *The Fellow.*

***Desert Orchid*, ridden by Richard Dunwoody, pictured during one of his four victories in the King George VI Chase.**

Run at Kempton over 3 miles   First Run 1937

		Jockey	Trainer	Owner	Odds
1937	**Southern Hero**	J Fawcus	G Evans	J V Rank	5/4
1938	**Airgead Sios**	T McNeill	V Tabor	Sir F Towle	4/1
1939/46	**No Race**				
1947	**Rowland Roy**	B Marshall	F Walwyn	A Boley	5/1
1948	**Cottage Rake**	A Brabazon	M V O'Brien	F Vickerman	13/8

The Fellow, ridden by A.Kondrat, takes the 1992 King George VI Chase to add to his victory of the previous year.

		Jockey	Trainer	Owner	Odds
1949	**Finnure**	R Francis	G Beeby	Lord Bicester	9/2
1950	**Manicou**	B Marshall	P Cazalet	HM The Queen	5/1
1951	**Statecraft**	A Grantham	P Cazalet	Mrs J Mildmay-White	100/6
1952	**Halloween**	F Winter	W Wightman	Contessa di Sant Elia	7/4
1953	**Galloway Braes**	R Morrow	A Kilpatrick	Lady Orde	9/4
1954	**Halloween**	F Winter	W Wightman	Contessa di Sant Elia	9/2
1955	**Limber Hill**	J Power	W Dutton	J Davey	3/1
1956	**Rose Park**	M Scudamore	P Cazalet	G Lawrence	100/6
1957	**Mandarin**	G Madden	F Walwyn	Mme K Hennessy	7/1
1958	**Lochroe**	A Freeman	P Cazalet	Mrs J Mildmay-White	7/2
1959	**Mandarin**	G Madden	F Walwyn	Mme K Hennessy	5/2
1960	**Saffron Tartan**	F Winter	D Butchers	G Westmacott	5/2
1961/62	**No Race**				
1963	**Mill House**	G W Robinson	F Walwyn	W Gollings	2/7
1964	**Frenchman's Cove**	S Mellor	H Thomson Jones	S Joel	4/11
1965	**Arkle**	P Taaffe	T Dreaper	Duchess of Westminster	1/7
1966	**Dormant**	J King	J W Kendrew	Mrs D W Kendrew	10/1
1967/68	**No Race**				
1969	**Titus Oates**	S Mellor	G W Richards	P Cussins	100/30
1970	**No Race**				
1971	**The Dikler**	B Brogan	F Walwyn	Mrs D August	11/2
1972	**Pendil**	R Pitman	F Winter	Mrs C Swallow	4/5
1973	**Pendil**	R Pitman	F Winter	Mrs C Swallow	30/100
1974	**Captain Christy**	R Coonan	P Taaffe	Mrs J Samuel	5/1
1975	**Captain Christy**	G Newman	P Taaffe	Mrs J Samuel	11/10
1976	**Royal Marshall II**	G Thorner	T Forster	J Sumner	16/1
1977	**Bachelor's Hall**	M O'Halloran	P Cundell	P Harris	9/2
1978	**Gay Spartan**	T Carmody	A Dickinson	M Armstrong	3/1
1979	**Silver Buck**	T Carmody	A Dickinson	Mrs C Feather	3/1
1980	**Silver Buck**	T Carmody	M Dickinson	Mrs C Feather	9/4
1981	**No Race**				
1982	**Wayward Lad**	J Francome	M Dickinson	Mrs S Thewlis	7/2
1983	**Wayward Lad**	R Earnshaw	M Dickinson	Mrs S Thewlis	11/8
1984	**Burrough Hill Lad**	J Francome	Mrs J Pitman	R S Riley	1/2
1985	**Wayward Lad**	G Bradley	Mrs M Dickinson	Mrs S Thewlis	12/1
1986	**Desert Orchid**	S Sherwood	D Elsworth	R Burridge	16/1
1987	**Nupsala**	A Pommier	F Doumen	Mrs R Fougedoire	25/1
1988	**Desert Orchid**	S Sherwood	D Elsworth	R Burridge	1/2
1989	**Desert Orchid**	R Dunwoody	D Elsworth	R Burridge	4/6
1990	**Desert Orchid**	R Dunwoody	D Elsworth	R Burridge	9/4
1991	**The Fellow**	A Kondrat	F Doumen	Marquesa de Moratalla	10/1
1992	**The Fellow**	A Kondrat	F Doumen	Marquesa de Moratalla	Evens

The Champion Hurdle

The legendary *Brown Jack*, who in 1928 beat *Blaris*, the previous year's winner of the Champion Hurdle. This was his last race over hurdles. In this picture, Steve Donoghue is up.

Continuing the policy of giving National Hunt participants a greater chance to run in weight-for-age events inaugurated by the Gold Cup in 1924, the Cheltenham executive decided to introduce a companion race in 1927. In truth, the Champion Hurdle Challenge Trophy was a grandiose title for a race which attracted only four runners and was worth £365 to the winner; the least valuable hurdle race at the meeting; but it was a case of principle rather than cash and the winner, *Blaris*, was certainly a worthy victor.

Blaris was a versatile animal who was equally able over fences and won eleven chases. He was ridden by George Duller, probably the best rider over hurdles ever seen, trained by former champion jockey Bill Payne who's grandson is now a successful Newmarket trainer, and owned by the formidable Mrs Hollins who chased Captain 'Tuppy' Bennet round the Aintree paddock with her umbrella after the gallant amateur had remounted Mrs Hollins' *Turkey Buzzard* no fewer than four times in the 1921 Grand National.

Brown Jack beat *Blaris* the following year, but on the advice of Steve Donoghue did not race over hurdles again and went on to a fabled career on the flat with Donoghue in the saddle. In the nineteen thirties, a lady just as formidable as Mrs Hollins was making her mark on the racing scene. In one of the great bloodstock deals of all time Miss Dorothy Paget bought *Golden Miller* and *Insurance* for £12,000. *Golden Miller* won five Gold Cups and *Insurance* took the Champion Hurdle in 1932 and 1933.

The post-war period saw the emergence of three superb hurdlers, *National Spirit, Hattons Grace* and *Sir Ken*. *National Spirit* had the distinction of defeating a future winner of the Prix de l'Arc de Triomphe when winning the first of his two victories, finishing a length to the good of *Le Paillon*, whose rider Alec Head had given away more ground than the winning margin by staying on the outside of the course.

Another purple patch originated in the late sixties with *Persian War's* three successive wins followed by *Bula, Comedy of Errors, Lanzarote, Night Nurse, Monksfield* and *Sea Pigeon*. The latter pair ran a series of epic contests in 1978, 1979, and 1980. Jumping the last together on all three occasions, *Monksfield* nipped clear to win by two lengths in 1978, but in 1979 the two fought a see-saw battle on the run-in with *Monksfield* again prevailing but only by a scrambled three-quarters of a length. In 1980, *Sea Pigeon* finally conquered the brave Irish horse by delaying his major challenge until after the last and winning by seven lengths.

As noted elsewhere, the word 'champion' is perhaps to easily bandied about, but in the case of the Champion Hurdle it is a true definition of the winner.

Run at Cheltenham over 2 miles First Run 1927

		Jockey	Trainer	Owner	Odds
1927	**Blaris**	G Duller	W Payne	Mrs H Hollins	11/10
1928	**Brown Jack**	L Rees	A Hastings	H Wernher	4/1
1929	**Royal Falcon**	F Rees	R Gore	Miss Williams-Bulkeley	11/2
1930	**Brown Tony**	T Cullinan	J Anthony	Mrs J de Selincourt	7/2
1931	**No Race**				
1932	**Insurance**	T Leader	A Briscoe	Miss D Paget	4/5
1933	**Insurance**	W Stott	A Briscoe	Miss D Paget	10/11
1934	**Chenango**	D Morgan	I Anthony	G Bostwick	4/9
1935	**Lion Courage**	G Wilson	F Brown	R Fox-Carlyon	100/8
1936	**Victor Norman**	H Nicholson	M Blair	Mrs M Stephens	4/1
1937	**Free Fare**	G Pellerin	E Gwilt	B Warner	2/1
1938	**Our Hope**	Capt R Harding	R Gubbins	R Gubbins	5/1
1939	**African Sister**	K Piggott	C Piggott	H Brueton	10/1
1940	**Solford**	S Magee	O Anthony	Miss D Paget	5/2
1941	**Seneca**	R Smyth	V Smyth	Sir M McAlpine	7/1
1942	**Forestation**	R Smyth	V Smyth	V Smyth	10/1
1943/44	**No Race**				
1945	**Brains Trust**	F Rimell	G Wilson	F Blakeway	9/2
1946	**Distel**	R O'Ryan	C Rogers	Miss D Paget	4/5
1947	**National Spirit**	D Morgan	V Smyth	L A Abelson	7/1
1948	**National Spirit**	R Smyth	V Smyth	L A Abelson	6/4
1949	**Hatton's Grace**	A Brabazon	M V O'Brien	Mrs M Keogh	100/7
1950	**Hatton's Grace**	A Brabazon	M V O'Brien	Mrs M Keogh	5/2
1951	**Hatton's Grace**	T Molony	M V O'Brien	Mrs M Keogh	4/1
1952	**Sir Ken**	T Molony	W Stephenson	M Kingsley	3/1

Sir Ken (3) on his way to victory in the 1953 Champion Hurdle. It was the second of three consecutive Champion Hurdle wins for the horse.

The vital last jump at the 1950 Champion Hurdle. *Hatton's Grace* (4) won the race after a mistake by *National Spirit* (extreme right).

		Jockey	Trainer	Owner	Odds
1953	**Sir Ken**	T Molony	W Stephenson	M Kingsley	2/5
1954	**Sir Ken**	T Molony	W Stephenson	M Kingsley	4/9
1955	**Clair Soleil**	F Winter	H R Price	G Judd	5/2
1956	**Doorknocker**	H Sprague	W Hall	C Nicholson	100/9
1957	**Merry Deal**	G Underwood	A Jones	A Jones	28/1
1958	**Bandalore**	G Slack	J Wright	Mrs D Wright	20/1
1959	**Fare Time**	F Winter	H R Price	G Judd	13/2
1960	**Another Flash**	H Beasley	P Sleator	J Byrne	11/4
1961	**Eborneezer**	F Winter	H R Price	B Pajgar	4/1
1962	**Anzio**	G W Robinson	F Walwyn	Sir T Ainsworth	11/2
1963	**Winning Fair**	Mr A Lillingston	G Spencer	G Spencer	100/9
1964	**Magic Court**	P McCarron	T Robson	J McGhie	100/6
1965	**Kirriemuir**	G W Robinson	F Walwyn	Mrs D Beddington	50/1
1966	**Salmon Spray**	J Haine	R Turnell	Mrs J Rogerson	4/1
1967	**Saucy Kit**	R Edwards	M H Easterby	K Adler	100/6

***Night Nurse*, the 1976 and 1977 Champion Hurdler.**

		Jockey	Trainer	Owner	Odds
1968	**Persian War**	J Uttley	C H Davies	H Alper	4/1
1969	**Persian War**	J Uttley	C H Davies	H Alper	6/4
1970	**Persian War**	J Uttley	C H Davies	H Alper	5/4
1971	**Bula**	P Kelleway	F Winter	E Edwards-Heathcote	15/8
1972	**Bula**	P Kelleway	F Winter	E Edwards-Heathcote	8/11
1973	**Comedy of Errors**	W Smith	F Rimell	E Wheatley	8/1
1974	**Lanzarote**	R Pitman	F Winter	Lord H de Walden	7/4
1975	**Comedy of Errors**	K White	F Rimell	E Wheatley	11/8
1976	**Night Nurse**	P Broderick	M H Easterby	R Spencer	2/1
1977	**Night Nurse**	P Broderick	M H Easterby	R Spencer	15/2
1978	**Monksfield**	T Kinane	D McDonogh	M Mangan	11/2
1979	**Monksfield**	D T Hughes	D McDonogh	M Mangan	9/4
1980	**Sea Pigeon**	J J O'Neill	M H Easterby	P Muldoon	13/2
1981	**Sea Pigeon**	J Francome	M H Easterby	P Muldoon	7/4
1982	**For Auction**	Mr C Magnier	M Cunningham	P Heaslip	40/1
1983	**Gaye Brief**	R Linley	Mrs M Rimell	Sheikh A A Khamsin	7/1
1984	**Dawn Run**	J J O'Neill	P Mullins	Mrs C Hill	4/5
1985	**See You Then**	S Smith Eccles	N Henderson	Stype Wood Stud Ltd	16/1
1986	**See You Then**	S Smith Eccles	N Henderson	Stype Wood Stud Ltd	5/6
1987	**See You Then**	S Smith-Eccles	N Henderson	Stype Wood Stud Ltd	11/10
1988	**Celtic Shot**	P Scudamore	F Winter	D Horton	7/1
1989	**Beech Road**	R Guest	G Balding	A Geake	50/1
1990	**Kribensis**	R Dunwoody	M Stoute	Sheikh Mohammed	95/40
1991	**Morley Street**	J Frost	G Balding	M Jackson Bloodstock Ltd	4/1
1992	**Royal Gait**	G McCourt	J Fanshawe	Sheikh Mohammed	6/1

The Queen Mother Champion Chase

It is to the late Lord Mildmay, one of the great Corinthian riders who's post-war achievements and popularity did much to establish modern National Hunt racing, that we owe Her Majesty Queen Elizabeth the Queen Mother's abiding interest in the sport. Staying at Windsor Castle for a Royal Ascot meeting, he persuaded the Queen as she then was to consider owning a jumper in partnership with her daughter, then Princess Elizabeth.

The first horse to race in the colours of the Princess was *Monaveen*, who won at Fontwell Park in October 1949. The animal was subsequently killed at Hurst Park in an attempt to win a second Queen Elizabeth Chase in 1950 but, undeterred the Queen Mother continued to patronise National Hunt racing, the horse running in the blue and buff colours of her family, the Earls of Strathmore.

The two mile Champion Chase was

***Dunkirk*, winner of the 1965 Queen Mother Champion Chase.**

first run in 1959, and re-named in honour of Her Majesty in 1980, the year of her eightieth birthday. There can be few more exciting sights than National Hunt racing at speed, and the race has never failed to thrill the packed Cheltenham stands on the second day of the March Festival.

The first winner was *Quita Que,* who had been runner-up in the Champion Hurdle in 1956 and 1957. The first of many dual winners was *Fortria,* also second in the Cheltenham Gold Cup in 1962 and 1963. *Dunkirk,* probably the most devastating two-mile chaser since the war, won in 1965 and *Flyingbolt,* once handicapped within two pounds of the mighty *Arkle,* followed up his 5/1 on success in 1966 with a close third in the Champion Hurdle the next day behind *Salmon Spray.* Those were the days!

Run at Cheltenham over 2 miles First Run 1959

		Jockey	Trainer	Owner	Odds
1959	**Quita Que**	J Cox	D Moore	Mrs D Brand	4/9
1960	**Fortria**	P Taaffe	T Dreaper	G Ansley	15/8
1961	**Fortria**	P Taaffe	T Dreaper	G Ansley	2/5
1962	**Piperton**	D Dick	A Thomlinson	A Thomlinson	100/6
1963	**Sandy Abbot**	S Mellor	G Owen	Mrs J McKechnie	5/1
1964	**Ben Stack**	P Taaffe	T Dreaper	Duchess of Westminster	2/1
1965	**Dunkirk**	D Dick	P Cazalet	W Whitbread	8/1
1966	**Flyingbolt**	P Taaffe	T Dreaper	Mrs T Wilkinson	1/5
1967	**Drinny's Double**	F Nash	R Turnell	P Mellon	7/2
1968	**Drinny's Double**	F Nash	R Turnell	P Mellon	6/1
1969	**Muir**	B Hannon	T Dreaper	W Willis	15/2
1970	**Straight Fort**	P Taaffe	T Dreaper	G Ansley	7/4
1971	**Crisp**	P Kelleway	F Winter	Sir C Manifold	3/1
1972	**Royal Relief**	W Smith	E Courage	E Courage	15/8
1973	**Inkslinger**	T Carberry	D Moore	Mrs M Jenney	6/1
1974	**Royal Relief**	W Smith	E Courage	E Courage	6/1
1975	**Lough Inagh**	S Barker	T Dreaper	A Martin	100/30
1976	**Skymas**	M Morris	J Lusk	M Magee	8/1
1977	**Skymas**	M Morris	J Lusk	M Magee	7/2
1978	**Hilly Way**	T Carmody	P McCreery	J Sweeney	7/1
1979	**Hilly Way**	T M Walsh	P McCreery	J Sweeney	7/1
1980	**Another Dolly**	S Morshead	F Rimell	I Urquhart	33/1
1981	**Drumgora**	F Berry	A Moore	D Monahan	25/1
1982	**Rathgorman**	K Whyte	M Dickinson	J Lilley	100/30
1983	**Badsworth Boy**	R Earnshaw	M Dickinson	D Armitage	2/1

		Jockey	Trainer	Owner	Odds
1984	**Badsworth Boy**	R Earnshaw	M Dickinson	D Armitage	8/13
1985	**Badsworth Boy**	R Earnshaw	Mrs M Dickinson	D Armitage	11/8
1986	**Buck House**	T Carmody	M Morris	Mrs S Purcell	5/2
1987	**Pearlyman**	P Scudamore	J Edwards	Mrs P Shaw	13/8
1988	**Pearlyman**	T Morgan	J Edwards	Mrs P Shaw	15/8
1989	**Barnbrook Again**	S Sherwood	D Elsworth	M Davies	7/4
1990	**Barnbrook Again**	H Davies	D Elsworth	M Davies	11/10
1991	**Katabatic**	S McNeill	A Turnell	Pell-mell Partners	9/1
1992	**Remittance Man**	J Osborne	N Henderson	J Collins	Evens

The Triumph Hurdle

As the starting prices indicate, the Triumph Hurdle as a betting prosposition is best left to those who have the benefit of a certificate of sanity signed by a doctor and two magistrates. None the less, this annual charge around Cheltenham always attracts a vigourous ante-post market and is keenly anticipated by racegoers and television viewers alike.

A Grade One Hurdle for four-year-olds only, it was first run at Hurst Park in 1939. The winner was the French trained *Grey Talk*. Given the original British philosophy that racing over hurdles was primarily a preparation for greater things over fences, it is not surprising that *Beaver II, Cantab, Kwannin, Clair Soleil, Abrupto* and *Grey Talk* were all bred across the Channel, where the French do not make a great distinction between the two schools of jump racing.

Prince Charlemagne gave a slightly porky Lester Piggott one of his twenty wins over hurdles in 1954, and when Hurst Park closed the race was moved to Cheltenham in 1965.

Since then, the Triumph has provided plenty of drama. The Chester Cup winner *Attivo* won after flattening the last flight in 1974, *Heighlin* gave David Elsworth an important early success in top company in 1980 after his nearest rival *Starfen*, possibly going the better, came a spectacular cropper at the last, and *Baron Blakeney* did his bit at 66/1 to put a then little known West Country trainer, on the map. His name is Martin Pipe.

Run at Cheltenham over 2 miles for 4 year-olds First Run 1939

		Jockey	Trainer	Owner	Odds
1939	**Grey Talk**	S Rochet	G Batchelor	J Hennessy	5/2
1940/49	**No Race**				
1950	**Abrupto**	R Mantelin	E Diggle	E Marchand	9/2
1951	**Blue Song II**	F Thirion	G Pelat	D Saint	6/1
1952	**Hoggar**	R Triboit	J Cunnington	M Fabiani	13/2
1953	**Claire Soleil**	F Winter	F Mathet	G Judd	8/1
1954	**Prince Charlemagne**	L Piggott	T Carey	L Lipton	11/4
1955	**Kwannin**	P Delfarguiel	A Head	Mme L Chataignoux	2/1
1956	**Square Dance**	M Scudamore	F Walwyn	Mrs V Cardy	13/2
1957	**Meritorius**	D Dillon	P Thrale	J Hart	20/1
1958	**Pundit**	H Sprague	S Ingham	G Baylis	5/2
1959	**Amazon's Choice**	J Gilbert	P Thrale	Miss M J Hindley	7/1
1960	**Turpial**	A Freeman	P Cazelet	Miss A T Hodgson	7/1
1961	**Cantab**	F Winter	H R Price	Miss E Chanelle	4/1
1962	**Beaver II**	J Gifford	H R Price	H R Price	100/6
1963/64	**No Race**				
1965	**Blarney Beacon**	G Ramshaw	R Smyth	F Laker	8/1
1966	**Black Ice**	H Beasley	A Thomas	A Crowther	9/2
1967	**Persian War**	J Uttley	B Swift	H Alper	4/1
1968	**England's Glory**	J Uttley	S Ingham	Mrs M Sherman	9/2
1969	**Coral Diver**	T Biddlecombe	F Rimell	B Jenks	3/1
1970	**Varma**	B Barker	M Masson	C Clore	100/7
1971	**Boxer**	J Uttley	R Smyth	Lord Blakenham	100/30
1972	**Zarib**	W Smith	F Rimell	Mrs A Hornby	16/1
1973	**Moonlight Bay**	J Haine	H R Price	Mrs J R Mullion	85/40
1974	**Attivo**	R Hughes	C Mitchell	P O'Sullevan	4/5
1975	**Royal Epic**	F McKenna	V Cross	R Head	20/1
1976	**Peterhof**	J J O'Neill	M W Easterby	H Gould	10/1
1977	**Meladon**	T Carberry	A J Maxwell	Mrs N Flynn	6/1
1978	**Connaught Ranger**	J Burke	F Rimell	J McGaughey	25/1
1979	**Pollardstown**	P Blacker	S Mellor	Mrs W Tulloch	12/1
1980	**Heighlin**	S Jobar	D Elsworth	Woodside Engineers	40/1
1981	**Baron Blakeney**	P Leach	M Pipe	Wheatley Leisure	66/1
1982	**Shiny Copper**	A Webb	Mrs N Smith	D Tyler	66/1
1983	**Saxon Farm**	M Perrett	S Mellor	A Birchall	12/1
1984	**Northern Game**	T Ryan	E O'Grady	F Conroy	20/1
1985	**First Bout**	S Smith Eccles	N Henderson	F Al Athel	5/1
1986	**Solar Cloud**	P Scudamore	D Nicholson	Mrs A McEwen	40/1
1987	**Alone Success**	S Smith Eccles	N Henderson	Sheikh A Dahlawi	11/1
1988	**Kribensis**	R Dunwoody	M Stoute	Sheikh Mohammed	6/1
1989	**Ikdam**	N Coleman	R J Holder	L B I Law (873) Ltd	66/1
1990	**Rare Holiday**	B Sheridan	D Weld	M Smurfit	25/1
1991	**Oh So Risky**	P Holley	D Elsworth	Oh So Risky Syndicate	14/1
1992	**Duke of Monmouth**	M Richards	S Sherwood	A Saeed	33/1

Run at Hurst Park 1939-1962

Billy Stott, who in 1933 rode *Golden Miller* to the second of five successive victories in the Cheltenham Gold Cup.

The Cheltenham Gold Cup

In the 1920s Liverpool reigned surpeme over all other National Hunt courses. The ace held by the Merseyside track was the Grand National. However, despite a prize, massive for the period, of £7,075 to the winner, it was only a handicap and no race can be considered a proper test if the poorest entrant is theoretically given as good a chance as the best. Aintree's principal condition race, the Champion Steeplechase, rarely attracted a competitive field, despite a prize of around £1,200.

In 1922, the Cheltenham executive under the chairmanship of F.H. Cathcart, who deservedly has a race named after him at the Festival, decided to frame a contest where the best could meet the best on level terms, with five-year-olds allowed 9lb. It was first run in 1924, decades before the introduction of overnight declarations including blinkers, jockeys and in flat racing, the draw. Newspapers could publish only the intended runners, with likely riders, which were described as 'probables'; the other entrants were listed as 'also engaged'.

All were entitled to run and even the racegoer did not know the definite runners until about twenty minutes before the race when they appeared in the number board. Off-course punters, either legally on credit or illegally in cash, had little chance of knowing the real intentions of owners or trainers.

On the day before the inaugural running of the Cheltenham Gold Cup, the probables included *Alcazar* trained by George Poole who retained the services of champion jockey Dick Rees. The horse had an outstanding record over park courses an was forecast at odds-on to beat *Conjuror 11*, third in the 1923 National and other Liverpool contenders *Old Tay Bridge*, *Forewarned* and *Gerald L.* The five-year-old *Red Splash* was not considered, although he had beaten *Old Tay Bridge* over three miles at Hawthorn Hill, admittedly receiving two stone and was a fresh horse.

Had the Gold Cup been a handicap, *Red Splash* would have received a similar amount from *Alcazar*, but at weight-for-age the margin was only 9lb. His trainer Fred Withington reckoned that his young horse, a May foal, was at a distinct disadvantage; moreover, he had been unable to secure the services of a suitable jockey, since Dick Rees who had partnered *Red Splash* at Hawthorn Hill was claimed for *Alcazar*.

When Withington left the course on Tuesday evening, he told the press that *Red Splash* was 'also engaged'. Arriving at the course the next day, he discovered that *Alcazar* would be saved for the Champion Chase at Liverpool in seventeen days time, which he duly won. The trainer snapped up Dick Rees to ride, declared *Red Splash* to run and the five-year-old held on to win by a head in a driving finish from *Conjuror II*.

One of only three five-year-olds to win the Gold Cup, including *Golden Miller*, *Red Splash* became unsound and never won again, but he bequeathed to National Hunt racing a never to be forgotten legacy, the Blue Ribbon of steeplechasing. By the early thirties, the Gold Cup was firmly established in its own right and racing at Cheltenham was no longer a mere stepping stone on the way to the glory and riches of Aintree. The rest, as the record shows, is history.

Golden Miller, **one of only three five-year-olds to win the Cheltenham Gold Cup, enjoyed consecutive victories from 1932 to 1936 inclsuive.**

Run at Cheltenham over 3 miles 2 furlongs   First Run 1924

		Jockey	Trainer	Owner	Odds
1924	**Red Splash**	F Rees	F Withington	H Wyndham	5/1
1925	**Ballinode**	E Leader	F Morgan	J C Bentley	3/1
1926	**Koko**	J Hamey	A Bickley	F Barbour	10/1
1927	**Thrown In**	Mr H Grosvenor	O Anthony	Lord Stalbridge	10/1
1928	**Patron Saint**	F Rees	H Harrison	F W Keen	7/2
1929	**Easter Hero**	F Rees	J Anthony	J H Whitney	7/4
1930	**Easter Hero**	T Cullinan	J Anthony	J H Whitney	8/11
1931	**No Race**				
1932	**Golden Miller**	T Leader	A Briscoe	Miss D Paget	13/2
1933	**Golden Miller**	W Stott	A Briscoe	Miss D Paget	4/7
1934	**Golden Miller**	G Wilson	A Briscoe	Miss D Paget	6/5
1935	**Golden Miller**	G Wilson	A Briscoe	Miss D Paget	1/2
1936	**Golden Miller**	E Williams	O Anthony	Miss D Paget	21/20
1937	**No Race**				
1938	**Morse Code**	D Morgan	I Anthony	D Part	13/2
1939	**Brendan's Cottage**	G Owen	G Beeby	Mrs A S Bingham	8/1
1940	**Roman Hackle**	E Williams	O Anthony	Miss D Paget	Evens
1941	**Poet Prince**	R Burford	I Anthony	D Sherbrooke	7/2
1942	**Medoc II**	H Nicholson	R Hobbs	Lord Sefton	9/2
1943/44	**No Race**				
1945	**Red Rower**	D Jones	Lord Stalbridge	Lord Stalbridge	11/4
1946	**Prince Regent**	T Hyde	T Dreaper	J V Rank	4/7
1947	**Fortina**	R Black	H Christie	Lord Grimthorpe	8/1
1948	**Cottage Rake**	A Brabazon	M V O'Brien	F Vickerman	10/1
1949	**Cottage Rake**	A Brabazon	M V O'Brien	F Vickerman	4/6

Morse Code, the winner, runs ahead of *Golden Miller* in the 1938 Cheltenham Gold Cup.

Tim Hyde unsaddling *Prince Regent* after his brilliant Gold Cup victory in 1946.

Gay Donald, surprise 33-1 winner of the 1955 Gold Cup, goes over the last fence alone to give jockey Tony Grantham his biggest and fourth success on the horse so far that season.

***Arkle*, with Pat Taaffe up, wins his third Gold Cup at Cheltenham in 1966.**

		Jockey	Trainer	Owner	Odds
1950	**Cottage Rake**	A Brabazon	M V O'Brien	F Vickerman	5/6
1951	**Silver Fame**	M Molony	G Beeby	Lord Bicester	6/4
1952	**Mont Tremblant**	D Dick	F Walwyn	Miss D Paget	8/1
1953	**Knock Hard**	T Molony	M V O'Brien	Mrs M Keogh	11/2
1954	**Four Ten**	T Cusack	J Roberts	A Strange	100/6
1955	**Gay Donald**	A Grantham	J Ford	P Burt	33/1
1956	**Limber Hill**	J Power	W Dutton	J Davey	11/8
1957	**Linwell**	M Scudamore	C Mallon	D Brown	100/9
1958	**Kerstin**	S Hayhurst	C Bewicke	G Moore	7/1
1959	**Roddy Owen**	H Beasley	D Morgan	Lord Fingall	5/1
1960	**Pas Seul**	W Rees	R Turnell	J Rogerson	6/1
1961	**Saffron Tartan**	F Winter	D Butchers	G Westmacott	2/1
1962	**Mandarin**	F Winter	F Walwyn	Mme K Hennessy	7/2
1963	**Mill House**	G W Robinson	F Walwyn	W Gollings	7/2
1964	**Arkle**	P Taaffe	T Dreaper	Duchess of Westminster	7/4

***L'Escargot*, ridden by Tom Carberry, won the Cheltenham Gold Cup for the second year running in 1971. Here, they clear the last fence well ahead of *Leap Frog*, who was second. *The Dikler* finished third.**

		Jockey	Trainer	Owner	Odds
1965	**Arkle**	P Taaffe	T Dreaper	Duchess of Westminster	30/100
1966	**Arkle**	P Taaffe	T Dreaper	Duchess of Westminster	1/10
1967	**Woodland Venture**	T Biddlecombe	F Rimell	H Collins	100/8
1968	**Fort Leney**	P Taaffe	T Dreaper	J Thomson	11/2
1969	**What a Myth**	P Kelleway	H R Price	Lady Weir	8/1
1970	**L'Escargot**	T Carberry	D Moore	R Guest	33/1
1971	**L'Escargot**	T Carberry	D Moore	R Guest	7/2
1972	**Glencaraig Lady**	F Berry	F Flood	P Doyle	6/1
1973	**The Dikler**	R Barry	F Walwyn	Mrs D August	9/1
1974	**Captain Christy**	H Beasley	P Taaffe	Mrs J Samuel	7/1
1975	**Ten Up**	T Carberry	J Dreaper	Duchess of Westminster	2/1
1976	**Royal Frolic**	J Burke	F Rimell	Sir E Hanmer	14/1
1977	**Davy Lad**	D T Hughes	M O'Toole	Mrs J McGowan	14/1
1978	**Midnight Court**	J Francome	F Winter	Mrs O Jackson	5/2
1979	**Alverton**	J J O'Neill	M H Easterby	Snailwell Stud Ltd	5/1
1980	**Master Smudge**	R Hoare	A Barrow	A Barrow	14/1
1981	**Little Owl**	A J Wilson	M H Easterby	R J Wilson	6/1
1982	**Silver Buck**	R Earnshaw	M Dickinson	Mrs C Feather	8/1
1983	**Bregawn**	G Bradley	M Dickinson	J Kennelly	100/30
1984	**Burrough Hill Lad**	P Tuck	Mrs J Pitman	R S Riley	7/2
1985	**Forgive'N'Forget**	M Dwyer	J Fitzgerald	T Kilroe & Sons	7/1
1986	**Dawn Run**	J J O'Neill	P Mullins	Mrs C Hill	15/8
1987	**The Thinker**	R Lamb	W A Stephenson	T McDonagh Ltd	13/2
1988	**Charter Party**	R Dunwoody	D Nicholson	Mrs C Smith	10/1
1989	**Desert Orchid**	S Sherwood	D Elsworth	R Burridge	5/2
1990	**Norton's Coin**	G McCourt	S Griffiths	S Griffiths	100/1
1991	**Garrison Savannah**	M Pitman	Mrs J Pitman	Autofour Engineering	16/1
1992	**Cool Ground**	A Maguire	G Balding	Whatcombe Manor Racing	25/1

The Grand National

The Grand National had its roots in underhanded dealing, a quarrel between partners and the financial support of the slave trade. It has been surrounded in controversy ever since, but now seems to have come to rest as 'the people's' race, a unique event which could not be staged anywhere else in the world but downtown Bootle.

The saga began when William Lynn, described as 'the best fish-cook in the world' opened the Waterloo Hotel in Liverpool. He was a keen sportsman and co-founder of the Waterloo Cup, combining his sporting and catering interests when he rented the grandstand at nearby Maghull racecourse and supplied the hungry and thirsty punters who attended the flat race track opened by John Formby in 1827.

Formby's course was laid out on land purchased by his father-in-law from the Earl of Sefton. Lynn was a member of the Maghull race committee in 1828, but the standard of racing was modest and Lynn formed plans of his own based on the success of the St Albans steeplechase course founded by a fellow hotelier, Tom Coleman. It was Coleman who had first realised the potential of steeplechasing as a spectator sport.

Lynn went behind Formby's back and did a deal with Lord Sefton's heir, Lord Molyneux, and leased the land adjoining Maghull in July 1828. The property was adjacent to the village of Aintree.

Lynn's plans were ambitious. Although at first limited to flat racing and alternating with Maghull for a few years, Lynn finally drove poor Formby out of business and the Racing Calendar recorded in 1835 that 'The proprietors of the Aintree and Maghull course have made an arrangement by which the races at both meetings will be run on the former course'.

Lynn now had control of both tracks and was free to frame his first steeplechase, to be observed by the gentry from his four tier stand erected in 1829 which incorporated extensive cellars for Lynn's wines; these were served in two separate drawing rooms, one for ladies the other for gentlemen.

There were ten runners for the prototype National, and *The Duke* was the winner ridden by Captain Becher in front of a huge crowd which had turned up to see the four mile chase over twenty fences and two hurdles extending over the old Formby course at Maghull.

There was plenty of money about with 162,000 tons of shipping registered on Merseyside, and Lynn thought that he only had to go up-market with his brainchild to make a killing. The 1836 race had carried the condition that the winner was to be sold for £200 'if demanded'. Clearly this had to be removed and in 1837 the race had lost the selling proviso and the added money had been increased to £180, as opposed to the £80 added in 1836, the additional £100 coming from the city of Liverpool.

Unhappily, by a rare error of commercial judgement, Lynn had decided to run on the day following Tom Coleman's 'Grand Annual' at St Albans which was then the top steeplechase in Britain. Only four runners turned up at Aintree and even *The Duke's* regular jockey Captain Martin Becher was absent and so Mr Henry Potts, a family friend of one of the horse's joint owners, took over and rode the winner of the first Grand National.

The following year, Liverpool Corporation withdrew financial support in the face of mounting criticism of steeplechasing by animal welfare groups headed by the Society for the Prevention of Cruelty to Animals, formed in the wake of the Ill Treatment of Horses Bill passed in 1823. The prime targets of the legislation were ruthless coachmen, carters and farmers, but many thought it hypocritical that 'gentlemen' whipping and spurring animals over walls and fences should escape prosecution in the name of sport.

Lynn sensibly modified the course, and a field of ten was attracted. *Sir William* ran out the winner but *The Duke* broke down, Aintree's first major casualty. The sun was setting for William Lynn as well, who quit in severe financial difficulties only three days before the 1839 race. Aintree passed into the control of a syndicate headed by Lord Stanley and including the Lords Derby, and Sefton and Lord George Bentinck, the principal racing administrator of the period.

It was not the first Grand National, but it was the first to attract really intense media coverage, the crowds boosted by the opening of the Liverpool to Manchester railway and the rapid spread of metalled roads pioneered by John Macadam. Lynn's old stand could not accommodate more than threequarters of the punters struggling to get in, and it was estimated that there were forty to fifty thousand racegoers on the course.

The race was won by *Lottery*, the perfect winner for the media mind given the risky nature of the event, and so the myth was born that the 1839 race was the first Grand National. It wasn't, but it did bring immortality to a couple of the outstanding riders of the time, *Lottery's* jockey Jem Mason and Captain Becher. Mason rode the winner, while Becher's mount *Conrad* dumped him in the brook which was forever to bear the gallant Captain's name. Emerging, Becher is said to have remarked to the effect that 'water is no damned use without brandy'.

However, the spectre of cruelty continued to haunt the race as it has done almost to the present day. The morning after the 1839 race the Editor of the Liverpool Mercury commented that he had 'heard with alarm and regret that it is in contemplation to establish steeplechasing (at Aintree) annually'. The writer went on to say that 'we would not decapitate them (the riders) but we would compell them to go through the prugatory of a steeplechase with sturdy drivers at their heels to urge them over hedge and ditch . . .and when they arrived at the finish they should do penance in white sheets or horse clothes in the church until they had confessed to their iniquities and promised to be more merciful to their animals'.

Despite this vehement, and not entirely unjustified local disapproval the race continued. In 1843 the National became a handicap, and the name changed from the Grand Liverpool Steeplechase to the Liverpool and National Steeplechase. In 1847 it was run as the Grand National Handicap Steeplechase for the first time.

It was also in 1843 that the National came under the administration of the Topham family. The association was to last for 130 years and saw the National rise to the pinnacle of National Hunt racing as the most sought after and greatest steeplechase in the world only to fall to the point of near extinction. In the seventies it was the bookmaking firm of Ladbrokes and the administrative skills of the late John Hughes that revived Aintree and the National, now safely in the hands of the Straker family, well known in northern and Scottish racing for many years.

It would be superfluous to detail all the exploits of the brave men, women and horses that have filled the record books over the years. In any case, they have been well chronicled elsewhere. Suffice to say that thankfully the Grand National is now as safe for horse and rider as can be and that the real champion is the race itself.

Run at Aintree over 4 miles 856 yards First Run 1837

		Jockey	Trainer	Owner	Odds
1837	**The Duke**	Mr H Potts	–	Mr Sirdefield	–
1838	**Sir William**	A McDonough	–	Mr Thompson	–
1839	**Lottery**	Jem Mason	G Dockeray	J Elmore	5/1
1840	**Jerry**	Mr B Bretherton	J Elmore	Mr Villebois	12/1
1841	**Charity**	Mr Powell	–	Lord Craven	14/1

Lottery, winner of the 1839 Grand National, only the third time the race had been run.

		Jockey	Trainer	Owner	Odds
1842	**Gay Lad**	T Olliver	–	J Elmore	7/1
1843	**Vanguard**	T Olliver	–	Lord Chesterfield	12/1
1844	**Discount**	Mr Crickmere	–	Mr Quartermaine	5/1
1845	**Cure-All**	Mr W Loft	W Loft	W Loft	–
1846	**Pioneer**	W Taylor	–	Mr Adams	–
1847	**Matthew**	D Wynne	J Courtenay	Mr Courtenay	10/1
1848	**Chandler**	Capt J Little	T Eskrett	Capt J Little	12/1
1849	**Peter Simple**	T Cunningham	T Cunningham	Mr Mason Jnr	20/1
1850	**Abd-el-Kader**	C Green	–	J Osborne	–
1851	**Abd-el-Kader**	T Abbot	–	J Osborne	7/1
1852	**Miss Mowbray**	Mr A Goodman	G Dockeray	T F Mason	–
1853	**Peter Simple**	T Olliver	T Olliver	Capt J Little	9/1
1854	**Bourton**	J Tasker	H Wadlow	W Moseley	4/1
1855	**Wanderer**	J Hanlon	–	Mr Dennis	25/1
1856	**Freetrader**	G Stevens	W Holman	W Barnett	25/1
1857	**Emigrant**	C Boyce	C Boyce	G Hodgman	10/1
1858	**Little Charley**	W Archer	W Holman	C Capel	100/6
1859	**Half Caste**	C Green	C Green	Mr Willoughby	7/1
1860	**Anatis**	Mr T Pickernell	W Holman	C Capel	7/2
1861	**Jealousy**	J Kendall	C Balchin	J Bennett	5/1
1862	**Huntsman**	H Lamplugh	H Lamplugh	Viscount de Namur	3/1
1863	**Emblem**	G Stevens	E Weever	Lord Coventry	4/1
1864	**Emblematic**	G Stevens	E Weever	Lord Coventry	10/1
1865	**Alcibiade**	Capt H Coventry	Cornell	B J Angell	100/7
1866	**Salamander**	Mr A Goodman	J Walters	Mr Studd	40/1
1867	**Cortolvin**	J Page	H Lamplugh	Duke of Hamilton	16/1
1868	**The Lamb**	Mr G Ede	B Land	Lord Poulett	9/1
1869	**The Colonel**	G Stevens	R Roberts	J Weyman	100/7
1870	**The Colonel**	G Stevens	R Roberts	M Evans	7/2
1871	**The Lamb**	Mr T Pickernell	C Green	Lord Poulett	11/2
1872	**Casse Tete**	J Page	A Cowley	E Brayley	20/1
1873	**Disturbance**	Mr J M Richardson	J M Richardson	Capt J Machell	20/1
1874	**Reugny**	Mr J M Richardson	J M Richardson	Capt J Machell	5/1
1875	**Pathfinder**	Mr T Pickernell	W Reeves	H Bird	100/6
1876	**Regal**	J Cannon	J Jewitt	Capt J Machell	25/1
1877	**Austerlitz**	Mr F G Hobson	R I'Anson	F G Hobson	15/1
1878	**Shifnal**	J Jones	J Nightingall	J Nightingall	7/1
1879	**The Liberator**	Mr G Moore	J Moore	G Moore	5/1
1880	**Empress**	Mr T Beasley	H Linde	P Ducrot	8/1
1881	**Woodbrook**	Mr T Beasley	H Linde	T Y L Kirkwood	11/2

Scene from the 1949 Grand National which was won by *Russian Hero*, a 66/1 outsider.

		Jockey	Trainer	Owner	Odds
1882	**Seaman**	Lord Manners	Capt J Machell	Lord Manners	10/1
1883	**Zoedone**	Count C Kinsky	W H P Jenkins	Count C Kinsky	100/7
1884	**Voluptuary**	Mr E P Wilson	W Wilson	H F Boyd	10/1
1885	**Roquefort**	Mr E P Wilson	A Yates	A Cooper	100/30
1886	**Old Joe**	T Skelton	G Mulcaster	A J Douglas	25/1
1887	**Gamecock**	W Daniels	J Gordon	E Jay	20/1
1888	**Playfair**	G Mawson	T Cannon	E W Baird	40/1
1889	**Frigate**	Mr T Beasley	M A Maher	M A Maher	8/1
1890	**Ilex**	A Nightingall	J Nightingall	G Masterman	4/1
1891	**Come Away**	Mr H Beasley	H Beasley	W G Jameson	4/1
1892	**Father O'Flynn**	Capt R Owen	G C Wilson	G C Wilson	20/1
1893	**Cloister**	W Dollery	A Yates	C G Duff	9/2
1894	**Why Not**	A Nightingall	W H Moore	C H Fenwick	5/1
1895	**Wild Man from Borneo**	Mr Joseph Widger	J Gatland	John Widger	10/1
1896	**The Soarer**	Mr D Campbell	W H Moore	W Hall-Walker	40/1
1897	**Manifesto**	T Kavanagh	W McAuliffe	H M Dyas	6/1
1898	**Drogheda**	J Gourley	R C Dawson	C G Adams	25/1
1899	**Manifesto**	G Williamson	W H Moore	J G Bulteel	5/1
1900	**Ambush II**	A Anthony	A Anthony	HRH the Prince of Wales	4/1
1901	**Grudon**	A Nightingall	B Bletsoe	B Bletsoe	9/1
1902	**Shannon Lass**	D Read	J Hackett	A Gorham	20/1
1903	**Drumcree**	P Woodland	Sir C Nugent	J S Morrison	13/2
1904	**Moifaa**	A Birch	W Hickey	S Gollan	25/1
1905	**Kirkland**	F Mason	E Thomas	F Bibby	6/1
1906	**Ascetic's Silver**	Mr A Hastings	A Hastings	Prince Hatzfeldt	20/1
1907	**Eremon**	A Newey	T Coulthwaite	S Howard	8/1
1908	**Rubio**	H B Bletsoe	F Withington	F Douglas-Pennant	66/1
1909	**Lutteur III**	G Parfrement	H Escott	J Hennessy	100/9
1910	**Jenkinstown**	R Chadwick	T Coulthwaite	S Howard	100/8
1911	**Glenside**	Mr J Anthony	Capt R Collis	F Bibby	20/1
1912	**Jerry M**	E Piggott	R Gore	Sir C Assheton-Smith	4/1
1913	**Covertcoat**	P Woodland	R Gore	Sir C Assheton-Smith	100/9
1914	**Sunloch**	W J Smith	T Tyler	T Tyler	100/6
1915	**Ally Sloper**	Mr J Anthony	A Hastings	Lady Nelson	100/8
1916	**Vermouth**	J Reardon	J Bell	P F Heybourne	100/8
1917	**Ballymacad**	E Driscoll	A Hastings	Sir G Bullough	100/9
1918	**Poethlyn**	E Piggott	H Escott	Mrs H Peel	5/1
1919	**Poethlyn**	E Piggott	H Escott	Mrs H Peel	11/4
1920	**Troytown**	Mr J Anthony	A Anthony	T Gerrard	6/1
1921	**Shaun Spadah**	F B Rees	G Poole	T M McAlpine	100/9

Above: Dick Francis in tears after the Queen Mother's *Devon Loch* threw him to the ground only 50 yards from the winning post in the 1956 Grand National. *Top right:* In happier times, *Devon Loch* pictured in December 1955. *Bottom right:* The winner of the 1967 Grand National, *Foinavon.*

		Jockey	Trainer	Owner	Odds
1922	**Music Hall**	L B Rees	O Anthony	H Kershaw	100/9
1923	**Sergeant Murphy**	Capt G H Bennett	G Blackwell	S Sanford	100/6
1924	**Master Robert**	R Trudgill	A Hastings	Lord Airlie	25/1
1925	**Double Chance**	Major J Wilson	F Archer	D Goold	100/9
1926	**Jack Horner**	W Watkinson	H Leader	A C Schwartz	25/1
1927	**Sprig**	T E Leader	T R Leader	Mrs M Partridge	8/1
1928	**Tipperary Tim**	Mr W P Dutton	J Dodd	H S Kenyon	100/1
1929	**Gregalach**	R Everett	T R Leader	Mrs M A Gemmell	100/1
1930	**Shaun Goilin**	T B Cullinan	F Hartigan	W H Midwood	100/8
1931	**Grakle**	R Lyall	T Coulthwaite	C R Taylor	100/6
1932	**Forbra**	J Hamey	T Rimell	W Parsonage	50/1
1933	**Kellsboro' Jack**	D Williams	I Anthony	Mrs F A Clark	25/1
1934	**Golden Miller**	G Wilson	A Briscoe	Miss D Paget	8/1
1935	**Reynoldstown**	Mr F Furlong	N Furlong	N Furlong	22/1
1936	**Reynoldstown**	Mr F Walwyn	N Furlong	N Furlong	10/1
1937	**Royal Mail**	E Williams	I Anthony	H Lloyd Thomas	100/6
1938	**Battleship**	B Hobbs	R Hobbs	Mrs M Scott	40/1
1939	**Workman**	T Hyde	J Ruttle	Sir A Maguire	100/8
1940	**Bogskar**	M A Jones	Lord Stalbridge	Lord Stalbridge	25/1
1941/45	**No Race**				
1946	**Lovely Cottage**	Capt R Petre	T Rayson	J Morant	25/1
1947	**Caughoo**	E Dempsey	H McDowell	J J McDowell	100/1
1948	**Sheila's Cottage**	A P Thompson	N Crump	J Procter	50/1
1949	**Russian Hero**	L McMorrow	G R Owen	W F Williamson	66/1
1950	**Freebooter**	J Power	R Renton	Mrs L Brotherton	10/1
1951	**Nickel Coin**	J A Bullock	J O'Donaghue	J Royle	40/1
1952	**Teal**	A P Thompson	N Crump	H Lane	100/7
1953	**Early Mist**	B Marshall	M V O'Brien	J H Griffin	20/1
1954	**Royal Tan**	B Marshall	M V O'Brien	J H Griffin	8/1
1955	**Quare Times**	P Taaffe	M V O'Brien	Mrs W Welman	100/9

***Red Rum*, ridden by Brian Fletcher, clears the last fence in the 1974 Grand National for his second successive victory in the race. It was the first time a horse had won successive Grand Nationals since *Reynoldstown* in 1935 and 1936.**

		Jockey	Trainer	Owner	Odds
1956	**E.S.B.**	D V Dick	F Rimell	Mrs L Carver	100/7
1957	**Sundew**	F Winter	F Hudson	Mrs G Kohn	20/1
1958	**Mr What**	A Freeman	Tom Taaffe	D J Coughlan	18/1
1959	**Oxo**	M Scudamore	W Stephenson	J E Bigg	8/1
1960	**Merryman II**	G Scott	N Crump	Miss W H S Wallace	13/2
1961	**Nicolaus Silver**	H R Beasley	F Rimell	C Vaughan	28/1
1962	**Kilmore**	F Winter	H R Price	N Cohen	28/1
1963	**Ayala**	P Buckley	K Piggott	P Raymond	66/1
1964	**Team Spirit**	G W Robinson	F Walwyn	J K Goodman	18/1
1965	**Jay Trump**	Mr C Smith	F Winter	Mrs M Stephenson	100/6
1966	**Anglo**	T Norman	F Winter	S Levy	50/1
1967	**Foinavon**	J Buckingham	J Kempton	C P T Watkins	100/1
1968	**Red Alligator**	B Fletcher	Denys Smith	J Manners	100/7
1969	**Highland Wedding**	E P Harty	G Balding	T H McCoy Jnr	100/9
1970	**Gay Trip**	P Taaffe	F Rimell	A J Chambers	15/1
1971	**Specify**	J Cook	J E Sutcliffe	F Pontin	28/1
1972	**Well To Do**	G Thorner	T Forster	T Forster	14/1
1973	**Red Rum**	B Fletcher	D McCain	N Le Mare	9/1
1974	**Red Rum**	B Fletcher	D McCain	N Le Mare	11/1
1975	**L'Escargot**	T Carberry	D Moore	R Guest	13/2

Red Rum **pictured after making history in 1977, when he won the Grand National for the third time. He had also finished second twice.**

		Jockey	Trainer	Owner	Odds
1976	**Rag Trade**	J Burke	F Rimell	P Raymond	14/1
1977	**Red Rum**	T Stack	D McCain	N Le Mare	9/1
1978	**Lucius**	B R Davies	G W Richards	Mrs D A Whitaker	14/1
1979	**Rubstic**	M Barnes	J Leadbetter	J Douglas	25/1
1980	**Ben Nevis**	Mr C Fenwick	T Forster	R C Stewart Jnr	40/1
1981	**Aldaniti**	R Champion	J Gifford	S N Embiricos	10/1
1982	**Grittar**	Mr C Saunders	F Gilman	F Gilman	7/1
1983	**Corbiere**	B de Haan	Mrs J Pitman	B Burrough	13/1
1984	**Hallo Dandy**	N Doughty	G W Richards	R Shaw	13/1
1985	**Last Suspect**	H Davies	T Forster	Duchess of Westminster	50/1
1986	**West Tip**	R Dunwoody	K M Oliver	P Luff	15/2
1987	**Maori Venture**	S Knight	A Turnell	H J Joel	28/1
1988	**Rhyme'N'Reason**	B Powell	D Elsworth	Miss J Reed	10/1
1989	**Little Polveir**	J Frost	G Balding	E Harvey	28/1
1990	**Mr Frisk**	Mr M Armytage	K Bailey	Mrs H Duffey	16/1
1991	**Seagram**	N Hawke	D Barons	Sir E Parker	12/1
1992	**Party Politics**	C Llewellyn	N Gaselee	Mrs D Thompson	14/1

·*Run at Gatwick 1916-1918*

The Whitbread Gold Cup

It is fitting that Sandown, the course which pioneered televised racing, should have staged the first commercially sponsored race. In 1939, the BBC suggested to the Sandown authorities that they should televise the Eclipse Stakes. The medium was still in its infancy and it is possible that either the Sandown stewards had not heard of television or regarded it as an amusement for the servants' hall. The offered facility fee of £15 was not enticing either, but in the wider social atmosphere of 1947, the project received a warmer welcome and the BBC transmitted two steeplechases and a hurdle race during the 1947-48 season.

The non-conformist conscience of the Corporation forbade any mention of betting, but the sport of National Hunt racing, with its evident dangers and vicarious thrills, proved to be a natural for television. The advent of commercial television in the middle of the next decade was the catalyst, and it was Colonel W.H.'Billy' Whitbread who first espyed the possibilities of combining shrewd public relations with the presentation of a top class steeplechase.

Col.Whitbread, a lifelong supporter of jumping who had himself completed the course in two Grand Nationals in the days when that was no mean achievement, founded the race which was to bear the name of the famous brewery of which he was chairman in 1957. The innovation was bold and some thought foolish, late April being a time when, apart from the meanderings of minor gaffs through the Bank Holiday season to the end of May, the National Hunt season was thought to be over after the Grand National.

However the flat racing enthusiasts who came to Sandown on 27 April 1957 were entranced by the one steeplechase on the card and cheered to the echo as *Much Obliged* and Johnny East beat *Mandarin* ridden by Gerry Madden in the inaugural race over three miles, five furlongs and seventy-five yards. The winning distance was a neck, with the usual nip and tuck finish up the Sandown Hill.

Significantly, it was at this time that the Grand National, for so many years the be-all and end-all of National Hunt racing was slipping swiftly into the decline which was to prove almost terminal. The foundation of the Whitbread and the Hennessy Gold Cups, together with the King George VI Chase and the Cheltenham Gold Cup provided a top class staying chaser with ample excuses to avoid the unnecessary hazards of Aintree, and still find fame and fortune.

The roll of honour is distinguished enough: *Mill House*, *Pas Seul*, *Arkle* and *Desert Orchid* all won under top weight, while *Larbawn* and *Diamond Edge* both won twice. Above all the Whitbread is not a race steeped in history which has lost its name for the expedience of commerical sponsorship, but an original which changed the face of British steeplechasing. Racing should raise a glass to them, coupled with the names of Hennessy and Mackeson (but not all in the same glass!)

Run at Sandown over 3 miles 5 furlongs 18 yards First Run 1957

		Jockey	Trainer	Owner	Odds
1957	**Much Obliged**	J East	N Crump	H Draper	10/1
1958	**Taxidermist**	Mr J Lawrence	F Walwyn	Mrs P Hastings	100/6
1959	**Done Up**	H Sprague	H R Price	J Baillie	100/6
1960	**Plummers Plain**	R Harrison	L Dale	F Clay	20/1
1961	**Pas Seul**	D V Dick	R Turnell	J Rogerson	8/1
1962	**Frenchman's Cove**	S Mellor	H Thomson Jones	S Joel	7/2
1963	**Hoodwinked**	P Buckley	N Crump	Lady Joicey	100/7
1964	**Dormant**	P Buckley	N Crump	Mrs D W-Kendrew	11/4
1965	**Arkle**	P Taaffe	T Dreaper	Duchess of Westminster	4/9
1966	**What a Myth**	P Kelleway	H R Price	Lady Weir	5/4
1967	**Mill House**	D Nicholson	F Walwyn	W Gollings	9/2
1968	**Larbawn**	J Gifford	M Marsh	M Marsh	8/1
1969	**Larbawn**	J Gifford	M Marsh	M Marsh	9/2
1970	**Royal Toss**	R Pitman	C Handel	C Handel	20/1
1971	**Titus Oates**	R Barry	G W Richards	P Cussins	11/1
1972	**Grey Sombrero**	W Shoemark	D Gandolfo	W Candwell	16/1
1973	**Charlie Potheen**	R Barry	F Walwyn	Mrs B Heath	11/4
1974	**The Dikler**	R Barry	F Walwyn	Mrs D August	5/1
1975	**April Seventh**	S Knight	R Turnell	Mrs B Meehan	16/1
1976	**Otterway**	J King	O Carter	O Carter	15/2
1977	**Andy Pandy**	J Burke	F Rimell	Mrs S Mulligan	4/1
1978	**Strombolus**	T Stack	P Bailey	M Buckley	7/1
1979	**Diamond Edge**	W Smith	F Walwyn	S Loughridge	7/1
1980	**Royal Mail**	P Blacker	S Mellor	J Begg	8/1
1981	**Diamond Edge**	W Smith	F Walwyn	S Loughridge	5/1
1982	**Shady Deal**	R Howe	J Gifford	G Hubbard	4/1
1983	**Drumlargan**	F Codd	E O'Grady	M Cuddy	11/1
1984	**Special Cargo**	K Mooney	F Walwyn	HM The Queen Mother	8/1
1985	**By the Way**	R Earnshaw	Mrs M Dickinson	Mrs C Feather	11/2
1986	**Plundering**	S Sherwood	F Winter	Mrs M Valentine	14/1
1987	**Lean Ar Aghaidh**	G Landau	S Mellor	Mrs W Tulloch	6/1
1988	**Desert Orchid**	S Sherwood	D Elsworth	R Burridge	6/1
1989	**Brown Windsor**	M Bowlby	N Henderson	W Shand Kydd	12/1
1990	**Mr Frisk**	Mr M Armytage	K Bailey	Mrs H Duffey	9/2
1991	**Docklands Express**	A Tory	K Bailey	R H Baines	4/1
1992	**Topsham Bay**	H Davies	D Barons	M Marsh	9/2

Run at Newcastle in 1973 over 3 miles 6 furlongs

Pat Taaffe on *Arkle* won the 1965 Whitbread Gold Cup under top weight.

Appendix — Wartime Racing

In 1914, when Europe was plunged into global war for the first time, it was inevitable that there should be a dramatic curtailment of racing but the Jockey Club considered that a minimal continuance of the sport was imperative if the thoroughbred breeding industry, which was inextricably linked to the future of the racehorse, was to survive.

Lloyd George's government, with a classical libertarian unthinking conscience which Harold Wilson would have envied, came to the conclusion 'that it was against public opinion that racing should be continued.' Seizing on the obvious loophole in this philosophy, namely that 'public opinion' had already voted with its feet as soldiers on leave and a war-torn Home Front flocked to the racecourses for a little light relief, Lord Jersey, the Senior Steward, backed by their lordships Durham, Crewe, Rosebery and Derby, supported by the Quarter-Master General and the Director of Remounts (who needed ex-racehorses for cannon-fodder), persuaded HM Government to allow the sport to continue. As Lord Rosebery pointed out, not even Napoleon had stopped racing in Britain.

And so the future of the Turf was preserved, albeit in a rather haphazard fashion. There was little difficulty with the classic races: the One Thousand Guineas and the Two Thousand Guineas belonged to Newmarket anyway, and it was simple enough to transfer The Oaks and The Derby to Headquarters. The good municipal burghers of Doncaster proved to be a little more intransigent, stipulating that no race called the St Leger could be run anywhere except at Town Moor, which was closed for the duration of hostilities.

Rightly rejecting this parochial point of view, the Jockey Club authorised a 'September Stakes' run over one and three-quarter miles at Newmarket and recognised as the St Leger, to the effect that *Pommern, Gay Crusader* and *Gainsborough,* winners in 1915, 1917 and 1918, were recorded as victors of the Triple Crown, having previously succeeded in the Two Thousand Guineas and the Derby.

Other arrangements in 1915 included a June Stakes at Newmarket, with the blessing of Epsom a substitute Coronation Cup, a Newmarket Gold Cup replacing the Ascot centrepiece with £1,000 added by the Ascot Authority, a Stewards' Handicap run at Newmarket with identical conditions to the Goodwood Stewards' Cup and a five furlong New Coventry Stakes, again with £1,000 added to the stakes by the Ascot Authority to stand in for what was then the premier two-year-old race in the Calendar.

In 1916, a substitute Lincolnshire Handicap, run over one mile at Lingfield and ingeniously named the Lincolnfield Handicap, was won by *Clap Gate,* sired by *Long Tom,* which suggests that the original owner Sir William Cooke was possessed of a sense of humour. *Clap Gate* must have been a useful horse and versatile, since he won the six-furlong Stewards' Handicap in 1915 for Sir William.

The New Coventry featured once again, as it would in 1917 and 1918 along with the June Stakes, the latter being over the Bunbury Mile in the last year of the war as the ground beyond the Choke Jade was unraceable, and the Stewards' Handicap.

Twenty years later, the storm clouds of war loomed once more, and the old objections voiced in 1917 against the continuance of racing were raised again. This time it was the late 'Manny' Shinwell (later Lord Shinwell) who quoted 'public opinion', but happily the Jockey Club, led by Lord Sefton, persuaded the Government to let the sport survive on a reduced scale. For their part, the Club encouraged owners to dispose of moderate animals, especially geldings, and it was agreed with the Ministry of Agriculture that the broodmare population should be reduced by 25 per cent.

Mr Shinwell and his Labour Party colleagues, who regarded the sport as (according to 'Hansard') 'an insane and unseemly spectacle' were informed in Parliament that if racing were suspended and the oats fed to the horses given to poultry, the saving would be one egg per head of the population once in four years. While Manny pondered the ideological implications for the masses, already — as in World War One — turning up in droves at the racetrack for rest and recuperation, the Jockey Club went ahead.

The Queen Mary Stakes for fillies was run throughout the war, at Newmarket after 1940 when racing was suspended in the face of possible invasion between June and September. Goodwood's Molecomb Stakes and the Sussex Stakes were run on the July course in 1941 and following the closure of York, the Nunthorpe, probably the most important all-aged handicap in the Calendar, also survived at Headquarters in 1942, 1943 and 1944. The good sprinter *Sugar Palm* won the Stewards' Handicap in 1942 and 1943, when the race was run at Windsor, and took the Nunthorpe in 1944.

Windsor featured strongly in the scenario of racing during World War Two. Not only did this course stage the Stewards' Cup substitute from 1942 to 1945, but also the July Stakes in 1943 and 1944. It is debatable as to whether the two-year-old races were actual substitutes for the real thing, although the distance and conditions were identical, especially as the 1943 race was run in two divisions.

However, the quality of the event was not diluted, and the division was almost certainly due to the size of the tricky Windsor figure-of-eight course as 28 horses took part, 19 in Division One and nine in Division Two.

The 'Newmarket Cesarewitch' was run at Headquarters over two miles 24 yards of the Summer Course, again truncated as in 1918 by military use. The classics were all staged at Newmarket, with the usual exception of the St Leger. Three runnings, 1942, 1943, 1944, graced the July Course, but the 1940 version was run at Thirsk on 23 November, the last day of the season, the 1941 event, was at Manchester, and York played host to the oldest classic in the Calendar in 1945.

Index

Race	Grade	Course	Page
Ascot Gold Cup	Group 1	Ascot	88
Ayr Gold Cup	Handicap	Ayr	183
Beefeater Gin Celebration Mile	Group 2	Goodwood	162
Beeswing Stakes	Group 3	Newcastle	124
Brigadier Gerard Stakes	Group 3	Sandown	48
Cambridgeshire Handicap	Handicap	Newmarket	201
Cesarewitch Stakes	Handicap	Newmarket	215
Challenge Stakes	Group 2	Newmarket	208
Champagne Stakes	Group 2	Doncaster	173
Champion Hurdle	Grade 1	Cheltenham	229
Champion Stakes	Group 1	Newmarket	212
Cheltenham Gold Cup	Grade 1	Cheltenham	234
Cherry Hinton Stakes	Group 3	Newmarket	112
Chester Cup	Handicap	Chester	36
Chester Vase	Group 3	Chester	34
Cheveley Park Stakes	Group 1	Newmarket	195
Cork & Orrery Stakes	Group 3	Ascot	87
Cornwallis Stakes	Group 3	Ascot	206
Coronation Cup	Group 1	Epsom	56
Coronation Stakes	Group 1	Ascot	79
Coventry Stakes	Group 3	Ascot	71
Craven Stakes	Group 3	Newmarket	18
Criterion Stakes	Group 3	Newmarket	102
Cumberland Lodge Stakes	Group 3	Ascot	186
Dante Stakes	Group 2	York	43
Dewhurst Stakes	Group 1	Newmarket	209
Diadem Stakes	Group 3	Ascot	190
Diomed Stakes	Group 3	Epsom	56
Doncaster Cup	Group 3	Doncaster	169
Duke of York Stakes	Group 3	York	44
Earl of Sefton Stakes	Group 3	Newmarket	17
Ebor Handicap	Handicap	York	153
Eclipse Stakes	Group 1	Sandown	106
Falmouth Stakes	Group 2	Newmarket	114
Fillies' Mile	Group 1	Ascot	188
Flying Childers Stakes	Group 2	Doncaster	181
Forte Mile	Group 2	Sandown	20
Fred Darling Stakes	Group 3	Newbury	12
Geoffrey Freer Stakes	Group 2	Newbury	147
Gimcrack Stakes	Group 2	York	156
Goodwood Cup	Group 3	Goodwood	136
Gordon Richards Stakes	Group 3	Sandown	20
Gordon Stakes	Group 3	Goodwood	125
Grand National	Grade 3	Aintree	239
Great Volligeur Stakes	Group 2	York	152
Greenham Stakes	Group 3	Newbury	13
Hardwicke Stakes	Group 2	Ascot	97
Haydock Park Sprint Cup	Group 1	Haydock	163
Hennessy Gold Cup	Grade 3	Newbury	225
Henry II Stakes	Group 3	Sandown	47
Horris Hill Stakes	Group 3	Newbury	218
Hungerford Stakes	Group 3	Newbury	146

Race	Grade	Course	Page
Irish Derby	Group 1	Curragh	103
Jersey Stakes	Group 3	Ascot	75
Jockey Club Cup	Group 3	Newmarket	203
Jockey Club Stakes	Group 2	Newmarket	32
John Porter Stakes	Group 3	Newbury	15
Juddmonte International Stakes	Group 1	York	149
July Cup	Group 1	Newmarket	119
July Stakes	Group 3	Newmarket	115
King Edward VII Stakes	Group 2	Ascot	73
King George V Stakes	Group 3	Goodwood	140
King George VI & Queen Elizabeth Stakes	Group 1	Ascot	122
King George VI Chase	Grade 1	Kempton	227
King's Stand Stakes	Group 2	Ascot	100
Kiveton Park Stakes	Group 3	Doncaster	172
Lancashire Oaks	Group 3	Haydock	109
Lanson Champagne Stakes	Group 3	Goodwood	136
Lincolnshire Handicap	Handicap	Doncaster	10
Lingfield Derby Trial Stakes	Group 3	Lingfield	40
Lockinge Stakes	Group 2	Newbury	45
Lowther Stakes	Group 2	York	160
Mackeson Gold Cup	Grade 3	Cheltenham	224
May Hill Stakes	Group 3	Doncaster	168
Middle Park Stakes	Group 1	Newmarket	197
Mill Reef Stakes	Group 2	Newbury	185
Molecomb Stakes	Group 3	Goodwood	141
Musidora Stakes	Group 3	York	41
Nassau Stakes	Group 2	Goodwood	144
Nell Gwyn Stakes	Group 3	Newmarket	16
Norfolk Stakes	Group 3	Ascot	94
November Handicap	Handicap	Doncaster	221
Nunthorpe Stakes	Group 1	York	158
One Thousand Guineas	Group 1	Newmarket	23
Ormonde Stakes	Group 3	Chester	39
Palace House Stakes	Group 3	Newmarket	33
Park Hill Stakes	Group 3	Doncaster	166
Portland Handicap	Handicap	Doncaster	164
Prestige Stakes	Group 3	Goodwood	161
Prince of Wales's Stakes	Group 2	Ascot	66
Princess Margaret Stakes	Group 3	Ascot	124
Princess of Wales's Stakes	Group 2	Newmarket	110
Princess Royal Stakes	Group 3	Ascot	205
Prix de l'Arc de Triomphe	Group 1	Longchamp	190
Queen Anne Stakes	Group 2	Ascot	64
Queen Elizabeth II Stakes	Group 1	Ascot	187
Queen Mary Stakes	Group 3	Ascot	77
Queen Mother Champion Chase	Grade 1	Cheltenham	231
Queen's Vase	Group 3	Ascot	84
Racing Post Trophy	Group 1	Doncaster	221
Ribblesdale Stakes	Group 2	Ascot	96

Richmond Stakes	Group 2	Goodwood	133
Rockfel Stakes	Group 3	Newmarket	212
Rose of Lancaster Stakes	Group 3	Haydock	146
Royal Hunt Cup	Handicap	Ascot	81
Royal Lodge Stakes	Group 2	Ascot	189
Sagaro Stakes	Group 3	Ascot	22
St James's Palace Stakes	Group 1	Ascot	68
St Leger	Group 1	Doncaster	175
St Simon Stakes	Group 3	Newbury	219
Scottish Classic	Group 3	Ayr	122
Select Stakes	Group 3	Goodwood	182
September Stakes	Group 3	Kempton	163
Solario Stakes	Group 3	Sandown	148
Steward's Cup	Handicap	Goodwood	127
Sun Chariot Stakes	Group 2	Newmarket	200
Supreme Stakes	Group 3	Goodwood	205
Sussex Stakes	Group 1	Goodwood	130
Temple Stakes	Group 2	Sandown	46
The Derby	Group 1	Epsom	49
The Oaks	Group 1	Epsom	58
Thresher Classic Trial	Group 3	Sandown	22
Triumph Hurdle	Grade 1	Cheltenham	233
Two Thousand Guineas	Group 1	Newmarket	23
Wartime Racing			247
Whitbread Gold Cup	Grade 3	Sandown	245
Wokingham Stakes	Handicap	Ascot	99
Yorkshire Cup	Group 2	York	43
Yorkshire Oaks	Group 1	York	150